LIVING
RELIGIONS

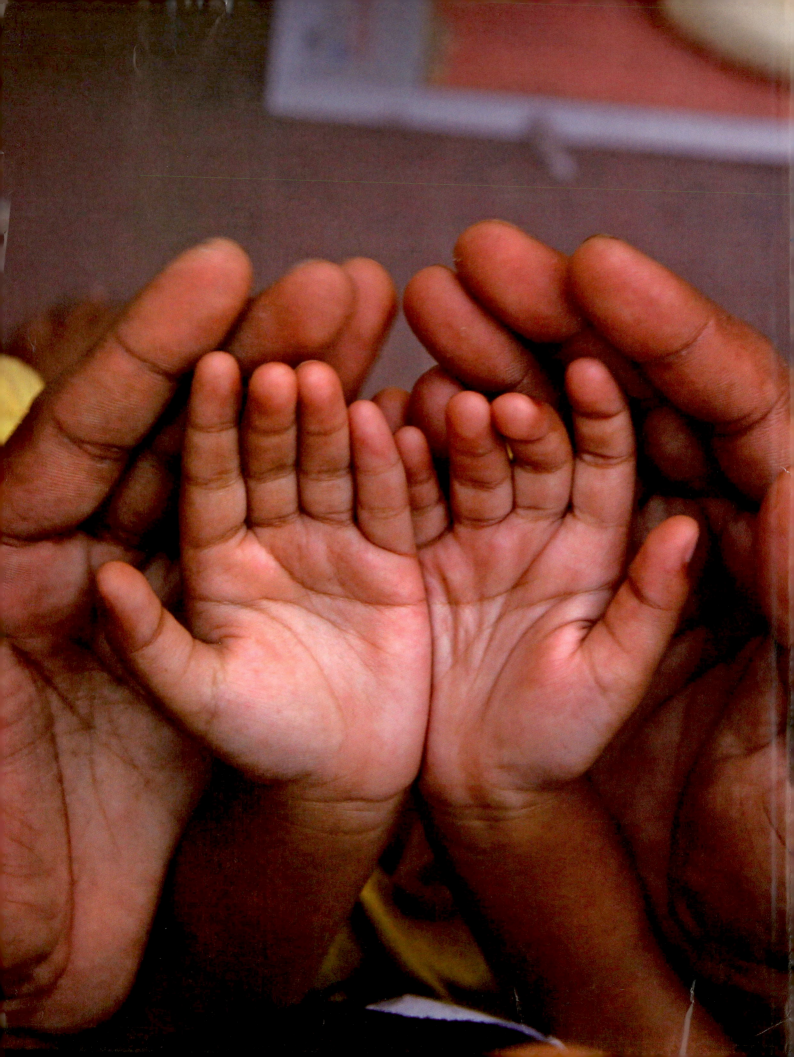

LIVING RELIGIONS

TENTH EDITION

MARY PAT FISHER • ROBIN RINEHART

CONSULTANTS

CAROL ANDERSON *Kalamazoo College*

GEORGE D. CHRYSSIDES *University of Birmingham, UK*

JAMES COX *University of Edinburgh*

MARTIN FORWARD *Aurora University*

MAXINE GROSSMAN *University of Maryland*

BRETT HENDRICKSON *Lafayette University*

JEFFERY D. LONG *Elizabethtown College*

NEELIMA SHUKLA-BHATT *Wellesley College*

PASHAURA SINGH *University of California*

JACK WASCHENFELDER *University of Alberta*

SIMON MAN-HO WONG *The Hong Kong University of Science and Technology*

HOMAYRA ZIAD *Trinity College, Connecticut*

PEARSON

Boston Columbus Indianapolis New York San Francisco
Amsterdam Cape Town Dubai London Madrid Milan Munich Paris Montréal Toronto
Delhi Mexico City São Paulo Sydney Hong Kong Seoul Singapore Taipei Tokyo

Editor-in-Chief: Sarah Touborg-Horn
Senior Sponsoring Editor: Helen Ronan
Editorial Assistant: Victoria Engros
Media Project Manager: Amanda Smith
Program Manager: Barbara Cappuccio
Project Manager: Marlene Gassler

Credits and acknowledgments borrowed from other sources and reproduced, with permission, in this textbook appear on pages 556–57.

Library of Congress Cataloging-in-Publication Data

Fisher, Mary Pat, 1943-
  Living religions / Mary Pat Fisher, Robin Rinehart ; consultants, Carol Anderson, Kalamazoo College, George D. Chryssides, University of Birmingham, UK, James Cox, University of Edinburgh, Martin Forward, Aurora University, Maxine Grossman, University of Maryland, Brett Hendrickson, Lafayette University, Jeffery D. Long, Elizabethtown College, Neelima Shukla-Bhatt, Wellesley College, Pashaura Singh, University of California, Jack Waschenfelder, University of Alberta, Simon Man-ho Wong, The Hong Kong University of Science and Technology, Homayra Ziad, Trinity College, Connecticut. -- Tenth Edition.
     pages cm
  Includes bibliographical references and index.
  ISBN 978-0-13-416897-5 -- ISBN 0-13-416897-6
1. Religions. I. Title.
  BL80.3.F57 2016
  200--dc23
                          2015022261

This book was designed and produced by Laurence King Publishing Ltd, London
www.laurenceking.com

Every effort has been made to contact the copyright holders, but should there be any errors or omissions, Laurence King Publishing Ltd would be pleased to insert the appropriate acknowledgment in any subsequent printing of this publication.

Picture Research: Ida Riveros
Design: Jo Fernandes
Production: Simon Walsh

Printed in Malaysia

Front cover: © CJG – Asia/Alamy
Frontispiece: GM Photo Images/Alamy
Page xiv: I. V. Chizhov

Student Edition:
ISBN-13: 978-0-13-416897-5
ISBN-10: 0-13-416897-6

Instructor's Review Copy:
ISBN-13: 978-0-13-416912-5
ISBN-10: 0-13-416912-3

À la Carte:
ISBN-13: 978-0-13-416907-1
ISBN-10: 0-13-416907-7

10 9 8 7 6 5 4 3 2 1

CONTENTS

CHAPTER 1

RELIGIOUS RESPONSES 1

CHAPTER 2

INDIGENOUS SACRED WAYS 33

CHAPTER 3

HINDUISM 72

CHAPTER 4

JAINISM 119

PREFACE

Religion is not a museum piece but a vibrant force in the lives of many people around the world today. *Living Religions* is a sympathetic approach to what is living and significant in the world's major religious traditions and in various new movements that are arising. This book provides a clear and straightforward account of the development, doctrines, and practices of the major faiths followed today. The emphasis throughout is on the personal consciousness of believers and their own accounts of their religion and its relevance in contemporary life.

What is new in this edition?

This tenth edition of *Living Religions* has been thoroughly revised and updated with the help of a wonderful co-author, Robin Rinehart, author of books on Asian religions, and Dean of the Faculty and Professor of Religious Studies at Lafayette College, Pennsylvania. In preparing the text we worked with an outstanding team of specialist consultants who provided detailed suggestions and resources for improving the text in the light of recent scholarship.

Old approaches to understanding and explaining religions are being increasingly challenged, so in this edition we have given special attention to sensitive issues raised by current scholarship and by voices from within the religions. Since the first edition of *Living Religions*, which was published in 1991, scholars have turned away from flat declarations that there are two distinct schools of Buddhism, for instance, for the reality is more fluid. Much more emphasis is being placed on cultural customs, popular spiritual practices, mixtures of religions, and varieties of religious ways, as opposed to distinct monolithic institutionalized religions, and this is reflected in new material woven throughout this edition. It is now more difficult to make sweeping generalizations about any religion, for they do not fit the facts that are coming to light.

Globalization

Globalization increasingly shapes our lives, altering cultures and bringing greater contact among people of different religions. It is harder than ever before to sort out reified individual religions. The effects of globalization are, therefore, examined in each chapter of this new edition.

Religion and violence

The crossing and merging of religious paths does not always lead to greater unity, however. Although appreciation and acceptance of the religious ways of others is increasing in some quarters, interactions between differing faiths are also leading to defensive hardening of boundaries. Sadly, the search for religious identity is being used politically to stoke fires of exclusivism and hatred. In the twenty-first century, as interest in religious participation grows, violence perpetrated in the name of religion is also growing. This tenth edition follows this disturbing trend, while making distinctions between the basic teachings of religions, none of which condones wanton violence, and the ways in which religions have been politicized. Every religion is struggling with its responses to modernity, including fundamentalist and exclusivist reactions to increasing pluralism within our societies, and these struggles are discussed in each chapter.

Economics

Tied together by globalization, people around the world have been affected by a widespread economic recession. The attitudes of religions toward economic issues, including greed, materialism, and the growing gap between rich and poor, are examined throughout this edition.

Environmental and societal change

People of many faiths are also looking at ways in which their religious practices and beliefs are interwoven with and affect the natural environment. This edition, therefore, includes material on religious approaches to contemporary ecological concerns, such as contamination from oil extraction that has devastated coastal areas in Nigeria and ominous signs of climate change everywhere. Many other social issues are being taken up by religious leaders. Examples in this edition include LGBT acceptance, structural injustice, corruption, HIV/AIDS, and female infanticide.

Women

This edition includes expanded coverage of women, with women's voices and contributions woven into the discussion of each religion. Feminist theologies now span decades of work and have reached the point of self-criticism, rather than focusing largely on criticism of traditional patriarchal attitudes that barred women from roles of spiritual power. Obstacles to women's expression of their spirituality still exist, however, and are discussed within the context of the various religious traditions.

This new edition also preserves and improves upon the features that make *Living Religions* special:

Personal interviews with followers of each faith provide interesting and informative first-person accounts of each religion as perceived from within the tradition. We have presented these first-person quotations from many people in "Living..." feature boxes, such as a new interview with a "spiritual but not religious" student in the United States, and also in excerpts woven throughout the text, such as new insights from a Yoruba dancer and a Jain nun. There are new interview boxes—which focus on how practitioners of each faith experience the beliefs and rituals of their tradition—in the Religious Responses and Daoism and Confucianism chapters. Each chapter opens with an emblematic quotation taken from this first-person material.

Sixteen Religion in Practice feature boxes portray the spiritual activities and beliefs of religious groups or individuals, such as the indigenous American sun dance and the Hindu sacred thread ceremony, providing fascinating insights into significant practices and festivals. A new Religion in Practice box in the Buddhism chapter gives a senior nun's explanation of death rites in Tibetan Buddhism, and a new box in the Judaism chapter follows the stories of an LGBT couple who are personally and professionally active in the Jewish community.

Eight Religion in Public Life feature boxes portray the spiritual roots of people who are making significant contributions to modern society, such as the Dalai Lama and Desmond Tutu. Two new Religion in Public Life boxes have been added in this tenth edition, featuring Malala Yousafzai, the 2014 Nobel Peace Prize winner who is courageously continuing to campaign for the right to education despite being shot by the Taliban in Pakistan; and the Assembly of the People of Kazakhstan, representing 130 different religious and ethnic groups who gather to jointly advise the Kazakhstani government on public issues.

Ten Teaching Story feature boxes contain tales that serve as take-off points for discussions about core values embedded in each faith.

An enhanced image program provides fifty-three new images, which, along with more than 200 existing images, help to bring religions to life. Many of the new photographs are Mary's own, from countries she has visited while doing personal research for this edition. Narrative captions offer additional insights into the characteristics and orientation of each tradition and the people who practice it. Five maps enhancing understanding of particular religions have been altered and improved for this edition.

Quotations from primary sources throughout the book give direct access to the thinking and flavor of each tradition. Attempts have been made to use accessible modern translations for easier understanding.

Pedagogical aids are included throughout the text. New Learning Objectives at the start of each chapter are designed to help students focus on key topics. To reinforce learning, these objectives appear as questions under section headings, and brief summaries of the main points are also included at the end of each chapter. Key Terms, defined and highlighted in boldface when they first appear for discussion, are included in an extensive glossary; many of these are also listed and defined at the end of each chapter for immediate understanding and

review. Useful guides to the pronunciation of many words are included in the glossary. Suggested reading lists of relevant books have been reinstated and updated for each chapter.

Chapter-by-chapter revisions

Chapter 1: Religious Responses has been revised and updated with increased reference to non-Western perspectives on the study of religion. The "Functional perspective: religion is useful" section has been revised with contentious assertions modified. The term "Ultimate Reality" has been used more consistently throughout the chapter as a way of referring to that which is central to all religions but known by many different names. The section on "Understandings of Ultimate Reality" now includes a discussion of humanism. New subheadings have been added for clarity in the sections "Ritual, symbol, and myth" and "The encounter between science and religion". The last section, "Lenses for studying religions," has been revised and made more relevant by including questions that students might ask themselves. A new interview box has been added featuring the views of a student who considers herself "spiritual but not religious," an increasingly common choice. New images in this chapter include an evocative photo of people praying in a traditional Daoist temple in Hong Kong, surrounded by the modern cityscape.

Chapter 2: Indigenous Sacred Ways has been revised with special attention to new ways of defining indigenous religions. Along with acknowledgment of the great cultural diversity among indigenous religious ways, there is also expanded discussion of commonalities. New topics explored include Yoruba dance experiences, spirit mediums, and conversion to Islam by Aboriginal people. Discussion of shamanism has been revised and the community-centered nature of indigenous ways has been brought into sharper focus. Discussions of contemporary issues now include the effects of ayahuasca tourism on local forest people in South America, eviction of Maasai for the sake of foreign tourism in Kenya, and Indian tribal people's attempts to block government allocation of forest land to coal-mining companies. New images include the popular Guelaguetza celebration in Oaxaca, Mexico, and an alarming photograph of the effects of oil spills on Ogoni land in Nigeria.

Chapter 3: Hinduism has been extensively reorganized for greater logic and easier understanding of this complex of religious ways. Hindu identity politics have come to the fore with successes of the BJP party in India, so the chapter includes questions of whether political success will lead to more exclusive or more inclusive versions of Hinduism. There are five new images in the chapter: an ancient stone carving representing the sun god, a float from a village procession with humans representing characters from the Ramayana, countless brass bells hung in gratitude to a popular local deity, a woman making auspicious designs of colored powders outside her home, and a photograph suggesting the great numbers of devotees who undertake the rigorous mountain trek to the Amarnath cave shrine.

Chapter 4: Jainism includes increased discussion of the relevance of Jainism today. Explanation of the role of the Tirthankaras is expanded, as is that of the role of nuns and laywomen in Jainism. A new feature box describes the meanings of the Jain symbol. The "World Jainism" section has also been updated and revised. The appeal of Jain meditation techniques for foreigners who travel to India to participate in special Preksha meditation camps is discussed, and there is a new image of this growing phenomenon. A new photo of a statue of Mahavir shows both his personal asceticism and the richly ornamental stone carvings with which Jain temples are often adorned.

Chapter 5: Buddhism has been extensively reorganized and revised in the light of recent scholarship, which stresses similarities more than differences between the various schools of Buddhism. Material on the Four Noble Truths and the Dharma has been clarified. New scholarship on the Mahayana tradition is incorporated, including the various canons and emphasis on rituals and monastic practices shared with Theravada. The Vajrayana section has also been updated to reflect new scholarship, and a new Religion in Practice box has been added on death rites in Tibetan Buddhism. "Buddhism in the West" has been amplified with new material on mindfulness teachings and practice. The "Socially engaged Buddhism" section is updated, with discussion on the goals of Buddhist development. Nine new images for this chapter include the huge One Million Monk Dhammakaya Temple in Thailand, Jizo statues for stillborn babies and aborted fetuses in Japan, a senior Tibetan nun teaching a hand position for meditation to a young nun, and the courageous Myanmar (Burma) opposition leader Aung San Suu Kyi.

Chapter 6: Daoism and Confucianism has new material on Daoist temples and practices in Hong Kong, where old traditions are popular among younger generations. The discussion of Confucian virtues has been expanded, for they are of increasing interest as having contemporary relevance. "Neo-Confucianism" has been revised with more information on Zhu Xi's work, and the spread of Neo-Confucianism to Korea and Japan. Material on the resurgence of Confucianism in twenty-first century China has been updated, and there is additional discussion of the contributions of Confucianism to the economic success of East Asian countries. A new Living Confucianism box has been added, featuring Simon Man-ho Wong of Hong Kong University of Science and Technology. Material on Falun Gong has been moved to the chapter on New Religious Movements, for both Daoists and Buddhists deny that the controversial movement is related to their religions. New images include a photo of a young woman making offerings to her ancestors at a Hong Kong ancestral hall and children participating in a lavish celebration of the birthday of Confucius in Qufu, his home city.

Chapter 7: Shinto has expanded sections on State Shinto and responses to the devastating 2011 tsunami, including revival of old rituals and festivals to improve relationships with the

kami. There are new images of a shrine festival organized by young people in the area hardest hit by the tsunami, and of sumo wrestling, which carries on traditions associated with Shinto beliefs.

The special section on **Zoroastrianism** has been updated to include modern-day pilgrimages to ancient holy places. A new photo illustrates pilgrims worshiping with fire at a sacred site at the base of a cliff in Iran.

Chapter 8: Judaism has been revised for clarity and chronology in the sections on biblical and rabbinic Judaism. Material on the Torah has been rewritten to provide a better explanation of the complexity of the Hebrew scriptures. Contemporary manifestations of Judaism have been updated with new material on Jewish Renewal and modern inclusion of LGBT Jews. A new Religion in Practice box has been added featuring prominent Jewish women who have married each other and who are educating their two children and other young people according to inclusivist values. New images in this chapter include a Torah study group in Israel, a family Seder, women celebrating Purim by reading the Book of Esther together, and Women of the Wall praying during their monthly Rosh Hadesh observance at the Western Wall.

Chapter 9: Christianity has been revised with special reference to contemporary features, issues, and scholarship. Discussion of popular Christianity includes additional information on veneration of relics and participation in pilgrimages. Coverage of the spread of Catholicism to South America, Asia, and Africa is expanded. Veneration of Mary is updated with its current manifestations. Contemporary issues including the plight of Christians amidst violence in the Middle East, sexual abuses by clergy, and ordination of women as bishops are discussed. This chapter also looks at liberalizing attempts by Pope Francis and the split in various denominations between traditionalists and modernizers. There is a new photo of Pope Francis and Ecumenical Patriarch Bartholomew from their historic meeting in Jerusalem to begin working together in areas of common concern. Other new photos include a painting of the Pentecost by a modern Chinese artist, a Posada procession for Christmas in California, Pope Francis greeting a little boy during his homily on grandparents, African Americans worshiping from the heart, and volunteers praying over relief supplies for malnourished children.

Chapter 10: Islam features updated material on contemporary Islam, particularly with reference to politics. Some of the quotations from the Qur'an are replaced with more recent translations, and there are more quotes by women. Information on hajj is expanded, and major Islamic holidays are described. The institution of the caliphate is explained, including its contemporary political relevance. Coverage of shari'ah is increased and fiqh (jurisprudence) explained. Financial and dietary principles are discussed. The militant activities of Boko Haram in Nigeria and IS (Islamic State) in Syria and Iraq are also discussed, along with repudiation of violence in the name of Islam by other Muslims. Malala Yousafzai, Nobel Peace Prize winner for her courageous support of education for girls in Pakistan, is the subject of a new Religion in Public Life box. New images include a closer photo of the cave of Hira where the Prophet undertook spiritual retreats, men doing their private prayers at an Indian mosque, a communal meal celebrating the end of Ramadan fasting in China, children dressed in their best clothes enjoying a sweet dish at the end of Eid al-Adha prayers, a better image of the interior of the Dome of the Rock, Eid al-Fitr in a Chinese mosque, and a screenshot from the website "Muslim Voices" with articles covering issues such as misunderstandings about Islam and being Muslim in America.

Chapter 11: Sikhism introduces the sant tradition as a feature of the environment in which Sikhism originated. Coverage of the Five Ks is expanded. Contemporary issues include discussion of hate crimes against Sikhs in the diaspora, including the Oak Creek incident in Wisconsin. There is a new image of reading from a large handwritten copy of the Guru Granth Sahib in the Golden Temple as a pilgrim listens reverently.

Chapter 12: New Religious Movements has been updated with discussion of the satirical Flying Spaghetti Monster movement and succession issues in the Unification movement since the death of Rev. Moon. Material on Falun Gong, previously in the Daoism and Confucianism chapter, is also included. There is a new image of a dramatic Agon Shu Shinto-Buddhist fire ceremony with discussion of combinations of several religions. The Chipko tree-hugging movement to save forests from destruction by vested interests is also illustrated and discussed.

Chapter 13: Religion in the Twenty-first Century opens with an updated pie chart on the percentages of people in the world practicing the various religions, including "nones." Religion is more in the news than ever before, often with reference to politically instigated clashes between people of different religions. Thus this chapter includes displacement of people in the Middle East by violent conflicts, fallout from the Iraq war and the Arab Spring, the spread of IS, recent tensions between Israelis and Palestinians, and the perceived need for radical cultural and political reform if such tensions are to be abated. At the same time, initiatives to improve harmony among people of different religions are growing. Thus the chapter describes efforts such as the Oasis of Peace community in Israel, and there is a new Religion in Public Life feature box on the Assembly of the People of Kazakhstan, which intentionally embraces all religious and ethnic groups. Discussion of serious social issues affecting the future of humanity includes responses to climate change and concern about structural evil embedded in capitalism and materialism. New images include a poster that scared Swiss citizens into voting to ban minarets on mosques, Israeli Jewish and Palestinian Arab children with a peace sign at their Oasis of Peace school, the Assembly of the People of Kazakhstan, and an interfaith Noah's Ark float in the huge People's Climate March in New York.

Acknowledgments

In order to try to understand each religion from the inside, Mary has traveled for many years to study and worship with devotees and teachers of all faiths, and to interview them about their experience of their tradition. People of all religions also come to the Gobind Sadan Institute for Advanced Studies in Comparative Religions, in New Delhi, where it is her good fortune to meet and speak with them about their spiritual experiences and beliefs. Robin has also traveled extensively while doing research on religions, especially in India, and her experiences and colleagues have been very helpful in improving our writings about the contemporary practice of religions.

In preparing this book, we have worked directly with consultants who are authorities in specific traditions and who have offered detailed suggestions and resources. For breadth of scholarship, a new group of consultants has been chosen for each edition. For this tenth edition, a number of extremely helpful and dedicated scholars have carefully reviewed the various chapters and made excellent suggestions for their improvement. They are Jack Waschenfelder, University of Alberta, Augustana Campus; James Cox, University of Edinburgh; Neelima Shukla-Bhatt, Wellesley College, Massachusetts; Jeffery D. Long, Elizabethtown College, Pennsylvania; Carol Anderson, Kalamazoo College, Michigan; Simon Man-ho Wong, the Hong Kong University of Science and Technology; Maxine Grossman, University of Maryland; Brett Hendrickson, Lafayette College, Pennsylvania; Homayra Ziad, Trinity College, Connecticut; Pashaura Singh, University of California,-Riverside; George D. Chryssides, University of Birmingham, UK; and Martin Forward, Aurora University, Illinois. All the consultants understood what makes *Living Religions* special and gave generously of their time and knowledge to help improve this edition. We are extremely grateful for their sensitive, knowledgeable, and enthusiastic help, and also for the assistance of the many scholars who have served as consultants to the previous editions and are acknowledged therein.

Many other people have helped with insights and resources. Among them are Kazumasa Osaha, Dima Kartunchikov, Darrol Bryant, Wang MinQin, John Smelcer, the Very Reverend Archbishop Benjamin, Naoyuki Ogi, Archie C. C. Lee, Lai Chi Tim, H. W. Wilson, Mr. Liu, Balkrishan Naik, Jabar Ali, Maria Petersson, Udita Panconcelli, Bert Gunn, Frank Kaufman, Tolegen Muhammedzhanov, Dina Zhuzdubayeva, Ernesto Kahan, Robert Chase, Valeria Porokova, Rev. Dr. Tobias Brandner, Shuhua, Ildar, Grigoriy Mozhnenko, Rajit Pal, Syed Zafar Mahmood, Jazz Anwar, Babl iKalha, Alison Byerly, Bob Cohn, and Youshaa Patel. We are very grateful to them all.

As always, Laurence King Publishing has provided us with excellent editorial help. Managing Director Laurence King and Chairman Nicholas Perren have been uncommonly supportive. Melanie Walker, Susie May, and Kara Hattersley-Smith have guided this edition through its development and production with brilliance, patience, and extraordinary helpfulness. Ida Riveros has worked hard to find the new illustrations that so enhance this edition. Designer Jo Fernandes has put everything together beautifully. And at Pearson, Sarah Touborg

Horn, Barbara Cappuccio, Marlene Gassler, Victoria Engros, and Amanda Smith have been ever encouraging.

Finally, Mary cannot adequately express her gratitude to her revered teacher, Baba Virsa Singh of Gobind Sadan. People of all faiths from all over the world came to him for his spiritual blessings and guidance. In the midst of sectarian conflicts, his place remains an oasis of peace and harmony, where permanent volunteers and visitors from ninety countries regard each other as members of one human family. May God bless us all to move in this direction.

Mary Pat Fisher
Gobind Sadan Institute for Advanced Studies
in Comparative Religions
Robin Rinehart
Lafayette College

The authors and Pearson would like to thank the following instructors who provided thoughtful guidance as reviewers:

William Abshire, Bridgewater College;
Jon Brammer, Three Rivers Community College;
Melinda Campbell, National University;
Gladys Childs, Texas Wesleyan University;
Barbara Darling-Smith, Wheaton College;
Marianne Ferguson, Buffalo State College;
Alison Jameson, Lehigh Carbon Community College;
Charles Johnson, Washtenaw Community College;
Ian MacKinnon, Lakeland Community College;
John McPhee, Marist College;
Chris Newcomb, Bethune-Cookman University;
Jonathan Webster, Radford University.

TEACHING AND LEARNING RESOURCES FOR LIVING RELIGIONS

Whether you want to enhance your lectures, create tests, or assign outside material to reinforce content from the text, you and your students will find the most comprehensive set of instructional materials available with *Living Religions, Tenth Edition*, to reinforce and enliven the study of world religions.

REVEL™
Educational technology designed for the way today's students read, think, and learn.

When students are engaged deeply, they learn more effectively and perform better in their courses. This simple fact inspired the creation of REVEL: an immersive learning experience designed for the way today's students read, think, and learn. Built in collaboration with educators and students nationwide, REVEL is the newest, fully digital way to deliver respected Pearson content.

REVEL enlivens course content with media interactives and assessments—integrated directly within the authors' narrative —that provide opportunities for students to read about and practice course material in tandem. This immersive educational technology boosts student engagement, which leads to better understanding of concepts and improved performance throughout the course.

Learn more about REVEL: http://www.pearsonhighered.com/revel/

Instructor's Manual with Tests
For each chapter in the text, this valuable resource provides a chapter outline, preview questions, lecture topics, research topics, and questions for classroom discussion. In addition, test questions in multiple choice and essay formats are available for each chapter.

Learn more at www.pearsonhighered.com

My Test
This computerized software allows instructors to create their own personalized exams, to edit any or all of the existing test questions, and to add new questions. Other special features of this program include random generation of test questions, creation of alternate version of the same test, scrambling question sequence, and test preview before printing. Learn more at www.pearsonhighered.com

PowerPoint Slides
These PowerPoint slides combine text and graphics for each chapter to help instructors convey anthropological principles in a clear and engaging way.

Learning Catalytics
A "bring your own device" student engagement, assessment, and classroom intelligence system. Question libraries for World Religions help generate classroom discussion, guide your lecture, and promote peer-to-peer learning with real-time analytics. Learn more at www.learningcatalytics.com

Build your own Pearson Custom course material: for enrollments of at least 25, the Pearson Custom Library allows you to create your own textbook by

- combining chapters from best-selling Pearson textbooks in the sequence you want
- adding your own content, such as a guide to local worship places, your syllabus, or a study guide you've created.

A Pearson Custom Library book is priced according to the number of chapters and may even save your students money. To begin building your custom text, visit www.pearsoncustomlibrary.com or contact your Pearson representative.

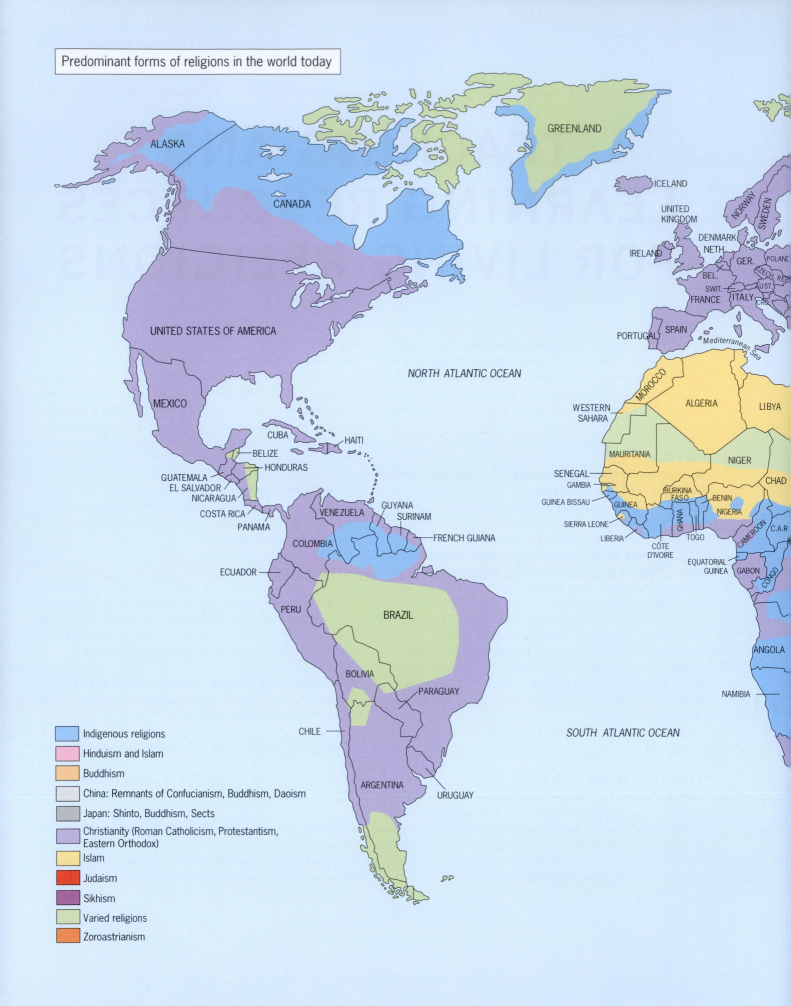

Predominant forms of religions in the world today

ALASKA

CANADA

GREENLAND

ICELAND

NORWAY · SWEDEN

UNITED KINGDOM

IRELAND · DENMARK · NETH. · GER. · POLAND

BEL. · CZECH REP.

SWIT. · AUST.

FRANCE · ITALY · CRO.

UNITED STATES OF AMERICA

PORTUGAL · SPAIN

Mediterranean Sea

NORTH ATLANTIC OCEAN

MEXICO

CUBA

HAITI

BELIZE

HONDURAS

GUATEMALA
EL SALVADOR
NICARAGUA

COSTA RICA

PANAMA

VENEZUELA

GUYANA
SURINAM

FRENCH GUIANA

COLOMBIA

ECUADOR

PERU

BRAZIL

BOLIVIA

PARAGUAY

CHILE

ARGENTINA

URUGUAY

MOROCCO

WESTERN SAHARA

ALGERIA

LIBYA

MAURITANIA

NIGER

SENEGAL

GAMBIA

GUINEA BISSAU

GUINEA

BURKINA FASO

CHAD

BENIN

NIGERIA

SIERRA LEONE

LIBERIA

CÔTE D'IVOIRE

GHANA

TOGO

CAMEROON

C.A.R

EQUATORIAL GUINEA

GABON

CONGO

ANGOLA

NAMIBIA

SOUTH ATLANTIC OCEAN

Indigenous religions

Hinduism and Islam

Buddhism

China: Remnants of Confucianism, Buddhism, Daoism

Japan: Shinto, Buddhism, Sects

Christianity (Roman Catholicism, Protestantism, Eastern Orthodox)

Islam

Judaism

Sikhism

Varied religions

Zoroastrianism

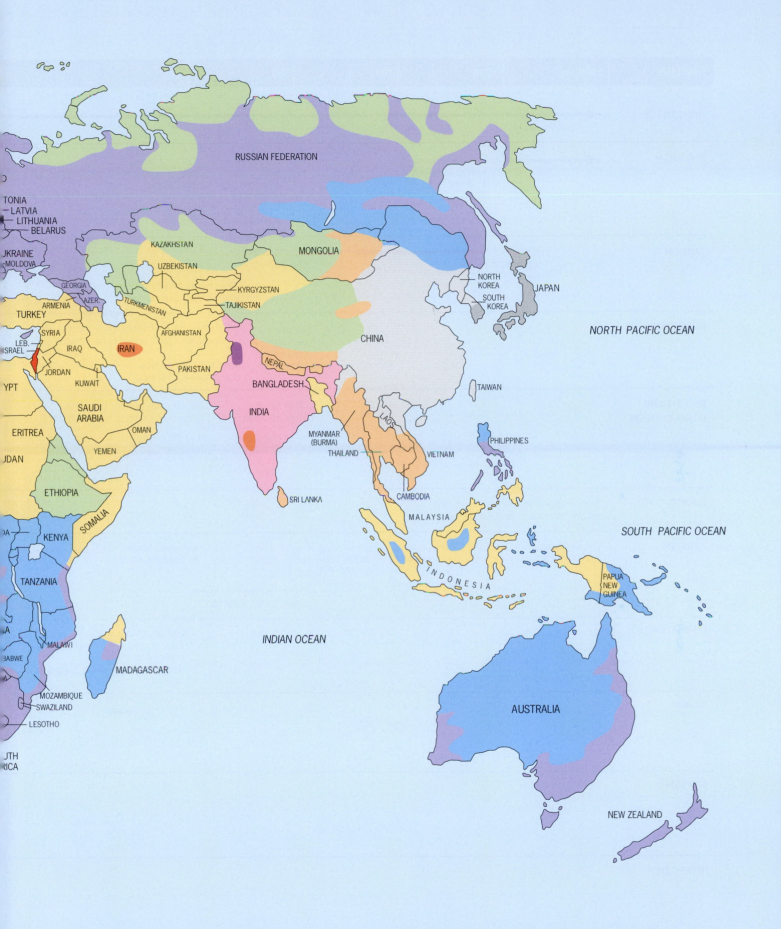

RUSSIAN FEDERATION

TONIA
LATVIA
LITHUANIA
BELARUS

UKRAINE
MOLDOVA

KAZAKHSTAN

MONGOLIA

GEORGIA
ARMENIA
AZER.
TURKMENISTAN
UZBEKISTAN
KYRGYZSTAN
TAJIKISTAN

TURKEY

SYRIA
LEB.
ISRAEL
IRAQ
JORDAN
KUWAIT

IRAN

AFGHANISTAN

PAKISTAN

CHINA

NORTH
KOREA
SOUTH
KOREA

JAPAN

NORTH PACIFIC OCEAN

YPT

SAUDI
ARABIA

OMAN

NEPAL

BANGLADESH

INDIA

TAIWAN

ERITREA

YEMEN

MYANMAR
(BURMA)

THAILAND

LAOS

VIETNAM

PHILIPPINES

JDAN

SRI LANKA

CAMBODIA

ETHIOPIA

MALAYSIA

SOUTH PACIFIC OCEAN

SOMALIA

DA

KENYA

INDONESIA

PAPUA
NEW
GUINEA

TANZANIA

MALAWI

BABWE

MADAGASCAR

INDIAN OCEAN

MOZAMBIQUE
SWAZILAND

LESOTHO

AUSTRALIA

JTH
RICA

NEW ZEALAND

TIMELINE	2000 BCE	1500	1000	500	1 CE
INDIGENOUS	←				
HINDUISM	←	According to some scholars, early Vedas first composed c.1500 BCE		*Ramayana* and *Mahabharata* in present form after 400 BCE	Code of Manu compiled 100–300 CE. Patanjali systematizes *Yoga Sutras* by 200 BCE
JAINISM		Series of 23 Tirthankaras before c.777 BCE →		Life of Mahavira 599–527 BCE. Digambaras and Shvetambaras diverge from 3rd century BCE	
BUDDHISM				Life of Gautama Buddha c.5th century BCE. Theravada Buddhism develops c.200 BCE–200 CE. King Ashoka spreads Buddhism c.258 BCE	Mahayana Buddhism develops 1st century CE
DAOISM AND CONFUCIANISM				Life of Laozi c.600–300 BCE. Life of Confucius c.551–479 BCE. Educational system based on Confucian Classics from 205 BCE. Life of Zhuangzi c.365–290 BCE	
SHINTO	Shinto begins in pre-history as local nature- and ancestor-based traditions				
JUDAISM	Life of Abraham c.1900–1700 BCE	Moses leads Israelites out of Egypt c.13th or 12th century BCE	David, king of Judah and Israel c.1010–970 BCE. First Temple destroyed; Jews exiled 586 BCE		Jerusalem falls to Romans 70 CE
CHRISTIANITY					Life of Jesus c.4 BCE–30 CE. Paul organizes early Christians c.50–60 CE. Gospels written down c.70–95 CE
ISLAM					
SIKHISM					
INTERFAITH					
	2000 BCE	**1500**	**1000**	**500**	**1 CE**

Ancient ways passed down and adapted over millennia ⟶

Tantras written down c.300

Bhakti movement 600–1800 ⟶

Life of Ramakrishna 1836–1886

Jain monks establish Jain centers outside India 1970s–1980s

Life of Songstan (c.609–650) who declares Buddhism national religion of Tibet

Persecution of Buddhism begins in China 845

Chan Buddhism to Japan as Zen 13th century

Buddhism spreads in the West 20th century

Full ordination of nuns from 23 countries 1998

Japan imports Confucianism to unite tribes into empire

Sung dynasty revives ritualistic Confucianism ("Neo-Confucianism")

Cultural Revolution attacks religions 1966–1976

Confucian revival in China; International Association of Confucianism established; Daoist sects and temples re-established 1990–2000

Shinto name adopted 6th century CE

State Shinto established 1868

Rabbinical tradition develops 1st to 4th centuries

Life of Maimonides 1135–1204

Expulsion of Jews from Spain 1492

The Holocaust 1933–1945 Independent state of Israel 1948

The Baal Shem Tov c.1700–1760

Israeli wall for separation from Palestinians 2003

Centralization of papal power after 800

Split between Western and Eastern Orthodox Churches 1054

Monastic orders proliferate 1300s

Protestantism established 1517

Spanish Inquisition established 1478

Second Vatican Council 1962–1965

Churches reopened in Soviet Union 1989

Life of Muhammad c.570–632

Spread of Islam begins 633 Sunni–Shi'a split c.682

Islam's cultural peak 750–1258

Akbar becomes Mughal emperor in India 1556

European dominance 1800s–1900s

Terrorism and counterterrorism increase 2001

Muslim resurgence and OPEC 1970s

Life of Guru Nanak 1469–1539

At death of Guru Gobind Singh (1708), living presence of the guru is embodied in Guru Granth Sahib (scriptures)

300th anniversary of Khalsa 1999

Mughal emperor Akbar initiates interfaith dialogues 1556–1605

First International Human Unity Conference 1974 Parliament of the World's Religions centenary celebrations 1993

CHAPTER 1

RELIGIOUS RESPONSES

"By calling myself spiritual but not religious, I can still acknowledge my belief that there may be higher powers of a divine nature without necessarily accepting just one belief system of an organized religious institution." Ivy DeWitt[1]

1.1 Explain what is meant by spirituality

1.2 Identify three perspectives used to explain the existence of religion

1.3 Differentiate between monotheistic, polytheistic, and nontheistic

1.4 Explain the significance of rituals, symbols, and myths in religions

1.5 Contrast absolutist with liberal interpretations of a religious tradition

1.6 Discuss the major positions that have emerged in the dialogue between science and religion since the nineteenth century

1.7 Describe how women are challenging the patriarchal nature of many institutionalized religions

1.8 Identify the factors that contribute to the negative aspects of organized religions

1.9 Summarize the different "lenses" used by scholars to study religion

Before sunrise, members of a Muslim family rise in Malaysia, perform their purifying ablutions, spread their prayer rugs facing Mecca, and begin their prostrations and prayers to Allah. In a French cathedral, worshipers line up for their turn to have a priest place a wafer on their tongue, murmuring, "This is the body of Christ, given for you." In a South Indian village, a group of women reverently anoint a cylindrical stone with milk and fragrant sandalwood paste and place

Jewish women praying at the Western Wall. Many scraps of paper with personal prayers are tucked into the cracks between the ancient stones.

around it offerings of flowers. The monks of a Japanese Zen Buddhist monastery sit cross-legged and upright in utter silence, which is broken occasionally by the noise of the *kyosaku* bat falling on their shoulders. On a mountain in Mexico, men, women, and children who have been dancing without food or water for days greet an eagle flying overhead with a burst of whistling from the small wooden flutes they wear around their necks. In Jerusalem, Jews tuck scraps of paper containing their personal prayers between the stones of the ancient Western Wall, which once supported their sacred Temple, while above that wall only Muslims are allowed to enter the Dome of the Rock to pray.

These and countless other moments in the lives of people around the world are threads of the tapestry we call **religion**. The word is probably derived from the Latin, meaning "to tie back," "to tie again." All of religion shares the goal of tying people back to something behind the surface of life—a greater reality, which lies beyond, or invisibly infuses, the world that we can perceive with our five senses.

Attempts to connect with or comprehend this greater reality have taken many forms. Many of them are organized institutions, such as Buddhism or Christianity. These institutions are complexes of such elements as leaders, beliefs, rituals, symbols, myths, scriptures, ethics, spiritual practices, cultural components, historical traditions, and management structures. Moreover, they are not fixed and distinct categories, as simple labels such as "Buddhism" and "Christianity" suggest. Each of these labels is an abstraction that is used in the attempt to bring some kind of order to the study of religious patterns that are in fact complex, diverse, ever-changing, and overlapping.

Attempts to define religion
What are the inner dimensions of religion?

The labels "Buddhism," "Hinduism," "Daoism," "Zoroastrianism," and "Confucianism" did not exist until the nineteenth century, though the many patterns to which they refer had existed for thousands of years. Professor Willard G. Oxtoby (1933–2003), founding director of the Centre for Religious Studies at the University of Toronto, observed that when Western Christian scholars began studying other religions, they applied assumptions based on the Christian model to other paths, looking for specific creedal statements of belief (a rarity in indigenous lifeways), a dichotomy between what is secular and what is sacred (not helpful in looking at the teachings of Confucius and his followers), and the idea that a person belongs to only one religion at a time (which does not apply in Japan, where people freely follow various religious traditions).

Not all religious behavior occurs within institutional confines. The inner dimensions of religion—such as experiences, beliefs, and values—can be referred to as **spirituality**. This is part of what is called religion, but it may occur in personal, noninstitutional ways, without the ritual and social dimensions of organized religions. Indeed there are growing numbers of people in the world today who describe themselves as "spiritual but not religious" (see box, p. 4). Personal spirituality without reference to a particular religious tradition permeates much contemporary artistic creation. Without theology, without historical references, such direct experiences are difficult to express, whether in words, images, or music. Contemporary artist Lisa Bradley says of her luminous paintings:

> *In them you can see movement and stillness at the same time, things coming in and out of focus. The light seems to be from behind. There is a sense of something like a permeable membrane, of things coming from one dimension to another. But even that doesn't describe it well. How do you describe truth in words?*[2]

Lisa Bradley, Passing Shadow, *2002.*

Religions can be dynamic in their effects, bringing deep changes in individuals and societies, for good or ill. As Professor Christopher Queen, world religions scholar from Harvard University, observes:

> *The interpersonal and political realms may be transformed by powerful religious forces. Devotion linking human and divine beings, belief in holy people or sacred space, and ethical teachings that shape behaviors and attitudes may combine to transform individual identities and the social order itself.*[3]

Frederick Streng (1933–1993), an influential scholar of comparative religion, suggested in his book *Understanding Religious Life* that the central definition of religion is that it is a "means to ultimate transformation." A complete definition of religion would include its relational aspect ("tying back"), its transformational potential, and also its political dimensions.

Current attempts to define religions may thus refer more to processes than to fixed independent entities. Professor of Religious Studies Thomas A. Tweed, for instance, proposes this definition in his book *Crossing and Dwelling: A Theory of Religion*:

> *Religions are confluences of organic-cultural flows that intensify joy and confront suffering by drawing on human and suprahuman forces to make homes and cross boundaries—terrestrial, corporeal, and cosmic. ...This theory is, above all, about movement and relation, and it is an attempt to correct theories [of religion] that have presupposed stasis and minimized interdependence.*[4]

Religion is such a complex and elusive topic that some contemporary scholars of religion are seriously questioning whether "religion" or "religions" can be studied at all, or whether the concept of religion itself is useful. They have determined that no matter where and at what point they try to define the concept, other parts will get away. Nonetheless, this difficult-to-grasp subject is central to many people's lives and has assumed great political significance in today's world,

LIVING RELIGIOUS RESPONSES

An Interview with Ivy DeWitt

 Ivy DeWitt is a recent college graduate who majored in both economics and religious studies. Raised in a traditional Baptist Church, she found that as she learned more about different religions, and asked questions about issues such as women's roles within religions, she no longer felt comfortable identifying herself as a member of one specific religious group. Now, like about eighteen percent of Americans, she describes herself as "spiritual but not religious,"[5] exploring her beliefs in an individualistic way rather than through set teachings and practices of a single religious organization. Ivy explains:

Being spiritual but not religious allows for a more individualized experience and expression of religion. Spirituality feels like an entirely personal experience in many ways to me, and being spiritual but not religious allows me to question and explore a variety of religious identities without feeling as though I'm constrained by a single religious institution. By calling myself spiritual but not religious, I can still acknowledge my belief that there may be higher powers of a divine nature without necessarily accepting just one belief system of an organized religious institution.

Ivy acknowledges the important role that religious organizations play in building a strong community, but found that her personal exploration of spirituality was more important to her:

I think of "religion" as having more to do with communities and institutions. Growing up as a Baptist Protestant Christian, I felt that the most important part of the religious experience was having strong ties to your group. I also believe another important aspect of religion is doctrines. While I acknowledge that people can have a variety of opinions within a single religion, and that views can also vary throughout branches of a religion, doctrines help to unify people under a central belief system, which can also be very important in holding a community together. In contrast, I think of spirituality as a more individualized experience, something that isn't defined by the specific teachings or practices of a particular religion. While many people associate spirituality with a greater sense of feeling or emotion than anything that comes about through being part of an organized religion, I don't necessarily agree. Religion and spirituality can overlap to create a wide sense of emotional experiences, but I like to associate spirituality with individual discovery. To me, spirituality is not just about emotional experience, but also about finding what your values are, and aligning them either with a religious identity or a personalized belief system.

Ivy first began to question whether her own evolving beliefs were compatible with what she was taught in school and church during high school:

I attended a non-denominational Protestant high school. I had questions about women's roles in church, and I wondered if my personal beliefs aligned with Protestant teachings on contemporary social issues. There were discussions within my communities about whether women could be pastors. I struggled to understand whether this implied that women and men had different spiritual capabilities, and if I agreed with that sentiment. I started to distance myself from the church as a way to decide what my own viewpoints were concerning women's rights and other social issues—and whether they aligned with the religious perspectives I had been raised with. I decided to identify as spiritual but not religious roughly about partway through my junior year of college. I began to realize that I didn't hold any set beliefs that I felt aligned with my religious tradition. Ultimately I decided that it didn't make sense for me to continue identifying as a Protestant, and the spiritual but not religious label seemed to capture how I felt at the time. I continue to use it now because I believe it is the most accurate description of my belief system. I care more about holding to my personal beliefs in relation to women's rights and social justice than the community or doctrinal aspects of religion. It's not that I believe the religious beliefs I grew up with are completely incongruent with my own, but at the moment identifying with a single religious community isn't reconcilable with other principles that I value.

For Ivy, spiritual experience does not follow from accepting a particular set of beliefs, but more from exploring many different religious traditions to see what inspires her.

Being spiritual but not religious allows me to navigate religious history while also navigating my own identity. I don't believe I'll ever finish navigating either one, which is why I enjoy how being spiritual has allowed me to do that free of any particular religious labels. Some people disagree with certain key tenets of their religion, but still remain a part of it. I think that they choose to focus on what they see as core principles of the tradition, in spite of whatever disagreements they have, and they may find it hard to give up being part of a religious community. I do think that spiritual but not religious people are to some extent missing out on some of the community-related parts of religion. But I believe that most people who identify as spiritual but not religious probably aren't looking for a community religious experience. Having participated in a religious community myself, I sincerely enjoy my current ability to explore different religious traditions and identities on my own without feeling tied to a specific institution.[6]

so it is important to try sincerely to understand it. In this introductory chapter, we will try to develop some understanding of religion in a generic sense—why it exists, its various patterns and modes of interpretation, its encounters with modern science, its inclusion or exclusion of women, and its potentially negative aspects—before trying in the subsequent chapters to understand the major traditions known as "religions" practiced around the world today.

Why are there religions?

What major theories have evolved to explain the existence of religion?

In many cultures and times, religion has been the basic foundation of life, permeating all aspects of human existence. In fact, in some cultures what we may now identify as "religion" has so permeated everything that it was not even identified as a particular category of human experience. But from the time of the European Enlightenment, religion has become in the West an object to be studied, rather than a basic fact of life. Cultural anthropologists, sociologists, philosophers, psychologists, and even biologists and neuroscientists have peered at religion through their own particular lenses, trying to explain what religion is, its function and purpose, and developing a wide range of methods for studying religion. In the following pages we will briefly examine some of the major theories that have evolved. They are not mutually exclusive.

Materialist perspective: humans invented religion

During the nineteenth and twentieth centuries, **scientific materialism** gained considerable prominence as a theory to explain the fact that religion can be found in some form in every culture around the world. The materialistic point of view is that the supernatural is invented by humans; only the material world exists.

An influential example of this perspective can be found in the work of the nineteenth-century philosopher Ludwig Feuerbach (1804–1872). He reasoned that deities are simply projections, objectifications of human qualities such as power, wisdom, and love onto an imagined cosmic deity outside ourselves. Then we worship it as Supreme and do not recognize that those same qualities lie within ourselves; instead, we see ourselves as weak and sinful. Feuerbach developed this theory with particular reference to Christianity as he had seen it.

Other scientific materialists believe that religions have been created or at least used to manipulate people. Historically, religions have often supported and served secular power. The nineteenth-century socialist philosopher Karl Marx (1818–1883), author of *The Communist Manifesto*, argued that a culture's religion—as well as all other aspects of its social structure—springs from its economic framework. In Marx's view, religion's origins lie in the longings of the oppressed. It may have developed from the desire to revolutionize society and combat exploitation, but in failing to do so it became otherworldly, an expression of unfulfilled desires for a better, more satisfying life:

> *Man makes religion: religion does not make man. ... The religious world is but the reflex of the real world. ... Religion is the sigh of the oppressed creature, the sentiment of a heartless world, and the soul of soulless conditions. It is the opium of the people.*[7]

According to Marx, not only do religions pacify people falsely, they may themselves become tools of oppression. For instance, he charged Christian authorities of his times with supporting "vile acts of the oppressors" by explaining them as due punishment of sinners by God. Other critics have made similar complaints against Asian religions that blame the sufferings of the poor on their own misdeeds in previous lives. Such interpretations and uses of religious teachings lessen the perceived need for society to help those who are oppressed and suffering. Marx's ideas thus led toward twentieth-century atheistic communism, for he had asserted, "The abolition of religion as the illusory happiness of the people is required for their real happiness."[8]

Many contemporary atheist thinkers have also adopted a materialist approach to religion, arguing that religious assertions about the supernatural, such as the existence of God, are testable hypotheses that cannot be proven.

Functional perspective: religion is useful

Another line of reasoning has emerged in the search for a theory explaining the universal existence of religions: They are found everywhere because they are useful, both for society and for individuals. Religions "do things" for us, such as helping us to define ourselves and making the world and life comprehensible to us. Functional explanations have come from many disciplines.

One version of the functional explanation is based on sociology. Pioneering work in this area was done by French sociologist Emile Durkheim (1858–1917). He proposed that humans cannot live without organized social structures, and that religion is a glue that holds a society together. Surely religions have the potential for creating harmony in society, for they all teach social virtues such as love, compassion, altruism, justice, and discipline over our desires and emotions. Political scientists Robert Putnam and David Campbell concluded from a survey of religiosity in the United States that people who are involved in organized religions are generally more generous toward their neighbors and more conscientious as citizens than those who do not participate in religions,[9] although critics have noted that it may be that the group affiliation that is part of religion is a better predictor of generosity than religious belief itself. The role of religion in the social process of identity formation at individual, family, community, and national levels is now being carefully examined, for people's identification with a particular religion can be manipulated to influence social change—either to thwart, moderate, or encourage it.

Biology also offers some functional reasons for the existence of religion. For instance, John Bowker, author of *Is God a Virus?*, asserts that religions are organized systems that serve the essential biological purpose of bringing people together for their common survival. To Bowker, religion is found universally because it protects gene replication and the nurturing of children. He proposes that because of its survival value, the potential for religiosity may even be genetically inherent in human brains.

Some medical professionals have found that religious faith may be good for our health. Research conducted by the Center for the Study of Religion/Spirituality and Health at Duke University found that those who attend religious services or read scriptures frequently are significantly longer lived, less likely to be depressed, less likely to have high blood pressure, and nearly ninety percent less likely to smoke. Many other studies have indicated that patients with strong faith recover faster from illness and operations. In contrast, however, some scholars have pointed out that some of the most religious regions of the world also have very high rates of disease, suggesting that it is not just religion but broader societal factors such as community support as well as access to health care that factor into overall wellbeing.

Many medical studies have also been done on the potential of prayer to heal illness, but results have been mixed. However, meditation has been proved to reduce mental stress and also to help develop positive emotions, even in the face of great difficulties. Citing laboratory tests of the mental calmness of Buddhists who practice "mindfulness" meditation, the Fourteenth Dalai Lama points out that:

> Over the millenniums, many practitioners have carried out what we might call "experiments" in how to overcome our tendencies toward destructive emotions. The

world today needs citizens and leaders who can work toward ensuring stability and engage in dialogue with the "enemy"—no matter what kind of aggression or assault they may have endured. If humanity is to survive, happiness and inner balance are crucial. We would do well to remember that the war against hatred and terror can be waged on this, the internal front, too.[10]

From the point of view of individual psychology, there are many explanations of the usefulness of religion. Psychoanalyst Sigmund Freud (1856–1938) suggested that religion fulfills neurotic needs. He described religion as a collective fantasy, a "universal obsessional neurosis"—a replaying of our loving and fearful relationships with our parents. Religious belief gives us a God powerful enough to protect us from the terrors of life, and will reward or punish us for obedience or nonobedience to social norms. From Freud's extremely sceptical point of view, religious belief is an illusion springing from people's infantile insecurity and neurotic guilt; as such it closely resembles mental illness.

On a more positive note, the twentieth-century psychoanalyst Erich Fromm (1900–1980) concluded that humans have a need for a stable frame of reference, and that religion fulfills this need. As Mata Amritanandamayi, a contemporary Indian spiritual teacher, explains:

Faith in God gives one the mental strength needed to confront the problems of life. Faith in the existence of God makes one feel safe and protected from all the evil influences of the world. To have faith in the existence of a Supreme Power and to live accordingly is a religion. When we become religious, morality arises, which, in turn, will help to keep us away from malevolent influences. We won't drink, we won't smoke, and we will stop wasting our energy through unnecessary gossip and talk. ... We will also develop qualities like love, compassion, patience, mental equipoise, and other positive traits. These will help us to love and serve everyone equally. ... Where there is faith, there is harmony, unity and love. A nonbeliever always doubts. ... He cannot be at peace; he's restless. ... The foundation of his entire life is unstable and scattered due to his lack of faith in a higher principle.[11]

For many, the desire for material achievement offers a temporary sense of purposefulness. But once achieved, material goals may seem hollow. Guru Tegh Bahadur, the Ninth Sikh Guru, said:

The whole world is just like a dream;
It will pass away in an instant,
Like a wall of sand,
[Though] built up and plastered with great care,
Which does not last even four days.
Likewise are the pleasures of mammon.[12]

Once this realization comes, a search for something more lasting and deeply meaningful may then arise.

Religions propose ideals that can radically transform people. Mahatma Gandhi (1869–1948) was an extremely shy, fearful child. His transformation into one of the great political figures of the twentieth century occurred as he meditated single-mindedly on the great Hindu scripture, the *Bhagavad-Gita*, particularly the second chapter, which he says was "inscribed on the tablet of my heart."[13] It reads, in part:

He is forever free who has broken
Out of the ego-cage of I and mine
To be united with the Lord of Love.
This is the supreme state. Attain thou this
And pass from death to immortality.[14]

People need inner strength for dealing with personal problems. Those who are suffering severe physical illness, privation, terror, or grief often turn to the divine for help. Conviction that Someone or Something that cannot be seen exists may be an antidote to the discomforting sense of being alone in the

Even in the midst of busy modern life, many people turn to Something they cannot see for spiritual help. These people are making food offerings in the popular Sik Sik Yuen Wong Tai Sin Daoist temple in Hong Kong in hope of spiritual healing for themselves or their loved ones.

universe. This isolation can be painful, even terrifying. The divine may be sought as a loving father or mother, or as a friend. Alternatively, some paths offer the way of self-transcendence. Through them, the sense of isolation is lost in mystical merger with the One Being, with the Ultimate Reality.

According to some Asian religions, the concept that we are distinct, autonomous individuals is an illusion; what we think of as "our" consciousnesses and "our" bodies is in perpetual flux. Thus, freedom from problems lies in accepting temporal change and devaluing the "small self" in favor of the eternal self. The ancient sages of India, whose teachings are preserved in the Upanishads, called this eternal self "the breathing behind breathing, the sight behind sight, the hearing behind hearing, the thinking behind thinking… "[15]

Buddhists see the problem of human existence differently. What humans have in common, they feel, is the suffering that comes from life's impermanence and our craving for it to remain the same. For Buddhists, reliance on an Absolute or God and the belief in a personal self or an Eternal Self only makes the suffering more intense. The solution is to let go of these ideas, to accept the groundlessness and openness of life, and to grow in clear awareness and humanistic values.

We may look to religions for understanding, for answers to our many questions about life. Is life just a series of random and chaotic incidents, or is there some meaning and order behind what is happening? Who are we? Why are we here? What happens after we die? Why is there suffering? Why is there evil? Is anybody up there listening? We have difficulty accepting the commonsense notion that this life is all there is. We are born, we struggle to support ourselves, we age, and we die. If we believe that there is nothing more, fear of death may inhibit enjoyment of life and make all human actions seem pointless. Confronting mortality is so basic to the spiritual life that, as the Christian monk Brother David Steindl-Rast observes, whenever monks from any spiritual tradition meet, within five minutes they are talking about death.

> *It appears that throughout the world man* [sic] *has always been seeking something beyond his own death, beyond his own problems, something that will be enduring, true and timeless. He has called it God, he has given it many names; and most of us believe in something of that kind, without ever actually experiencing it.*
>
> *Jiddu Krishnamurti*[16]

For those who find security in specific answers, some religions offer **dogma**—systems of doctrines proclaimed as absolutely true and accepted as such, even if they lie beyond the domain of one's personal experiences. Absolute faith provides some people with a secure feeling of rootedness, meaning, and orderliness in the midst of rapid social change. Religions may also provide rules for living, governing everything from diet to personal relationships. Such prescriptions may be seen as earthly reflections of the order that prevails in the cosmos. Some religions, however, encourage people to explore the perennial questions by themselves, and to live in the uncertainties of not knowing intellectually, breaking through old concepts until nothing remains but truth itself.

Faith perspective: Ultimate Reality exists

From the point of view of religious faith, there truly is an underlying reality that cannot readily be perceived. Human responses to this Ultimate Reality have been expressed and institutionalized as the structures of some religions.

How have people concluded that there is some supreme, Ultimate Reality, even though they may be unable to perceive it with their ordinary senses? Some simply accept what has been told to them or what is written in their holy books. Others have come to their own conclusions.

One path to faith is through deep questioning. Martin Luther (1483–1546), father of the Protestant branches of Christianity, recounted how he searched for faith in God through storms of doubt, "raged with a fierce and agitated conscience."[17] Jnana yoga practitioners probe the question "Who am I?" Gradually they strip away all of what they are not—for instance, "I am not the body, I am not the thinking"—and dig even into the roots of "I," until only pure Awareness remains.

The human mind does not function in the rational mode alone; there are other modes of consciousness. In his classic study *The Varieties of Religious Experience*, the philosopher William James (1842–1910) concluded:

Sufi dervishes in Sudan chant names of God's qualities as a way to God-realization.

Our normal waking consciousness, rational consciousness as we call it, is but one special type of consciousness, whilst all about it, parted from it by the flimsiest of screens, there lie potential forms of consciousness entirely different. … No account of the universe in its totality can be final which leaves these other forms of consciousness quite disregarded.[18]

To perceive truth directly, beyond the senses, beyond the limits of human reason, beyond blind belief, is often called **mysticism**. George William Russell (1867–1935), an Irish writer who described his mystical experiences under the pen name "AE," was lying on a hillside:

not then thinking of anything but the sunlight, and how sweet it was to drowse there, when, suddenly, I felt a fiery heart throb, and knew it was personal and intimate, and started with every sense dilated and intent, and turned inwards, and I heard first a music as of bells going away … and then the heart of the hills was opened to me, and I knew there was no hill for those who were there, and they were unconscious of the ponderous mountain piled above the palaces of light, and the winds were sparkling and diamond clear, yet full of colour as an opal, as they glittered through the valley, and I knew the Golden Age was all about me, and it was we who had been blind to it but that it had never passed away from the world.[19]

Encounters with this ordinarily unseen, Ultimate Reality are given various names in spiritual traditions: **enlightenment**, **realization**, illumination, satori, **awakening**, self-knowledge, **gnosis**, ecstatic communion, "coming home." Such a state may arise spontaneously, as in near-death experiences in which people seem to find themselves in a world of unearthly radiance, or may be induced by meditation, fasting, prayer, chanting, drugs, or dancing.

Many religions have developed meditation techniques that encourage intuitive wisdom to come forth. Whether this wisdom is perceived as a natural faculty within or an external voice, the process is similar. The consciousness is initially turned away from the world and even from one's own feelings and thoughts, letting them all go. Often a concentration practice, such as watching the breath or staring at a candle flame, is used to collect the awareness into a single, unfragmented focus. Once the mind is quiet, distinctions between inside and outside drop away. The seer becomes one with the seen, in a fusion of subject and object

A sense of the presence of the Great Unnamable may burst through the seeming ordinariness of life. (Samuel Palmer, The Rising of the Skylark, 1839, National Museum of Wales.)

through which the inner nature of things often seems to reveal itself.

Kabir, a fifteenth-century Indian weaver who was inspired alike by Islam and Hinduism and whose words are included in Sikh scripture, described the cosmic dimensions of this inner awakening:

> *The flute of the Infinite is played without ceasing, and its sound is love:*
> *When love renounces all limits, it reaches truth.*
> *How widely the fragrance spreads! It has no end, nothing stands in its way.*
> *The form of this melody is bright like a million suns: Incomparably sounds the vina, the vina of the notes of truth.*[20]

> *[The "flash of illumination" brings] a state of glorious inspiration, exaltation, intense joy, a piercingly sweet realization that the whole of life is fundamentally right and that it knows what it's doing.*
>
> *Nona Coxhead*[21]

Our ordinary experience of the world is that our self is separate from the world of objects that we perceive. But this dualistic understanding may be transcended in a moment of enlightenment in which the Real and our awareness of it become one. The *Mundaka Upanishad* says, "Lose thyself in the Eternal, even as the arrow is lost in the target." For the Hindu, this is the prized attainment of liberation, in which one enters into awareness of the eternal reality. This reality is then known with the same direct apprehension with which one knows oneself. The Sufi Muslim **mystic** Abu Yazid in the ninth century CE said, "I sloughed off my self as a snake sloughs off its skin, and I looked into my essence and saw that 'I am He.'"[22]

An alternative kind of spiritual experience brings one into contact with what the German professor of theology Rudolf Otto (1869–1937) called the "Wholly Other." Otto referred to this as **numinous**—a nonrational, nonsensory experience of that which is totally outside the self and cannot be described. In his landmark book *The Idea of the Holy*, Otto wrote of this mysterious experience as the heart of religion. It brings forth two general responses in a person: a feeling of great awe or even dread and, at the same time, a feeling of great attraction. These responses, in turn, have given rise to the whole gamut of religious beliefs and behaviors.

Though ineffable, the nature of religious experience that leads to faith is not unpredictable, according to the research of Joachim Wach (1898–1955), a German scholar of comparative religion. In every religion, it seems to follow a certain pattern: (1) It is an experience of what is considered Ultimate Reality; (2) It involves the person's whole being; (3) It is the most shattering and intense of all human experiences; and (4) It motivates the person to action, through worship, ethical behavior, service, and sharing with others in a religious grouping.

Understandings of Ultimate Reality

What are the different ways in which the nature of Ultimate Reality has been understood?

In the struggle to understand what the mind cannot readily grasp, individuals and cultures have come to rather different conclusions. Mircea Eliade (1907–1986) was a very influential scholar who helped to develop the field of **comparative religion**. This discipline attempts to understand and compare religious patterns found around the world. He used the terms "sacred" and "profane": The **profane** is the everyday world of seemingly random, ordinary, and unimportant occurrences. The **sacred** is the realm of extraordinary, apparently purposeful, but generally imperceptible forces. In the realm of the sacred lies the source of the universe and its values. However relevant this dichotomy may be in describing some religions, there are some cultures that do not make a clear distinction between the sacred and the profane. Many indigenous peoples who have an intimate connection with their local landscape feel that spiritual power is everywhere; there is nothing that is not sacred. Trees, mountains, animals—everything is perceived as being alive with sacred presence.

Another distinction made in the study of comparative religion is that between "immanent" and "transcendent" views of sacred reality. To understand that reality as **immanent** is to experience it as present in the world. To understand it as **transcendent** is to believe that it exists outside of the material universe (e.g., "God is out there").

The nature of Ultimate Reality is another area in which we find great differences among religious traditions. Many people perceive the sacred as a personal being, as Father, Mother, Teacher, Friend, Beloved, or as a specific deity. Religions based on one's relationship to a Divine Being are called **theistic**. If the being is worshiped as a singular form, the religion is called **monotheistic**. If many attributes and forms of the divine are

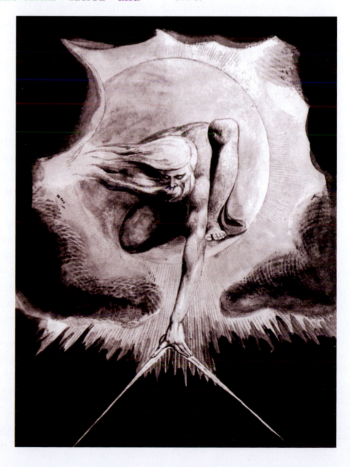

The concept of God as an old man with a beard who rules the world from the sky has been supported by the art of patriarchal monotheistic traditions, such as William Blake's frontispiece to "Europe," The Act of Creation, 1794.

EXCLUSIVISM VS. UNIVERSALISM

A Letter from I. H. Azad Faruqi

In this letter, the highly respected Muslim scholar Dr. I. H. Azad Faruqi, Professor of Islamic Studies and Honorary Director of the Centre for the Study of Comparative Religions and Civilizations, Jamia Milia Islamia, New Delhi, gives his views on exclusivist and universalist standpoints.

Despite the attitude of the majority of the followers of world religions justifying the claims of exclusive nature found in almost all world religions, there are sufficient grounds in the scriptures of these traditions which allow a universalistic interpretation of the phenomenon of the multiplicity of religions. That is, the scriptures of the various world religions within themselves contain the elements which can be interpreted to claim a viewpoint looking at various religious traditions as so many paths leading to the same Goal.

Secondly, almost all world religions contain a vision of a Supreme Reality, which ultimately is considered beyond the categories of the rational thought, Incomprehensible and Unlimited. Thus, by their own admission these traditions appear to claim their vision of, and approach to, the Supreme Reality as short of exhausting It, and limited to a particular view of It.

Otherwise also, although almost all the basic truths and aspects of religious life are represented in each of the religious traditions, each of these traditions tends to emphasize certain dimensions of the religious experience more than others. And these particular accentuations, at the core of the spiritual experience of these traditions, *are the factors which appear to determine the special hue or distinctiveness of these traditions. Thus, each of the different religious traditions can be claimed to express some particular aspects of the Ultimate Reality which, in spite of its myriad manifestations, remains unfathomable and far beyond the sum of all Its expressions. Seen from this perspective, the uniqueness of each religious tradition, and Its particular experience of the Supreme Reality, should no more remain as a hindrance in the cordial relations amongst them, as the usual case has been hitherto. Rather, these very particularities and distinctions would turn into the grounds for mutual attraction between them.*

Thirdly, the individualistic claims of various religions can be taken as true only in a relative sense. Each of the religious traditions being a close and complete world in itself, these are bound to claim their particular standpoints as absolute. Perhaps these could not develop into self-sufficient traditions in their own right without their exclusivist claims of being the only truly guided ones. But today, in the pluralistic societies of modern times, the claims of these traditions having the monopoly of the Supreme Truth can be considered as relatively absolute only, if the term of a relative absolute can be permitted. That is, we can attempt to approach and study these traditions on their own grounds, with a more humble attitude, and let them speak from within their own world, while being aware that this is only one world out of many such worlds.[23]

Buddhism is sometimes referred to as a nontheistic religion, for its beliefs do not refer to a personal deity. Practitioners try to perceive the impermanence and interdependence of all things.

emphasized, the religion may be labeled **polytheistic**. Religions that hold that beneath the multiplicity of apparent forms there is one underlying principle or substance are called **monistic**.

Ultimate Reality may also be conceived in **nontheistic** terms, as a "changeless Unity," as "Suchness," or simply as "the Way." There may be no sense of a personal Creator God in such understandings; in nontheistic traditions, Ultimate Reality may instead be perceived as impersonal.

Some people believe that the Ultimate Reality is usually invisible but occasionally appears visibly in human **incarnations**, such as Christ or Krishna, or in special manifestations, such as the flame Moses reportedly saw coming from the center of a bush but not consuming it. Or the deity that cannot be seen may be described in human terms. Christian theologian Sallie McFague thus writes of God as "lover" by imputing human feelings to God:

God as lover is the one who loves the world not with the fingertips but totally and passionately, taking pleasure in its variety and richness, finding it attractive and valuable, delighting in its fulfilment. God as lover is the moving power of love in the universe, the desire for unity with all the beloved.[24]

Throughout history, there have been **exclusivist** religious authorities—in other words, those who claim that they worship the only true deity and label all others as "pagans" or "nonbelievers." For their part, the others apply similar negative epithets to them. When these rigid positions are taken, often to the point of violent conflicts or forced conversions, there is no room to consider the possibility that all may be talking about the same indescribable thing in different languages or referring to different aspects of the same unknowable Whole—a position which may be called **universalism**.

Atheism is the belief that there is no deity. Atheists may reject theistic beliefs because they seem to be incompatible with the existence of evil in the world, or because there is little or no concrete proof that God exists, or because they reject the concept of God as an old man in the sky, or because theistic beliefs seem unscientific, or because they inhibit human independence. In 2009, atheists in Britain mounted a major campaign to put up

billboards and signs on buses proclaiming, "There's probably no God. Now stop worrying and enjoy your life." A movement called "New Atheism" is attacking religious faith as being not only wrong, but actually evil because it can be used to support violence. As we will see throughout this book, extremist religious views have indeed been used throughout history to justify political violence and oppression. One of the leading figures in the New Atheism movement is Richard Dawkins, Oxford Professor of the Public Understanding of Science and author of *The Selfish Gene* and *The God Delusion*. Around him a debate is raging about whether science itself is fully "scientific," in the sense of being totally objective, or whether it is a culturally shaped enterprise based on unproven assumptions— the same criticism that its atheistic proponents make about religious faith.

Agnosticism is not the denial of the divine but the feeling "I don't know whether it exists or not," or the belief that if it exists it is impossible for humans to know it. Religious scepticism has been a current in Western thought since classical times; it was given the name "agnosticism" in the nineteenth century by T. H. Huxley, who stated its basic principles as a denial of metaphysical beliefs and of most (in his case) Christian beliefs since they are unproven or unprovable, and their replacement with scientific method for examining facts and experiences.

Humanism is an approach to life that focuses on humans' responsibility to lead ethical lives and work for the good of all humanity without any belief in the supernatural.[25] There is also **secularism**, in which people go about their daily lives without any reference to religion: All focus is on material life. This trend is particularly pronounced in contemporary Europe.

These categories are not mutually exclusive, so attempts to apply the labels can sometimes confuse us rather than help us understand religions. In some polytheistic traditions there is a hierarchy of gods and goddesses with one highest being at the top. In Hinduism, each individual deity is understood as an embodiment of all aspects of the divine. In the paradoxes that occur when we try to apply human logic and language to that which transcends rational thought, a person may believe that God is both a highly personal being and also present in all things. Or mystics may have personal encounters with the divine and yet find it so unspeakable that they say it is beyond human knowing. The Jewish scholar Maimonides (1135–1204) asserted that:

> *the human mind cannot comprehend God. Only God can know Himself. The only form of comprehension of God we can have is to realize how futile it is to try to comprehend Him.*[26]

Jaap Sahib, the great hymn of praises of God by the Tenth Sikh Guru, Guru Gobind Singh, consists largely of the negative attributes of God, such as these:

Atheists in Britain ran a large-scale campaign to advertise their point of view, posting large signs proclaiming "There's probably no God. Now stop worrying and enjoy your life" on buses and in public places.

Father Bede Griffiths emphasized the common elements found in all religions.

Salutations to the One without colour or hue,
Salutations to the One who hath no beginning.
Salutations to the Impenetrable,
Salutations to the Unfathomable …
O Lord, Thou art Formless and Peerless
Beyond birth and physical elements. …
Salutations to the One beyond confines of religion. …
Beyond description and Garbless
Thou art Nameless and Desireless.
Thou art beyond thought and ever Mysterious.[27]

Some people believe that the aspect of the divine that they perceive is the only one. Others feel that there is one being with many faces, that all religions come from one source. Bede Griffiths (1906–1993), a Catholic monk who lived in a community in India attempting to unite Asian and Western traditions, was one who thought that if we engage in a deep study of all religions we will find their common ground:

In each tradition the one divine Reality, the one eternal Truth, is present, but it is hidden under symbols. … Always the divine Mystery is hidden under a veil, but each revelation (or "unveiling") unveils some aspect of the one Truth, or, if you like, the veil becomes thinner at a certain point. The Semitic religions, Judaism and Islam, reveal the transcendent aspect of the divine Mystery with incomparable power. The oriental religions reveal the divine Immanence with immeasurable depth. Yet in each the opposite aspect is contained, though in a more hidden way.[28]

Ritual, symbol, and myth

Why are rituals, symbols, and myths important in religions?

Many of the phenomena of religion are ways of worship, symbols, and myths. Worship consists in large part of attempts to express reverence and perhaps to enter into communion with that which is worshiped or to request help with problems such as ill health, disharmony, or poverty. Around the world, rituals, sacraments, prayers, and spiritual practices are used to create a sacred atmosphere or state of consciousness necessary to convey the requests for help, to bring some human control over things that are not ordinarily controllable (such as rainfall), to sanctify and explain the meaning of major life stages such as birth, puberty, marriage, and death, or to provide spiritual instruction.

Ritual

When such actions are predictable and repeated rather than spontaneous, they are known as **rituals.** Group rituals may be conducted by priests or other ritual specialists or by the people themselves. There may be actions such as recitation of prayers, chants, scriptures or stories, singing, dancing, sharing of food, spiritual purification by water, lighting of candles or oil lamps, and offerings of flowers, fragrances, and food to the divine. Professor Antony Fernando of Sri Lanka explains that when food offerings are made to the deities:

Even the most illiterate person knows that in actual fact no god really picks up those offerings or is actually in need of them. What people offer is what they own. Whatever is owned becomes so close to the heart of the owner as to become an almost integral part of his or her life. Therefore, when people offer something, it is, as it were, themselves they offer. … Sacrifices and offerings are a dramatic way of proclaiming that they are not the ultimate possessors of their life and also of articulating their determination to live duty-oriented lives and not desire-oriented lives.[29]

Music, chants, and other kinds of sound play very significant roles in religious rituals, whether it is the noisy bursting of firecrackers to scare away unwanted spirits at Chinese graves or choral singing of *Kyrie Eleison* (Lord have mercy) in a sublime composition by the eighteenth-century composer Johann Sebastian Bach. Ethnomusicologist Guy Beck identifies many purposes for which sacred sounds may be used in religions: to ask for favors or blessings, to ask forgiveness for sins, to praise and thank the Creator, to chase away demons, to invoke the presence and blessings of deities, to make prayerful requests, to develop a mood of inner quietude or repentance, to purify the worshiper, to paint pictures of a future state of being, to create communion between the human and divine worlds, to teach doctrines, to create states of ecstasy and bliss, to empty and then fulfill, to invigorate, and to express jubilation.[30] The effects of sounds on mind and heart are so touching that sacred texts or messages are often chanted or sung rather than simply read or recited. Speaking from a theistic point of view, nineteenth-century musicologist Edmund Gurney reflected:

> *The link between sound and the supernatural is profound and widespread. ...*
> *If we are believers, then we can believe that the spirit is moving us in our ritual*
> *music. Ritual sound makes the transcendent immanent. It is at the same time*
> *ours, our own sounds pressing in around us and running through us like a*
> *vital current of belief, molding us into a living interior that is proof against the*
> *unbelieving emptiness that lies around.[31]*

Paintings and other forms of art have also inspired religious experience. John Damascus of Byzantium (*c.* 675–749 CE) proclaimed:

> *Paintings are the books of the illiterate. They distract those who look at them with*
> *a silent voice and sanctify life. ... If I have no books I go to church, pricked as by*
> *spines by my thoughts; the flower of painting makes me look, charms my eyes as*
> *does a flowering meadow and softly distils the glory of God in my soul.[32]*

Symbol

What religions attempt to approach may be considered beyond human utterance. Believers build statues and buildings through which to worship the divine, but these forms are not the divine itself. Because people are addressing the invisible, it can be suggested only through metaphor. Deepest consciousness cannot speak the language of everyday life; what it knows can be suggested

Places of worship are often designed as visual symbols of religious ideals. The Baha'i Temple in New Delhi was crafted in the shape of a lotus, symbol of beauty and purity rising divinely above stagnant water, and its nine-sided structure symbolizes the unity of all world religions.

only in **symbols**—images borrowed from the material world that are similar to ineffable spiritual experiences. For example, attempts to allude to spiritual merging with Ultimate Reality may borrow the language of human love. The great thirteenth-century Hindu saint Akka Mahadevi sang of her longing for union with the Beloved by using powerful symbolic language of self-surrender:

> *Like a silkworm weaving her house with love*
> *From her marrow and dying in her body's threads*
> *Winding tight, round and round, I burn*
> *Desiring what the heart desires.*[33]

Tracing symbols throughout the world, researchers find many similarities in their use in different cultures. Ultimate Reality is often symbolized as a Father or Mother, because it is thought to be the source of life, sustenance, and protection. It is frequently associated with heights, with its invisible power perceived as coming from a "place" that is spiritually "higher" than the material world. The sky thus becomes heaven, the abode of the god or gods and perhaps also the pleasant realm to which good people go when they die. A vertical symbol—such as a tree, a pillar, or a mountain—is understood as the center of the world in many cultures, for it gives physical imagery to a connection between earth and the unseen "heavenly" plane. The area beneath the surface of the earth is often perceived as an "underworld," a rather dangerous place where life goes on in a different way than on the surface.

Some theorists assert that in some cases these common symbols are not just logical associations with the natural world. Most notably, the psychologist Carl Jung (1875–1961) proposed that humanity as a whole has a collective unconscious, a global psychic inheritance of archetypal symbols from which geographically separate cultures have drawn. These archetypes include such symbolic characters as the wise old man, the great mother, the original man and woman, the hero, the shadow, and the trickster.

Extended metaphors may be understood as **allegories**—narratives that use concrete symbols to convey abstract ideas. The biblical book attributed to the Hebrew prophet Ezekiel, for instance, is full of such allegorical passages. In one he says that God's spirit led him to a valley full of dry bones. As he watched and spoke as God told him, the bones developed flesh and muscles, became joined together into bodies, and rose to their feet. The voice of God in the scripture explains the allegorical meaning: the bones represent the people of Israel, who have been abandoned by their self-serving leaders and become scattered and preyed upon by wild beasts, like the sheep of uncaring shepherds. God promises to dismiss the shepherds, raise the fallen people and restore them to the land of Israel, where they will live peacefully under God's protection (Ezekiel 34–37). Such allegories may assume great significance in a people's self-understanding.

This symbolic representation of a World Tree comes from 18th-century Iran. It is conceived as a tree in Paradise, about which the Prophet Muhammad reportedly said, "God planted it with His own hand and breathed His spirit into it."

Myth

Symbols are also woven together into **myths**—the symbolic stories that communities use to explain the universe and their place within it. Like many cultures, Polynesians tell a myth of the world's creation in which the world was initially covered with water and shrouded in darkness. When the Supreme Being, Io, wanted to rise from rest, he uttered words that immediately brought light into the darkness. Then at his word the waters and the heavens were separated, the land was shaped, and all beings were created. Myths may purport to explain how things came to be as they are, perhaps incorporating elements of historical truth, and in any case are treated as sacred history.

Joseph Campbell (1904–1987), who carried out extensive analysis of myths around the world, found that myths have four primary functions: mystical (evoking our awe, love, wonder, gratitude); cosmological (presenting explanations of the universe based on the existence and actions of spiritual powers or beings); sociological (adapting people to orderly social life, teaching ethical codes); and psychological (opening doors to inner exploration, development of one's full potential, and adjustment to life cycle changes). Understood in these senses, myths are not falsehoods or the works of primitive imaginations; they can be deeply meaningful and transformational, forming a sacred belief structure that supports the laws and institutions of the religion and the ways of the community, as well as explaining the people's place within the cosmos. Campbell paid particular attention to myths of the hero's journey, in which the main character is separated from the group, undergoes hardships and initiation, and returns bearing truth to the people. Such stories, he felt, prepare and inspire the listener for the difficult inward journey that leads to spiritual transformation:

> It is the business of mythology to reveal the specific dangers and techniques of the dark interior way from tragedy to comedy. Hence the incidents are fantastic and "unreal": they represent psychological, not physical, triumphs. The passage of the mythological hero may be overground, [but] fundamentally it is inward—into depths where obscure resistances are overcome, and long lost, forgotten powers are revivified, to be made available for the transfiguration of the world.[34]

Absolutist and liberal responses to modernity

How do absolutist and liberal interpretations of a tradition differ?

Traditional religious understandings are under increasing pressure from the rapidly growing phenomenon of globalization. Complex in its dynamics and manifestations, **globalization** has been defined by Global Studies Professor Manfred Steger as "the expansion and intensification of social relations and consciousness across world-time and world-space."[35] Local cultures and community ties have rapidly given way to hybrid homogenized patterns that have evolved in countries such as the United States. "McDonaldization" of the world, fueled by ever faster and more accessible means of communication and transportation, transnational corporations, free trade, urbanization, and unrestrained capitalism, has made deep inroads into traditional local cultural ways. As a result, there is increasing tension between those who want to preserve their traditional ways and values and those who open doors to change.

Within each faith people may thus have different ways of interpreting their traditions. The **orthodox** stand by an historical form of their religion, strictly following its established practices, laws, and **creeds**. Those who resist contemporary influences and affirm what they perceive as the historical core of their religion could be called **absolutists**. In our times, many people feel that their identity as individuals or as members of an established group is threatened by the sweeping changes brought by modern global industrial culture. The breakup of family relationships, loss of geographic rootedness, decay of clear behavioral codes, and loss of local control may be very unsettling. To find a stable footing, to attempt to preserve their distinctive identity as a people in the face of modernity and secularization, some people may try to stand on selected religious doctrines

Angels Weep

Wherever there is slaughter of innocent men, women, and children for the mere reason that they belong to another race, color, or nationality, or were born into a faith which the majority of them could never quite comprehend and hardly ever practice in its true spirit; wherever the fair name of religion is used as a veneer to hide overweening political ambition and bottomless greed, wherever the glory of Allah is sought to be proclaimed through the barrel of a gun; wherever piety becomes synonymous with rapacity, and morality cowers under the blight of expediency and compromise, wherever it be—in Yugoslavia or Algeria, in Liberia, Chad, or the beautiful land of the Sudan, in Los Angeles or Abuja, in Kashmir or Conakry, in Colombo or Cotabato—there God is banished and Satan is triumphant, there the angels weep and the soul of man cringes; there in the name of God humans are dehumanized; and there the grace and beauty of life lie ravished and undone.

*Dr. Syed Z. Abedin, Director of the
Institute for Muslim Minority Affairs,
Jeddah, Saudi Arabia*[36]

or practices from the past. Religious leaders may encourage this trend toward rigidity by declaring themselves absolute authorities or by telling the people that their scriptures are literally and exclusively true. They may encourage antipathy or even violence against people of other religious traditions.

The term **fundamentalism** is often applied to this selective insistence on parts of a religious tradition and to highly negative views of people of other religions. This use of the term is misleading, for no religion is based on hatred of other people and because those who are labeled "fundamentalists" may not be engaged in a return to the true basics of their religion. A Muslim "fundamentalist" who insists on the veiling of women, for instance, does not draw this doctrine from the foundation of Islam, the Holy Qur'an, but rather from historical cultural practice in some Muslim countries. A Sikh "fundamentalist" who concentrates on externals, such as wearing a turban, sword, and steel bracelet, overlooks the central insistence of the Sikh Gurus on the inner rather than outer practice of religion.

A further problem with the use of the term "fundamentalism" is that it has a specifically Protestant Christian connotation. The Christian fundamentalist movement originated in the late nineteenth century as a reaction to liberal trends, such as historical-critical study of the Bible, which will be explained below. Other labels may, therefore, be more cross-culturally appropriate, such as "absolutist," "extremist," or "reactionary," depending on the particular situation.

Those who are called religious **liberals**, also sometimes called progressives, take a more flexible approach to religious tradition. They may see scriptures as products of a specific culture and time rather than the eternal voice of truth, and may interpret passages metaphorically rather than literally. If activists, they may advocate reforms in the ways their religion is officially understood and practiced.

While absolutists tend to take their scriptures and received religious traditions as literally true, liberals have for several centuries been engaged in a different approach to understanding their own religions and those of others: **historical-critical studies**. These are academic attempts to reconstruct the historical life stories of prophets and their cultures as opposed to legends about them, and to subject their scriptures to objective analysis. Such academic study of religion neither accepts nor rejects the particular truth-claims of any religion.

Non-faith-based methods of **exegesis** (critical explanation or interpretation of texts) reveal that "sacred" scriptures may include polemics against opponents of the religion, myths, cultural influences, ethical instruction, later interpolations, mistakes by copyists, literary devices, factual history, and genuine spiritual inspiration. This process began with historical-critical study of the Bible at the end of the eighteenth century and has expanded to include scriptures of other traditions, such as the Holy Qur'an of Islam, the Dao de jing of Daoism, and Buddhist and Hindu texts.

One area of research is to try to determine the original or most reliable form of a particular text. Another focus is ferreting out the historical aspects of the text, with help from external sources such as archaeological findings, to determine the historical setting in which it was probably composed, its actual author or authors, and possible sources of its material, such as oral or written traditions. Such research may conclude that material about a certain period may have been written later and include perspectives from that later period, or that a text with one person's name as author may actually be a collection of writings by different people. A third area of research asks, "What was the intended audience?" A fourth examines the language and meanings of the words. A fifth looks at whether a scripture or passage follows a particular literary form, such as poetry, legal code, miracle story, allegory, parable, hymn, narrative, or sayings. A sixth focuses on the **redaction**, or editing and organizing, of the scripture and the development of an authorized **canon** designed to speak not only to the local community but also to a wider audience. Yet another approach is to look at the scripture in terms of its universal and contemporary relevance, rather than its historicity.

Although such research attempts to be objective, it is not necessarily undertaken with sceptical intentions. To the contrary, these forms of research are taught in many seminaries as ways of reconciling faith with reason. Nevertheless, such analyses may be seen as offensive and/or false by orthodox believers. In any case, they are not perfect, for there are gaps in the available data and they can be interpreted in various ways. Scriptures also serve different purposes in different traditions, and these differences must be understood.

The encounter between science and religion
What major positions have emerged in the dialogue between science and religion?

Like religion, science is also engaged in searching for universal principles that explain the facts of nature. The two approaches have influenced each other since ancient times, when they were not seen as separate endeavors. In both Asia and the West, there were continual attempts to understand reality as a whole.

Historical background

In ancient Greece, source of many "Western" ideas, a group of thinkers who are sometimes called "nature philosophers" tried to understand the world through their own perceptions of it. By contrast, Plato (c. 427–347 BCE) distrusted the testimony of the human senses. He thus made a series of distinctions: between what is perceived by the senses and what is accessible through reason, between body and soul, appearance and reality, objects and ideas. In Plato's thought, the soul was superior to the body, and the activity of reason preferable to the distraction of the senses. This value judgment dominated Western thought through the Middle Ages, with its underlying belief that all of nature had been created by God for the sake of humanity.

In the seventeenth century, knowledge of nature became more secularized (that is, divorced from the sacred) as scientists developed models of the universe as a giant machine. Its ways could be discovered by human reason, by studying its component parts and mathematically quantifying its characteristics. However, even in discovering such features, many scientists regarded them as the work of a divine Creator or Ruler. Isaac Newton (1642–1727), whose gravitational theory shaped modern physics, speculated that space is eternal because it is the emanation of "eternal and immutable being." Drawing on biblical quotations, Newton argued that God exists everywhere, containing, discerning, and ruling all things.

During the eighteenth-century Enlightenment, rational ways of knowing were increasingly respected, with a concurrent growing scepticism toward claims of knowledge derived from such sources as divine revelation or illuminated inner wisdom. The sciences were viewed as progressive; some thinkers attacked institutionalized religions and dogma as superstitions. According to scientific materialism, which developed during the nineteenth and twentieth centuries, the supernatural is imaginary; only the material world is real.

The old unitary concepts of science and religion received another serious challenge in 1859, when the naturalist Charles Darwin (1809–1882) published *On the Origin of Species*, a work that propounded the theory of evolution by natural selection. Darwin demonstrated that certain genetic mutations give an organism a competitive advantage over others of its species. As evolutionary biology has continued to develop since Darwin through genetic research, it shows that those carrying advantageous genes statistically produce more offspring that survive to breed themselves, so the percentage of the new gene gradually increases in the gene pool. Evolutionary studies are revealing more and more evidence of what appear to be gradual changes in organisms, as recorded in fossil records, footprints, and genetic records encoded in DNA. According to evolutionary biology theory, over great lengths of time such gradual changes have brought the development of all forms of life. The theory of natural selection directly contradicted a literal understanding of the biblical Book of Genesis, in which God is said to have created all life in only six days. By the end of the nineteenth century, all such beliefs of the Judeo-Christian tradition were being questioned.

Science and religion: recent developments

However, as science has progressed during the twentieth and twenty-first centuries, it has in some senses moved back toward a more nuanced understanding of religious belief. Science has always questioned its own assumptions and theories, and scientists have given up trying to find absolute certainties. From

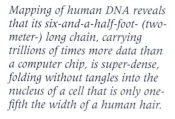

Mapping of human DNA reveals that its six-and-a-half-foot- (two-meter-) long chain, carrying trillions of times more data than a computer chip, is super-dense, folding without tangles into the nucleus of a cell that is only one-fifth the width of a human hair.

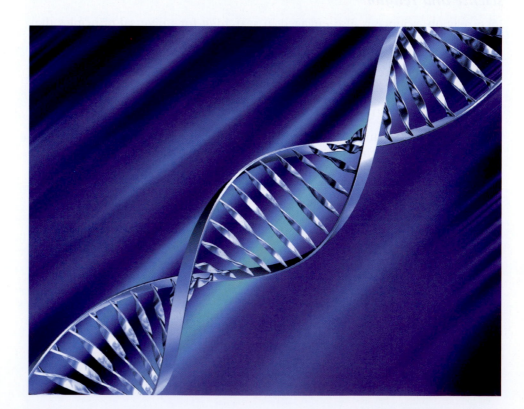

The Hubble space telescope reveals an unimaginably vast cosmos, with billions of galaxies in continual flux. The Eagle nebula shown here is giving birth to new stars in "pillars of creation" which are six trillion miles (ten trillion kilometers) high.

contemporary scientific research, it is clear that the cosmos is mind-boggling in its complexity and that what we perceive with our five senses is not ultimately real. For instance, the inertness and solidity of matter are only illusions. Each atom consists mostly of empty space with tiny particles whirling around in it. These subatomic particles—such as neutrons, protons, and electrons—cannot even be described as "things." Theories of quantum mechanics, in trying to account for the tiniest particles of matter, uncovered the Uncertainty Principle: that the position and velocity of a subatomic particle cannot be simultaneously determined. These particles behave like energy as well as like matter, like waves as well as like particles. Their behaviors can best be described in terms of a dynamic, interdependent system that includes the observer. As physicist David Bohm (1917–1994) put it, "Everything interpenetrates everything."[37]

Our own bodies appear relatively solid, but they are in a constant state of flux and interchange with the environment. Our eyes, ears, noses, tongues, and skin do not reveal absolute truths. Rather, our sensory organs may operate as filters, selecting from a multidimensional universe only those characteristics that we need to perceive in order to survive. Imagine how difficult it would be simply to walk across a street if we could see all the electromagnetic energy in the atmosphere, such as X-rays, radio waves, gamma rays, and infrared and ultraviolet light, rather than only the small band of colors we see as the visible spectrum. Though the sky of a starry night appears vast to the naked eye, the giant Hubble telescope placed in space has revealed an incomprehensibly immense cosmos whose limits have not been found. It contains matter-gobbling black holes, vast starmaking clusters, intergalactic collisions, and cosmic events that happened billions of years ago, so far away that their light is only now being captured by the most powerful instruments we have for examining what lies far beyond our small place in this galaxy. We know that more lies beyond what we have yet been able to measure. And even our ability to conceive of what we cannot sense may perhaps be limited by the way the human brain is organized.

As science continues to question its own assumptions, various new hypotheses are being suggested about the nature of the universe. "Superstring theory" proposes that the universe may not be made of particles at all, but rather of tiny vibrating strings and loops of strings. According to superstring theory, whereas we think we are living in four dimensions of space and time, there may be at least ten dimensions, with the unperceived dimensions "curled up" or "compactified" within the four dimensions that we can perceive. According to another current theory, the cosmos is like a soccer ball, a finite closed system with many facets.

New branches of science are finding that the universe is not always predictable, nor does it always operate according to human notions of cause and effect. Physicist Murray Gell-Mann says that we are "a small speck of creation believing it is capable of comprehending the whole."[38] And whereas scientific models of the universe were until recently based on the assumption of stability and equilibrium, physicist Ilya Prigogine observes that "today we see instability, fluctuations, irreversibility at every level."[39]

Physicist Hans-Peter Dürr, winner of the Right Livelihood Award (often described as the "Alternative Nobel Prize"), describes the dilemma that these discoveries pose to human understanding:

> *We found out that matter is not existent. At the beginning, there is only something which changes. How can something which is in-between create something which can be grasped? ... We are part of the same organism which we cannot talk about. If I explain it, try to catch it with language, I destroy it. The Creation and the Creator cannot be seen as separate. There is only oneness.*[40]

> *The most beautiful and profound emotion that we can experience is the sensation of the mystical. It is the sower of all true science. He to whom this emotion is a stranger, who can no longer wonder and stand rapt in awe, is as good as dead. To know that what is impenetrable to us really exists, manifesting itself as the highest wisdom and the most radiant beauty which our dull faculties can comprehend only in their most primitive forms—this knowledge, this feeling is at the center of true religiousness. ... A human being is part of the whole. ... He experiences himself, his thoughts and feelings as something separated from the rest—a kind of optical delusion of his consciousness. ... Our task must be to free ourselves from this prison by widening our circle of compassion to embrace all living creatures, and the whole [of] nature in its beauty.*
>
> *Albert Einstein*[41]

In the work of physicists such as David Bohm, physics approaches **metaphysics**—philosophy based on theories of subtle realities that transcend the physical world. Bohm described the dimensions we see and think of as "real" as the *explicate* order. Behind it lies the *implicate* order, in which separateness resolves into unbroken wholeness. Beyond may lie other subtle dimensions, all merging into an infinite ground that unfolds itself as light. This scientific theory is very similar to descriptions by mystics from all cultures about their intuitive experiences of the cosmos. They speak of realities beyond normal human perceptions of space and time. The Hindu term "*Brahma*," for instance, means "vast"—a vastness perceived by sages as infinite dimensions of a Supreme Consciousness that started without any material and then Itself became the Creation. In the realization of Guru Nanak, first of the Sikh Gurus, God is "*Akal Murat*"—Reality that transcends time.

When Science Approaches Religion

Theoretical physicist Paul Davies (b. 1946) has won the Templeton Prize, a prestigious international award for contribution to thinking about religion. He suggests that science approaches religion when it asks fundamental questions:

If you are a biologist and you get stuck, you might go to a chemist to help you out. If a chemist gets stuck, you might get a physicist. If you're a physicist and you get stuck, there's nowhere to go except theology, because physics is the most basic science. It's at the base of the explanatory pyramid upon which everything else is built. It deals with the fundamental laws of nature. And that inevitably prompts us to ask questions like, "Why those laws? Where have they come from? Why are they mathematical? What does it mean? Could they be different?" Clearly these are questions on the borderline between science and philosophy, or science and theology.

The early scientists perceived this natural order and its hidden mathematical content, and they thought it derived from a creator-being. What happened in the centuries that followed was that science accepted the existence of a real order in nature. You can't be a scientist if you don't believe that there is some sort of order that is at least in part comprehensible to us. So you have to make two enormous assumptions—which don't have to be right. But to be a scientist, you've got to believe they're true. First, that there is a rational order in nature. Second, that we can come to understand nature, at least in part. What an extraordinary thing this is to believe in! There is a rational, comprehensible order in nature. Science asserts that the world isn't arbitrary or absurd.

If I use the word "God," it is not in the sense of a super-being who has existed for all eternity and, like a cosmic magician, brings the universe into being at some moment in time on a whimsical basis. When I

refer to "God," it is in the sense of the rational ground in which the whole scientific enterprise is rooted. The God I'm referring to is not really a person or a being in the usual sense. In particular, it is something that is outside of time. That is a very significant issue, and one on which there can be a very fruitful exchange, in my opinion, between physics and philosophy.

Almost all of my physics colleagues, and scientists from other disciplines, even if they would cast themselves as militant atheists, are deeply inspired by the wonder, the beauty, the ingenuity of nature, and the underlying, law-like mathematical order.

It could be that there are some things that are simply going to be forever beyond scientific enquiry—not because we're lacking the money or the expertise or something of that sort, but because there are inherent limits to how far rational enquiry can take us. If science leaves us with mystery, is there a way that we can come to know about the world, about existence, not through scientific enquiry but through some other method? I'm open-minded as to whether that is the case. I'm talking here about revelatory or mystical experiences, where somehow the answer is grasped—not through rational enquiry, nor through experimentation, but by "knowing" in some internal sense.

Nothing I have said deals with the sort of issues we struggle with in daily life, which are ethical and moral issues. The weakness of restricting to a God who's just some sort of abstract, mathematical, rational ground for the world is that it doesn't provide us with any sort of moral guidance. Most people turn to religion not because they want to understand how the universe is put together, but because they want to understand how their own lives are put together, and what they should do next. You don't go to a physicist to ask about right and wrong.[42]

Science is moving beyond its earlier mechanical models toward more dynamic biological models. For instance, James Lovelock has proposed the Gaia Theory of the earth as a complex, self-regulating organism of sorts, but he does not see it as the work of any Grand Planner. He explains:

> Gaia theory sees the earth as a complete system made up of all the living things. … The whole of that constitutes a single system that regulates itself, keeps the climate constant and comfortable for life, keeps the chemical composition of the atmosphere so that it's always breathable. [The earth] is not alive like an animal. What I am implying is alive in the sense of being able to regulate itself. It's a system that evolved automatically, without any purpose, foresight, or anything. It just happened and has been in existence now for about three and a half to four billion years.[43]

In the United States, the conservative Christian community has objected to mechanistic scientific theories of biological evolution, preferring **Creationism**, the concept of intentional divine creation of all life forms. **Intelligent design** theory has been cited to support the religious concept of Creationism. According to intelligent design theorists, scientific discoveries of the complexities and perfections of life can be said to prove the existence of an Intelligent Designer. For instance, if the weak force in the nucleus of an atom were a small fraction weaker, there would be no hydrogen in the universe—and thus no water. Biologists find that the natural world is an intricate harmony of beautifully elaborated, interrelated parts. Even to produce the miniature propeller that allows a tiny bacterium to swim, some forty different proteins are required.

The intelligent design movement concludes that there must be a Creator. However, science is a method of proposing testable hypotheses and testing them, whereas the intelligent-design hypothesis is not testable. In 2005, the judge in a landmark case in Dover, Pennsylvania, ruled that intelligent design could not be recommended to ninth-grade biology students because intelligent design does not qualify as science—unless the definition of science is changed to include supernatural explanations—and because the First Amendment of the Constitution prevents government officials from imposing any particular religion or religious belief.

In the current dialogue between science and religion, four general positions have emerged. One is a conflict model, which is most apparent in issues such as creation, with some scientists rejecting any form of supernatural agency and some religionists holding onto faith in a Creator God whose existence cannot be proved by scientific method. A second position is that science and religion deal with separate realms. That is, religions deal with matters such as morality, hope, answers to philosophical questions ("Why are we here?"), and ideas about life after death, whereas science deals with quantifiable physical reality. In this position, a person can live with "two truths," and neither side is required to venture into the other's domain. A third position is that of dialogue, in which scientists and religious believers can find common ground in interpreting religious propositions as metaphors and bases for the moral use of scientific research. Claims to absolute truth are softened on each side. A fourth position is that of integration, in which science and religion overlap. One example is illustrated by the boxed excerpt from physicist Paul Davies; another is what is sometimes called "creation theology," referring to scientific enquiries by people who believe in a creative deity or deities. Environmentalist Ellen Bernstein explains this exploration from a Jewish perspective:

> Creation theology refers to any kind of reflection on God and the world as a whole, or the elements of the world. It is interested in the nature of nature, and the nature of humanity, and the interplay of the two. It understands God as the continual, creative Presence in the world. … Jews who accept the logic of evolution theory should be relieved to learn that embracing a theology of creation in no way requires a suspension of rational thought or scientific integrity.[44]

At the cutting edge of research, scientists themselves find they have no ultimate answers that can be expressed in scientific terms.

Women in religions

How are women today challenging the patriarchal nature of many institutionalized religions?

Another long-standing issue in the sphere of religion is the exclusion of women in male-dominated systems. Most institutionalized religions are **patriarchal**, meaning that men lead like father figures. Women are often relegated to the fringes of religious organizations, given only supporting roles, thus reflecting existing social distinctions between men and women. In some cases, women are even considered incapable of spiritual realization or dangerous to men's spiritual lives. Founders of religion have in many cases attempted to temper cultural restraints on women. Jesus, for example, apparently included women among his close disciples, and the Prophet Muhammad gave much more respect to women than had been customary in the surrounding culture. However, after the founders, the institutions that developed often reverted to exclusion and oppression of women, sometimes giving a religious stamp of approval to gender imbalances.

Although women are still barred from equal spiritual footing with men in many religions, this situation is now being widely challenged. The contemporary feminist movement includes strong efforts to make women's voices heard in the sphere of religion. Women are trying to discover their own identity, rather than having their identities defined by others, and to develop full, purposeful lives for themselves and their families. Scholars are bringing to light the histories of many women who have been religious leaders. Feminists are challenging patriarchal religious institutions that have excluded women from active participation. They are also challenging gender-exclusive language in holy texts and authoritarian masculine images of the divine. Their protests also go beyond gender issues to question the narrow and confining ways in which religious inspiration has been institutionalized. Many Buddhist centers in the West and some in Asia are run by women, and female scholars are having a major impact on the ways that

Even when denied access to public leadership roles in religions, women have been spiritually influential as mothers, nurses, Sunday-school teachers, and the like.

Buddhist teachings are being understood. At prestigious Christian seminaries in the United States, women preparing for the ministry now outnumber men and are radically transforming views of religion and religious practice. Many women are deeply concerned about social ills of our times—violence, poverty, ecological disaster—and are insisting that religions be actively engaged in ensuring human survival, and that they be life-affirming rather than punitive in approach.

Even in traditional roles, women are redefining themselves as important spiritual actors. Buddhist practitioner Jacqueline Kramer observes:

> The life occupation of mothering and homemaking has been both glorified and demeaned, but seldom has it been seen as the valid spiritual path it can be. Yet, the practices the mothers engage in, day in and day out—selfless service, generosity, letting go, developing a deep love for all beings, patience, faith, and mindfulness—are the way of practice for monks and nuns of all the world's wisdom traditions.[45]

Negative aspects of organized religions

What factors contribute to the negative aspects of organized religions?

Tragically, religions have often split rather than unified humanity, have oppressed rather than freed, have terrified rather than inspired. Institutionalization of religion is part of the problem. As institutionalized religions spread the teachings of their founders, there is the danger that more energy will go into preserving the outer form of the tradition than into maintaining its inner spirit. Max Weber (1864–1920), an influential early twentieth-century scholar of the sociology of religion, referred to this process as the "routinization of charisma." **Charisma** is the rare quality of personal magnetism often ascribed to founders of religion. When the founder dies, the center of the movement may shift to those who turn the original inspirations into routine rituals, dogma, and organizational structures.

Since the human needs that religions answer are so strong, those who hold religious power are in a position to dominate and control their followers. In fact, in many religions leaders are given this authority to guide people's spiritual lives, for their perceived wisdom and special access to the sacred are valued. Because religions involve the unseen, the mysterious, these leaders' teachings are not verifiable by everyday physical experience. They must more often be accepted on faith and it is possible to surrender to leaders who are misguided or unethical. Some religious leaders have used the power of their positions to exploit their followers financially, physically, or emotionally. Religious leaders, like secular leaders, may not be honest with themselves and others about their inner motives. They may mistake their own thoughts and desires for divine guidance.

Another potential problem is exaggeration of guilt. Religions try to help us make ethical choices in our lives, to develop a moral conscience. But in people who already have perfectionist or paranoid tendencies, the fear of sinning and being punished can be exaggerated to the point of neurosis or even psychosis by blaming, punishment-oriented religious teachings. If people try to leave their religion for the sake of their mental health, they may be haunted with guilt that they have done a terribly wrong thing. Religions thus have the potential for wreaking psychological havoc on their followers.

Still another potentially negative use of religion is escapism. Because some religions, particularly those that developed in Asia, offer a state of blissful contemplation as the reward for spiritual practice, the faithful may use religion to escape from their everyday problems. Psychologist John Welwood observes that Westerners sometimes embrace Asian religions with the unconscious motive of avoiding their unsatisfactory lives. He calls this attempt "spiritual bypassing."

Because religions can exert such a strong hold on their followers—by their fears, their desires, their deep beliefs—they are potential centers for political power. When Church and state are one, the belief that the dominant national religion is the only true religion may be used to oppress those of other beliefs within the country. Religion may also be used as a rallying point for wars against other nations, casting the desire for control as a holy motive. Throughout history, huge numbers of people have been killed in the name of eradicating "false" religions and replacing them with the "true" religion. Rather than uniting us all in bonds of love, harmony, and mutual respect, this approach has often divided us with barriers of hatred and intolerance.

In our times, dangerous politicized polarizations between religions are increasing in some areas, albeit cooling off in others. Some of the most worrisome conflicts are pitting Christians and Jews against Muslims to such an extent that some have predicted a catastrophic "clash of civilizations." No religion has ever sanctioned violence against innocent people, but such political clashes have given a holy aura to doing just that, posing a grave threat to life and peace. Sadism, terrorism, wars over land and resources, political oppression, and environmental destruction can all be given a thin veneer of religious sanctification, thus obscuring their evil aspects.

His Highness the Aga Khan, spiritual leader of Isma'ili Shi'a Muslims, maintains that the real problem today is a "clash of ignorance."[46] This is not the time to think of the world in terms of superficial, rigid distinctions between "us" and "them." It is the time when we must try to understand each other's beliefs and feelings clearly, carefully, and compassionately, and bring truly religious responses into play. To take such a journey does not mean forsaking our own religious beliefs or our scepticism. But the journey is likely to broaden our perspective and thus bring us closer to understanding other members of our human family.

Lenses for studying religions

How can the study of religions be approached?

Scholars of different disciplines have their own lenses through which they attempt to describe and explain religions. Some studies focus on the history of religious institutions; others may address the psychological experience of religion. Some scholars devote themselves to the careful study of religious texts, while others conduct their research by observing religious practices. Some scholars have explored one particular religion deeply; others have sought to compare themes, concepts, and practices across different religions. In recent years, scholars have used feminist critical approaches to explore how religions have defined gender; they have used postcolonial theories to investigate how the experience of colonialism and imperialism has continued to have an impact on some religions; scholars interested in issues of gender and sexuality have focused on how religious texts and ideologies have helped to shape attitudes about gender expectations and sexual norms.

Regardless of the disciplinary lens or lenses that are used in studying religion, there are also important questions to ask about our own perspectives. Do we view our own religion through the same lens as we view others? Is it possible to be objective about one's own religion, or about the religions of others? Is it indeed possible to be completely objective about religion as we study it? To what extent might our own beliefs and practices affect our ability to understand those of others? Are accounts that come from inside or outside a religion more reliable? Should we strive for empathy, or adopt a more critical approach? These are complex questions to which there may not be definitive answers, but they are very important questions to keep in mind as we undertake our study of living religions. In addition to exploring various scholarly perspectives, we will try to listen carefully to individuals of all faiths as they tell their own stories.

Key terms

absolutist Believing in one's received traditions as completely and exclusively true.

agnosticism Belief that if there is anything beyond this life it is impossible for humans to know it.

allegory Narrative using symbols to convey abstract ideas.

atheism Belief that there is no deity.

awakening Full awareness of invisible Reality.

charisma Magnetic attraction, a quality often ascribed to spiritual leaders.

comparative religion A discipline that attempts to compare and understand patterns found in different religious traditions.

Creationism Belief that all life was created by God.

dogma Doctrines proclaimed as absolutely true by religious institutions.

enlightenment Wisdom that is thought to come from direct experience of Ultimate Reality.

exclusivism Belief that one's own tradition is the only true religion and that others are invalid.

fundamentalism Insistence on what is perceived as the historical form of one's religion.

gnosis Intuitive knowledge of spiritual realities.

humanism An approach to life focusing on humans' responsibility to lead ethical lives without belief in the supernatural.

immanent Present in the visible world.

incarnation Physical embodiment of the divine.

intelligent design Theory that scientific discoveries prove the existence of an all-encompassing Designer, since they reveal complexities that seem to be beyond chance or evolutionary process.

liberal Taking a flexible, nondogmatic approach.

metaphysics Philosophy based on theories of subtle realities that transcend the physical world.

monotheism Belief that there is only one deity.

mysticism The intuitive perception of spiritual truths beyond the limits of reason.

myth A symbolic story expressing ideas about reality or spiritual history.

orthodox Strictly standing by received traditions.

polytheism Belief that there are many deities.

profane Worldly, secular, as opposed to sacred.

realization Personal awareness of the existence of Unseen Reality.

redaction Editing and organization of a religion's scriptures.

religion A particular response to dimensions of life considered sacred, as shaped by institutionalized traditions.

ritual Repeated, patterned religious act.

sacred The realm of the extraordinary, beyond everyday perceptions, the supernatural, holy.

scientific materialism Belief that only the material world exists and that the supernatural is only imagined by humans.

secularism Personal disregard of religion; government policy of not favoring one religion.

spirituality Any personal response to dimensions of life that are considered sacred.

symbol Visible representation of an invisible reality or concept.

theism Belief in a deity or deities.

transcendent Spiritual reality that exists apart from the material universe.

universalism Acceptance that truth may be found in all religions.

Suggested reading

Asad, Talal, *Genealogies of Religion: Discipline and Reasons of Power in Christianity and Islam*, Baltimore, Maryland: Johns Hopkins University Press, 1993. A fascinating study of the development of the concept of religion in the West.

Barbour, Ian. G., *Religion and Science: Historical and Contemporary Issues*, New York: HarperOne, 1997. Engaging, accessible introduction to past and present debates regarding religion and science.

Braun, Willi and Russell T. McCutcheon, eds, *Guide to the Study of Religion*, London: Cassell, 2000. A series of short articles on key topics in the study of religion, organized around the themes of description, explanation, and location.

Browning, Don and M. Christian Green, eds, *Sex, Marriage, and Family in World Religions*, New York: Columbia University Press, 2009. A collection of primary texts with introductions outlining how the major world religions have addressed issues of sex and family.

Campbell, Joseph with Bill Moyers, *The Power of Myth*, New York: Doubleday, 1988. More brilliant comparisons of the world's mythologies, with deep insights into their common psychological and spiritual truths.

Capra, Fritjof, *The Tao of Physics*, third edition, Boston: Shambhala, 1991. A fascinating comparison of the insights of Eastern religions and contemporary physics.

Carter, Robert E., ed., *God, The Self, and Nothingness—Reflections: Eastern and Western*, New York: Paragon House, 1990. Essays from major Eastern and Western scholars of religion on variant ways of experiencing and describing Ultimate Reality.

Dawkins, Richard, *The God Delusion*, Boston: Houghton Mifflin and London: Transworld (Bantam Press), 2006. Controversial arguments against belief in a personal God by a leading atheistic evolutionary biologist.

Eliade, Mircea, trans. Rosemary Sheed, *Patterns in Comparative Religion*, Lincoln, Nebraska: University of Nebraska Press, 1958, 1996. A classic study of beliefs, rituals, symbols, and myths from around the world.

Eliade, Mircea, *The Sacred and the Profane: The Nature of Religion*, New York: Harcourt, 1959. A good basic introduction to Eliade's theories of sacred space and sacred time.

Fisher, Mary Pat, *Women in Religion*, New York: Pearson Longman, 2007. Many women's stories and analysis of how each major religion has included or excluded them.

Fuller, Robert C., *Spiritual But Not Religious*, New York and Oxford: Oxford University Press, 2001. An introduction to an increasingly prominent trend.

Harris, Sam, *Waking Up: A Guide to Spirituality without Religion*, New York: Simon and Schuster, 2014. One of the leading "new atheists" argues that meditation can be valuable for those who otherwise reject religion.

Hick, John, *An Interpretation of Religion*, New Haven: Yale University Press, 1992. A leading philosopher of religion offers a rational justification for seeing the major world religions as culturally conditioned forms of response to the great mystery of Being.

Juergensmeyer, Mark and Margo Kitts, eds, *Princeton Readings in Religion and Violence*, Princeton: Princeton University Press, 2011. A wide-ranging anthology of key readings on the relationship between religion and violence, from both scholars and religious texts.

King, Ursula, *Women and Spirituality: Voices of Protest and Promise*, second edition, University Park, Pennsylvania: Pennsylvania State University Press, 1993. Excellent cross-cultural survey of feminist theology and spiritual activism.

Marty, Martin E. and R. Scott Appleby, *The Fundamentalism Project*, five volumes, Chicago: University of Chicago Press, 1991–2000. Scholarly analyses of fundamentalist phenomena in all religions and around the globe.

McCutcheon, Russell T., *Manufacturing Religion: The Discourse on Sui Generis Religion and the Politics of Nostalgia*, New York and Oxford: Oxford University Press, 1997. Critique of the comparative study of religions as isolated phenomena without social and historical contexts.

McGrath, Alister E., *Dawkins' God: Genes, Memes, and the Meaning of Life*, Oxford: Blackwell, 2005. A biochemist and Christian theologian refutes Richard Dawkins's criticism of religion.

Otto, Rudolf, *The Idea of the Holy*, second edition, London: Oxford University Press, 1950. An important exploration of "nonrational" experiences of the divine.

Paden, William E., *Interpreting the Sacred: Ways of Viewing Religion*, Boston: Beacon Press, 1992. A gentle, readable introduction to the complexities of theoretical perspectives on religion.

Pals, Daniel L., *Nine Theories of Religion*, third edition, New York and Oxford: Oxford University Press, 2014. Accessible introduction to anthropological, sociological, and psychoanalytical theories of religion.

Sharma, Arvind, ed., *Women in World Religions*, Albany, New York: State University of New York Press, 1987. Analyses of the historical and contemporary place of women in each of the major religions.

Smart, Ninian, *Worldviews: Crosscultural Explorations of Human Beliefs*, Upper Saddle River, New Jersey: Prentice Hall, 2000. In-depth exploration of many dimensions of religious ideologies that influence beliefs around the world.

Stone, Merlin, *When God was a Woman*, San Diego, California: Harcourt Brace Jovanovich, 1976. Pioneering survey of archaeological evidence of the early religion of the Goddess.

Ward, Keith, *God, Chance and Necessity*, Oxford: Oneworld Publications, 1997. A leading Christian theologian critiques scientific theories that deny the existence of God.

Ward, Keith, *The Case for Religion*, Oxford: Oneworld Publications, 2004. An attempt to justify and define religion in historical contexts and also contemporary understandings.

1.1 Explain what is meant by spirituality

The inner dimensions of religion, such as experiences, beliefs, and values, can be referred to as spirituality. This is part of what is called religion, but it may occur in personal, noninstitutional ways, without the ritual and social dimensions of organized religions.

1.2 Identify three perspectives used to explain the existence of religion

During the nineteenth and twentieth centuries, scientific materialism gained prominence as a theory to explain the fact that religion can be found in some form in every culture around the world. The materialistic point of view is that the supernatural is invented by humans; only the material world exists.

According to the functional perspective, religions are found everywhere because they are useful, both for society and individuals. The faith perspective believes that there is an underlying reality that cannot readily be perceived. Human responses to this Ultimate Reality have been expressed and institutionalized as the structures of some religions.

1.3 Differentiate between monotheistic, polytheistic, and nontheistic

Religions based on one's relationship to a Divine Being are called theistic. If the being is worshiped as a singular form, the religion is called monotheistic. If many attributes and forms of the divine are emphasized, the religion may be labeled polytheistic. In nontheistic traditions Ultimate Reality may be perceived without a personal deity or deities.

1.4 Explain the significance of rituals, symbols, and myths in religions

Rituals, such as recitation of prayers and scriptures, singing, dancing, sharing of food, lighting of candles, and making offerings, are the predictable and repeated acts used in worship to express reverence and perhaps to enter into communion with what is worshiped or to request help. Symbols are images borrowed from the material world; visible representations of an invisible reality or concept. Through the use of metaphor, they help connect believers with the Ultimate Reality. Myths are the symbolic stories that communities use to explain the universe and their place within it. They have four primary functions: mystical, cosmological, sociological, and psychological.

1.5 Contrast absolutist with liberal interpretations of a religious tradition

Within each faith people may have different ways of interpreting their tradition. Those who resist contemporary influences and affirm what they perceive as the historical core of their religion (selected doctrines and practices from the past) could be called absolutists. Such people are also sometimes called fundamentalists, though this term is problematic. Those who are called religious liberals take a more flexible approach to religious tradition. They may see scriptures as products of a specific culture and time rather than the eternal voice of truth, and may interpret passages metaphorically rather than literally.

1.6 Discuss the major positions that have emerged in the dialogue between science and religion since the nineteenth century

In 1859 Charles Darwin's *On the Origin of Species* propounded the theory of evolution by natural selection and directly contradicted a literal understanding of the biblical Book of Genesis. As science has progressed, it has in some senses moved back to a more nuanced understanding of religious belief. It continues to question its own assumptions, with various new hypotheses being suggested about the nature of the universe. "Superstring theory" proposes that the universe may not be made of particles at all and that there may be at least ten dimensions of time and space. New branches of science are finding that the universe is not always predictable, nor does it always operate according to human notions of cause and effect.

In the United States, the conservative Christian community has objected to mechanistic scientific theories of biological evolution, preferring Creationism—the concept of intentional divine creation in all life forms. Intelligent design—the theory that scientific discoveries prove the existence of an all-encompassing Designer—has been cited in support of Creationism.

1.7 Describe how women are challenging the patriarchal nature of many institutionalized religions

Although women are still barred from equal spiritual footing with men in many religions, this situation is now being challenged. Scholars are bringing to light the histories of many women who have been religious leaders and feminists are challenging patriarchal religious institutions that have excluded women from active participation as well as gender-exclusive language in holy texts and authoritarian masculine images of the divine.

1.8 Identify the factors that contribute to the negative aspects of organized religions

Those who hold power in institutionalized religions are in a position to dominate and control their followers, which can lead to problems. When Church and state are one, the belief that the dominant national religion is the only true religion may be used to oppress those of other beliefs within the country. Religion may also be used as a rallying point for wars against other nations and faiths, casting the desire for control as a holy motive. Another negative aspect is the exaggeration of guilt, which gives religions the potential to wreak psychological havoc on their followers. Escapism, in which the faithful may use religion to escape from their everyday problems, is another potentially negative use of religion.

1.9 Summarize the different "lenses" used by scholars to study religion

Studies of religion can focus on the history of religious institutions or address the psychological experience of traditions. Scholars may devote themselves to the careful study of religious texts or conduct their research by observing religious practices. Some scholars have explored one particular religion deeply, while others have sought to compare themes, concepts, and practices across different religions. In recent years, scholars have used feminist critical approaches to explore how religions have defined gender. They have also used postcolonial theories to investigate how the experience of colonialism and imperialism has continued to have an impact on some religions. Those scholars interested in issues of gender and sexuality have focused on how religious texts and ideologies have helped to shape attitudes about gender expectations and sexual norms.

CHAPTER 2

INDIGENOUS SACRED WAYS

"I am a child of both worlds. Despite being a university professor, and one who has embraced modernity, I am still a Maasai girl deep down." Damaris Parsitau[1]

2.1 Outline the challenges faced by scholars in understanding indigenous sacred ways

2.2 Explain the cultural diversity of indigenous groups

2.3 Describe the circle of right relationships

2.4 Identify the different spiritual specialists in indigenous sacred ways

2.5 Summarize group and individual observances in indigenous sacred ways

2.6 Illustrate how the processes of globalization are affecting indigenous peoples

2.7 Discuss how development projects have affected indigenous peoples and how they have responded

Here and there around the globe, pockets of people still follow local sacred ways handed down from their remote ancestors but adapted to contemporary circumstances. They are often referred to by religious scholars as **indigenous** peoples. In common parlance, "indigenous" means "native to a place," but some of these groups have actually migrated or been displaced from somewhere else. This is thus a somewhat catch-all label used to distinguish these local groups from worldwide religions. Despite their great variety, "indigenous peoples" have two characteristics in common: Their spiritual beliefs, rituals, and social practices are centered on their own ancestors, and they relate to a specific geographic place. Their distribution around the world, suggested in the map overleaf, reveals a fascinating picture, with many indigenous groups surviving in the midst of industrialized societies, but with globalization processes altering their traditional lifeways.

Indigenous peoples comprise at least four percent of the world's population. Some who follow the ancient spiritual traditions still live close to the earth in nonindustrial, small-scale cultures; some do not. In some places, such as parts of Africa and India, many traditional spiritual practices and ways of understanding have been retained, albeit influenced by modernity and global religions. In other places, the ways that indigenous peoples may refer to as their "original instructions" on how to live have almost been lost under the onslaught of genocidal colonization, conversion pressures from global religions, mechanistic materialism, and the destruction of their natural environments by the global economy of limitless consumption. In those cases, much of the ancient visionary wisdom has disappeared. To seek paying jobs and modern comforts such as electricity, people have shifted from their natural environments into urban settings. In the southwestern United States, there are few traditionally trained elders left and few young people willing to undergo the lengthy and rigorous training necessary for spiritual leadership in these sacred ways. Nevertheless, in many places there is now a renewal of interest in these traditions among the people, fanning hope that what they offer will not be lost.

> *To what extent can [indigenous groups] reinstitute traditional religious values in a world gone mad with development, electronics, almost instantaneous transportation facilities, and intellectually grounded in a rejection of spiritual and mysterious events?*
>
> *Vine Deloria, Jr.*[2]

Understanding indigenous sacred ways
What challenges have scholars faced in understanding indigenous sacred ways?

Outsiders have known or understood little of the indigenous sacred ways, many of which have long been practiced only in secret. In Mesoamerica, the ancient teachings have remained hidden for 500 years since the coming of the conquistadores, passed down within families as a secret oral tradition. The Buryats living

The approximate distribution of indigenous groups mentioned in this chapter.

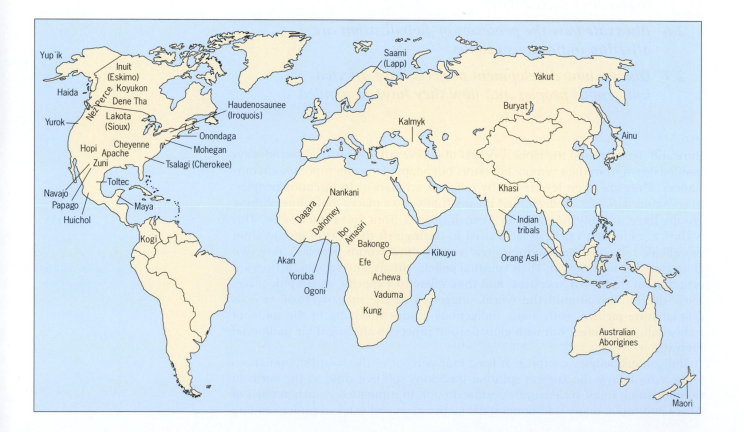

Uluru (Ayers Rock), a unique mass rising from the plains of central Australia, has long been considered sacred by the Aboriginal groups of the area, and in its caves are many ancient paintings.

near Lake Baikal in Russia were thought to have been converted to Buddhism and Christianity centuries ago; however, almost the entire population of the area gathered for indigenous ceremonies on Olkhon Island in 1992 and 1993.

In parts of Aboriginal Australia, the indigenous teachings have been underground for 200 years since white colonialists and Christian missionaries appeared. As Aborigine Lorraine Mafi Williams explains:

> We have stacked away our religious, spiritual, cultural beliefs. When the missionaries came, we were told by our old people to be respectful, listen and be obedient, go to church, go to Sunday school, but do not adopt the Christian doctrine because it takes away our cultural, spiritual beliefs. So we've always stayed within God's laws in what we know.[3]

Not uncommonly, the newer global traditions have been blended with the older ways. For instance, Buddhism as it spread often adopted existing customs, such as the recognition of local deities. Now many indigenous people practice one of the global religions while still retaining many of their traditional ways.

Until recently, those who attempted to ferret out the native sacred ways had little basis for understanding them. Many were anthropologists who approached spiritual behaviors from the nonspiritual perspective of Western science or else the Christian understanding of religion as a means of salvation from sinful earthly existence—a belief not found among most indigenous peoples. There is a great difference between the conceptual frameworks of the religions of Africa and the thinking of Western scholars. Knowing that researchers from other cultures did not grasp the truth of their beliefs, native peoples have at times given them information that was incorrect in order to protect the sanctity of their practices from the uninitiated.

Academic study of traditional ways is now becoming more sympathetic and self-critical, however, as is apparent in this statement by Gerhardus Cornelius Oosthuizen, a South African scholar:

> [The] Western worldview is closed, essentially complete and unchangeable, basically substantive and fundamentally non-mysterious; i.e. it is like a rigid

programmed machine. ... This closed worldview is foreign to Africa, which is still deeply religious. ... This world is not closed, and not merely basically substantive, but it has great depth, it is unlimited in its qualitative varieties and is truly mysterious; this world is restless, a living and growing organism.[4]

Indigenous spirituality is a **lifeway**, a particular approach to all of life. It is not a separate experience, like meditating in the morning or going to church on Sunday. Spirituality ideally pervades all moments. As an elder of the Huichol in Mexico puts it:

Everything we do in life is for the glory of God. We praise him in the well-swept floor, the well-weeded field, the polished machete, the brilliant colors of the picture and embroidery. In these ways we prepare for a long life and pray for a good one.[5]

In most native cultures, spiritual lifeways are shared orally. Oral transmission has been used in all religions, but in indigenous religions oral transmission rather than written scripture remains the main way of sharing and carrying on the traditions. The people create and pass on songs, proverbs, myths, riddles, short sayings, legends, art, music, and the like. This helps to keep the indigenous sacred ways dynamic and flexible rather than fossilized. It also keeps the sacred experience fresh in the present. Oral narratives may also contain clues to the historical experiences of individuals or groups, but these are often carried from generation to generation in symbolic language. The symbols, metaphors, and humor are not easily understood by outsiders but are central to a people's understanding of how life works. To the Maori of New Zealand, life is a continual dynamic process of becoming in which all things arise from a burst of cosmic energy. According to their creation story, all beings emerged from a spatially confined liminal state of darkness in which the Sky Father and Earth Mother were locked in eternal embrace, continually conceiving but crowding their offspring until their children broke that embrace. Their separation created a great burst of light, like wind sweeping through the cosmos. That tremendously freeing, rejuvenating power is still present and can be called upon through rituals in which all beings—plants, trees, fish, birds, animals, people—are intimately and primordially related.

The lifeways of many small-scale cultures are tied to the land on which they live and their entire way of life. They are most meaningful within this context. Many traditional cultures have been dispersed or dismembered, as in the forced emigration of slaves from Africa to the Americas. Despite this, the dynamism of traditional religions has made it possible for African spiritual ways to transcend space, with webs of relationships still maintained between the ancestors, spirits, and people in the diaspora, though they may be practiced secretly and are little understood by outsiders.

Despite the hindrances to understanding of indigenous forms of spirituality, the doors to understanding are opening somewhat in our times. The traditional elders are very concerned about the growing potential for planetary disaster. Some are beginning to share their basic values, if not their esoteric practices, in hopes of preventing industrial societies from destroying the earth.

Cultural diversity

Why are indigenous groups culturally diverse?

In this chapter we are considering the faithways of indigenous peoples as a whole. However, behind these generalizations lie many differences in social contexts as well as in religious beliefs and practices. There are hundreds of different indigenous traditions in North America alone, and at least fifty-three different ethnolinguistic groups in the Andean rainforests. And Australian Aboriginal lifeways, which are some of the world's oldest surviving cultures, traditionally included more than 500 different clan groups, with differing beliefs, living patterns, and languages.

Indigenous traditions have evolved within materially as well as religiously diverse cultures. Some are descendants of civilizations with advanced urban technologies that supported concentrated populations. When the Spanish conqueror Hernán Cortés took over Tenochtitlán (which now lies beneath Mexico City) in 1519, he found it a beautiful, clean city with elaborate architecture, indoor plumbing, an accurate calendar, and advanced systems of mathematics and astronomy. Former African kingdoms were highly culturally advanced with elaborate arts, such as intricate bronze and copper casting, ivory carving, goldworking, and ceramics. In recent times, some Native American tribes have become quite materially successful via economic enterprises, such as gambling complexes.

The indigenous community of Acoma Pueblo—built on a high plateau in New Mexico—live in what may be the oldest continuously occupied city in the United States.

Among Africa's innumerable ethnic and social groupings, there are some indigenous groups comprising millions of people, such as the Yoruba of West Africa and the Ashanti of Ghana. Even though they are so large as to be considered "nations," these groups can be labelled indigenous because they are located in one region, their stories of origin relate to how their ancestors came to occupy that land, and they are bound by lines of kinship, even though these may be mythical. At the other extreme are those few small-scale cultures that still maintain a survival strategy of hunting and gathering. For example, some Australian Aborigines continue to live as mobile foragers, though restricted to government-owned stations. A nomadic survival strategy necessitates simplicity in material goods; whatever can be gathered or built rather easily at the next camp need not be dragged along. But material simplicity is not a sign of spiritual poverty. The Australian Aborigines have complex **cosmogonies**, or models of the origins of the universe and their purpose within it, as well as a working knowledge of their own bioregion.

Some traditional peoples live in their ancestral enclaves, though not untouched by the outer world. The Hopi people have continuously occupied a high plateau area of the southwestern United States for between 800 and 1,000 years; their sacred ritual calendar is tied to the yearly farming cycle. By contrast, tribal peoples have lived in India for thousands of years, but the forests they now occupy may not have been their primary homelands. There is evidence that they once lived in the hills and plains but were marginalized by higher-caste Hindus and then British colonizers, and the only place left for them was the forests. Since the twentieth century even the forests have been taken over for "development" projects and encroached upon by more politically and economically powerful groups, rendering many of the seventy-five million Indian tribespeople landless laborers.

Other indigenous peoples visit their sacred sites and ancestral shrines but live in more urban settings because of job opportunities. The people who participate in ceremonies in the Mexican countryside include subway personnel, journalists, and artists of native blood who live in Mexico City.

In addition to variations in lifestyles, indigenous traditions vary in their adaptations to dominant religions. Often native practices have become interwoven with those of global religions, such as Buddhism, Islam, and Christianity. In Southeast Asia, household Buddhist shrines are almost identical to the spirit houses in which the people still make offerings to honor the local spirits. In Africa, the spread of Islam and Christianity saw the introduction of new religious ideas and practices into indigenous sacred ways. The encounter transformed indigenous religious thought and practice but did not supplant it; indigenous religions preserved some of their beliefs and ritual practices but also adjusted to the new sociocultural milieu. The Dahomey tradition from West Africa was carried to Haiti by African slaves and called **Vodou**, from *vodu*, one of the names for the chief nonhuman spirits. Forced by European colonialists to adopt Christianity, worshipers of Vodou secretly fused their old gods with their images of Catholic saints. More recently, emigrants from Haiti have formed diaspora communities of Vodou worshipers in cities such as New York, New Orleans, Miami, and Montreal, where Vodou specialists are often called upon to heal sickness and use magic to bring desired changes. In Australia, some Aboriginal people are converting to Islam for various reasons. These include honouring their roots among ancestors who intermarried with Muslim traders from Indonesian islands or cameleers from Afghanistan, political activism against social injustice, and the search for a positive identity. Conversion does not necessarily mean abandoning their traditional culture. As one convert explains:

> *Islam recognises tribes and nations. It gives you identity, a purpose. It doesn't just say, "You're Muslim, that's it." It says yes, all Muslims are the same, but it does recognise we belong to different tribes and nations, so it doesn't do what Christianity did to a lot of Aboriginal people [which] was try and make them like white people. ... Islam allows you your identity, your tribe and nation, and that is quoted in the Quran.*[6]

Despite their different histories and economic patterns, and their geographical separation, indigenous sacred ways have some characteristics in common. Similarities found among the myths and symbols of geographically separate peoples can be partly accounted for by global diffusion through trade, travel, communications, and other kinds of contact. Perhaps from ancient contact across land-bridges that no longer exist, there are similarities between the languages of the Tsalagi in the Americas, Tibetans, and the aboriginal Ainu of Japan. There are also basic similarities in human experience, such as birth and death, pleasure and pain, and wonderment about the cosmos and our place in it. Cognitive scientists of religion also relate similarities in symbols and stories to shared human environmental conditions and the way the human mind functions. For instance, in all cultures, people tend to project human qualities onto plants, animals, and inanimate things and cross boundaries of this-worldly logic, developing belief in beings or forces that operate in extraordinary ways in the midst of ordinary time and space. People's relationships to, and the concepts surrounding, these symbols are not inevitably the same. Nevertheless, the following sections look at some recurring themes in the spiritual ways of diverse indigenous cultures. These tendencies are not unique to indigenous religions, for they appear in other religions as well, but they may be particularly prominent in indigenous lifeways.

The circle of right relationships
What is the circle of right relationships?

For many indigenous peoples, everything in the cosmos is intimately interrelated. These interrelationships originate in the way everything was created. To Australian Aborigines, before time began there was land, but it was flat and devoid of any features. Powerful ancestral beings came forth from beneath the surface and began moving around, shaping the land as they moved across it. In this "Dreamtime," the ancestral figures also created groups of humans to take care of the places that had been created. The people thus feel that they belong to their native place in an eternal sacred relationship.

A symbol of unity among the parts of this sacred reality is a circle. This is not used by all indigenous people; the Navajo, for instance, regard a completed circle as stifling and restrictive. However, many other indigenous peoples hold the circle sacred because it is infinite—it has no beginning, no end. Time is circular rather than linear, for it keeps coming back to the same place. Life revolves around the generational cycles of birth, youth, maturity, and physical death,

Among the gentle Efe pygmies of the Ituri Forest in the Democratic Republic of Congo (formerly Zaire), children learn to value the circle by playing the "circle game." With feet making a circle, each child names a circular object and then an expression of roundness (the family circle, togetherness, "a complete rainbow").

the return of the seasons, the cyclical movements of the moon, sun, stars, and planets. Rituals such as rites of passage may be performed to help keep these cycles in balance.

To maintain the natural balance of the circles of existence, most indigenous peoples have traditionally been taught that they must develop right relationships with everything that is. Their relatives include the unseen world of spirits, the land and weather, the people and creatures, and the power within.

Relationships with spirit

The cosmos is thought to contain and be affected by numerous divinities, spirits, and also ancestors. For many indigenous groups, ancestors are the closest and most important spirits. Death is not an end; connection continues between the spirit of the dead person and the living relatives. To the Nankani of northern Ghana, ancestors have been delegated the power to take care of the needs and quarrels of their descendants, since they know and understand them well. For the Amasiri people of southeast Nigeria, the relationship of ancestors with the living is so intimate that the dead person may be buried in the floor of the home. During a funeral, mourners beg the parent not to forget them—to always remember and protect them.

Traditional Africans understand that the person is not an individual, but a composite of many souls—the spirits of one's parents and ancestors—resonating to their feelings. Rev. William Kingsley Opoku, International Coordinator of the African Council for Spiritual Churches, says:

> *Our ancestors are our saints. Christian missionaries who came here wanted us to pray to their saints, their dead people. But what about our saints? ... If you are grateful to your ancestors, then you have blessings from your grandmother, your grandfather, who brought you forth.*[7]

Continued communication with the "living dead" (ancestors who have died within living memory) may include libation rituals in which food and drink are offered to the ancestors, acknowledging that they are still in a sense living and engaged with the people's lives. For the Nankani, female ancestors are represented by pots within the house decorated with bangles; male ancestors are represented by pots placed outside the house. The guidance and protection of the ancestors is essential. Failure to keep in touch with them is a dangerous oversight, which may bring misfortunes to the family.

Australian Aborigines understand their environment as concentric fields of subtle energies. (Nym Bunduk, 1907–1974, Snakes and Emu.)

Many unseen powers are perceived to be at work in the material world. In addition to ancestors, some of these are perceived without form, as mysterious presences, who may be benevolent or malevolent. Others are perceived as having more definite, albeit invisible, forms and personalities. These may include deities with human-like personalities, the nature spirits of special local places, such as venerable trees and mountains, animal spirit helpers, personified elemental forces, or the *nagas,* known to the traditional peoples of Nepal as invisible serpentine spirits who control the circulation of water in the world and also within our bodies.

The Dagara of Burkina Faso in West Africa are familiar with the *kontombili,* who look like humans but are only about one foot (thirty centimeters) tall, because of the humble way they express their spiritual power. Other West African groups, descendants of ancient hierarchical civilizations, recognize a great pantheon of deities, the *orisa* or *vodu,* each the object of special worship. The *orisa* are embodiments of the dynamic forces in life, such as Oya, powerful goddess of change, experienced in winds; Osun, *orisa* of fresh waters, associated with sweetness, healing, love, fertility, and prosperity; Olokun, ruler of the mysterious depths of consciousness; Shango, a former king who is now honored as the stormy god of electricity and genius; Ifa, god of wisdom; and Obatala, the source of creativity, warmth, and enlightenment. At the beginning of time, in Yoruba cosmology, there was only one godhead, described by psychologist Clyde Ford as "a beingless being, a dimensionless point, an infinite container of everything, including itself."[8] According to the mythology, this being was smashed by a boulder pushed down by a rebellious slave, and broke into hundreds of fragments, each of which became an *orisa.* According to some analysts, *orisa* can also be seen as archetypes of traits existing within the human psyche. Their ultimate purpose—and that of those who pay attention to them as inner forces—is to return to that presumed original state of wholeness.

Many indigenous traditions also worship a Supreme Being who they believe created the cosmos. This being is known by the Lakota as "Great Mysterious" or "Great Spirit." African names for the being are attributes, such as "All-powerful," "Creator," "the one who is met everywhere," "the one who exists by himself," or "the one who began the forest." To traditional Buryats of Russia, the chief power in the world is the eternally blue sky, Tengry. The Supreme Being is often referred to by male pronouns, but in some groups the Supreme Being is a female. Some tribes of the southwestern United States call her "Changing Woman"—sometimes young, sometimes old, the mother of the earth, associated with women's reproductive cycles and the mystery of birth, the creatrix. Many traditional languages make no distinction between male and female pronouns, and some see the divine as androgynous, a force arising from the interaction of male and female aspects of the universe. In the religions of Africa, the Supreme Being—whether singular or plural— may have human-like qualities, but no gender. This great Source is so awesome that no images are used to represent it. An Inuit spiritual adept described his people's experience of:

> a power that we call Sila, which is not to be explained in simple words. A great spirit, supporting the world and the weather and all life on earth, a spirit so mighty that [what it says] to mankind is not through common words, but by storm and snow and rain and the fury of the sea; all the forces of nature that men fear. But Sila has also another way of [communicating]; by sunlight and calm of the sea, and little children innocently at play, themselves understanding nothing. … When all is well, Sila sends no message to mankind, but withdraws into endless nothingness, apart.[9]

Deity may be conceived as either male or female in indigenous religions. In Navajo belief, divinity is personified as both Father Sky and Mother Earth. In this traditional sand-painting, Father Sky is on the left, with constellations and the Milky Way forming his "body." Mother Earth is on the right, with her body bearing the four sacred plants: squash, beans, tobacco, and corn.

African myths suggest that the High God was originally so close to humans that they became disrespectful. The All-powerful was like the sky, they say, which was once so close that children wiped their dirty hands on it, and women (blamed by men for the withdrawal) broke off pieces for soup and bumped it with their sticks when pounding grain. Although southern and central Africans believe in a high being who presides over the universe, including less powerful spirits, they consider this being either too distant, too powerful, or too dangerous to worship or call on for help.

It cannot therefore be said that indigenous concepts of, and attitudes toward, a Supreme Being are necessarily the same as that which Western monotheistic religions refer to as God or Allah. In the religions of Africa, much more emphasis tends to be placed on the transcendent dimensions of everyday life and doing what is spiritually necessary to keep life going normally. The spirits are thought to be available to those who seek them as helpers, as intermediaries between the people and the power, and as teachers. A right relationship with these spirit beings can be a sacred partnership. Seekers respect and learn from them; they also purify themselves in order to engage their services for the good of the people.

Teachings about the spirits also help the people to understand how they should live together in society. Professor Deidre Badejo observes that in Yoruba tradition there is an ideal of balance between the creativity of women, who give and sustain life, and the power of men, who protect life. Under various internal and external pressures, this balance has swung toward male dominance, but

YORUBA TEACHING STORY

Osun and the Power of Woman

Olodumare, the Supreme Creator, who is both female and male, wanted to prepare the earth for human habitation. To organize things, Olodumare sent the seventeen major deities. Osun was the only woman; all the rest were men. Each of the deities was given specific abilities and specific assignments. But when the male deities held their planning meetings, they did not invite Osun. "She is a woman," they said.

However, Olodumare had given great powers to Osun. Her womb is the matrix of all life in the universe. In her lie tremendous power, unlimited potential, infinities of existence. She wears a perfectly carved, beaded crown, and with her beaded comb she parts the pathway of both human and divine life. She is the leader of the *aje*, the powerful beings and forces in the world.

When the male deities ignored Osun, she made their plans fail. The male deities returned to Olodumare for help. After listening, Olodumare asked, "What about Osun?" "She is only a woman," they replied, "so we left her out." Olodumare spoke in strong words, "You must go back to her, beg her for forgiveness, make a sacrifice to her, and give her whatever she asks."

The male deities did as they were told, and Osun forgave them. What did she ask for in return? The secret initiation that the men used to keep women in the background. She wanted it for herself and for all women who are as powerful as she is. The men agreed and initiated her into the secret knowledge. From that time onward, their plans were successful.[10]

the stories of feminine power (see Box) and the necessity for men to recognize it remain in the culture, teaching an ideal symmetry between female and male roles. In many indigenous cultures, women appear as powerful beings in myths and they are thought to have great ritual power.

Kinship with all creation

In addition to the unseen powers, all aspects of the tangible world are believed to be imbued with spirit. Josiah Young III explains that in African traditional religion, both the visible and the invisible realms are filled with spiritual forces:

The visible is the natural and cultural environment, of which humans, always in the process of transformation, are at the center. The invisible connotes the numinous field of ancestors, spirits, divinities, and the Supreme Being, all of whom, in varying degrees, permeate the visible. Visible things, however, are not always what they seem. Pools, rocks, flora, and fauna may dissimulate invisible forces of which only the initiated are conscious.[11]

Within the spiritually charged visible world, all things may be understood as spiritually interconnected. Everything is therefore experienced as family. In African traditional lifeways, "we" may be more important than "I," and this "we" often refers to a large extended family and ancestral village, even for people who have moved to the cities. In indigenous cultures, the community is paramount, and it may extend beyond the living humans in the area. Many traditional peoples know the earth as their mother. The land one lives on is part of her body, loved, respected, and well known. Oren Lyons, an elder of the Onondaga Nation Wolf Clan, speaks of this intimate relationship:

[The indigenous people's] knowledge is profound and comes from living in one place for untold generations. It comes from watching the sun rise in the east and set in the west from the same place over great sections of time. We are as familiar with the lands, rivers and great seas that surround us as we are with the faces of our mothers. Indeed we call the earth Etenoha, our mother, from whence all life springs. ... We do not perceive our habitat as wild but as a place of great security and peace, full of life.[12]

Some striking feature of the natural environment of an area—such as a great mountain or canyon—may be perceived as the center from which the whole world was created. Such myths heighten the perceived sacredness of the land. Western Tibet's Mount Kailash, high in the Himalayas, is seen by the indigenous people of that area as the center of the earth, a sacred space where the earthly and the supernatural meet. The Western Apache remember vivid symbolic narratives about the exploits of people in specific places in their environment and contemplate them to make their minds smooth, steady, and resilient. Dudley Patterson's grandmother taught him:

> *Wisdom sits in places. It's like water that never dries up. You need to drink water to stay alive, don't you? Well, you also need to drink from places. You must remember everything about them. You must learn their names. You must remember what happened at them long ago. You must think about it and keep on thinking about it. Then your mind will become smoother and smoother. Then you will see danger before it happens. You will walk a long way and live a long time. You will be wise. People will respect you.*[13]

Because of the intimate relationship indigenous peoples have with their particular environments, forced removal from that environment can be devastating. When pushed onto the most marginal lands by colonizers, nation-states, or multinational companies that regard land as a valuable commercial resource rather than a sacred place, indigenous peoples may feel they have lost their own identity. New Zealand traditional elders, who were systematically forced off their ancestral homeland from the nineteenth century onward, explain:

> *It is important to know where we come from, to know where we belong. To identify who I am I identify my mountain, my river, my lands, our tribal and subtribal community. Knowing these things helps to bring about and to keep together the healing, the wellbeing of our people. We have suffered the loss of our lands, our connection to the land. We belong to the mountains, to the sea, to the forest. With the loss of the land, there has been a tremendous alienation from who we are. As a people we are currently in a renaissance, in a reclamation of our cultural identity, our land works, our traditional practices, our healing methods, because without these things we become a lost people, we become invisible, we become submerged into the dominant culture.*[14]

An indigenous earthwork in Ohio represents a snake and an egg, symbols of fertility and transformation. The spiral in the snake's tail may be an appreciative symbol of the life force and wisdom inherent in the earth.

In contrast to the industrial world's attempts to own and dominate the earth, native peoples consider themselves caretakers of their mother, the earth. Some are now raising their voices against the destruction of the environment, warning of the potential for global disaster. Nepali shamans who have undertaken the difficult pilgrimage to Lake Mansarovar at the base of revered Mount Kailash report that the lake level is low and the spirits are unhappy. Their prophecies indicate difficult times ahead unless we humans take better care of our planetary home. Some indigenous visionaries say they hear the earth crying. Contemporary Australian Aboriginal elder Bill Neidjie speaks of feeling the earth's pain:

I feel it with my body,
with my blood.
Feeling all these trees,
all this country ...
If you feel sore ...
headache, sore body
that mean somebody killing tree or grass.
You feel because your body in that tree or earth. ...
You might feel it for two or three years.
You get weak ...
little bit, little bit ...
because tree going bit by bit ...
dying.[15]

Many traditional peoples learn a sense of reverence for, and kinship with, the natural world, as suggested in this image from Botswana created by Elisabeth Sunday.

Rocks, bodies of water, and mountains—considered inanimate by other peoples—are personified as living beings. Before one can successfully climb a mountain, one must ask its permission. Visionaries can see the spirits of a body of water, and many traditional cultures have recognized certain groves of trees as places where spirits live, and where spiritual specialists can communicate with them. As a Pit River Indian explained, "Everything is alive. That's what we Indians believe."[16]

All creatures may be perceived as kin, endowed with consciousness and the power of the Great Spirit. Many native peoples have been raised with an "ecological" perspective: They know that all things depend on each other. They are taught that they have a reciprocal, rather than dominating, relationship with all beings. Children learn from their elders that just as they have family relationships with humans, other living things are also like family members. They have intimate spiritual connections with trees, birds, animals, fish, reptiles—all creatures—and are taught that they can and should communicate with them, for their mutual benefit. All are to be approached with caution and consideration. If one must cut down a tree or kill an animal, one must first explain one's intentions and ask forgiveness. Those who harm nature may themselves be harmed in return. Tribal peoples of Madhya Pradesh in central India will avoid killing a snake, for they feel that its partner would come after them to seek revenge. When a Buryat cuts a tree to build a house, he must first offer milk, butter, rice, and alcohol to the spirits of the forest and ask their forgiveness. In 1994, a half-French, half-Buryat businessman returned to Buryatia and started to build a guesthouse in a picturesque place that had long been considered sacred to the god Huushan-baabay. When the businessman began cutting trees, he was warned by the traditional people that he would not be successful. Nonetheless, he proceeded and finished the guesthouse. Three months later, it burned down.

Respect is always due to all creatures, in the indigenous worldview. The Yup'ik of southwestern Alaska know animals as thinking, feeling fellow beings. In fact, they may be even more sensitive and aware than humans. No one should handle the geese's eggs or goslings, lest the human smell should frighten the adults and they abandon the babies, to be eaten by predators. In Yup'ik belief, if humans treat animal populations carefully as guests, they will come back in plentiful numbers the following year to intentionally offer themselves to the Yup'ik hunters.

In the challenging environment of the Koyukon people of northern Canada, all interactions between humans and animals are conducted carefully according to a respectful moral code so that the animals will allow themselves to be caught. The animal spirits are very easily offended, not by animals being killed but by disrespect shown to the animals or their remains. Killing must be done prayerfully and in a way that does not cause suffering to the animal; wounded animals must be found and put out of their misery. If displeased, the spirits can bring bad luck in the hunt for that species or perhaps illness or even death for the hunters. But if humans maintain good relationships with the animals, they will give themselves freely to the hunters and keep coming back year after year. It is the natural world that is dominant, not humans.

There are many stories of indigenous peoples' relationships with nonhuman creatures. Certain trees tell the healing specialists which herbs to use in curing the people. Australian Aboriginal women are adept at forming hunting partnerships with dogs. Birds are thought to bring messages from the spirit world. The Ainu people of Japan learned to heed the cries of foxes when a tsunami was coming, and thus moved to higher ground to save themselves. A crow, a wild yak, and a pack of silver wolves revealed the sacred path to Mount Kailash in Tibet. A Hopi elder said he spent three days and nights praying with a rattlesnake. "Of course he was nervous at first, but when I sang to him he recognized the warmth of my body and calmed down. We made good prayer together."[17]

Relationships with power

Another common theme in indigenous lifeways is developing an appropriate relationship with spiritual energy.

All animals have power, because the Great Spirit dwells in all of them, even a tiny ant, a butterfly, a tree, a flower, a rock. The modern, white man's way keeps that power from us, dilutes it. To come to nature, feel its power, let it help you, one needs time and patience for that. … You have so little time for contemplation. … It lessens a person's life, all that grind, that hurrying and scurrying about.

Lame Deer, Lakota Nation[18]

In certain places and beings, the power of spirit is believed to be highly concentrated. It is referred to as *mana* by the people of the Pacific islands. This is the vital force that makes it possible to act with unusual strength, insight, and effectiveness.

Tlakaelel, a spiritual leader of the descendants of the Toltecs of Mexico, described how a person might experience this power when looking into an obsidian mirror traditionally made to concentrate power:

When you reach the point that you can concentrate with all your will, inside there, you reach a point where you feel ecstasy. It's a very beautiful thing, and everything is light. Everything is vibrating with very small signals, like waves of music, very smooth. Everything shines with a blue light. And you feel a sweetness. Everything is covered with the sweetness, and there is peace. It's a sensation like an orgasm, but it can last a long time.[19]

Sacred sites may be recognized by the power that believers feel there. Some sacred sites have been used again and again by successive religions, either to capitalize on the energy or to co-opt the preceding religion. Chartres Cathedral in France, for instance, was built on an ancient ritual site. In New Zealand, the traditional Maori people know of the revivifying power of running water, such as waterfalls (now understood by scientists as places of negative ionization, and which do indeed have an energizing effect). The Maori elders have told the public of the healing power of a certain waterfall on North Island; the area is now dedicated to anyone who needs healing.

Because power can be built up through sacred practices, the ritual objects of spiritually developed persons may have concentrated power. Special stones and animal artefacts may also carry power. A person might be strengthened by the spiritual energy of the bear or the wolf by wearing sacred clothing made from its fur. Power can also come to one through visions, or by being given a sacred pipe or the privilege of collecting objects into a personal sacred bundle.

In some cultures women are thought to have a certain natural power; men have to work harder for it. Women's power is considered mysterious, dangerous, uncontrolled. It is said to be strongest during menstruation. Women are secluded during their menstrual periods in many cultures, not necessarily because they are considered polluting. Among the Yurok of northern California, houses have a separate back room for women who are menstruating so that they can concentrate on their inner selves, becoming inwardly stronger and purified by the flow of blood. In certain rituals in which both men and women participate, women's menstrual blood is often thought to diminish or weaken the ritual or the men's spiritual power. In most Native American nations that have sweat lodge ceremonies for ritual purification, menstruating women are not allowed to enter the lodge. A few cultures, such as the Ainu of Japan, have prized menstrual blood as a potent offering returned to the earth.

Gaining power is both desirable and dangerous. If misused for personal ends, it becomes destructive and may turn against the person. To channel spiritual power properly, native peoples are taught that they must live within certain

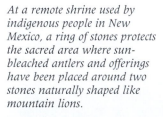

At a remote shrine used by indigenous people in New Mexico, a ring of stones protects the sacred area where sun-bleached antlers and offerings have been placed around two stones naturally shaped like mountain lions.

strict limits. Those who seek power or receive it unbidden are supposed to continually purify themselves of any selfish motives and dedicate their actions to the good of the whole.

Spiritual specialists
What types of spiritual specialists are there in indigenous sacred ways?

In a few remaining hunting and gathering tribes, religion is a relatively private matter. Each individual has direct access to the unseen. Although spirit is invisible, it is considered a part of the natural world. Anyone can interact with it spontaneously, without complex ceremony and without anyone else's aid.

More commonly, however, the world of spirit is thought to be dangerous. Although everyone is expected to observe certain personal ways of worship, such as offering prayers before taking plant or animal life, many ways of interacting with spirit are thought to be best left to those who are specially trained for the roles. These specialists are gradually initiated into the secret knowledge that allows them to act as intermediaries between the seen and the unseen.

Storytellers and other sacred roles

Specialists' roles vary from one group to another, and the same person may play several of these roles. One common role is that of storyteller. Because the traditions are oral rather than written, these people must memorize long and complex stories and songs so that the group's sacred traditions can be remembered and taught, generation after generation. The orally transmitted epics of the indigenous Ainu of Japan are up to 10,000 "lines" long. Chants of the Yoruba *orisa* comprise 256 "volumes" of 800 long verses each. Unlike written texts, stories are told in context, as performances that change as they are told. They may be told for entertainment, for social or moral purposes, or for rituals such as dances in which deities manifest.

Yoruba chants about the *orisa* include an explanation of the genesis of the earth, with its center in what is now the Nigerian city of Ife. When time began, where the earth now exists there was only a vast watery area, with a dim and misty atmosphere, the domain of Olokun. The other *orisa* lived in an upper world of light until Obatala decided to go down to see if some solid land could be created so that the *orisa* could inhabit the earth. He had a sacred chain of gold made for his descent, and carried a shell of sand, a white hen, a palm nut, and a black cat. He climbed down to the watery world by means of the chain, but it was too short. Thus he poured the sand downward and then released the hen, who by scratching in the sand created the contours of the earth. Obatala settled on the land and planted his palm nut, which flourished and sent its seed far and wide, developing the plant life of the earth. At first he was alone, with only the black cat as his companion, but as the story continues, many things happen, accounting for the features of the earth and its inhabitants as we know them today. The golden chain is a common mythological symbol of a World Axis connecting heaven and earth; the palm tree also commonly appears in myths of the World Tree, giver and protector of the first forms of life on earth.

Such stories are important clues to understanding the universe and one's place in it. What is held only in memory cannot be physically destroyed, but if a tribe is small and all its storytellers die the knowledge is lost. This happened on a large scale during contacts with colonial powers, as indigenous people were killed by war and imported diseases. Professor Wande Abimbola, who has tried to preserve the oral tradition of the Yoruba, has made thousands of tapes of the chants, but there are few people who can understand and interpret their meaning. Loss of traditional languages is not only a loss of cultural identity; it is a loss of symbolic layers of meaning embedded in languages.

A storyteller of the Kung people of Botswana entertains an audience while passing on the oral teachings of the distant past.

There are also contemporary bards who carry the energy of ancient traditions into new forms. In Africa, poets are considered "technicians of the sacred," conversing with a dangerous world of spirits. Players of the "talking drums" are highly valued as communicators with the spirits, ancestors, and Supreme Being. As the Akan of Ghana say:

> *The thumb, finger with mouth, wake up and speak!*
> *The thumb armed with sticks for drumming*
> *Is more loquacious and more eloquent*
> *Than a human being sleeping;*
> *Wake up and come!*[20]

Drumming creates a rhythmic environment in which the people can draw close to the unseen powers. By counterposing basic and complex cross-rhythmic patterns with a "return beat," Yoruba drummers create a tension that draws listeners into the unfilled spaces between the beats.

"Tricksters" such as foxes often appear in the stories of indigenous traditions. They are paradoxical, transformative beings. Similarly, sacred clowns may endure the shame of behaving as fools during public rituals in order to teach the people through humor. Often they poke fun at the most sacred of rituals, keeping the people from taking themselves too seriously. A sacred fool, called *heyoka* by the Lakota, must be both innocent and very wise about human nature, and must have a visionary relationship with spirit as well.

> *Life is holiness and everyday humdrum, sadness and laughter, the mind and the belly all mixed together. The Great Spirit doesn't want us to sort them out neatly.*
>
> *Leonard Crow Dog, Lakota medicine man*[21]

Another coveted role is that of being a member of a secret society in which one can participate by initiation or invitation only, whether to enhance one's prestige or to draw closer to the spirit world. When serving in ceremonial capacities, members often wear special costumes to hide their human identities and help them take on the personas of spirits they are representing. In the religions of Africa, members of secret societies periodically appear as impersonators of animal spirits or ancestors, demonstrating that the dead are still watching the living, warning transgressors and protecting the village. The all-male Oro secret society in some Yoruba tribes uses this authority to enforce male domination, fearsomely "roaring" by swinging a piece of wood on a cord.

Women also have their secret societies. Among Aboriginal peoples of Australia, the men's and women's groups initiate members into separate but interrelated roles for males and females. For instance, when boys are separated from the tribe for circumcision by the men's secret society, the women's secret society has its own separation rituals and may stage mock ritual fights with the men's society. But men's and women's rituals ultimately refer to the eternal Dreaming, in which there is no male/female differentiation.

Sacred dancers likewise make the unseen powers visible. Body movements are a language in themselves expressing the nature of the cosmos, a language that is understood through the stories and experiences of the community. Yvonne Daniel describes the dance of the Yoruba goddess Oya, as she learned it in Cuba: First the dancer makes a foot pattern that indicates all the directions and all spheres of being, to slow drum-beats. Oya being associated with wind and dynamic change, she then shifts from this powerfully balanced base into a canter and then a gallop, and finally to the fierce tornado of a fighting buffalo. To the sound of aggressive *tuitui* music, she hurls herself into a pattern of "three huge, percussive torso undulations that alternate side to side. Literally on top of this, the arms, which have been carrying the *iruke* [fly-whisk], finish the pattern by slashing downward from high in the air to at least hip height, alternately on each side."[22] Through her movements, she teaches the community about female strength, modeling "vivacious power."[23]

In some socially stratified societies there are also priests and priestesses. These are specially trained and dedicated people who carry out the rituals that ensure proper functioning of the natural world, and perhaps also communicate with particular spirits or deities. Though West African priests or priestesses may have part-time earthly occupations, they are expected to stay in a state of ritual purity and spend much of their time in communication with the spirit being, paying homage and asking for guidance.

Indigenous groups may be led by people who combine spiritual and social duties. The Cheyenne Nation of the North American plains is believed to have been established by its visionary hero, Sweet Medicine, in the 1700s. One of its salient features is a council of forty-four men chosen from various groups in the Cheyenne family to be peace chiefs. When they join the council, the peace chiefs are to make a complete break with their past, in which they might have been warriors, and give up violence as a means of settling disputes. Instead, they have been instructed by Sweet Medicine that, if there are any fights, "You are to do nothing but take your pipe and smoke."[24] The chiefs meet to arbitrate disputes by smoking the peace pipe together; the goal is to smoke the pipe with their enemies. The chiefs' homes also become places of refuge, for they are to help the people however they can. At a community meal, they are the last to be fed.

Mystical intermediaries

There are other distinctive spiritual specialists found among many indigenous peoples. They are called by many names. The Siberian and Saami word "**shaman**" is often used as a generic term for those who offer themselves as mystical intermediaries between the human community and the spirits, attempting to use them for various needs of the community, such as ensuring the success

Shaman Maria Amanchina of Siberia outside the hut she uses for healing. Maria repeatedly became seriously ill until she accepted her spiritual powers and began serving people as a healer.

of the hunt or curing illnesses. Such people are able to enter alternate realities, moving in and out of time and space that is different from ordinary time and space. Archaeological research has confirmed that shamanic methods are extremely ancient—at least 20,000 to 30,000 years old. Shamanic ways are remarkably similar around the globe.

There are also spirit mediums who undergo possession by spirits for the sake of others. A spirit medium is possessed by a spirit and usually does not remember what goes on during the possession. The medium is a conduit but does not control the spirit that inhabits him or her. Such a person may become ill and nearly die until a religious specialist diagnoses the cause as the need for a spirit to make the person his or her medium. A shaman, by contrast, attempts to control the spirits.

Other intermediaries include **"medicine people"** who have special healing skills. There are many kinds of **medicine**. One is the ability to heal physical, psychological, and spiritual problems. Techniques used include physical approaches to illness, such as therapeutic herbs, sweat-bathing, massage, cauterization, and sucking out toxins. But the treatments are given to the whole person—body, mind, and spirit, with emphasis on healing relationships within the group—so there may also be divination, prayer, chanting, and ceremonies in which group power is built up and spirit helpers are called in. If an intrusion of harmful power, such as the angry energy of another person, seems to be causing the problem, the medicine person may attempt to suck it out with the aid of spirit helpers and then dry-vomit the invisible intrusion into a receptacle.

These healing methods are now beginning to earn respect from the scientific medical establishment. Organizations of registered spiritual healers practice in recognized clinics in Russia, Korea, and China. In the United States, medicine people are permitted to attend indigenous patients in some hospitals, and the National Institute of Mental Health has paid Navajo medicine men to teach young Indians the ceremonies that have often been more effective than Western psychiatry in curing the mental health problems of Navajos.

In addition to healing, certain mystical intermediaries are thought to have gifts such as being able to talk with plants and animals, control the weather, see and communicate with the spirit world, and prophesy. A gift highly developed in Africa is that of divination, using techniques such as reading patterns supposed to be revealed by a casting of cowrie shells. According to Mado Somé of the Dagara, "Divination is a way of accessing information that is happening now, but not right where you live. ... The cowrie shells work like an intermediary between us and the other world."[25] Since everything is interrelated, divination is a system for finding the point at which harmony has been disrupted and how the break can be healed.

Whatever the mode of operation, these mystical intermediaries may be helpers to society, using their skills to benefit others. They are not to be confused with sorcerers, who practice black magic to harm others or promote their own selfish ends, interfering with the cosmic order. Spiritual power is neutral; its use depends on the practitioner. What Native Americans call "medicine power" does not originate in the medicine person. Black Elk explained:

> Of course it was not I who cured. It was the power from the outer world, and the visions and ceremonies had only made me like a hole through which the power could come to the two-leggeds. If I thought that I was doing it myself, the hole would close up and no power could come through.[26]

The role of shaman may be hereditary or it may be recognized as a special gift. Either way, training is rigorous. In order to work in a mystical state of ecstasy, moving between ordinary and non-ordinary realities, shamans must experience physical death and rebirth. Uvavnuk, an Inuit shaman, was spiritually initiated when she was struck by a lightning ball. After she revived, she had great power, which she dedicated to serving her people.

Other potential mystical intermediaries undergo rituals of purification, isolation, and bodily torment until they make contact with the spirit world. Igjugarjuk from northern Hudson Bay chose to suffer from cold, starvation, and thirst for a month in a tiny snow hut in order to draw the attention of Pinga, a helping female spirit:

> My novitiate took place in the middle of the coldest winter, and I, who never got anything to warm me, and must not move, was very cold, and it was so tiring having to sit without daring to lie down, that sometimes it was as if I died a little. Only towards the end of the thirty days did a helping spirit come to me, a lovely and beautiful helping spirit, whom I had never thought of; it was a white woman; she came to me whilst I had collapsed, exhausted, and was sleeping. But still I saw her lifelike, hovering over me, and from that day I could not close my eyes or dream without seeing her. ... She came to me from Pinga and was a sign that Pinga had now noticed me and would give me powers that would make me a shaman.[27]

For many mystical intermediaries, initiation into the role is not a matter of their own choice. The spirits enter whom they will. Often it is a person with unusual spiritual sensitivity who is chosen for this sacred work. Some people try to resist their calling but it is reportedly very difficult to do so because the spirits persist. Two men who were called as shamans in Nepal tried to get the spirits to leave them by praying to them, performing special worship ceremonies, and finally even carrying manure around to make themselves undesirable. But when some of their relatives and animals died, they surrendered and their rigorous initiation program began. When people resist the call, they themselves may become very sick and nearly die. Nevertheless, some who are called do not want to become spiritual intermediaries because the role would require them to give up their ordinary lives and take on heavy spiritual responsibilities, as well as go through difficult training that sometimes takes them to the edge of death.

Traditional diviners in Mali rake sand and leave it overnight. The tracks of animals that run over it are interpreted the next day for information the client seeks.

A shaman in Senegal invokes the power of a spirit and then, as its vehicle, sprays energized water onto a girl who needs healing.

LIVING INDIGENOUS SACRED WAYS

An Interview with Nadezhda Ananyevna Stepanova

One of the remaining traditional shamans of Buryatia, Nadezhda Ananyevna Stepanova comes from a family of very powerful shamans. Her mother tried to prevent her from becoming a shaman. Buddhist lamas had spread the impression that shamans were to be avoided, saying that they were ignorant, primitive servants of dark, lower spirits. The reputation of shamans has also been recently damaged by pseudo-shamans—some of whom have certain extrasensory powers and others of whom are simply cheats. But when a shaman receives a true spiritual call, to deny that pull is dangerous. Nadezhda explains:

As a child I knew when I would fall ill, and I could repeat by heart anything the teacher said or anything I read in a book, but I thought that was normal. When I was twenty-six, I was told I would be a shaman, a great shaman. When I told Mother, she said, "No, you won't." She took a bottle, went to her native town, and then came back. "Everything will be taken away; you won't become a shaman," she said. I didn't understand. The year I was said to become a shaman, I became seriously ill, and Mother was paralyzed. Usually paralyzed people have high blood pressure, but hers was normal. The doctors were surprised, but I understood then: We were both badly ill because she went against the gods.

Nobody could heal me. Then one seer said, "You must cure." I replied, "I don't know anything about curing." But a voice inside me said, "If you don't become a shaman, you will die. You will be overrun by a lorry with a blue number." I began to collect materials about medicine, about old rites. Then I could do a lot, for all we need is seeing and feeling. I was initiated by the men shamans of all the families, each praying to his god in a definite direction, for every god has his direction. I sat in the middle. Every shaman asked his gods to help me, to protect me, to give me power. The ritual was in early March. It was very frosty and windy, and I was only lightly dressed, but I wasn't cold at all. The wind didn't touch me. I sat motionless for about four hours, but I was not cold.

I began to cure. It is very difficult. You go through pain, through the tears of children and adults. I am able to see whether I will be able to cure a specific

person. The main thing to me is to help a person if I can. I pray to my gods, ask them for mercy, I ask them to pay attention, to help. I feel the pain of those who come to me, and I want to relieve it. I have yodo—*bark from a fir tree scratched by a bear; its smoke purifies. I perform rituals of bringing back the soul; often they work. My ancestors are very close to me; I see them as well as I see you.*

Last year in the island Olkhon in Lake Baikal, there was a great gathering of shamans from Tchita, Irkutsk, Ulan-Ude, Yakutiya, and Buryatia to pray to the great spirits of Baikal about the well-being and prosperity of the Buryat land. For a long time these spirits were not turned to. They were forgotten by the people, and they fell asleep. They could not take an active part in the life of people; they could not help them any more. Teylagan, *the prayer of the shamans for the whole Buryatia, was to awaken the great spirits.*

It was a clear, clear sunny day, without a cloud. When the prayer began, it started to rain. It was a very good sign. There had been a long drought before. The Olkhon shamans had tried to call rain, but they couldn't. But when everyone gathered and three sheep were sacrificed, then they could, and the shamans of that district were grateful.

We had always prayed to thirteen northern nainkhats, *the great spirits of this area. But when the Buddhists came, persecution began, and people prayed secretly, only for their families. They could not pray for the whole Buryat Nation, and they did not. They forgot. Shamans were killed. Then the atheistic Soviet regime tried to make us forget the faith, and we forgot. The most terrible thing about them was that they wanted to make people forget everything, to live by the moment and forget their roots. And what is man without roots? Nothing. It is a loss of everything. That is why now nobody has compassion for anybody. Now we are reaping the fruit: robbery, drinking, drugs. This is our disaster. That is why we must pray to our own gods.*

When we had the teylagan, *on the first day three blue pillars rose from earth to the sky—it was a prayer to Ehon-Bahve, the head spirit of Baikal, and to all three gods. The second day we prayed to the bird-god, and there were very many birds flying and a rainbow in the sky."*[28]

In addition to becoming familiar with death, a potential mystical intermediary must undergo lengthy training in spiritual techniques, the names and roles of the spirits, and secrets and myths of the tribe. Novices are taught both by older shamans and reportedly by the spirits themselves. If the spirits do not accept and teach the shaman, he or she is unable to carry the role.

The helping spirits that contact would-be mystical intermediaries during the death-and-rebirth crisis become essential partners in their sacred work. Often it is a spirit animal who becomes the shaman's guardian spirit, giving him or her special powers. The shaman may even take on the persona of the animal while working. Lapp shamans metamorphosed into wolves, reindeer, bears, or fish.

To enter parallel realities an altered state of consciousness is needed. Techniques for entering this state are the same around the world: drumming, rattling, singing, dancing, and in some cases hallucinogenic drugs. The effect of these influences is to open what the Huichol shamans of Mexico call the *nar-ieka*—the doorway of the heart, the channel for divine power, the point where human and spirit worlds meet. It is often experienced and represented artistically as a pattern of concentric circles.

The "journey" then experienced by mystical intermediaries is typically into the Upperworld or the Lowerworld. To enter the latter, they descend mentally through an actual hole in the ground, such as a spring, hollow tree, cave, animal burrow, or special ceremonial hole regarded as a navel of the earth. These entrances typically lead into tunnels that, if followed, open into bright landscapes. Reports of such experiences include not only what the journeyer saw but also realistic physical sensations, such as how the walls of the tunnel felt during the descent.

The shaman enters into the alternate landscape, encounters beings there, and may bring something back if it is needed by the client. This may be a lost guardian spirit or a lost soul, brought back to revive a person in a coma. The mystical intermediary may be temporarily possessed by the spirit of departed relatives so that an afflicted patient may finally clear up unresolved tensions with them that are seen as causing illness. Often a river must be crossed as the boundary between the world of the living and the world of the dead. A kindly old man or woman may appear to assist passage through the Lowerworld. In cultures that have subdued the indigenous ways, this mystical process is retained only in myths, such as the Greek story of Orpheus in the underworld.

Group observances

What group and individual observances do indigenous sacred ways follow?

Indigenous ways are community-centered. Through group rituals, traditional people not only honor the sacred but also affirm their bonds with each other and all of creation. Humans can help to maintain the harmony of the universe and thus, for example, ensure success in the hunt or harvest by their ritual observances. Rituals often take people out of everyday consciousness and into awareness of the presence of the sacred. In such altered states, participants may also experience a heightened group consciousness that powerfully binds individuals together as a community.

Rituals tend to follow certain patterns everywhere. Some honor major points in the human life cycle, such as birth, naming, puberty, marriage, and death. These rites of passage assist people in the transition from one state to another and help them become aware of their meaningful contribution to life. When a Hopi baby is twenty days old, it is presented at dawn to the rays of Father Sun for the first time and officially given a name. Its face is ritually cleansed with sacred cornmeal, a ceremony that will be repeated at death for the journey to the Lowerworld.

The Sun Dance Way of Self-Sacrifice

Sacrificing oneself for the sake of the whole is highly valued in most indigenous traditions. Through purification ceremonies, the people attempt to break through their small selves in order to serve as clear vehicles for the energy of the Great Spirit. In the Americas a powerful ceremony for these purposes is the sun dance. Among the Oglala Lakota, participants may dance for four days without food or water, looking at the sun and praying for blessings for the people. They say the ceremony as they practice it was first given to them through a vision received by a man named Kablaya.

In diverse forms, sun dances are now performed at many sites each spring and summer, most of them on the midwestern and northern plains of North America. In theory, only those who have had visions that they should perform the dance should do so. Some come in penance, for purification; others offer themselves as vehicles to request blessings for all people or for specific people who need help. It is not considered proper to dance for one's own needs.

Dancers make a commitment to do the dance for a certain number of times. Some sun dances include women dancers; some who dance are children. Non-indigenous people are generally barred from dancing.

The power of the sun dance requires that everything be handled in a sacred way. Dancers must do vision quests and purify themselves in sweat lodges before the ceremony begins. In spite of thirst and exhaustion, those in some sun dances continue to participate in sweat lodges each day of the dance. A tree is chosen to be placed at the center of the circle (among the Lakota, it is always a cottonwood, which when cut crosswise reveals a multipointed star pattern representing the sun). The tree's sacrifice is attended with ritual prayers. Participants may string prayer flags onto its branches before it is hoisted in the center of the dancing circle.

During the dance itself, the participants are guided through patterns with symbolic meanings. The choreography varies from one group to another. The Sioux sun dancers do not move around the circle except to shift slightly during the day so that they are always facing the sun. In Mexico the patterns continually honor the powers of the four directions by facing each one in turn.

As they dance, the dancers blow whistles traditionally made from the wing bones of the spotted eagle, but now often whittled from hollow sticks. When giving instructions for the dance, Kablaya reportedly

Sacred tree at the center of an area prepared for a Mexican version of the sun dance: Tonal Mitotianilitzli. Cloth strips tied to the tree carry prayers for the people.

explained, "When you blow the whistle always remember that it is the voice of the Spotted Eagle; our Grandfather, Wakan Tanka, always hears this, for you see it is really His own voice."[29]

At a recent sun dance held in Mexico, one participant* reports:

When the energy of the Dancers was probably at their lowest and most exhausted, nearing the end of a very long and hot and sunny day, an eagle flew overhead and kept circling the Dance for maybe five minutes, flying back and forth, and again and again to the sound of the Dancers' whistles and the Huehuetl drum. It brought tears to the eyes of many. The Dancers just kept whistling and saluting and greeting the huge and graceful bird. I have often seen an eagle fly over our circle during the Dance for a minute, but never have we seen one just keep circling and returning so long. It was truly breathtaking, like a message from the Creator that all was well, and our prayers were heard.

A group of people support the dancers by singing special sacred songs and beating a large drum. If their energy flags, so does that of the dancers. A woman sun dancer says that after a while, "The drum is no longer outside of you. It is as if in you and you don't even know that you're dancing." The dancers also support each other in ways such as using the feathers they carry to fan those whose energy seems low. There may also be communal vision ceremonies.

Each dancer is the carrier of a sacred pipe. Between rounds, the pipes may be shared with group onlookers who are led into the circle and who pass them around among the dancers to strengthen them with the power of the smoke.

Nondancers may also be led into the circle for a special healing round on the third or fourth day. By that time, the dancers have been so purified and empowered that they can all act as healers, using their eagle feathers as instruments to convey the divine power.

The suffering that each dancer willingly undergoes is heightened during piercing. For those whose visions suggest it—and whose tribes use piercing, for some do not—at some point during the dance incisions are made in the skin of their chest, back, or arms and sharpened sticks are inserted. There are then various ways of tearing through the skin. One reserved for chiefs is to drag buffalo skulls from ropes attached to the piercing sticks, symbolizing their carrying of the burdens of the people. More often, ropes are thrown over the trees and attached to the piercing sticks. Each person who pierces is then pulled upward, "flying" by flapping eagle wings, until the sticks break through the skin. It is thought that the more a person asks to do when making the sacrifice the more difficult it will be to break free. One Lakota dancer was instructed in a vision that he should be hung from the tree for a whole night. They had to pierce him in many places in order to distribute his weight, and then pull him down in the morning.

Why must the dance involve so much suffering? A Lakota sun dancer explains, "Nobody knows why, but suffering makes our prayers more sincere. The sun dance tests your sincerity, pushes your spirit beyond its limits." And as the dance goes on, many of the dancers transcend their physical agony and experience an increasing sense of euphoria. A Mexican dancer explains:

It's not pain. It's ecstasy. We get the energy from the sun and from the contact with Mother Earth. You also feel the energy of the eagles [who often fly overhead], all the animals, all the plants that surround you, all the vegetation. That energy comes to sustain you for the lack of food and water. Also when you smoke the pipe it serves as food or energy; the smoke feeds you energy so that you can continue. And every so often we put our palms to the sun to receive the energy from the sun. You can feel it in your whole body, a complete bath of energy.

*Names of individual dancers interviewed are not given here, to preserve their privacy and the sacredness of the dance.

In Oaxaca, Mexico, where more than half of the population is from indigenous cultures, perpetuation of those cultural traditions is encouraged by the annual Guelaguetza celebration. It showcases regional traditional dances and values of sharing, community, and reciprocity.

Girls commonly go through a special ceremony marking their first menstruation, which signals the end of childhood and preparation for becoming wives and mothers. For both boys and girls, the rituals of reaching puberty typically involve separation from the community, then a transition phase in which they are secluded with no clear identity and prepared for adulthood, and finally a third phase in which they are reincorporated into the community with a new adult identity. Boys' initiation rites may include ritual circumcision. Madonna Swan of the Lakota reports that she was secluded in part of her grandmother's cabin for her first moon ceremony, and that each day her grandmother would coach her in domestic skills and ethical principles. Her grandmother and mother daily bathed her in water with purifying sage and green cedar, and prayed for her in this fashion:

> *Grandfathers above and in the four directions, make Madonna a good woman. Help her to treat guests with hospitality. Grandfathers, help her to be a good worker. Grandfathers, and Maka Ina (Mother Earth), help Madonna to be a good mother. I pray that the food she cooks in her life will be good for those that eat it. Grandfathers, help her to be a good wife and live with the same man all her life. Grandfathers, bless her with healthy children.[30]*

There are also collective rituals to support the group's survival strategies. In farming communities these include ways of asking for rain, of ensuring the growth of crops, and of giving thanks for the harvest. Ritual dramas about the beginnings and sacred history of the people engage performers and spectators on an emotional level through the use of special costumes, body paint, music, masks, and perhaps sacred locations. These dramas provide a sense of orderly interface among humans, the land, and the spiritual world. They also dramatize mysticism, drawing the people toward direct contact with the spirit world. Those who have sacred visions and dreams are supposed to share them with others, often through dramatization.

Plains Indians observe sacred pipe ceremonies. According to legend, the Plains Indians were given the sacred pipe by White Buffalo Calf Woman as a tool for communicating with the mysteries and understanding the ways of life. The bowl of the pipe represents the female aspect of the Great Spirit, the stem the male aspect. When they are ritually joined, the power of the spirit is thought to be present as the pipe is passed around the circle for collective communion with each other and with the divine.

Groups also gather for ritual purification and spiritual renewal of individuals. Indigenous peoples of the Americas "smudge" sites and possessions, cleansing them with smoke from special herbs, such as sage and sweetgrass. Many groups make an igloo-shaped "sweat lodge" into which hot stones are carried. People huddle together in the dark around the stone pit. When water is poured on the stones, intensely hot steam sears bodies and lungs. Everyone prays earnestly. Lakota medicine man and spiritual leader Leonard Crow Dog says of the *inipi* (sweat lodge):

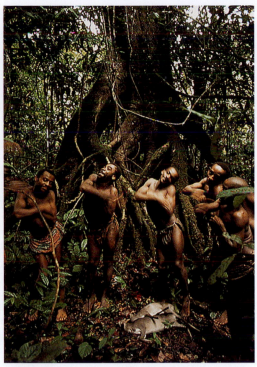

> The inipi *is probably our oldest ceremony because it is built around the simplest, basic, life-giving things: the fire that comes from the sun, warmth without which there can be no life;* inyan wakan, *or* tunka, *the rock that was there when the earth began, that will still be there at the end of time; the earth, the mother womb; the water that all creatures need; our green brother, the sage; and encircled by all these, man, basic man, naked as he was born, feeling the weight, the spirit of endless generations before him, feeling himself part of the earth, nature's child, not her master.*[31]

To the Efe pygmies of the Ituri Forest in the Democratic Republic of Congo, the Great Spirit is embodied in the forest itself, a benevolent presence that is both Mother and Father. Men perform a dance of gratitude to the forest for the animal food it provides.

Pilgrimages to sacred sites are often communal. Buryats gather on top of Erde, the mountain where the spirit of the earth lives, and all join hands to encircle it; a great energy is said to appear in the huge circle. The Huichol Indians of the mountains of western Mexico make a yearly journey to a desert they call Wirikuta, the Sacred Land of the Sun. They feel that creation began in this place. And like their ancestors, they gather their yearly supply of peyote cactus at this sacred site. Peyote has the power to alter consciousness: It is a spirit who helps them to communicate with the spirit world.

When indigenous groups are broken up by external forces, they lose the cohesive power of these group rituals. Africans taken to the New World as slaves lost not only their own individual identity but also their membership in tight-knit groups. In an attempt to re-establish a communal sense of shared spiritual traditions among African Americans, in 1966 Professor Maulana Ron Karenga created Kwanzaa, a contemporary end-of-year group celebration based on indigenous African "first fruits" harvest festivals. To explore their growth over the past year, participants look at their own experiences of the "seven principles"—unity, self-determination, collective work, family centeredness, purpose, creativity with limited resources, and confidence—and reward each other for progress by giving gifts.

In West Africa, the gods and the spirits of the dead appear to the living in masquerades. The mysteries of spirit are made semi-visible by costumed initiates.

Individual observances

In indigenous sacred ways, individuals may also experience a personal connection with the spirits, but the ways of doing so are shaped by community traditions. The people acknowledge and work with the spirits in ways dictated by communal norms. For instance, when searching for herbs, a person is not to take the first plant found;

This altar in the home of a Mexican healer illustrates the blending of indigenous ways with those of later religions. The serpent, masks, vegetables, eggs, and "bird's nest" derive from indigenous sacred ways, but are juxtaposed with Christian symbols.

an offering is to be made to it, with the prayer that its relatives will understand one's needs. Guardian spirits and visions may be sought by ordinary individuals, as well as by specialists. The shaman may have more spirit helpers and more power, but in some indigenous cultures, visionary experiences and opportunities for worship may be available to all. Indigenous traditions have therefore sometimes been called "democratized shamanism."

Temples to the spirits may exist, but one can also worship them anywhere. Wande Abimbola observes:

> Big temples aren't necessary to worship the orisa, even though there are temples for most orisa in Africa. If you are a devotee of Ifa, you can carry the objects of Ifa in your pocket. If you want to make an offering to Ogun, put any piece of iron on the floor and make an offering to it.[32]

To open themselves for contact with the spirit world, individuals in some indigenous cultures undergo a **vision quest**. After ritual purification, they are sent alone to a sacred spot to cry to the spirits to help them in their journey. Prepuberty or the onset of puberty is commonly thought to be the best time for vision quests, for children are closest to the spirit world. Among the Dene Tha' of northwestern Alberta, Canada, children are informally encouraged to go out to the bush before the age of puberty and spend time alone, seeking a spirit helper:

> When you are young, you go alone in the bush and you stay there and an animal comes to you. He talks to you just like we do now [sitting next to each other], and he tells you about him and with his power he gives you his power to heal other people. With it you heal people. If it tells you all how he is from beginning to end, you help someone, you cure him. If he does not tell everything, and you do not know all about him, then, when you help someone, you cure him, but you get the sickness.[33]

Adults may also make vision quests before undertaking a sacred mission, such as the sun dance. Indigenous Mexican leader Tlakaelel described the vision quest as he observed it:

You stay on a mountain, desert, or in a cave, isolated, naked, with only your sacred things, the things that you have gained, in the years of preparation—your eagle feathers, your pipe, your copal *[tree bark used as incense]. You are left alone four days and four nights without food and water. During this time when you are looking for your vision, many things happen. You see things move. You see animals that come close to you. Sometimes you might see someone that you care about a lot, and they're bringing water. You feel like you're dying of thirst, but there are limits around you, protection with hundreds of tobacco ties. You do not leave this circle, and this vision will disappear when they come to offer the water or sometimes they will just drop it on the ground. Or someone comes and helps you with their strength and gives you messages.*[34]

One is not supposed to ask for a vision for selfish personal reasons. The point of this individual ordeal, which is designed to be physically and emotionally stressful, is to ask how one can help the people and the planet. Moreover, it occurs within the context of the local and communal group tradition.

Globalization

How has globalization affected indigenous peoples?

Local spiritual traditions have suffered immensely from the onslaught of globalization processes. Many people are seeing the land they are supposed to be caretakers of taken over by others who have destroyed the natural environment; they are losing their grounding in local communities and lifeways, losing their languages, being devalued and suppressed by global religions, and becoming embroiled in nonlocal economic systems.

Sadly, traditional spiritual wisdom has been largely obliterated in many parts of the world by those who wanted to take the people's lands or save their souls with some other path to the divine. Under the slogan "Kill the Indian and save the man," the American founder of the boarding-school system for native children took them away from their families at a young age and transformed their cultural identity, presenting the native ways as inferior and distancing the children from normal participation in the traditional sacred life. They were exposed to the "modern" worldview, which does not believe in miracles, supernatural healings, or divine intervention—thus contradicting thousands of years of received wisdom in their own tradition.

A similar policy of attempted acculturation was conducted between the 1880s and 1960s with Australian Aboriginal children. Taken away from their parents by force, the "stolen generation" were often abused or used as slaves. Five children of Eliza Saunders were taken away by social workers while she and her husband were looking for employment. One of her children, the Green Party politician Charmaine Clarke, managed to run away from foster care after eleven years and rejoin her mother, but Clarke says of her missing family history, "When myself and my brothers and sisters go home, we five have to sit there quite mute and just listen, observe. Because we were never there."[35] In 1998, Australian citizens tried to apologize for this "attempted genocide," with some 300,000 signatures in Sorry Books and hundreds of emotional multiracial ceremonies in churches, schools, and cities across Australia.

In Africa, despite globalized social contexts, traditional religion is still strong among some groups, such as the Yoruba, whose priest-diviners are still respected, and to whom the *orisa* reportedly contacted in trance still reveal the nearness and importance of the invisible forces. However, in contemporary urban African areas, the traditional interest in the flow of the past into the present, with value placed on the intensity of present experience, has been rapidly replaced by a Westernized view of time in which one is perpetually anxious about the future. This shift has led to severe psychological disorientation and social and political instability. Those whose spiritual cultures have been merged with world religions such as Islam, Buddhism, or Christianity are now examining the

The Orang Asli of Malaysia: Traditions Being Lost

In peninsular Malaysia, at least 147,000 indigenous people known as the Orang Asli (original peoples) still maintain some of their traditional ways. Among them are a subgroup known as the Jakun, inhabitants of what was once an extensive peat swamp forest. Traditionally the Jakun lived by hunting and gathering, as well as cultivating small plots temporarily before moving on after harvesting the crops. They lived simply, with great respect for the forest, the forest animals, and the invisible spirits around them. Now, however, much of the peat swamp forest has been logged, drained, and converted into oil palm or rubber plantations. Destruction of the sponge-like peat swamp forest has brought increased flooding to the Jakuns' traditional home along the Bebar River, so severe that the Department of Orang Asli Affairs shifted them to a permanent settlement on higher ground in Kampung Simpai. Their children have been sent to distant boarding schools along with Malay children; there they are exposed to popular culture, and have become very fond of televisions, cell phones, and Western clothing. The Orang Asli remain one of the poorest sectors within Muslim-majority Malaysia.

In the past, the lives of the Jakun were governed by a series of taboos. For example, they were not to chop down unfamiliar trees or joke or shout in the forest, lest the spirit of a tree might possess or curse them. No animals thought to have the quality of *badi* (sacred spirits or spirits of the dead) should be killed or harmed, lest those spirits might retaliate in a manner resembling the way in which the animal was harmed.

Through these and other such taboos, the people were traditionally taught to live carefully, always mindful of the spirits around them. Thus they behaved respectfully everywhere, whether in the forest, in the river, or at home. Abu Bin Le, a fifty-three-year-old man who is now helping in the Heritage Garden Project sponsored by the European Commission and the United Nations Development Program to document and conserve indigenous medicinal plants and promote sustainable use of the forest, decries the loss of reverence among the younger generations:

Kids these days do not believe because [the dire results of breaking taboos] have not happened during their lifetime. The forests surrounding our village are gone, so there are no spirits left. Maybe just a few, but not as many as in the old days. Back then, we had forests, vast tracts of forests. Many spirits dwelled in the forests. Now that the forests are gone, it is unlikely that it would happen. When there were many spirits, we could not break taboos.

Seventeen-year-old Habib feels little connection to the spirits of the forests. He says:

It is not instilled in us. Besides, there isn't much of a forest left anyway, just acres of oil palm plantation. I remember when the forests still surrounded our houses when I was young.

Despite the loss of many traditional taboos, certain precautions are still followed, such as one prescribing that children are not to be scolded or teased to the point where they cry uncontrollably. Children are treated gently because many of the younger generations remember or heard of a dangerous storm which followed the breaking of the taboo about teasing children. Twenty-four-year-old Ann, great-granddaughter of the late village *bomoh* (shaman), was there when the storm happened:

Piran, who was then a little boy, was playing with a frog, but then his uncle took the frog away from him. He started crying and was inconsolable. All of a sudden, out of nowhere, there was thunder. The sky became dark and it started to pour. Piran's mother quickly grabbed Piran and ran towards her house, but it was as if the lightning was trailing them from behind. They ran into a local shaman's house who quickly performed jampi *[communication with the spirits]. At once, the rain stopped and the sky became clear and sunny again.*

Sanisah Dep, thirty-eight-year-old granddaughter of the late village *bomoh*, was also there:

I was horrified by what I saw. It was like a storm, but it was different from the usual storms we have here. As she ran, it was as if a group of dark clouds was hovering over her, chasing her. The uncle was teasing the child, so it happened. Now whatever the children want, we try to give or we pacify the child immediately.

In older times, there were *bomohs* who knew how to heal people, how to communicate with the spirits, and how to conduct the necessary rituals. But few of these elders are left. Sanisah lived next door to her grandfather, the village *bomoh*, and is certain that his death in 1997 was a result of his being unable to perform the obligatory ceremony to please the spirits:

Grandfather was an old man, in his eighties. Even so, he was still very strong, and was as fit as a fiddle. He was the village head and shaman, and many people respected him and sought his advice and help. Then early in 1997 the forest surrounding our houses was cleared to make way for Phase 2 of the community oil palm plantation. He was very upset with the village committee for clearing the forest behind his house, as he had asked them to spare a small portion of the forest, for this was where he did the bela kampung *ritual for the wellbeing of his family and the village. He warned them that if they cleared the area where he conducted the* bela kampung, *the spirits would be angry and there could be repercussions later on. No one listened to him and the forest was cleared and the oil palm planted.*

About two to three months after that, Grandfather was still hale and hearty and called all his grandchildren and great-grandchildren to a small feast in his house. All of a sudden, Grandfather gave a loud cry; he said that his head was very painful. I ran to get help. When I returned, I saw him sprawled on the floor of his house, his face tilted sideways, stiff. Unable to talk, he gestured to us to find his shaman tools so that he could perform jampi. *We did not know where he kept them, as he never told us. Unable to help him, we rushed him to the hospital, about 40 kilometers away, but he died upon reaching it. The doctors told us that his kidneys were damaged. I am not convinced, as Grandfather was very healthy. This happened all of a sudden, shortly after failing to perform the* bela kampung *when the time was due.*

Now there is no *bomoh* left in Kampung Simpai. There is still a *bomoh* in a nearby village, however, and his help was called for in November 2006 when a twelve-year-old Jakun girl contracted dengue hemorrhagic fever. The doctors at the nearest hospital said there was little chance of her recovery. To save her, her family took her to the *bomoh*. The girl recovered. She observed all traditional taboos until a special *putus ubat* ceremony was held for the whole extended family, to complete the healing and thank the spirits. Its climax was bathing of the girl and her father with coconut water mixed with water over which the *bomoh* had done *jampi*. In the photo shown here, the girl's maternal aunt is holding a knotted coconut leaf used in healing rituals, representing the suffering and disease that needed to be purged from the patient's body. The patient tore it into two, marking the end of her illness.

Although earlier generations lived with little chance for work, with even rice a luxury, some of the old people are nostalgic about the past. Abu says:

We Orang Asli open up small portions of the forest for our swidden plots, say ten acres. But now the plantations have opened up thousands of acres of forest. It's so vast that one cannot see anything but oil palm. I remember hearing birds chirping and monkeys making funny noises. Our community was not only a community of people, but also of animals. We do miss the sounds of the animals in the morning. All we hear now is the rumbling of the lorries carrying the oil palm fruit.[36]

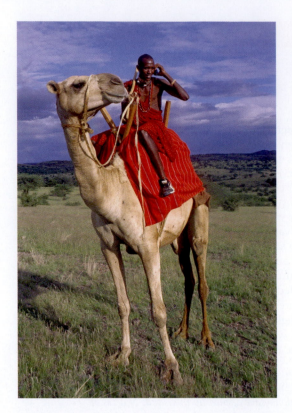

Many Maasai men have resisted globalization in terms of clothing and pastoral lifestyle, but nevertheless live in the modern world, complete with cell phones.

relationship of their earlier tradition to the intercultural traditions. African scholars have noted, for instance, that to put God in the forefront, as Christians do, does violence to the greater social importance of ancestor spirits in the religions of Africa.

However, indigenous groups have not just suffered passively and become extinct. They are negotiating with modernity and globalization in various ways. In some cases, contact with the rest of the world has been turned to advantage without loss of the traditional culture. The Dene Tha' now live in houses built by the government and ride snowmobiles instead of their traditional dog sleds, but as hunters they still seek spiritual aid from "animal helpers" and find important meaning and guidance in their visionary experiences. In a Maasai village near Nairobi in Kenya, elders started a small museum. In a traditional hut, they collected various Maasai artefacts—such as spears, swords, iron ore, shields, knives, hides and skins, gourds, and beadwork—in a bid to preserve their culture and traditions and, at the same time, use the museum as a tourist attraction to create income for community development. African-derived religions are increasingly appropriating new communication technologies to transmit their ideologies outside Africa, as in Internet websites such as OrishaNet.org.

Indigenous sensitivities are also playing a role in environmental preservation. In Kenya, local indigenous communities, when faced with the threat of destruction of their sacred forest of Ruiga, managed to protect the land from illegal logging and human encroachment by having it designated a natural monument under the Antiquities and Monuments Act. One of the world's best-preserved indigenous forests, Ruiga has traditionally been protected by the local people through myths and taboos. For instance, cutting trees within the forest was forbidden because it was thought that if a tree were cut, it would bleed and cry, and also bring a curse on the family of the person who cut it. Children were taught that there was a deep but invisible lake in the heart of the forest; any trespassers would probably drown in it. Now a community-based organization is charged with protecting, conserving, and preserving the sacred forest, and also with guiding visitors from around the world who come to see it.

On the other hand, there may be strong resistance to selling sacred knowledge to outsiders. While indigenous traveling teachers are swamped with eager students from other cultures who are fascinated with shamanism, elders of the Lakota tribes have urged all indigenous nations to use every means possible to prevent the exploitation of their spiritual traditions by "'the New Age movement,' 'the men's movement,' 'neo-paganism cults,' 'shamanism' workshops—a scandalous assortment of pseudo-Indian charlatans, 'wannabes,' commercial profiteers, cultists and 'New Age shamans.'"[37] Stories of the visionary benefits of the Amazonian plant brew ayahuasca have brought hordes of foreigners to Peru—where it is legal—to engage in vision-seeking experiences that were traditionally monitored by shamans. Now the area is full of pseudo-shamans and resorts that are exploiting the financial potential of this sacred practice, sometimes with fatal results. This new phenomenon raises issues of how foreigners and local people have reinvented, adopted, and transformed the indigenous spiritual traditions and what effects these changes are having on the local forest people and ethnic cultural revival. Even outsiders who value the sacred teachings may disrupt or alter the indigenous practices. Osage theologian George Tinker describes what has often happened in North America:

> *The first Indian casualty today in any such New Age spiritual-cultural encounter is most often the strong deep-structure cultural value of community and group cohesion that is important to virtually every indigenous people. ... Well-meaning New Agers drive in from New York and Chicago or fly in from Austria and*

Denmark to participate in annual ceremonies originally intended to secure the well-being of the local, spatially configured community. These visitors see little or nothing at all of the reservation community, pay little attention to the poverty and suffering of the people there and finally leave having achieved only a personal, individual spiritual high.[38]

Development issues

How have indigenous peoples responded to development projects?

Contemporary economic development schemes are not necessarily having positive effects in indigenous cultures. The Nankani understand that *malgo* (development) to benefit the people is an eternal process, but one in which the spiritual connection with spirits, family, and community must be maintained as the "root to hold on to and to be held."[39]

In collision or collusion with larger societies, indigenous peoples have often been victims of disastrous development projects. In the United States, reservations on which thousands of Navajos and Hopis were living were found to be sitting on the largest coal deposit in the country—the 4,000-square-mile (10,000-square-kilometer)"Black Mesa." In 1966, the Navajo and Hopi tribal councils signed agreements allowing Black Mesa to be strip-mined by utility companies to provide electricity for southwestern cities, and, presumably, economic development for the tribes. Since then the sacred land has been devastated, ancient archaeological and burial sites have been destroyed, thousands of Navajos have been displaced, surface and ground water have been contaminated, and aquifers are drying up as 1.3 billion gallons (five billion liters) of pure water per year have been used to pump the coal slurry to a power plant hundreds of miles away. It is now thought that the government-established tribal councils—themselves not considered genuine representatives of the tribal peoples—were being advised by an attorney who was secretly employed by the coal company. Indigenous groups are pressing for legal action that would impose limits on future damage to the area and curb tactics being used to pressurize the indigenous people. Cherokee attorney Jace Weaver points out that there are difficulties in protecting the rights of indigenous people on religious grounds because the legal definition of "religion" is limited. He writes, "Lacking a concept of the holy, our legal system finally is incapable of comprehending Native religious freedom and land claims."[40]

In the heart of India, tribal peoples of Madhya Pradesh are trying to block government allocation of more than a million acres (400,000 hectares) of forest land to coal-mining companies. In Tanzania, Maasai people are trying to prevent eviction from their land for the sake of foreign tourists who would shoot the lions and leopards. In Zimbabwe, thousands of traditional self-sufficient Vaduma people were displaced when their ancestral lands were flooded to create a huge artificial lake for irrigating an area hundreds of miles away. Jameson Kurasha of the University of Zimbabwe describes the effects on the Vaduma:

When the "idea" of development was imposed on them, families were separated by a massive stretch of water. Now the Murinye Mugabe families are alienated from each other. They are now peoples without a tangible past to guide and unite them because their past [i.e. ancestors] are either buried or washed away by the lake. They are basically a people without a home to point to. The separation has left a cultural damage that will never be restored.[41]

In Malaysia, the indigenous Orang Asli people and anthropologists, sociologists, and development workers who are familiar with their situation feel that the Malaysian government is intentionally but discreetly forcing the people from their traditional homelands so that it can appropriate the timber-rich land. So long as the Orang Asli live in the forests, especially if they are granted land rights to their ancestral lands, the individual state governments cannot get access to

For the Ogoni of Nigeria, oil extraction by multinational companies for decades without environmental protection has brought devastating effects.

the timber revenues. Critics think this is why the government is making efforts to "integrate" the Orang Asli into Malay culture in the name of "development," including relocation, education, and Islamization, in order to detach them from their spiritual affinity to their land.

Exploitation by multinational companies of the natural resources on land occupied by indigenous groups has sometimes been cloaked in talk of helping the local economy, but often the results have been devastating for indigenous peoples, spiritually as well as economically. In Nigeria, oil production accounts for eighty-seven percent of the government's foreign revenue. Multinational companies' activities to extract the oil have for decades involved burning the waste gases, dumping waste products, leaks from oil pipelines, and oil slicks, causing extensive destruction of animal and plant life, soil damage, air and water pollution, and health problems among the indigenous peoples. The efforts of one severely affected group, the Ogoni, to protest this situation were met with harassment, and ultimately the leaders were killed by the government. The Ogoni have continued their opposition nevertheless. Not only have their traditional lifeways been disrupted with the destruction of their environment, but also, more significantly from their point of view, they feel they must try to protect their ancestors' graves on their homesteads, plus their sacred groves and natural holy places. They feel their ancestors will not forgive them if they do not stand up to the oil business's desecration of their graves and sacred sites.

Modern development schemes—as well as outright plunder of natural resources for profit—are being called into question by land-based traditional peoples around the world, and attempts have begun to re-establish the validity of the ancient wisdom. In India, officials in the Ministry of Environment and Forests are acknowledging that the remaining sacred groves of the indigenous peoples are treasure houses of biodiversity and should not be destroyed. In such areas, it is often the shamans who teach the tribal people the importance of protecting the trees and vegetation.

Some indigenous peoples feel that their traditional sacred ways are not only valid, but actually essential for the future of the world. They see these understandings as antidotes to mechanistic, dehumanizing, environmentally destructive ways of life. Rather than regarding their ancient way as inferior, intact groups such as the Kogi of the high Colombian rainforest feel they are the elder brothers of all humanity, responsible for keeping the balance of the universe and re-educating their younger brothers who have become distracted by desire for material gain.

Damaris Parsitau

Having come from the Maasai tribe in Kenya and now being a professor at the University of Egerton, Damaris Parsitau is looked up to as a mentor for Maasai girls and women. When she makes scholarly presentations at international academic conferences (she is shown here at a conference in Oxford, UK), she helps to dispel stereotypes of Maasai as being primitive because these tall, proud people have traditionally lived as nomadic pastoralists and only recently were persuaded to abandon their traditions of training young men as warriors. Many still refuse to wear Western clothing. Damaris explains that her life straddles both worlds:

I am not living a traditional Maasai lifestyle, although I feel like I am a true Maasai woman. My grandparents practiced Maasai culture and tradition. To date, some of my relatives still practice traditional culture. Having said this, it is important to note that I am a child of both worlds. I was brought up by my parents who practiced some aspects of Maasai traditional culture and a bit of modernity. My mother was a Presbyterian and I was baptized in this church at the age of twelve. My father was more of a traditional man who embraced modernization. He sent his children to school, built a modern house for his family, but also kept a large herd of cattle, sheep, and goats and owned huge tracts of land where his livestock grazed.

Yet despite being a university professor, and one who has embraced modernity, I am still a Maasai girl deep down. What does being a Maasai mean to me? I am proud of my Maasai culture and tradition. It is my heritage, my identity, and who I am. It has given me my roots, a sense of belonging and community, and I take great pride in my cultural and traditional heritage. I speak my mother tongue (Maa) and love Maasai food—milk, meat (although I love my vegetables as well)—and mode of dress. Occasionally I don my Maasai attire during functions like weddings, graduation ceremonies, fundraising activities, and other community-based events.

I have raised my children as Maasai and I try to pass on to them some of our best cultural aspects as a minority group—a sense of community, respect for others, kindness, and compassion. For example, being mean and unkind to others is frowned upon, and people are encouraged to eat together and share what they have with others. Children are taught to respect each other, elders, seniors, women, and the weak. My parents opened their home to many needy people and my father was engaged in community work, while my mother worked with women. I have passed these values to my children, and we do what we can to help others. I have taught them to respect people irrespective of whether they are poor or rich, good-looking or not. I abhor prejudice of all kinds and am not willing to judge others on account of race, ethnicity, class, color, etc.

Stories of tradition are taught and followed in our family. Once a year we all meet so that our children can know and connect with each other and learn from each other. However, as an educated Maasai woman, I come across many stereotypes. Many people find it hard to believe that I am Maasai and many wonder how a woman from such a "primitive" tribe is so well-schooled and intelligent, well-traveled, and teaches at university. The Maasai are regarded as unschooled, backward, and primitive because they resist modernization and Westernization. But I am amazed at how smart and knowledgeable indigenous people are and how they connect powerfully with nature and their spirituality. For example, the Maasai are well known all over Kenya for their knowledge of indigenous medicines for treating both humans and animals.

My Maasai culture and background enables me to respect and even embrace other people's cultures, traditions, and spiritualities. I practice yoga and meditation for relaxation—not very Maasai-like. Yet I don't see much conflict between being a Maasai woman and a modern woman at the same time.[42]

The International Council of Thirteen Indigenous Grandmothers has been created as a project of the Center for Sacred Studies in Guerneville, California. The grandmothers form a global alliance for prayer, education, and healing of the earth for the sake of the next seven generations. From left to right, they are Clara Shinobu Iura and Maria Alice Campos Freire (Amazonian rainforest, Brazil), Margaret Behan (Arapaho/Cheyenne, Montana, USA), Rita Pitka Blumenstein (Yup'ik, Alaskan tundra, USA), Beatrice Long Visitor Holy Dance and Rita Long Visitor Holy Dance (Oglala Lakota, Black Hills, South Dakota, USA), Bernadette Rebienot (Omyene, Gabon, Africa), Mona Polacca (Havasupai/Hopi/Tewa, Arizona, USA), Agnes Baker Pilgrim (Takelma Siletz, Grants Pass, Oregon, USA), Julieta Casimiro (Mazatec, Huautla de Jimenez, Mexico), Flordemayo (Maya, highlands of Central America/New Mexico), Aama Bombo/Buddhi Maya Lama (Tamang, Nepal), and Tsering Dolma Gyaltong (Tibetan).

Differences of opinion and lifestyle between native people who live traditionally and those who have embraced industrial materialistic culture have led to rifts within the communities. There are people for and against selling mineral rights to community land for economic gain. Some indigenous people also question the ethics of developing gambling casinos as a base for economic self-sufficiency. But gaming has interesting precedents in many world religions and was traditionally part of sacred rites in many indigenous cultures. Ceremonial throwing of dice has been symbolically associated with the cycles of death and rebirth, and the movement of the sun, moon, and stars. The chance turn of the dice or wheel of fortune often appears in myths as a metaphor for balance in the continual shifts between happiness and sorrow. Gaming rituals were used by some tribes to help the movement of the seasons and the shifts between night and day, to influence the weather, to assist in hunting, and to restore health. Addictive gambling is a different matter, for it can be disastrous for individuals and their families.

In traditionally matriarchal societies, some women's groups are trying to save traditional social structures. The Igbo-speaking peoples (also known as Ibo)—numbering more than thirty million in Nigeria and the diaspora—have a basically matriarchal social structure and theology. Theirs has traditionally been an economy of co-operation and exchange, with the land associated with dead ancestors and therefore never to be sold. With particular reference to the Igbo, Adi Amadiume, Professor of African Studies at Dartmouth College, New Hampshire, proposes a theory of matriarchal versus patriarchal economics:

> *It is the relational matriarchal model that contains the ideal economic theory of African traditional religions; this is a theory of community, exchange, reciprocity, and sharing. This relational matriarchal theory is based on the ideology of* Umunne, *those who share the spirit of common motherhood, who eat out of one pot, and are bound by the prohibition of* Ibenne, *a taboo of same blood where love and not self-interest rules. ... Social values of exchange are better expressed in matriarchy than in linear patriarchy because patriarchy promotes competition rather than exchange.*[43]

Women played a major role in trying to resist colonial invasion. Igbo and neighboring Ibibio matriarchs led the Women's War of 1929 against the destructive effects of a cash-crop economy, taxation, and capitalist market forces, as well as the religious and social marginalization of women. Today, Igbo women are fighting against patriarchal state and international structures, including the World Bank and International Monetary Fund, to resist what they regard as culture-fragmenting competitive economic policies.

Personal visions and ancient prophecies about the dangers of a lifestyle that ignores the earth and the spiritual dimensions of life are leading native elders around the world to gather internationally and raise their voices together. They assert indigenous spiritual insights and observations about the state of the planet, political matters, and contemporary lifestyle issues.

Indigenous elders who are now speaking out seek converts not to their path but to a respect for all of life, which they feel is essential for the harmony of the planet. A respected elder of the Hopi Nation, the late Thomas Banyacya, made a stirring appeal to the United Nations in 1992, in which he explained Hopi prophecies about our times. According to the prophecies, the creator made a perfectly balanced world but when humans turned away from spiritual principles for selfish reasons, the world was destroyed by earthquakes. The few survivors developed the second world, but repeated their mistakes, and the world was destroyed by the Ice Age. The few people who survived spoke one language and developed high technologies but when they turned away from natural laws and spiritual principles, the third world was destroyed by a great flood, which is remembered in the ancient stories of many peoples. Now we are living in the fourth world. According to Hopi time lines, we are in the final stages of decay. Showing a rock drawing of part of the Hopi prophecy, Thomas Banyacya explained:

There are two paths. The first with high technology but separate from natural and spiritual law leads to these jagged lines representing chaos. The lower path is one that remains in harmony with natural law. Here we see a line that represents a choice like a bridge joining the paths. If we turn to spiritual harmony and live from our hearts we can experience a paradise in this world. If we continue only on this upper path, we will come to destruction.[44]

Key terms

cosmogony A model of the origins of the universe.
indigenous Native to an area.
lifeway An entire approach to living in which sacred and secular are not separate.
medicine person An indigenous healer.
orisa Yoruba term for a deity.
shaman A man or woman who has undergone spiritual ordeals and can communicate with the spirit world to help the people.
vision quest A solitary ordeal undertaken to seek spiritual guidance about one's mission in life.

Suggested reading

Adogame, Afe, Ezra Chitando, and Bolaji Bateye, eds, *African Traditions in the Study of Religion in Africa: Emerging Trends, Indigenous Spirituality and the Interface with other World Religions*, Farnham, Surrey, UK: Ashgate Publishing, 2012. Studies of African religions by African scholars.

Amenga-Etego, Rose Mary, *Mending the Broken Pieces: Indigenous Religion and Sustainable Rural Development in Northern Ghana*, Trenton: Africa World Press, 2011. Study of a particular African indigenous tradition to determine the relationship of its spiritual ways with modern development.

Basso, Keith H., *Wisdom Sits in Places: Landscape and Language among the Western Apache*, Albuquerque: University of New Mexico Press, 1996. Interesting first-person ethnographic study of the meanings that Apache people attach to their environment.

Bell, Diane, *Daughters of the Dreaming*, second edition, Minneapolis: University of Minnesota Press, 1993. A pioneering study of Australian Aboriginal women, by an anthropologist who lived among them.

Berger, Julian, *The Gaia Atlas of First Peoples: A Future for the Indigenous World*, New York: Anchor Books, 1990. An illustrated survey of contemporary survival issues facing the indigenous people of many lands, with particular reference to threats to their environment from invading cultures.

Bongmba, Elias Kifon, *The Wiley-Blackwell Companion to African Religions*, Chichester, West Sussex, UK: Wiley-Blackwell, 2012. A comprehensive review written by leading experts on African religions.

Cox, James L., ed., *Critical Reflections on Indigenous Religions*, Farnham, Surrey, UK: Ashgate Publishing, 2013. Essays sorting out methodological issues in the study of indigenous religions that have arisen from using Western models of understanding.

Cox, James L., *From Primitive to Indigenous: The Academic Study of Indigenous Religions*, Farnham, Surrey, UK: Ashgate Publishing, 2007. Critique of the history of academic study of indigenous religions, with case studies.

Eliade, Mircea, trans. Willard Trask, *Shamanism: Archaic Techniques of Ecstasy*, London: Routledge & Kegan Paul, 1964. The first scholarly book to examine shamanism as an authentic religious form rather than as an anthropological oddity.

Erdoes, Richard and Alfonso Ortiz, *American Indian Myths and Legends*, New York: Pantheon Books,1984. A classic collection of stories from eighty North American tribes that offers insights into traditional perceptions and lifeways.

Ewen, Alexander, *Voice of Indigenous Peoples*, Santa Fe, New Mexico: Clear Light Publishers, 1994. Speeches and writings from indigenous speakers at the 1992 United Nations Human Rights Day, analyzing the political conditions facing indigenous peoples.

Ford, Clyde, *The Hero with an African Face: Mythic Wisdom of Traditional Africa*, New York: Bantam, 2000. Sensitive exploration of mythological clues to traditional African beliefs.

Gill, Sam D., *Native American Religions*, Belmont, California: Wadsworth, 1982, 2004. Academic survey of indigenous sacred ways in the United States.

Gleason, Judith, *Oya: In Praise of an African Goddess*. San Francisco: HarperSanFrancisco, 1993. Dynamic study of the complex of beliefs surrounding the Yoruba goddess Oya.

Goulet, Jean-Guy A., *Ways of Knowing: Experience, Knowledge, and Power among the Dene Tha*, Lincoln: University of Nebraska Press, 1998. Attempt by an anthropologist to directly experience and then explain to others the contemporary lifeways of these traditional people in northern Canada.

Grim, John, ed., *Indigenous Traditions and Ecology: The Interbeing of Cosmology and Community*, Cambridge, Massachusetts: Harvard University Press, 2001. One of the excellent volumes of the series "Religions of the World and Ecology," this volume traces environmental themes across many different indigenous cultures.

Halifax, Joan, *Shamanic Voices: A Survey of Visionary Narratives*, New York: E. P. Dutton, 1979, and Harmondsworth: Penguin, 1980. Firsthand accounts of shamanistic visionary experiences.

Harvey, Graham, *Indigenous Religions: A Companion*, London and New York: Continuum International Publishing, 2000. Scholarly articles about specific cultures, attempting to transcend the tendency to understand indigenous religions in terms of concepts taken from other religions.

Jakobsen, Merete Demant, *Shamanism: Traditional and Contemporary Approaches to the Mastery of Spirits and Healing*, Providence, Rhode Island: Berghahn, 1999. A specific historical study of shamanism in Greenland, which the author then compares with neo-shamanic practices associated with contemporary "Core Shamanism."

Magesa, Laurenti, *African Religion: The Moral Traditions of Abundant Life*, Maryknoll, New York: Orbis Books, 1997. An African Catholic theologian describes African traditional beliefs and practices as teachings about how to live meaningfully and harmoniously.

Mbiti, John S., *African Religions and Philosophy*, second edition, Oxford: Heinemann, 1999. A classic study of traditional African religions from an African point of view, including a strong critique of earlier anthropological perspectives.

Nelson, Richard K., *Make Prayers to the Raven: A Koyukon View of the Northern Forest*, Chicago: University of Chicago Press, 1986. Careful explanations of the close interrelationships between people and the rest of the natural world among these people of the western Canadian forest and tundra.

Onnudottir, Helena, Adam Possamai, and Bryan S. Turner, *Religious Change and Indigenous Peoples: The Making of Religious Identities*, Farnham, Surrey, UK: Ashgate

Publishing, 2013. Survey of conversion by indigenous people in Australia and New Zealand to global religions, especially Islam.

Olupona, Jacob K., ed., *African Spirituality: Forms, Meanings and Expressions*, New York: Crossroad Publishing Company, 2000. Studies of spiritual themes in the religions of Africa and how they have become integrated with Christian and Muslim influences.

Ponniah, K. James, *The Dynamics of Folk Religion in Society: Pericentralisation as Deconstruction of Sanskritisation*, New Delhi: Serials Publications, 2011. Unraveling of the interrelationships between tribal beliefs and global "Hinduism" in southern India.

Prasad, Archana, *Against Ecological Romanticism: Verrier Elwin and the Making of an Anti-Modern Tribal Identity*, second edition. Gurgaon, India: Three Essays Collective, 2011. A new look at romantic ideas about tribal life and ecology in India.

Smelcer, John, *The Raven and the Totem: Traditional Alaskan Native Myths*. Anchorage: Salmon Runn/Todd communications, 1992. Collection of myths from twenty indigenous Alaskan groups.

St. Pierre, Mark and Tilda Long Soldier, *Walking in the Sacred Manner*, New York: Simon and Schuster, 1995. First-person accounts of Plains Indian women's spiritual roles.

Weaver, Jace, ed., *Native American Religious Identity: Unforgotten Gods*, Maryknoll, New York: Orbis Books, 1998. Essays examining facets of contemporary religious identities among Native Americans.

2.1 Outline the challenges faced by scholars in understanding indigenous sacred ways

Many indigenous sacred ways, such as those in Mesoamerica, have long been practiced only in secret. In most native cultures, people create and pass on traditions, myths, songs, and sayings orally, and there are no scriptures of the sort that other religions are built around. Until recently, those who attempted to ferret out the native sacred ways had little basis for understanding them and approached spiritual behaviors from the nonspiritual perspective of Western science or else the Christian understanding of a religion as a means of salvation from sinful earthly existence (a belief not found among most indigenous peoples). Realizing that researchers did not grasp the truth of their beliefs, native peoples have sometimes hindered Western scholars by giving them incorrect information in order to protect the sanctity of their practices.

2.2 Explain the cultural diversity of indigenous groups

While indigenous sacred ways have some characteristics in common, there are many differences in the lifestyles, religious beliefs, and practices among indigenous peoples. In North America alone there are hundreds of different indigenous traditions, and Australian Aboriginal lifeways included more than 500 different clan groups. Among Africa's innumerable ethnic and social groupings, there are some indigenous groups comprising millions of people, such as the Yoruba, and others that are small-scale. All of these indigenous peoples have different geographies, histories, and economic patterns. Some traditions have evolved within materially and technologically advanced cultures; others have had to adapt to dominant religions such as Buddhism, Islam, and Christianity. While some indigenous peoples continue to live as mobile foragers or in their ancestral enclaves, others live in more urban settings because of job opportunities, but visit their sacred sites and ancestral shrines.

2.3 Describe the circle of right relationships

For many indigenous peoples, everything in the cosmos is intimately interrelated. They feel that they belong to their native place in an eternal sacred relationship. Some hold the circle as a sacred symbol because it has no beginning nor end. To maintain the natural balance of the circles of existence, most indigenous peoples have traditionally been taught they must develop right relationships with spirits and spiritual energy.

Many indigenous traditions worship a Supreme Being, while others recognize a great pantheon of deities. Communication with ancestors is also important to some traditions, particularly in Africa. All aspects of the tangible world are believed to be imbued with spirit and interconnected, and respect is thus due to all creatures and the natural environment. Developing an appropriate relationship with spiritual energy is also a common theme in indigenous lifeways, and the power of spirit is believed to be highly concentrated in certain sacred sites and beings.

2.4 Identify the different spiritual specialists in indigenous sacred ways

In many indigenous cultures, ways of interacting with spirit are thought best left to those who are specially trained. Specialists' roles vary from one group to another, but one common role is that of the storyteller who must memorize long and complex stories and songs so that the group's sacred traditions can be remembered and taught. Another coveted role is that of being a member of a secret society, either by initiation or invitation, enabling the person to draw closer to the spirit world. Sacred dancers also make the unseen powers visible and in some socially stratified societies there are priests and priestesses who carry out rituals. Other spiritual specialists include shamans, who offer themselves as mystical intermediaries between the human community and the spirits, attempting to use them for various needs of the community, such as ensuring the success of the hunt or curing illnesses. There are also spirit mediums, who undergo possession by spirits for the sake of others, and medicine people, who have special healing skills.

2.5 Summarize group and individual observances in indigenous sacred ways

Through group rituals, traditional people not only honor the sacred but also affirm their bonds with each other and all of creation. Ceremonies are performed to maintain natural balance and to ensure success in the hunt or harvest. Some groups honor major points in the human life cycle, such as birth, naming, marriage, death, and particularly puberty. There are also collective rituals to support the group's survival strategies and ritual dramas about the beginnings and sacred history of the people. Groups also gather for ritual purification and spiritual renewal of individuals, and pilgrimages to sacred sites are often communal.

It is considered important for each person to experience a personal connection with the spirits and worship is made through offerings and prayers. Individuals in many indigenous cultures undergo a vision quest in which, after ritual purification, they are sent alone to a sacred spot to cry to the spirits to help them in their journey.

2.6 Illustrate how the processes of globalization are affecting indigenous peoples

Indigenous peoples are seeing the land of which they are supposed to be caretakers taken over by others who have destroyed the natural environment. They are losing their grounding in local communities and lifeways, losing their languages, being devalued and suppressed by global religions, and becoming embroiled in nonlocal economic systems. Traditional spiritual wisdom has been largely obliterated in many parts of the world by those who wanted to take the people's lands or save their souls with some other path to the divine.

2.7 Discuss how development projects have affected indigenous peoples and how they have responded

In collision or collusion with larger societies, indigenous peoples have often been victims of disastrous modern development projects, as well as of the outright plunder of natural resources for profit. The results of these schemes have been spiritually and economically devastating. In the United States, indigenous groups are pressing for legal action to impose limits on future damage to sacred land and ancient archaeological sites destroyed by coal mining. In Nigeria, the Ogoni have protested against multinational companies' extraction of oil, which has caused pollution, destruction of the environment, and health problems. In the heart of India, tribal peoples of Madhya Pradesh are trying to block government allocation of more than a million acres (400,000 hectares) of forest land to coal-mining companies.

Personal visions and ancient prophecies about the danger of a lifestyle that ignores the earth and spiritual dimensions of life are also leading native elders around the world to gather internationally and raise their voices: speaking out to seek converts not to their path but to a respect for all of life.

CHAPTER 3

HINDUISM

"Beyond all these things is that same existence, that same primordial frequency." Somjit Dasgupta[1]

3.1 **Explain the origins and significance of the Vedas**

3.2 **Illustrate how the epics and Puranas represent the Supreme**

3.3 **Compare and contrast Shaktas, Shaivas, and Vaishnavas**

3.4 **Describe the major philosophical systems**

3.5 **Outline the main public and private rituals in Hinduism**

3.6 **Discuss the issue of defining Hindu identity in modern India**

In the Indian subcontinent there has developed a complex variety of religious paths. Some of these paths are relatively unified religious systems, such as Buddhism, Jainism, and Sikhism. Most of the other Indian religious ways have been categorized together as if they were a single tradition under the name "Hinduism." This term is derived from a name applied by foreigners to the people living in the region of the Indus River, and was introduced in the nineteenth century under colonial British rule as a category for census-taking.

This labeling and interpretation of Indian religious traditions by non-Indians is currently a hotly debated issue. Some Indians now assert that Western analysis of Hinduism has been carried on by outsiders who were biased against Indian culture, or who presumed that all religions can be studied according to Western religious categories. Even the Hindi word "**dharma**," often translated into English simply as "religion," refers to a broad complex of meanings, encompassing duty, natural law, social welfare, ethics, health, wealth, power, fulfillment of desires, and transcendental realization. Furthermore, Hinduism is not easily separated fully from other dharmic traditions that have arisen in India, including Buddhism, Jainism, and Sikhism, for there has been extensive cross-pollination among them.

The spiritual expressions of Hinduism range from extreme **asceticism** to extreme sensuality, from the heights of personal devotion to a deity to the heights of abstract philosophy, from metaphysical proclamations of the one-ness behind the material world to worship of images representing a multiplic-ity of deities. According to tradition, there are actually 330 million deities in India. The feeling is that the divine has countless faces.

The extreme variations within Hinduism are reflections of its great age. Few of the myriad religious paths that have arisen over the millennia have been lost. They continue to co-exist in present-day India. Some scholars of religion argue that these ways are so varied that there is no central tradition that can be called Hinduism proper.

In villages, where the majority of Indians live, worship of deities is quite diverse and does not necessarily follow the more reified and philosophical Brahmanic tradition that is typically referred to as "Hinduism." Since it is not possible here to trace all these diffuse, widely scattered strands in their complex historical development, we will instead explore the main facets of the Brahmanic tradition thematically: its philosophical and metaphysical elements, then its devotional and ritual aspects, and, finally, its features as a way of life. These are not in fact totally separate categories, but we will separate them somewhat for clarity. Afterward, we will look at global and political aspects of the contemporary practice of Hinduism.

Philosophical and metaphysical origins
What are the origins and significance of the Vedas?

The Brahmanic tradition can be traced back to the Vedic age, thousands of years ago. The metaphysical beliefs in the Vedas were elaborated into various schools of thought by philosophers and sages. These beliefs were brought forth experientially by various methods of spiritual discipline.

> *Truth is one; sages call it by various names.*
>
> *Rig Veda*

The Indus Valley civilization

Many of the threads of Hinduism may have existed in the religions practiced by the early Dravidian peoples of India. There were also advanced urban centers in the Indus Valley from about 2500 BCE, or even earlier, until 1500 BCE. Major fortified cities with elaborate plumbing and irrigation systems and paved, right-angled streets have been found by archaeologists at Harappa, Mohenjo-Daro, Dholavira, and other sites; the culture they represent is labeled the Indus Valley civilization.

According to theories advanced by eighteenth- and nineteenth-century European scholars, the highly organized cultures of the Indus Valley and other parts of the subcontinent were overrun by lighter-skinned nomadic invaders from some homeland to the north, whose peoples also spread westward and developed European civilizations. The theory argued that the **Vedas**, the religious texts often referred to as the foundations of Hinduism, were the product of the invaders and not of indigenous Indians, or perhaps a combination of both cultures.

The theory of an invasion of, and religious influence on, the Indus Valley civilization by "Aryans" from the north was based largely on linguistic similarities between classical European languages such as Latin and Greek to **Sanskrit**, the ancient language in which the Vedas were composed. Similarities were also noted between Vedic religious traditions and those of the ancient Iranian Zoroastrian faith. However, the word "**Aryan**" is used in the Vedas to mean a noble person who speaks Sanskrit and practices the Vedic rituals. It is not a racial category. Nevertheless, the idea of an invasion of the Indus Valley by "Aryans" persisted until recent times, when it has become the subject of intense research by scholars of historical linguistics, archaeology, anthropology, and textual analysis. There is as yet no confirmed evidence of what actually happened, and the "**Aryan Invasion Theory**" is strongly contested by many scholars who think there is no proof to support it.

The Indian subcontinent includes areas that are now politically separate from India. The Indus Valley, for instance, lies in what is now the Muslim state of Pakistan. Another Muslim state was carved out of the eastern portion of India in 1947, and became the independent state of Bangladesh in 1971.

The relationship of the Vedas to the Indus Valley sites is also unclear. The early Vedas seem to have been composed by agropastoral people, whereas the Indus Valley civilization was primarily urban-centered. Despite claims by some Indian historians that the Vedas may be of great antiquity, Western Indologists generally continue to think that the early Vedas began to be compiled when the Indus Valley civilization was in decline, approximately 1500 BCE. The Indus script has not yet been deciphered, so there is no way of knowing if it is related to the Sanskrit of the Vedas.

There are, however, some similarities between artefacts of the Indus Valley civilization and religious practices associated with Hinduism. Narrative scenes and figures on seals and pottery include representations of trees with what appear to be deity figures, suggesting that worship may have taken place in natural settings under trees considered sacred—such as the peepul tree, which even in contemporary India is thought to be so sacred that it should not be cut down, even when its great trunk threatens walls and buildings. There are male figures apparently seated in meditation, some of them with horns, which have been interpreted as evidence of ancient practice of yogic postures or worship of the deity Shiva. There are also many decorated female figurines, which may indicate worship of a goddess. Researchers find evidence of many levels of religious practice, from local cults to what may have been established state religions of the elite.

TIMELINE

Hinduism

BCE *c.* 8000–6000	According to Indian tradition, Vedas heard by rishis, carried orally
c. 3102	According to Indian tradition, beginning of Kali Yuga; Vishnu incarnates as Vyasa, who compiles the Vedas
c. 2500–1500	Indus Valley civilization
c. 1500	According to some scholars, early Vedas first composed
c. 900–700	*Brahmanas* compiled
c. 600–100	Upanishads compiled
c. 400 BCE–200 CE	*Ramayana* (present form)
c. 400 BCE–400 CE	*Mahabharata* (present form)
by 200	Patanjali systematizes yoga sutras [Indian tradition: yoga practices are ancient, indigenous]
100–300 CE	Code of Manu compiled
c. 300	Tantras written down [Indian tradition: Tantras are as old as the Upanishads]
500–1500	Puranas compiled
c. 600–1800	Bhakti movement flourishes
711	Arrival of Islam in India
by *c.* 788–829	Shankara reorganizes Vedanta
c. 800–900	*Bhagavata Purana* written down
1556–1707	Mughal Empire
1828	Brahmo Samaj revitalization begins
1836–1886	Life of Ramakrishna
1857–1947	British rule of India
1869–1948	Life of Mahatma Gandhi
1875	Arya Samaj reform begins
1947	Independence; partition of India and Pakistan
1948	Assassination of Mahatma Gandhi
1992	Demolition of Babri Mosque
2002	Violence erupts again over attempts to build Rama Temple at Ayodhya
2011	Anna Hazare fasts to advocate Lokpal or anti-corruption bill
2013	Lokpal Act passed by Indian parliament

The Vedas

Although their origins and antiquity are still unknown, the Vedas themselves can be examined. They are a revered collection of ancient sacred hymns praising the deities and exploring the nature of the cosmos. According to orthodox Hindus, the Vedas are not the work of any humans; they were revealed to sages, and transmitted orally from teacher to student. They are considered *shruti* texts—those that have been revealed, rather than written by mortals. They are the breath of the eternal, as "heard" by the ancient sages, or **rishis**, and later compiled by Vyasa. The name "Vyasa" means "Collector." He was traditionally considered to be one person, but some scholars think it likely that many people were acting as compilers. Most scholars agree that the Vedas were composed and redacted over a period of roughly a thousand years, *c.* 1500 BCE to 500 BCE.

The Vedas are thought to transcend human time and are thus as relevant today as they were thousands of years ago. The **Gayatrimantra**, a verse in a Vedic hymn, is still chanted daily by the devout as the most sacred of prayers:

> *Aum [the primordial creative sound],*
> *Bhurbhuvah Svah [the three worlds: earth, atmosphere, and heaven],*
> *Tat Savitur Varenyam,*
> *Bhargo Devasya Dheemahi [adoration of the glory, splendor, and grace that*
>   *radiate from the Divine Light that illuminates the three worlds],*
> *Dhiyo Yo Nah Prachodayat [a prayer for liberation through awakening of the*
>   *light of the universal intelligence].*[2]

The oldest of the known Vedic scriptures—and among the oldest of the world's existing scriptures—is the **Rig Veda**. This praises and implores the blessings of the **devas**—the controlling forces in the cosmos, deities who consecrate every part of life. The major devas included **Indra** (god of thunder and bringer of welcome rains), **Agni** (god of fire), **Soma** (associated with a sacred drink, **soma**), and **Ushas** (goddess of dawn). The devas included both opaque earth gods and transparent deities of the sky and celestial realms. But behind all the myriad aspects of divinity, the sages perceived one unseen reality. This reality, beyond human understanding, ceaselessly creates and sustains everything that exists, encompassing all time, space, and causation.

The Rig Veda is the first of four collections of which the Vedas are comprised. The other three also contain hymns and sacred sounds to be recited while making offerings to the deities by means of a sacrificial fire. These sounds are thought to carry great power, for they are based on the sound vibrations by which the cosmos was created and sustained.

Other ancient *shruti* texts include the *Brahmanas* (directions about performances of the ritual sacrifices to the deities), *Aranyakas* ("forest treatises" by sages who went to the forests to meditate as recluses), and **Upanishads** (teachings from highly realized spiritual masters). The principal Upanishads are thought to have developed last, around 600 to 100 BCE. They represent the mystical insights of rishis who sought the ultimate, unseen reality through their meditations in the forest. Many people consider these philosophical and metaphysical reflections the cream of Indian thought, among the highest spiritual literature ever written. They were not taught to the masses but rather were reserved for advanced seekers of spiritual truth. Emphasis is placed not on outward ritual performances, as in the earlier texts, but on inner experience as the path to realization and immortality.

The rishis, through the discovery of meditative practices leading to higher states of consciousness, experienced the presence of an infinite reality beyond conventional awareness, as experienced through the five senses. The rishis called this unseen but all-pervading ultimate reality **Brahman**, the Unknowable: "Him the eye does not see, nor the tongue express, nor the mind grasp."[3]

Surya Deva, the Vedic god of the sun, is still worshiped in many temples throughout India. This stone image of Surya Deva is revered in an 8th century temple near Binsar in the Himalayan foothills.

Vedic worship with fire is still significant in contemporary rituals. Fire ceremonies may be conducted by Hindu pandits to invoke the blessings of the Unseen.

The joyous discovery of the rishis was that they could find Brahman as the subtle self or soul (**atman**) within themselves. One of the rishis explained this relationship thus:

> *In the beginning there was Existence alone—One only, without a second. He, the One, thought to himself: Let me be many, let me grow forth. Thus out of himself he projected the universe, and having projected out of himself the universe, he entered into every being. All that is has its self in him alone. Of all things he is the subtle essence. He is the truth. He is the Self. And that, … THAT ART THOU.*

> *Chandogya Upanishad*[4]

When one discovers the inner self, atman, and thus also its source, Brahman, the self merges into its transcendent source, and one experiences unspeakable peace and bliss.

The Upanishads express several doctrines central to all forms of Hinduism. One is **reincarnation**. In answer to the universal question, "What happens after we die?" the rishis taught that the soul leaves the dead body and enters a new one. One takes birth again and again in countless bodies—perhaps as an animal or some other life form—but the self remains the same. Birth as a human being is a precious and rare opportunity for the soul to advance toward its ultimate goal of liberation from rebirth and merging with the ultimate reality or Brahman.

Karma is an important related concept. Karma means action, and also the consequences of action. Every act we make, and even every thought and every desire we have, shapes our future experiences. Our life is what we have made it. And we ourselves are shaped by what we have done: "As a man acts, so does he become. … A man becomes pure through pure deeds, impure through impure deeds."[5] Not only do we reap in this life the good or evil we have sown; they also follow us after physical death, affecting our next incarnation. Ethically, this is a strong teaching, for our every move has far-reaching consequences.

The ultimate goal, however, is not creation of good lives by good deeds, but a clean escape from the karma-run wheel of birth, death, and rebirth, or **samsara**. To escape from samsara is to achieve **moksha**, or liberation from the limitations of space, time, and matter through realization of the ultimate reality. Many life-times of upward-striving incarnations are required to reach this transcendence of earthly miseries. This desire for liberation from earthly existence is one of the underpinnings of classical Hinduism, and of Buddhism as well.

Theistic foundations

How is the Supreme represented in the epics and Puranas?

In ancient Vedic times, elaborate fire sacrifice rituals were created, controlled by **Brahmins** (priests). Specified verbal formulas, sacred chants, and sacred actions were to be used by the priests to invoke Brahman, the all-pervading reality, the breath behind all of existence. After a period when Brahmanic ritual and philosophy dominated, the **bhakti**, or devotional, approach came to prominence around 600 CE. It opened spiritual expression to both *shudras* (a **caste** of manual laborers and artisans) and women, and has been the primary path of the masses ever since. It may also have been the initial way of the people, as it is difficult to pray to the impersonal Absolute referred to in the Upanishads, for it is form-less and is not totally distinct from oneself. More personal worship of a Divine Being can be inferred from the goddess and Shiva-like low reliefs found in the archaeological sites of ancient India. Worship of major deities probably persisted during the Vedic period and was later given written expression. Eventually bhakti—intense devotion to a personal manifestation of Brahman—became the heart of Hinduism as the majority of people now experience it.

The epics and Puranas

Personal love for a deity flowered in the spiritual literature that followed the Vedas. Two major classes of scriptures that arose after 500 BCE (according to Western scholarship) were the epics and the **Puranas**. These long heroic narra-tives and poems popularized spiritual knowledge and devotion through national myths and legends. They were particularly useful in spreading Hindu teachings to the masses at times when Buddhism and Jainism—movements born in India but not recognizing the authority of the Vedas—were winning converts.

In contrast to the rather abstract depictions of the ultimate reality in the Upanishads, the epics and Puranas represent it as a supreme being, or rather as various human-like deities, with richly detailed stories about their lives and relationships. As T. M. P. Mahadevan explains:

> The Hindu mind is averse to assigning an unalterable or rigidly fixed form or name to the deity. Hence it is that in Hinduism we have innumerable god-forms and countless divine names. And, it is a truth that is recognized by all Hindus that obeisance offered to any of these forms and names reaches the one supreme God.[6]

Two great epics, the *Ramayana* and the *Mahabharata*, present the Supreme usually as Vishnu, who intervenes on earth during critical periods in the cosmic cycles. In the inconceivable vastness of time as reckoned by Hindu thought, each world cycle lasts 4,320,000 years. Two thousand of these world cycles are the equivalent of one day and night in the life of Brahma, the Creator god. Each world cycle is divided into four ages, or *yugas*.

Dharma—moral order in the world, and people's duty to act in accord with that order—is natural in the first age. The second age is like a cow standing on three legs; people must be taught their proper roles in society. During the darker third age, revealed values are no longer recognized, people lose their altruism and willingness for self-denial, and there are no more saints. The final age, **Kali Yuga**, is as imbalanced as a cow trying to stand on one leg. The world is at its worst, with egotism, ignorance, recklessness, and war rampant. According to Hindu time reckoning, we are now living in a Kali Yuga period that began in 3102 BCE. Such an age is described thus:

A local parade celebrating the events of the Ramayana, *including Ravana's abduction of Sita and his mortally wounding the brave old eagle who tried to save her.*

> *When society reaches a stage where property confers rank, wealth becomes the only source of virtue, passion the sole bond of union between husband and wife, falsehood the source of success in life, sex the only means of enjoyment, and when outer trappings are confused with inner religion ...*[7]

Each of these lengthy cycles witnesses the same turns of events. The balance inexorably shifts from the true dharma to dissolution and then back to the dharma as the gods are again victorious over the anti-gods. The Puranas list the many ways that Vishnu has incarnated in the world when dharma is decaying, to help restore virtue and defeat evil. For instance, Vishnu is said to have incarnated great **avatars** such as Krishna and Rama to help uplift humanity. It is considered inevitable that Vishnu will continually return in answer to the pleas of suffering humans. It is equally inevitable that he will meet with resistance from "demonic forces," which are also part of the cosmic cycles.

Ramayana The epics deal with the eternal play of good and evil, symbolized by battles involving the human incarnations of Vishnu. Along the way, they teach examples of the virtuous life—responsibilities to others as defined by one's social roles. One is first a daughter, son, sister, brother, wife, husband, mother, father, or friend in relationship to others, and only secondarily an individual.

The *Ramayana*, a long poetic narrative in the Sanskrit language thought to have been compiled between approximately 400 BCE and 200 CE, is attributed to the bard Valmiki. Probably based on old ballads, it is much beloved and is acted out with great pageantry throughout India every year. It depicts the duties of relationships, portraying ideal characters, such as the ideal servant, the ideal brother, the ideal wife, the ideal king. In the story, Vishnu incarnates as the virtuous prince Rama in order to kill Ravana, the ten-headed demon king of Sri Lanka. Rama is heir to his father's throne, but the mother of his stepbrother compels the king to banish Rama into the forest for fourteen years. A model of morality, Rama goes willingly, observing that a son's duty is always to obey his parents implicitly, even when their commands seem wrong. He is accompanied into the ascetic life by his wife Sita, the model of wifely devotion in a patriarchal society, who refuses his offer that she should remain behind in comfort.

Rama and Lakshman shoot arrows into the breast of the demon Ravana, with Hanuman and the monkeys in the background. (North India, c. 19th century.)

Eventually Sita is kidnapped by Ravana, who woos her unsuccessfully in his island kingdom and guards her with all manner of terrible demons. Although Rama is powerful, he and his half brother Lakshman need the help of the monkeys and bears in the battle to get Sita back. Hanuman the monkey becomes the hero of the story. He symbolizes the power of faith and devotion to overcome our human frailties. In his love for the Lord he can do anything. The bloody battle ends in single-handed combat between Ravana and Rama. Rama blesses a sacred arrow with Vedic **mantras** and sends it straight into Ravana's heart. In what may be a later addition to the poem, when Rama and Sita are reunited he accuses her of infidelity, so to prove her innocence she undergoes an ordeal by fire in which Agni protects her. Another version of the *Ramayana*, perhaps as elaborated by later ballad-singers, has Rama ordering Sita into the forest because his subjects are suspicious of what may have happened while she was in Ravana's captivity. She is abandoned near the ashram of Valmiki. There she takes shelter and gives birth to twin boys. Years later, Valmiki and the sons attend a great ritual conducted by King Rama, and the boys sing the *Ramayana*. There is an emotional reunion of the children with their father. Thereupon Sita, a daughter of the earth, begs the earth to receive her if she has been faithful to Rama. With these words, she becomes a field of radiance and disappears into the ground:

> *O Lord of my being, I realize you in me and me in you. Our relationship is eternal. Through this body assumed by me, my service to you and your progeny is complete now. I dissolve this body to its original state.*
> *Mother Earth, you gave form to me. I have made use of it as I ought to. In recognition of its purity may you kindly absorb it into your womb.*[8]

Mahabharata The other famous Hindu epic is the *Mahabharata*, a Sanskrit poem of more than 100,000 verses. Perhaps partly historical, it may have been composed between 400 BCE and 400 CE. The plot concerns the struggle between the sons of a royal family for control of a kingdom near what is now Delhi. The story teaches the importance of sons, the duties of kingship, the benefits of ascetic practice and righteous action, and the qualities of the gods. In contrast to the

TEACHING STORY

Hanuman, the Monkey Chief

Hanuman was of divine origin and legendary powers, but he was embodied as a monkey, serving as a chief in the monkey army. When Rama needed to find his wife Sita after Ravana abducted her, he turned to the monkey king for help. The monkey king dispatched Hanuman to search to the south.

When the monkeys reached the sea dividing India from Sri Lanka they were dismayed, because monkeys do not swim. A vulture brought word that Sita was indeed on the other side of the water, a captive of Ravana. What to do? An old monkey reminded Hanuman of the powers he had displayed as an infant and told him that he could easily jump to Lanka and back if only he remembered his power and his divine origin.

Hanuman sat in meditation until he became strong and confident. Then he climbed a mountain, shook himself, and began to grow in size and strength. When at last he felt ready he set off with a roar, hurling himself through the sky with eyes blazing like forest fires.

When Hanuman landed in Lanka he shrunk himself to the size of a cat so that he could explore Ravana's forts. After many dangerous adventures, he gave Sita the message that Rama was preparing to do battle to win her back, and then he jumped back over the sea to the Indian mainland.

During the subsequent battle of Lanka, Rama and his half brother Lakshman were mortally wounded. Nothing would save them except a certain herb that grew only in the Himalayas. In his devotion to Rama, Hanuman flew to the mountains, again skirting danger all the way. But once he got there he could not tell precisely which herb to pick, so he uprooted the whole mountain and carried it back to Lanka. The herb would be effective only before the moon rose. From the air, Hanuman saw the moon about to clear the horizon so he swallowed the moon and reached Lanka in time to heal Rama and Lakshman.

After the victory, Rama rewarded Hanuman with a bracelet of pearls and gold. Hanuman chewed it up and threw it away. When a bear asked why he had rejected the gift from God, Hanuman explained that it was useless to him since it did not have Rama's name on it. The bear said, "Well, if you feel that way, why do you keep your body?" At that, Hanuman ripped open his chest, and there were Rama and Sita seated in his heart, and all his bones and muscles had "Rama, Rama, Rama" written all over them. Hanuman serves as a symbol of strength and fervent devotion.

---

idealized characters in the *Ramayana*, the *Mahabharata* shows all sides of human nature, including greed, lust, intrigue, and the desire for power. It is thought to be relevant for all times and all peoples. A serial dramatization of the *Mahabharata* has drawn huge television audiences in contemporary India. The *Mahabharata* teaches one primary ethic: that the happiness of others is essential to one's own happiness. This consideration of others before oneself is a central dharmic virtue.

The eighteenth book of the *Mahabharata*, which may have originally been an independent mystical poem, is the *Bhagavad-Gita* (Song of the Supreme Exalted One). Krishna, revered as a manifestation of the Supreme, appears as the charioteer of Arjuna, who is preparing to fight on the virtuous side of a battle that will pit family members against one another, thus occasioning a treatise about the conflict that may arise between our earthly duties and our spiritual aspirations.

Before they plunge into battle, Krishna instructs Arjuna in the arts of self-transcendence and realization of the eternal. The instructions are still central to Hindu spiritual practice. Arjuna is enjoined to withdraw his attention from the impetuous demands of the senses, ignoring all feelings of attraction or aversion. This will give him a steady, peaceful mind. He is instructed to offer devotional service and to perform the prescribed Vedic sacrifices, but for the sake of discipline, duty, and example alone rather than reward—to "abandon all attachment to success or failure ... renouncing the fruits of action in the material world."[9]

Actually, Krishna says those who do everything for love of the Supreme transcend the notion of duty. Everything they do is offered to the Supreme, "without desire for gain and free from egoism and lethargy."[10] Thus they feel peace, freedom from earthly entanglements, and unassailable happiness.

Lord Krishna and Arjuna discuss profound philosophical questions in a battle chariot, as represented in this archway above the sacred Ganges River in Rishikesh.

This yogic science of transcending the "lower self" by the "higher self" is so ancient that Krishna says it was originally given to the sun god and, through his agents, to humans. But in time it was lost, and Krishna is now renewing his instructions pertaining to "that very ancient science of the relationship with the Supreme."[11] He has taken human form again and again to teach the true religion:

> Whenever and wherever there is a decline in religious practice [dharma] … and a predominant rise of irreligion—at that time I descend Myself.
> To deliver the pious and to annihilate the miscreants, as well as to re-establish the principles of religion, I advent Myself millennium after millennium.[12]

Krishna says that everything springs from his Being:

> There is no truth superior to Me. Everything rests upon Me, as pearls are strung on a thread. …
> I am the taste of water, the light of the sun and the moon, the syllable om in Vedic mantras; I am the sound in ether and ability in man. …
> All states of being—goodness, passion or ignorance—are manifested by My energy. I am, in one sense, everything—but I am independent. I am not under the modes of this material nature.[13]

This supreme Godhead is not apparent to most mortals. The deity can be known only by those who love him, and for them it is easy, for they remember him at all times: "Whatever you do, whatever you eat, whatever you offer or give away, and whatever austerities you perform—do that … as an offering to Me." Any small act of devotion offered in love becomes a way to him: "If one offers Me with love and devotion a leaf, a flower, fruit, or water, I will accept it."[14]

The Puranas The Puranas are an ancient compendium of mythological narratives on the origins of the cosmos, life, deities, and humanity; stories of legendary or canonical heroes; and the actions of divine beings. Theology is often implicit in the puranic stories. The major Puranas are based on theologies of Vishnu, Shiva, and Shakti expressed through complex narratives. They were probably compiled between 500 and 1500 CE. There are a total of eighteen major Puranas—six about Vishnu, six about Brahma, and six about Shiva. These narratives popularize the more abstract philosophical teachings found in the

Vedas and Upanishads by giving them concrete form. Of the Puranas, the most well known and loved is the *Bhagavata Purana*, which includes the life story of Krishna. Most Western Indologists think it was written about the ninth or tenth century CE, but according to Indian tradition it was one of the works written down at the beginning of Kali Yuga by Vyasa.

In the *Bhagavata Purana*, the supreme personality of Godhead is portrayed first in its vast dimensions—the Being whose body animates the material universe:

> *His eyes are the generating centers of all kinds of forms, and they glitter and illuminate. His eyeballs are like the sun and the heavenly planets. His ears hear from all sides and are receptacles for all the Vedas, and His sense of hearing is the generating center of the sky and of all kinds of sound.*[15]

This material universe we know is only one of millions of material universes. Each is like a bubble in the eternal spiritual sky, arising from the pores of the body of Vishnu, and these bubbles are created and destroyed as Vishnu breathes out and in. This cosmic conception is so vast that it is impossible for the mind to grasp it. It is much easier to comprehend and adore Vishnu in his incarnation as Krishna. Whereas he was a wise teacher in the *Bhagavad-Gita*, Krishna of the *Bhagavata Purana* is a much-loved child, raised by cowherds in an area called Vrindavan near Mathura on the Yamuna River.

Devotional traditions

How do Shaktas, Shaivas, and Vaishnavas differ?

From the deities praised in the Vedas, to those whose stories are narrated in the epics and Puranas, to countless regional and local deities, Hinduism has many ways of expressing the multifaceted nature of divinity. Among Hindus, there are three major groupings: **Shaktas**, who worship a Mother Goddess, **Shaivas**, who worship the god Shiva, and **Vaishnavas**, who worship the god Vishnu. Each devotee has his or her own "chosen deity," but will honor others as well. The three groupings are not hard and fast boundaries. Ultimately, some Hindus rest their faith in one genderless deity with three basic aspects: creating, preserving, and destroying, in continuing cosmic cycles.

Shaktas

An estimated fifty million Hindus worship some form of the goddess, whose great power is called **shakti**. Some Shaktas follow a Vedic path; some are more independent of Vedic tradition. Worship of the feminine aspect of the divine probably dates back to the pre-Vedic ancient peoples of the Indian subcontinent. The goddess may be worshiped both as a singular, supreme being representing the totality of deity, eternal creator, preserver, and destroyer, and as a figure who appears in multiple forms. The mythology of the goddess is related in many of the Puranas, and there are multiple regional goddess traditions as well.

The general term "**Devi**" may be used to refer generically to the goddess in all her forms, understood as the supreme Divine Mother, the totality of all the energy of the cosmos. Sri Swami Sivananda of the Divine Life Society explains that it is quite natural to regard the Divine as Mother:

> *To the child, in the mother is centered a whole world of tenderness, of love, of nourishment and of care. It is the ideal world from where one draws sustenance, where one runs for comfort, which one clings to for protection and nourishment; and there he gets comfort, protection and care. Therefore, the ideal of love, care and protection is in the conception of the mother.*[16]

Devi is known by many names, and is thought to have many manifestations. Among them are benign, extremely powerful, and even fierce forms. The goddess **Durga** is often represented as a beautiful woman with a gentle face but ten

Lakshmi is often pictured standing gloriously upon a lotus flower, bestowing coins of prosperity and flanked by elephants signifying her royal power.

arms holding weapons with which she vanquishes the demons who threaten the dharma; she rides a lion. She is the blazing splendor of God incarnate, in benevolent female form.

Kali is the goddess in her fierce form. She may be portrayed dripping with blood, carrying a sword and a severed head, and wearing a girdle of severed hands and a necklace of skulls symbolizing her aspect as the destroyer of evil. What appears as destruction is actually a means of transformation. With her merciful sword she cuts away all personal impediments to realization of truth for those who sincerely desire to serve the Supreme. At the same time, she opens her arms to those who love her. Some of them worship her with blood offerings from animal sacrifices, but some shakti temples are now doing away with this practice, at the behest of animal lovers.

Another popular great goddess is **Lakshmi**, who embodies wealth, generosity, good fortune, beauty, and charm. She is often depicted as a radiant woman sitting on a waterborne lotus flower. The lotus floats pristine on the water but has its roots in the mud, thus representing the refined spiritual energy that rises above worldly contamination. The goddess **Saraswati** is associated with knowledge, the arts, and music and also with the great river Saraswati that once flowed parallel to the Indus River in the cradle of the Indus Valley civilization. The Saraswati River dried up long ago, probably contributing to the decline of that ancient civilization.

From ancient times, worship of the divine female has been associated with worship of nature, particularly great trees and rivers. The Ganges River is considered an especially sacred female presence, and her waters, flowing down from the Himalayas, are thought to be extraordinarily purifying. Pilgrims bathe in Mother Ganga's waters, facing the sun at sunrise, and corpses or the cremated ashes of the dead are placed in the river so that their sins will be washed away.

The goddess is worshiped in many forms. At the village level, especially in southern India, local deities are most typically worshiped as goddesses. They may not be perceived as taking human-like forms; rather, their presence may be represented by round stones, trees, yantras (a linear image with complex cosmic symbolism), or small shrines without images. These local goddesses are intimately concerned with village affairs, unlike the more distant great goddesses of the upper class, access to whose temples was traditionally forbidden to those of low caste.

Sacred texts called **Tantras** instruct worshipers how to honor the feminine divine according to practices that may have been in existence since before 2500 BCE. Ways of worship include concentration on yantras, meditation with the hands in mudras (positions that reflect and invoke a particular spiritual reality), **kundalini** practices to raise spiritual energy up the spine, and use of mantras. One such text gives a thousand different "names" or attributes of the Divine Mother as mantras for recitation, such as these: "*Sri mata* (She who is the auspicious Mother), *Sri maha rajni* (She who is the Empress of the Universe) ... *Raga svarupa pasadhya* (She who is holding the rope of love in Her hand) ... *Mada nasini* (She who destroys pride), *Niscinta* (She who has no anxiety about anything), *Nir ahankara* (She who is without egoism) … *Maha virya* (She who is supreme in valor), *Maha bala* (She who is supreme in might), *Maha buddhih* (She who is supreme in intelligence)."[17]

In contrast to ascetic forms of Hinduism that denigrate the material world as a lower, impermanent form of reality, Tantra celebrates worldly as well as spiritual aspects of life. The body is appreciated as the vehicle for spiritual realization, and the whole earth is regarded as the sacred manifestation of the goddess. In the most extreme "left-handed" forms, tantric rites intentionally subvert orthodox Hindu notions of purity and impurity through the use of five things traditionally considered defiling: meat, fish, parched grain, wine, and sexual intercourse in which the woman is worshiped as the goddess. Describing this path, which is only considered appropriate for advanced initiates who have personally experienced the omnipresence of the divine, Professor Rita D. Sherma, Executive Director of the School of Philosophy and Religious Studies, Taksha University, writes:

> The panca-tattva *[ritual of the five elements] ritual's conflation of the sacred and the profane would be highly offensive to the Hindu sensibility and run counter to all normative models of purity and impurity, sanctity and desecration in the Hindu consciousness. It seems that the element of shock inherent in the ritual becomes itself a highly potent catalyst capable of catapulting the mind out of its familiar dualistic thought patterns and into the realm of unity consciousness. By partaking of five defiling things in the setting of the meditative ritual, the aspirant affirms their underlying purity and shatters the cognitive processes of the unenlightened mind that fractionalizes all life into myriad brittle distinctions. No difference remains between the clean and unclean, the sacred and the profane, purity and impurity. All phenomena take on the glow of divine power and presence.*[18]

Shakti worship has also been incorporated into worship of the male gods. Each is thought to have a female consort, with whom he is often portrayed in close embrace, signifying the eternal unity of male and female principles in the oneness of the divine. Here the female is often conceived as the life-animating force; the transcendent male aspect is inactive until joined with the productive female energy.

A Shaiva sadhu meditates in the Himalayas at the source of the holy Ganges River.

Feminist scholars are particularly interested in the significance of reverence for shakti. Many see this belief cluster as a positive valuation of the feminine that has the potential to empower women, even though the lives of many poor women in India are not free. Others see wider philosophical implications that have not yet been fully explored, in which the fullness of the feminine principle includes *prakriti*—the natural material world of the universe; shakti—the creative Power that pervades it; and **maya**—the ever-changing, differentiating, and self-veiling qualities of the omnipresent unity.

Shaivas

Shiva is a personal, many-faceted manifestation of the attributeless supreme deity. In older systems he is one of the three major aspects of deity: Brahma (Creator), Vishnu (Preserver), and Shiva (Destroyer). Shaivas nevertheless worship him as the totality, with many aspects. As Swami Sivasiva Palani, Shaivite editor of *Hinduism Today*, explains: "Shiva is the unmanifest; he is creator, preserver, destroyer, personal Lord, friend, primal Soul," and he is the "all-pervasive underlying energy, the more or less impersonal love and light that flows through all things."[19] Shiva is sometimes depicted dancing above the body of the demon he has killed, reconciling darkness and light, good and evil, creation and destruction, rest and activity in the eternal dance of life.

Shiva and Parvati's embrace symbolizes the unity of masculine and feminine energies.

Shiva as Lord of the Dance, trampling the demon of evil and bearing both the flame of destruction and the drum of creation. One of his two free hands gestures "Fear not"; the other points to his upraised foot, denoting bliss.

Shiva is also the god of yogis, for he symbolizes asceticism. He is often shown in austere meditation on Mount Kailash, clad only in a tiger skin, with a snake around his neck. The latter signifies his conquest of the ego. In one prominent story, it is Shiva who swallows the poison that threatens the whole world with darkness, neutralizing the poison by the power of his meditation.

Shiva has various shaktis, or feminine consorts. He is often shown with his devoted spouse, **Parvati**. Through their union, cosmic energy flows freely, seeding and liberating the universe. Nevertheless, they are seen mystically as eternally chaste. Shiva and his shakti are also expressed as two aspects of a single being. Some sculptors portray Shiva as androgynous, with both masculine and feminine physical traits. Tantric belief incorporates an ideal of balance of male and female qualities within a person, leading to enlightenment, bliss, and worldly success as well. This unity of male and female is often expressed abstractly, as a **lingam** within a **yoni**, a symbol of the female vulva.

The lingams used in worship of Shiva are naturally occurring or sculpted cylindrical forms honored since antiquity in India (and apparently in other cultures as well, as far away as Hawai'i). Those shaped by nature, such as stones polished by certain rivers, are most highly valued, with rare natural crystal lingams considered especially precious. Tens of thousands of devotees each year undergo dangerous pilgrimages to certain high mountain caves to venerate large lingams naturally formed of ice. While the lingam sometimes resembles an erect phallus, most Shiva-worshipers focus on its symbolic meaning, which is abstract and asexual. They see the lingam as a nearly amorphous, "formless" symbol for the unmanifest, transcendent nature of Shiva—that which is beyond time, space, cause, and form—whereas the yoni represents the manifest aspect.

Shaivism encompasses traditions that have developed outside Vedic-based Brahmanism. These include sects such as the Lingayats, who wear a stone

lingam in remembrance of Shiva as the One Undivided Being. Their ancient ways of Shiva worship underwent a strong reform movement in the twelfth century, refusing caste divisions, Brahminical authority, and consideration of menstruating women as polluted. They practice strict vegetarianism and regard men and women as equals.

Another branch is represented by the sixty-three great Shaiva saints of Tamil Nadu in southern India, who from the seventh century CE onward expressed great love for Shiva. They experienced him as the Luminous One, present everywhere in subtle form but apparent only to those who love him. For this realization, knowledge of the scriptures and ascetic practices are useless. Only direct personal devotion will do. The Tamil saint Appar sang:

> *Why chant the Vedas, hear the shastras' lore? …*
> *Release is theirs, and theirs alone,*
> *Whose heart from thinking of its Lord shall never depart.*[20]

Shiva and Parvati's son Ganesh, a deity with the head of an elephant, guards the threshold of space and time and is therefore invoked for his blessings at the beginning of any new venture. Ganesh was the subject of an extraordinary event that happened in temples in many parts of India, as well as in Hindu temples in other parts of the world. On 21 September 1995, devotees reported that statues of Ganesh began drinking milk from spoons, cups, and even buckets offered by devotees. Scientists suggested explanations such as mass hysteria or capillary action in the stone. However, the phenomenon lasted only one day.

Vaishnavas

Vishnu is beloved as the tender, merciful deity. In one myth, a sage was sent to determine who was the greatest of the gods by trying their tempers. The first two, Brahma and Shiva, he insulted and was soundly abused in return. When he found Vishnu the god was sleeping. Knowing of Vishnu's good-naturedness, the sage increased the insult by kicking him awake. Instead of reacting angrily, Vishnu tenderly massaged the sage's foot, concerned that he might have hurt it. The sage exclaimed, "This god is the mightiest, since he overpowers all by goodness and generosity!"

The auspicious blessings of Ganesh are invoked for all occasions. Here his image has been painted on a wall before a marriage celebration.

Vishnu has been worshiped since Vedic times and came to be regarded as the Supreme as a person. In Vaishnava iconography, the world is continually being reborn on a lotus growing out of Vishnu's navel. Vishnu is often associated with his consort, Lakshmi (whom Shaktas worship as a goddess in her own right). According to ideas appearing by the fourth century CE, Vishnu is considered to have appeared in many earthly incarnations, some of them animal forms. Many deities have been drawn into this complex, in which they are interpreted as incarnations of Vishnu. Most beloved of his purported incarnations have been Rama, subject of the *Ramayana* (see p. 79), and Krishna (see p. 81). However, many people still revere Krishna without reference to Vishnu.

Popular devotion to Krishna takes many forms. If Krishna is regarded as the transcendent Supreme Lord, the worshiper humbly lowers himself or herself. If Krishna is seen as master, the devotee is his servant. If Krishna is loved as a child, the devotee takes the role of loving parent. If Krishna is the divine friend, the devotee is his friend. And if Krishna is the beloved, the devotee is his lover. The latter relationship was popularized by the ecstatic sixteenth-century Bengali saint, scholar, and social reformer Shri Chaitanya, who adored Krishna as the flute-playing lover. Following Shri Chaitanya, the devotee makes himself (if a male) like a loving female in order to experience the bliss of Lord Krishna's presence. It is this form of Hindu devotion that was carried to America in 1965, organized as the International Society for Krishna Consciousness, and then spread to other countries. Its followers are known as Hare Krishnas.

Major philosophical systems
What are three of the most prominent philosophical systems related to the Vedas?

In addition to the Vedas and texts such as the epics and Puranas, elaborate philosophical systems were developed long ago in India. Those associated with Brahmanic Hindu tradition all have certain features in common:

1 All have deep roots in the Vedas and other scriptures but also in direct personal experiences of the truth through meditation.
2 All hold ethics to be central to orderly social life. They attribute suffering to the law of karma, thereby suggesting incentives to more ethical behavior.
3 All hold that the ultimate cause of suffering is people's ignorance of the Self, which is omniscient, omnipotent, omnipresent, perfect, and eternal.

Two other major philosophical systems born in India—Jainism and Buddhism—do not acknowledge the authority of the Vedas but nevertheless draw on many of the same currents as Hinduism. Prominent among the philosophical systems that are related to the Vedas are **Samkhya**, **Advaita Vedanta**, and **yoga**.

Samkhya

The Samkhya system, though undatable, is thought to be the oldest in India. Its founder is said to be the semi-mythical sage Kapila. Its principles appear in Jainism and Buddhism from the sixth century BCE, so the system probably preceded them and may be of pre-Vedic origin.

The highly analytical Samkhya system holds that the material universe consists of three essential qualities. They are *sattva* (fine, illuminated, balanced), *rajas* (active, passionate), and *tamas* (heavy, inert, coarse). Interaction and tension between the equilibrium of *sattva*, the activity of *rajas*, and the resistance to action of *tamas* govern the development of the world. The interaction of these qualities is a key factor in some Indian systems of diet and medicine.

Advaita Vedanta

Advaita (nondualist) Vedanta is generally **monistic**, positing a single reality. It is based on the Upanishads: Its founder is said to be Vyasa, systematizer of the Vedas. The eminent philosopher Shankara reorganized the teachings many centuries later, probably between the eighth and ninth centuries CE.

Whereas one view of the Upanishads is that the human self (atman) is an emanation of Brahman, Shankara insisted that the atman and Brahman are actually one. According to Shankara, our material life is an illusion. It is like a momentary wave arising from the ocean, which is the only reality. Ignorance consists in thinking that the waves are different from the ocean. The absolute spirit, Brahman, is the essence of everything, and it has no beginning and no end. It is the eternal ocean of bliss within which forms are born and die, giving the false appearance of being real.

That which makes us think the physical universe has its own reality is maya, the power by which the Absolute veils itself. Maya is the illusion that the world as we perceive it is real. Shankara uses the metaphor of a coil of rope that, at dusk, is mistaken for a snake. The physical world, like the rope, does actually exist but we superimpose our memories and subjective thoughts upon it. Moreover, he says, only that which never changes is truly real. Everything else is changing, impermanent. In ignorance we think that we exist as individuals, superimposing the notion of a separate ego-self on the underlying absolute reality of pure being, pure consciousness, pure bliss. It is a mistake to identify with the body or the mind, which exist but have no unchanging reality. When a person reaches transcendent consciousness, the oneness of reality is experienced.

In recent times, some Hindu thinkers have advocated an approach called neo-Vedanta, arguing that while many Hindus approach the ultimate reality through worship of various gods and goddesses, at its pinnacle Hindu practice aims toward recognition of one's union with the singular supreme Brahman.

Yoga

From ancient times, people of the Indian subcontinent have practiced spiritual disciplines designed to clear the mind and support a state of serene, detached awareness. The practices for developing this desired state of balance, purity, wisdom, and peacefulness of mind are known collectively as yoga. It means "yoke" or "union"—referring to union with the true Self, the goal described in the Upanishads. While to many Westerners the term "yoga" may evoke images of stretches and poses for relaxation, the forms of yoga developed in India involve far more.

The sages distinguished four basic types of people and developed yogic practices that are particularly suitable for each type, in order that each can attain the desired union with the Self. For meditative people, there is **raja yoga**, the path of mental concentration. For rational people, there is **jnana yoga**, the path of rational inquiry. For naturally active people, there is **karma yoga**, the path of right action. For emotional people, there is **bhakti yoga**, the path of devotion.

Raja yoga Some believe that the **sadhanas**, or practices of raja yoga, were known as long ago as the Neolithic Age and were practiced in the Indus Valley culture. By 200 BCE, a yogi named Patanjali (or perhaps a series of people taking the same name) had described a system for attaining the highest consciousness through raja yoga—the path of mental concentration. Patanjali's *Yoga Sutras* is a book of 196 terse sayings called **sutras**. These include such observations as:

> *"From contentment comes the attainment of the highest happiness."*
> *"From penance comes destruction of impurities, thence the perfection of the body and the senses."*
> *"From study comes communion with the desired deity."*
> *"From the profound meditation upon Isvara [God] comes success in spiritual absorption."*[21]

In kundalini yoga, the body is thought to exist within a field of energy, which is most concentrated at the major chakras—subtle centers along the vertical axis of the body.

Yogic adepts have developed extreme control of their bodies to amplify meditation efforts.

Yogis say that it is easier to calm a wild tiger than it is to quiet the mind, which is like a drunken monkey that has been bitten by a scorpion. The problem is that the mind is our vehicle for knowing the Self. If the mirror of the mind is disturbed, it reflects the disturbance rather than the pure light within. The goal of yogic practices is to make the mind absolutely calm and clear.

Patanjali distinguishes eight "limbs" of the yogic path: moral codes expressed in terms of abstentions and observances, physical conditioning, breath control, sense control, concentration, meditation, and the state of peaceful spiritual absorption (**samadhi**).

The moral and ethical principles that form the first limb of yogic practice are truth, nonviolence, nonstealing, continence, non-covetousness, cleanliness, contentment, burning zeal, self-study, and devotion to God. The second limb consists of **asanas**—physical postures used to cleanse the body and develop the mind's ability to concentrate. Regulated breathing exercises are also used to calm the nerves and increase the body's supply of **prana**, or invisible life energy. Breath is thought to be the key to controlling the flow of this energy within the subtle energy field surrounding and permeating the physical body. Its major pathway is through a series of **chakras**, or subtle energy centers, along the spine. The ideal is to raise the energy from the lowest, least subtle chakra at the base of the spine to the top of the head and open the highest, most subtle chakra there, leading to the bliss of union with the Sublime. This evolved state is depicted as a thousand-petaled lotus, effulgent with light.

In addition to these practices using the body and breath, Indian thought has long embraced the idea that repetition of certain sounds has sacred effects. It is said that some ancient yogic adepts could discern subtle sounds and that mantras (sacred formulas) express an aspect of the divine in the form of sound vibration. The sound of the mantras was believed to evoke the reality they named. The language used for these verbal formulas since ancient times was Sanskrit. It was considered a re-creation of the actual sound-forms of objects, actions, and qualities, as heard by ancient sages in deep meditation.

Chanting sacred syllables is thought to still the mind and attune the devotee to the Divine Ground of Existence. Indians liken the mind to the trunk of an elephant, always straying restlessly here and there. If an elephant is given a small stick to hold in its trunk, it will hold it steadily, losing interest in other objects. In the same way, the mantra gives the restless mind something to hold, quieting it by focusing awareness in one place. If chanted with devoted concentration, the mantra may also invoke the presence and blessings of the deity.

Many forms of music have also been developed in India to elevate a person's attunement and may go on for hours if the musicians are spiritually absorbed.

Another way of steadying and elevating the mind is concentration on some visual form—a candle flame, the picture of a saint or guru, the **OM** symbol representing the sacred mantra aum, the sound that first manifested creation, or yantras. Large yantras are also created as designs made of colorful seeds for ritual invocations of specific deities.

One-pointed concentration ideally leads to a state of meditation. In meditation, all worldly thoughts have dissipated. Instead of ordinary thinking, the clear light of awareness allows insights to arise spontaneously as flashes of illumination.

The OM symbol, representing the original sound of creation, is topped by the sun and the moon, harmonized opposites. To chant OM is to commune with this cosmic sound vibration.

The ultimate goal of yogic meditation is samadhi: a super-conscious state of union with the Absolute. Swami Sivananda attempts to describe it:

Words and language are imperfect to describe this exalted state. ... Mind, intellect and the senses cease functioning. ... It is a state of eternal Bliss and eternal Wisdom. All dualities vanish in toto. ... All visible merge in the invisible or the Unseen. The individual soul becomes that which he contemplates.[22]

Jnana yoga The path of rational inquiry—jnana yoga—employs the rational mind rather than trying to transcend it by concentration practices. In this path, ignorance is considered the root of all problems. Our basic ignorance is our idea of our selves as being separate from the Absolute. One method is continually to ask, "Who am I?" The seeker discovers that the one who asks the question is not the body, not the senses, not the mind, but something eternal beyond all these. The guru Ramana Maharshi explains:

> After negating all of the above-mentioned as "not this," "not this," that Awareness which alone remains—that I am. … The thought "Who am I?" will destroy all other thoughts, and, like the stick used for stirring the burning pyre, it will itself in the end get destroyed. Then, there will arise Self-realization.[23]

In the *jnana* path, the seeker must also develop spiritual virtues (calmness, restraint, renunciation, resignation, concentration, and faith) and have an intense longing for liberation. The ultimate wisdom is spiritual rather than intellectual knowledge of the self.

Karma yoga In contrast to these ascetic and contemplative practices, another way is that of helpful action in the world. Karma yoga is service rendered without any interest in its fruits or results and without any personal sense of giving. The yogi knows that the Absolute performs all actions, and all actions are gifts to the Absolute. This consciousness leads to liberation from the self in the very midst of work.

Classical Indian music is based on inner spiritual communion with the divine.

Bhakti yoga The final type of spiritual path is the one embraced by most Hindus. It is the path of devotion to a personal deity, bhakti yoga. For the *bhakta* (devotee), the relationship is that of intense love. Bhakta Nam Dev described this deep love in sweet metaphors:

> Thy Name is beautiful, Thy form is beautiful, and very beautiful is Thy love, Oh my Omnipresent Lord.
>   As rain is dear to the earth, as the fragrance of flowers is dear to the black bee, and as the mango is dear to the cuckoo, so is the Lord to my soul.
>   As the sun is dear to the sheldrake, and the lake of Man Sarowar to the swan, and as the husband is dear to the wife, so is God to my soul.
>   As milk is dear to the baby and as the torrent of rain to the mouth of the sparrow-hawk who drinks nothing but raindrops, and as water is dear to the fish, so is the Lord to my soul.[24]

Mirabai, a fifteenth-century princess, was married to a ruler at a young age, but from her childhood she had been utterly devoted to the deity Krishna. Her poetry expresses her single-minded love for her beloved:

> Everything perishes,
> sun, moon, earth, sky, water, wind,
> everything.
> Only the One Indestructible remains.
> Others get drunk on distilled wine,
> in love's still I distil mine;
> day and night I'm drunk on it
> in my Lover's love, ever sunk …
> I'll not remain in my mother's home,
> I'll stay with Krishna alone;
>   He's my Husband
>   and my Lover,
>   and my mind is
>   at his feet forever.[25]

When Mirabai continued to spend all her time in devotions to Krishna, an infuriated in-law tried to poison her. It is said that Mirabai drank the poison while laughingly dancing in ecstasy before Krishna; in Krishna's presence the poison seemed like nectar to her and did her no harm. The Beloved One is said to respond and to be a real presence in the fully devoted *bhakta*'s life.

Traditional bhakti narratives are rich in earthly pleasures. The boy Krishna mischievously steals balls of butter from the neighbors and wanders garlanded with flowers through the forest, happily playing his flute. Between episodes of carefree bravery in vanquishing demons that threaten the people, he playfully steals the hearts of the *gopis*, the cowherd girls. His favorite is the lovely Radha, but through his magical ways he multiplies himself so that each girl thinks he dances with her alone. Each is so much in love with Krishna that she feels she is one with him and desires only to serve him. Swami Vivekananda explains the spiritual meaning of the *gopis*' divine love for Krishna, which is:

> *too holy to be attempted without giving up everything, too sacred to be understood until the soul has become perfectly pure. Even the Gita, the great philosophy itself, does not compare with that madness, for in the Gita the disciple is taught slowly how to walk towards the goal, but here is the madness of enjoyment, the drunkenness of love, where disciples and teachers and teachings and books … everything has been thrown away. What remains is the madness of love. It is forgetfulness of everything, and the lover sees nothing in the world except that Krishna, and Krishna alone.*[26]

Eventually Krishna is called away on a heroic mission, never returning to the *gopis*. Their grief at his leaving and their intense longing for him serve as models for the bhakti path—the way of extreme devotion. In Hindu thought, the emotional longing of the lover for the beloved is one of the most powerful vehicles for concentration on the Supreme Lord.

In the bhakti path, even though the devotee may not transcend the ego in samadhi, the devotee's whole being is surrendered to the deity in love. The

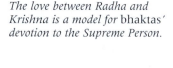

The love between Radha and Krishna is a model for bhaktas' *devotion to the Supreme Person.*

nineteenth-century saint Ramakrishna explained why the bhakti way is more appropriate for most people:

> As long as the I-sense lasts, so long are true knowledge and Liberation impossible. … [But] how very few can obtain this Union [Samadhi] and free themselves from this "I"? It is very rarely possible. Talk as much as you want, isolate yourself continuously, still this "I" will always return to you. Cut down the poplar tree today, and you will find tomorrow it forms new shoots. When you ultimately find that this "I" cannot be destroyed, let it remain as "I" the servant.[27]

The Hindu way of life
What is puja?

Although there is no single founder, devotional tradition, or philosophy which can be said to define Hinduism, everyday life is so imbued with spiritually meaningful aspects that spirituality is never far from one's mind. Those we will examine here include rituals, castes and social duties, life stages, homage to the guru, rituals, fasting, prayer, auspicious designs, reverence paid to trees and rivers, pilgrimages, and religious festivals.

Castes, duties, and life goals

Life in India continues to be shaped to a considerable extent by hierarchies and inequalities derived from **jati** (thousands of groups denoted by shared geographical origin, language, food practices, common customs and beliefs, occupations, and endogamy—marriage only within their group) and **varna** (a more general traditional fourfold division of labor that ultimately became hereditary). Both aspects of this complex situation are imprecisely referred to by the English word "caste."

The varnas seem to date back to the Vedic age. Because the Vedic sacrifices were a reciprocal communion with the gods, priests who performed the public sacrifices had to be carefully trained and maintain high standards of ritual purity. Those so trained—the Brahmins—comprised a special occupational group. The orderly working of society included a clear division of labor among four major occupational groups, which later became entrenched as hereditary castes. These occupational categories applied to men; women were automatically associated with their father's or husband's varna. The Brahmins were the priests and philosophers, specialists in the life of the spirit. The next group, later called **Kshatriyas**, were the nobility of feudal India: kings, warriors, and vassals. Their general function was to guard and preserve the society; they were expected to be courageous and majestic. *Vaishyas* were the economic specialists: farmers and merchants. The *shudras* were the manual laborers and artisans. Lower than these original four varnas were those "outcastes," who came to be considered "**untouchables**." They carried out work such as removing human waste and corpses, sweeping streets, and working with leather from the skins of dead cows—occupations that made their bodies and clothing abhorrent to others. Over time, Vedic religion was increasingly controlled by the Brahmins, and contact between castes was limited. Varna membership became hereditary. The caste system became a significant aspect of Indian life, although many Hindus questioned its rules, particularly with respect to spiritual capabilities. Many medieval bhakti poets of low caste challenged the restrictions that kept them out of temples, asserting that the gods accepted sincere devotion even from those of the lowest status. Since the nineteenth century, many Hindu leaders and groups have challenged and rejected caste distinctions. Mahatma Gandhi renamed the lowest caste *Harijans*, "the children of God." Finding this designation condescending, a segment of this population who are pressing for better status and opportunities now refer to themselves as **Dalits** (oppressed).

Anna Hazare

 He lives in a small, bare room annexed to a temple in a rural Indian village and holds no public office, but by his tremendous efforts and the force of his moral authority he has been able to make deep changes at all levels of Indian government. By 2011, when he undertook a fast unto death for a national bill challenging corruption by government officials, his name was a household word throughout India.

"Anna" is what the people call him; he was born Kisan Baburao Hazare in 1940. One of seven children, he grew up in poverty. He left school in seventh grade to try to earn some money to help the family. He began selling flowers in Mumbai, but fell into bad company and wasted his income on vices. He joined the Indian Army in 1960, but became so depressed by the lonely life of a truck driver that he considered suicide.

In 1965 during the war between India and Pakistan, Hazare's truck was bombed, killing everyone but him. Later when he was serving in insurgent Nagaland, he was the only survivor of an attack by Naga terrorists. He began to think that his life was precious and that God was saving him for a reason. Then while sitting in the New Delhi railway station, he saw a book by Swami Vivekananda, *Call to the Youth for Nation Building*. He began to read Vivekananda's books and also the writings of Mahatma Gandhi and his follower, Acharya Vinoba Bhave. Under these influences, he decided to give his life to improve society. In 1974, he returned to his native village, Ralegan Siddhi in Maharashtra.

At that time, eighty percent of the villagers were barely surviving on only one meal a day. Thefts and fights were commonplace. Perceiving that the most critical immediate need was for water, Anna began motivating the villagers to build canals, check-dams, percolation tanks, contour trenches, and drip irrigation, and to plant trees. As the water table was replenished, farmers became self-sufficient in grain production and no longer needed to leave the village in search of work. Related projects in dairy improvement brought farmers a tenfold increase in income. Encouraging the principle of *shramdan* (offering of voluntary labor), Hazare unified the villagers in undertaking various social projects, such as constructing a school and renovating the temple. To attack the scourge of alcoholism, he held a meeting in the temple in which the villagers

decided to close down shops selling liquor and ban drinking in the village. Using the temple as the site for these decisions gave them the stamp of religious commitments. He also encouraged social mixing among all jatis at community celebrations and helped Dalits to rise economically. Ultimately Hazare extended the Ralegan Siddhi model to seventy-five villages of the area, for which in 1992 he was given one of India's highest civilian awards.

Hazare's program of improving society reached the regional and state level, with the passage of laws such as a Prohibition Act by which if twenty-five percent or more of the women in an area voted to ban liquor, licenses of liquor sellers would be canceled. He won the right for locally chosen bodies to make decisions for local improvement. Traveling throughout his state of Maharashtra to inform and mobilize the people, he was able to force statewide and ultimately national legislation giving citizens the Right to Information, by which they could challenge lapses and corruption, which exists at all levels of government in India.

Using his own body as a vehicle to force needed changes, Hazare has undertaken many indefinite hunger strikes, refusing to eat until his demands are met. In 2011, he undertook another such fast in the capital, joined by huge crowds and cheered on by millions of citizens throughout India, to force passage of a strong Lokpal bill, which would institute an independent ombudsman authorized to investigate charges of corruption. The Lokpal Bill finally passed in 2013. Highly respected for his honesty and determination, Hazare shares a simple philosophy:

Educational institutions are not enough to make good citizens. Every home should become an educational centre. Indulgence causes disease whereas sacrifice leads to accomplishment. When the person learns to see beyond his self-interest, he begins to get mental peace. One who performs all worldly functions and still remains detached from worldly things is a true saint. Salvation of the self is part of salvation of the people. It is impossible to change the village without transforming the individual. Similarly, it is impossible to transform the country without changing its villages. If villages are to develop, politics must be kept out. ... Some of the crucial junctures of history demand that we live up to our national values and ideals; not living up to those values and ideals is like a living death.[31]

In 1948 the stigma of "untouchability" was legally abolished, though many caste distinctions still linger in modern India. Marriage across varna lines, for instance, is still usually disapproved of and families typically try to maintain jati endogamy when arranging marriages.

Caste distinctions are now being treated as a human rights issue. Since 1935, under British rule, there have been measures to reserve special quotas in government jobs and politics for those of Scheduled Castes (lists of the lowest jatis subject to discrimination—the former "untouchables"). Many religious groups and social welfare organizations have tried to eliminate discriminatory practices based on caste divisions. Theories of the origins of caste distinctions are being hotly debated by scholars in India and abroad. Numerous Dalit Hindus have converted to Christianity, Buddhism, and Islam—religions that do not recognize caste differences. A highly educated Dalit leader, Dr. B. R. Ambedkar (1891–1956) became chairman of the drafting committee for the Indian Constitution and independent India's first law minister, and was instrumental in getting anti-discrimination clauses written into the Constitution. He inspired Dalits to get better education, and shortly before his death, he led half a million "untouchable" Hindus to convert to Buddhism.

The division of labor represented by the varnas is part of Hinduism's strong emphasis on social duties and sacrifice of individual desires for the sake of social order. The Vedas, other scriptures, and historical customs have all conditioned the Indian people to accept their social roles. These were set out in religious–legal texts such as the Code of Manu, compiled 100–300 CE. In it are laws governing all aspects of life, including the proper conduct of rulers, dietary restrictions, marriage laws, daily rituals, purification rites, social laws, and ethical guidance. It prescribed hospitality to guests and the cultivation of such virtues as contemplation, truthfulness, compassion, nonattachment, generosity, pleasant dealings with people, and self-control. It condemned "untouchables" to living outside villages, eating only from broken dishes. On the other hand, the code proposed charitable giving as the sacred duty of the upper castes, and thus provided a safety net for those at the bottom of this hierarchical system. And common practice did not necessarily follow the religious–legal texts. Whereas the Code of Manu barred *shudras* from owning land, in South India many *shudras* were apparently wealthy and influential landowners. The code prescribed a subservient status to women, but some ancient temples contain stone carvings commemorating women who had endowed them with money in their own names.

Hospitality to human guests is a duty for people of all castes. To turn someone away from your door without feeding him or at least offering him a drink of water is a great sin, for every person is the deity incarnate. Ceremonies are often held for making offerings to a deity and feeding the public. The head of the household may, toward the end of his life, engage the services of a number of Brahmins to help complete the requisite 24,000,000 repetitions of the *Gayatrimantra* during his lifetime. Beggars take advantage of belief in sacrifice by saying that those who give to them will be blessed. But the most important sacrifices are considered to be inner sacrifices—giving one's entire self over to the Supreme Reality.

Hinduism also holds up four major goals that define the good life. One is dharma, or carrying out one's responsibilities and duties, for the sake of social and cosmic order. A second is *artha*, or success in worldly activities, including the pursuit of wealth and advantage. A third is *kama*, which refers to love and sensual pleasures, and also to aesthetic expression. Many other religious paths regard eroticism as an impediment to spiritual progress, but the *Mahabharata* proposes that dharma and *artha* both arise from *kama*, because without desire and creativity there is no striving. The fourth and ultimate goal of life is moksha, or liberation from the cycle of death and rebirth. Its attainment marks the end of all the other goals.

Sacred Thread Ceremony

When a boy from an upper-caste Hindu family reaches a certain age he may be formally initiated into Vedic rites and invested with a sacred thread. Although, according to Hindu canonical texts, the sacred thread is meant to be worn by all three upper castes, today the ceremony is associated only with the Brahmin community.

The rites involved are lengthy and detailed, for the boy must be taught many ancient Vedic rituals. He is initiated in the presence of his relatives, with his father and several pandits playing the major roles in his training, and his mother and other female relatives playing minor roles. Traditionally, this began the *brahmacharya* (student) stage of life, after which he would enter an ashram to study at the feet of his guru until the next stage of his life, during which he would marry and become a householder. Nowadays it is more likely that he will live at home with his parents, but he will at times be involved in sacred rituals, and will always be aware of his special caste status because beneath his outer clothes he will be wearing his sacred thread.

The ceremony may last four to five hours. Once the sacred thread is placed over the boy's left shoulder by his father and the pandits, his training in Vedic rites begins. For instance, he is taught how to pray using Vedic mantras, how to hold his fingers while eating or doing *pranayama* (the yoga of breathing), and how to carry on *havan* (*homa*) fire rituals. His hair is shaved above his forehead to reveal the shining of his inner third eye. He is bathed and dressed in a new dhoti, and then carried to the place of the sacred fire by his maternal uncle, while his aunts wave a tray of red-dyed water before him as an auspicious omen. Three white stripes are painted on his forehead and arms, vertical

if he is a devotee of Vishnu or horizontal to identify him as a devotee of Shiva. He washes his father's feet to show his reverence and affection, and then daubs colored powders on them to seek his father's blessings. After formally requesting his father to give him the ancient Gayatri mantra, he, his father and mother, and the pandit huddle under a cloth so that he can receive the mantra in secret. When they emerge, his relatives throw flowers and rice grains, symbolizing longevity and prosperity, over him.

The boy is then given a branch from a *palaasa* tree, which symbolizes the trees under which the ancient rishis used to sit. A *tilak* of vermilion is rubbed on his forehead and he is wrapped in a turmeric-dyed cloth, symbolizing purity. He is taken outside to learn how to look at the sun without having his retinas burned, by interlacing his fingers before his eyes.

After prostrating before the sacred fire, he prostrates before his mother, who blesses him. Then he goes to each of his female relatives with a tray, symbolically begging them for alms, for if he had entered an ashram he would have been begging daily for his food. The net result of his initiation is a strengthening of his identity and confidence as a member of what has traditionally been considered the highest spiritual caste in India, pledged to uphold dharma in everything he does.

Left: Ram (Vijay Krishna Ramaswamy), age eight, receives his sacred thread in the ancient monastery established by Shankara in the ninth century CE: Sharada Peetam in Karnataka. Center: Carried by his uncle, Ram is painted with horizontal stripes identifying him as a devotee of Shiva. Right: Ram washes his father's feet with water poured by his mother.

Life stages

The process of attaining spiritual realization or liberation is thought to take at least a lifetime, and probably many lifetimes. Birth as a human being is prized as a chance to advance toward spiritual perfection. In the past, spiritual training was usually available to upper-caste males only; women and *shudras* were excluded. Spiritual training for men has historically been preceded by an initiation ceremony in which the boy received the **sacred thread**, a cord of three threads to be worn across the chest from the left shoulder.

A Brahmin male's lifespan was ideally divided into four periods of approximately twenty-five years each. For the first twenty-five years he is a chaste student at the feet of a teacher. Next comes the householder stage, during which he is expected to marry, raise a family, and contribute productively to society. After this period, he starts to detach himself from worldly pursuits and to turn to meditation and scriptural study. By the age of seventy-five, he is able to withdraw totally from society and become a **sannyasin**.

Living as a renunciate, the sannyasin is a contemplative who cuts himself off from wife and family, declaring, "No one belongs to me and I belong to no one." Some sannyasins take up residence in comfortable temples. Others wander alone with only a water jar, a walking staff, and a begging bowl as possessions; some of them wear no clothes. In silence, the sannyasin is supposed to concentrate on practices that will finally release him from samsara into cosmic consciousness.

The majority of contemporary Hindu males do not actually follow this path of four periods but many Hindus still become sannyasins. Some of them have renounced the world at a younger age and joined a monastic order, living in an **ashram**, a retreat community that has developed around a teacher.

For a woman, the ideal stages of life are daughter, wife, and, if her husband should die before her, widow. The woman is to be protected first by her father, then her husband, then her eldest son. Brahminic Hinduism does not advocate that women become sannyasins, but today an estimated fifteen percent of the renouncers in India are female. While classical Hindu texts do not fully detail women's religious obligations, Hindu women are actively involved in a wide range of religious activities.

The guru

Nearly every practicing Hindu seeks to place himself or herself at the feet of a spiritual teacher, or **guru**. The title "guru" is applied to venerable spiritual guides. Gurus do not declare themselves as teachers; people are drawn to them because they have achieved spiritual status to which the seekers aspire. Gurus are often regarded as enlightened or "fully realized" individuals. A guru does not provide academic instruction. Rather, he or she gives advice, example, and encouragement to those seeking enlightenment or realization.

Anyone and everyone cannot be a guru. A huge timber floats on the water and can carry animals as well. But a piece of worthless wood sinks, if a man sits on it, and drowns him.

Ramakrishna[29]

Many gurus migrated to the West to spread Hindu teachings there. Paramahansa Yogananda's book Autobiography of a Yogi *continues to attract Western followers to Indian religious traditions.*

When seekers find their guru, they love and honor him or her as their spiritual parent. The guru does not always behave as a loving parent; often disciples are treated harshly, to test their faith and devotion or to strip away the ego. True devotees are nevertheless grateful for opportunities to serve their guru, out of love. They often bend to touch his or her feet, partly out of humility and partly because great power is thought to emanate from a guru's feet. Humbling oneself before the guru is considered necessary in order to receive the teaching. A metaphor commonly used is that of a cup and a pitcher of water. If the cup (the disciple, or chela) is already full, no water (spiritual wisdom) can be poured into it from the pitcher (the guru). Likewise, if the cup is on the same level as the pitcher, there can be no pouring. What is necessary is for the cup to be empty and below the pitcher; then the water can be freely poured into the cup.

Rituals

From the cradle to the cremation ground, the Hindu's life is wrapped up in rituals. There are sixteen rites prescribed in the ancient scriptures to purify and sanctify the person in his or her journey through life, including rites at the time of conception, the braiding of the pregnant mother's hair, birth, name-giving, beginning of solid foods, starting education, investing boys with a sacred thread, first leaving the family house, starting studies of Vedas, marriage, and death. The goal is to continually elevate the person above his or her basically animal nature.

Public worship—**puja**—is usually performed by *pujaris*, or Brahmin priests (typically male), who are trained in Vedic practices and in proper recitation of Sanskrit texts. They conduct worship ceremonies in which the sacred presence is made tangible through devotions employing all the senses. Shiva-lingams may be anointed with precious substances, such as ghee (clarified butter), honey, or sandalwood paste, with offerings of rosewater and flowers. In a temple, devotees may have the great blessing of receiving **darshan** (visual contact with the divine) through the eyes of the images. The cosmos is viewed as a vibrational field, and therefore the chanting of mantras, blowing of a conch shell, and ringing of bells create vibrations thought to have positive effects. Incense and flowers fill the area with uplifting fragrances. *Prasad*, food that has been sanctified by being offered to the deities and/or one's guru, is passed around to be eaten by devotees, who experience it as sacred and spiritually charged.

In temples, the deity image is treated as if it were a living king or queen. Fine-haired whisks may be waved before it, purifying the area for its presence. Aesthetically pleasing meals are presented on the deity's own dishes at appropriate intervals; fruits must be perfect, without any blemishes. During visiting hours the deity holds court, giving audience to devotees. In the morning, the image is ritually bathed and dressed in sumptuous clothes for the day; at night, it may be put to rest in bedclothes. If it is hot, the deity takes a nap in the afternoon, so arrangements are made for its privacy. For festivals, the deity is

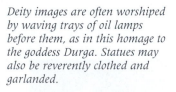

Deity images are often worshiped by waving trays of oil lamps before them, as in this homage to the goddess Durga. Statues may also be reverently clothed and garlanded.

carefully paraded through the streets. In Puri's Ratha Yatra, huge crowds of ecstatic devotees pull and push three massive chariots bearing flower-bedecked deities after their yearly bath with perfumed water. More than a million worshipers seek darshan of the colossal statues as their chariots are pulled along the parade route. The largest of these teak chariots bears Lord Jagannath; it is 45 feet (13.7 meters) high, with sixteen wooden wheels. Its ponderous journey has entered English vocabulary, misspelled as "juggernaut."

Loving service to the divine makes it real and present. The statue is not just a symbol of the deity; the deity may be experienced through the statue, reciprocating the devotee's attentions. According to Swami Sivasiva Palani:

It is thought that the subtle essences of these things given in devotion are actually absorbed by the divine, in an invisible and rather mystical process. It's as though we are feeding our God in an inner kind of way. It's thought that if this is done properly, with the right spirit, the right heartfulness, the right mantras, that we capture the attention of the personal Lord and that he actually communes with us through that process, and we with him. Of course, when I say "us" and "him" I connote a dualism that is meant to be transcended in this process.[30]

Ritual fire ceremonies around a **havan**, or sacred fire place, are also conducted by Brahmin pandits (teacher-scholars), following ancient Vedic traditions. The Vedic principle of sacrifice was based on the idea that generous offerings to a deity will be rewarded. Fruits, fragrances, mixtures of herbs and grains, and ghee are placed in the fire as offerings to the deities, invoked and praised by chants, with offerings conveyed by Agni, the god of fire. According to Vedic science, fire is a medium of purification and transformation, and havan (as the ritual is also called) is expected to purify the environment and the participants. Such havans may be conducted in celebration of a particular deity, or at the behest of a patron for the sake of his health or good fortune.

Death ceremonies are also carried out by fire, as the body is cremated soon after death. Carefully washed, rubbed with fragrant sandalwood paste, and dressed in fresh clothes, it is wrapped in white sheets and carried on a wooden stretcher to a burning ground. Male relatives and well-wishers place flowers on the shrouded body and then logs are stacked around it to make a fierce fire. Pandits may chant Vedic verses designed to cleanse it and assist the soul's release from the body and its passage to the spiritual realm. The senior mourner—usually the eldest surviving son—carries a clay pot of water around the body three times, gradually pouring out the water, then dashes the pot to the ground, a dramatic and emotional moment signifying the end of the earthly body. It is also he who then lights the pyre. Alternatively, the shrouded body may be placed in an electric crematorium. Once the burning of the body is complete, survivors take the remaining bits of bone and ash for ritual immersion in the waters of a holy river.

In addition to public puja ceremonies conducted by pandits, home puja is an important aspect of Hindu life. Nearly every Hindu home in India has a shrine with pictures or small statues of various deities, and many have a prayer room set aside for worship. For puja, ritual purity is emphasized; the time for prayer and offerings to the deities is after the morning bath or after one has washed in the evening. Puja is an everyday observance, although among orthodox families

Two of the huge chariots in the annual Ratha Yatra in Puri.

An Interview with Somjit Dasgupta

In Hinduism, many forms of dance, song, and instrumental music have evolved as means of spiritual expression. Somjit Dasgupta is a very accomplished Indian musician whose ragas softly played on the stringed sarod touch a deep place in the soul. His words reflect the importance attached to teacher–pupil lineages in Hindu classical music tradition, and also the reverence that Hindus may feel for their guru:

My Guru was Radhikamohan Maitreya, whose main instrument was the sarod. For music, there has been no distinction between Hindu or Muslim tradition. When the Muslim rulers came here, they preached from the ashrams. Some of the old Hindu musicians were converted and joined the Muslim courts. And some of the Persian musicians who accompanied the sultans learned Indian classical music. By and by, some court instruments were born. But the old instruments were still there, and some of the essence of meditation was carried to the courts.

In our old Sanskrit texts, it is written, "There is no education, no learning beyond music." In the Indian tradition, it is sangeet—*collective worship and singing.*

Meditation was there in other parts of the world also, but it was very special in this part of the world. Meditation means to sit and see within yourself. Once I asked my Guru, "What did you achieve in your life? You are highly regarded by almost all the big musicians. They touch your feet, but you are sitting here. You did not play in public concerts. We have our Gurubhais [pupils of the same Guru] all over the world, but what I feel is that you are not very famous. What have you achieved?" He said, "Nobody ever asked me that. But this is a little boy [I was only fourteen at the time]. I will answer that later."

After I passed through school and entered college, one day he said "Acha, Somjit, one day you asked me one thing. I was telling you many things regarding the social status of men and women and such things, but I also told you about this soil, which can give the world the things that come from the spiritual light."

Then he told me, "What do you mean by sound? Sound is some cluster of frequencies that you are hearing. In that way, I am Radhikamohan Maitreya: I am a cluster of frequencies. My body is constructed out of that particular frequency. And you are Somjit Dasgupta. Some other set of frequencies created you.

That's why your self and my self are joined in different ways, giving us different personalities. But our aim is to go back to the primordial frequency, through this sadhana, this spiritual practice. Everybody in every sadhana has to go through music. The Ramayana *and the* Mahabharata *were sung; all the saints could sing. With our finger touch, by Guru's grace, our aim is to reach that primordial frequency. And there, there is no myself. No self is there. That is eternity. There is no 'you' and 'other' feeling. This thing my Guru gave me. I cannot say it is an achievement. It is as though you are going back to your father's place. It's a huge joy, joy, and joy." I asked, "What is there?" Then he said, "Some day I will tell you. You asked me, and after four years I am saying this to you. I will tell you later what is there."*

Then he told me about one song, which says, "The same single Omkar *[a name referring to the Ultimate Reality as primordial vibration] is spread throughout the world. It has no form, no dimensions. In the primordial frequency there is nothing, nobody, only* Omkar. *When I see That personally, I enjoy That personally, I feel That personally, then only can I think about the Almighty."*

He also told me about another song from the dhrupad *musical tradition, a song which contains the seed, the essence. It says, "Chaitanya—the primordial sensations, presence, and sensitivity within me—is eternal, and very calm and quiet. Bindu is where you touch to experience that Chaitanya. When you are touching your instrument, that is your touching point. Beyond all these things is that same existence, that same primordial frequency."*

He taught me fourteen songs about the Guru, containing the inner essence of dharma. One says, "There is no knowledge beyond the Guru. There is no spiritual practice, no meditation beyond the Guru. All kinds of inner enlightened knowledge finish in eternity: There my Guru stays, with all the blessings."

Our work is not to perform on the stage or anything like that. It is that whatever you get from your Guru, your entire existence is to pass that on, so that this teaching can go on and on and on, and give that essence for the future. Maybe a very worthy person can come who can achieve something much more than me, if I keep this teaching intact. So the main thing is to keep this teaching alive. The rest is up to the Guru, and up to the Almighty.[31]

menstruating women are considered unclean and are not allowed to approach the shrines. Otherwise, women as well as men carry on puja in their homes. Typically, a small oil lamp and a smoldering stick of incense are reverently waved before the deities' images to please them with light and fragrance. If the devotee or family has a guru, a picture of him or her is usually part of the shrine.

Fasts, prayers, and auspicious designs

Orthodox Brahmins and also common people observe many days of fasting and prayer, corresponding to auspicious points in the lunar and solar cycles or times of danger, such as the months of the monsoon season. The ancient practice of astrology is so highly regarded that some couples choose birth by Caesarean section for the purpose of selecting the most auspicious moment for their child's birth. Women may make vows to particular deities and then keep regular fasts for various ends, such as the health and success of family and children.

Many expressions of Indian spirituality, particularly in rural areas, are not encapsulated within Brahmanic traditions but rather have a timeless existence of their own. Such, for instance, are the homemade designs daily laid out before homes at dawn. They are created by women to protect their household by inviting a deity such as the goddess Lakshmi. Typically made of edible substances, such as rice flour, the designs are soon dismantled by insects and birds, but this is of no concern for they help to fulfill the dharmic requirement that one should feed 1,000 souls every day.

Golu Devata, known as god of justice and fulfiller of wishes, is a popular local deity in the lower Himalayas. Devotees pledge to offer bells when their prayers are granted.

A South Indian woman prepares patterns of colored powders outside her home to bring spiritual protection and good fortune for her family.

Reverence of trees and rivers

Practices such as worship under large trees stretch back into prehistory and are apparent in archaeological evidence from the Indus Valley civilization. Such worship continues at countless small shrines today. In some rural areas, trees are thought to have great capacity for absorbing suffering, so sometimes people are first "married" to trees in order to improve the fortunes of their families who are facing difficulties. There is a strong taboo against cutting certain sacred tree species, such as the peepul tree, which sprouts wherever it can gain the slightest foothold, often in stone or brick walls, even on the sides of buildings. Whole tracts of virgin forest are kept intact by villagers in some parts of India. There they reverently protect both animal and plant life with the understanding that the area is the home of a deity. These sacred groves are now viewed by environmentalists as important islands of biological diversity.

Not only forests but also hilltops, mountains, and river sources are often viewed as sacred and their natural environment is thus protected to a certain extent. Water is revered for its life-sustaining and purifying force. Most Indian rivers, most famously the Ganges, are regarded as goddesses. The Narmada River is one of India's most sacred. Its banks are lined with thousands of temples devoted to Mother Narmada and Lord Shiva. Pilgrims reverently circumambulate the entire 815-mile (1,312-kilometer) length of the river, from its source in central India to its mouth in the Gulf of Khambhat, and back again. However, the river and its huge watershed are the subjects of the world's largest water development scheme. The highest of the dams is under construction, creating a reservoir with a final proposed height of over 450 feet (138 meters). When the reservoir is filled, some 245 villages will be submerged, temples and all. The idea is to capture the water and divert it to drought-ridden areas to benefit people there. Yet the inhabitants of the watershed that will be inundated are closely linked to their local sacred landscape. One of them explains, "Our gods cannot move from this place. How can we move without them?"[32] Fierce conflicts have been raging since 1990 between environmentalists and social activists who are fighting the high dams, claiming they will adversely affect at least one million people in the watershed for the sake of vested interests elsewhere, and modernists who regard such high dams, as Nehru said, as "the secular temples of modern India."[33]

A devotee prays before taking a holy bath in the sacred Ganges River.

High dams are not the only threat to sacred rivers. Construction and waste dumping have polluted rivers even up to the headwaters of the sacred Ganges high in the Himalayas. Religious practices themselves may lead to high levels of water pollution. Mass bathing on auspicious occasions is accompanied by wastes, such as butter oil, flowers, and human excreta (contrary to scriptural injunctions about proper behavior in sacred rivers). The remains of dead bodies reverently immersed in the sacred rivers may be incompletely cremated. Immersion of images of Ganesh or Durga on holy days as a symbol of purification has become a major source of water pollution. In one year alone, ritual immersion of idols in Kolkata added to the Hooghly River an estimated seventeen tons of varnish and thirty-two tons of paints, which contained manganese, lead, mercury, and chromium.[34] There are now efforts in many Indian cities to use more environmentally friendly materials for religious objects.

Pilgrimages

Pilgrimages to holy places and sacred rivers are thought to be special opportunities for personal purification and spiritual elevation. Many holy sites in India are associated with events in the epics and Puranas, and thus visiting them is a means of expressing devotion to the deities associated with the place. Shaktas trek to *shaktipithas*; these fifty-one

Millions of Hindus undertake difficult pilgrimages to worship at mountain shrines each year.

pilgrimage spots on the Indian subcontinent are thought to mark abodes of the goddess or places where parts of her body now rest. The god Krishna spent much of his childhood in Vrindavan and the area surrounding it, and pilgrims visit Vrindavan to see the sites traditionally associated with events in his life. Similarly, millions of pilgrims yearly undertake strenuous climbs to remote mountain sites that are thought to be blessed by the divine. One of the major pilgrimage sites is Amarnath Cave. At an altitude of 11,090 feet (3,380 meters) in the Himalayas of Kashmir, ice has formed a giant stalagmite, which is highly revered as a Shiva lingam. Pilgrims may have been trekking to this holy place in the high Himalayas for up to 3,000 years. The 14,800-foot (45-kilometer) foot-path over a glacier is so dangerous that 250 people were killed by freak storms and landslides in 1996, but in subsequent years tens of thousands of devotees have continued to undertake the pilgrimage.

The places where great saints and teachers have lived also automatically become places of pilgrimage, during their lives and after they pass on. It is felt that their powerful vibrations still permeate and bless these sites. One such place is the holy mountain of Arunachala in southern India. The great saint Ramana Maharshi (1879–1951) lived there so absorbed in Ultimate Consciousness that he neither talked nor ate and had to be force-fed by another holy man. But the needs of those who gathered around him drew out his compassion and wisdom, and he spontaneously counseled them on their spiritual needs.

Festivals

Hinduism honors the divine in so many forms that almost every day a religious celebration is being held in some part of India. Sixteen religious holidays are honored by the central government so that everyone can leave work to join in the throngs of worshipers. The holidays are calculated partially on a lunar calendar, so dates vary from year to year. Most Hindu festivals express spirituality in its happiest aspects. Group energy attracts the gods to overcome evils, and humorous abandon helps merrymakers to forget their fears.

Janmashtami is often celebrated by placing an image of baby Krishna in a decorated swing. Everyone takes turns to pull the cord and lovingly rock Krishna.

Holi

The jolliest of all Hindu festivals is Holi, celebrated at the time of winter's death and the advent of spring. It falls on the first full moon of the lunar month Phagun (late February or early March in the solar calendar). The major activity is throwing colored powder or squirting water paint with wild abandon. This may not seem spiritual when measured by the standards of more staid religions, and people may not even be sure exactly what is being celebrated. Indeed, the same wild flinging of paint is given different meanings in different parts of India, illustrating the great variety of ways that are collectively referred to as "Hinduism."

Apparently Holi has been celebrated since prehistoric times. The earliest colors were made from natural plants that are also used in traditional Ayurvedic medicine to ward off viral fevers and colds, such as yellow-dyeing turmeric powder. Psychologically, Holi's effect is rejuvenating and harmonizing, as social taboos are transcended and people from all levels rub or throw paint on each other. This is a major, albeit temporary, change from the usual taboos according to which males and females, high and low castes, do not touch each other. Women have free license on this day to beat men with sticks and throw buckets of mud on them—a role reversal they adopt with great hilarity.

Vaishnava devotees relate Holi to the story of Prahlad, a young follower of Vishnu. His father was Hiranyakashipu, king of demons. Hiranyakashipu became so proud that he attacked heaven and earth and demanded that everyone worship him instead of the gods. However, his own son Prahlad persisted in worshiping Vishnu. Hiranyakashipu tried to get him

killed by poison, by elephants, and by snakes, but Prahlad survived all the attacks. Then Hiranyakashipu enlisted the help of his sister Holika, who had a magic shawl that protected its wearer from fire. He ordered Prahlad to sit on his aunt's lap in a fire, expecting his son to burn to death while Holika in her shawl would be unharmed. Instead, the shawl flew off Holika and onto Prahlad, who had prayed to Vishnu for safety. Thus many Vaishnavas begin their Holi celebration by building big fires to rejoice over the burning of the demoness Holika, for whom the festival is named.

Krishna worshipers associate Holi with the love of Radha for Krishna, especially in spring, the season of love. It is thought that Krishna played Holi mischievously with the *gopis*, and when he criticized Radha because her skin was not as dark as his, his mother put Holi colors on her face to darken it.

Yet another Krishna legend has been linked with Holi. According to this, at the time of Krishna's birth his uncle Kans, king of winter, ordered that all babies be murdered to avoid Krishna's future threat to his power. A demoness was sent to suckle Krishna to death, but Krishna, recognizing her, instead sucked out all her lifeblood, whereupon she died. Some Krishna worshipers therefore burn the demoness in effigy as well as spraying colors, singing, and dancing to celebrate Holi at the onset of spring.

To Shiva worshipers, Holi commemorates a story about Shiva. According to this, Kamadeva, god of love, was implored by Parvati to help her get Shiva's attention. Shiva was deep in meditation when Kamadeva shot his weapon at him. At this, Shiva opened his third eye (the all-seeing eye in the center of the forehead), whose gaze was so powerful that Kamadeva was burned to ashes. He was later restored to life at Parvati's request, and Shiva and Parvati were married. In this story, winter is the time of meditation, and the coming of spring signals fertile new life and fulfillment.

Backed by a variety of legends, Holi is celebrated with such vigor that some revelers take it as an excuse for drunken and destructive behavior. Furthermore, environmental groups are now pointing out that the industrial dyes used for Holi powder can be quite toxic. However, like those who are trying to educate the public not to shoot off fireworks on Divali to avoid extreme air pollution, these groups have had little effect on people's exuberant, carefree ways of celebrating the Hindu holidays.

Holi is the riotously joyful celebration of the death of winter and the return of colorful spring. Its many attributed meanings illustrate the great diversity within Hinduism (see Box, facing page).

In August or September, Vaishnavas celebrate Krishna's birthday (Janmashtami). Devotees fast and keep vigil until midnight, retelling stories of Krishna's life or reading his enlightened wisdom from the *Bhagavad-Gita*. In some places Krishna's image is placed in a cradle and lovingly rocked. Elsewhere, pots of milk, curds, and butter are strung high above the ground to be seized by young men who form human pyramids to get to them. They romp about with the pots, drinking and spilling their contents like Krishna, playful stealer of the milk products he loved.

At the end of summer, Ganesh is honored, especially in western and southern India, during Ganesh Chaturthi. Special potters make elaborate clay images of the jovial elephant-headed remover of obstacles, son of Parvati, who formed him from her body's dirt and sweat and set him to stand guard while she bathed. When he wouldn't let Shiva in, her angry spouse smashed the boy's head into a thousand pieces. Parvati demanded that the boy be restored to life with a new head, but the first one found was that of a baby elephant. To soothe Parvati's distress at the peculiarity of the transplant, Shiva granted Ganesh the power of removing obstacles. The elephant-headed god is now the first to be invoked in all rituals. After days of being sung to and offered sweets, the Ganesh images are carried to a body of water and bidden farewell, with prayers for an easy year.

In different parts of India the first nine or ten days of Ashvina, the lunar month corresponding to September or October, are dedicated either to Durga Puja (in which elaborate images of the many-armed goddess celebrate her powers to vanquish the demonic forces) or to Dussehra (which marks Rama's nine nights of worshiping Durga before killing Ravana on the tenth day). The theme of both Durga Puja and Dussehra is the triumph of good over evil.

Divali, the happy four-day festival of lights, is twenty days later, on the night of the new moon. Variously explained as the return of Rama after his exile, the puja of Lakshmi (goddess of wealth, who visits only clean homes), and the New Year of those following one of the Indian calendars, it is a time for tidying business establishments and bringing financial records up to date, cleaning houses and illuminating them with oil lamps, wearing new clothes, gambling, feasting, honoring clay images of Lakshmi and Ganesh, and setting off fireworks, often to the point of severe air pollution.

Initially more solemn is Mahashivaratri, a day of fasting and a night of keeping vigil to earn merit with Shiva. During the ascetic part of the observance, many pilgrims go to sacred rivers or special tanks of water for ritual bathing. Shiva lingams and statues are venerated, and the faithful stay awake throughout the night, chanting and telling stories of their Lord.

Every few years, millions of Hindus of all persuasions gather for Kumbha Mela. It is held alternately at four sacred spots where drops of the holy nectar of immortality are said to have fallen. On one day in 2013, in what has been recorded as one of the largest ever gatherings of human beings for a single purpose, an estimated thirty million people amassed at the point near Allahabad where the Yamuna River meets the sacred Ganges and the invisible Saraswati, the sacred river that dried up long ago but is still considered invisibly present. There they took a purifying bath in icy waters on the most auspicious date, as determined by astrologers. Among

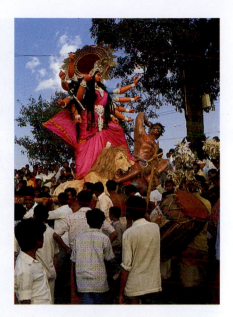

At the end of Durga Puja, images of the ten-armed vanquisher of evil are carried to the river and consigned to the deep, so that she may return to her mate Shiva, who awaits her in the Himalayas.

In the villages of India, all-night singing of sacred songs often marks special holidays. Women have their own repertoire and improvisations.

Bridges are constructed over the Ganges River at Haridwar to help accommodate huge crowds during the Kumbha Mela.

the Kumbha Mela pilgrims are huge processions of ascetic **sadhus** from various orders, many of whom leave their retreats only for this festival. They gather to discuss religious matters and also social problems, which sometimes leads to revisions of Hindu codes of conduct. At the 2013 Kumbha Mela, activist groups promoted the welfare of female children and brought attention to environmental issues.

Women's religious roles

At the level of spiritual ideals, the female is highly venerated in Hinduism, compared to many other religions. Women are thought to make major contributions to the good earthly life, which includes dharma (order in society), marital wealth (by bearing sons in a patriarchal society), and the aesthetics of sensual pleasure. Women are auspicious beings, mythologically associated with wealth, beauty, splendor, and grace. As sexual partners to men, they help to activate the spiritualizing life force. No ceremonial sacrifice is complete unless the wife participates as well as the husband.

In the ideal marriage, husband and wife are spiritual partners. Marriage is a vehicle for spiritual discipline, service, and advancement toward a spiritual goal. Men and women are thought to complement each other, although the ideal of liberation has traditionally been intended largely for the male.

Women were not traditionally encouraged to seek liberation through their own spiritual practices. A woman's role is usually linked to that of her husband, who takes the position of her god and teacher. For many centuries, there was even the hope that a widow would choose to be cremated alive with her dead husband in order to remain united with him after death.

In early Vedic times, women were relatively free and honored members of Indian society, participating equally in important spiritual rituals. But because of social changes, by the nineteenth century wives had become like servants of the husband's family. With expectations that a girl will take a large dowry to a boy's family in a marriage arrangement, girls are such an economic burden that female babies may be intentionally aborted or killed at birth. There are also cases today of women being beaten or killed by the husband's family after their dowry has been handed over—an atrocity that occurs in various Indian communities, not only among Hindus.

Nevertheless, many women in contemporary India have been well educated, and many have attained high political positions. As in the past, women are also considered essential to the spiritual protection of their families, for they are thought to have special connections with the deities. Married women carry on daily worship of the deities in their homes, and also fasts and rituals designed to bring good health, prosperity, and long life for their family members.

There have also been many women who have left their prescribed family duties and achieved such high levels of spiritual realization that they have been revered as saints and gurus. The bhakti approach to the divine produced many such women. For example, Andal (725–755 CE) was a South Indian Alvar—a group known for its poet mystics. Andal was so overcome with love for Vishnu that she refused to marry anyone else. Her **hagiography** (idealized biography of the life of a saint) maintains that she merged into the deity after being mystically married to Him. Many Vaishnava temples thus have an image of Andal next to that of Vishnu.

Akka Mahadevi was a thirteenth-century bhakti poet saint in the radical South Indian Virashaiva movement, which rejected Brahmin patriarchy and casteism. Its founder, Basava, had renounced his Brahmin identity and taught that women—because of their creative and nurturing powers—and people of lower castes—because they are not constrained by wealth or worldly power— are closer to God than Brahmin males. This movement gave rise to many great women saints. Akka Mahadevi was so devoted to Shiva that she refused marriage to any man:

> I have fallen in love, O mother, with the Beautiful One,
> Who knows no death, knows no decay, and has no form. …
> Fling into the fire the husbands who are subject to death
>   and decay.[35]

After escaping from a forced marriage, the beautiful Akka Mahadevi lived alone as an ascetic amid the streams and mountains of a holy area linked with Shiva. Her rejection of the life of a traditional wife was so total that she lived naked. She was an early advocate of the equality of women and of women's right to spiritual and social liberation.

A more recent renowned female saint in the bhakti tradition was Mirabai (see p. 91). Like many women saints, she was at first considered mad as well as socially deviant as she danced on the streets in ecstasy, describing herself as "defiant of worldly censure or family shame," behavior considered totally unfitting for her status as a Rajasthani princess. But her songs, like those of Andal and Akka Mahadevi, continue to be widely sung in rural India.

The tantric traditions and texts suggest that there have been many women adepts who have transmitted tantric doctrines. There are references, for instance, to yoginis who are either solitary ascetics known for their enlightened wisdom or consorts of male tantric masters, worthy of the same respect as the male gurus. In tantric literature, worshipers are encouraged to identify with the inner shakti, as the Universal Goddess. This is considered easier and more natural for those who are already in women's

Akka Mahadevi, a saint who lived alone and naked in the mountains.

bodies. Some of the most remarkable Hindu teachers today are women who understand themselves as embodiments of the goddess and see all people as their children.

Hinduism has thus given rise to many renowned female spiritual teachers over the millennia. Among the most famous of recent times was Anandamayi Ma (1896–1982, "Blissful Mother"), a guru from Bengal who was born in a very poor orthodox Brahmin family. Often seen sitting in a state of spiritual absorption as a child, but nonetheless scrupulously carrying out all her domestic chores, she was married at a young age to a kind young man. Their marriage was never consummated for when he tried to approach her, he received a powerful electric shock. When she was twenty years old, she began spontaneously adopting advanced yogic postures and reciting ancient Sanskrit texts and mantras that she had never learned from any human teacher. She was suspected of being possessed, and exorcists were called, but they were unsuccessful in stopping her spiritual expressions; one exorcist even experienced severe pain until Ma healed him. An inner voice told her that the power manifesting in her was "Your Shakti. You are everything." Ma later explained, "I realized that the Universe was all my own manifestation."[36] When she was twenty-two, she was guided to give herself mantra initiation, thus adopting the roles of both guru and disciple. People began flocking to her for darshan, healing, and spiritual counseling. Detached from worldly concerns and thoughts, she ate very little and ultimately stopped feeding herself, so her devotees tried to hand-feed her. Following only the inner guidance, in total disregard for cultural and religious mores—especially restrictions on women—she sometimes gave brilliant teachings in Vedanta philosophy (even though she was nearly illiterate), traveled unpredictably, attracted stray animals by her aura of love, and reportedly manifested siddhis (spiritual powers) such as appearing at several places at the same time, changing her size, helping people at distant locations, multiplying food, and transforming people by her joyous and peaceful presence. Ultimately millions of people became her followers, regarding her as the goddess in human form, but she reportedly did not consider herself a guru, nor did she recognize anyone as her disciples—she saw only Herself everywhere.

Similarly, Mataji Nirmala Devi (1923–2011) was regarded by her devotees as an incarnation of the primal shakti. She is now venerated as divine by her followers in more than 200 countries. And as we will see later, Amritanandamayi ("Amma") is one of the world's most famous contemporary saints, with millions of followers and extensive charitable activities to take care of her "children."

Hinduism in the modern world

Why is Hindu identity an important issue in modern India?

Hinduism did not develop in India in isolation. Christianity may have put down roots in India as long ago as 70 CE. Muslims began taking over certain areas beginning in the eighth century CE; during the sixteenth and seventeenth centuries a large area was ruled by the Muslim Mughal emperors. Islam and Hinduism generally co-existed, despite periods of intolerance, along with Buddhism and Jainism, which had also grown up within India. Indian traders carried some aspects of Hinduism to Java and Bali, where it survives today with a unique Balinese flavor.

As the Mughal Empire went into decline, European colonialists gradually moved in. Ultimately the British dominated, and in 1857 India was officially placed under direct British rule. Christian missionaries set about attempting to correct abuses they perceived in certain Hindu practices, such as widow-burning and the caste system. But they also taught those who were being educated in their schools that Hinduism was "intellectually incoherent and ethically unsound."[37] Some Indians believed them and drifted away from their ancient tradition.

Modern movements

Many other Indians, however, sought to revitalize and in some cases change aspects of religious practice that had come under criticism, rather than abandoning their traditions altogether. To counteract Western influences, Mahatma (Great Soul) Gandhi (1869–1948) encouraged grassroots nationalism, emphasizing that the people's strength lay in awareness of spiritual truth and in nonviolent resistance to military or industrial oppression. He claimed that these qualities were the essence of all religions, including Hinduism, which he considered the universal religion.

In addition to being made a focus for political unity, Hinduism itself was revitalized by a number of spiritual leaders. One of these was Ramakrishna (1836–1886), who was a devotee of the Divine Mother in the form of Kali. Eschewing ritual, he communicated with her through intense love. He experimented with many different forms of religious practice. These brought him spiritual powers, spiritual insight, and reportedly a visible brilliance, but he longed only to be a vehicle for pure devotion:

> I seek not, good Mother, the pleasures of the senses! I seek not fame! Nor do I long for those powers which enable one to do miracles! What I pray for, O good Mother, is pure love for Thee—love for Thee untainted by desires, love without alloy, love that seeketh not the things of the world, love for Thee that welleth up unbidden out of the depths of the immortal soul![38]

Ramakrishna, the great 19th-century mystic, recognized the divine as being both formless and manifested in many forms, and also as transcending both form and formlessness.

Ramakrishna worshiped the divine through many Hindu paths, as well as Islam and Christianity, and found the same One in them all. Intoxicated with the One, he had continual visions of the Divine Mother and ecstatically worshiped her in unorthodox, uninhibited ways. For instance, once he fed a cat some food that was supposed to be a temple offering for the Divine Mother, for she revealed herself to him in everything, including the cat. He also placed his spiritual bride, Sarada Devi, in the chair reserved for the deity, honoring her as the Great Goddess.

> Do not care for doctrines, do not care for dogmas, or sects, or churches, or temples; they count for little compared with the essence of existence in each [person], which is spirituality. … Earn that first, acquire that, and criticize no one, for all doctrines and creeds have some good in them.
>
> Ramakrishna[39]

Vivekananda was a brilliant spiritual teacher who brought Hinduism to the attention of the West when he spoke at the World Parliament of Religions in 1893. When he returned to India, he founded a mission to spread the teachings of his teacher, Ramakrishna.

The pure devotion and universal spiritual wisdom that Ramakrishna embodied inspired what is now known as the Ramakrishna Movement, or the Vedanta Society. A famous disciple, named Vivekananda (1863–1902), carried the message of Hinduism to the world beyond India and excited so much interest in the West that Hinduism became a global religion. He also reintroduced Indians to the profundities of their great traditions. He taught detachment from material perspectives, in favor of evolved spiritual understanding:

> What we want is neither happiness nor misery. Both make us forget our true nature; both are chains, one iron, one gold; behind both is the Atman, who knows neither happiness nor misery. These are states, and states must ever change; but the nature of the soul is bliss, peace, unchanging.[40]

Within India Hinduism has also been influenced by reform movements such as Brahmo Samaj and Arya Samaj. The former defended Hindu mysticism and bhakti devotion to an immanent deity. The latter advocated a return to what it saw as the purity of the Vedas, rejecting image worship, devotion to a multiplicity of deities, priestly privileges, and popular rituals.

In addition to religious reform movements, Hindu tradition is currently

Dharmic Principles: The Swadhyaya Movement

Today there are said to be twenty million people in 100,000 villages in India who are beneficiaries of a silent social revolution based on the principles of the ancient Hindu scriptures, especially the *Bhagavad-Gita*. The movement is called Swadhyaya. The term means "self-study," using traditional scriptural teachings to critically analyze oneself in order to improve.

The work began in the 1950s, as scriptural scholar Pandurang Shastri Athavale, known by his followers as "Dada" (elder brother), determined that the *Gita* was "capable of resolving the dilemmas of modern man and solving the problems of material life, individual and social."[41] He founded a school near Mumbai, refusing to accept any financial help from the government or outside funding agency, insisting that "those institutions which depend upon others' favors are never able to achieve anything worthwhile or carry out divine work."[42] He named the buildings for the ancient sages who have inspired people to live according to Vedic principles. It was they who recognized that within each person is a divine spark whose realization gives them the energy and guidance with which to uplift themselves. As Dada once observed, the sage who wrote the *Ramayana* is:

> virtually urging us to take Rama—the awareness that the Lord is with us and within us all the time—to every home and every heart, as this alone will provide the confidence and the strength to the weakest of the weak and will bring joy and fragrance into the life of every human being.[43]

Realization of the divine within themselves also leads to realization of the divine within others, which is the beginning of social harmony and co-operation.

The principle upon which Dada's social development work is centered is bhakti, or selfless devotion. He inspired his students to pay devotional visits to towns and villages in Gujarat state. They carried their own food and asked for nothing from the people. They simply met the inhabitants one to one and spoke of the divine love which made them reach out to distant places. After years of regular visits and assurance that gratefulness to God and brotherly love was developing among the villagers, the villagers allowed them to build simple hut temples of local materials, devotional places for people of all castes and creeds.

In gratitude toward the in-dwelling God for being present when they go to their farms, giving them energy to work, *swadhyayees* feel that God is entitled to a share in the produce. They therefore bring a portion of their income to the hut temples to be distributed among the most needy, as the benevolence of God.

Believing in work as worship, the villagers were also inspired to set aside a portion of land to be farmed in common, as "God's farm." All give a certain number of days of volunteer service on the farm, in grateful service to God. The harvests are treated as "impersonal wealth." One-third of the money is distributed directly to the needy; two-thirds are put into a community trust for long-term needs to help people stand on their own feet.

The movement spreads from village to village, as missionaries who have seen the positive results of the program voluntarily go to other areas to tell the people there about it. When Swadhyaya volunteers first appeared in fishing villages on India's west coast, they found the people were spending what income they had on gambling and liquor. Now, the same people place a portion of their earnings from fishing and navigation at the feet of God, as it were. They have created such a surplus that they have been able to purchase community fishing boats. These are manned by volunteers on a rotation basis, with everyone eager to take a turn, and the income is distributed impersonally as God's graceful beneficence to those in need.

In addition, *swadhyayees* have created "tree temples," in which trees are planted in formerly barren lands, and have developed cultural programs, sports clubs, family stores, dairy produce centers, children's centers, centers for domestic skills, and discussion centers for intellectuals and professionals. Through water-harvesting by recharging more than 90,000 wells and constructing more than 500 percolation tanks, *swadhyayees* by their own skill and labor are generating additional annual farm produce worth some 300 million US dollars for small and medium-sized farmers. They have also introduced soakpit systems for disposal of household drainwater and refuse, thus improving village hygiene and health.

Throughout the growing network of *swadhyayees*, there is no hierarchy and no paid staff. Those whose lives have been improved by inner study and devotional service become enthusiastic volunteers and living demonstrations that people are happiest when dharmic principles are placed ahead of self-interest.

being challenged by social reform movements facing issues of gender, caste, poverty, pollution, and corruption. Feminists are criticizing the traditional ideal that all women should marry and dedicate themselves to serving and obeying their husbands. Ecofeminists are encouraging recognition of the sacredness and interdependence of all life, as found in tantric and goddess traditions, rather than exclusionary brahmanic philosophies of purity and superiority that are blamed for exploitation of women, marginalized people, animals, and the earth. Dalit activists are attacking old caste distinctions that tend to keep them marginalized and poor. And the Indian government is challenging huge depositories of money, gold, silver, and jewels found in the treasuries of certain extremely wealthy temples and gurus.

Global Hinduism

Hinduism is also experiencing vibrant growth beyond the Indian subcontinent, partly among expatriates and partly among converts from other faiths. During the British Empire, Hindus along with other Indians were sent as indentured laborers to other parts of the Empire. After India achieved its independence in 1947, in the post–World War II period waves of Indian laborers and professionals left India to work abroad, rebuilding war-torn areas, developing stunning modern communities on the former sands of the Gulf States, and providing skilled services such as medicine and information technology. Hindus now live in more than 150 countries. When Hindus have gathered abroad, they have often tended to develop a heightened awareness of their Hindu identity, as they find themselves in the minority. Many have pooled their resources to build temples in order to preserve their traditions and their identity. But since Hinduism is so multifaceted, there have been disagreements over which deities should be worshiped in the temples. There has thus been a trend toward a less sectarian, generalized version of Hinduism, as well as some adjustments in traditions to the new geographic and cultural environments into which Hindus have moved.

Hindus in the diaspora, along with other people of Asian heritage, have sometimes experienced discrimination, disenfranchisement, violence, temple destruction, and forced conversions by members of majority communities. Even within Asia, such problems have occurred in areas where Hindus are in the minority, including Bangladesh, Pakistan, Sri Lanka, and Malaysia. In the West, people of Abrahamic religions have historically had difficulty in understanding the complexities of Hindu traditions which are different from their own, and have sometimes decried them as "evil" and "demonic." In 2011, there was an attempt to ban the *Bhagavad-Gita* in Russia, where it was alleged that the scripture promotes social discord and hatred of non-Hindus. There have also been instances of deep insults to Hindu sensitivities by Western companies, with the manufacture of products such as footwear or toilet seats featuring pictures of Hindu deities.

Nevertheless, Hindu philosophy and practices have left indelible imprints on other cultures. To cite a few examples in the United States, the nineteenth-century Transcendental poets Ralph Waldo Emerson, Henry David Thoreau, and Walt Whitman were deeply influenced by "Hindoo" texts, attracted to Upanishadic conceptions of ultimate reality as well as Hindu mythology. Swami Vivekananda had a major impact when he addressed the 1893 Parliament of World Religions in Chicago. After the band The Beatles encountered Maharishi Mahesh Yogi in Rishikesh in the 1960s, many Hindu references began to make their way into Western popular culture. Teachers of yoga and meditation have spread those practices widely, often as self-help and physical-culture techniques divorced from their spiritual roots.

Hinduism has also been spread globally by gurus who have exported its teachings. For the past hundred years, many self-proclaimed gurus have left India to develop followings in other countries. Some were discovered to be fraudulent, with scandalous private behavior or motives of wealth and power.

Despite increased Western wariness of gurus, some of the exported movements have continued to grow.

Many non-Indians discovered Hinduism by reading *Autobiography of a Yogi*, by Paramahansa Yogananda (1893–1952). The book describes his intriguing spiritual experiences with Indian gurus and also explains principles of Hinduism in loving fashion. Yogananda traveled to the United States and began a movement, the California-based Self-Realization Fellowship, which has survived his death and is still growing, with centers, temples, and living communities in forty-six countries. Their first goal, as set forth by Paramahansa Yogananda, is to "disseminate among the nations a knowledge of definite scientific techniques for attaining direct personal experience of God."[44]

Another example of an exported movement is the Netherlands-based Transcendental Meditation (TM) movement, begun by Maharishi Mahesh Yogi (d. 2008) in the 1960s. For a fee of thousands of dollars, his disciples teach people secret mantras and assert that repeating the mantra for twenty minutes twice each day will bring great personal benefits. These range from enhanced athletic prowess to increased satisfaction with life. By paying more, advanced practitioners can also learn how to "fly"—that is, how to take short hops into the air while sitting cross-legged. The organization claims a success rate of sixty-five percent in ending drug and alcohol addiction and asserts that groups of yogic "fliers" temporarily lowered crime rates in Washington, D.C., and conflicts in West Asia, claims that have not been independently verified. Although not as visible as in its heyday, TM is an extensive global organization, complete with luxurious health spas in Europe, a Vedic "theme park" near Niagara Falls in Canada, Vedic-based development projects in Africa, colleges, universities, and Maharishi Schools of Management in many countries, an ashram for 10,000 people in India, and ongoing plans to build large "peace palaces" near cities around the world where people could receive training in TM and thus help to bring peace in the collective unconscious of the world, through the "Maharishi effect."

Another success story is ISKCON, the International Society for Krishna Consciousness. In 1965, the Indian guru A. C. Bhaktivedanta Swami Prabhupada

Devotees of Lord Krishna ecstatically sing his praises in Western settings—here, in London.

arrived in the United States, carrying the asceticism and bhakti devotion of Shri Chaitanya's tradition of Krishna worship from India to the heart of Western materialistic culture. Adopting the dress and diet of Hindu monks and nuns, his initiates lived in temple communities. Their days began at 4 a.m. with meditation, worship, chanting of the names of Krishna and Rama, and scriptural study, with the aim of turning from a material life of sense gratification to one of transcendent spiritual happiness. During the day, they chanted and danced in the streets to introduce others to the bliss of Krishna, distributed literature (especially Swami Prabhupada's translation of the *Bhagavad-Gita*), attracted new devotees, and raised funds. Despite schisms and scandals, the movement has continued since Swami Prabhupada's death in 1977, and is growing in strength in various countries, particularly in India and eastern Europe. In England, followers have turned a great mansion into a huge ISKCON temple, which also serves Indian immigrants as a place to celebrate major festivals.

Mata Amritanandamayi comforts a man after he has been operated on for a brain tumor and also embraces his father with her left arm.

Some contemporary gurus are also enjoying great global popularity. One of the most famous at present is Mata Amritanandamayi, a seemingly tireless, motherly saint from South India who takes people from all walks of life into her arms. In large-scale gatherings around the world, the "hugging saint" may embrace up to 70,000 people at a stretch, through the night and into the next day. She encourages her "children" to find personal solace and compassion for others through worship of the divine in any form. Many of her followers regard "Amma" herself as the personification of the Divine Mother.

Hindu identity

As Hinduism is reaching around the world, some Hindu academics and organizations in the diaspora—especially DANAM (Dharma Academy of North America, which is initiating a new field known as Dharma Studies)—are defining their identity in broad terms, as being part of a process of interrelated development among the dharma traditions that arose on the Indian subcontinent. At the same time, some Hindu groups within India are narrowing their identity and giving Hinduism a nationalistic thrust. In particular, the RSS—Rashtriya Svayamsevak Sangh—arose early in the twentieth century, espousing Hindu cultural renewal in order to combat the ills of modernity and return to an idealized past referred to as "Rama Rajya," the legendary kingdom of Lord Rama, when Hindu virtues were maintained by a perfect ruler. This movement gave organized expression to the ideals of V. D. Savarkar, who wrote of an ancient Hindu nation and *Hindutva* (Hinduness), excluding Muslims and Christians as aliens in India, in contrast to historical evidence that what is called Hinduism is a noncentralized, evolving composite of variegated ways of worship.

Secularism is officially established by India's constitution, which recognizes the multicultural, multireligious fabric of the country and does not confer favored political status on any religion. But according to what could be called Hindu "fundamentalists," in the name of secularism people are being robbed of their religious values and identity, which the RSS, the religious organization Vishva Hindu Parishad (VHP), and political parties such as the Bharatiya Janata Party (BJP) say they are trying to restore.

The RSS maintains tens of thousands of branches in Indian villages and cities, where Hindu men and boys meet for group games, songs, lectures, and prayers to the Hindu nation, conceived as the Divine Mother. The leader of the RSS has publicly urged throwing all Christian missionaries out of India and has asserted that all Indians are actually Hindus. There are estimated to be 12,000 RSS schools in India in which children are educated according to the Hindutva agenda.

A major focus of these activities has been the small town of Ayodhya, which according to Hindu mythology is the birthplace of Lord Rama. According to Hindutva belief, Babur, the Muslim Mughal ruler, had the main temple commemorating Rama's birthplace torn down and the Babri Mosque built on its ruins. Firm believers attempted to take matters into their own hands and redress this perceived insult to their holy place. In 1992, some 200,000 Hindus managed to enter Ayodhya and tear down the Babri Mosque. This act was followed by a spate of Hindu–Muslim violence throughout India. In 2010, a high court ruling divided the disputed land into three parts, two for Hindu groups and one for the Sunni board managing mosques, a decision that brought temporary peace in the area but may be contested.

Political affiliates of the RSS—particularly the BJP—have become very powerful in Indian politics. It was the leading party in the central government in power in 2002 when one coach of a train carrying volunteers who were seeking to illegally construct a new temple in Ayodhya caught fire in the state of Gujarat and was surrounded by a presumably Muslim mob. Inside the coach, fifty-nine Hindus burned to death, a horror that was followed by terrible inter-religious violence. Perhaps 2,000 people, most of them Muslims, were killed by mobs while local officials did little to stop them. In the 2014 elections, the BJP won a majority of seats in the Indian parliament, and Narendra Modi, who was chief minister of Gujarat when the 2002 riots took place, became prime minister of India. Modi's critics have argued that he did not do enough to stop the riots. Modi's 2014 campaign focused more on economic development than Hindutva; in a television interview, he once explained that Hindutva means that all dharmas are equal, and cited the Rig Vedic verse that "Truth is one, sages call it by various names."[45] Some critics worry, however, that a BJP-majority government may at some point seek to implement a less accepting form of Hindutva. Observers also point out that Modi comes from a lower caste, and that his rise to power is indicative of changing attitudes in India.

The Vishva Hindu Parishad is now pursuing a dual goal of reviving Hinduism in India and the diaspora, while at the same time encouraging respect for all religions. The definition of a Hindu, according to VHP guidelines, includes this quality: "[A] Hindu is one … who evinces equal respect and adoration to all religious and spiritual creeds and sects founded from time to time by great divine souls of sublime, noble character."[46] Balkrishan Naik, Joint General Secretary of Vishwa Hindu Parishad, explains,

We feel that dharma-based cultures are inclusive, not exclusive. We want to respect all as they are, that they should preserve their identity, and co-operate with each other. Diversity is their beauty; diversity is growth. It should be promoted, not suppressed. Why does the conflict come? A human being says, "Mine alone is the best, and others are not; I want that others should follow me. They should lose their identity, and they should get submerged in my identity." That egoistic, aggressive attitude is the main reason for struggle. Pride and egotism should be replaced with love, with affection, gratefulness, sympathy.[47]

Balkrishan Naik is alluding to perceptions that Christians are trying to convert Indians from Hinduism to Christianity by offering social services for the poor such as schools and hospitals. An estimated fifty percent of all Christians in India were formerly of low-caste origin. Opposition to Christian conversion has sometimes turned quite violent, as it did in 2008, when the homes of thousands of Indian Christians in the state of Orissa were burned, apparently by Hindu extremists.

Tensions also continue to run high between Hindus and Muslims in Kashmir, where efforts to achieve Kashmiri independence from India often pit Hindus and

Muslims against each other. Nevertheless, although tensions between religions exist in many regions of India, what predominates is the spirit of accommodation with which the various communities have lived side by side for hundreds of years.

The Indian Supreme Court has formally defined Hindu beliefs in a way that affirms universality rather than exclusiveness. Drawing upon the works of Hindu and Western scholars, the court defined the basic concepts of Hinduism as:

1 acceptance of the Vedas as the highest authority in religious and philosophical matters;
2 a spirit of tolerance and willingness to understand and appreciate others' points of view, based on the realization that truth is many-sided;
3 acceptance of belief in an endless succession of vast periods of creation, maintenance, and dissolution of the world;
4 belief in rebirth and pre-existence;
5 recognition of many ways or means to salvation;
6 there may be many gods worshipped, and there are Hindus who do not believe in worshiping idols;
7 no definite set of philosophical concepts, unlike other religions.[48]

Mahatma Gandhi, the father of independent India, asserted that Hinduism's special identity lies in its inclusiveness, dynamism, and continuing search for truth:

Hinduism is a living organism liable to growth and decay, and subject to the laws of Nature. It is and is not based on scriptures. It does not derive its authority from one book. It takes a provincial form in every province, but the inner substance is retained everywhere. The Vedas, the Upanishads, the Smritis *[authoritative but nonrevealed scriptures], the Puranas, and the* Itihasas *[historical epics] did not arise at one and the same time. Each grew out of the necessities of particular periods. Hinduism abhors stagnation. Every day we add to our knowledge of the power of* Atman, *and we shall keep on doing so.*[49]

Key terms

asana Yogic posture.
ashram A usually ascetic spiritual community of followers gathered around their guru.
atman The individual soul.
avatar An incarnation of a deity.
bhakti Intense devotion to a personal manifestation of Supreme Reality.
Brahman The Supreme Reality.
Brahmin Priest or member of the priestly caste.
caste Originally an occupational category; hereditary classes into which people are born.
chakra A subtle energy center in the body.
Dalit "Oppressed"; name used by some people formerly considered untouchables.
darshan Visual contact with the divine.
deva A deity.
dharma Moral order, duty, righteousness, religion.
guru Spiritual teacher.
Kali Yuga The present degraded era.
karma Our actions and their effects on this life and lives to come.
mantra A sound or phrase chanted to evoke sound vibration of one aspect of creation or to praise a deity.
moksha Liberation.
prana The invisible life force.
puja Ritual worship.
reincarnation After death, rebirth in a new life.

rishi A sage.

Shaiva Worshiper of Shiva.

Shakta Worshiper of the divine in female form.

samsara The worldly cycle of birth, death, and rebirth.

sannyasin Renunciate spiritual seeker.

Sanskrit The ancient language of the Vedas.

secularism The constitutional principle of not giving favored status to any religion.

shakti Feminine divine power.

sutra Terse spiritual teaching.

Tantra A sacred esoteric text with spiritual practices honoring the divine in female form.

Upanishads The philosophical part of the Vedas.

Vaishnava Worshiper of Vishnu or one of his manifestations, such as Krishna.

Vedas Revered ancient scriptures.

yoga Practices for union with the true Self.

Suggested reading

The *Bhagavad-Gita*, available in numerous translations. Central teachings about how to realize the immortal soul and the nature of dharma.

Bryant, Edwin, *The Quest for the Origins of Vedic Culture: The Indo-Aryan Migration Debate*, Oxford: Oxford University Press, 2001. Detailed survey of the complex interdisciplinary, international debates about the origins of Vedic civilization.

Chapple, Christopher Key and Mary Evelyn Tucker, eds, *Hinduism and Ecology*, Cambridge, Massachusetts: Harvard University Press, 2000. Perceptive contemporary essays about the relationship between various Hindu paths and environmental protection.

Eck, Diana, *Darsan: Seeing the Divine Image in India*, second edition, Chambersburg, Pennsylvania: Anima Books, 1985. A lively explanation of deity images and how the people of India respond to them.

Eck, Diana, *India: A Sacred Geography*, New York: Harmony Books, 2012. An introduction to India's sacred geography, from rivers to gods such as Shiva, Shakti, Vishnu, and Krishna, with discussion of pilgrimage.

Jayakar, Pupul, *The Earth Mother*, New Delhi: Penguin Books, 1989. Explorations of ways of worshiping the goddess in rural India.

Lopez, Donald S., Jr., ed., *Religions of India in Practice*, Princeton, New Jersey: Princeton University Press, 1995. An interesting anthology of popular texts with contemporary rather than stereotypical understandings, primarily from Hinduism but also including Buddhist, Jain, and Sikh material.

Pechilis, Karen, ed., *The Graceful Guru: Hindu Female Gurus in India and the United States*, Oxford: Oxford University Press, 2004. Essays on some of the leading female Hindu gurus of recent times.

Pintchman, Tracy, ed., *Women's Lives, Women's Rituals in the Hindu Tradition*, Oxford: Oxford University Press, 2007. Essays on women's rituals and experiences in different regions of India.

Prabhavananda, Swami, *Spiritual Heritage of India*, Madras: Sri Ramakrishna Math, undated. Classic explanation of Indian spirituality and philosophy since the Vedic age by a disciple of Ramakrishna.

Ramaswamy, Krishnan, Antonio de Nicolas, and Aditi Banerjee, *Invading the Sacred: An Analysis of Hinduism Studies in America*, New Delhi: Rupa and Company, 2007. A critique of how Western scholars have portrayed Hinduism.

Ramaswamy, Vijaya, *Walking Naked: Women, Society, Spirituality in South India*, Shimla, India: Indian Institute of Advanced Study, 1997. Groundbreaking study of movements in which women were able to transcend social restrictions and give free expression to their spirituality.

Rinehart, Robin, ed., *Contemporary Hinduism: Ritual, Culture, and Practice*, Santa Barbara, California: ABC/CLIO, 2004. A very accessible, carefully explained introduction to Hindu culture.

Singh, Karan, *Essays on Hinduism*, New Delhi: Ratna Sagar, 1987 and 1990. An excellent and concise introduction to the many facets of Hinduism, interpreted in modern terms.

Sondhi, Madhuri Santanam, *Modernity, Morality and the Mahatma*, New Delhi: Haranand Publications, 1997. A brilliant analysis of Indian responses to the challenges of modernity, including the contributions of many religious figures.

Thapar, Romila, Jonathan Mark Kenoyer, Madhav M. Deshpande, Shereen Ratnagar, *India: Historical Beginnings and the Concept of the Aryan*, Delhi: National Book Trust, 2006. Essays surveying current archaeological, linguistic, and social research into the Aryan invasion theory.

3.1 Explain the origins and significance of the Vedas

The origins and antiquity of the Vedas (the religious texts often referred to as the foundations of Hinduism) are still unknown, but most scholars agree that they were composed and redacted over a period of roughly a thousand years, *c.* 1500 BCE to 500 BCE.

The Vedas are a revered collection of ancient sacred hymns, praising the deities and exploring the nature of the cosmos. According to orthodox Hindus, the Vedas are not the work of any humans; they were revealed to sages, and transmitted orally from teacher to student. They are considered *shruti* texts—those which have been revealed, rather than written by mortals. The Rig Veda—the oldest and the first of four collections of which the Vedas are composed—praises and implores the blessings of the devas (controlling forces in the cosmos, deities who consecrate every part of life). Behind all these myriad aspects of divinity the sages perceived one ultimate, unseen reality that ceaselessly creates and sustains everything.

The Upanishads, a part of the Vedas that focuses on philosophical questions, contain teachings from highly realized spiritual masters reserved for advanced seekers of spiritual truth.

3.2 Illustrate how the epics and Puranas represent the Supreme

The epics and Puranas arose after 500 BCE and popularized knowledge and devotion through myths and legends. In contrast to the rather abstract depictions of the absolute reality in the Upanishads, the epics and Puranas represent the Supreme as a person, or rather as various human-like deities, with richly detailed stories about their lives and relationships. The two great epics—the *Ramayana* and *Mahabharata*—present the Supreme usually as Vishnu, who intervenes on earth during critical periods in the cosmic cycle. The Puranas list the many ways that Vishnu has incarnated in the world when dharma—moral order in the world—is decaying, to help restore virtue and defeat evil. For instance, Vishnu is said to have incarnated great avatars such as Krishna and Rama to help uplift humanity. The major Puranas are also based on theologies of Shiva and Shakti.

3.3 Compare and contrast Shaktas, Shaivas, and Vaishnavas

Of all the deities worshiped by Hindus, there are three major groupings. The Shaktas worship some form of the goddess (whose great power is called shakti). Some of these Shaktas follow a Vedic path. The general term "Devi" may be used to refer generically to the goddess in all her forms, understood as the supreme Divine Mother, the totality of all the energy of the cosmos. From ancient times, worship of the divine female has been associated with worship of nature, particularly trees and rivers. Sacred texts called Tantras instruct worshipers how to honor the feminine divine.

Shaivas worship the god Shiva, a personal, many-faceted manifestation of the attributeless supreme deity. Shiva has various shaktis, or feminine consorts; he is often shown with his devoted spouse Parvati. Lingams—naturally occurring or sculpted cylindrical forms—have been used in the worship of Shiva since antiquity in India. Shaivism encompasses traditions that have developed outside Vedic-based Brahmanism, including sects such as the Lingayats, who wear a stone lingam in remembrance of Shiva as the One Undivided Being.

Vaishnavas worship the god Vishnu, beloved as the tender, merciful deity. Vishnu has been worshiped since Vedic times and came to be regarded as the

Supreme as a person. He is often associated with his consort Lakshmi (whom Shaktas worship as a goddess in her own right). Rama and Krishna are generally understood to be incarnations of Vishnu in earthly forms.

3.4 Describe the major philosophical systems

In addition to the Vedas, and texts such as the epics and Puranas, elaborate philosophical systems were developed long ago in India. Among the most prominent of these are Samkhya, Advaita Vedanta, and yoga. The highly analytical Samkhya system holds that the material universe consists of three essential qualities. They are *sattva* (fine, illuminated, balanced), *rajas* (active, passionate), and *tamas* (heavy, inert, coarse). Interaction and tension between the equilibrium of *sattva*, the activity of *rajas*, and the resistance to action of *tamas* govern the development of the world. The interaction of these qualities is a key factor in some Indian systems of diet and medicine.

Advaita Vedanta is generally monistic, positing a single reality and based on the Upanishads. The goal of Advaita Vedanta is the realization that the self is Brahman.

Yoga is a spiritual discipline designed to clear the mind and support a state of serene, detached awareness. There are four paths of yogic practices, designed to help different types of people attain the desired union with the Self: raja yoga (path of mental concentration), jnana yoga (path of rational inquiry), karma yoga (path of right action), and bhakti yoga (the path of devotion).

3.5 Outline the main public and private rituals in Hinduism

There are sixteen rites prescribed in the ancient scriptures to purify and sanctify a person in his or her journey through life, such as investing boys with a sacred thread in a special ceremony.

Public worship—puja—is usually performed by *pujaris*, or Brahmin priests, who conduct ceremonies. In a temple, devotees may have the great blessing of receiving darshan (visual contact with the divine) through the eyes of the images. Ritual fire ceremonies around a havan, or sacred fire place, are also conducted by Brahmin pandits. Death ceremonies are carried out by fire, as the carefully washed and prepared body is cremated after death. In addition to public puja ceremonies, nearly every home in India has a shrine with pictures or small statues of various deities. Home puja is an everyday observance: A small oil lamp and a smoldering stick of incense are reverently waved before the deities' images to please them.

Orthodox Brahmins and common people also observe many days of fasting and prayer, corresponding to auspicious points in the lunar and solar cycles. Trees and rivers, such as the Ganges, are revered as sacred places. Pilgrimages to holy sites, such as Amarnath Cave, also provide opportunity for personal purification and spiritual elevation.

3.6 Discuss the issue of defining Hindu identity in modern India

As Hinduism is reaching around the world, some Hindu groups within India are narrowing their identity and giving Hinduism a nationalistic thrust. In particular, the RSS (Rashtriya Svayamsevak Sangh) espouses Hindu cultural renewal in order to combat the ills of modernity and to restore the religious values and identity that they believe secularism (officially established by India's constitution) has taken from the people. Political affiliates of the RSS—particularly the BJP (Bharatiya Janata Party)—have become very powerful in Indian politics. At the same time, some Hindus in India and in the diaspora are defining their identity in broad terms, as being part of a process of interrelated development among the dharma traditions that arose on the Indian subcontinent.

CHAPTER 4

JAINISM

"The practice is that you have to look upon worldly things as the seer. You are not to be involved in them, because through attachment with worldly things you land up with all those problems that are existing in the world. If you detach yourself, you become only a seer, and then you attach yourself with the self only." M. P. Jain[1]

4.1 *Explain the Jain belief about the Tirthankaras*

4.2 *Define the principles of nonviolence, nonattachment, and nonabsolutism*

4.3 *Describe the key Jain spiritual practices*

4.4 *Summarize the Jain diaspora*

Although the majority of Indians who are religious continue to follow the Hindu paths, Mother India has given birth to several other religions that are not based on the Vedas. One of them is Jainism, which has approximately 4.5 million adherents. Until recently, it has been little known outside India. Even within India it is practiced by only a small minority. Yet its **ascetic** (austere, detached from worldly comforts) teachings offer valuable clues to our global survival. It is becoming recognized as a complete and fruitful path with the potential for uplifting human awareness and inculcating high standards of personal ethics. For example, it has never condoned war or the killing of animals for any reason. Jain teachings recognize that we humans are imperfect, but hold out the promise that through careful control of our senses and thoughts we can attain perfection, freedom, and happiness. Despite having a relatively small number of followers, Jainism has exerted an enormous influence upon both Hinduism and Buddhism. In addition to its distinctive contributions to global culture in the form of its teaching of nonviolence and its ecological wisdom, Jainism is also an important key to understanding Hinduism and Buddhism.

The Tirthankaras and ascetic orders

Who are the Tirthankaras?

What is now called Jainism stretches far back into antiquity. Its major teacher for this age is Mahavira or Mahavir (The Great Hero). He was a contemporary of the Buddha and died approximately 527 BCE. Like the Buddha, he was the prince of a **Kshatriya** clan and renounced his position and his wealth at the

Mahavira is said to have become so detached from worldly concerns that he shed his clothes as well as his royal status. Jains nevertheless often honor him by surrounding his statues with lavish marble designs.

age of thirty to wander as a spiritual seeker. The austerities he undertook while meditating without clothes in the intense summer heat and winter cold are legendary. He often undertook total fasts of at least two days, not even drinking water. In Jain scriptures it is written that six times he fasted for two months at a time, and once he fasted for six months straight.[2] Swarms of mosquitoes and ants often bit him. Humans also tormented him. He was repeatedly arrested and mistreated by officials who mistook him for a common thief, not recognizing him as the son of their king. In places where he was meditating, often in a standing position, villagers are said to have treated him miserably to make him leave:

Once when he [sat in meditation], his body unmoving, they cut his flesh, tore his hair, and covered him with dirt. They picked him up and then dropped him, disturbing his meditational postures. Abandoning concern for his body, free from desire, the Venerable One humbled himself and bore the pain.[3]

Finally, after twelve years of meditation, silence, and extreme fasting, Mahavira achieved liberation and perfection. For thirty years until his death at Pava, he spread his teachings. His community is said to have consisted of 14,100 monks, 36,000 nuns, and 310,000 female and 150,000 male lay followers. They came from all castes, as Jainism does not officially acknowledge the caste system.

The Jain teachings are not thought to have originated with Mahavira, however. He is considered the last of twenty-four **Tirthankaras** of the current cosmic cycle. The Tirthankaras are called "Fordmakers," for they create a crossing or "ford" across the river of rebirth to the further shore of liberation. In Jain cosmology, the universe is without beginning or end. Eternally, it passes through long cycles of progress and decline. At the beginning of each downward cycle, humans are happy, long-lived, and virtuous; they have no need for religion. As these qualities decline, Tirthankaras must create religion in order to steer people away from the growing evil in the world.

Hagiographies of the Tirthankaras are major sources of ethical instruction and inspiration for Jains. The first Tirthankara introduced civilizing social institutions, such as marriage, family, law, justice, and government, taught the arts of agriculture, crafts, reading, writing, and mathematics, and built villages, towns, and cities. Twenty-three more Tirthankaras followed over a vast expanse of time. The twenty-second is generally acknowledged by scholars as an historic figure, Lord Krishna's cousin, renowned for his compassion toward animals. The twenty-third Tirthankara, a prince who became an extreme ascetic and a great preacher, lived from 877 to 777 BCE. His traditional hagiographies bear interesting resemblances to those of the Buddha, such as his terrific confrontation with Mara (Death) while meditating, after which he emerged serene and omniscient. In Jain iconography, which may derive from prehistoric myths, this twenty-third Tirthankara is typically shown protected by a multi-headed snake forming a canopy over his head.

The extreme antiquity of Jainism as a non-Vedic, indigenous Indian religion is well documented. Ancient Hindu and Buddhist scriptures refer to Jainism as an existing tradition that began long before Mahavira.

After Mahavira's death, his teachings were not written down because the monks lived without possessions; they were initially carried orally. In the third century BCE, the great Jain saint Bhadrabahu predicted that there would be a prolonged famine where Mahavira had lived, in what is now Bihar in northeast India. He led some 12,000 monks to southern India to avoid the famine, which lasted for twelve years. When they returned, they discovered that two major changes had been introduced by the monks who had remained. One was relaxation of the requirement of nudity for monks; the other was the convening of a council to edit the existing Jain texts into a canon of forty-five books.

Eventually the two groups split into the **Digambaras**, who had left and did not accept the changes, and the **Shvetambaras**, who had stayed near Mahavira's original location. Digambara (sky-clad) monks wear nothing at all, symbolizing innocence and nonattachment. They do not consider themselves "nude"; rather, they have taken the environment as their clothing. They have only two possessions: a gourd for drinking water and a broom of feathers dropped by peacocks. The broom is used to sweep the ground before they walk on it, to avoid harming any creatures. The Shvetambara (white-clad) monks and nuns wear simple white cloth robes: They do not feel this prevents them from attaining liberation.

The two orders also differ over the subject of women's abilities. Digambaras believe that women cannot become so pure that they could rise to the highest heaven or so impure that they would be reborn in the lowest hell; they cannot renounce clothes and be naked; they cannot be such skillful debaters as men; they are of inferior status in society and in the monastic order. They can be liberated only if they are reborn in a man's body. Shvetambaras feel that women are capable of the same spiritual achievements as men, and that the nineteenth Tirthankara was a woman. In truth, even Shvetambara nuns are of lower status than monks, but they still comprise the great majority of Jain nuns. Of today's approximately 6,000 Jain nuns, fewer than 100 are Digambaras.

The existence of thriving orders of female ascetics—which include many skillful teachers and counselors and which have apparently always outnumbered male ascetics—is unique in India. In Brahmanic Hindu tradition, women were never allowed to be mendicants and marriage was considered obligatory. Whereas previously most Jain nuns had been widows, today most are young women who have never married, for Jains now consider the ascetic vocation an honorable alternative to marriage for females. Nuns may be regarded as heroes for their renunciate practices, such as extensive fasting. Jain laywomen who undertake long fasts are also honored, and their families may proudly display photo albums of their many fasts.

Jain nuns at the feet of a monolithic fifty-foot (seventeen-meter) statue of Bahubali (thought to be the great renunciate son of the first Tirthankara), also shown in miniature in the foreground. During a famous ceremony that takes place once every twelve years, a succession of offerings is poured over the statue from a scaffolding above. These include sugarcane juice, milk, turmeric, herbs, sandal, saffron, gold and silver flowers, precious stones, and, at the end, flowers showered from a helicopter.

Freeing the soul: the ethical pillars
What are the three basic principles Jains adopt to avoid accumulating karma?

In the midst of a world of decline, as they see it, Jains are given great room for hope. The *jiva*—the individual's higher consciousness, or soul—can save itself by discovering its own perfect, unchanging nature and thus transcend the miseries of earthly life. Jains, like Hindus and Buddhists, believe that we are reborn again and again until we finally free ourselves from **samsara**, the wheel of birth and death.

The gradual process by which the soul learns to extricate itself from the lower self and its attachments to the material world involves purifying one's ethical life until nothing remains but the purity of the *jiva*. In its true state, it is fully omniscient, shining, potent, peaceful, self-contained, and blissful. One who has thus brought forth the highest in his or her being is called a **Jina** (a "winner" over the passions), from which the term Jain is derived. The Tirthankaras were Jinas who helped others find their way, by teaching inspiring spiritual principles.

Karma

Jains believe that the universe is without beginning and that it has no creator or destroyer. Our lives are therefore the results of our own deeds; only by our own efforts can we be saved. Padma Agrawal explains:

> In Jainism, unlike Christianity and many Hindu cults, there is no such thing as a heavenly father watching over us. To the contrary, love for a personal God would be an attachment that could only bind Jainas [Jains] more securely to the cycle of rebirth. It is a thing that must be rooted out.[4]

The world operates by the power of nature, according to natural principles. Jains do believe in gods and demons, but the former are subject to the same ignoble passions as humans. In fact, one can only achieve liberation if one is in the human state, because only humans can clear away karmic accumulations on the soul. Like Hindus and Buddhists, Jains believe that our actions influence the future course of our current life, and of our lives to come. But in Jain belief, **karma** is actually subtle matter—minute particles that we accumulate as we act and think. Until it frees itself from karmas, the mundane soul wanders about through the universe in an endless cycle of deaths and rebirths, instantly transmigrating into another kind of being upon the death of its previous body. Acharya Shri Kund Kund, a great ancient Jain teacher, asserted: "Nowhere

TEACHING STORY

The Story of Bahubali

Rishabha, the first Tirthankara of the current cosmic cycle, had 100 sons from one wife and one son, Bahubali, from the other. He gave his eldest son, Bharata, the lion's share of his inheritance. Bharata was eager to be the supreme king, and he wanted his other brothers, who had been given smaller portions of land, to come under his subjugation. All the people surrendered to his sovereignty, except for Bahubali, who refused to surrender his kingdom. He said to Bharata, "You are independent, I am independent. Why should I come under your rule?"

The armies of the two sides were drawn up on the battleground. The wise men from the two sides came forth and said, "In the clash of two brothers, millions of people will be killed. Millions of innocent people will be killed to satisfy the egos of two brothers. Why should this happen?" So it was decided that the two would fight it out between themselves. They would fight in three ways to see who was defeated.

First, they looked into each other's eyes, concentrating until one looked away. Bahubali defeated Bharata in this combat. Then they fought under water, and again Bahubali was victorious. Thirdly, Bahubali picked up Bharata physically and held him overhead, ready to dash him to the ground. That is how he got the name Bahubali—"He whose arms are very powerful."

As Bahubali was holding Bharata aloft, a thought crossed his mind: "Whom am I throwing? My own brother. For what? For this parcel of land? For this kingdom? Only for that, I would kill my brother?" He put Bharata down.

At that point, Bahubali felt like renouncing the world. He ceased to make war, and he went into meditation. For twelve years he meditated, standing. Vines grew on his legs. Snakes made their homes around his body. Many people tried to convince him to come out of his meditation, but he was unmoved. Nevertheless, he could not attain ultimate liberation.

Rishabha, his father, was asked why Bahubali was not attaining liberation. From his omniscient knowledge, Rishabha said that just before Bahubali started his meditation, he had a thought left in his mind: "I am standing on my brother's soil." So Bharata went and prayed to him: "This soil is universal, not yours or mine." The moment that thought entered Bahubali's mind he was liberated.

throughout the space in the entire universe is there any place in its course where the mundane soul has not taken birth in many forms, big and small."[5]

Birth as a human is the highest stage of life, short of liberation. One should therefore lose no time in this precious, brief period in human incarnation, for within it lies the potential for perfection.

To perfect and purify themselves as quickly as possible, Jains try to eliminate within themselves any false mental impressions, negative tendencies, or passions, and to develop pure thoughts and actions. Through this process, the veils of karma are lifted and the soul experiences more and more of its natural luminosity. In the highest state of perfection, known as *kevala*, the liberated being has "boundless vision, infinite righteousness, strength, perfect bliss, existence without form, and a body that is neither light nor heavy."[6]

The three basic principles that Jains adopt to avoid accumulating karma are nonviolence (**ahimsa**), nonattachment (*aparigraha),* and nonabsolutism (*anekantwad).*

Ahimsa

The principle of nonviolence—ahimsa—is very strong in Jain teachings, and through Jainism it also influenced Mahatma Gandhi. Jains believe that every centimeter of the universe is filled with living beings, some of them minute. A single drop of water contains 3,000 living beings. All of them want to live. Humans have no special right to supremacy; all things deserve to live and evolve as they can. To kill any living being has negative karmic effects.

It is difficult not to do violence to other creatures. Even in breathing, Jains feel, we inhale tiny organisms and kill them. Observant Jains avoid eating after sunset, so as not to eat unseen insects that might have landed on the food, and some Jain ascetics wear a cloth over their mouth to avoid inhaling any living organisms.

The higher the life form, the heavier the karmic burden of its destruction. The highest group of beings are those with many senses, such as humans, gods, and higher animals. Lower forms have fewer senses. The "one-sensed" beings have only the sense of touch. They include plants and the earth-bodies in soil, minerals, and stones, the water-bodies in rivers and lakes, fire-bodies in fires and lightning, and wind-bodies in winds and gases. The Jain sutras describe the suffering of even these one-sensed beings: It is like that of a blind and mute person who cannot see who is hurting him or express the pain.

> *All breathing, existing, living, sentient creatures should not be slain, nor treated with violence, nor abused, nor tormented, nor driven away. This is the pure, unchangeable, eternal law … Correctly understanding the law, one should arrive at indifference for the impressions of the senses, and not act on the motives of the world.*
>
> *Akaranga Sutra, IV: Lesson 1*[7]

Jains are therefore strict vegetarians, and they treat everything with great care. In Delhi, Jain benefactors have established a unique charitable hospital for sick and wounded birds. Great attention is paid to their every need, and their living quarters are air-cooled in the summer. Some Jains also go to markets where live animals are usually bound with wire, packed into hot trucks, and driven long distances without water to be killed for meat. To try to save the animals from suffering, they buy them and then attempt to raise them in comfort. Even to kick a stone while walking is to injure living beings. Jains are keenly aware that we may cause violence even through the clothes we buy. Many Jains thus eschew both leather and silk. Layman R. P. Jain tells how he felt when he learned how silk is made:

Jain Purification

A central Jain practice undertaken both by laypeople and by ascetics has for thousands of years been used for freeing the soul from internal impurities. Anger, pride, deceit, and greed are lasting stains that must be completely eradicated if the soul is to realize its true nature: pure consciousness, infinite knowledge, and bliss. Even a momentary realization of this state brings a feeling of great inner purity and calmness and a longing to return to it permanently. The ritual for achieving this inner purification is known as *samayika*.

Jain laypeople usually undertake this practice in the evening, after work and a meal. They sit in a quiet and solitary place, remove excess clothing, sit cross-legged on a mat, and chant formulas to cleanse and pacify their mind. These begin with a pledge to renounce all harmful activities, followed by requesting forgiveness:

> *I ask forgiveness of all beings,*
> *may all beings forgive me.*
> *I have friendship with all beings,*
> *and I have hostility with none.*[8]

They reach out mentally to all life forms, saying:

> *Friendship toward all beings,*
> *Delight in the qualities of virtuous ones,*
> *Utmost compassion for affected beings,*
> *Equanimity towards those who are not*
> *   well-disposed towards me,*
> *May my soul have such dispositions forever!*[9]

Then follow verses that commit the person to renouncing food, bodily desires, and passions for the period of the meditation, persisting in equanimity, come what may. The meditation ends with the universal Jain prayer:

> *Cessation of sorrow*
> *Cessation of karmas*
> *Death while in meditation,*
> *Attainment of enlightenment.*
> *O holy Jina! friend of the entire universe,*
> *   let these be mine, for*
> *I have taken refuge at your feet.*

> *I used to wear silk. On my eighteenth birthday I was telling one of my distant relatives not to eat chocolate because it had egg powder in it. He said, "Turn around—you're wearing silk. What are you preaching? Do you know that to make one yard of silk, nearly fifty thousand to one hundred thousand silkworms are boiled alive? To wear silk is a sin!" When I learned that is the way natural silk is made, I said, "R. P. Jain, what are you doing to your own soul? Shame on you!" From that day, I took a vow never in my life to wear natural silk.*[10]

Ahimsa also extends to care in speaking and thinking, for abusive words and negative thoughts can injure another. The revered ascetic Acharya Tulsi (1914–1997) explained:

> *A non-violent man is he who does not in the least discriminate between rich and poor or between friend and foe. … Non-violence is the best guarantee of humanity's survival and progress. A truly non-violent man is ever awake and is incapable of harbouring any ill will.*[11]

One's profession must also not injure beings, so most Jains work at jobs considered harmless, such as banking, education, law, and publishing. Agriculture is considered harmful, for in digging one harms minute organisms in the earth; in harnessing bullocks to plows one harms not only the bullock but also the tiny life forms on its body. Monks and nuns must move slowly with eyes downward, to avoid stepping on any being. In general, they will do the least harm if they devote their time to sitting or standing in meditation rather than moving around.

Global violence is of increasing concern, and here, too, Jains have great wisdom to offer. The late Acharya Tulsi taught that self-restraint is essential for the sake of world peace. He said:

Individual desire and ego are perennial human traits. Whenever they have been conjoined with power, there has been a general increase in war hysteria leading to the repetition of bloody and violent events in history. The reason why moral values have been held in the highest esteem is that they transform this evil combination of desire, ego and power into courteous humility. The history of the human race has been far more honorable and full of freedom during periods of such transformation. ... The fact cannot be ignored that the fate of the politicians is finally in the hands of the people. Even though it is generally true that it is the former who ultimately decide war and peace, the awakened conscience of the people is bound to ensure one day that a handful of over-ambitious people are not allowed to play with the future of mankind by imposing wars on them. The way to universal peace lies in our adherence to the precept of self-restraint.[12]

Aparigraha

Another central Jain ideal is nonattachment to things and people. One should cut one's living requirements to a bare minimum. Possessions possess us; their acquisition and loss drive our emotions. Digambara monks wear no clothes; the Tirthankaras are always depicted as naked, and therefore free. Even attachments to our friends and relatives bind us to samsara. We are to live helpfully and consciously within the world but not be drawn into its snares.

Aparigraha, or nonacquisitiveness, is considered the way to inner peace. If we can let go of things and situations, moment by moment, we can be free. A Jain nun of the Rajasthan desert, Samani Sanmati Pragya, belongs to an order in which the nuns' clothing and bedding is limited to four white saris, one white shawl, and one woolen cloth. She explains:

In the winter we do not have a quilt for warmth at night, for it would be too bulky to carry. In the summer we use no fan. It is so hot that we cannot sleep at night. We bear any kind of circumstances. In fact, we remain very happy. Our happiness comes from inside.[13]

Aparigraha is of value to the world community as well. Contemporary Jains point out that their principle of limiting consumption offers a way out of the global poverty, hunger, and environmental degradation that result from unequal grasping of resources by the wealthy.

Anekantwad

The third central principle is *anekantwad* ("manifold aspects"), a nonabsolutist perspective. Jains try to avoid anger and judgmentalism, remaining open-minded by remembering that any issue can be seen from many angles, all partially true. They tell the story of the blind people who are asked to describe an elephant. The one who feels the trunk says an elephant is like a tree branch. The one grasping a leg argues that an elephant is like a pillar. The one feeling the ear asserts that an elephant is like a fan. The one grasping the tail insists that an elephant is like a rope. And the one who encounters the side of the elephant argues that the others are wrong; an elephant is like a wall. Each has a partial grasp of the truth.

In the Jain way of thinking, the fullness of truth has many facets. Shree Chitrabhanu describes the results of eliminating false impressions and allowing the pure consciousness to flow in:

Once you have closed the open gates, dried up the polluted water, and cleaned out all the debris, then you can open them again to receive the fresh, clean rainfall. What is that rainfall? It is the flow of maitri—*pure love, compassion, and communication. You feel free. ... See how easily you meet people when there is no feeling of greater or lesser, no scar or bitterness, no faultfinding or criticism.*[14]

Spiritual practices
How do ordinary followers practice Jainism?

Jainism is an ascetic path and thus is practiced in its fullest by monks and nuns. In addition to practicing meditation, monks and nuns adopt a life of celibacy, physical penance and fasting, and material simplicity. They may sleep on the bare ground, cardboard, or wooden slabs, and are expected to endure any kind of weather with indifference. At initiation, their hair may be pulled out by the roots. Lest they become attached to any place, they cannot stay long anywhere. They must learn to accept social disapproval, to depend on others for their food, and to feel no pride at being more spiritually advanced than others.

Jain monks and nuns carry ahimsa to great extremes in their wariness of injuring one-sensed beings. Among the many activities they must avoid are digging in the ground (because of the earth-bodies there); bathing, swimming, or walking in the rain (because of the water-bodies they might injure); using flush toilets (which do violence to the water-bodies in an inordinate amount of water); extinguishing or lighting fires (because even to light a fire means that a fire-body will eventually be destroyed); fanning themselves (to avoid sudden changes in air temperature that would injure air-bodies); and walking on vegetation or touching living plants.

Jain nun Prasannamati Mataji explains:

People think of our life as harsh, and of course in many ways it is. But going into the unknown world and confronting it without a single rupee in our pockets means that differences between rich and poor, educated and illiterate, all vanish, and a common humanity emerges. As wanderers, we monks and nuns are free of shadows from the past. This wandering life, with no material possessions, unlocks our souls. There is a wonderful sense of lightness, living each day as it comes, with no sense of ownership, no weight, no burden. Journey and destination became one, thought and action became one, until it is as if we are moving like a river into complete detachment.[15]

Difficult to conquer is oneself; but when that is conquered, everything is conquered.

Uttaradhyayana Sutra 9.34–36

Most householders cannot carry renunciation as far as monks and nuns, but they can nonetheless purify and perfect themselves. Jain homes and temples are typically scrupulously clean, diets are carefully vegetarian, and medicines are prepared without cruel testing on animals. The mind and passions are also to be willingly controlled. Twelve "limited" vows are to be undertaken by Jain laypeople, the major ones being the first five:

Jain monks and nuns are celibate ascetics. This 15th-century illustrated text of Mahavira's last teachings shows a monk resisting the attractions of women.

- *The vow of nonviolence.*
- *The vow of truthfulness.*
- *The vow of not taking anything that has not been given.*
- *The vow of renouncing any sexual activity outside of marriage.*
- *The vow of limiting one's possessions.*
- *The vow of limiting the geographic area of nonvirtuous activities.*
- *The vow of limiting the quantity of things one will use.*
- *The vow of abstaining from purposeless harmful activities.*
- *The vow of meditation and reading scriptures for at least forty-eight consecutive minutes in a day.*
- *The vow to further reduce for a fixed period the area of nonvirtuous activities.*
- *The vow of fasting and living like an ascetic for a certain period.*
- *The vow of giving necessary articles to monks and nuns.*

In all spheres of life, Jains are taught to limit the harm they do to themselves, to others, and to the environment. Acharya Mahaprajna (1920–2010) pointed to many facets of violence in the world and taught that violence can only be overcome through profound individual transformation:

> *Purity of life, peacefulness and compassion are the foremost requirements of a civilized society. Reform cannot come until one achieves the capacity to withstand pain, oppression and hardship.*[16]

Practicing strict ethics and self-control, Jains are often quite successful and trusted in their professions. Many Jains have thus become wealthy. Because of the religion's emphasis on nonpossessiveness, wealthy Jains are often philanthropists.

Lay Jains are divided into those who worship at temples and those who do not. For those who worship in temples, Jain philanthropists have built very ornate temples, which are kept immaculately clean. Within the temples, the Tirthankaras are honored through images. They all look alike, for the perfect soul is nonparticularized; symbols such as the bull, always shown with the first Tirthankara, are used to help worshipers identify each of the twenty-four. The worshiper's feeling is one of reverence rather than supplication; the Tirthankaras are elevated beyond the human plane and are not available as helpers. They are instead models for one's own life, and since there can be no divine intervention there is not a great emphasis on priesthood. Laypeople can carry out

In Jain worship, images of the Tirthankaras are ideally to be venerated without expectation of help or a personal response to prayers.

worship services themselves, either alone or in groups. People pay their respects before images of the Tirthankaras with offerings and by waving lamps, but do not expect any reciprocation from them. Liberation from samsara is a result of personal effort, often portrayed by a symbolic diagram laid out with rice grains. Acharya Tulsi expressed the Jain point of view: "The primary aim of dharma is to purify character. Its ritualistic practices are secondary."[17]

> *Just as a fire quickly reduces decayed wood to ashes, so does an aspirant who is totally absorbed in the inner self and completely unattached to all external objects shake to the roots, attenuate, and wither away his* karma-*body.*
>
> *Samantabhadra, Aptamimamsa 24–7*

The ultimate spiritual practice in Jainism is fasting unto death at the end of life. This tradition has been observed for several thousand years as an honorable final cleansing of one's karmic burden by ceasing to kill living beings. The discipline requires many years of previous ascetic practice. It is not considered suicide, which is forbidden in Jainism. A classic text, *Ratnakarandaka Sravakaschara*, describes the practice, which is known as *Sallekhana* (thinning out of existence) by Digambaras and as *Santhara* (passing over) by Shvetambaras:

> *Prior to the adoption of the vow one should give up all love, hatred and attachment to possessions, with a pure mind, and obtain forgiveness of one's relations while also forgiving them oneself. One should give up grief, fear, anguish, attachment and keep oneself engaged in meditation. Then he should give up gradually food, then liquid and even water. During the observance of the vow one should not commit any of the transgressions.*[18]

The only circumstances under which a Jain can undertake the ultimate fast are very old age, terminal illness, famine, or dire calamity. Despite the strict conditions imposed, this ancient practice is now controversial and is being legally

The Jain Symbol

The new Jain symbol adopted in 1974 has "ahimsa" inscribed on an open palm, symbolizing fearlessness and nonviolence toward all creatures. The circle in the palm represents the cycle of reincarnation, and the twenty-four spokes represent the teachings of the twenty-four Tirthankaras, which can liberate one from the cycle of reincarnation. The words written below mean "Live and let live." The swastika above the hand is a very positive symbol for Jains, Hindus, and Buddhists, representing prosperity and auspiciousness. For Jains, its four limbs also represent the four parts of the Jain community (monks, nuns, laymen, and laywomen) and the four types of rebirth (deity, human, animal, and hell-being). The swastika was appropriated by the Nazis—but reversed—because of Hitler's preoccupation with occult symbolism and his belief that this ancient symbol would lead him to victory. The three dots symbolize insight, knowledge, and conduct. The crescent and dot above symbolize the liberated soul in the highest region of the universe.

परस्परोपग्रहो जीवानाम्

challenged in India as a form of suicide. But it is not perceived as such by Jains. Dr. Shugan Jain, chairman of the International School for Jain Studies in Delhi, explains the philosophy of "pious death":

> It is not that you want to die. We say, "The body is not cooperating with me to observe my religious duties. So since this body is not helping me, I want to leave it. And after death, I will acquire a new body. If I have detachment, then hopefully my new body will be better and stronger so that I can perform more religious duties." The most important thing is faith in the eternity of the soul and its capability to achieve super-soul status: liberation from worldly transmigration. This is the faith you must have. If you don't believe in the soul or if you don't believe in birth after death, and don't see the world as a place of misery, then this practice will not be tenable for you. You will say it is suicide.[19]

Festivals and pilgrimages

With their emphasis on self-discipline and self-perfection, Jains do not celebrate their holy days as jubilantly as Hindus. Even the festival days are characterized by meditation, renunciation, fasting, scriptural study, and hymns. However, these activities are undertaken with enthusiasm and dedication.

Divali, which Hindus celebrate with lights and fireworks, is for Jains an occasion for a three-day fast and an entire night spent reciting hymns and meditating on Mahavira, who is said to have attained liberation on Divali. The fifth day after Divali is set aside for the worship of pure knowledge. One of the activities is cleaning and worshiping of the books in religious libraries.

Among all Jain festivals, the most important is Paryushan Mahaparva, the annual festival of atonement. Many Jains undertake an eight-day fast, while listening to scriptural readings and lectures about ethical living, particularly the virtue of forgiveness. The final day is celebrated as Forgiveness Day. People seek forgiveness from anyone toward whom they feel hatred or enmity and try to give up these negative karmic burdens, adopting instead feelings such as compassion, contentment, equanimity, and sharing. Jagdish Prasad Jain, president of the Jain Mission in New Delhi, explains:

> One can perform these other activities beneficial to others only when there is renunciation of excessive attachment or sense of mine-ness to material objects, subsidence of the passion of greed, i.e. acquisitiveness and exploitation of others, which are often the cause of enmity and hatred on the part of others. Thus, the virtues of humility, honesty or straightforwardness and purity of mind, including freedom from greed, are dovetailed into forgiveness. One is asked to renounce or minimize the four passions of anger, pride, deceit and greed, which are the real enemies of the purity of the soul and which stand in the way of peace and happiness of the individual as also social well-being.[20]

Pilgrimages to sacred sites are also very popular forms of Jain spiritual practice. Individuals, families, or groups may travel long distances to worship at famous sites, many located on hills or mountains in beautiful natural environments. Many of these are in Bihar, south of the Indian border with Nepal. Bihar is considered the cradle of Jainism, for it was here that twenty of the twenty-four Tirthankaras, including Mahavira, are thought to have achieved liberation. Some areas in western India are also rich in intricately carved Jain temples and pilgrimage places. And in South India there is a colossal statue of Bahubali which was carved out of solid rock in 980 CE. His feet—the most accessible part, as well as the focus of reverence in Indian culture—are daily bathed as a devotional ritual. Every twelve to fifteen years, a huge scaffold is erected so that pots of water, sandalwood fragrance, coconut, and sugar can be poured over the fifty-foot (seventeen-meter) statue. This special ceremony draws enormous crowds of worshipers. Construction of temples continues today, keeping alive ancient traditions of intricate stone-carving.

World Jainism

How has Jainism spread from India since the twentieth century?

Through the centuries, Jainism managed to survive as a small minority within largely Hindu India. Today there are approximately 4.5 million Jains worldwide. From ancient times, lay Jains travelled outward from India as traders, to areas such as East Africa, Central Asia, Turkey, and China, However, most of the outward migration by Jain businesspeople and professionals has happened during the last half-century. Since the twentieth century, Jainism has been carried as a religion by several teachers. One of them, Shree Chitrabhanu, was for twenty-nine years a monk who walked barefoot over 30,000 miles of Indian soil to teach Jain principles to the populace. When he was invited to address interfaith conferences in Switzerland and the United States in 1970 and 1971, his controversial decision to attend in person marked the first time in Jain history that a Jain monk had traveled outside India. He then established Jain meditation centers in the United States, Brazil, Canada, Kenya, the United Kingdom, and India.

Acharya Shri Sushil Kumar (1926–1994) likewise established Jain centers in the United Kingdom and the United States as well as in India. He pointed out that the Jain scriptures consider as "Jains" all those who practice Jain principles:

> *If somebody is a real symbol of non-violence, love, compassion, peace, harmony, oneness, then he is the perfect Jain. We can't convert any Jains, but you can convert your habits, your mind.*[21]

Many Jains live outside India now, owing to emigration to North America, Europe, East Africa, and elsewhere. Approximately 120,000 Jains live in North America, where there are more than one hundred Jain organizations and thirty-six Jain temples or combined Jain–Hindu temples, many of them constructed of marble in elaborate Rajasthani style. At the same time, young people are encouraged by media and peer pressures to drink alcohol, eat meat, and live irresponsibly for the sake of fun, trends that are affecting the young generation in India as well.

Nevertheless, wherever they have gone, the highly literate Jain emigrants have kept in touch with their Indian roots and have established sociocultural associations. In England, Jains have organized the Institute of Jainology, under whose auspices some thirty scholars worked to prepare the Jain Declaration on Nature and ancient Jain texts are being translated into modern English. Jain Studies are also going on at the renowned School of Oriental and African Studies at the University of London, and in the United States a perpetual Bhagwan Mahavir Chair for Jain Studies has been endowed at Florida International University. Sectarian divisions are less prominent in the diaspora than in India, and in North America the organization JAINA has been established as a federation encouraging co-operation among sixty-five Jain associations.

In North American culture, acceptance of religious diversity has brought increased beliefs in karma, rebirth, and vegetarianism among the general populace, so these Jain principles no longer seem strange to non-Jains. But the traditional Jain qualities of individual asceticism and renunciation seem to be giving way to focus on environmentalism, animal rights, vegan diet, nonviolence, and interfaith activities. This trend is especially pronounced among the second-generation young people. Some see the ascetic practices as old-fashioned and incompatible with modern lifestyles. If people work into the night, for instance, it is not possible to eat dinner before sunset.

The extreme asceticism modeled by monks and nuns in India is not visible outside the country, since they can only travel on foot. However, in 1980 Acharya Tulsi created new orders of "semi-monks" and "semi-nuns" who are allowed to travel abroad in order to spread Jain teachings and who are less bound by time-consuming restrictions that limit their time for teaching. For instance, they are allowed to gather all their food from one house rather than

Acharya Tulsi (1914–1997)

An Interview with M. P. Jain

M. P. Jain is the director of Motilal Banarsidass Publishing Company, a venerable publisher of books about Indian religions and culture. He is one of five brothers who live together in New Delhi as an extended family, all involved in the family publishing business along with their married children. He speaks of the difficulty of the lay practice of Jainism:

Very few people are really practicing the true Jainism—not even the monks. Jain tradition speaks of two aspects: the self and the non-self. Non-self is everything that is destroyable, whether your body, your ideas, your house, your business, or your eatables. Non-self cannot be possessed. The self, the jivatma, is eternal. It moves from one body to another body after birth and rebirth. Thus that is the permanent thing, but people do not understand this. They love only those things that are non-self, and non-self is absolutely impermanent.

To consider all non-self things impermanent and detach yourself from them is very difficult, because in all previous births we have been loving non-self things. This is a habit; there is no habit of concentrating on the self. That requires a lot of spiritual practice. Only then can you divert yourself from non-self to self. The practice is that you have to look upon worldly things as the seer. You are not to be involved in them, because through attachment with worldly things you land up with all those problems that are existing in the world. If you detach yourself, you become only a seer, and then you attach yourself with the self only. Then you can achieve something.

In business, most people's main purpose is to make money somehow, by wrong or right methods. But I don't agree. One should try to be as fair as possible.

Renunciation has to be done happily. One must be mentally happy, physically happy, and happy in activities. Only then can one achieve the goal. As a father, I can only tell my family that this is the way, but it is very hard to make them do it. Only through punye—good deeds which one has done in previous births—can you renounce. You have to change from the prevalent way. Only one like Mahatma Gandhi, who walked alone, can change from the prevalent way. He had those punye, so he could walk alone and thousands of people followed him.

I have a spiritual teacher. He is an unassuming person, absolutely unknown. He is like a monk, living in the Himalayas. I see him only once a year when he passes through Delhi on his way to meet his mother.

I go to the temple every day. I worship there, reciting some mantras and doing some rituals. There is a sense of pleasure and a sense of duty. It is essential because I have understood the importance of worshiping those who have attained the highest level of renunciation. If you worship greater people, those who have attained nirvana, you will get the same peace that they have attained. Our guru inspired us to do so. From our family, about twenty percent of us go to the temple every day, including my mother, who is still practicing Jainism to a great extent.

We support the monks and nuns by providing them the things that they need, like clothes, food, and travel arrangements. They do not travel in vehicles, but when they walk from one station to another, they need a rickshaw for their belongings and a servant to escort them so that they go to the right place. But things are changing. The older monks and nuns have started traveling in wheelchairs; someone pushes them.

My wife, my mother, and I do not eat after sunset, because in food preparation, drinking water, and so forth there is more death of jivas after sunset than before sunset. Some jivas cannot be seen; some can be seen. It depends on their size. One should try to save them as much as one can. That is the reason one should not travel during night, because in the night they are many, and in the sunlight they are less.

As for mosquitoes, I try to keep my room as clean as possible so that the mosquitoes do not show up. If they come, you have to turn on the air-conditioner, take a blanket, and sleep under that. There is no question of killing them. It is better to bear the mosquitoes to be on the safe side, because killing is no answer. If you kill, that is very harmful, because if you kill one soul you kill your own soul also.[22]

taking only a tiny amount from each of many houses (a restriction that was intended to lessen the burden on any one householder). Acharya Tulsi also inspired the development of the Jain Vishva Bharati Institute, a university in the Rajasthani desert where research into Jain traditions is being conducted, "to promote and propagate the high ideals of Anekant (nonabsolutist outlook), Ahimsa (nonviolence), Tolerance and Peaceful Co-existence for the weal of mankind." Its students are modeling and teaching these principles in many settings, both in India and abroad. The Institute explains:

> There is no dearth of universities and institutes throughout the world. They are fulfilling the aims of education by awarding degrees for getting jobs and orienting the students in the fields of Science, Arts, and Commerce. Though this type of education leads to the advancement of science and technology and sharpens the intellect of students, it also increases the tendency of materialistic possession, which demands indiscriminate fulfillment of wants, leading to an erosion of rules, code of conduct, moral values and the ethical content from human life. The prevalent educational system has inadvertently neglected character-building and the attainment of emotional balance, without which human beings, with all their high intellectual accomplishments, cannot co-exist peacefully.[23]

Acharya Tulsi also began the Anuvrat Movement in 1949, to enlist people of all faiths and nationalities to commit themselves to *anuvrats* (small vows). He developed these to help people rejuvenate strong moral standards of self-restraint in the midst of an ethically unhealthy society. The small vows include: Avoid willful killing of any innocent creature, refrain from attacks and aggression and work instead for world peace and disarmament, avoid discrimination on the basis of caste or race, eschew religious intolerance, avoid false business and political practices, limit acquisition of possessions, eschew addictive substances, and avoid wasting water or cutting down trees.

In 1995, Acharya Tulsi renounced even his own position as the leader of his order by installing Acharya Mahapragya (1920–2010) as his successor. Acharya Tulsi and Acharya Mahapragya developed a system which they called "Preksha Meditation," for teaching people of all backgrounds and religions transformation of thoughts, development of "right emotions," and efficient use of mind and body. It includes yogic practices that lead to impartial awareness of breath, physical sensations, emotions, and urges, and thus ideally to a purified state of constant equanimity in which karmas do not accumulate. Hundreds of thousands of people from many countries have participated in Preksha Meditation camps thus far.

International Preksha meditation camp in progress in Rajasthan, India.

Acharya Mahapragya's self-description was an indication of the internal qualities that keep Jain faith alive:

I am an ascetic. My asceticism is not bound by inert rituals. … I follow a tradition, but do not treat its dynamic elements as static. I derive benefit from the scriptures, but do not believe in carrying them as a burden. … In my consciousness there is no bondage of "yours and mine." It is free from it. My spiritual practice is not to "worship" truth, but to subject it to minute surgery. The only mission of my life is boundless curiosity to discover truth. … It is not an external accoutrement. Like a seed it is sprouting out of my being.[24]

Key terms

ahimsa Nonviolence, a central Jain principle.

anekantwad Jain principle of nonabsolutism, because truth has many aspects.

aparigraha Nonacquisitiveness, a major Jain principle.

ascetic Austere, detached from worldly comforts.

Digambara A highly ascetic order of Jain monks who wear no clothes.

Jina A fully perfected human.

jiva The soul.

karma Subtle matter or particles that accumulate on the soul as a result of one's thoughts and actions.

samsara The continual round of birth, death, and rebirth.

Shvetambara Jain order of monks who are less ascetic than the Digambara.

Tirthankaras The great enlightened teachers in Jainism, of whom Mahavira was the last in the present cosmic cycle.

Suggested reading

Chapple, Christopher, ed., *Jainism and Ecology: Non-violence in the Web of Life*. Cambridge, Massachusetts: Center for the Study of World Religions. 2002. Scholars examine possibilities of bringing Jain principles to bear on contemporary environmental issues.

Jain, Jagdish Prasad "Sadhak," *Fundamentals of Jainism*, New Delhi: Radiant Publishers, 2005. Examination of the ancient roots of Jain tradition, according to literary and archaeological sources, plus Jain ethics and philosophy.

Jain, Prakash C., *Jains in India and Abroad: A Sociological Introduction*, New Delhi: International School for Jain Studies, 2011. Comprehensive information about Jains living outside India, plus summary of Jain history, beliefs, and practices.

Jaini, Padmanabh S., *The Jaina Path of Purification*, Berkeley: University of California Press, 1979. An appreciative, scholarly analysis of the Jaina path.

Jaini, Padmanabh S., ed., *Collected Papers on Jaina Studies*, Delhi: Motilal Banarsidass Publishers, 2000. In-depth look at contemporary issues in Jain scholarship and practice.

Kumar, Acharya Sushil, *Song of the Soul*, Blairstown, New Jersey: Siddhachalam Publishers, 1987. Insights into Jain mantra practice, as taught by a twentieth-century monk.

Long, Jeffery D., *Jainism: An Introduction*, London and New York: I. B. Tauris & Co. Ltd, 2010 Introduction to beliefs, practices, and history of Jainism, with special attention to the principle of relativity and contemporary relevance for the West.

Muller, F. Max, ed., *Jaina Sutras*, vols XLV and XXII of *Sacred Books of the East*, Oxford: Clarendon Press, 1884 and 1895. Engaging translations of various sorts of *sutras*, including both philosophical treatises and rules of conduct for Jain ascetics.

Nyayavijayaji, Munisri, trans. Nagin J. Shah, *Jaina Philosophy and Religion*, Delhi: Motilal Banarsidass Publishers, 1998. A renowned twentieth-century monk's comprehensive tome describing the major aspects of Jain philosophy, liberation practices, logics, metaphysics, and ethics in contemporary terms.

Pániker, Agustín, trans. David Sutcliffe, *Jainism: History, Society, Philosophy and Practice*, Delhi: Motilal Banarsidass Publishers, 2010. Cosmology, mythology, social and religious context, texts, philosophy, practices, and orders within Jainism.

Rankin, Aidan, *The Jain Path: Ancient Wisdom for the West,* Hampshire, UK: John Hunt Publishing, 2006. Jainism described for a Western audience as clues to a global paradigm shift.

Suri, Amrtacandra, English translation by Barend Faddegon, *The Pravacana-sara of Kund-Kund with the commentary Tattva-dipika,* Fremont, California: Jain Publishing Company, Inc., 1935, reprinted. Terse writings of the ancient Jain sage, Acharya Kund-Kund, with commentaries.

Tobias, Michael, *Life Force: The World of Jainism,* Berkeley, California: Asian Humanities Press, 1991. A highly appreciative and readable account of Jain practices and philosophy by a Western observer.

Vallely, Anne, *Guardians of the Transcendent: An Ethnography of a Jain Ascetic Community,* Toronto: University of Toronto Press, 2002. The ascetic lives of Jain nuns in a Rajasthan community, described and analyzed by a participant observer.

4.1 Explain the Jain belief about the Tirthankaras

Jainism's major teacher, Mahavira (d. *c.* 527 BCE), a contemporary of Buddha, is considered the last of twenty-four Tirthankaras (great enlightened teachers) of the current cosmic cycle. In Jain cosmology, the universe is without beginning or end and eternally passes through cycles of progress and decline. It is the Tirthankaras' role in periods of decline to create religion in order to steer people away from the growing evil in the world. The first Tirthankara introduced civilizing social institutions, such as marriage, family, law, justice, and government, and built villages, towns, and cities.

In the third century BCE, Mahavira's followers split into two groups: the Digambaras, an ascetic order of monks who wear nothing at all (symbolizing innocence and nonattachment), and the Shvetambaras, monks and nuns who wear simple white robes. Shvetambaras believe that the nineteenth Tirthankara was a woman.

4.2 Define the principles of nonviolence, nonattachment, and nonabsolutism

Until a mundane soul frees itself from karmas (minute particles that we accumulate as we act and think), Jains believe that it wanders about through the universe in an endless cycle of deaths and rebirths. To avoid accumulating karma, Jains adopt three basic principles. Nonviolence (ahimsa) is the belief that all living things deserve to live and evolve as they can. Jains are thus strict vegetarians and treat everything with great care. Nonattachment (*aparigraha*) is considered the way to inner peace; by letting go of things and situations, moment by moment, we can be free. Nonabsolutism (*anekantwad*) involves trying to avoid anger and judgmentalism, and remaining open-minded by remembering that any issue can be seen from many angles, all partially true.

4.3 Describe the key Jain spiritual practices

Jainism is an ascetic path and practiced in its fullest by monks and nuns. In addition to practicing meditation, they adopt a life of celibacy, physical penance and fasting, and material simplicity.

Most householders cannot carry renunciation as far as monks and nuns but nonetheless try to purify and perfect themselves. Jain homes and temples are typically scrupulously clean, diets are carefully vegetarian, and medicines are prepared without cruel testing on animals. In all spheres of life, Jains are taught to limit the harm they do to themselves, to others, and to the environment. People pay their respects before images of the Tirthankaras with offerings and by waving lamps. Festivals, such as Divali and Paryushan Mahaparva (the annual festival of atonement), are characterized by meditation, renunciation, scriptural study, and hymns. Pilgrimages to sacred sites are also popular. The ultimate spiritual practice is the now-controversial fasting unto death at the end of life, a discipline that requires many years of previous ascetic practice and one that may only be undertaken because of very old age, terminal illness, famine, or dire calamity.

4.4 Summarize the Jain diaspora

Since the twentieth century, Jainism has been carried to the outside world by teachers such as Shree Chitrabhanu and Acharya Shri Sushil Kumar, who established Jain centers in the United States, Brazil, Canada, Kenya, the United Kingdom, and India. In 1980 Acharya Tulsi (who began the Anuvrat Movement in 1949) created new orders of "semi-monks" and "semi-nuns" who are allowed to travel abroad in order to spread Jain teachings.

Many Jains also now live outside India owing to emigration to North America, Europe, East Africa, and elsewhere. In the diaspora, the traditional Jain qualities of individual asceticism and renunciation seem to be giving way to focus on environmentalism, animal rights, vegan diet, nonviolence, and inter-faith activities—a trend particularly pronounced among the second-generation young people.

CHAPTER 5

BUDDHISM

"What changed with Buddha's teaching is that now I'm not thinking about myself. I think more about others. I realized that everybody is interconnected. We are not alone." Naoyuki Ogi[1]

5.1 **Tell the story of the Buddha's enlightenment**

5.2 **Define the Four Noble Truths and the Noble Eightfold Path to liberation**

5.3 **Differentiate between Theravada and Mahayana Buddhism**

5.4 **Identify the schools of Mahayana in East Asia**

5.5 **Contrast Vajrayana with Theravada and Mahayana Buddhism**

5.6 **Describe the major Buddhist festivals**

5.7 **Discuss the growing popularity of Buddhism in Western societies**

5.8 **Outline the emerging focus on social problems in contemporary Buddhist practice**

About the same time that Mahavira was teaching the Jain path, the man who became known as the Buddha preached another alternative to the ritual-oriented Brahmanism of India. The Buddha taught about earthly suffering and its cure. Many religions offer comforting supernatural solutions to the difficulties of earthly life. Early Buddhism was quite different: It held that liberation from suffering depends on our own efforts. The Buddha taught that by understanding how we create suffering for ourselves we can become free.

The effort involved in having to take responsibility for our own happiness and our own liberation may seem daunting and unlikely to attract many followers. On the contrary, the Buddha's teachings spread far and wide from India throughout Asia, becoming the dominant religious tradition in many countries. The Buddha's teachings have been meaningful to some as a profound system of philosophy and to others as a system of religious practice or way of life. As Buddhism spread to new lands, it took new forms, often reflecting earlier local traditions. These new forms might include devotional practices, mystical elements, and appeals to the various Buddhas and bodhisattvas for protection and blessing. Now, more than 2,500 years after the Buddha's death, the path that he taught is attracting considerable interest in Western countries, where its psychological and meditative aspects are often emphasized.

The life and legend of the Buddha
How did the Buddha gain enlightenment?

Although the Buddha was apparently an historical figure, what we know about him is derived from stories passed down over time through generations of followers. His prolific teachings were probably not collected in written form until several hundred years after his death. In the meantime, they were apparently transmitted orally, chanted from memory by monks, groups of whom were responsible for remembering specific parts of the teachings.

Only a few factual details of the Buddha's life have been retained. While stories about his life are abundant in authorized Buddhist texts, these stories were never organized into a unified canonical biography. Extant complete biographies of the Buddha date from four centuries after his passing. These texts venerate the Buddha as a legendary hero, and were written by storyteller poets rather than historians. An example of such a sacred biography is Ashvaghosa's famous **epic**, the *Buddhacharita* (Acts of the Buddha), probably composed in the second century CE.

The one who became the Buddha (a generic term meaning "Awakened One") was reportedly born near what is today the border between India and Nepal. He was named Siddhartha Gautama, meaning "wish-fulfiller" or "he who has reached his goal." It is said that he lived for more than eighty years during the fifth century BCE, though his life may have extended either into the late sixth or early fourth century. His father was apparently a wealthy landowner serving as one of the chiefs of a Kshatriya clan, the Shakyas, who lived in the foothills of the Himalayas. The family name, Gautama, honored an ancient Hindu sage whom the family claimed as ancestor or spiritual guide. His mother, Maya, is said to have given birth to him in the garden of Lumbini near Kapilavastu. The epics embellish his birth story as a conception without human intercourse, in which a white elephant carrying a lotus flower entered his mother's womb during a dream. He is portrayed as the reincarnation of a great being who had been born many times before and took birth on earth once again out of compassion for all suffering beings.

According to legend, the child was raised in the lap of luxury, with fine clothes, white umbrellas for shade, perfumes, cosmetics, a mansion for each

The region where Siddhartha grew up is in full view of the high peaks of the Himalayas.

TIMELINE

Buddhism

c. 5th–4th century BCE	Life of Gautama Buddha
c. 258 BCE	Indian King Ashoka embraces Buddhism, spreads it outward
c. 200 BCE–200 CE	Development of Theravada in Sri Lanka and Southeast Asia
c. 29 BCE	Pali Canon written down in Sri Lanka
c. 50 CE	Buddhism carried to China and then Southeast Asia
1st century	Development of Mahayana Buddhism; spread of Perfection of Wisdom scriptures
c. 2nd century	Ashvaghosha writes *Acts of the Buddha*
c. 150–250	Life of Nagarjuna, who develops "emptiness" philosophy
c. 550	Buddhism enters Japan; becomes state religion of Korea
589–845	Peak of Chinese Buddhism
600s	Songtsan declares Buddhism the national religion of Tibet; Chan School begins in China
700s	Buddhist monasteries established in Tibet; Thai Buddhism begins
845	Persecution of Buddhism begins in China
1079–1153	Life of Milarepa
1198	Nalanda University destroyed; Buddhism disappears in India
1200–1253	Life of Dogen, who spreads Zen Buddhism in Japan
1222–1282	Life of Nichiren; Pure Land and Nichiren sects founded in Japan
c. 1300–1500	Buddhism declines in Korea, succeeded by Islam in Indonesia
1700s	Colonial occupation of Sri Lanka, Burma, Laos, Cambodia, Vietnam
1893	Buddhist missionaries star at World's Parliament of Religions, Chicago; Western study of Buddhist literature begins
1956	Revival of Buddhism among India's "untouchables"
1959	Dalai Lama escapes to India; persecution of Buddhism in China and Tibet
1960s on	Rise of Engaged Buddhism
1970s on	Popularity of Buddhist ideas and practices in the West
1989, 1991	Nobel Peace Prizes to Dalai Lama, Aung San Suu Kyi
1998	Full ordination of 135 nuns from 23 countries
2010	Aung San Suu Kyi freed from house arrest in Myanmar (Burma)

season, the company of female musicians, and a harem of dancing girls. He was also trained in martial arts and married to at least one wife, Yashodhara, who bore a son. Despite this life of ease, Siddhartha was reportedly unconvinced of its value. As the legend goes, the gods arranged for him to see "four sights" that his father had tried to hide from him: a bent old man, a sick person, a dead person, and a mendicant seeking lasting happiness rather than temporal pleasure. Seeing the first three sights, he was dismayed by the impermanence of life and the existence of old age, suffering, and death. The sight of the monk piqued his interest in a life of renunciation. As a result, at the age of twenty-nine Siddhartha renounced his wealth, left his wife and newborn son (whom he had named Rahula, meaning "fetter"), shaved his head and donned the coarse robe of a wandering ascetic. He embarked on a wandering life in pursuit of a very difficult goal: finding the way to total liberation from suffering.

Many Indian **sannyasins** were already leading the homeless life of poverty and simplicity that was considered appropriate for seekers of spiritual truth. Although the future Buddha later developed a new spiritual path that departed significantly from Brahmanic tradition, he initially tried traditional methods. He headed southeast to study with a Brahmin teacher who had many followers, and then with another who helped him reach an even higher mental state.

Unsatisfied, still searching, Siddhartha reportedly underwent six years of extreme self-denial techniques: nakedness, exposure to great heat and cold, breath retention, a bed of brambles, severe fasting. Finally he acknowledged that this extreme ascetic path had not led to enlightenment. He described his appearance after a long and strenuous period of fasting:

Because I ate so little, all my limbs became like the knotted joints of withered creepers; because I ate so little, my protruding backbone became like a string of balls; because I ate so little, my buttocks became like a bullock's hoof; because I ate so little, my gaunt ribs became like the crazy rafters of a tumbledown shed; because I ate so little, the pupils of my eyes appeared lying low and deep in their sockets as sparkles of water in a deep well appear lying low and deep.[2]

Siddhartha then shifted his practice to a Middle Way that rejected both self-indulgence and self-denial. He revived his failing health by accepting food once more and began a period of reflection. On the night of the full moon in the sixth lunar month, it is said that he sat in deep meditation beneath a tree in a village now called Bodh Gaya, and finally experienced supreme awakening. After passing through four states of serene contemplation, he recalled all his previous lives. Then he had a realization of the wheel of repeated death and

The Buddha is traditionally thought to have given his first sermon, laying out the basic principles he had realized, in the Deer Park at Sarnath, to ascetics with whom he had previously engaged in severe austerities.

rebirth, in which past good or bad deeds are reflected in future lives. Finally, he realized the cause of suffering and the means for ending it. After this experience of awakening or enlightenment, it is said that he was radiant with light.

According to legend, Siddhartha was tempted by Mara, the personification of evil, to keep his insights to himself, for they were too complex and profound for ordinary people to understand. But the Buddha compassionately determined to set the wheel of the Dharma in motion and began by teaching in Sarnath, in the Deer Park. He then spent decades walking and teaching ever-increasing groups of followers all over northern India. The Enlightened One's teachings and personality were apparently so compelling that many people were transformed simply by meeting him. Gradually he became known as "Shakyamuni Buddha," the "sage of the Shakya clan." Out of the abundant and varied scriptures later attributed to Shakyamuni Buddha, historians agree on the validity and centrality of a core of teachings that became known as the **Dharma** (in the **Pali** dialect: *Dhamma**) that he taught: the Four Noble Truths, the Noble Eightfold Path, the Three Marks of Existence, and other guidelines for achieving liberation from suffering. In Buddhist usage, the term Dharma is especially focused on what is proper or right, while in Hinduism, dharma is often more focused on duty.

The newly awakened Buddha walked across northern India for forty-five years as a mendicant with an alms bowl, giving teachings and advice to people of all backgrounds and religions. Many young men decided to become monks (**bhikshus**; Pali: *bhikkhus*), emulating his life of poverty and spiritual dedication. Many others adopted his teachings but continued to live as householders.

The **Sangha**—the monastic order that developed from the Buddha's early disciples—accepted people from all castes and levels of society. The Buddha's stepmother, Mahaprajapati, who had raised him after the death of his mother, and his wife, Yashodhara, became **bhikshunis** (Pali: *bhikkhunis*), members of the order of nuns that the Buddha founded. After the death of his father, King Shuddhodana, the Buddha's stepmother requested permission to enter the Sangha. When the Buddha hesitated to admit her, she and 500 women from the court shaved their heads, put on yellow robes, and walked a great distance to Vaishali where he was, and made the same request. At last he agreed, reportedly on the condition that Mahaprajapati observe eight special rules, a story that has been used to justify the subordination of nuns to monks, regardless of seniority. The Buddha's alleged reluctance to admit women to the Sangha is today a matter of much speculation. Some think that later monks may have added the rules or that the eight special rules were laid down with the monks' weaknesses in mind. Be this as it may, in the context of patriarchal Indian society, for women to leave their homes and become itinerant mendicants would probably have been perceived as socially disruptive, as well as difficult for women of the court. According to Hindu social codes, a woman could not lead the renunciate life and could achieve spiritual salvation only through personal devotion, especially devotion to her husband. By contrast, the Buddha asserted that women were as capable as men of achieving enlightenment.

Traditional accounts of the Buddha's death at the age of eighty are evidence of his selfless desire to spare humankind from suffering. His last meal, served by a blacksmith, inadvertently included some poisonous mushrooms or perhaps spoiled pork. Severely ill and recognizing his impending death, the Buddha pushed on to his next teaching stop at Kushinara. He sent word to the blacksmith not to feel remorse or blame himself, for his offering of food accrued great merit. When the Buddha reached his destination he lay down on a stone couch. As his monks came to pay their last respects, he urged them to tend to their own spiritual development:

* Buddhist terms have come to us both in Pali, an Indian dialect first used for preserving the Buddha's teachings (the Buddha himself probably spoke a different ancient dialect), and in Sanskrit, the language of Indian sacred literature. For instance, the Pali *sutta* (aphorism) is equivalent to the Sanskrit *sutra*. In this chapter Sanskrit will be used, as it is more familiar to Westerners, except in the section on Theravada, which uses Pali.

You must be your own lamps, be your own refuges. … A monk becomes his own lamp and refuge by continually looking on his body, feelings, perceptions, moods, and ideas in such a manner that he conquers the cravings and depressions of ordinary men and is always strenuous, self-possessed, and collected in mind.[3]

He designated no successor and appointed no one to lead the order. But the Buddhist teachings and the monastic order survived and spread widely. His cousin and closest helper, Ananda, explained that before passing away the Buddha made it clear that his followers should take the Dharma and ethical discipline as their support. Followers should study the Dharma, put it into practice, and be able to defend it in the face of criticism.

Be the master of your own mind.

The Buddha[4]

In his last discourse, the Buddha reportedly explained to his disciples:

The true Buddha is not a human body—it is Enlightenment. A human body must die, but the Wisdom of Enlightenment will exist forever in the truth of the Dharma, and in the practice of the Dharma.[5]

Nevertheless, after cremation of the Buddha's body, seven pieces of his bones and teeth were collected and greatly revered. It is said that these relics were given to messengers from seven clans, who built dome-shaped reliquaries called stupas to commemorate the Buddha's passing, or final liberation (*parinirvana;* Pali: *parinibbana*). The Buddha's death is memorialized by images in which he is serenely lying on his side. These stupas and images became the focus of great devotion to the Buddha. Inscriptions dating back to the third century BCE or even earlier show that both monastics and laypeople made pilgrimages to these sacred sites. Standing before them, followers sense that the Buddha is present there.

The Buddha's final liberation into nirvana when he physically died is symbolized by this enormous Sri Lankan statue that depicts him serenely lying down with eyes closed to the world.

The Dharma

What are the Four Noble Truths and the Noble Eightfold Path to liberation?

Buddhism is often described as a nontheistic religion. There is no personal God who creates the world or to whom prayers can be directed. Although gods are mentioned in Buddhist texts, as when they make the "four sights" appear to young Siddhartha, they are not able to help people attain spiritual awakening. Buddhists who attended the 1993 Parliament of the World's Religions in Chicago found it necessary to explain to people of other religions that they do not worship the Buddha:

> *Shakyamuni Buddha, the founder of Buddhism, was not God or a god. He was a human being who attained full Enlightenment through meditation and showed us the path of spiritual awakening and freedom. Therefore, Buddhism is not a religion of God. Buddhism is a religion of wisdom, enlightenment and compassion. Like the worshippers of God who believe that salvation is available to all through confession of sin and a life of prayer, we Buddhists believe that salvation and enlightenment are available to all through removal of defilements and delusion and a life of meditation. However, unlike those who believe in God who is separate from us, Buddhists believe that Buddha which means "one who is awake and enlightened" is inherent in us all as Buddha nature or Buddha mind.[6]*

Unlike other Indian sages, the Buddha did not focus on descriptions of an unseen reality, the nature of the soul, life after death, or the origin of the universe. He said that curiosity about such matters was like a man who, having been wounded by a poisoned arrow, refused to get it pulled out until he was told the caste and origin of his assailant, his name, his height, the color of his skin, and all details about the bow and arrow. In the meantime, he died.

> *Being religious and following* dhamma *has nothing to do with the dogma that the world is eternal; and it has nothing to do with the other dogma that the world is not eternal. For whether the world is eternal or otherwise, birth, old age, death, sorrow, pain, misery, grief, and despair exist. I am concerned with the extinction of these.[7]*

The Buddha spoke of his teachings as a raft to take us to the farther shore, rather than a description of the shore or something to be carried around once we get there. The farther shore is **nirvana** (Pali: *nibbana*), or liberation, the goal of spiritual effort; the planks of the raft are insights into the truths of existence and teachings about the path to liberation.

The Four Noble Truths

In his very first talk on Dharma at Sarnath, the Buddha set forth the Four Noble Truths, the foundation for all his later teachings:

1 The truth of pain and suffering.
2 The truth of the arising of pain.
3 The truth of the cessation of pain.
4 The truth of the path to end pain: the Noble Eightfold Path.

The Buddha was neither pessimistic nor optimistic about our human condition, but realistic. Sri Lankan monk and scholar Walpola Rahula spoke of the Buddha as "the wise and scientific doctor for the ills of the world."[8] In the Four Noble Truths, the Buddha diagnosed the human condition and proposed a cure, one step at a time. The Buddha's First Noble Truth is the existence of *dukkha*: pain, suffering, and dissatisfaction. At some time or another, we all experience grief, unfulfilled desires, sickness, old age, physical pain, mental anguish, and eventually death. We may be happy for a while, but even when we feel happiness, it may be tinged with fear for we know that this happiness does not last. Even our personal identity is impermanent. What we regard as a "self" is an ever-changing bundle of fleeting feelings, sense impressions, ideas, and evanescent physical matter. Unlike some of the Hindu renunciates of his day, the Buddha found no evidence for an eternal soul. One moment of identity leads to the next like one candle being lit from another, but no two moments are the same.

The Second Noble Truth is that the origin of *dukkha* is craving and clinging—to sensory pleasures, to fame and fortune, for things to stay as they are or for them to be different—and attachment to things and ideas. The Buddha taught that craving leads to suffering because of ignorance: We fail to understand the true, constantly changing nature of the things we crave. We grasp at things and hold on to life as we want it to be, rather than seeing things as they are, in a constant state of flux.

In Buddhism, unhappiness is understood as the inevitable companion of happiness. Sunshine gives way to rain, flowers wilt, friends die, and our bodies eventually age and decay. As the contemporary monk Ajahn Sumedho points out, "trying to arrange, control and manipulate conditions so as to always get what we want, always hear what we want to hear, always see what we want to see, so that we never have to experience unhappiness or despair, is a hopeless task."[9]

To remedy this situation, the Buddha taught awareness of the Three Marks of Existence: *dukkha*, **anitya** (Pali: *anicca*, impermanence), and **anatman** (Pali: *anatta*, no self). According to this revolutionary and unique doctrine, there is no separate, permanent, or immortal self; instead, a human being is an impermanent composite of interdependent physical, emotional, and cognitive components. Insight into *anatman* is spiritually valuable because it reduces attachment to one's mind, body, and selfish desires. Even pain is useful, because it helps us to see things as they really are. When we realize that everything changes and passes away, moment by moment, we become aware that nothing in this world is permanent and independently existent. There are only momentary configurations within a continual process of change. As Venerable Ajahn Chah of Thailand explained to a dying woman:

> *Having been born we get old and sick and then we die, and that's totally natural and normal. As soon as we're born, we're dead. It's a little funny to see how at a death people are so grief-stricken and distracted, fearful and sad, and at a birth how happy and delighted. I think if you really want to cry, then it would be better to do so when someone's born. Just think, "This is the way things are." Right now nobody can help you; there is nothing that your family and your possessions can do for you. All that can help you now is the correct awareness.[10]*

Once we have grasped these basic facts of life, we can be free in this life, and free from another rebirth. Ajahn Sumedho explains:

> *When you open the mind to the truth, then you realize there is nothing to fear. What arises passes away, what is born dies, and is not self—so that our sense of being caught in an identity with this human body fades out. We don't see ourselves as some isolated, alienated entity lost in a mysterious and frightening universe. We don't feel overwhelmed by it, trying to find a little piece of it that we can grasp and feel safe with, because we feel at peace with it. Then we have merged with the Truth.[11]*

The Third Noble Truth is that *dukkha* will cease when craving and clinging cease. In this way, illusion ends, insight into the true nature of things dawns, and nirvana is achieved. One lives happily and fully in the present moment, free from self-centeredness and full of compassion. One can serve others purely, without thought of oneself. The Fourth Noble Truth is that craving and suffering can be extinguished by following the Noble Eightfold Path—a path of ethical conduct, concentration, and wisdom.

To be free from clinging to thinking and feeling is nirvana—the highest, supreme happiness.

Maha Ghosananda[12]

The Noble Eightfold Path to liberation

The Buddha set forth a systematic approach so that human beings could extricate themselves from suffering and achieve the final goal of liberation. The Noble Eightfold Path offers ways to purify the mind of afflictive emotions and avoid unwholesome actions. By following this path, we can live a happy life and also create the causes for a favorable rebirth. Ultimately, the path leads to freedom from the cycle of death and rebirth, and the peace of nirvana.

The first aspect of the Noble Eightfold Path is right understanding—comprehending reality correctly through deep realization of the Four Noble Truths. Initially, this means seeing through illusions, such as the idea that wealth and possessions can bring happiness. Gradually we learn to question old assumptions in the light of the Four Noble Truths. Everything we do and say is ultimately produced by the mind. The Buddha said that if our mind is defiled and uncontrolled, suffering will follow us just as a chariot follows a horse. If our mind is purified and well trained, then our actions will be wholesome and we will naturally experience happiness and well-being.

The second aspect is right thought or intention. The Buddha's teachings help us to uncover any afflictive emotions that affect our thinking, such as selfish desires or a tendency to hide our imperfections. As we discover and purify mental defilements such as self-interest, our thinking becomes free from the limitations of self-centeredness—relaxed, clear, and open, and this in turn helps us to act in positive ways.

The third aspect is right speech. The Buddha taught his followers to relinquish the propensity to lie, gossip, speak harshly, or engage in divisive speech, and instead to use communication in the service of truth and harmony. He also advised us to speak to ourselves and others in a positive way: "May you be well and happy today."

The fourth aspect is right action, which begins with observing the five basic precepts for ethical conduct: to avoid destroying life, stealing, sexual misconduct, lying, and intoxicants. Beyond these, all actions should be based on clear understanding. "Unwholesome deeds," said the Buddha, are those "done from motives of partiality, enmity, stupidity, and fear."[13]

The fifth is right livelihood—making sure that one's way of making a living does not violate the five precepts. One should choose a profession or line of work that does not cause harm to others or disrupt social harmony.

Right effort, the sixth aspect, means striving continually to eliminate the impurities of the mind and diligently cultivating wholesome actions of body, speech, and mind. Joyful effort is the antidote to laziness.

The seventh aspect, right mindfulness, is a distinctive feature of the Buddhist path. The way to liberation requires discipline and the cultivation of awareness, moment to moment. The *Dhammapada* (The Path of Dhamma), an early compilation of the Buddha's teachings, includes this pithy injunction:

Check your mind.
Be on your guard.
Pull yourself out
as an elephant from mud.[14]

The eighth aspect, right meditation, applies mental discipline to quiet the mind and develop single-pointed concentration. The Buddha explained that the mind is "subtle, invisible, treacherous."[15] Skillful means are therefore needed to understand and control its restless nature. When the mind is completely stilled, it becomes a quiet pool in which the true nature of things is clearly reflected. The various schools of Buddhism that developed over the centuries have taught different techniques of meditation, but this basic principle remains the same.

> *Try to be mindful, and let things take their natural course. Then your mind will become still in any surroundings, like a clear forest pool. All kinds of wonderful, rare animals will come to drink at the pool, and you will clearly see the nature of all things. You will see many strange and wonderful things come and go, but you will be still. This is the happiness of the Buddha.*
>
> *Ajahn Chah, meditation master, Wat Pa Pong, Thailand*[16]

The wheel of birth and death

Buddhist teachings about rebirth are significantly different from those of Hindu orthodoxy, for there is no eternal, independently existing soul to be reborn. In Buddhism, each phenomenon or event acts as a cause that sets another into

The Wheel of Life. In the center are animals representing the three root afflictions: attachment, aversion, and delusion. The next circle shows the fate of those with good karma (white background on left) and bad karma (black background on right). The third circle represents the spheres of existence, from the gods to the infernal regions. The outer rim shows the chain of cause and effect. Grasping the wheel is a monster representing impermanence and death.

motion. This sequence of spiritual cause and effect is called **karma** (Pali: *kamma*), the "action" of body, speech, and mind. The impressions of our virtuous and nonvirtuous actions shape our experience moment by moment. When we die, this process continues, passing on the flame to a new life in a realm of existence that reflects our past karma.

This wheel of birth and death operates primarily because of the three root afflictions: attachment or greed, aversion or hatred, and delusion or ignorance. The opposites of these afflictions—nongreed (such as generosity, renunciation for others' sake), nonhate (such as friendliness, compassion, and patience), and nondelusion (such as mental clarity and insight)—act as causes to ultimately leave the circle of birth and death.

In Buddhist thought, not only do sentient beings take birth many times, but they also take on many different forms, creating an interconnected web of life. This has important implications for one's relationships with all life. One text explains:

TEACHING STORY

The Great Ape Jataka Tale

When Brahmadatta was king of Benares, the Buddha took birth among the apes and became the powerful king of the 80,000 monkeys living near the Ganges. Overhanging the river there was a great mango tree, with huge and delicious fruits. When ripe, some fell on the ground and some fell into the river. Eating these mangoes with his monkeys, the Great Being foresaw that those that fell into the water would some day bring danger to the herd. He ordered that all the mangoes growing on branches over the river should be plucked when very small and discarded. However, one fruit was hidden by an ant's nest. When it was ripe, it fell into the nets which the king's fishermen had placed into the river. When they pulled out the ambrosial fruit, they took it to the king in Benares. When he tasted it, he developed a great craving for more and insisted on being taken to the tree from which it came.

A flotilla of boats brought the king to the great mango tree. Camping beneath it, he ate mangoes to his heart's delight. At midnight, the Great Being and his monkeys came and leapt from branch to branch above, eating the mangoes. The king woke up and saw them. He ordered his men to surround the tree and prepare to shoot arrows at the monkeys so that they could feast on mangoes and monkey flesh the following day.

Terrified, the monkeys appealed to the Great Being for help. He told them not to be afraid, for he would save their lives. So saying, he at once climbed to one of the branches over the river and then made a tremendous leap across the wide river to the opposite bank. There he cut a long bamboo shoot which he calculated would be long enough to reach across the river. Lashing it to a bush on the farther shore, he lashed the opposite end of the bamboo to his waist and then made a terrific leap back toward the mango tree where the monkeys were cowering in fear for their lives. The shoot being slightly short, he grabbed an overhanging branch so that his own body's length filled the remaining distance. He signaled to the monkeys that they were to run across his body and then the bamboo shoot in order to escape to the other shore. Paying their obeisances to the Great Being and asking his forgiveness, the 80,000 monkeys ran across him to safety. In the process, one of the monkeys [later reborn as Devadatta, a cousin of the Buddha who repeatedly tried to undermine him] took the opportunity to leap from an upper branch onto the great ape's back, breaking his heart.

After all the monkeys had crossed to safety, the wounded Great Being was left alone, hanging from the tree. The king, who had watched the whole thing, was struck by the greatness of his self-sacrifice for the sake of his monkeys. At daybreak, he ordered his people to gently bring the great ape down from the tree, bathe him, rub his body with fine oil, dress him in yellow, and lay him to rest. Sitting beside the great ape, the king questioned him about his action. The Great Being explained to him that no worry or death could trouble him, and that he had acted for the welfare of all those whom he governed, as an example for the king to emulate. After thus advising the king, the Great Being died. King Brahmadatta ordered funeral ceremonies due to a king for him, and then had a shrine built at the place of his cremation and had his skull inlaid with gold, which he then enshrined at Benares. According to the instructions of the Great Being, Brahmadatta then became a very righteous ruler and a traveler to the Bright World.

When the Buddha told this Jataka Tale, he revealed that the human king was Ananda, and that the ape-king was himself.

In the long course of samsara *[cycle of death and rebirth], there is not one among living beings with form who has not been mother, father, brother, sister, son, or daughter, or some other relative. Being connected with the process of taking birth, one is kin to all wild and domestic animals, birds, and beings born from the womb.*[17]

It is said that the Buddha remembered all his past lives and told stories about them to illustrate moral lessons. Hundreds of these stories have been collected as the Jataka Tales, or birth stories of the Buddha's past lives as a **bodhisattva** (one dedicated to liberating others from suffering). The one recounted here, "The Great Ape Jataka Tale" (see Box, facing page), illustrates not only the Buddhist path as a way of personal development but also its importance in establishing moral guidelines for monastics, laity, and rulers alike.

In Buddhist cosmology, there are multiple possible states of existence, including hell beings, hungry ghosts, animals, humans, and gods. Whether interpreted as psychological metaphors or metaphysical realities, all these states of rebirth are imperfect and impermanent. Sentient beings take birth again and again, caught up in this cycle of **samsara**, repeatedly experiencing birth, aging, suffering, and death as a result of their actions and mental defilements. Finally, by purifying their minds of greed, hatred, ignorance, and other delusions, they are able to achieve nirvana, or liberation from cyclic existence and suffering.

Nirvana

The goal of Buddhist practice is nirvana, which literally means "extinguishing," often explained as the extinguishing of the fires of the three root afflictions of attachment, aversion, and delusion, which brings about the end of *dukkha* and the cycle of rebirth. To end the cycle of *dukkha*, one must end all craving and lead a life free of attachment that has no karmic consequences. One enters a state that the Buddha called "quietude of heart,"[18] "a state beyond grasping, beyond aging and dying,"[19] "the unborn, … undying, … unsorrowing, … stainless, the uttermost security from bonds."[20] For the **arhant** (Pali: *arhat, arahat*), a worthy one, who has found nirvana in this life:

> *No suffering for him*
> *who is free from sorrow*
> *free from the fetters of life*
> *free in everything he does.*
> *He has reached the end of his road. …*
>
> *Like a bird invisibly flying in the sky,*
> *he lives without possessions,*
> *knowledge his food, freedom his world,*
> *while others wonder. …*
>
> *He has found freedom—*
> *peaceful his thinking, peaceful his speech,*
> *peaceful his deed, tranquil his mind.*[21]

When an arhant dies, individuality disappears and the being enters the ultimate state of nirvana. Given that the Buddha taught there is no eternal soul to escape the cycle of death and rebirth, it is hard to conceptualize this ultimate state of nirvana. The Buddha explained that rather than trying to speculate about the exact nature of nirvana, one should focus on doing those things that lead to it. His teaching emphasized following the path to nirvana, and not being sidetracked by questions that do not help one to progress. To illustrate this point, he

A Buddhist monk practices meditation to calm and purify his mind.

remained silent when he was asked what happens to an arhant after death. Instead, he picked up a handful of leaves from the forest floor and asked his disciples which were more numerous, the leaves in his hand or those in the forest. When they replied, "Very few in your hand, lord; many more in the grove," he said:

> *Exactly. So you see, friends, the things that I know and have not revealed are more than the truths I know and have revealed. And why have I not revealed them? Because, friends, there is no profit in them; because they are not helpful to holiness; because they do not lead from disgust to cessation and peace, because they do not lead from knowledge to wisdom and nirvana.*[22]

The spread of Buddhism

What are the key similarities and differences between Theravada and Mahayana Buddhism?

After the Buddha attracted a group of disciples, he began to send them out in all directions to help teach the Dharma. Two hundred years after the Buddha died, a powerful Indian king named Ashoka led a huge military campaign to extend his empire. After he saw the tremendous loss of life on both sides, he reportedly felt great remorse, became a practicing Buddhist, and began to espouse non-violence. He had inscriptions written on rocks and pillars throughout his empire teaching the Dharma, with an emphasis on developing an attitude of social responsibility. Under King Ashoka's leadership, Buddhism was disseminated throughout the kingdom and outward to other countries, beginning its development as a global religion. As the Buddha's teachings expanded and adapted to local cultures, various schools developed, sometimes because of different interpretations of the monastic code, and sometimes because of differences of opinion regarding practice or how to interpret the Buddha's teaching. There are narratives that describe the spread of Buddhism from northern Indian schools of Buddhism, as well as from the schools that were established in southern India. There are also first-person accounts of Chinese monks who traveled throughout Buddhist lands in the first millennium CE. All these narratives depict a rich diversity of Buddhist practices and teachings. Nonetheless, though monks of various schools had different ways of expressing the Buddha's teachings, they still shared a common set of religious practices, rituals, and rules that defined monastic life for monks and nuns. These different expressions of the Buddha's teachings have become known as the branches of **Theravada** (initially, one school from a branch of Buddhism that Mahayana Buddhists derogatorily called Hinayana, or the "Lesser Vehicle," but now generally understood as a branch in its own right), **Mahayana**, and **Vajrayana** Buddhism, but the similarities in practices were, and remain, far greater than the differences in the beliefs between the different branches.

After Ashoka's death, advanced study and dissemination of Buddhist philosophy and culture were highly developed in great Buddhist universities, such as Nalanda in northeastern India, which was founded in the second century CE. Other universities were founded in this same region in the eighth century, and were largely devoted to the study of Tibetan Buddhism, but still attracted scholars from different schools of Buddhism as well as from China and other countries. All of these universities had royal patrons, and consisted of huge complexes with libraries and lecture halls, and curricula that covered everything from linguistics to music, architecture, and science. Monks from different schools lived together at these universities, copying texts, studying for advanced degrees, and composing commentaries and treatises. However, eventually Brahmins reasserted their political influence and Buddhists were persecuted in some parts of India. With the growing popularity of devotional movements within Hinduism, Buddhism was already in decline by the time of the twelfth-century Muslim incursions

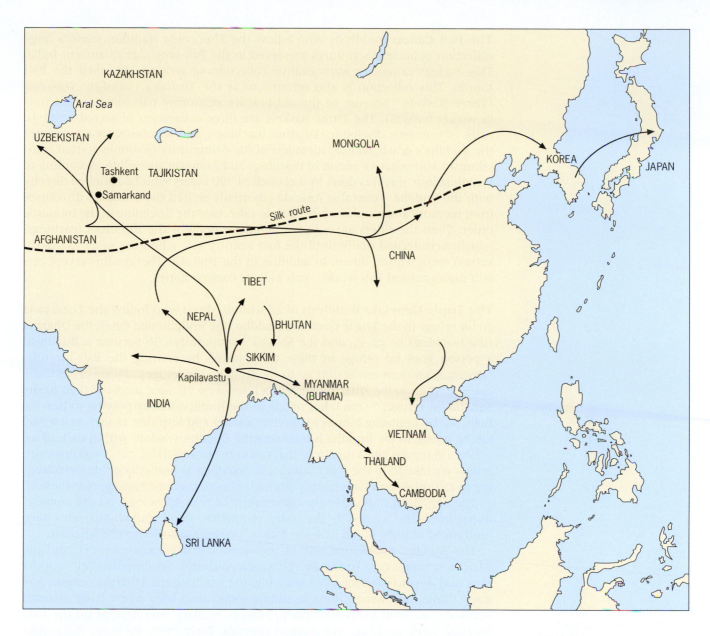

into India, and never became the dominant religion in the Buddha's homeland, although some monasteries remained active until the sixteenth century.

Of the earliest Buddhist schools, only the one today known as Theravada (Way of the Elders) survives. The Theravada branch is prevalent in Southeast Asian countries such as Sri Lanka, Myanmar (Burma), Thailand, Cambodia, and Laos. The schools that developed somewhat later are collectively known as Mahayana (Great Vehicle). Mahayana schools gradually became dominant in Nepal, Tibet, China, Korea, Mongolia, Vietnam, and Japan. The Vajrayana branch became dominant in Tibet. Followers of all these forms of Buddhism share many ideas and practices in common, and are in general agreement about the Four Noble Truths, the Noble Eightfold Path, and the teachings about karma, samsara, and nirvana.

Theravada: mindfulness

Theravada Buddhists study the early scriptures in Pali, honor the life of renunciation, and follow mindfulness and insight meditation teachings. These characteristics are more obvious among intellectuals and monastics; ordinary laypeople tend to be devotional in their practices, although in recent times there have also been efforts to promote meditation among Theravada laypeople.

Buddhism spread in all directions from India but had nearly disappeared in India itself by the 13th century CE.

The Pali Canon Buddhists who follow the Theravada tradition study a large collection of ancient scriptures preserved in the Pali language of ancient India. This ancient canon, or authoritative collection of writings, is called the **Pali Canon**. This collection is also referred to as the **Tipitaka** (Sanskrit: *Tripitaka*, "Three Baskets," because of the old practice of storing palm-leaf manuscripts in wicker baskets). The Three Baskets are three collections of sacred writings: rules of monastic discipline, Dharma teachings, and scholastic treatises. After the Buddha's death, leading members of the community of monks started compiling an authoritative canon of teachings and monastic discipline. According to Buddhist lore, this was done by a council of 500 elders who had studied directly with the Buddha. Venerable Ananda reportedly recited the Buddha's discourses from memory and another close disciple rehearsed the discipline of the monastic order. Then the elders agreed on a definitive body of the Buddha's teachings, which were recited orally until the first century BCE, when the *suttas* (Sanskrit: sutras) were written down. In addition to the Tipitaka, Theravadins accept certain noncanonical Pali works, such as later commentaries.

The Triple Gem Like Buddhists of all schools, those who follow the Theravada go for refuge in the **Triple Gem**: the Buddha (the Enlightened One), the Dharma (the teachings he gave), and the Sangha (community). To become a Buddhist, a person goes for refuge in these three jewels by reciting the Pali formula: "*Buddham saranam gacchami* [I go to the Buddha for refuge], *dhammam saranam gacchami* [I go to the Dharma for refuge], *sangham saranam gacchami* [I go to the Sangha for refuge]." One takes refuge in the Buddha not by praying to him for help, but by honoring him as a supreme teacher and inspiring model. In a sense, taking refuge in the Buddha is honoring the Buddha-wisdom within each of us.

The Dharma is like a medicine that can cure our suffering, but it will not work unless we take it. In the Pali Canon, it is described as immediate, timeless, leading to calmness, and known only through direct experience and personal effort.

The Sangha is ultimately the community of realized beings; on the conventional level, the Sangha is the order of bhikkhus and bhikkhunis who have renounced worldly life in order to follow, preserve, and share the Dharma.

The Buddha established one of the world's first monastic orders, and the Sangha remains very strong in Theravada countries. To simplify their worldly lives and devote themselves to studying and teaching the Dharma, monks and nuns shave their heads, dress in simple robes, own only a few basic material items, eat no solid foods after noon, practice celibacy, and depend on the laity for their food, clothing, and medical supplies. Early every morning the monks set forth with an alms bowl, and laypeople regard it as a merit-making opportunity to offer food to them. The monks reciprocate by offering spiritual guidance, chanting blessings, and performing various social services, including offering advice and education.

Buddhist monasteries are at the center of village life, not isolated, as one might imagine. The monasteries are left open, and people come and go throughout the day. The monks hold a revered social position as models of self-control, kindness, and intelligence. In Thailand, it is common for young men to take temporary vows as monks—often for the duration of the rainy season when little farmwork can be done. They wear saffron robes, set forth with shaven heads and alms bowls, and receive religious instruction while practicing a life of simplicity.

Buddhist monks make daily rounds with their begging bowls seeking food from laypeople, who serve them with reverence, as in this scene in Laos.

Some 135 women from twenty-three countries received full ordination as Buddhist nuns at Bodh Gaya in 1998, helping to revive orders of bhikkhunis.

In contrast to the monks, there has traditionally been little social support for Buddhist nuns in Southeast Asia. Provisions were made during the time of the Buddha for women monastics to live in their own monasteries, practicing the same lifestyle as monks, but the order of fully ordained nuns (bhikkhunis) disappeared completely in Theravadin countries about a thousand years ago. Many of the early Buddhist scriptures take an egalitarian position toward women's capacity for wisdom and attainment of nirvana, but spiritual power has remained in the hands of monks and there has been little opportunity for nuns to take positions of teaching and leadership.

Over time, some of the monks and the texts they edited became somewhat sexist. Because Buddhist monks are celibate, they are not allowed to come into direct contact with women, and many believe that women are hindrances to monks' spiritual development. Feminist scholars object to this interpretation. Thai Buddhist Venerable Dhammananda, for instance, asserts:

Newly ordained monks who have not had much experience with practice and are very weak in their mental resolve may be easily swayed by sensual impulses, of which women are the major attraction. Even if no women are present, some monks still create problems for themselves by images of women they have in their minds. Women are not responsible for the sexual behavior or imaginings of men; the monks themselves must cope with their own sensual desires. Enlightened ones are well-fortified against such mental states and are able to transcend gender differences. The Buddha himself found no need to avoid women, because women no longer appeared to him as sexual objects. He was well-balanced and in control of his mental processes.[23]

There are now attempts to revive full ordination for nuns in Theravadin countries. A landmark event occurred in 1998, when 135 nuns from many countries received full ordination in Bodh Gaya. According to the code of discipline, ordination of nuns is possible only if a quorum of both ordained monks and nuns is present. In China, Taiwan, Japan, and Korea orders of fully ordained nuns have continued, and therefore it was possible to assemble the requisite number of ten bhikkhus and ten bhikkhunis in Bodh Gaya. However, not all Theravadin monks accept the nuns' ordination as legitimate.

Meditation The Theravada tradition preserves a wide variety of meditation techniques for cultivating the mind, derived from the early Buddhist teachings. The two major forms of meditation practice are *samatha* (calm abiding) and vipassana (insight). The practice begins with increasing one's attentiveness to a specific object to focus the mind and achieve calm abiding. One then proceeds to the practice of vipassana to develop insight into *dukkha*, *anicca*, and *anatta*, the three marks of existence.

As taught by the famous Burmese meditation master Mahasi Sayadaw (1904–1982), vipassana practice begins by simply watching one's breath as it flows in and out, focusing attention on the rise and fall of the abdomen. To keep the mind concentrated on the present movement, rather than being distracted by uncontrolled, conditioned responses, one continually makes concise mental notes of what is happening: "rising" and "falling." Other vipassana masters suggest observing a point on the upper lip as the breath goes in and out of the nostrils, posting one's attention like a gatekeeper at that point. Despite the attempt to hold the restless mind to one point, inevitably other thoughts and feelings arise in the restless mind. As they arise, one simply notes these thoughts and feelings—"imagining," "wandering," "remembering"—and returns one's attention to the rising and falling of the breath. Bodily sensations are handled in the same way, noting "itching," "tight," "tired," and so on, as they arise, but maintaining an observer's attitude rather than letting one's mental equanimity be disturbed by reacting to the sensations. Periods of sitting meditation are alternated with periods of walking meditation, during which one notes the movements of the body in great detail: "lifting," "moving," and "placing." If ecstatic states or visions arise in the process of meditation, one simply notes them and lets them pass away without attachment. In the same way, emotions that arise are simply observed, accepted, and allowed to pass away, without evaluating them as "good" or "bad." As Buddhist teacher Joko Beck mentions, ordinarily it is very easy to get caught up and stuck in our emotions:

> *Everyone's fascinated by their emotions because we think that's who we are. We're afraid that if we let our attachment to them go, we'll be nobody. Which of course we are! When you wander into your ideas, your hopes, your dreams, turn back—not just once but ten thousand times if need be, a million times if need be.*[24]

Dukkha (suffering and dissatisfaction), *anicca* (impermanence), and *anatta* (no eternal self)—become apparent during the process of meditation. As one continues the practice, the mind becomes calm, clear, attentive, flexible, and free from the disturbances of likes and dislikes. The next step is to carry this same type of mindfulness over into every activity of everyday life.

Devotional practices In addition to the contemplative and philosophical traditions described above, many lay Buddhists and also many monastic practitioners of Theravada Buddhism in Southeast Asia are likely to turn to the Buddha in devotion, taking refuge in his protective presence and power. Temples, halls, and roadside shrines have been built with images of the Buddha before which people bow, light candles, burn incense, offer flowers, press bits of gold leaf onto the images, and make aspirations and prayers. Some monastics and intellectuals—including Protestant Christians who became interested in Buddhist studies in the late nineteenth century—have labeled such practices antithetical to the spirit of Buddhism, which they understand as rationalistic, philosophical, non-ritualistic, noniconic, and nontheistic. Despite the increasing commercialization of Buddhist imagery, some commentators are now trying to trace the history of image-oriented worship. Devotional practices are so widespread and so influential in popular Buddhist practice that scholars have begun to examine them as perhaps being part of the mainstream of Buddhism after all.

A key text in this regard is the *Mahaparinibbana Sutta*, a Pali scripture that describes the Buddha's cremation and the dispersal of his relics. The text also deals with the issue of devotionalism, recounting that, before his death, the Buddha recommended the commemoration of his relics alongside dedicated practice of the Dharma: "Whoever lays wreaths or puts sweet perfumes and colors ... with a devout heart, will reap benefit and happiness for a long time."[25] Simultaneously, the text advocates devotion to the Dharma as a way of respect-

ing, revering, and paying homage to the Buddha. When lay Buddhists recite the refuge formula, taking refuge in the Buddha, the Dharma, and the Sangha, they may experience this refuge not merely as a philosophical idea, but as a way of connecting with the timeless presence of the Buddha.

In one popular ritual in northern Thailand, a network of threads attached to a large statue of the Buddha is used in special ceremonies to conduct his spiritual power to the Sangha, holy water, amulets, or new images to be consecrated. The 108 squares formed overhead by the strings are believed to form a magical cosmos whose sacred energy touches the earth through cords hanging downward. People may wrap these cords around their heads during the chanting of sutras by monks and thus receive spiritual blessings.

To consecrate new images of the Buddha, monks initially seal them by closing the eyes with beeswax and covering the heads with cloth. Throughout the night, they chant, meditate, and teach about the Buddha and the Dharma as a way to train their minds and also consecrate the images. In the process, the members of the Sangha are also drawn into a strong sense of unity with the Buddha, the Dharma, and each other. At sunrise, the coverings are removed from the images, and they are offered milk and sweet rice; in a sense, they are now living presences.

Similarly, followers may consider the Buddha's power to be present in his relics—bits of hair, nails, teeth, bones, and ashes from his cremated body. Such relics or images of the Buddha may be placed in **stupas**, reliquary mounds reaching toward the sky—a practice perhaps derived from earlier indigenous spiritual traditions. For instance, a tiny bone chip believed to be a **relic** of the Buddha is enshrined at Doi Suthep Temple in Chiang Mai in Thailand. To share this sacred relic with the people, the ruler is said to have placed it on the back of a white elephant—a legendary symbol of the Buddha—in the belief that the elephant would choose the best place for the temple. The elephant climbed a nearby hill until it reached the auspicious spot and went down on its knees. Today, flocks of pilgrims climb the 290 steps to the temple and request blessings by acts such as

Stupas, such as these bell-shaped monuments in Borobudur, Java, may house relics or statues of the Buddha and are sacred places for pilgrimage.

A relic purported to be a tooth of the Buddha is so revered that it is carried on an elephant palanquin in a huge yearly procession in Sri Lanka.

pressing squares of gold leaf onto an image of the Buddha, lighting three sticks of incense to honor the Triple Gem, lighting candles, and offering flowers. So great are the powers associated with relics that huge processions carrying what is thought to be the Buddha's tooth relic have been used by the governments in Sri Lanka and Myanmar (Burma) to legitimize their claims to temporal power.

There is no evidence of worship of images of the Buddha during his lifetime. Early Buddhist art depicts only an empty seat under the bodhi tree where the Buddha attained enlightenment or symbols representing other events in his life: a lotus flower or elephant for his birth, a wheel or two deer kneeling before a throne for his first sermon. What was thought to be the Buddha's last footprint impressed into a stone was later worshiped by King Ashoka, and its replicas also became objects of worship. Images of the Buddha himself were not used until the first century BCE at the earliest, and were not standardized until about the fifth century CE.

Now cherished images of the Buddha proliferate in temples and roadside shrines. The shrines are almost identical to the indigenous spirit shrines that are still quite common in Thailand, where Buddhism is frequently combined with indigenous spirituality and Brahmanism. These physical images are a reminder of the Buddha's teachings and give a sense of his protective, guiding presence. In Southeast Asia, aspects of Theravada Buddhism are often adopted by shamans for greater efficacy in healing rituals. In Sri Lanka, the *yakeduras* invoke the power of the Buddha and the Dharma to ward off evil spirits and help cure spiritually afflicted people. In the cosmic hierarchy, the Buddha and the Dharma are considered powerful and therefore useful in subduing lesser forces. During healing rituals, patients listen to Buddhist stories to help free themselves from afflictions and obtain protection by the power of the mind. Even monks are regarded as magical protectors of sorts, and followers frequently request chanted blessings for protection.

As in all Buddhist cultures, Buddhist temples are important centers for community identity and integration. There the monks not only teach the Dharma, but also preside over agricultural festivals to improve the harvest, ceremonies to assist the dead to achieve a better rebirth, and ceremonies to invoke the blessings of the deities. All these events generate a festive atmosphere and communal joy. The monks and nuns help the people accumulate merit or spiritual benefits and share them with others. Ashin Nyana Dipa, a monk from Myanmar (Burma), explains the idea of transferring merit:

When we concentrate, our mind is purified. The purified mind can transmit, for it is stable. I can share if I have already done good deeds for the people, such as teaching them vipassana. *It is like a wire: Without wire, electricity cannot pass. The wire is concentration; the electricity is loving-kindness. We have to use concentration and send benefits with loving-kindness. You have a bank account, so I put something into your bank account to fill it. Like a candle, one gives light to another. Then the light is more and more. My light will not be reduced; it will be more and more. You also get more; I also get more. Sometimes when I meditate, I see your face in my mind. When I see your face, I want to see your face happy, I don't want you to be in trouble. So I'm sending, sending my merits: "Let it be good."*[26]

The One Million Monk Dhammakaya Temple in Thailand.

Mahayana: compassion and wisdom

Additional Buddhist practices and teachings began to appear in a wide range of scriptures from the early centuries CE. These further developments in thought and practice gradually evolved into what is called Mahayana, the Great Vehicle. The Mahayana scriptures emphasize the practice of compassion and wisdom by both monastics and laypeople, toward the goal of liberating all sentient beings from *dukkha*. The Mahayana traditions honor all the teachings set forth in the Pali Canon and, in addition, accept the extensive Mahayana literature originally found in Sanskrit and later translated into Chinese, Tibetan, and other languages, eventually leading to the development of canons for five different Mahayana schools. This literature praises the deeds and qualities of innumerable Buddhas and bodhisattvas, and inspires practitioners to develop the compassion and wisdom needed to become bodhisattvas and eventually Buddhas themselves.

The Mahayana scriptures emphasize the importance of religious experience. For the Mahayanist, the Dharma is the source of a transformative experience that awakens the quest for enlightenment as the greatest value in life and seeks to embody the Dharma in every aspect of life. Each of the many schools within Mahayana offers a special set of methods, or "skillful means," for awakening. These methods are quite varied, but the Mahayana traditions share many common characteristics. The Mahayana traditions also share many rituals and monastic practices with the Theravada school.

Bodhisattvas An early Mahayana scripture, the *Lotus Sutra*, defended its seemingly innovative ideas by claiming that earlier teachings were skillful means for those with lower capacities. The idea is that the Buddha geared his teaching to

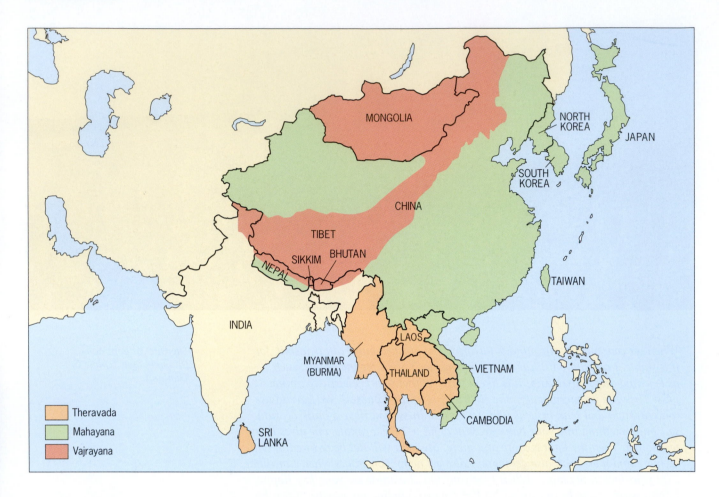

Map showing the approximate distribution of forms of Buddhism in the world today.

his audience, and that his teachings were presented in different ways and at different levels of completeness in accordance with the readiness of his audience to understand them.

One of the most significant new interpretations introduced by the *Lotus Sutra* regards the Eternal Buddha. According to the *Lotus Sutra*:

> *Common people believe that Buddha was born a prince and learned the way to Enlightenment as a mendicant; actually, Buddha has always existed in the world which is without beginning or end.*
>
> *As the Eternal Buddha, He has known all people and applied all methods of relief.*
>
> *There is no falsity in the Eternal Dharma which Buddha taught, for He knows all things in the world as they are, and He teaches them to all people. ...*
>
> *Buddha alone truly and fully knows the world as it is and He never says that it is true or false, or good or evil. He simply portrays the world as it is.*
>
> *What Buddha does teach is this: "That all people should cultivate roots of virtue according to their natures, their deeds, and their beliefs."*[27]

The *Lotus Sutra* and other new Mahayana scriptures also taught that there was a higher goal than the arhant's achievement of liberation, namely, to aspire to become a bodhisattva. Theravada Buddhists use the term bodhisattva to refer to the Buddha in his past lives and up to the time he attained enlightenment. Mahayana Buddhists speak of the bodhisattva as a being who has taken a vow to become fully enlightened in the future—a fully awakened Buddha—and who will assist others in their liberation as they work to complete their vow. The *Lotus Sutra* says that all beings have the capacity for Buddhahood and are destined to attain it eventually. Both monastics and laity are urged to take the bodhisattva vow and work to become fully enlightened. Today Mahayana Buddhists in East

Asia express this commitment in the Four Great Bodhisattva Vows compiled in China in the sixth century CE by Tiantai Zhiyi, founder of the Tiantai School:

Beings are infinite in number, I vow to save them all;
The obstructive passions are endless in number, I vow to end them all;
The teachings for saving others are countless, I vow to learn them all;
Buddhahood is the supreme achievement, I vow to attain it.

His Holiness the Fourteenth Dalai Lama, representing the Tibetan Buddhist tradition, says:

The motivation to achieve Buddhahood in order to save all sentient beings is really a marvelous determination. That person becomes very courageous, warm-hearted, and useful in society.[28]

Soen Nakagawa-roshi, from the Japanese Zen tradition, says:

You are not just here for yourself alone, but for the sake of all sentient beings. Keep your mind pure and warm.[29]

The concept of the selfless bodhisattva is not just an ideal for earthly conduct; numerous bodhisattvas are believed to be present and available to hear the devotees' petitions. As emanations of wisdom and compassion, they are sources of inspiration and blessing on the path to Buddhahood. For karmic purification and removal of inner obstructions to enlightenment and bodhisattvahood, aspirants are taught to practice the Ten Perfections (*Paramitas*): generosity, morality, renunciation, transcendental wisdom, energy and diligent effort, patience and forbearance, truthfulness, determination, loving kindness, and serene equanimity.

The most popular bodhisattva in East Asia is Avalokiteshvara (known as Guanyin in China, Kannon in Japan), who symbolizes compassion and extends blessings to all. Although he is depicted as male in India, the *Lotus Sutra* says that this bodhisattva takes whatever form is needed to help others, and lists thirty-two examples. In East Asia, Avalokiteshvara is typically depicted as female, often as the bestower or protector of young children. In one hand, she holds a vase with the nectar of compassion; in the other, she holds a willow branch symbolizing her healing powers. An image of the bodhisattva holding a baby has become especially popular in East Asia as a source of inspiration and blessing for women and children. She may also be depicted standing serenely atop a dragon in a turbulent ocean. The storm-tossed ocean and dragon are symbols of the upheavals of life and within our minds. Guanyin is therefore a model of the inner strength, equilibrium, and self-control with which these turbulences can be mastered.

Guanyin, "hearer of cries," bodhisattva of mercy, as depicted in statues in a Hong Kong temple.

Many Buddhists anticipate the coming of Maitreya, the Buddha of the future, to re-establish the purity of the Dharma. This statue of Maitreya is in Thiksi Monastery, Ladakh.

The Three Bodies of Buddha The Theravada tradition emphasizes that the Buddha is an historical figure who taught the Dharma as a guide to liberation from suffering, then died like any other human being, leaving behind a body of teachings. By contrast, in the Mahayana tradition, the Buddha came to be regarded as the embodiment of enlightened awareness. Metaphysically, the Buddha is said to be an immanent presence in the universe with three aspects, or "bodies." The first aspect is the formless enlightened wisdom of a Buddha; the second is the body of bliss of a Buddha, an aspect that communicates the Dharma to bodhisattvas; and the third is the

Jizo is a much-loved bodhisattva in Japan. One of his new forms is Mizuko Jizo, the guardian of unborn, stillborn, aborted, and miscarried babies, whose parents seek his protection for them by adorning small Jizo statues.

emanation body, whereby a Buddha manifests in countless forms to help liberate suffering beings. It was in such an emanation body that the Buddha appeared for a time on the earth as the historical figure Shakyamuni Buddha.

In Mahayana, the Buddhas are seen to embody perfect purity, boundless compassion, omniscient wisdom, and many other enlightened qualities. Although some may interpret the Buddhas and bodhisattvas as metaphors for various aspects of enlightened awareness, others regard them as living presences that are able to impart blessings and guidance to those who call on them. Both Theravada and Mahayana are nontheistic, in that the existence or nonexistence of gods is not a primary concern, yet ordinary people are inclined to seek help from them in times of need.

Mahayana scriptures portray Buddhas and bodhisattvas moving swiftly through intergalactic space and time, appearing in multiple forms at different world systems simultaneously. In the Tibetan tradition, for example, the Fourteenth Dalai Lama is regarded as a human emanation of Avalokiteshvara, the bodhisattva of compassion. Many Tibetan monks, nuns, and laypeople followed him into exile after the communist takeover of Tibet and have set up a community in the mountains of northern India, in Dharamsala, to be near him. Practitioners are not to be attached to these appearances, but receive teachings and draw great inspiration from them.

Emptiness As in Theravada, the Mahayana schools understand ultimate reality as the true nature of things. This "suchness" is not an absolute, but the absence of a permanent, independent reality. In accordance with the universal law of cause and effect, all conditioned phenomena arise and perish continuously, and therefore lack true existence. In the Udana scripture from the Pali Canon, the Buddha states, "O monks, there is an unborn, undying, unchanging, uncreated. If it were not so, there would be no point to life, or to training." But here the Buddha is referring to nirvana, a nonregressive state of liberation from mental afflictions, suffering, and rebirth, rather than to an eternal, independently existing reality.

Shunyata, meaning emptiness or voidness, is the most complex and profound of the Mahayana teachings. The concept of shunyata was elaborated by the Indian philosopher Nagarjuna around the second and third century CE on the basis of the Perfection of Wisdom scriptures. According to Nagarjuna, compounded things have no independent existence and no eternal reality. All composite phenomena arise and pass away, dependent on causes and conditions. The world of phenomena is therefore empty of true or inherent existence, even though we may mistakenly experience the world as real in everyday, conventional life. Nagarjuna wrote that while on the conventional level, the Four Noble Truths are real, for *dukkha* is a part of human life, on the ultimate level even the Four Noble Truths are empty, devoid of any inherent or permanent existence. Insight into emptiness is similar to the insight into no-self that arises when we observe the arising and passing away of the elements of mind and body during vipassana meditation. Insight into emptiness also arises by understanding the dependent nature of thought constructs and freeing our minds from fixed concepts.

Everything being empty, there is nothing to cling to, so one who realizes emptiness is free to experience reality directly and to be compassionate without attachment. The concepts of selflessness and emptiness help practitioners understand things "as they are" and also help them overcome attachment to things, including attachment to concepts.

Some people may wonder: If everything is ultimately empty, what is the point of action? The teaching on emptiness does not mean we do nothing, but that we are not attached to the results of our actions. Emptiness is always paired with compassion, skillful means, and the wish to benefit all living beings. Zen teacher Dainin Katagiri advised:

> Broadly speaking, without desire, how can we survive in this world? Using our knowledge, we consider carefully what to do next. And then whatever we decide to do, let's just do it, do our best to accomplish it from the beginning to the end. That's all we have to do. Immediately, see the result and accept it. Just continue to sow good seeds from moment to moment.[30]

The Perfection of Wisdom scriptures that celebrate the liberating experience of emptiness are foundational texts for most Mahayana schools. What is distinctive and startling about Mahayana is the application of the idea of emptiness to all things. Even the teachings of the Buddha and emptiness itself are empty of true existence. In the *Heart Sutra*, which is recited in all Mahayana schools, the core doctrines of traditional Buddhism are also deconstructed. Avalokiteshvara sees that the five aggregates of a person (form, feelings, perceptions, karmic formations, and consciousness) are empty of true existence, because they exist in relation to and dependent on other phenomena. With this realization, the bodhisattva becomes free of delusion. Next, birth and death, purity and defilement, increase and decrease are understood to be empty; the six sense objects, the six sense organs, and the six types of consciousness are empty; life and death are empty; the Four Noble Truths and Eightfold Path are empty. Even knowledge and attainment are proclaimed to be empty. With this "perfection of wisdom," there are no obstacles and no fear. Having seen through the illusion of true existence of even the core Buddhist teachings, one attains nirvana. In the *Heart Sutra*, this realization culminates in the mantra: *Gate, Gate, paragate, parasamgate, bodhi, svaha!* ("Gone, gone, gone beyond, gone completely beyond, awakened, so be it!"). As Professor David Chappell observed:

> The systematic emptying of the central doctrines of the tradition is unparalleled in religious history. (Imagine a Christian saying that the Ten Commandments and Lord's Prayer and Apostles' Creed are empty!) And yet, insight into the impermanence of all things, and their connectedness, gives Mahayana a self-critical profundity and an inclusive acceptance of diversity, which provides balance in the midst of movement, and peace in the midst of compassion.[31]

Mahayana in East Asia
What Mahayana schools developed in East Asia?

Buddhism was transmitted from India to China beginning around the first century CE and thence to Korea, Japan, and Vietnam. The major schools of East Asian Buddhism are part of the Mahayana branch. Many of these schools have also absorbed elements from other East Asian religions, such as Daoism, Korean shamanic practices, and Shinto.

Chan and Zen: the great way of enlightenment

Around the fifth century CE, according to tradition, a South Indian monk named Bodhidharma traveled to a monastery in northern China, where he reportedly spent nine years in silent meditation, "facing the wall." He became recognized as the first patriarch of the radical path that came to be called Chan Buddhism, from the Sanskrit word *dhyana*, meaning meditation. Although traditional accounts of Bodhidharma's life and contributions may not be completely factual, they illustrate the emphasis on meditation and direct insight that characterize the Mahayana school of Chan Buddhism, which became the most successful form of Buddhism in China. Bodhidharma's legendary practice became emblematic of a firm determination to reach enlightenment through sitting meditation. In lines attributed to Bodhidharma, Chan Buddhism is described as:

> *Directly pointing to the human mind,*
> *Achieving Buddhahood by seeing one's nature.*[32]

The Chan school was transmitted to Japan, where it is known as **Zen**. Zen claims to preserve the essence of the Buddha's teachings through direct experience, triggered by mind-to-mind transmission of the Dharma. Instead of focusing on scriptures, Buddhas, and bodhisattvas, Zen emphasizes direct insight into the true nature of one's own mind, to reveal one's own Buddha nature. Direct insight results from **zazen** (sitting meditation). "To sit," said the Sixth Zen Patriarch, "means to obtain absolute freedom and not to allow any thought to be caused by external objects. To meditate means to realize the imperturbability of one's original nature."[33]

A 16th-century Zen rock garden with raked gravel in the Daitoki-Ji temple complex in Kyoto. The garden is to be contemplated as a miniature and symbolic landscape of mountains, islands, land, and sea.

The Great Way is not difficult
for those who have no preferences.
When love and hate are both absent
everything becomes clear and undisguised.
Make the smallest distinction, however,
and heaven and earth are set infinitely apart.

Sengtsan[34]

In Zen, instructions in the manner of sitting are quite rigorous to avoid distracting the mind: One must maintain an upright posture and not move during the meditation period. Skillful means are then applied to make the mind one-pointed and clear. The initial practice is simply to watch and count each inhalation and exhalation from one to ten, starting over from one if anything other than awareness of the breath enters the mind. Although this practice sounds simple, the mind is so restless that many people must work for months before finally getting to ten without having to start over. Getting to ten is not really the goal; the goal is the process itself, the process of recognizing what comes up in the mind and gently letting it go without attachment or preferences.

As one practices zazen, undisturbed by phenomena, one becomes inwardly calm and the natural mind is revealed in its original purity. This "original mind" is spacious and free, like an open sky. Thoughts and sensations may float through it like clouds, but they then disappear, leaving no trace. What remains

Major Branches of Buddhism

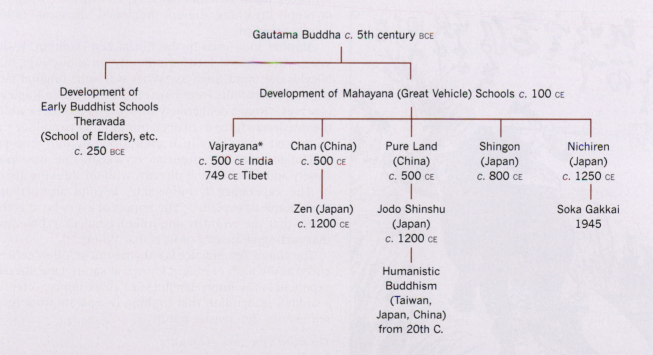

Gautama Buddha *c.* 5th century BCE

Development of
Early Buddhist Schools
Theravada
(School of Elders), etc.
c. 250 BCE

Development of Mahayana (Great Vehicle) Schools *c.* 100 CE

Vajrayana*
c. 500 CE India
749 CE Tibet

Chan (China)
c. 500 CE

Pure Land
(China)
c. 500 CE

Shingon
(Japan)
c. 800 CE

Nichiren
(Japan)
c. 1250 CE

Zen (Japan)
c. 1200 CE

Jodo Shinshu
(Japan)
c. 1200 CE

Soka Gakkai
1945

Humanistic
Buddhism
(Taiwan,
Japan, China)
from 20th C.

* Although some scholars classify Vajrayana as a form of Mahayana Buddhism, many consider it a separate branch.

The tea ceremony in Japan is a ritual way of inculcating direct awareness, simplicity, and self-restraint.

In the 12th century, Chinese Chan (Japanese Zen) masters developed a series of ten images that suggest the seeker's path to enlightenment. The image of an ox is used to represent the untamed mind. In this, the sixth image of the series, the seeker has found and tamed the ox—a metaphor for spiritual practice—and now comfortably rides upon it, playing his flute.

is insight into "thusness," the true nature of things. In some Zen schools, this perception of thusness comes in a sudden burst of insight, or *kensho*.

When the mind is calm, action becomes spontaneous and natural. Zen practitioners are taught to rest in the natural simplicity of their own **Buddha-nature**. It is said that two Zen monks, on gaining a glimpse of enlightenment, ran naked through the woods scribbling on rocks. On the other hand, the Zen tradition links spontaneity with intense, disciplined concentration. In the art of calligraphy, the perfectly spontaneous brushstroke is executed with the whole body in a single breath, yet this is the outcome of years of attentive practice. Being fully present in the moment—when pouring tea, being aware only of pouring tea—is simplicity itself. Whether painting, serving tea, sweeping, or simply breathing, the unconditioned "thusness" of life is fully revealed.

Another tool, used in the Rinzai Zen tradition, is the **koan**. Attention is focused ardently on a question that boggles the mind, such as "What was your original face before your parents were born?" As Roshi Philip Kapleau observes, "Koans deliberately throw sand into the eyes of the intellect to force us to open our Mind's eye and see the world and everything in it undistorted by our concepts and judgments." To concentrate on a koan, one must look closely and experience it directly, without thinking about it. The experience is immediate, beyond abstractions. Roshi Kapleau explains, "The import of every koan is the same: that the world is one interdependent Whole and that each separate one of us is that Whole."[35]

The aim of Zen practice is enlightenment, often experienced as the flash of insight known as **satori**. One directly experiences the interrelatedness of all existence, often in a sudden recognition that nothing is separate from oneself. As one Zen master put it:

The moon's the same old moon,
The flowers exactly as they were,
Yet I've become the thingness
Of all the things I see![36]

All aspects of life become, at the same time, utterly precious and utterly empty, "nothing special." This paradox cannot be grasped intellectually; it can only be realized through direct intuitive awareness.

Pure Land: devotion to Amitabha Buddha

Chan/Zen is a practice of inner awareness with close attention given to every action and requires years of disciplined meditation. Other forms of Buddhist practice developed in India and East Asia that had greater appeal. One of the most popular Buddhist Mahayana schools in East Asia is **Pure Land** Buddhism. At times of great social upheaval (for instance, when the government became corrupt and society was falling apart), it was widely thought that people had become so degenerate that it was nearly impossible for them to attain enlightenment through their own efforts.

Under the circumstances, many became devoted to Amitabha Buddha, the Buddha of Boundless Light. It was believed that Amitabha (**Amida** in Japanese) was previously a prince who vowed to attain enlightenment. After he did so, he used his pure virtue to manifest a Pure Land of Bliss for all those who called his name. In Japan, the original abstract Indian Buddhist concept of a Pure Land in the west to which devotees return after death became more concrete. The Japanese had an ancient tradition of worshiping mountains as destinations which the dead ascend and from which deities descend to earth. They began to depict Amida riding on billowing clouds over the mountains and welcoming his dying devotees.

Amida Buddha (center) depicted beyond the mountains, ready to welcome dying devotees to the Pure Land.

Jodo Shinshu: the True Pure Land In the thirteenth century, the Japanese monk Shinran broke with monastic tradition by marrying. He emphasized the principle that salvation comes through repeating the name of Amida Buddha—the *nembutsu*, *"Namu-amida-butsu"*—with sincere trust and devotion, not by separating oneself from society. The Jodo Shinshu, or "True Pure Land," school developed by Shrinran's followers became a major Buddhist movement throughout the world. Unlike other Buddhist sects in Japan, it did not mix its beliefs with those of Shinto, nor did its practitioners accept donations for prayers and blessings. It became the most popular form of Buddhism practiced in Japan. It is the most popular Buddhist school among Japanese immigrants and their descendants in North America, with well-established communities also in Europe, Australia, and Africa.

Nichiren: salvation through the *Lotus Sutra*

While some Buddhists in Japan despaired of achieving enlightenment through their own efforts and therefore relied on the grace of Amida Buddha, others stressed the importance of striving to enlighten not only ourselves but also society. One example was a thirteenth-century fisherman's son who named himself Nichiren. For Nichiren, the highest truths of Buddhism were embodied in the *Lotus Sutra*'s compilation of parables, verses, and descriptions of innumerable beings who practiced the Buddha's teachings. Nichiren gave particular attention to two of these beings: the Bodhisattva of Superb Action, who staunchly devotes himself to spreading the Perfect Truth, and the Bodhisattva Ever-Abused, who is persecuted because of his insistence, with unshaken conviction, that each person is potentially a Buddha. Nichiren himself was repeatedly abused by the authorities, but persisted in his efforts to reform Buddhism in Japan and spread what he considered its purified essence, the bodhisattva ideal, to the world. The phrase chanted by Nichiren and his followers, *"Namu myoho rengekyo,"* pays homage to the *Lotus Sutra*. Today it is chanted by Nichiren monks, nuns, and laypeople for hours. The chant is thought to slowly reveal the profound meaning of the *Lotus Sutra* and to work inwardly, beyond thought.

In our time, some Nichiren followers undertake long peace walks. In one peace effort sponsored by Nipponzan Myohoji in 1995, people walked from Auschwitz in Poland to Hiroshima and Nagasaki in Japan, to commemorate the fiftieth anniversary of the end of World War II, making a plea for nonviolence and respect for all of life. They beat hand-drums while chanting *"Namu myoho rengekyo,"* and bowed to the Buddha in each person they met, whether friendly or not, as a contribution to world peace. The founder of Nipponzan Myohoji, the Most Venerable Nichidatsu Fujii, strongly influenced Gandhi's doctrine of nonviolence. Before he passed away in 1985 at the age of 100, he explained:

> *We do not believe that people are good because we see that they are good, but by believing that people are good we eliminate our own fear and thus we can intimately associate with them. To believe in the compassionate power of the Supreme Being which we cannot see is a discipline in order to believe in the invisible good in others.*[37]
>
> *Civilization has nothing to do with having electric lights, airplanes, or manufacturing atomic bombs. It has nothing to do with killing human beings, destroying things or waging war. Civilization is to hold one another in mutual affection and respect.*[38]

The chanting of *"Namu myoho rengekyo"* has led to more than seventy Peace Pagodas being built in many countries, with donated materials and labor, by people of all faiths who pray for world peace and the elimination of all weapons.

Soka Gakkai International is another important offshoot of Nichiren's movement, which is based in Japan but has millions of members around the world. Its founders call for a peaceful world revolution through transformation of individual consciousness. They combine the central practice of chanting *"Nam myoho*

An Interview with Naoyuki Ogi

Naoyuki Ogi is a young writer and translator now working in Tokyo at a society dedicated to propagating the teachings of Buddha. He is very kind and generous in devoting his time and energy to help others. He explains:

I'm in the fourteenth generation of a Buddhist family. I was born in the temple family of Choshoji temple. All my ancestors were Buddhist priests. In ten years when I'm forty I will be the abbot of my temple. I want to have a good relationship with the members. I want to help them realize the good life and the truth in life, and I will try to ease their suffering. I want to make the temple the center of the community. That's my dream.

When Japan faced a financial crisis, everybody had to save their money. People couldn't go abroad. But then they realized: We don't need to go outside, because we have such a rich culture in our country.

To me, Amida Buddha is the invisible supporting Power. My experience goes back to my childhood. I loved my grandmother. It's because of her that I encountered the teaching of Buddha. She passed away when I was only ten years old. I was so sad. A guy came to greet me. He said, "You know how to greet, how to speak, how to sit up straight, just like your grandmother." Then I realized how Buddha's teachings light our lives. Buddha's power, Buddha's light may be an invisible support in my life, in my kindness.

I don't ask Amida Buddha for anything for myself. I just give appreciation. I say, "I give thanks for the teaching of Buddha. I thank you for helping my life, supporting my life." That's the meaning of reciting the name of Amida Buddha which originally means immeasurable life and light.

I have a small Buddhist altar in my room. Every morning and every evening before going to bed, I recite the name of Amida Buddha and express my appreciation by saying "Namu Amida Butsu" (I take refuge in Amida Buddha). In the morning I say, "Thank you very much for making me alive this morning," and then I try to live that day with gratitude as much as possible. And then before going to bed, I try to reflect on myself. Sometimes I'm so selfish, so I try to be selfless for the next day.

I can be called a Buddhist priest. When I was twenty years old, I went to Nishiyama Betsuin temple to get the qualification of Buddhist priest of Jodo Shinshu (Shin Buddhist) tradition. I shaved my hair and I got ordained. On special occasions—such as memorial services or funerals—I wear ceremonial robes for rituals, but usually I don't, because now I am working as a businessman.

Almost 100 families belong to my temple in my hometown. That means probably at least 300 people are supporting my temple, so I have to take care of them—by rituals, by counseling. For me they're not just members of the temple, they're more like family. But it is difficult for temple families to support themselves in the countryside because of the depopulation of their villages. In Japan, temple income depends on donations from temple members. This tradition used to be taken over by the next generations, but young people started to move to big cities like Tokyo to get jobs, discarding their agriculture-related family works. They do not come back to their hometown and do not care about any Buddhist tradition. Countryside temples are losing members, and many temples might be closed in the future. Since my temple is quite small and doesn't have many members, my parents have to work outside the temple to financially support and renovate the dilapidated temple. However, they share the teachings of Shinran in their jobs and in the communities they serve, and many people have come to trust them and often visit my temple to get advice and support from my parents when trouble arises. As the fourteenth-generation abbot of my temple, I want to spend my time serving the people of my area by sharing the message of Buddha. However, in order to financially support my temple, I am going to establish a Buddhist translation company.

Today people are very busy, but they need more time to reflect on themselves. They need more invisible body. Before the earthquake, people just depended on materialism. Material results were everything to them. After the earthquake, they came to depend more on the invisible body—on kindness, on spiritual stuff. I think they need time to reflect on themselves through spiritual practice. Also they need to cultivate their spiritual thoughts, their spiritual ideas, because that may be helpful for them when they face a lot of problems. They have to train their hearts.

Because of Buddha's teachings, my heart has changed a lot. I want to share this wonderful experience with everybody, so that other people might be able to experience what I received. What changed with Buddha's teaching is that now I'm not thinking about myself. I think more about others. I realized that everybody is interconnected. We are not alone. That's why I want to help open other people's blind eyes, so they may realize how wonderful a life we are living.[39]

rengekyo" with modern social activism in areas such as humanitarian relief, environmental awareness, human rights, literacy, and cultural and interfaith exchanges. Members are encouraged to develop their "unlimited potential" for hope, courage, and altruism.

Another new branch of Buddhism inspired by the *Lotus Sutra* is Rissho Kosei-kai, founded in Japan in the 1930s by Rev. Nikkyo Niwano and Myoko Naganuma. They sought to bring the message of the *Lotus Sutra* to the world in practical ways in order to encourage happiness and peace. Members chant the *Lotus Sutra* every day, skip a meal several times a month and donate the money for aid and peace projects, and meet twice a month in circles to discuss ways of applying the Buddha's teachings to specific problems in their own lives. Based on the *Lotus Sutra*'s understanding of the Eternal Buddha as the "great life-force of the universe,"[40] Rissho Kosei-kai tries to co-operate with people and organizations of other religions. Its mission statement asserts:

> *Truth is universal and all religions are manifestations of it. All life springs from the same source, and thus all people are related and belong to one family. The* Lotus Sutra *declares that everyone is inherently imbued with the bodhisattva wish.*[41]

The organization therefore is very active in international inter-religious activities.

> *The Bodhisattva loves all living beings as if each were his only child.*
>
> *Vimalakirtinirdesha Sutra 5*

Vajrayana: the indestructible path
How does Vajrayana differ from Theravada and Mahayana Buddhism?

Although some scholars classify it as a form of Mahayana Buddhism, many consider Vajrayana a separate branch. Followers of Vajrayana call it the "third turning" of the wheel of Dharma (with the early schools that included Theravada being the first, and the Mahayana schools the second). Vajrayana developed in India, was transmitted to Tibet, and has also historically been practiced in Nepal, Bhutan, Sikkim, and Mongolia. Currently it is practiced throughout the Tibetan diaspora and increasingly in North America and Europe, where it is one of the most popular forms of Buddhism practiced by Westerners.

Prior to the introduction of Buddhism from India, the mountainous Tibetan region was home to a shamanic religion called Bön. In the seventh century CE a particularly powerful Tibetan king named Songtsan became interested in Buddhism and sent a group of students to India to study it. The journey from Tibet to India was extremely difficult and many of these emissaries died in the searing heat of the Indian plains. Only one member of a second group survived the arduous trip across the Himalayas, returning with many Sanskrit texts. After some of these works were translated into Tibetan, Songtsan declared Buddhism the national religion and encouraged Buddhist virtues in his subjects. Bön proponents are said to have sabotaged the new religion, until finally a tantric adept, Padmasambhava, was invited to Tibet in the eighth century CE. Eventually, it is said, Guru Padmasambhava subdued and converted the local Bön deities and, along with his consort Yeshe Tsogyal, firmly established Buddhist teachings in Tibet. Although the Tibetans' understanding of Buddhism was no doubt influenced by earlier beliefs, and elements such as the use of prayer flags and an emphasis on practices for the dying may reflect Bön concerns, the Tibetans spent many centuries attempting to understand the Indian Buddhist teachings as purely as possible.

RELIGION IN PUBLIC LIFE

His Holiness the Dalai Lama

Surely one of the best known and most loved spiritual leaders in the world, His Holiness the Fourteenth Dalai Lama is a striking example of Buddhist peace and compassion. Wherever he goes, he greets everyone with evident delight. Even when addressing an audience of thousands, he looks around the hall with a broad, childlike grin, which seems directed to each person individually. His example is all the more powerful because he is the leader in exile of Tibet, a small nation that experienced extreme oppression and suffering during the twentieth and twenty-first centuries.

The simplicity of His Holiness's words and bearing belie his intellectual power. His Holiness was a peasant child just two years old in 1937 when he was located and carefully identified as the reincarnation of the thirteenth Dalai Lama. He was formally installed as the fourteenth Dalai Lama when he was only four and a half years old, thus becoming the spiritual and temporal ruler of Tibet. He was raised and rigorously educated in the Potala in Lhasa, capital of Tibet. One of the world's largest buildings, with more than 1,000 rooms, the Potala contained large ceremonial halls, thirty-five chapels, meditation cells, government storehouses, national treasures, a complete record of Tibetan history and culture in 7,000 volumes, plus thousands of illuminated volumes of the Buddhist scriptures. The young Dalai Lama was educated according to the traditional Tibetan Buddhist system, which stressed an extensive and profound method for developing the mind to acquire many kinds of knowledge and also to practice advanced Buddhist meditation techniques.

Such a rigorous grounding in religious education and practice, maintains the Dalai Lama, brings steadiness of mind in the face of any misfortunes. He says:

Humanitarianism and true love for all beings can only stem from an awareness of the content of religion. By whatever name religion may be known, its understanding and practice are the essence of a peaceful mind and therefore of a peaceful world. If there is no peace in one's mind, there can be no peace in one's approach to others, and thus no peaceful relations between individuals or between nations.[42]

The Dalai Lama's equanimity of mind was seriously challenged by the Chinese invasion and oppression of his small country. In 1959, when he escaped from Tibet to India in hopes of preventing bloodshed during a widespread popular revolt against the Chinese, Tibet was home to more than 6,000 monasteries. Only twelve of them were still intact by 1980. It is said that at least one million Tibetans died as a direct result of the Chinese occupation. Violence and suppression of the religion, culture, and people of Tibet continue today as millions of Chinese settlers fill the country.

In the face of the overwhelming military power of the Chinese, and armed with Buddhist precepts, the Dalai Lama has persistently tried to steer his people away from violent response to violence. Asserting that "Non-violence is the only way. … It's a slower process sometimes, but a very effective one," he explains:

Practically speaking, through violence we may achieve something, but at the expense of someone else's welfare. That way, although we may solve one problem, we simultaneously seed a new problem. The best way to solve problems is through human understanding, mutual respect. On one side make some concessions; on the other side take serious consideration about the problem. There may not be complete satisfaction, but something happens. At least future danger is avoided. Non-violence is very safe.[43]

The Dalai Lama has been an enthusiastic advocate for dialogue between religious practitioners and scientists, particularly with respect to efforts to study the effects of meditation and other spiritual practices. While slowly, patiently trying to influence world opinion so that the voice of Tibet will not be extinguished by Chinese might, the Dalai Lama has established an entire government in exile in Dharamsala, India, in the Himalayas. There he and Tibetan refugees have built schools, orphanages, hospitals, craft co-operatives, farming communities, monasteries, libraries, and institutes for preserving traditional music, drama, dance, painting, and medicine. From this base, he has traveled tirelessly around the world in an effort to keep the voice of Tibet alive. Although he relinquished his role as political leader in 2011, he remains the spiritual leader of Tibetan Buddhists and is recognized as one of the greatest moral leaders of our time. His quintessentially Buddhist message to people of all religions is that only through kindness and compassion toward each other and the cultivation of inner peace shall we survive as a species.

A senior Tibetan Buddhist nun teaches a complicated mudra to a young nun in Zanskar in the Indian Himalayas.

The Indian Buddhism that was transmitted to Tibet included elements of tantra—ancient esoteric teachings and practices that could have been in existence in India since before 2500 BCE. These ways emphasize visualization, ritual, mantras, mudras (hand positions during meditation), mandalas (sacred diagrams), and union of male and female energies for spiritual liberation, all under the strict guidance of a teacher. Lay Buddhists picked up these practices not only to invoke the aid of celestial Buddhas and bodhisattvas but also to help in spiritual awakening and attainment of Buddhahood.

As Indian Buddhism was carried to Tibet, there was a period of decline in the tenth century CE, when some misinterpreted the tantric teachings. A teacher named Atisha was invited from the great center of Buddhist learning at Nalanda, India, to set things right. Under Atisha, Tibetan Buddhism became a complex path with three stages, said to have been prescribed by the Buddha. The first stage is quieting the mind and relinquishing attachments through meditation practice, as emphasized in the early Buddhist teachings. The second stage is intensive training in compassion and wisdom, as emphasized in the Mahayana teachings. The third stage is the advanced esoteric path called Vajrayana (the diamond vehicle) or **Tantrayana**, a rigorous, accelerated path to nurture enlightenment within a single lifetime.

Vajrayana aspirants are guided through a series of tantric practices by qualified teachers, or **lamas**. Some of these teachers are recognized as incarnate bodhisattvas and are carefully trained from a young age to help others advance toward enlightenment.

> *The masses have their heads on backwards. If you want to get things right, first look at how they think and behave, and consider going the opposite way.*[44]
>
> *Lama Drom Tonpa, eleventh century*

Vajrayana initiates practice **deity yoga**: meditating on themselves in the form of a Buddha or bodhisattva in order to embody the enlightened qualities that the practitioner wishes to manifest. These radiant forms are themselves imagined and therefore lacking true existence, but meditating on them is considered a

Death rites in Tibetan Buddhism

Venerable Tenzin Dadon, a Bhutanese nun, describes traditions surrounding death in the Tibetan Buddhist tradition:

Traditionally Tibetan Buddhists have not celebrated birthdays. People don't even know their birth date; they only know the year. Now, however, many young people have picked up Western ways and are expecting that their birthdays be celebrated. But according to the traditions, people's death anniversaries are celebrated rather than their birth anniversaries.

When a dying person is almost going, a high lama, a monk or nun, or if they're not available, a lay practitioner is brought to read The Tibetan Book of the Dead *into the ear of the person. The book is read part by part every day for forty-nine days following the death to guide the deceased. When the book is read, it tells the person not to be afraid, and to know that it is because of our own mental delusions that we seem to see darkness or ghosts or lights of different colors. It also tells them which color of light to follow. Some colors of light will take the deceased toward hell, others toward animal birth, others toward the realms of gods and semi-gods, etc.*

People also prepare themselves for death while they are living by practicing phowa—*transference of consciousness. It not only helps us, but by practicing it we are also able to help those who are passing away. We visualize the Buddha Amitabha above our crown and visualize ourselves in* dakini *[a female deity who transmits wisdom about secret teachings] form. We visualize that our consciousness lies in the heart of the* dakini. *We eject our consciousness through our crown up to the Buddha, through his feet and up to his heart. If we are doing this for ourself, we then bring it back into ourselves, and then back up to his heart, which is transferring consciousness. If we are doing it for the dying person or one who has just passed away, we visualize them as a* dakini *(also with the Buddha Amitabha above our crown); the only difference is we don't visualize their consciousness coming back again. If we have practiced* phowa *our whole life, then when we are dying we don't have to worry. We eject our consciousness to Amitabha Buddha, and this is how people go very peacefully.*

When a person is dying we don't let people touch them because we want the consciousness to leave through the crown. Otherwise the consciousness will be drawn somewhere else. I always carry around my neck a vial with a little bit of sand from a sand mandala to put on the person's crown at the time of death. Or sometimes people will pull a hair from the top of the crown to draw the consciousness there. When the outer breath is gone—the clinical death—the person has not yet died. It takes a few hours for the inner breath to go.

During the first forty-nine days after a death, in addition to reading from The Tibetan Book of the Dead, *people pray every seven days for the consciousness because every seven days it passes away again and looks for a place to be reborn. If it doesn't get rebirth, it stays in the Bardo, an intermediate state. Up until the forty-ninth day, the family pray and offer butter lamps, give charity, and do many good actions to show the dead one the proper path to a better rebirth. Buddhahood is the ultimate goal, otherwise to be reborn in Buddha Amitabha Pure Land, and if not at least in precious human rebirth. On the forty-ninth day, the lama will burn the name of the person and the painted photo of that person, to help them understand that they have passed away, to separate their consciousness from the body, and to ask them to leave their relatives.*

When a person dies, we don't encourage crying and mourning by the relatives. If the people do that the consciousness will not be able to see anything, will not be able to find the path, and will have a lot of anger and fear. Our prayers are like the sun, and the butter lamps also help to light the way for them to the right path. If they are peaceful, they will be able to think of the good deeds they have done when they were living. If instead there is quarreling among the family after they die, they see all that. They will feel lots of anger and hatred, which will lead to a lower rebirth. They can see everything, but they can't touch us or feel us as they are formless. We must be very quiet and peaceful at their death so that their mind is not disturbed

Each year after the death for at least three years, monks and nuns and higher lamas are invited to the home. They do a lot of prayers and offer butter lamps. They make an image of the deceased person, and when they offer food we mention the person by name. We believe that once people have passed away, their consciousness will travel nine times faster and they are nine times more intelligent than in life. We only have to mention their name, and they will be there.[45]

One of the most beloved of Tibetan Buddhist deities is Tara. She is savior and mother of the world; she protects us and helps us to achieve our spiritual longings. (Detail of Tibetan thangka, 18th/19th century, tempera on cotton.)

way to understand one's own true nature. Some of these meditational deities are shown in wrathful form, such as Mahakala, defender of the Dharma, while others, such as Tara, are shown in peaceful form.

The highest Vajrayana practices use the subtle vital energies of the body to transform the mind. A very subtle and profound state of consciousness is produced after lengthy practice; when the "gross mind" is neutralized, the "subtle mind" manifests powerfully as "the clear light of bliss." This innermost subtle mind of clear light is the true empty quality of one's own mind. Once it is realized, one is said to be capable of attaining Buddhahood in a single lifetime. The Seventh Dalai Lama of Tibet (1708–1757) gave this perspective:

Even the most seemingly evil person has the primordial clear light mind at the heart of his or her existence. Eventually the clouds of distortion and delusion will be cleared away as the being grows in wisdom, and the evil behavior that emanates from these negative mindsets will naturally evaporate. That being will realize the essential nature of his or her own mind, and achieve spiritual liberation and enlightenment.[46]

The practices used to transform the mind are also believed to enable supernormal powers such as levitation, clairvoyance, meditating continuously without sleep, and warming the body from within while sitting naked in the snow. Milarepa, the famous Tibetan poet-saint, whose enlightenment was won through great austerities, once sang this song:

*Blissful within, I don't entertain
The notion "I'm suffering,"
When incessant rain is pouring outside.*

*Even on peaks of white snow mountains
Amidst swirling snow and sleet
Driven by new year's wintry winds
This cotton robe burns like fire.*[47]

One of the highest practitioners of tantric Vajrayana was a woman, Yeshe Tsogyel, the consort of Padmasambhava, the powerful tantric adept who had helped bring Buddhism to Tibet. According to a semihistorical biography written by an eighteenth-century tantric monk, Yeshe Tsogyel was very beautiful but wanted only a life of spiritual seeking. Her father nonetheless sent her out to be grabbed by rival suitors, from whom she escaped, but she was ultimately taken by the king. As the king's greatest desire was for spiritual liberation, he offered her to Padmasambhava in exchange for his precious spiritual guidance. The two, Padmasambhava and Yeshe Tsogyel, were said to have practiced tantra together in a remote cave, developing their extraordinary spiritual powers in an "ecstatic dance of delight." Eventually Yeshe Tsogyel went alone to practice severe austerities on the edge of a glacier, where she faced the intense wind and cold without any clothing or food. When she returned to Padmasambhava after a year, he reportedly said:

*O yogini who has mastered the Tantra,
The human body is the basis of the accomplishment of wisdom
And the gross bodies of men and women are equally suited,
But if a woman has strong aspiration, she has higher potential.*[48]

For centuries, Vajrayana was highly developed in Tibet, with an estimated 100,000 monks and nuns by the early twentieth century. However, communist Chinese overran Tibet between 1950 and 1959, destroying countless ancient monasteries and scriptures and killing an estimated one-sixth of the population over decades of occupation. The beloved Fourteenth Dalai Lama, spiritual and political leader of Tibet, escaped to India in 1959. The town of Dharamsala in the mountains of northern India where he established his headquarters has become

Tibetan Buddhists' full-length prostrations are so arduous that many have to strap on wooden pads and canvas shields to protect their bodies.

a magnet for spiritual seekers. Despite persecution, religious practice and meaning still pervade every aspect of Tibetan life, from house-raising to fervent pilgrimages. Monks and laypeople alike meditate on *thangkas* and **mandalas**, visual aids to concentration and illumination, which portray Buddhas and bodhisattvas and representations of an ideal universe. A favorite practice is the chanting of mantras, especially *"Om mani padme hum,"* the mantra of Avalokiteshvara, the bodhisattva of compassion. This mantra evokes an awareness of the sufferings of sentient beings in different states of existence and compassion for all living beings from within the heart of each of us. To help manifest this compassion, mantras are repeatedly recited, written thousands of times, spun in prayer wheels, and printed on prayer flags so that the blessings of the mantra extend in all directions as they blow in the wind. In addition to Tibet, Vajrayana is practiced throughout the Himalayan region and beyond: in Nepal, Bhutan, Sikkim, Ladakh, Mongolia, and parts of Russia. Tibetan lamas in exile have also spread the Tibetan Buddhist tradition to Western countries, Southeast Asia, and Taiwan, where it has gained many adherents.

Buddhist festivals

How do the different forms of Buddhism celebrate the Buddha's life?

Since Buddhism has evolved into different forms in different countries, most of its festivals are not uniformly celebrated. The most important Buddhist festival is *Vesak*, which according to Theravadins marks the Buddha's birth, enlightenment, and death, all of which were said to have miraculously occurred on the same day. For Mahayana Buddhists, *Vesak* marks the day of the Buddha's enlightenment. Vajrayana Buddhists celebrate four distinct days commemorating the Buddha's conception, birth, enlightenment, and death. According to the lunar calendar, the Buddha is said to have been born on the full moon of the month *Vaisakha*, the second month of the Indian calendar, which falls in April and May. In general, devout Buddhists gather at temples or monasteries before dawn to hear stories about the Buddha's life, to wash images of him, to make offerings of flowers, candles, and incense, and carefully to observe the Five Precepts, including refraining from any kind of killing. In several Buddhist-majority countries, slaughterhouses and liquor shops are closed for the holiday by government decree. In Sri Lanka, thousands of insects, birds, and animals

Vesak, Buddha's birthday, being celebrated in Seoul, Korea, with a lantern festival.

are released as a symbolic act of liberation of all beings who are unwillingly imprisoned or tortured.

In Japan, Shakyamuni Buddha's birthday (*Hana Matsuri*) is celebrated in early April, coinciding with the blooming of cherry blossoms. The happy celebrations follow the traditional story in which birds sang, flowers bloomed, and there was a sweet rain from the heavens when he was born in the garden of Lumbini. The baby is said to have taken seven steps in each of the four directions, raised one hand to the sky and pointed downward with the other, and proclaimed his noble greatness and his mission of bringing peace to all suffering beings. In Buddhist temples, statues of a child in this pose are placed under flower-bedecked canopies representing the garden of Lumbini, and children pour sweet tea brewed from hydrangea flowers over the image of the little Buddha, symbolizing the sweet rain. There are also parades with images of the baby Buddha, a white elephant representing his mother's dream of an elephant just before he was born, and children wearing traditional Japanese clothes and carrying cherry blossoms.

On the full moon day of the third lunar month, *Magha* (approximately March), some Buddhists celebrate Magha Puja Day, also known as "Sangha Day." It commemorates a major event early in the Buddha's teachings in which, after giving the sermon to his first disciples at the Deer Park in Sarnath, he went to the capital city of Rajagaha and preached to the king and more than 1,000 citizens. His sermon was so convincing that most took refuge in the new teaching, and the king donated a beautiful bamboo grove for the Sangha's use.

With the monsoon comes the rainy-season retreat for monks and nuns, during a period when it is traditionally difficult to walk through the countryside. In some countries young laymen may temporarily enter the Sangha and live as monks for a while to consecrate their passage into adulthood. What happens during the rainy-season retreat varies according to the teacher's instructions, but it is designed to turn one's mind away from worldly concerns and back to calm inner reflection. Vietnamese nun Cue Nguyen describes her rainy-season retreat pattern:

I spend most of my day writing in a diary, reflecting upon myself and the world. Only in calm water do things reflect faithfully. I observe nature, people, listen carefully to the crickets and the fallen leaves as if they are the most important things now.[49]

After the rainy-season retreat, laypeople may ceremoniously offer new robes and other necessities to the monks and nuns, understanding that they are thereby earning spiritual merit.

Many other days are celebrated on local and national levels, such as the Festival of the Tooth in Sri Lanka honoring the Buddha's tooth relic, which is normally hidden within a series of caskets in a special temple but is on this day paraded through the streets on the back of a richly decorated elephant (see p. 154). In Thailand, there is a special Festival of Floating Bowls on the full moon night of the twelfth lunar month. Bowls made of leaves and flowers with candles and incense sticks are floated upon the water of rivers and canals, which are especially full at this time. As people let them go, they feel that their bad luck is floating away.

Buddhism in the West

Which factors may account for the growing popularity of Buddhism in Western societies?

Images of the Buddha are now enshrined around the world. The path to enlightenment that first gained currency in India has gradually spread to Western countries as well as throughout Asia. Wherever Asian Buddhists traveled, they carried Buddhism into their new surroundings. In the middle of the nineteenth century, Chinese workers migrated to California as the gold rush and railways opened up employment opportunities. In their new surroundings they built temples to Guanyin and Amitabha. In the late nineteenth century, Japanese workers migrated to Hawai'i as plantation workers and to the West Coast of the United States. Wherever they settled, they invited priests of various Buddhist schools from Japan. The largest school, Jodo Shinshu, gradually formed an organization called Buddhist Churches of America.

By the end of the century, Western Orientalists and occultists had developed considerable interest in Buddhism. The landmark 1893 World's Parliament of Religions in Chicago included a large delegation of Buddhist teachers from Japan, and some from China, Thailand, and Sri Lanka. One of the leading figures, Anagarika Dharmapala from Sri Lanka, announced that just as King Ashoka had twenty-four centuries earlier spread Buddhism from India to teach Asia "the noblest lessons of tolerance and gentleness,"[50] the Buddhists had come bringing the same message to the West. Overflow crowds collected to hear their discourses.

During the twentieth century, North American and European countries became vibrant centers of Buddhism. Scholars today are studying Buddhist traditions at a variety of universities and many people are interested in learning Buddhist meditation practices. The exodus of Buddhists from Tibet since 1959, including many high lamas, has led to the establishment of Tibetan Buddhist centers in many Western countries as well as in Southeast Asia and India, the Dalai Lama's home in exile, where more than 100,000 Tibetan refugees now live. Several hundred thousand Westerners now have some spiritual involvement with Tibetan Buddhism.

More than 400 Zen meditation centers are also flourishing in North America alone, and there are many Zen monasteries that give training in zazen and offer a monastic lifestyle as a permanent or temporary alternative to the stress and confusion of modern life.

Intensive vipassana meditation retreats lasting up to three months are held in Theravada centers such as the Insight Meditation Society in rural Barre, Massachusetts. Theravadin teachers from Southeast Asia and Europe make frequent visits to conduct retreats, and American teachers who have undertaken rigorous training in Southeast Asia under traditional meditation masters are also emerging as respected teachers. An American monk named Venerable Sumedho, who trained in traditional Theravada Buddhism in Thailand, has established

Life in a Western Zen Monastery

Side by side in still rows, with birdsong and sunlight streaming in through the tall windows, sit the monks and laypeople of Zen Mountain Monastery. For thirty-five-minute blocks, separated by periods of attentive walking, they support each other by practicing zazen together in silence. With this group structure, many find it easier to carry on the rigorous discipline of serious Zen training than they would by themselves.

This particular monastery, located in the Catskill Mountains near Mount Tremper, New York, reflects the changing face of religion in the United States. More than 100 years ago the main building was handcrafted of stone as a Benedictine monastery; later it became a Lutheran summer camp. Now, back to back with Christ on the cross on the outside of the building is a statue of the Buddha on the altar inside the *zendo*. The monastery houses ordained monastics (including women) who have taken lifetime vows of service, novices and postulants in training (an aspect adopted

from Western monasticism), lay residents who stay for up to a year, and groups of people who come for special retreats and classes. These are primarily professionals and family people from the mainstream culture, rather than the hippies who embraced Buddhism in the 1960s and 1970s. They do not come for a comfortable vacation, for zazen is hard work and the teachers are dedicated to creating snags that help people discover the places where they are not free. They are expected to practice intensely and then leave, carrying what they have learned back into the world. As Geoffrey Shugen Arnold, Sensei, who received Dharma transmission in 1997, says, "If Zen doesn't work in the world, it's not working." In addition to long sessions of silent sitting and walking, Dharma talks by the resident Zen master, and private coaching by the monks, monastery residents participate in structured nontheistic liturgical services designed to foster attentiveness and appreciation. They chant in Japanese and English, with

John Daido Loori Roshi (1931–2009), founder of Zen Mountain Monastery, an American ordained in both authentic Zen lineages.

frequent bowing to each other, to their meditation cushions, and to the Buddha on the altar, in solidarity with all beings and gratitude for the teachings. The late abbot John Daido Loori, who was born a Catholic, noted that liturgy reflects the innards of a religion: "In Catholicism, cathedrals are awe inspiring, the chants expansive; in Zen the form is simple and the chanting is grounded, not otherworldly."

The rest of the day is devoted to taking care of the buildings and 200-acre (80-hectare) nature sanctuary, mindfulness practice done in silence, body practice, Zen art practices, academic study, and work practice. Those with office jobs combine ancient and modern skills: They sit cross-legged on low cushions before their computers to prepare news, music, and interviews for their online radio station WZEN.org, and use calligraphic skills to hand-letter signs. Meals are simple and include coarse breads donated by a nearby whole-grain bakery. Every action—even brushing one's

teeth—is treated as practice, in the sense of bringing total attentiveness to the sacredness of even the most "mundane" activity, teaching that enlightenment takes place in one's everyday experience.

Following the lead of their former teacher Daido, who was at once highly disciplined in mind-to-mind Dharma transmission and down-to-earth, approachable, compassionate, and married, monastery residents are human, playful, and loving. The women "monks" shave their heads when they get ordained and keep their hair very short thereafter, but that is considered a freedom rather than self-sacrificing asceticism.

From training in flower arranging or Aikido to exploring the relevance of Buddhist principles in the workplace, Zen Mountain Monastery's programs are oriented toward one central goal: the personal experience of enlightenment and its application in the twenty-first-century world.

The stillness of the zendo *at Zen Mountain Monastery.*

Oriyoki, *a ceremonial meal, at Zen Mountain Monastery.*

Buddhism has spread around the world. Venerable Tenzin Palmo from England, who spent twelve years in a cave in the Himalayas, is standing sixth from the left with Buddhist nuns from Switzerland, India, Nepal, Mongolia, Singapore, Sri Lanka, Australia, Vietnam, the Netherlands, and the United States during a gathering of Daughters of the Buddha in Mongolia.

monastic forest communities and meditation centers in England, Switzerland, Italy, and the United States. In contrast to the low profile of Buddhist women in Asia, many Buddhist centers in the West are led by women, who are explaining traditional Buddhist teachings to Westerners in fresh, contemporary ways. Some are exemplars of dedicated spiritual practice, such as Tenzin Palmo, a British woman who became a Tibetan Buddhist nun and lived alone for twelve years in a cave located 13,200 feet (4,000 meters) high in the Himalayas, undergoing tremendous austerities in the quest for enlightenment.

The Vietnamese monk Venerable Master Thich Nhat Hanh now lives in exile in southern France, conducting retreats for both women and men in a community called Plum Village. When he travels internationally, large audiences gather and derive inspiration from his teachings. He speaks simply, using familiar examples, and emphasizes bringing the awareness fostered by meditation into everyday life, rather than making spirituality a separate compartment of one's life. He says:

> *When we walk in the meditation hall, we make careful steps, very slowly. But when we go to the airport, we are quite another person. We walk very differently, less mindfully. How can we practice at the airport and in the market?*[51]

Buddhism is often embraced by people in the West because they long for peace of mind in the midst of a chaotic materialistic life. The Buddhist concept of "mindfulness" has become especially popular, and there are many mindfulness teachings and practices that take inspiration from Buddhist tradition but present mindfulness in a secular context, from mindfulness workshops for corporate and business leaders to formal programs such as Mindfulness Based Stress Reduction.

Many psychotherapists are studying Buddhism for its insights into the mind and human suffering. Richard Clarke, who was both a psychotherapist and a Zen teacher, and founded the Living Dharma Center in Massachusetts, proposed that a discipline such as Zen should be part of the training of counselors and therapists:

> *Emptiness is … the source of infinite compassion in working with people: to really feel a person without any agenda, to be spacious to that person, to will that they be the way they are. When a person experiences that in someone's presence, then*

they can drop away those things that they've invented to present themselves with. Those faces, those armors, those forms of the self become unnecessary.[52]

Are Westerners able to achieve enlightenment by taking Buddhist workshops here and there? Particularly in the case of Tibetan Buddhist practices, Westerners often want to be initiated into the most highly advanced teachings without taking time for years of patient practice and being inwardly transformed by the step-by-step foundational teachings. Can teachings developed within a specific cultural context be directly transplanted into the soil of an entirely different culture? Most Westerners who are adopting Buddhist practices are living in highly materialistic societies with different priorities and values, rather than in traditional Buddhist cultures or monastic settings. In their impatience to get results, many shop around from one teacher to the next and experiment with one practice after another, rather than persisting with one path over a long time. As Alan Wallace remarks:

In Tibetan society, fickleness is considered to be one of the worst of vices, while reliability, integrity, trustworthiness, and perseverance are held in high regard.

So a few of the finest lamas are now refusing even to come to the West. Some are feeling—given the brevity and preciousness of human life—that devoting time to people with such fickleness and so little faith is time not very well spent.[53]

Another crucial issue is how to train teachers for the West. Two large Tibetan Buddhist organizations from the Gelukpa order have opened nearly 600 centers for study and meditation around the world but do not have enough fully trained lamas to staff all of them. Traditional training takes up to twenty-five years of rigorous study and debate of the finer points of Buddhist philosophy, logic, meditation, cosmology, psychology, and monastic life. Close guidance by an advanced teacher has traditionally been considered essential, but this is not possible for all Western aspirants, given the shortage of qualified teachers and the language problems entailed.

Given the differences in culture, background, and motivation, are Western students and their teachers in the process of creating new forms of Buddhism adapted to Western ways? How authentic are these new forms? Some observers feel that Western Buddhism, with its emphasis on inner practice rather than outer forms, is actually closer to what they construe as the core of early Buddhism than are later developments in the East. Contemporary Western Buddhists tend to be oriented to the goal of achieving enlightenment by their own efforts, which is reportedly what the Buddha prescribed for his followers, and are searching for ways to achieve that goal, though sometimes hoping to do so with minimum effort. Whether or not Western Buddhism conforms to early patterns, it seems to be evolving in new directions with some people in the West remaking Buddhism in their own image. For instance, the British Buddhist Stephen Batchelor argues in his book *Buddhism Without Beliefs* that the West needs a Buddhism stripped of belief in rebirth and karma. He emphasizes instead a secularized version, an "existential, therapeutic and liberating agnosticism."[54]

Another important difference between Western Buddhism and historical developments in Asia is the Western tendency to support equal participation of women, as renunciates, teachers, and lay practitioners. In recent years, Buddhists in Asia, confronted by modernization, consumerism, globalization, and new social attitudes, are taking directions similar to those of Western Buddhists.

Since 1987, Buddhist women from Asia and the West have joined hands and held international gatherings to enhance the role of women in Buddhism. Sakyadhita (Daughters of the Buddha), the International Association of Buddhist Women, is working to improve conditions for women's Buddhist education, practice, ordination, and training as teachers of Buddhism. Sakyadhita's conferences bring together women and men, lay and ordained, from different traditions to exchange ideas on meditation, peace-building, and women's roles in contemporary Buddhist practice. The 2008 Sakyadhita conference in Mongolia highlighted Buddhist women's achievements in recent years as well as persistent inequalities in education and ordination. The 2011 Sakyadhita conference in Bangkok paid tribute to eminent Buddhist women in the past and in contemporary society, with panels on issues such as leadership and lineage, stereotypes of women, global sustainability, and new directions for Buddhist social transformation. In 2013, the Bhutan Nuns Foundation held an international nuns conference, with nuns from different traditions discussing the Buddhist nuns' role in contemporary society. Karma Lekshe Tsomo, founder of Sakyadhita and also the Jamyang Foundation, which tries to increase educational opportunities for Buddhist nuns, says, "There are 300 million Buddhist women in the world. They have tremendous potential, goodwill, and energy to work for peace and the benefit of humanity."[55]

Socially engaged Buddhism

How is Buddhism responding to social problems in the world today?

An emerging focus in contemporary Buddhist practice is the relevance of Buddhism to social problems. Contrary to popular assumptions, the Buddha did not advise people to permanently leave society to seek their own enlightenment. Sri Lankan Buddhist monk Walpola Rahula (1907–1997) explained:

> It may perhaps be useful in some cases for a person to live in retirement for a time in order to improve his or her mind and character, as preliminary moral, spiritual, and intellectual training, to be strong enough to come out later and help others. But if someone lives an entire life in solitude, thinking only of their own happiness and salvation, without caring for their fellow beings, this surely is not in keeping with the Buddha's teaching which is based on love, compassion, and service to others.[56]

Buddhism, like other world religions, has always been engaged with the wider society and political life. In Thailand, for instance, the king is the bearer of the Buddhist heritage, and thus has sacred legitimization. But Thailand also has a tradition of socially conscious lay practice of Buddhism. The renowned Thai monk Buddhadasa Bhikkhu (1906–1993) was a great critic of capitalism, teaching that it increases egoism and selfishness, thus causing distress both to the individual and to society.

In Vietnam, Thich Nhat Hanh and other socially active Buddhists refused to take sides with the governments and military movements of either North Vietnam or South Vietnam during the Vietnam War, for they felt that both were oppressing the common people and also exploiting American soldiers. All were victims of an ideological conflict between Communism and anti-Communism. Buddhists worked hard to bring a negotiated end to the war, and helped the suffering people as best they could by evacuating villagers caught in the midst of battles, helping to rebuild damaged buildings, taking care of orphans, and providing medical care to people from all sides. They believed that all life is precious and interdependent—violence and suffering affect everyone. Thus they meditated to generate selfless compassion, according to the teachings of the Buddha, who said:

> Hatred is never appeased by hatred. It is appeased by love. This is an eternal law. Just as a mother would protect her only child, even at the risk of her own life, even so let one cultivate a boundless heart towards all beings. Let one's thoughts of boundless love pervade the whole world.[57]

However, Buddhism's link with politics has not always been entirely altruistic. In Sri Lanka, a selective interpretation of Theravada Buddhist tradition was used to bolster nationalistic sentiments among the Sinhalese Buddhist majority against the Tamil (mostly Hindu and Muslim, as well as Christian) minority in a conflict that had been going on for 2,000 years. As in many contemporary fundamentalist movements elsewhere, a chauvinistic, rigid version of religious identity developed in response to rapid colonization, modernization, and Westernization. The reaffirmation of Buddhist identity became a tool of ethnic oppression of the minority, leading to a violent separatist movement among the Tamils and ultimately civil strife which disrupted life on the island from 1983 to 2009. Since 2012, there have been clashes between Buddhists and the Muslim-minority Rohingya people in Myanmar (Burma), with the monk Wirathu speaking out against Muslims and supporting campaigns designed to force Muslims to leave Myanmar.

In general, however, the Buddha's emphasis on compassion has prevailed, and even when Buddhists have been social activists, they have tended to be guided by Buddhist principles of nonviolence, compassion, and social justice. In this posture, some contemporary Buddhists have tried to correct injustice, oppression, famine, cruelty to animals, nuclear testing, warfare, and environmental devastation. Thai Buddhist activist and founder of the International Network of Engaged Buddhists, Sulak Sivaraksa (b. 1933), has challenged traditional models of economic development, explaining that:

> *The goals of Buddhist development are equality, love, freedom, and liberation. The means for achieving these lie within the grasp of any community—from a village to a nation—once its members begin the process of reducing selfishness. To do so, two realizations are necessary: an inner realization concerning greed, hatred, and delusion, and an outer realization concerning the impact these tendencies have on society and the planet.*[58]

Ajahn Pongsak, a Thai Buddhist monk, was so troubled by the devastation of the northern Thai forests that he rallied 5,000 villagers to reforest an area by building a tree nursery, terracing the eroded hillsides, planting nearly 200,000 seedlings, laying irrigation pipes, and fencing the area to protect the new trees. He taught them the importance of a respectful relationship with the forest as their own home, their own parent. He says:

> *A mind that feels no gratitude to the forest is a coarse mind indeed—without this basic* siladhamma *[moral teaching], how can a mind attain enlightenment? … The times are dark and* siladhamma *is asleep, so it is now the duty of monks to reawaken and bring back* siladhamma. *Only in this way can society be saved.*[59]

Maha Ghosananda courageously led peace marches through Khmer Rouge territory, and, as leader of the decimated population of Buddhist monks in post-communist Cambodia, helped to revive the religion and the country.

Cambodians are in the process of recovering from decades of a culture of terror in which the Khmer Rouge murdered more than one million people. Buddhists have played major roles in peacemaking and rebuilding the country, promoting nonviolent responses to violence. The monks of Buddhism for Development, for instance, have gone to the villages and cities to carry out community development projects, emphasizing the Dharma of physical development, moral development, spiritual development, and intellectual development. The most instrumental figure has been Venerable Maha Ghosananda (1929–2007), whose entire family was killed during the Pol Pot regime. In addition to political initiatives, he led many peace marches of monks, nuns, and laypeople through areas infested with landmines, and counseled people facing issues such as domestic violence, HIV/AIDS, deforestation, and dire poverty. He urged:

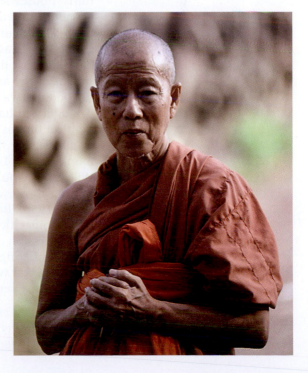

> *We must remove the landmines in our hearts which prevent us from making peace—greed, hatred and delusion. We can overcome greed with the weapon of generosity; we can overcome hatred with the weapon of loving kindness; we can overcome delusion with the weapon of wisdom. …*[60]

Aung San Suu Kyi (b. 1945) is internationally famous for her nonviolent resistance to oppression in her home country, Myanmar (Burma).

We must find the courage to leave our temples and enter the temples of human experience, temples that are filled with suffering. If we listen to the Buddha, Christ, or Gandhi, we can do nothing else. The refugee camps, the prisons, the ghettos and the battlefields will then become our temples.[61]

Another notable example of the use of Buddhist teachings as an antidote to violence is Aung San Suu Kyi, leader of the National League for Democracy in Myanmar. Her father was assassinated in the attempt to bring democracy to the people, and she has been an outspoken advocate of democratic social change, repeatedly exposing herself to danger and ill health from continual house arrest or imprisonment. When she was freed from house arrest in 2010, she spoke of

the most dangerous kind of politics: the politics of dissent. You do not ask [NLD workers] if they have ever been to prison. You ask them how many times they have been to jail. Their weapons are their faith, their armour is their passion, our passion. What is the cause to which we are so passionately dedicated as to forego the comforts of a conventional existence? We are dedicated to the defence of the right of individuals to free and truthful life. [For a dissident] freedom from fear does not have to be complete. It only has to be sufficient to enable us to carry on; and to carry on in spite of fear requires tremendous courage.[62]

Living by Buddhist principles to counteract fear and cope with government oppression, Aung San Suu Kyi observes:

It would be difficult to dispel ignorance unless there is freedom to pursue the truth unfettered by fear. With so close a relationship between fear and corruption it is little wonder that in any society where fear is rife corruption in all forms becomes deeply entrenched. The effort necessary to remain uncorrupted in an environment where fear is an integral part of everyday existence is not immediately apparent to those fortunate enough to live in states governed by the rule of law. Where there are no such laws, the burden of holding the principles of justice and common decency falls on the ordinary people.[63]

In Taiwan, Buddhist values mixed with Confucian civil ethics and Daoism have helped to support freedom and democracy. The Engaged Buddhist thrust is evident in Taiwan in several new Mahayana organizations that are attempting to create a Pure Land in this world, rather than waiting for the afterlife. Among these is Tzu Chi, founded by Venerable Cheng Yen in 1966 with donations from thirty housewives. A self-educated nun, Venerable Cheng Yen now heads an efficient bureaucracy with five million members in forty-five countries, who are following and teaching the bodhisattva path by providing volunteer services such as disaster relief, medicine, education, environmental protection, and bone-marrow donor registry. As they work, they sing hymns about the joy of serving. They are taught to regard all of humanity as their own family, true to the bodhisattva vow.

Buddhism had largely declined in India but then returned during the twentieth century as a vehicle for overcoming caste distinctions which had made life so difficult for those considered "untouchables," now called Dalits. A Buddhist monk named Lokanatha, for example, wrote a pamphlet entitled "Buddhism Will Make You Free," and addressed it to the "Depressed Classes" of India. Among those who were influenced by this message was Dr. B. R. Ambedkar (1891–1956). Born an "untouchable" Hindu, he was the chief architect of India's new democratic constitution, and built into it many provisions designed to end the oppression of the traditional Hindu caste system. In his personal search for a religion offering freedom and dignity to all human beings, he chose Buddhism. Dr. Ambedkar wrote that he was presented with a book on the Buddha when he was the first person from the lowest caste to graduate from high school:

That opened my eyes to Buddhism, and I have read voraciously on the topic ever since. Whatever I have achieved, I owe to the Buddha. I find thorough equality and superb humanism in Buddhism.[64]

When Dr. Ambedkar publicly converted shortly before his death, he was the inspiration for almost half a million Dalits to do likewise. Despite this, he openly questioned and changed certain Buddhist teachings.

In "Ambedkarite Buddhism," the emphasis is on active social engagement, helping the people, rather than renunciation and meditation. Dr. Ambedkar prescribed twenty-two vows for his followers, including denouncing belief in Hindu deities and social inequality, and replacing these with affirmations such as "I shall believe in the equality of man," "I shall endeavor to follow the noble eight-fold path and practice compassion and loving-kindness in everyday life," and "I solemnly declare and affirm that I shall hereafter lead my life according to the principles and teachings of the Buddha and his Dhamma." Various Ambedkarite organizations are trying to propagate these vows on a large scale in India, particularly to help erase the traumas of casteism. Ambedkar Buddhists generally reject the Buddhist idea that a person's birth into a particular social class is a result of karma from previous lives. This version of Buddhism based in social activism has been informally called "Navayana," (new vehicle), comprising what some consider a fourth branch of Buddhism.

Buddhism has also been adopted for political purposes in India. Politicians in some areas have tried to promote Dalit liberation through Buddhism and respect for Dr. Ambedkar, whose statue now appears in many towns. Since the Dalits comprise a large vote bank, it is uncertain whether the intention is sincerely to instill Buddhist ideals in them or rather to gain their votes. In the most populous state in India, Uttar Pradesh, the merger of Buddhist religion and politics is particularly controversial. The chief minister up to 2012, a Dalit politician named Mayawati, spent millions of rupees on public monuments honoring the Buddha, Dr. Ambedkar, and local politicians, including herself, affirming that these public works would engender public pride and economic development. Among her projects were the renovation of the ancient Buddhist pilgrimage sites—including Kapilvastu, Sarnath, and Kushinagar, the places of the Buddha's birth, first sermon, and death—and Gautam Buddha University, with its schools of humanities and social sciences, management, information technology, law and social justice, biotechnology, engineering and design, and Buddhist studies and civilization. While critics point to the persistence of poverty in Uttar Pradesh, Mayawati's supporters likened her building projects to those of the ancient King Ashoka, who coined the expression *dharma vijaya*, "the victory of righteousness."

Summarizing the work of Engaged Buddhists, Thich Nhat Hanh said:

Once there is seeing, there must be acting. We must be aware of the real problems of the world. Then, with mindfulness, we will know what to do, and what not to do, to be of help.[65]

Sulak Sivaraksa explains that socially engaged Buddhism does not mean promoting Buddhism per se:

The presence of Buddhism in society does not mean having a lot of schools, hospitals, cultural institutions, or political parties run by Buddhists. It means that the schools, hospitals, cultural institutions, and political parties are permeated with and administered with humanism, love, tolerance, and enlightenment, characteristics which Buddhism attributes to an opening up, development, and formation of human nature. This is the true spirit of nonviolence.[66]

Even when one intends to be nonviolent in one's approach to life, difficult ethical questions may still arise. For example, contemporary scholars of Buddhist medical ethics are trying to determine how best to apply Buddhist principles to

A celebration around a statue of Dr. Ambedkar in honor of his birthday is mixed with political-party banners. Dr. Ambedkar inspired many Dalits to convert to Buddhism in order to overcome the oppression caused by the traditional Hindu caste system.

issues such as abortion, reproductive technologies, genetic engineering, organ transplants, suicide, coma patients, and euthanasia.

Buddhism is thus as relevant today, and its insights as necessary, as in the fifth century BCE, when the one who became Shakyamuni Buddha renounced a life of ease to save all sentient beings from suffering.

Key terms

anatman (Pali: *anatta*) The principle that there is no eternal self.

anitya (Pali: *anicca*) Impermanence.

arhant (Pali: *arhat* or *arahat*) A "worthy one" who has followed the Buddha's path to liberation.

bhikshu (Pali: *bhikkhu*; feminine: bhikshuni or *bhikkuni*) A monk or nun who renounces worldliness for the sake of following the path of liberation and whose simple physical needs are met by lay supporters.

bodhisattva A person who is dedicated to liberating others from suffering.

deity yoga Vajrayana meditation on a deity in order to develop his or her qualities.

Dharma (Pali: *Dhamma*) The teachings and laws for conduct given by the Buddha.

dukkha Discomfort, suffering, frustration, disharmony.

karma (Pali: *kamma*) Actions; the law of cause and effect.

kensho A sudden experience of enlightened awareness.

koan A question used by Zen teachers to boggle the student's mind and thus liberate direct awareness.

lama A high Vajrayana teacher.

Mahayana The "Great Vehicle," the branch of Buddhist schools that stress the altruistic wish to become perfectly awakened in order to free all living beings from suffering.

nirvana Liberation from mental afflictions, suffering, and rebirth.

Pali Canon Ancient Buddhist scriptures written in Pali and considered authoritative.

samsara Cyclic existence; the continual round of birth, death, and rebirth.

Sangha The monastic community; more broadly, a Dharma community.

stupa Monument containing Buddhist relics or images.

shunyata The doctrine of voidness, emptiness.

Theravada The remaining of the early schools of Buddhism, which adheres to the earliest scriptures.

Triple Gem The Buddha, the Dharma, and the Sangha.

Vajrayana A branch of Buddhism practiced in the Tibetan diaspora that incorporates deity yoga, mantras, mudras (hand gestures), and mandalas to achieve awakening; sometimes included as a school of the Mahayana branch.

vipassana Insight. A meditation technique for developing insight into *dukkha, anicca,* and *anatta.*

zazen Sitting meditation, in Zen schools.

Zen A Chinese and Japanese Mahayana school emphasizing that all things have Buddha-nature, which can only be grasped when one escapes from the intellectual mind.

Suggested reading

Carter, John Ross and Mahinda Palihawadana (trans.), *The Dhammapada: The Sayings of the Buddha*, Oxford: Oxford University Press, 2000. A basic book of sayings attributed to the Buddha that covers the essentials of the Dharma in memorable, pithy verses.

Conze, Edward, I. B. Horner, David Snellgrove, and Arthur Waley, ed. and trans., *Buddhist Texts through the Ages*, Oxford: Oneworld Publications, 1995. A fine collection of Buddhist scriptures translated from Pali, Sanskrit, Chinese, Tibetan, and Japanese.

Eppsteiner, Fred, ed., *The Path of Compassion: Writings on Socially Engaged Buddhism*, Berkeley, California: Parallax Press, 1988. A highly readable and relevant collection of essays by leading contemporary Buddhist teachers about the ways in which Buddhism can be applied to social problems.

Fields, Rick, *How the Swans Came to the Lake: A Narrative History of Buddhism in America*, Boston: Shambhala, 1986. The multifaceted story of Buddhism's transfer to the United States.

Fremantle, Francesca, and Chogyam Trungpa, trans., *The Tibetan Book of the Dead*, Boston and London: Shambhala Publications, 1975. The classic Tibetan Buddhist scripture on the projections of the mind and the practices of deity yoga to attain enlightenment.

Friedman, Lenore, *Meetings with Remarkable Women: Buddhist Teachers in America*, Boston and London: Shambhala Publications, 1987. Wisdom from Buddhist traditions shared in very personal, perceptive interviews.

Ghosananda, Maha, *Step by Step*, Berkeley, California: Parallax Press, 1992. Accessible and touching explanations of basic Buddhist doctrines.

Gross, Rita M., *Buddhism after Patriarchy*, Albany, New York: State University of New York Press, 1993. A feminist reconstruction of Buddhist history, revealing its core of gender equality but later overlays of sexism, plus analysis of key Buddhist concepts from a feminist point of view.

Habito, Ruben, *Experiencing Buddhism: Ways of Wisdom and Compassion*, Maryknoll, New York: Orbis Books, 2005. Clear and sensitive exploration of various ways in which Buddhists are attempting to practice the Buddha's teachings, especially in the contemporary world.

Hanh, Thich Nhat, *The Heart of the Buddha's Teaching: Transforming Suffering into Peace, Joy, and Liberation*, New York: Broadway Books, 1998. In simple, compassionate language, the famous Vietnamese monk explains the efficacy of Buddhist teachings for dealing with today's problems.

Heine, Steven and Charles S. Prebish, *Buddhism in the Modern World: Adaptations of an Ancient Tradition*, New York: Oxford University Press, 2003. Essays examining how specific schools of Buddhism have adapted to contemporary challenges and yet maintained their links with tradition.

Jerryson, Michael K. and Mark Juergensmeyer, eds, *Buddhist Warfare*, New York: Oxford University Press, 2010. A collection of essays challenging popular conceptions of Buddhism as wholly peaceful, exploring instances in which Buddhists have been involved in warfare.

Kaza, Stephanie and Kenneth Kraft, *Dharma Rain: Sources of Buddhist Environmentalism*, Boston and London: Shambhala, 2000. Classic and contemporary texts integrating Buddhist spirituality with environmental awareness and activism.

Levine, Stephen, *A Gradual Awakening*, Garden City, New York: Doubleday, 1979 and London: Rider & Company, 1980. Gentle, poetic presentation of vipassana techniques in their relevance to contemporary life.

Lopez, Donald S., Jr., ed., *Buddhism in Practice*, Princeton: Princeton University Press, 1995. Annotated translation of original sources dealing with Buddhist practice around the world, organized around the Triple Jewels of Buddha, the Dharma, and the Sangha.

Lopez, Donald S., Jr., ed., *A Modern Buddhist Bible: Essential Readings from East and West*, Boston: Beacon Press, 2002. An anthology of original writings by modern Buddhist teachers trying to revive original Buddhist traditions of meditation and spirituality.

Lopez, Donald S., Jr., *The Story of Buddhism: A Concise Guide to its History and Teachings*, San Francisco: HarperSanFrancisco, 2001. An introduction incorporating the latest scholarship.

Mackenzie, Vicki, *Cave in the Snow*, London: Bloomsbury Publishing, 1999. Fascinating story of a Western woman who spent twelve years alone in a Himalayan cave to concentrate on intense meditation practices and achieve enlightenment in a woman's body.

Mitchell, Donald W., *Buddhism: Introducing the Buddhist Experience*, New York and Oxford: Oxford University Press, 2002. Detailed descriptions of general and culture-specific manifestations of Buddhism.

Niwano, Nikkyo, trans. Richard L. Gage, *Lifetime Beginner*, Tokyo: Kosei Publishing Co., 1978. Fascinating stories from the life of the founder of Rissho Kosei-kai, as he tried to put the *Lotus Sutra* into practice in the midst of great difficulties.

Powers, John, *A Bull of a Man: Images of Masculinity, Sex, and the Body in Indian Buddhism*, Cambridge, Massachusetts: Harvard University Press, 2009. Study of how portrayals of the Buddha in Indian Buddhism emphasized virility.

Queen, Christopher, Charles Prebish, and Damien Keown, eds, *Action Dharma: New Studies in Engaged Buddhism*, London: Routledge, 2003. Articles on both the theory and practice of Buddhist involvement in contemporary social and political causes.

Queen, Christopher S. and Sallie B. King, eds, *Engaged Buddhism: Buddhist Liberation Movements in Asia*, Albany: State University of New York Press, 1996. A thorough survey of contemporary Buddhist activism in Asian countries.

Rahula, Walpola Sri, *What the Buddha Taught*, New York: Grove Press, 1974. The classic introduction to Buddhist teachings—an accurate and clear guide through the complexities of Buddhist thought and practice, with representative texts.

Reynolds, Frank E. and Jason A. Carbine, eds, *The Life of Buddhism*, Berkeley: University of California Press, 2000. Attempts to analyze Buddhist ways in their cultural and historical contexts.

Sivaraksa, Sulak, *Seeds of Peace: A Buddhist Vision for Renewing Society*, Berkeley, California: Parallax Press, 1992. A renowned Thai social activist examines the "politics of greed" and issues involved in the transformation of society, from the point of view of Buddhist ideals.

Suzuki, Shunryu, *Zen Mind, Beginner's Mind*, New York and Tokyo: Weatherhill, 1970. A beautiful book, leading one gracefully and seemingly simply through the paradoxes of Zen.

Tsomo, Karma Lekshe, ed., *Out of the Shadows: Socially Engaged Buddhist Women*, Delhi: Sri Satguru Publications, 2006. Realistic in-depth expressions of Buddhist women's experiences in many cultures, and their efforts to uphold the Dharma therein.

5.1 Tell the story of the Buddha's enlightenment

Siddhartha Gautama, who became the Buddha, was reportedly born near what is today the border between India and Nepal and lived for more than eighty years, most likely during the fifth century BCE. On being shown "four sights" that his wealthy father tried to hide from him, Siddhartha renounced his wealth, left his wife and newborn son, shaved his head and wore the robe of a wandering ascetic. He embarked on a wandering life in pursuit of finding the way to total liberation from suffering.

Siddhartha studied first with several Brahmin teachers and then underwent six years of extreme self-denial techniques, but this extreme ascetic path did not lead to enlightenment. He then changed to a Middle Way that rejected both self-indulgence and self-denial, and finally experienced a supreme a wakening. He had a realization of the wheel of repeated death and rebirth, in which past good or bad deeds are reflected in future lives. He realized the cause of pain and the means for ending it. He subsequently spent decades walking and teaching ever-increasing groups of followers all over northern India.

5.2 Define the Four Noble Truths and the Noble Eightfold Path to liberation

The Buddha's core teachings became known as the Dharma and included the Four Noble Truths, the Noble Eightfold Path, the Three Marks of Existence, and other guidelines for achieving liberation from suffering.

The Four Noble Truths form the foundation for all the Buddha's later teachings. The first Noble Truth is the truth of pain and suffering (*dukkha*); the second is the arising of pain; the third is the cessation of pain; and the fourth is the path to end pain.

The Noble Eightfold Path offers ways to purify the mind of afflictive emotions and avoid unwholesome actions. Ultimately the path leads to freedom from the cycle of death and rebirth, and the peace of nirvana (egoless state of bliss). The aspects of the path are: right understanding, right thought or motivation, right speech, right action, right livelihood, right effort, right mindfulness, right meditation.

5.3 Differentiate between Theravada and Mahayana Buddhism

Followers of Theravada and Mahayana Buddhism share many ideas and practices in common, and are in general agreement about the Four Noble Truths, the Noble Eightfold Path, and the teachings about karma (actions), samsara (cyclic existence), and nirvana.

Theravada (Way of the Elders) is the only earliest school to survive and is prevalent in Southeast Asian countries such as Sri Lanka, Burma, Thailand, Cambodia, and Laos. Theravada Buddhists study the early scriptures in Pali, honor the life of renunciation, and follow mindfulness and insight meditation teachings.

The schools that developed somewhat later are collectively known as Mahayana (Great Vehicle) and gradually became dominant in China, Nepal, Tibet, China, Korea, Mongolia, Vietnam, and Japan. The Mahayana scriptures emphasize the practice of compassion and wisdom by both monastics and lay-people, toward the goal of liberating all sentient beings from *dukkha*.

5.4 Identify the schools of Mahayana in East Asia

Chan Buddhism, with its emphasis on meditation and direct insight, became the most successful form of Buddhism in China from the fifth century CE. The Chan school was transmitted in the thirteenth century CE to Japan, where it is known as Zen. Instead of focusing on scriptures, Buddhas, and bodhisattvas (those dedicated to liberating others from suffering), Zen emphasizes direct insight into the true nature of one's own mind, to reveal one's own Buddha nature.

One of the most popular Buddhist schools in East Asia is Pure Land Buddhism, which centers on faith in Amitabha Buddha (Amida in Japanese), who promised to welcome believers to the paradise of the Pure Land (a metaphor for enlightenment). In Japan there is also the Nichiren school, inspired by the *Lotus Sutra*, which stresses the importance of striving to enlighten not only ourselves but also society.

5.5 Contrast Vajrayana with Theravada and Mahayana Buddhism

Although some scholars classify it as a form of Mahayana Buddhism, many consider Vajrayana a separate branch. Followers of Vajrayana call it the "third turning" of the wheel of Dharma. Vajrayana developed in India, was transmitted to Tibet in the eighth century CE, and is currently practiced throughout the Tibetan diaspora and increasingly in North America and Europe.

In contrast to Theravada and Mahayana Buddhism, which emphasize cyclic existence, Vajrayana is an esoteric path that offers the possibility of attaining Buddhahood in a single lifetime. It incorporates deity yoga, mantras, mudras (hand gestures), and mandalas (a symmetrical image used for meditation) to achieve awakening.

5.6 Describe the major Buddhist festivals

For Theravadins the most important festival is Vesak, which marks on one day the Buddha's birth, enlightenment, and death. For Mahayana Buddhists, Vesak marks the day of the Buddha's enlightenment. Vajrayana Buddhists celebrate four distinct days commemorating the Buddha's conception, birth, enlightenment, and death. Some Buddhists also celebrate Magha Puja Day, which commemorates a major event early in the Buddha's teachings.

5.7 Discuss the growing popularity of Buddhism in Western societies

During the twentieth century, North American and European countries became vibrant centers of Buddhism. The exodus of Buddhists from Tibet since 1959 has led to the establishment of Tibetan Buddhist centers in many Western countries. More than 400 Zen monasteries are flourishing in North America. Monks and teachers, such as Venerable Master Thich Nhat Hanh, conduct retreats for both men and women in meditation centers in North America and Europe.

Buddhism is often embraced by people in the West because they long for peace of mind in the midst of a chaotic materialistic life. The Buddhist concept of "mindfulness" has become especially popular, and there are many mindfulness teachings and practices that take inspiration from Buddhist tradition but present mindfulness in a secular context. Western Buddhists emphasize inner practice rather than outer forms and tend to be oriented to the goal of achieving enlightenment by their own efforts. There is also a tendency to support equal participation of women, as renunciates, teachers, and lay practitioners.

5.8 Outline the emerging focus on social problems in contemporary Buddhist practice

In general, Buddhist social activists have tended to be guided by Buddhist principles of nonviolence, compassion, and social justice. In Cambodia, Buddhists have played major roles in peacemaking and rebuilding the country. Another notable example of the use of Buddhist teachings as an antidote to violence is Aung San Suu Kyi, leader of the National League for Democracy in Myanmar (Burma)—an outspoken advocate of democratic social change. In Taiwan, Buddhist values mixed with Confucian civil ethics and Daoism have helped to support freedom and democracy.

In India, Buddhism returned during the twentieth century as a vehicle for overcoming the caste distinctions that had made life so difficult for those considered "untouchables" (Dalits). Dr. B. R. Ambedkar, an "untouchable" Hindu who publicly converted to Buddhism shortly before his death, was the chief architect of India's new democratic constitution. In "Ambedkarite Buddhism" the emphasis is on active social engagement, helping the people, rather than on renunciation and meditation.

CHAPTER 6

DAOISM AND CONFUCIANISM

"It is very hard to find a true sage who through his self-cultivation has perfectly combined himself with Heaven, or the transcendent Dao, or ultimate reality—whatever you may call it." Simon Man-ho WONG*[1]

6.1 Describe the ancient Chinese tradition of ancestor worship and the concept of cosmic balance

6.2 Identify the basic principles for life in harmony with Dao

6.3 Outline the practices associated with popular religion and organized Daoism

6.4 Explain the increasing interest in Daoist practices and philosophy in the West

6.5 Outline the major teachings of Confucius

6.6 Define Neo-Confucianism

6.7 Discuss the ways in which Confucianism is being adapted to modern concerns in mainland China and other parts of East Asia

While India was giving birth to Hinduism, Jainism, and Buddhism, three other major religions were developing in East Asia. Daoism and Confucianism grew largely in China, and later spread to Japan and Korea; Shinto is considered distinctively Japanese. In this chapter we will explore the two that developed in China from similar roots but with different emphases: Daoism and Confucianism. Buddhism also spread to East Asia, where its encounter with Chinese traditions developed its world-affirming qualities. Buddhism is now the most common religion in China. There are also popular religious practices and beliefs that persist alongside, and mixed with, the more formalized religious ways, even as China becomes highly modernized and economically progressive.

* Traditionally, the Chinese surname is mentioned before the first name, but where a Chinese person has adapted the Western way of citing his or her surname last then the Western tradition will be used. For clarity, we have given the surname in capital letters at first mention.

In East Asia, religions that will be treated as separate entities in this chapter and the following one are, in fact, more subtly blended and practiced. Daoism and Confucianism, though they may seem quite opposite to each other, co-exist as complementary value systems in East Asian societies, and a person's thought and actions may encompass both streams. The idea of distinct religions is not prominent in Chinese thought. Even though scholars may trace the historical threads of Daoism, Confucianism, and Buddhism, Chinese people tend to refer to their religious practices simply as "worshiping," and temples may include images from more than one of the "Three Teachings."

In this chapter we will be transliterating Chinese words according to the contemporary Pinyin system, which has replaced the older Wade-Giles system. Thus "Daoism" is the Pinyin transliteration; "Taoism" was the earlier Wade-Giles transcription of the same word. When terms are first introduced in this chapter, the Wade-Giles equivalent—which is still found in many English books—will be given in parenthesis.

Ancient traditions

Why are ancestor worship and cosmic balance important?

Chinese civilization is very old and continuous. By 2000 BCE, people were living in settled agrarian villages in the Yellow River Valley, and also in areas of southern China, with musical instruments and skillful work in bronze, silk, ceramics, and ivory. Interpretations of archaeological findings suggest that elements still present in Chinese religious ways, both popular and institutionalized, were practiced there as long ago as this.

Worship and divination

There is prehistorical evidence of worship of ancestors. Their graves were lined up in rows near villages and provided with funeral offerings such as ornaments, pottery, and tools, suggesting belief in an afterlife in which they could use them. Perhaps then, as now, the spirits of deceased ancestors were thought

Chinese gravesites built in places considered auspicious are littered with the wrappers of firecrackers used to tell the dead and other spirits that the living have not forgotten them, for they are very kind and filial, and also to request them not to hurt those who are alive.

- The Five Great Mountains of Daoism

RUSSIA

MONGOLIA

CHINA

Beijing

• Hengshan

Yellow River

Confucianism by 3rd–4th century CE

NORTH KOREA

JAPAN

Seoul   SOUTH KOREA

Qufu

• Tai Shan

Confucianism by 7th century CE

birthplace of Confucius, c.551 BCE
birthplace of Mengzi, c.390 BCE

traditional birthplace of Laozi

• Hua Shan   • Song Shan

TIBET

Jiming

Yangtze River

Changsha

• Hengshan

Wuyuan

Taipei

birthplace of Zhu Xi, 1130–1200 CE

NEPAL

BHUTAN

TAIWAN

INDIA

discovery of oldest Dao de jing

• Hong Kong

BURMA

Historic sites of Daoism and Confucianism.

to remain closely bonded to their living descendants for some time. Chinese tradition requires that respect be paid to the ancestors—especially the family's founding ancestor and those recently deceased—through funerals, mourning rites, and then continuing sacrifices. These sacred rituals of ancestor worship are called *li*. They are essential because the ancestors will help their descendants if treated with proper respect, or cause trouble if ignored.

It appears that in addition to ancestors early Chinese people worshiped a great variety of invisible spirits. Plants, animals, rivers, stones, mountains, stars, cosmic forces—in popular religion, all parts of the natural world are vitalized by cosmic energy and many are personified, honored, and consulted as deities. From the earliest historical dynasty, the Shang (*c.* 1600–1046 BCE), archaeological evidence indicates that kings and their priests were making regular sacrifices, not only to ancestors but also to deities living in the earth, water, and air. Wine for them was poured onto the earth, jade thrown into rivers, and grains and animal flesh burned on outdoor altars.

From ancient times, there was also belief in a great variety of demons (such as a thorn demon and a water-bug demon) and the ghosts of people who had not been properly honored after their death. These beings were seen as causing so much mischief that many efforts were made to thwart them, ultimately including evil-deflecting charms, gongs, firecrackers, appeals through spirit mediums, spirit walls to keep them from entering doorways, exorcisms, prayers, incense, and fasts.

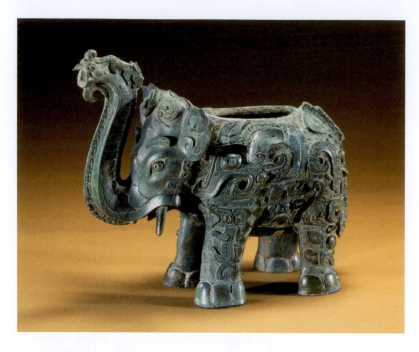

This bronze wine vessel from the Shang dynasty is richly ornamented with mystical beings and energies, including dragons, snakes, a tiger, wind, and thunderclouds. According to Professor Minqin WANG of Hunan University, dragons were revered as noble, heavenly animals who helped people by producing clouds and rain. Eventually the dragon became the symbol of the emperor, and Chinese people regarded themselves as descendants of the dragons, who are ready to sacrifice themselves to serve others.

The spiritual activities of the common people of the Shang period are not definitely known, but it seems clear that kings played very significant religious roles as chief priests for their kingdoms. They sought the help of their aristocratic ancestors and deities by a process of divination through the medium of oracle bones. These were large flat bones onto which the divining specialist scratched questions posed by the king, such as whether or not the sacrifices had been properly performed, whether hunting or military campaigns would be successful, whether or not the coming period would be favorable, and how to interpret dreams. Touching the bones with a hot poker made them crack, forming patterns that the diviner interpreted as useful answers from the ancestors or deities. Kings had the questions and answers inscribed onto the bones, which were maintained as part of the royal archives.

During the reign of the Shang kings, there was a highest god, above deified humans, deities of the local environment, royal ancestors, and gods and goddesses of the cosmic forces. This highest god was **Shangdi** (**Shang Ti**) the Lord-on-High. He was understood as a masculine deity who ruled over important phenomena such as the weather, crops, battles, and the king's health. It was the king who was chiefly responsible for maintaining harmony between the transcendent realm of gods and ancestors and the earthly world.

During the Zhou (Chou) dynasty (c. 1046–221 BCE), which overthrew the Shang, the rulers continued to play major spiritual roles. However, the focus shifted from Shangdi to Tian, a more impersonal power controlling the universe. Though typically translated as "Heaven," the character *tian* has also been translated as "Supreme Ultimate" and "One above man." It may also be used to refer to the high god of the Chou dynasty, derived from the word for "sky." Its precise meaning is not agreed upon, but it became an important point of reference for rulers as well as philosophers.

The emperors of the ruling dynasty then developed the idea of the "Mandate of Heaven" which justified their rule. This was the belief that Heaven responds to human virtue and, specifically, that it endows rulers with the authority to rule based on their virtue. It can also remove the mandate when a ruler's virtue declines. Rulers have a moral duty to maintain the welfare of the people and a spiritual duty to conduct respectful ceremonies for Heaven, Earth, and ancestors. These obligations would later become significant aspects of Confucian thought.

Cosmic balance

In ancient Chinese tradition the universe arises from the interplay of yin and yang. They are modes of energy commonly represented as interlocking shapes, with dominance continually shifting between the dark, receptive yin mode and the bright, assertive yang mode.

In addition to ancestors, deities, and Heaven, there has long existed in China a belief that the cosmos is a manifestation of an impersonal self-generating physical–spiritual substance called **qi** (**ch'i**). It is basically the "stuff" of which all things that exist are composed. It has two aspects, whose interplay causes the ever-changing phenomena of the universe. **Yin** is the dark, receptive, "female" aspect; **yang** is the bright, assertive, "male" aspect. Men and women have both aspects within themselves. Wisdom lies in recognizing their ever-shifting, but regular and balanced, patterns and moving with them. This creative rhythm of the universe is called the **Dao** (**Tao**), or "way." As traditionally diagramed, yin and yang interpenetrate each other (represented by small circles). As soon as one aspect reaches its fullest point, it begins to diminish, while at the same time its polar opposite increases.

TIMELINE

Daoism and Confucianism

	DAOISM	CONFUCIANISM
BCE Legendary Yellow Emperor		
Shang dynasty (c. 1600–1046 BCE)	Ancient traditions of worship and divination	Ancient traditions of worship and divination
	DAOISM	**CONFUCIANISM**
Zhou dynasty (c. 1046–221 BCE)	c. 600–300 Author(s) of *Dao de jing* c. 365–290 Life of Zhuangzi	c. 551–479 Life of Confucius c. 390–305 Life of Mengzi c. 340–245 Life of Xunzi
Qin dynasty (221–206 BCE)	Immortality movements Queen Mother of the West cult	Confucian scholars suppressed, books burned
Han dynasty (206 BCE–220 CE)	Early religious Daoist sects Celestial Master tradition begins	Confucian Classics used as training for government officials
Tang dynasty CE (618–907)	Mutual influences between Daoism and Buddhism 748 Daoist Canon first compiled	Some Buddhist sects reach peak, then are persecuted Confucianism makes comeback
Song dynasty (960–1280)	*Taiji quan* appears Northen Daoist sects flourish	Neo-Confucianism 1130–1200 Life of Zhu Xi
1900	1911 Last imperial dynasty overthrown	1911 Last imperial dynasty overthrown Confucianism rejected as official state ideology
1950	Daoist Association of China (White Cloud Monastery, Beijing)	1949–1976 Mao Zedong and Communist Party take control of China; Mao's "Red Book" replaces Confucian Classics
Cultural Revolution (1966–1976)	Temples and books destroyed	Temples and books destroyed
1980		1989 Students' requests refused at Tiananmen Square
1990–2015	Daoist sects, temples re-established First Daoist Grand Ritual Popular faith and practices	Confucian Classics reintroduced in schools Confucius's birthday celebrated Hundreds of Confucius Institutes set up globally Huge statue of Confucius installed in Tiananmen Square and then taken down

The hexagram Sheng is a visual symbol of the various meanings attached to "Pushing Upward."

Nothing is outside of this process. As modern Confucian scholar TU Weiming explains:

All modalities of being, from a rock to Heaven, are integral parts of a continuum which is often referred to as the "great transformation." Since nothing is outside of this continuum, the chain of being is never broken. … The continuous presence of qi in all modalities of being makes everything flow together as the unfolding of a single process. Nothing, not even an almighty creator, is external to this process.[2]

To harmonize with the cosmic process, the ancients devised many forms of divination. One system developed during the Zhou dynasty was eventually written down as the *Yijing* (*I Ching*), or *Book of Changes*. It is a common source for both Daoism and Confucianism and is regarded as a classic text in both traditions. The *Yijing* was highly elaborated with commentaries by scholars beginning in the Han dynasty (206 BCE–220 CE). To use this subtle system, one respectfully purifies the divining objects—such as yarrow stalks or coins, whose manipulations will yield either odd numbers signifying yin or even numbers signifying yang. The person asks a question, casts the objects six times, and then consults the *Yijing* for the symbolic interpretation of the yin–yang combinations.

The pattern of throws is diagramed in the *Yijing* as a hexagram, with yin represented as a broken line and yang by a straight line. For example, hexagram number 46, called "Sheng," or "Pushing Upward," has been likened to a tree emerging from the earth, growing slowly and invisibly:

Thus the superior person of devoted character
Heaps up small things
In order to achieve something high and great.[3]

Another set of commentaries is based on the two trigrams within the hexagram. In the case of hexagram 46, the upper pattern of three yin lines can be interpreted as devotion and yielding, and the lower pattern of two yang lines above one yin line suggests gentleness. According to the commentaries, these nonaggressive qualities will ultimately lead to supreme success.

By studying and systematizing the ways of humans and of nature, the ancient Chinese tried to order their actions so that they might steer a coherent course within the changing cosmos. They recognized that any extreme action will produce its opposite as a balancing reaction, and thus they strived for a middle way of discretion and moderation.

From these roots gradually developed two contrasting ways of harmonizing with the cosmos—the more mystically religious ways, which are collectively called Daoism, and the more political and moral ways, which are known as Confucianism. Like yin and yang, they interpenetrate and complement each other, and are themselves evolving dynamically.

Daoism—the way of nature and immortality
What are the basic principles for life in harmony with Dao?

Daoism is as full of paradoxes as the Buddhist traditions it influenced: Chan, or Zen, Buddhism. It has been adored by Westerners who seek a carefree, natural way of life as an escape from the industrial rat race. Yet beneath its precepts of the simple life in harmony with nature is a tradition of great mental and physical discipline. As developed over time, some Daoist scriptures counsel indifference about birth and death; others teach ways of attaining physical immortality. These variations developed within an ancient tradition that had no name until it had to distinguish itself from Confucianism. "Daoism" is actually a label invented by scholars and awkwardly stretched to cover a philosophical (or **"literati"**) tradition, a multitude of self-cultivation and longevity techniques, and an assortment of religious sects, which probably developed at least in part from the early philosophical texts and practices. Popular religious practices such as home worship of the kitchen god have often mixed with Daoist elements, although institutional Daoism has tried to distance itself from popular religion, seeing itself as a much higher form of religion, with gods who occupy higher heavens.

Teachings of Daoist sages

Aside from its general basis in ancient Chinese ways, the specific origin of Daoist philosophy and practices is unclear. In China, tradition attributes the publicizing of these ways to the Yellow Emperor, who supposedly ruled from 2697 to 2597 BCE. He was said to have studied with an ancient sage and to have developed meditation, health, and military practices based on what he learned. After ruling for 100 years, he ascended to heaven on a dragon's back and became one of the Immortals.

Over the millennia the classic philosophical, or literati, form of Daoism has been pursued by intellectuals and artists, who explore the concepts about the Dao expressed in ancient texts and perhaps also try to apply them to their social and political environment in the effort to create a condition of harmony known as the Great Peace. The two most salient texts of the classic Daoist tradition are the *Dao de jing* and the *Zhuangzi*.

The *Dao de jing* (*Tao te Ching*, "The Classic of the Way and its Power") has been translated many times into Western languages, including more than 100 English translations, for its ideas are not only fascinating but also elusive for translators. According to tradition, the book was written for a border guard by Laozi (Lao-tzu), a curator of the royal library of the Zhou dynasty, when he left society for the mountains at the reported age of 160. The guard had recognized Laozi as a sage and begged him to leave behind a record of his wisdom. Laozi reportedly complied by inscribing the 5,000 words now known as the *Dao de jing*. This is traditionally said to have happened during the sixth century BCE, with Laozi somewhat older than Confucius. But archaeological finds date the earliest existent version of the *Dao de jing* to 350 BCE and suggest it was an alternative to Confucianism. Many scholars think it was an oral tradition, derived from the teachings of several sages, and question whether there was ever a single person corresponding to the name Laozi (Old Master).

Laozi, one of the major conveyors of the Daoist tradition, is often depicted as a humorous old man riding off into the mountains after reportedly drawing the 5,000 characters of the Dao de jing.

The book's central philosophy is a practical concern with improving harmony in life. It says that one can best harmonize with the natural flow of life by being receptive and quiet. These teachings were elaborated more emphatically and humorously by a sage named Zhuangzi (Chuang-tzu) (c. 365–290 BCE). Unlike Laozi, whose philosophy was addressed to those in leadership positions, Zhuangzi asserted that the best way to live in a chaotic, absurd civilization is to become detached from it.

At the heart of Daoist teachings is the idea of Dao, the "unnamable," the "eternally real."[4] Modern-day master Da Liu asserts that Dao is so ingrained in Chinese understanding that it is a basic concept that cannot be defined, like "goodness." Moreover, Dao is a mystical reality that cannot be grasped by the mind. The *Dao de jing* says:

> *The way that can be spoken of*
> *Is not the constant way;*
> *The name that can be named*
> *Is not the constant name.*
> *The nameless was the beginning of heaven and earth;*
> *The named was the mother of the myriad creatures.*[5]

Another chapter of the *Dao de jing* is more explicit about the mysterious Unnamable:

> *There is a thing confusedly formed,*
> *Born before heaven and earth.*
> *Silent and void*
> *It stands alone and does not change,*
> *Goes round and does not weary.*
> *It is capable of being the mother of the world.*
> *I know not its name*
> *So I style it "the way."*
> *I give it the makeshift name of "the great."*[6]

Although we cannot describe the Dao, we can live in harmony with it. Ideally, says Laozi:

> *Humans model themselves on earth,*
> *Earth on heaven,*
> *Heaven on the way,*
> *And the way on that which is naturally so.*[7]

There are several basic principles for the life in harmony with Dao. One is to experience the transcendent unity of all things, rather than separation. This realization can only be attained when one ceases to feel any personal preferences. Daoism is concerned with direct experience of the universe, accepting and co-operating with things as they are, not with setting standards of morality, nor with labeling things as "good" or "bad." Zhuangzi asserts that herein lies true spirituality:

> *Such a man can ride the clouds and mist, mount the sun and moon, and wander beyond the four seas. Life and death do not affect him. How much less will he be concerned with good and evil!*[8]

The Daoist sage takes a low profile in the world. He or she is like a valley, allowing everything needed to flow into his or her life, or like a stream. Flowing water is a Daoist model for being. It bypasses and gently wears away obstacles rather than fruitlessly attacking them, effortlessly nourishes the "ten thousand things" of material life, works without struggling, leaves all accomplishments behind without possessing them.

This is the uniquely Daoist paradox of *wu wei*—"actionless action," or taking no intentional or invasive action contrary to the natural flow of things. *Wu wei* is spontaneous, creative activity proceeding from the Dao, action without ego-assertion, letting the Dao take its course. Zhuangzi uses the analogy of a butcher whose knife always stays sharp because he lets his hand be guided by the makeup of the carcass, finding the spaces between the bones where a slight movement of the blade will glide through without resistance. Even when difficulties arise, the sage does not panic and take unnecessary action.

> To know yet to think that one does not know is best;
> Not to know yet to think that one knows will lead to difficulty.
>
> *Laozi*[9]

The result of *wu wei* is noninterference. Much of Laozi's teaching is directed at rulers, that they might guide society without interfering with its natural course. Nothing is evil, but things may be out of balance. The world is naturally in harmony; Dao is our original nature. But according to tradition, the Golden Age of Dao declined as humans departed from the "Way." "Civilization," with its intellectual attempts to improve on things and its rigid views of morality, actually leads to world chaos, the Daoists warn. How much better, Laozi advises, to accept not-knowing, moving freely in the moment with the changing universe.

Daoism places great value on withdrawal from the madding crowd to a contemplative life and love of nature. The classic Daoist seeks to find the still center, to save energy for those times when action is needed, and to take a humble, quiet approach to life. As asserted in a fourth-century BCE essay on inner training:

> The vitality of all people inevitably comes from their peace of mind.
> When anxious, one loses this guiding thread; when angry,
>   one loses this basic point.
> When one is anxious or sad, pleased or angry, the Way has no place to settle. …
> That mysterious vital energy within the mind, one moment it arrives,
>   the next it departs.
> So fine nothing can be contained within it, so vast nothing can be outside it.
> The reason we lose it is because of the harm caused by agitation.[11]

The ethical effects of such a philosophy are designed to harmonize humanity with the cosmos. Heaven, earth, and humanity all arise from the same source, the Dao, ultimate reality of the cosmos. Coming from the same source, all things

TEACHING STORY

Three in the Morning

Whether you point to a little stalk or a great pillar, a leper or the beautiful Hsi-shih (Xi Shi), things ribald and shady or things grotesque and strange, the Way makes them all into one. ... Only the man of far-reaching vision knows how to make them into one. So he has no use [for categories], but relegates all to the constant. The constant is the useful; the useful is the passable; the passable is the successful; and with success, all is accomplished. He relies upon this alone, relies upon it and does not know he is doing so. This is called the Way.

But to wear out your brain trying to make things into one without realizing that they are all the same—

this is called "three in the morning." What do I mean by "three in the morning"? When the monkey trainer was handing out acorns, he said, "You get three in the morning and four at night." This made all the monkeys furious. "Well, then," he said, "you get four in the morning and three at night." The monkeys were all delighted. There was no change in the reality behind the words, yet the monkeys responded with joy and anger. Let them, if they want to. So the sage harmonizes with both right and wrong and rests in Heaven the Equalizer.

Zhuangzi[10]

on earth are to be loved and allowed to exist and develop according to their nature. As the sage GE Hong (283–343 CE) writes in the *Inner Chapters of the Master who Embraces Simplicity*, "Universal Dao acts on noninterference [*wu wei*], that is, lets everything be natural, no matter what relationship among them and how different they are." Along with the motto "Dao follows what is natural," the Daoist feels "I am one with all things."

The only thing to be pursued is Dao, rather than material gain or fame. Laozi says:

> The five colours make man's eyes blind; ...
> Goods hard to come by
> Serve to hinder his progress.[12]

By contrast, he says:

> I have three treasures
> Which I hold and cherish.
> The first is known as compassion,
> The second is known as frugality,
> The third is known as not daring
>   to take the lead in the empire. ...
> There is no disaster greater than
>   not being content;
> There is no misfortune greater
>   than being covetous.
> Hence in being content, one will
>   always have enough.[13]

Furthermore, according to Daoist ideals, there should not be a great gap between the rich and the poor. Just as Heaven makes adjustments between surpluses and deficiencies, the rich should desire to share with the poor. But as Laozi observes:

> Who is there that can take what he himself
>   has in excess and offer this to the empire?
> Only he who has the way.[14]

Popular religion and organized Daoism

What practices are associated with popular religion and organized Daoism?

Popular religion and organized Daoism became considerably intertwined over the centuries when Daoist specialists took charge of spiritual tasks such as alchemy, faith healing, and the use of talismans, which seem to have existed from ancient times in China. But some of the folk practices have also survived as independent traditions outside of formal Daoist frameworks.

People may believe in invisible spirits who are involved in their destinies, so out of both fear and respect they want to make sure to worship them properly. Burning incense and making offerings have been ways of communicating with them since antiquity. In temple worship, these practices have become institutionalized, with detailed ritual instructions and a priesthood to carry them out. However, folk practices may transcend the restrictions of classic Daoism, with variations such as making offerings of nonvegetarian foods. LIU Zhongyu, of a branch of the Dragon Gate sect of the Complete Perfection lineage in Hong Kong, pragmatically explains, "In fact, it is forbidden in Daoism to give things such as pig's heads as offerings. But as the people have long been doing so, Daoism has to let things take their own course."[15]

Letting things take their own course has long included the art of **feng shui**, or geomancy—determining natural flows of qi through the earth, as

Chinese artists captured the flows of qi through mountains, water, and trees in their paintings.

revealed by the flows of wind and water. Although awareness of these flows probably arose from shamanistic folk traditions, it sometimes became the province of specialists. By observing the contours of the land and the flows of wind and water, specialists in feng shui can reportedly determine the best places for the harmonious placement of a temple, dwelling place, or grave. By examining the flow of qi within a dwelling, they decide on the optimal placement of furniture and wall decorations.

Deities arising from folk traditions have in some cases become part of the Daoist pantheon. One of the most familiar deities in popular Chinese traditions is the kitchen god. Although his worship usually takes place at the family level in the home where he lives, he was at one time listed in official Daoist spirit pedigrees as the Great Emperor and Controller of Destinies of the Eastern Kitchen. According to folk belief, the kitchen god sits in a corner of the kitchen watching the family's doings so that he can make an annual report about their virtues and failings to the Jade Emperor. Sometimes, humorous ruses are used to ensure that he does not give a bad report. One is to make an offering before he sets off for Heaven that is so intoxicating that he forgets about the family's flaws. Another is to offer him some sweet maltose that is so sticky that he cannot open his mouth to speak when he meets the Jade Emperor.

The ancient practice of worshiping certain people as divine, appointed to heavenly office after they have died, is also encompassed by organized Daoism. For example, during the Song dynasty a virtuous girl who had received talismans and esoteric teachings from a Daoist master was thought to have saved her father and brother with her spiritual powers when their boat capsized.

Near the end of the Chinese lunar year, performers in Shanxi province carry on a traditional dragon dance in a festival honoring the kitchen god.

Other miraculous interventions also became attributed to her. After she died at a young age, a temple was erected in her honor. Her cult thence spread along the southeast coast of China, and by the twelfth century she was recognized by the imperial court as a nationally important deity to whom sacrifices were to be performed all over the country. Her importance grew as various titles were given to her by imperial decrees. In 1683, she was declared the "Consort of Heaven" (*Tianhou*, or *Tien-hou*), but most people continue to call her by the familiar name *Mazu* (Ma-tsu) (Grandma).

In popular practice, people vow to do a good deed if their prayer request is granted. Accordingly, they may offer incense, candles, or food to the deities to redeem the vow once they feel the deities have blessed them with success. Sometimes the vow-redeeming promises are more elaborate, such as releasing a captive animal, or sculpting a statue of a deity. Many people vow to do some kind of performance to please the deities, often including singing, dancing, music, or beating drums. Some such performances are organized on a large scale, as performance fairs at temples.

As in ancient times, Chinese villages make collective offerings to the local spirits or organize processions in which the spirits visit the local region, bless them, and protect them from harm such as epidemics. The images of the deities from the temple are put in palanquins (or today, trucks) and carried in the procession. Talismans are also made for protection, with the written characters presumed to have magical power to control the spirits.

Inner alchemy

In contrast to popular practices, an elite thread of ancient traditions that have also become interwoven with Daoism involves inner alchemy: individual spiritual practices for the sake of inner transformation, self-cultivation, longevity, and perhaps immortality. Daoist texts refer to powerful ascetic practices traditionally passed down secretly from teacher to pupil. The teachers lived in the mountains; great Daoist teachers are said to be still hidden in the remote mountains of China and Korea.

The aim of the longevity practices is to use the energy available to the body in order to become strong and healthy, and to intuitively perceive the order of the universe. Within our body is the spiritual micro-universe of the "three treasures" necessary for the preservation of life: generative force (*jing*), vital life force (*qi*), and spirit (*shen*). These three are said to be activated with the help of various methods: breathing techniques, vocalizations, vegetarian diets, gymnastics, absorption of solar and lunar energies, sexual techniques, visualizations, and meditations.

The process of "inner alchemy" involves circulating and transmuting *jing* energy from the lower body into qi energy and then to *shen* energy to form what is called the Immortal Fetus, which an adept can reportedly raise through the Heavenly Gate at the top of the head and thus leave their physical body for various purposes, including preparation for life after death. In addition, the adept learns to draw the qi of heaven and earth into the micro-universe of the body, unifying and harmonizing inner and outer.

> *The secret of the magic of life consists in using action in order to attain non-action.*
>
> The Secret of the Golden Flower[16]

One of the goals of esoteric Daoist practice is to separate the Immortal Fetus from the body so that the former can operate independently, both before and after death.

In contrast to physical practices to lengthen life and lead to immortality, Zhuangzi had counseled indifference to birth and death: "The True Man of ancient times knew nothing of loving life, knew nothing of hating death. He emerged without delight; he went back in without a fuss. He came briskly, he went briskly, and that was all."[17] Laozi referred enigmatically to immortality or long life realized through spiritual death of the individual self, the body and mind transmuted into selfless vehicles for the eternal. As Professor Huai-Chin NAN notes, people who are interested in Daoist practices:

> *usually forget the highest principles, or the basis of philosophical theory behind the cultivation of Tao [Dao] and the opening of the ch'i [qi] routes for longevity. … Longevity consists of maintaining one's health, slowing down the ageing process, living without illness and pain, and dying peacefully without bothering other people. Immortality does not mean indefinite physical longevity; it indicates the eternal spiritual life.*[18]

A quiet contemplative life in natural surroundings, with peaceful mind, health-maintaining herbs, healthy diet, practices to strengthen the inner organs and open the meridians (subtle energy pathways known to Chinese doctors), and meditations to transmute vital into spiritual energy, does bring a marked tendency to longevity. Chinese literature and folk knowledge contain many references to venerable sages thought to be centuries old. They live hidden in the mountains, away from the society of others, and are said to be somewhat translucent. The most famous of the legendary long-lived are the Eight Immortals, humans who were said to have gained immortality, each with his or her own special magical power.

Since ancient times, one of the most revered celestial beings has been the Queen Mother of the West. She guards the elixir of life and is the most wondrous incarnation of yin energy. The Daoist canon also includes the writings of some female Daoist sages who undertook the great rigors of Daoist meditation practices and reportedly mastered the processes of inner transformation. In her mystical poetry, the twelfth-century female sage SUN Bu-er describes the ultimate realization:

> *All things finished.*
> *You sit still in a little niche.*
> *The light body rides on violet energy,*
> *The tranquil nature washes in a pure pond.*
> *Original energy is unified, yin and yang are one;*
> *The spirit is the same as the universe. …*[19]

Daoist sects

Institutionalization of such ancient, esoteric, and popular practices into distinctive religious movements, with revealed texts, detailed rituals, and priests serving as ritual specialists, developed as the Han dynasty (206 BCE–220 CE) was declining amid famine and war. An array of revelations and prophecies predicted the end of the age and finally led to the rise of religious/political organizations.

In 184 CE, inspired by a vision of Great Peace, hundreds of thousands of followers of a leader who was known as a faith healer and advocate of egalitarian ideas rebelled in eight of China's twelve provinces; their rebellion took several years to suppress and presaged the fall of the Han dynasty. Simultaneously, in western China, Zhang Daoling (Chang Tao-ling) had a vision in which he was appointed representative of the Dao on earth and given the title Celestial Master. He advocated similar practices of healing by faith and developed a quasi-military organization of religious officials, attracting numerous followers. The older Han religion had involved demons and exorcism, belief in an afterlife, and a god of destinies, who granted fortune or misfortune based on heavenly records of good and bad deeds. These roles were now ascribed to a pantheon of celestial deities, who in turn were controlled by the new Celestial Master priesthood led by Zhang's family. This hereditary clergy performed imperial investitures as well as village festivals, with both men and women serving as libationers in local dioceses. After the sack of the northern capitals early in the fourth century, the Celestial Masters and other aristocrats fled south and established themselves on Dragon-Tiger Mountain in southeast China. Today the **Celestial Masters** tradition is thriving in Taiwan and Hong Kong, and the movement is also being revived in mainland China.

In approximately 365 CE another aristocratic family in exile in southern China began receiving revelations from a deceased member, Lady Wei. These revelations of the names and powers of newly discovered deities, meditation methods, alchemy, and rituals were recorded in exquisite calligraphy and transmitted to a few advanced disciples. This elite group of celibates, who resided on Mount Mao, called their practices "**Highest Purity Daoism**." They looked down on the Celestial Masters tradition as crude, and they avoided village rituals and commoners. Instead, they focused on meditations for purifying the body with divine energies so as "to rise up to heaven in broad daylight." Although the Highest Purity Daoism did not reach the mass of the people, its texts and influence continue to be revered today as the elite tradition of organized Daoism.

In the late fourth century, another group arose in the wake of Highest Purity: the Numinous Treasure school. It assimilated many elements of Buddhism, creating a medley of new meditation practices, divine beings, rituals, scriptures, heavens, rebirth, and hells. This tradition was in turn succeeded in the twelfth century by **Complete Perfection**, which has been the dominant monastic school ever since. It unites Daoist inner alchemy with Chan Buddhist meditation and Confucian social morality, harmonizing the three religions. Actively monastic, it focuses on meditation and nonattachment to the world. Today its major center is the White Cloud Monastery in Beijing, the headquarters of the government-approved Daoist Association of China. Complete Perfection is also the foundation for most Hong Kong Daoist temples and martial arts groups.

The many revealed scriptures of Daoist movements were occasionally compiled and canonized by the court. The present Daoist canon was compiled in 1445 CE. Containing about 1,500 sophisticated scriptures, it has begun to be studied by non-Daoist scholars in recent decades. It includes a wealth of first-hand accounts by mystical practitioners—poems of their visionary shamanistic journeys, encounters with deities, advanced meditation practices, descriptions of the perfected human being, methods and elixirs for ascending to heavenly realms and achieving immortality, and descriptions of the Immortals and the heavenly bureaucracies. The rituals and inner cultivation practices of the canon are in use today, and the immense pantheon of deities that has evolved is represented by a great variety of images.

The Lantern Festival

Popular religious practices of ancient origin survive in China today as happy festivals. One of the favorites is the Lantern Festival, the end of Chinese New Year celebrations. These begin on the twenty-third or twenty-fourth day of the twelfth month of the lunar year, which is thought to be the day the gods go to heaven to offer their respects to the supreme deity, the Jade Emperor. One of them is the kitchen god making his report about the family, which will determine their fortunes in the year to come. The New Year begins in the spring, as the earth comes back to life and ploughing and sowing of fields can start again. In preparation for the coming year, houses are thoroughly cleaned to remove any bad luck, and doors and windows may be painted and decorated with auspicious inscriptions. People happily visit each other with offerings of gifts and flowers, and attempt to clear all their debts. Families may wake early on the second or fifth day of the first lunar month to set off firecrackers to welcome the Magic Horse of Wealth to their home.

The climax of the celebrations—the Lantern Festival—occurs on the night of the fifteenth day of the first lunar month. People roam joyfully through the streets carrying, and looking at, a great array of paper lanterns, and enjoying lion dances, dragon dances, parades, plays, fireworks, acrobatics, and sticky sweet rice balls. Owners of the lanterns may write riddles on them, and those who successfully solve them are given small prizes. It is a cultural festival thought to have sacred origins, but there are various understandings of what is being celebrated. Lanterns may illustrate popular subjects or may be decorated with scenes of the Immortals—or else of Buddhas and bodhisattvas.

According to one legend, the Jade Emperor in heaven was so upset because a town had killed his beloved goose that he determined to destroy the town with fire. But the townspeople, warned by a fairy, lit so many lanterns that from above the town appeared to be on fire. Feeling that his anger had already been avenged, the Jade Emperor did not send the firestorm. From then on, people celebrated their rescue by carrying lanterns on the first full moon of the year.

Another explanation features the god of Heaven worshiped by people in ancient China. It was he who controlled the fate of the world, as he had sixteen dragons and could therefore send famine, plagues, droughts, or calamities. The emperor would therefore request him to send only good weather and good health to the people of the kingdom. During the Han dynasty, an emperor dedicated a night of great celebrations to the god of Heaven, and the tradition has continued.

Yet another story revolves around the Heavenly Official Who Gives Blessings. His birthday is the fifteenth day of the first lunar month. Because he likes all sorts of entertainment, the people decorate lanterns and offer many amusements in the hope of being blessed with good fortune.

Whatever the explanation, people are entertained by great cultural festivals in the name of pleasing the gods. A description of the Lantern Festival from the Song dynasty listed dozens of dancing troupes, including the Cloud Holders, the Sword Players, the Wedding Players, the Clothes washers' Songs, the Bamboo Horses, the Camels and Elephants, and the Deities and Ghosts, plus twenty-four puppet troupes such as the Land Dragon Boats and the Lantern Kickers. The celebrations and the lanterns became more and more elaborate and now, with the aid of modern electronics, people happily enjoy spectacular entertainments.

At death either Daoist or Buddhist priests may be hired by families to perform rituals to help the deceased. Every temple has a side shrine to Tudi Gong (T'u-ti Kung), the local earth god, lowest member of the celestial hierarchy, who can transport offerings to deceased loved ones.

Daoism today

Which Daoist practices are of increasing interest in the West?

Historically, whenever the central Chinese government has been strong, it has tended to demand total allegiance to itself as a divine authority and to challenge or suppress competing religious groups. Since the Han dynasty, Chinese emperors were called "Son of Heaven," and their families claimed to have received the Mandate of Heaven when it was taken away from the previous dynasty. Confucian scholars were suppressed and their books were burned by the Qin (Ch'in) dynasty (221–206 BCE), shamans were forbidden during the Han dynasty, Buddhists were persecuted during the Tang dynasty, the Taiping rebellion of the nineteenth century attempted to purge China of Daoism and Buddhism, and during the Cultural Revolution of 1966 to 1976 zealous young Red Guards destroyed Daoist, Buddhist, and Confucian temples and books. However, during the economic liberalization that began in the late twentieth century in mainland China, in spite of an atheistic communist ideology temples were maintained as historic sites, pilgrimages to temples in natural sites and religious tourism have been encouraged, and an explosion of temple building has occurred.

All forms of Daoist practice are still actively undertaken today, in communist mainland China, Taiwan, Hong Kong, Korea, and Chinese communities overseas. Chinese temples combine Confucian, Buddhist, and Daoist elements, but the liturgies tend to be Daoist.

Both Daoist and Buddhist groups continue to be recipients of new revelations and scriptures. These texts, known as "precious scrolls," emanate from deities such as the Golden Mother of the Celestial Pool. It is believed that in the past the Divine Mother sent Buddha and Laozi as her messengers but that now the crisis of the present world requires her direct intervention.

Starting in the 1980s, a few ancient Daoist practitioners in China tried to teach groups of young students so that the disciplines could be continually transmitted. They met with many bureaucratic obstacles within communist China but received considerable support from Chinese communities and scholars

Making food offerings for ancestors in the ancestral hall of Fung Ying Sin Temple, Hong Kong.

abroad. The Communist Party is still officially anti-religious, espousing the Marxist theory that religion will die out as unnecessary in a socialist state, but in fact there is a great resurgence of religious practice of all sorts, both in the countryside and in the cities. After the violent attempts of the Cultural Revolution to stamp out religion, shrines and halls for worship of clan ancestors are sprouting and many new Daoist and Buddhist temples, Muslim mosques, and Christian churches are being built. Temples are busy with worshipers, including people trying to find clues to their future by casting divining sticks after praying before the image of a deity. Party policy seems to have turned toward the pragmatic view that traditional religious and cultural traditions can perhaps play a "positive role" in building social stability in the midst of rapid social and economic change. Religious organizations must register with the government and operate under government control. There are hundreds of local Daoist associations in the provinces of China, as well as the Daoist Association of China, centered in the White Cloud Monastery in Beijing. Its stated goals include promoting:

Daoist nun HUANG Zhi An (left) organized a nunnery where women are trained in traditional arts and Daoist spiritual practices.

> *the mutual adaptation between Daoism and socialist society. The association is to participate in the building of the socialist modernizations, and devote itself to the maintenance of the stability of society, the unification of the country, and the peace of the world.*[20]

Daoist nuns and monks are of equal status. HUANG Zhi An, head nun of the Daoist Temple in Hengshan, Hunan Province, collected funds to help rebuild the temple and monastic complex—which also includes a Buddhist monastery and a temple of both religions combined—and to build a center for training nuns in the classical arts, including chanting, music, and practices to develop qi. Her speech, gestures, and actions are natural and spontaneous, like those of an energetic child, and yet she presides over solemn, ritualized chanting by the nuns. When asked to explain this combination of opposites, she says simply of Daoist practice, "It's like democracy: There has to be a combination of freedom and also rules for confining freedom, or else there is chaos."[21]

Hong Kong has long been home to many Daoist temples and activities. The Peng Ying Xian Guan (Fung Ying Seen Koon) branch of Complete Perfection Daoism began early in the twentieth century as an attempt by two Dragon Gate priests to develop a secluded holy place for self-cultivation, as a cure for decaying social morality. Now the organization sponsors a free clinic, a school, lectures for teaching the Dao, training classes for priests and study of rites and scriptures, and rituals to pray for blessings and redeem lost souls. Worship at Daoist temples is so popular in Hong Kong that in places there are attempts to limit the amount of incense worshipers use in hope of pleasing the deities. For instance, the Sik Sik Yuen Wong Tai Sin Temple, where many people believe that their prayer requests are being answered, has printed a brochure that advises worshipers:

> *The spirit of Taoism is that we should respect and protect nature and be considerate. … It is sufficient that worshippers offer a stroke of incense with three sticks to express their sincere devotion to Gods. Be careful not to burn enormous or a large amount of incense, which may pollute the environment and nature.*[22]

Attempting to unite Daoists and promote social welfare, the Hong Kong Taoist Association is developing schools to combine education with Daoist enlightenment and character-building, giving lectures encouraging morality, building and

On Chinese New Year, Hong Kong temples are filled with worshipers who burn incense sticks to pay homage to the spirits.

repairing Daoist temples, and organizing festivals observed by all Daoist temples such as Seven-Day-and-Night Rituals for Accumulating Merits for the sake of the prosperity and peace of Hong Kong and harmony in the world. Similar Daoist associations now exist in Taiwan, Malaysia, and Singapore

Academic study of Daoism is intensifying with the help of such Daoist religious organizations, university scholars, social science research institutes, and cultural and artistic institutions. The Chinese government's Center for Religious Studies carries on activities such as a major project to republish the entire Daoist canon with extensive explanatory material from current research. A series of international conferences on Daoist Studies has been held not only in China and Hong Kong, but also in Bavaria, Boston, and Los Angeles.

Daoist ideas are also being promoted to help curb the environmental and social damage that has resulted in China from rapid industrialization. ZHOU Zhongzhi, Director of the Center of Business Ethics Study in Shanghai Normal University, describes the ecological principles embedded in Daoist thought:

> *Through interaction and interdependence, humans and nature constitute a harmonious and unified system, [but] it is possible to lead to inharmoniousness of human and nature, even burst into ecological crisis, if man becomes insatiable and conscienceless.*[23]

According to Zhou, application of Daoist principles would lead people to limit their consumer desires and foster compassionate giving, countering the growing disparities between rich and poor.

Interest in Daoist practices and philosophy has boomed in the West from the middle of the twentieth century. By now there are many masters and centers in the United States. They include organized religious institutions, societies for self-cultivation, and practitioners of techniques for spiritual development, health, and longevity. Tours of Daoist temples and sacred mountains in China are also offered by American Daoist Studies scholars, including visits to a huge new statue of Laozi on Mount Qingcheng in western China. In the Western popularization of Daoism, classic Daoist texts are even being used by businesses to teach management practices.

Many people outside China are now benefiting from acupuncture therapy, which is based on the idea that qi flows through the body in channels, or meridians. Needle stimulation or burning of herbs above specific points along the meridians is successfully used to cure or alleviate many ailments. Traditional

Many Chinese gather to do taiji quan *together at sunrise in public spaces, such as this promenade in Shanghai.*

Chinese herbal medicine is also of increasing interest, as are energy training practices. Of these, *Taiji quan* (**T'ai chi ch'uan**) was developed in the eighteenth century as a training for martial arts. It is still practiced today by many Chinese at dawn and dusk for their health. It looks like slow swimming in the air, with continual circular movement through a series of dance-like postures. They are considered manifestations of the unobstructed flow of qi through the body. According to the *Taiji Quan Classics*, "In any action the entire body should be light and agile and all of its parts connected like pearls on a thread."[24] *Taiji quan* is often physically beneficial in controlling blood pressure, muscular co-ordination, and balance, and thus is useful to elderly people.

In the early twentieth century, a sickly tuberculosis patient cured himself by practicing the energy training disciplines from an old Daoist inner alchemical text describing traditional meditation and longevity techniques. He learned to detect the inner movements of qi within himself and then wrote about them in contemporary biomedical terms. Others also thence became interested in the traditional health exercises. The self-cultivation systems they popularized are now generally known as **qigong** (**ch'i-kung**) and are widely used in China and elsewhere to cure diseases, increase physical vitality, and improve concentration.

Confucianism—the practice of virtue

Which virtue did Confucius feel could save society?

To trace a different strand of East Asian religion, we return to the sixth century BCE, which was a period of great spiritual and intellectual flourishing in many cultures. It roughly coincided with the life of the Buddha, the Persian Empire, the Golden Age of Athens, the great Hebrew prophets, and in China with the life of another outstanding figure. Westerners call him Confucius and his teaching Confucianism. His family name was Kong; the Chinese honored him as Kong Fuzi (Master Kong) and called his teaching **Rujiao** (the teaching of the scholars). Rujiao did not begin with Confucius. Rather, it is based on the ancient Chinese beliefs in Heaven, ancestor worship, and the efficacy of rituals. Confucius developed from these roots a school of thought that emphasizes the cultivation of moral virtues and the interaction between human rulers and Heaven, with political involvement as the way to transforming the world. This philosophy became highly influential in China and permeated the cultures of East Asia, where it is still prevalent, despite great political changes. It exists not only as a school of thought but also as the practice of religious ethics and today includes both traditional and newly invented rituals

For 2,000 years, the strands classified by Western scholars as Daoism, Buddhism, and Confucianism have co-existed in China, contributing mutually to the culture. Both Daoism and Buddhism emphasize the ever-changing nature of things in the cosmos, whereas Confucianism focuses on ways of developing a just and orderly society. This is the Confucian way of connecting human beings to the transcendent—yet also immanent—moral will of Heaven.

Individuals often harmonize the apparently opposite characteristics of Daoism and Confucianism in their own lives and feel no need to identify themselves as followers of only one religious path. For example, elderly Daoist Master An speaks on one hand of the fact that he and his fellows sweep the temple when they feel like it—"We're not caught up in routines"—and on the other of the ways that his father's teaching of Confucian maxims shaped his life:

> My father was very cultured and adamant about teaching us the true Tao. He mastered the classics, and would write out quotations all the time. Over on the wall there is a quotation by Confucius he wrote:
>
> "If I'm not generous with those below me,
> If I'm disrespectful toward the proprieties,
> Or if I do not properly mourn at a funeral,
> How can I have self-esteem?"
>
> He'd paste these quotations on our wall above the bed. I'd turn my head and there it was, sinking in my brain. ... Confucius also said, "One who seeks the Tao cannot be deficient in manners."[25]

Professor YU Yingshi explains that Daoism and Confucianism can co-exist because in Chinese tradition there are no major divisions between mind and matter, utopian ideals and everyday life:

> For Chinese, the transcendental world, the world of the spirit, interpenetrates with the everyday world though it is not considered identical to it. ... So mundane human relationships are, from the very beginning, endowed with a transcendental character.[26]

Master Kong's life

Confucius was born in approximately 551 BCE, during the Zhou dynasty, into a family whose ancestors had been prominent in the previous dynasty. They had lost their position through political struggles, and his father, a soldier, died when the boy was only three years old. Although the young boy was determined to be a scholar, the family's financial straits necessitated his taking such humble work as overseeing granaries and livestock. He married at the age of nineteen and had at least two children. His mother died when he was twenty-three, and during three years of mourning he lived ascetically and studied ancient ceremonial rites (*li*) and imperial institutions. When he returned to social interaction, he gained some renown as a teacher of *li* and of the arts of governing.

It was a period of political chaos, with the stability of the early Zhou dynasty giving way to disorder. As central power weakened, feudal lords held more power than kings of the central court, ministers assassinated their rulers, and sons killed their fathers. Confucius felt that a return to classical rites and standards of virtue was the only way out of the chaos, and he unsuccessfully sought rulers who would adopt his ideas. He then turned to a different approach: training young men to be wise and altruistic public servants. He is said to have had 3,000 disciples, of whom seventy-two became known for their wisdom and virtue, and who collected and spread his teachings. Confucius proposed that the rulers should perform classical rites and music properly so that they would remain of visibly high moral character and thus inspire the common people to be virtuous. He thus instructed his students in the "Six Classics" of China's cultural heritage: the *Yijing*, poetry, history, rituals, music and dance, and the Spring and Autumn Annals of events in his state, Lu. According to tradition, it was Confucius who edited older documents pertaining to these six areas and put them into the form now known as the Confucian Classics. There are now only five; the treatises on music were either destroyed or never existed. One of the five Classics is *The Book of Rites*, whose contents include not only ritual instructions but also philosophical discourses such as the *Great Learning* and the *Doctrine of the Mean*. Of his role, Confucius claimed only: "I am a transmitter and not a creator. I believe in and have a passion for the ancients."[27]

In addition to reviving the Confucian Classics, Confucius so inspired his disciples that they put together excerpts from what he had taught them as the *Analects of Confucius*. The terse sayings include what appears to be a sort of autobiographical statement:

> *The Master said, "At fifteen I had set my will upon learning. At thirty, I stood firm. At forty, I had no doubts. At fifty, I knew the will of Heaven. At sixty, I heard it with a listening ear. At seventy, I could follow my heart's desires without overstepping what was right.*[28]

In other words, after learning about the Way of Heaven, ultimately he manifested it in his own life.

Confucius's work and teachings were considered relatively insignificant during his lifetime. After his death in 479 BCE, interstate warfare increased, ancient family loyalties were replaced by large and impersonal armies, and personal virtues were replaced by laws and state control. After the brutal reunification of China by the Qin dynasty, however, rulership required a more cultured class of bureaucrats who could embody the virtues advocated by Confucius. In the second century BCE the Confucian Classics thus became the basis of training for the scholar-officials who were to serve in the government. The life of the gentleman-scholar devoted to proper government became the highest professed ideal. Eventually temples were devoted to the worship of Confucius himself as the model for unselfish public service, human kindness, and scholarship. However, the official state use of the Confucian Classics can be seen as a political device to give the government a veneer of civility.

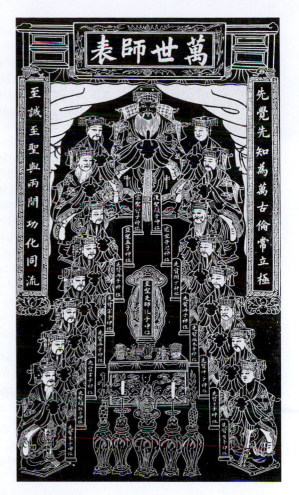

Confucianism idealized gentleman-scholars, who became the highest class in China until the 20th-century revolution.

The Confucian virtues

As codified during the Han dynasty (206 BCE–220 CE), there are five cardinal virtues encouraged by Confucius: humaneness, righteousness and justice, civility (ritual propriety), wisdom, and faithfulness. Foremost among these virtues that Confucius felt could save society was **ren (jen)**. Translations of this central term include "humaneness," "innate goodness," "love," "benevolence," "perfect virtue," and "human-heartedness."

> *The Noble Person does not, even for the space of a single meal, act contrary to goodness. In moments of haste, he cleaves to it. In seasons of danger, he cleaves to it.*
>
> *The Analects, IV:5*

The modern Chinese character for *ren* is a combination of "two" and "person," conveying the idea of relationship. Those relationships emphasized by

Confucians are the interactions between parent and child, older and younger siblings, husband and wife, ruler and subject, and friend and friend. In all but the last of these relationships, the first is considered superior to the second. Each relationship is nonetheless based on distinct but mutual obligations and responsibilities. At the top, the ruler models himself on Heaven, serving as a parent to the people and linking them to the larger cosmic order through ritual ceremonies. Confucius says that this was the source of the greatness of Yao—a sage king of *c.* 2357 BCE: "It is Heaven that is great and Yao who modeled himself upon it."[29]

In Confucius's ideal world, there is a reciprocal hierarchy in which each knows his place and respects those above him. As the *Great Learning* states it, peace begins with the moral cultivation of the individual and order in the family. This peace extends outward to society, government, and the universe itself like circular ripples in a pond.

In chapter IV of the *Analects*, Confucius describes the rare person who is utterly devoted to *ren* as one who is not motivated by personal profit but by what is moral, is concerned with self-improvement rather than public recognition, is ever mindful of parents, speaks cautiously but acts quickly, and regards human nature as basically good.

The prime exemplar of *ren* should be the ruler. Rulers were urged to rule not by physical force or coercion but by the example of personal virtue:

> *Confucius said: If a ruler himself is upright, all will go well without orders. But if he himself is not upright, even though he gives orders they will not be obeyed. ... One who governs by virtue is comparable to the polar star, which remains in its place while all the stars turn towards it."*[30]

Asked to define the essentials of strong government, Confucius listed adequate troops, adequate food, and the people's trust. But of these, the only true necessity is that the people have faith in their rulers. To earn this faith, the ruling class should "cultivate themselves," leading lives of virtue and decorum. They should continually adhere to *ren*, always reaching upward, cherishing what is right, rather than reaching downward for material gain.

In addition to the five classic virtues, Confucius emphasized filial piety to parents. According to Confucian doctrine, there are three grades of filial piety: The lowest is to support one's parents, the second is not to bring humiliation to one's parents and ancestors, and the highest is to glorify them. In the ancient *Book of Rites*, as revived by Confucius, deference to one's parents is scrupulously defined. For instance, a husband and wife should go to visit their parents and parents-in-law, whereupon:

> *On getting to where they are, with bated breath and gentle voice, they should ask if their clothes are (too) warm or (too) cold, whether they are ill or pained, or uncomfortable in any part; and if they be so, they should proceed reverently to stroke and scratch the place. They should in the same way, going before or following after, help and support their parents in quitting or entering (the apartment). In bringing in the basin for them to wash, the younger will carry the stand and the elder the water; they will beg to be allowed to pour out the water, and when the washing is concluded, they will hand the towel. They will ask whether they want anything, and then respectfully bring it. All this they will do with an appearance of pleasure to make their parents feel at ease.*[31]

Confucius also supported the ancient Chinese custom of ancestor worship, as an extension of filial piety—indeed, as the highest achievement of filial piety.

Confucius said relatively little about the supernatural, preferring to focus on the here-and-now: "While you are not able to serve men, how can you serve the ghosts and spirits?"[32] He made a virtue of *li* (the rites honoring ancestors and deities), suggesting that one make the sacrifices with the feeling that the spirits were present. The rites should not be empty gestures; he recommended that they be outwardly simple and inwardly grounded in *ren*. His teachings clearly have a religious underpinning: that life is to be cultivated in a way that brings one into rapport with the ultimate religious authority of Heaven. He refers to Heaven as a given. For instance:

> The Master said, "I would prefer not speaking." Tzu-kung said, "If you, Master, do not speak, what shall we, your disciples, have to record?" The Master said, "Does Heaven speak? The four seasons pursue their courses, and all things are continually being produced, but does Heaven say anything?"[33]

Although Confucius did not speak much about an unseen Reality, he asserted that *li* are the earthly expressions of the natural cosmic order. Everything should be done with a sense of propriety. Continually eulogizing the Noble Person (*junzi*) of China's ancient high civilization as the model, Confucius used examples such as the way of passing someone in mourning. Even if the mourner were a close friend, the *junzi* would assume a solemn expression and "lean forward with his hands on the crossbar of his carriage to show respect; he would act in a similar manner towards a person carrying official documents."[34] Even in humble surroundings, the proprieties should be observed: "Even when a meal consisted only of coarse rice and vegetable broth, [the *junzi*] invariably made an offering from them and invariably did so solemnly."[35]

Confucianism after Confucius

What was the significance of Neo-Confucianism?

The Confucian tradition has been added to by many later commentators. Two of the most significant were Mengzi (Mencius) and Xunzi (Hsun Tzu), who differed in their approach.

A little over a hundred years after Confucius died, the "Secondary Sage" Mengzi (Meng Tzu, commonly latinized as Mencius) was born. During his lifetime (*c.* 390–305 BCE) Chinese society became even more chaotic. Like his predecessor, the Secondary Sage tried to share his wisdom with embattled rulers, but to little avail. He, too, took up teaching, based on stabilizing aspects of the earlier feudal system.

Mengzi's major addition to the Confucian tradition was his belief in the inherent goodness of human nature. Mengzi emphasized the moral duty of rulers to govern by the principle of humanity and the good of the people. If rulers are guided by profit motives, this self-centered motivation will be reflected in all subordinates and social chaos will ensue. On the other hand, "When a commiserating government is conducted from a commiserating heart, one can rule the whole empire as if one were turning it in one's palm."[36] This is a natural way, says Mengzi, for people are naturally good: "The tendency of human nature to do good is like that of water to flow downward."[37] Heaven empowers the righteous, for there is a direct connection between the goodness of human nature and the nature of Heaven. Learning is therefore ideally a process of coming to understand the Way of Heaven.

Another follower of Confucius quite disagreed with this assessment. This was Xunzi, who seems to have been born when Mengzi was an old man. Xunzi argued that human nature is naturally self-centered and that Heaven is impersonal, operating according to natural laws rather than intervening on the side of good government or responding to human wishes ("Heaven does not suspend the winter because men dislike cold"[38]). Humans must hold up their own end. Their natural tendency, however, is to envy, to compete, and to desire personal gain and sensual pleasure. The only way to constrain these tendencies is to teach and legally enforce the rules of *li* and *yi* (righteous conduct). Rituals help people to limit their desires and create social order. Though naturally flawed, humans can gradually attain sagehood by persistent study, patience, and good works and thereby form a co-operative triad with Heaven and Earth.

Xunzi's careful reasoning provided a basis for the new legalistic structure of government. The idealism of Mengzi was revived much later as a Chinese response to Buddhism and became required for the civil-service examinations from the thirteenth to the early twentieth centuries. However, their points of agreement are basic to Confucianism: The appropriate practice of virtue is of great value; humans can attain this through self-cultivation; and study and emulation of the ancient sages are the path to harmony in the individual, family, state, and world, with proper relationships between Heaven, Earth, and humans.

These basic points situate Confucianism within the academic category that can be referred to as "religion," if religion is defined broadly as Frederick Streng did: "a means to ultimate transformation."[39] All things considered, Confucian Studies Professor Rodney L. Taylor concludes: "The key to the religious interpretation of Confucianism lies in the role of Heaven, not just as an authority for the stability of society, but as a source of religious authority and inspiration for the individual."[40] The goal of Confucian learning is to become a sage, fully cultivating one's inner virtues and always acting according to righteousness, in accord with the Way of Heaven.

The state cult

Since ancient times, as we have seen, rulers have been regarded as the link between Earth and Heaven. This understanding persisted in Chinese society, but Confucius and his followers had elaborated the idea that the ruler must be virtuous for this relationship to work. During the Han dynasty, Confucius's teachings were at last honored by the state. The Han scholar DONG Zhongshu (Tung Chung-shu, c. 179–c. 104 BCE) set up an educational system based on the Confucian Classics. He used Confucian ideals to unite the people behind the ruler, who himself was required to be subject to Heaven.

During the Han dynasty, the traditional *Book of Rites* and *Etiquette and Ritual* were reconstructed, with an increased emphasis on offerings, as practiced since ancient times. These rites were thought to preserve harmony between humans, Heaven, and Earth. At the family level, offerings were made to propitiate the family ancestors. Government officials were responsible for ritual sacrifices to beings such as the gods of fire, literature, cities, mountains, waters, the polar star, sun, moon, and former rulers, and also to Confucius. The most important ceremonies were performed by the emperor, to give thanks and ask blessings from Heaven, Earth, gods of the land and agriculture, and the dynastic ancestors. Of these, the highest ritual was the elaborate annual sacrifice at the white marble Altar of Heaven by the emperor. He was considered Son of Heaven, the "high priest of the world." Both he and his large retinue prepared themselves by three days of fasting and keeping vigil. In a highly reverent atmosphere, he then sacrificed a bull, offered precious jade, and sang prayers of gratitude to the Supreme.

Neo-Confucianism

Buddhism and Daoism became very popular during the period of disunity that followed the fall of the Han dynasty, and Confucianism declined. But during the Song dynasty (960–1280 CE), Confucianism was revived, on the premise that Buddhism and Daoism had brought moral and thus political weakness into Chinese society. This revised version is referred to by Western scholars as **Neo-Confucianism**. Chinese people know it by a term meaning "metaphysical thought," or "the learning of principle."

Under Neo-Confucian influence, the civil service examination system became fully developed as the chief means of attaining government positions. In addition to the five Confucian Classics, the *Four Books* (the *Analects*, the *Mencius*, the *Great Learning*, and the *Doctrine of the Mean*) formed the core of Confucian education. Its greatest proponent was the scholar ZHU Xi (Chu Hsi, 1130–1200 CE), who developed a curriculum running from elementary classes to higher education. This approach lasted for centuries, up to the beginning of the twentieth century. ZHU Xi's book *Family Rituals* was also reprinted for hundreds of years

An Interview with Simon Man-ho Wong

Simon Man-ho WONG is Associate Professor of Chinese Philosophy and Religion at Hong Kong University of Science and Technology. He is soft-spoken and very careful to be truthful in his words. As he explains, he is striving toward the Confucian goal of being a sage, but has not reached it:

I would say that it is hard to find a real spiritual teacher in Confucianism. Maybe some contemporary Neo-Confucians can be somewhat regarded as spiritual teachers, but they are not perfect. They are not sages. In fact, through the whole Confucian tradition, only Confucius and some kings in the ancient past can be regarded as sages. It is very hard to find a true sage who through his self-cultivation has attained a perfect stage of morality, who is perfect in his personality. By perfect personality, we mean that he has perfectly combined himself with Heaven, or the transcendent Dao, or ultimate reality—whatever you may call it.

According to some explanations in the Confucian tradition, the transmission of this ultimate reality was lost for hundreds of years. After that, some Confucianists discovered it again. This was the beginning of Neo-Confucianism. Some scholars say that the contribution of the Neo-Confucians is that they developed a kind of metaphysical attitude for Confucianism: Through your self-cultivation, you fully manifest your own liangzhi, *your innate knowing. This is actually the universal mind, the metaphysical reality of the universe, or your "real self." People like me who read the classics and the works of the Neo-Confucians are somehow affected by these teachings and we try to do some self-cultivation. It is very difficult to find a sage now. So we just learn from the ancient texts, Confucian classics, and also the works by some Confucian gentlemen. We try to learn from them and attempt self-cultivation to attain the stage of being a sage. I think it is possible for people to strive to become sages.*

When I was young, I had started to ask questions about life, the meaning of life, such as "What happens to me after death?" Then I tried to find the answer. One day my teacher in secondary school told me a story, and I was affected by it. He told me about a famous novel in China called Journey to the West. *A central character in it, the Monkey King, has hairs, and every time he picks hairs from his body, they grow into little monkeys. We are like the little monkeys, my teacher said. The little monkeys just play in the world, without understanding, without knowing that they actually come from the mother monkey, the Monkey King.*

Eventually some of the monkeys get tired and want to go back. They have the awareness, "Somehow I have to go back to my mother, to the Monkey King." And they go back to the body of their mother, which is the Monkey King. So this is what we call the purpose of life.

When I heard this story I was very much influenced by the meaning behind it: The purpose of our life is to go back to our source, to the origin of our lives. It was a Buddhist story, so I started from Buddhism. Later when I entered university I took some courses about Confucianism. I studied works of the Neo-Confucians, the works of Mencius and Confucius, and I came to love Confucianism. The real idea behind Confucianism is to ask you to go back to your self. I think to some extent all religions have this common element—they ask people to return to their origin.

Now that I am a professor in a university, I am supposed to have some kind of objective attitude toward what I teach. The students all know that I believe in that kind of teaching of Confucianism and Buddhism, but I try to make myself appear to be a person who keeps himself at a distance from the religion that I am teaching. Nevertheless, they all know that I am in that tradition by the way that I teach. Sometimes they come to me and ask some questions about life. I am very happy to answer the questions. We always need people to understand all wisdom and then convey the message to people in modern language. This is my mission, I think, the only thing that I can do.

I have done my own interpretation of the text of Laozi, the Dao de jing. *I find that I can somehow integrate all the eighty chapters of Laozi into one concept. That concept is Laozi's own concept, which is wu wei—non-doing. This is the key concept in understanding the whole of Laozi. What is meant by not doing? Not doing doesn't mean literally not doing anything—just sitting there. Absolutely not. My explanation is that you do something without attachment to the doing. If you are in a state of wu wei, you are always in connection with your true self, the origin of your self. So in every behavior, every action, every interaction between yourself and the world and other people, you are always in this state, without losing contact with your origin. If you are in this state without losing contact with the origin of your life, you will find that life is very simple. You may be very busy taking care of all kinds of things, but it is as if you have done nothing.*

I don't think I have touched the Dao yet. I know it theoretically, but I try my best to get in touch with this thing. I don't think I have already attained this stage of touching this, getting in touch with my origin. I am working on this.[41]

The Hall for Prayer for Good Harvests, part of the Temple of Heaven complex in Beijing, built from 1406 to 1420 for the emperor's annual prayer to Heaven for good crops. The same complex includes the white marble Altar of Heaven, where the emperor made sacrifices for favorable weather each year.

as the standard reference for rituals of ancestor worship and life-cycle events. His system is still being studied and developed by Confucian scholars in many countries.

Neo-Confucian thinkers also further developed the metaphysical basis for Confucianism: The individual is intimately linked with all of the cosmos. According to ZHANG Zai's (Chang Tsai) *Western Inscription*:

> *Heaven is my father and earth is my mother and even such a small creature as I finds an intimate place in their midst. Therefore, that which extends throughout the universe I regard as my body and that which directs the universe I regard as my nature. All people are my brothers and sisters and all things are my companions. The great ruler [the emperor] is the eldest son of my parents [Heaven and Earth], and the great ministers are his stewards. … To rejoice in Heaven and to have no anxiety—this is filial piety at its purest.*[42]

By becoming more humane one can help to transform not only oneself but also society and even the cosmos. The Neo-Confucianists thus stressed the importance of meditation and dedication to becoming a sage.

Confucian women had previously been expected to take a subordinate role in the family and in society, but at the same time to be strong, disciplined, wise, and capable in their relationships with their husbands and sons. While ZHU Xi maintained patriarchal traditions, he affirmed that women are innately endowed with the same classic moral virtues of humaneness, righteousness, propriety, wisdom, and faithfulness as men, and he encouraged education for women.

As Chinese culture spread to Korea and thence to Japan, Neo-Confucianism found fertile soil in these countries. Neo-Confucian thought became quite prominent in Korea, with an emphasis on education of scholar-officials and filial piety in the family. In Japan, Neo-Confucian ideals influenced development of scholar-samurai warriors and intense loyalty to the emperor.

Confucianism in the modern world
How is Confucianism being adapted to modern concerns in mainland China and other parts of East Asia?

The performance of state rituals was a time-consuming and major part of government jobs, carried out on behalf of the people. But as China gradually opened to the West in recent centuries, a reaction set in against these older ways, and the last of the imperial dynasties was overthrown in 1911. In the 1920s republic, science and social progress were glorified by radical intellectuals who were opposed to all the old systems. Under the communist regime established in 1949, Communism took the place of religion, attempting to transform the society by secular means. Party chairman MAO Zedong (Mao Tse-tung, 1893–1976) was venerated almost as a god, with the "Little Red Book" of quotations from Chairman Mao replacing the Confucian Classics.

During the Cultural Revolution (1966–1976), Confucianism was attacked as one of the "Four Olds"—old ideas, culture, customs, and habits. The Cultural Revolution attempted to destroy the hierarchical structure that Confucianism had idealized and to prevent the intellectual elite from ruling over the masses. Contrary to the Confucian virtue of filial piety, young people even denounced their parents at public trials, and scholars were made objects of derision. An estimated one million people were attacked. Some were killed, some committed suicide, and millions suffered.

Mao said that he had hated Confucianism from his childhood. What he so disliked was the intellectual emphasis on the study of the Classics, the "superstitious" rituals, and the oppression of the lowest members of hierarchical Chinese society—women and peasants. He urged peasants to overthrow all authoritarian traditions, including religion. Nevertheless, in some respects, Confucian morality continued to form the basis of Chinese ethics. Mao particularly emphasized the (Confucian) virtues of selfless service to the people and of self-improvement for the public good:

> *All our cadres, whatever their rank, are servants of the people, and whatever we do is to serve the people. How then can we be reluctant to discard any of our bad traits?*[43]

For decades, communist China prided itself on being the most law-abiding country in the world. But in recent decades there has been a rise in crime and official corruption. The society has changed abruptly since China opened its doors to the West in 1978, undermining what remained of traditional Confucian virtues. The government blames the influx of materialistic values, resulting from the indiscriminating embrace of the underside of Western culture and the rapid shift toward a free market economy. In 1989, ZHAO Ziyang (Chao Tzu-yang), then Communist Party leader, urged officials to maintain Confucian discipline (without naming it that) in the midst of the changes: "The Party can by no means allow its members to barter away their principles for money and power."[44] But when the people picked up this cry, aging leaders chose to suppress popular calls for greater democracy and an end to official corruption; they did so in the name of another Confucian value: order in society.

For their part, the intellectuals of the democracy movement had tried to do things in the proper way but were caught on the horns of the poignant Chinese dilemma. Under Confucian ethics, it has been the continuing responsibility of scholars to play the role of upright censors. On the other hand, scholars had to remain loyal to the ruler, for they were subjects and observing one's subservient position as a subject preserved the security of the state. The leaders of the democracy movement tried to deal with this potential conflict by ritualized, respectful action: In 1989 they formally walked up the steps of the Great Hall of the People in Tiananmen Square to present their written requests to those in power. But they were ignored and brutally suppressed.

Despite his own denunciation of religion, Chairman Mao himself is becoming revered as a semi-deified father figure or bodhisattva. Statues of him are on sale at his homestead in Hunan Province, and many people have his image hanging in their cars.

Now, in twenty-first-century China, as noted earlier, popular and intellectual interest in various religions is increasing. Evangelical Christianity has grown so vigorous that China is now home to the second largest evangelical Christian community in the world, and there are more Catholics in China than in Ireland. Buddhists account for the majority of religious adherents, with 320,000 nuns and monks in 16,000 Chinese temples and monasteries. Islam is strong in northwest China, home of most of China's eighteen million Muslims. The Communist Party is still officially atheistic but is showing signs of regarding religions as having a certain social usefulness. At the same time, it also attempts to control religious activities and beliefs through its Religious Affairs Bureau and police. While Confucianism is not yet recognized as a "religion"—the five religions officially permitted in China being government-approved forms of Buddhism, Islam, Daoism, Protestantism, and Catholicism—its philosophy and ethics are attracting new government attention. Old Confucius temples throughout the country have been renovated and since 2004 official celebrations of Confucius's birthday have been held therein. In Qufu, birthplace of Confucius, the enormous Confucius Temple complex, Confucius Mansions (consisting of 450 halls, rooms, and buildings from the sixteenth century), and Confucius Forest with tombs of Confucius and his descendants reportedly receive more than four million visitors a year. Qufu now calls itself "The Holy City of the Orient" and a lavish museum and park with a statue of Confucius that is almost as high as the Statue of Liberty are being constructed. The government also sponsors hundreds of "Confucian Institutes" on university campuses and "Confucius classrooms" in elementary and secondary schools around the world for the study of Chinese culture and language. Some critics worry that these Chinese government-sponsored institutes and classrooms are expressions of "soft power" that inhibit free discussion of politically sensitive topics related to China.

Alongside the development of Communism, since the 1920s there has been intellectual interest in analyzing Confucianism not as an historical artefact but as a model that is relevant to modern life, with the potential to contribute significantly to cultural identity, economic progress, social harmony, and a personal sense of the meaning of human life. Some of these "New Confucian" scholars are even promoting the idea of Confucianism as a state religion that would support moral reconstruction.

Confucianism may inform capitalistic behavior as well as Marxist communism. There is now talk of "Capitalist Confucianism"—business conducted according to Confucian ethics such as humanity, trustworthiness, sincerity, and altruism. As Professor YAO Xinzhong explains:

> *Free choice is the foundation of modern society, and the pre-condition of market economy. However, freedom without responsibility would result in the collapse of the social network and in the conflict between individuals and between individuals and society, and would lead to the sacrifice of the future in order to satisfy short-term needs. This has become a serious challenge to human wisdom and to human integrity. In this respect, Confucianism can make a contribution to a new moral sense, a new ecological view and a new code for the global village.*[45]

Confucian values are also being reappraised as a significant addition to holistic education. In them is imbedded the motivation to improve oneself and become a responsible and ethical member of one's family and society. Thus the Neo-Confucians developed multistage learning programs that extend beyond the years of formal schooling. The seventeenth-century Confucian text *Rules for Students and Children*, a manual for developing Confucian virtues, has become quite popular in today's China. Students read it in elementary schools, and there are also online versions such as cartoons and videos. Confucian-based civil-service examinations are being partially reintroduced in the selection of public servants. Earlier castigated as "feudal institutions," Confucian academies are now being described as fine centers for learning.

Children participating in grand celebrations of Confucius's birthday in his home city of Qufu.

Chinese authorities are also reviving aspects of the religious cult of Confucius, such as gala celebrations of his birthday in Qufu, partly for the sake of tourism. But official ambivalence about Master Kong remains, as indicated in the erection of a thirty-one-foot- (9.5-meter-) high statue of him in Tienanmen Square in Beijing and then the mysterious removal of the statue four months later in April 2011.

After the ravages of the Cultural Revolution, only a few hundred Confucian temples remained in China, but now approximately forty of them have been declared "national cultural heritage sites." Visitors may come to admire the historical architecture or to perform religious rituals such as burning incense, bowing or kneeling before a statue or tablet of Confucius, and praying in some fashion. A contemporary innovation is the introduction of prayer cards on which people write their requests. These are then placed on shelves outside the main temple hall or on branches of trees. So many people are now praying in this way that in order to protect the trees the cards have to be frequently removed and stored elsewhere. The prayers are typically requests to Confucius for blessings such as success in exams, health, good relationships, and prosperity.

In the moral and spiritual vacuum left after the demise of fervent Maoism, Confucianism may also help restore a sense of holy purpose to people's lives. The traditional feeling was that the Mandate of Heaven gives transcendent meaning to human life. Professor TU Weiming, a modern Confucian, explains:

We are the guardians of the good earth, the trustees of the Mandate of Heaven that enjoins us to make our bodies healthy, our hearts sensitive, our minds alert, our souls refined, and our spirits brilliant. ... We serve Heaven with common sense, the lack of which nowadays has brought us to the brink of self-destruction. Since we help Heaven to realize itself through our self-discovery and self-understanding in day-to-day living, the ultimate meaning of life is found in our ordinary, human existence.[46]

This desire for meaning in modern life is so strong that in 2006, when a media professor from Beijing Normal University, Ms. YU Dan, broadcast a seven-day series of lectures about the teachings of Confucius on the state-owned national television network, she instantly became famous. The book then compiled from her lectures sold ten million copies in its first year alone. Her accessible introduction to Confucian teachings draws on quotes from the sages, folk tales, scenes from everyday life, and her own observations as a person "immersed in the spring" of Confucian values. She concludes:

Our ultimate aim is to let the key principles of Confucius enter into our hearts, uniting heaven, earth, and humankind in a perfect whole, and giving us infinite strength. In China today we often say that for a nation to survive and prosper, heaven must smile on it, the earth must be favorable to it, and its people must be at peace. It is to this harmonious balance that Confucius can lead us today.[47]

Confucianism in East Asia

Countries and city-states near China that have historically been influenced by China politically and culturally—particularly Japan, Taiwan, South Korea, Hong Kong, and Singapore—are also permeated by Confucian values. These countries have been so successful economically in recent years that there has been considerable research into how Confucian ethics may have contributed to their economic ascent. Some commentators have concluded that the Western model is individualistic, whereas these areas have brought to business practice a Confucian-influenced culture that stresses stable life of the family and larger clan, respect for the wisdom of elders, respect for education, interest in the common good, hard work, and long-term sustainable growth.

Confucianism—in particular, ZHU Xi's Neo-Confucianism—was adopted as the official state ideology of Korea by the Choson dynasty in 1392. State examinations were based on Zhu Xi's school of principle and officials tried to practice it both in ritual and in everyday life. The highly aristocratic Choson dynasty, which lasted until 1910, loved Confucian rituals; the elite even changed their marriage rites to mirror Zhu's prescriptions. They claimed to be more Confucian

Some Confucian rites are still observed today in South Korea. These people making offerings in Chungdak-dong village have maintained a traditional Confucian lifestyle for hundreds of years.

than the Chinese. Few South Koreans now consider themselves adherents of Confucianism as a religion, but lectures and special events are nonetheless being sponsored by hundreds of local Confucian institutes to promote Confucian teachings. In some cases, Confucianism is associated with particular clans in East Asia, and thus with political favoritism. Some of the Korean institutes are politically conservative and oppose women's efforts to revise family laws.

Confucianism entered Japan during the seventh century when Chinese political thought and religious ideas first began to have significant influence there. It left its mark on the first constitution of Japan, on the arrangement of government bureaucracy, and in the educational system. From the twelfth to the sixteenth century, Confucianism was studied in Zen Buddhist monasteries. Neo-Confucian schools in Japan attempted to balance "quiet sitting" (meditation) with moral action in the world. In quietude the Way of Heaven could be discerned and truth understood, so that a person could act in the proper way. Then from the seventeenth to the nineteenth century, Confucianism began to spread more widely among the people of Japan because of its adoption as an educational philosophy in public and private schools. Confucian moral teachings became the basis for establishing proper human relationships in the family and in Japanese society. At the higher level, the Tokugawa shogunate in 1600 adopted Confucianism as an official ideology for forming a stable new government. As in Japanese tradition, the emperor was thought to be of divine origin; beneath him in the hierarchy were the shoguns, feudal lords, samurais, and hereditary local government. Rather than loyalty to the family, as in Chinese Confucianism, Japanese were trained to revere the emperor above all. Both Confucianism and Shinto were manipulated by the Japanese military in the period before World War II to inculcate a nationalist expansionist ideology. More in keeping with the original motives of Confucianism, some scholars have observed that Japan's notably effective modernization is partly due to values derived from Confucianism. These values include a high regard for diligence, consensus, education, moral self-cultivation, frugality, and loyalty.

Confucian organizations in Hong Kong, Taiwan, and other parts of East Asia are also attempting to restore religious versions of Confucianism, such as the worship of Confucius himself or study of the Confucian Classics.

Dr. Mary Evelyn Tucker, noted scholar of East Asian studies and the relationships between religions and the environment, concludes that Confucianism is not outdated. Rather, it can be seen as quite relevant now and for the future as well, for "It aims to promote flourishing social relations, effective educational systems, sustainable agricultural patterns, and humane political governance within the context of the dynamic, life-giving processes of the universe."[48]

Key terms

Celestial Master Daoist tradition with hereditary lineage of priests representing celestial deities.

Complete Perfection A monastic tradition combining inner alchemy, meditation, and social morality.

Dao (Tao) The way or path; the Nameless.

feng shui The art of architecture that harmonizes with natural energy flows.

Highest Purity Daoism An elite tradition of celibates who meditate on purification of the body for spiritual elevation.

li Ceremonies, rituals, and rules of proper conduct, in the Confucian tradition.

literati Intellectuals and scholars.

Neo-Confucianism Confucianism stressing the importance of self-cultivation and dedication to becoming a sage, established during the Chinese Song dynasty.

qi (ch'i) The vital energy in the universe and in our bodies according to Chinese cosmology and the Chinese sciences.

ren Humanity, benevolence—the central Confucian virtue.

wu wei In Daoism, "actionless action," in the sense of taking no action contrary to the natural flow.

yang In Chinese philosophy, the bright, assertive, "male" energy in the universe.

yin In Chinese philosophy, the dark, receptive, "female" energy in the universe.

Suggested reading

Adler, Joseph A., *Chinese Religious Traditions*, Upper Saddle River, New Jersey: Prentice Hall, 2002. Very clear introduction to the complexes of ancient and popular practices, Confucianism, Daoism, and Buddhism.

Bell, Daniel A., *China's New Confucianism: Politics and Everyday Life in a Changing Society*, Princeton: Princeton University Press, 2008. Interesting insights on the re-emergence of Confucianism in contemporary China.

Berthrong, John H. and Evelyn Nagai, *Confucianism: A Short Introduction*, Oxford: One World, 2000. An accessible survey of Confucianism as a holistic system covering all aspects of life and affecting people throughout East Asia.

Chau, Adam Yuet, *Miraculous Response: Doing Popular Religion in Contemporary China*, Stanford, California: Stanford University Press, 2005. Research into the revival of folk traditions and temple rituals in contemporary China.

Ching, Julia, *Chinese Religions*, Maryknoll, New York: Orbis Books, 1993. Survey of the history of the many religious strands in Chinese culture.

de Bary, William Theodore and Irene Bloom (vol. 1), and William Theodore de Bary and Richard Lufrano (vol. 2), *Sources of Chinese Tradition*, second edition, New York: Columbia University Press, 1999. Useful commentaries and extensive texts from Confucian and Daoist schools.

Dao de jing, attributed to Laozi, available in numerous translations, including the English translation by D. C. Lau, London: Penguin Books, 1963, and the English translation by Victor H. Mair, New York: Bantam Books, 1990.

The I Ching, translated into German by Richard Wilhelm and thence into English by Cary Baynes, third edition, Princeton, New Jersey: Princeton University Press, 1967. Insights into the multiple possibilities of the interplay of yin and yang in our lives.

Kindop, Jason and Carol Lee Hamrin, eds, *God and Caesar in China: Policy Implications of Church–State Tensions*, Washington, D. C.: The Brookings Institution, 2004. A survey of China's struggles to control religions throughout history, with particular reference to recent Party efforts to compromise with the burgeoning public interest in religion.

Kohn, Livia, *The Taoist Experience*, Albany, New York: State University of New York Press, 1993. Interesting translations of ancient and more recent texts covering the various aspects of Daoism.

Kohn, Livia, *Daoism and Chinese Culture*, Cambridge, Massachusetts: Three Pines Press, second edition, 2004. Concise survey of different forms of Daoism in chronological order, considering comparative aspects and providing additional bibliography.

Lau, D. C., *Confucius: The Analects*, London and New York: Penguin Classics, 1979. Classic English translation of the central teachings of Confucius.

Lopez, Donald S., ed., *Religions of China in Practice*, Princeton, New Jersey: Princeton University Press, 1996. Excellent articles illustrating the overlap between Confucianism, Daoism, and Buddhism in traditional and contemporary practice, with translations of original texts.

Mencius, trans. D. C. Lau, New York: Viking Penguin, 1970.

Sommer, Deborah, ed., *Chinese Religions: An Anthology of Sources*, New York and Oxford: Oxford University Press, 1995. Interesting primary source material from Daoist, Confucian, Buddhist, and communist writings about religious topics.

Sun, Anna, *Confucianism as a World Religion: Contested Histories and Contemporary Realities*, Princeton and Oxford: Princeton University Press, 2013. Intellectual history of the theory that Confucianism is a "world religion."

Taylor, Rodney, trans. James Legge, *Confucius, the Analects: The Path of the Sage*, Woodstock, Vermont: Skylight Paths Publishing, 2011. Selections from the *Analects* of Confucius, with comments about their meaning.

Taylor, Rodney, *The Religious Dimensions of Confucianism*, Albany: State University of New York Press, 1990. A collection of essays dealing with the question of whether Confucianism is a religion.

Tu Weiming, ed., *Confucian Traditions in East Asian Modernity: Moral Education and Economic Culture in Japan and the Four Mini-Dragons*, Cambridge, Massachusetts: Harvard University Press, 1996. A now-classic study of the theory that Confucian values undergird economic success stories in East Asia.

Tu Weiming and Mary Evelyn Tucker, *Confucian Spirituality*, 2 vols, New York: Crossroad Publishing Company, 2003–2004. Eastern and Western scholars analyze Confucianism as a spiritual path.

Tucker, Mary Evelyn and John Berthrong, *Confucianism and Ecology: the Interrelation of Heaven, Earth, and Humans*, Cambridge, Massachusetts: Harvard University Press, 1998. Interesting articles from a major series of conferences probing the relationships between particular religious teachings and the environment.

Watson, Burton, *Chuang Tzu: Basic Writings*, New York: Columbia University Press, 1964. An engaging translation of major writings by Zhuangzi, with an introduction that is particularly helpful in dealing with this paradoxical material.

Wilson, Thomas A., ed., *On Sacred Grounds: Culture, Society, Politics, and the Formation of the Cult of Confucius*, Cambridge, Massachusetts: Harvard University Asia Center, 2002. Articles by Chinese and Western scholars tracing factors contributing to the development of Confucianism as a state cult.

Wong, Eva, *The Shambhala Guide to Taoism*, Boston: Shambhala Press, 1996. Introduction to the synthesis of Daoism, Buddhism, and Confucianism in China, Daoist history, techniques, and rites.

Yang, Fenggang, *Religion in China: Survival and Revival under Communist Rule*, Oxford: Oxford University Press, 2012. Exploration of how religions have survived the Cultural Revolution in China and re-emerged in vigorous forms despite communist controls.

6.1 Describe the ancient Chinese tradition of ancestor worship and the concept of cosmic balance

Archaeological findings suggest that Chinese religious ways, both popular and institutionalized, were practiced as long ago as 2000 BCE. Chinese tradition requires that respect must be paid to the ancestors (especially the family's founding ancestor and those recently deceased) through funerals, mourning rites, and then continuing sacrifices. These sacred rituals of ancestor worship are called *li* and are essential because the ancestors will help their descendants if respected but cause trouble if ignored. Kings, in their roles as chief priests, sought the help of their aristocratic ancestors and deities by a process of divination through the medium of oracle bones (large flat bones on which the king's questions were scratched).

There has also long existed in China a belief that the cosmos is a manifestation of an impersonal self-generating substance called qi, which has two aspects: yin, the dark, receptive "female" aspect, and yang, the bright, assertive "male" aspect. Wisdom lies in recognizing their ever-shifting, but regular and balanced, patterns and moving with them. This creative rhythm of the universe is called the Dao, or "way." To harmonize with the cosmic process, the ancients devised many forms of divination. One system developed during the Zhou dynasty was eventually written down as the *Yijing*, or *Book of Changes*, and became a common source for both Daoism and Confucianism.

6.2 Identify the basic principles for life in harmony with Dao

There are several basic principles for the life in harmony with Dao. One is to experience the transcendent unity of all things, rather than separation. This realization can only be attained when one ceases to feel any personal preferences. Another principle is *wu wei*—"actionless action," or taking no intentional or invasive action contrary to the natural flow of things. The result of *wu wei* is noninterference. Daoism also places great value on a contemplative life and love of nature. As all things on earth come from the same source, Daoists believe that they are to be loved and allowed to exist and develop according to their nature. Also according to Daoist ideals, there should be no great gap between rich and poor.

6.3 Outline the practices associated with popular religion and organized Daoism

Despite the intertwining of popular religion and organized Daoism over the centuries, some folk practices have survived. People may believe in invisible spirits who are involved in their destinies, and burn incense and make offerings to them out of respect and fear, vowing to do a good deed if their prayer request is granted. The art of feng shui (or geomancy)—determining and harmonizing with natural flows of qi through the earth—is also practiced.

In organized Daoism, Daoist specialists have taken charge of spiritual tasks such as inner alchemy (individual spiritual practices for the sake of inner transformation, self-cultivation, longevity, and perhaps immortality), faith healing, and the use of talismans (made for protection from spirits). In temple worship, priests carry out rituals. Deities arising from folk traditions have also become part of the Daoist pantheon (such as the kitchen god) and the ancient practice of worshiping certain people as divine is also encompassed by organized Daoism.

6.4 Explain the increasing interest in Daoist practices and philosophy in the West

From the middle of the twentieth century, interest in Daoist practices and philosophy has boomed in the West. There are now many masters and centers in the United States, including organized religious institutions, societies for self-cultivation, and practitioners of techniques for spiritual development, health, and longevity. Many people outside China are now benefiting from acupuncture therapy and traditional Chinese herbal medicine, and energy training practices, such as *Taiji quan*, are of increasing interest.

6.5 Outline the major teachings of Confucius

Confucius was born *c.* 551 BCE, during the Zhou dynasty, a period of political chaos. The only way out of this chaos, he believed, was a return to classical rites and standards of virtue. Foremost among the virtues he felt could save society was *ren* (humanity, benevolence). The prime exemplar of *ren* should be the ruler. Confucius urged rulers to rule not by physical force or coercion but by the example of personal virtue. The ruling class should also "cultivate themselves," adhering to *ren* by reaching upward and cherishing what is right, rather than reaching downward for material gain. Confucius also supported the ancient Chinese custom of ancestor worship as an extension of filial piety, another important aspect of *ren*.

6.6 Define Neo-Confucianism

Neo-Confucianism was the revived version of Confucianism that appeared during the Song dynasty (960–1280 CE). It was based on the premise that Buddhism and Daoism, which had become popular during the period of disunity following the fall of the Han dynasty (220 CE), had brought moral and thus political weakness into Chinese society.

Under Neo-Confucian influence, the civil-service examination system became fully developed as the chief means of attaining government positions. An educational curriculum, which lasted until the beginning of the twentieth century, was developed based on the five Confucian Classics and the *Four Books*. Neo-Confucian thinkers also further developed the metaphysical basis for Confucianism: The individual is intimately linked with all of the cosmos. The Neo-Confucianists thus stressed the importance of meditation and dedication to becoming a sage.

6.7   Discuss the ways in which Confucianism is being adapted to modern concerns in mainland China and other parts of East Asia

Today in China, Confucianism is being analyzed not as an historical artefact but as a tradition that is relevant to modern life, with the potential to contribute significantly to cultural identity, economic progress, social harmony, and a personal sense of the meaning of human life. There is now talk of "Capitalist Confucianism"—business conducted according to Confucian ethics such as humanity, trustworthiness, sincerity, and altruism. Confucian values are also being reappraised as a significant addition to holistic education. In them is embedded the motivation to improve oneself and become a responsible and ethical member of one's family and society. In the moral and spiritual vacuum left after the demise of fervent Maoism, Confucianism may also help to restore a sense of holy purpose to people's lives.

Countries in East Asia that have historically been influenced by China politically and culturally are also permeated by Confucian values. These countries have been so successful economically in recent years that there has been considerable research into how Confucian ethics may have contributed to their economic ascent. In contrast to the competitive, individualistic Western model, these areas have brought to business practice a Confucian-influenced culture that stresses stable life of the family and larger clan, respect for the wisdom of elders, respect for education, interest in the common good, hard work, and long-term sustainable growth.

CHAPTER 7

SHINTO

"People come to shrines because these are sacred places from ancient times where people have come to pray. And other people want to go where people are gathered." Hitoshi Iwasaki[1]

7.1 Explain the importance of the natural world in the roots of "Shinto"

7.2 Outline the elements of Confucianism and Buddhism that have been blended with Shinto

7.3 Discuss the reasons why Shinto has been so closely tied to Japanese nationalism

7.4 Define what is meant by "Sect Shinto" and give an example

7.5 Summarize the main aspects of contemporary Shinto

Japan has embraced and adapted many religions that originated in other countries, but also has its own local traditions closely tied to nature, the native land, and its rulers. Under relatively recent historical circumstances, these have been referred to collectively as "Shinto." However, according to current scholarship, Shinto is not a single self-conscious religious tradition but rather an overarching label applied to ways of honoring the spirits in nature, ancestor veneration, "folk" religious practices such as divination and taboos, local rites and festivals, imperial myths, nationalism, and universalistic teachings.

Many modern Japanese combine practices derived from various religious streams, each of which offers something different. Confucianism has informed organizations and ethics, Buddhism and Christianity offer ways of understanding suffering and the afterlife, traditional veneration of ancestors links the living to their family history, and the ways called "Shinto" lead people to worship and pray for blessings at shrines and participate in popular cultural festivals. However, in Japan an unusual situation has arisen: Religious participation is high, but affiliation to institutional religions is low. While almost ninety percent of the people annually visit their ancestors' graves, seventy-five percent have either a Buddhist or a Shinto altar in their home, seventy percent visit a Shinto shrine during the first three days of the New Year, more than sixty percent believe in an "unseen higher power," almost fifty percent say they believe in deities or buddhas, and more than thirty percent engage a Shinto priest to purify new cars or building plots, only thirty percent of the population say that they belong to any institutional religion.[2]

The roots of "Shinto"

Why is kinship with nature linked with Shinto?

Shinto is not easily identified as a "religion" in the Western sense for it has no single founder, no orthodox canon of sacred literature, and no explicit code of ethical requirements. The meanings of its rituals are unknown by many who practice them. In ancient times, individual clans apparently worshiped a particular deity as their own ancestor, along with other unseen beings and natural forces, but such worship was localized until the eighth century CE, when the term "Shinto" came into use to distinguish indigenous Japanese ways from Buddhism and other imported religions. The label "Shinto" was formed from the words *shin* (divine being) and *do* (way). The major chronicles of "Shintoism" were written down—the *Kojiki* (compiled 712 CE) and *Nihongi* (720 CE)—but contemporary scholars do not regard them as uniquely Japanese, for they seem to be greatly influenced by Buddhist, Confucian, Korean, and Chinese thought. These chronicles combine myths, historical facts, politics, and literature and are not generally revered as sacred scriptures. The *Kojiki* seems to be aimed at conferring spiritual legitimacy on the Imperial Throne by allegedly documenting the divine origins of the imperial lineage. The legendary founder and first emperor of Japan, Jimmu, is described as a descendant of Amaterasu, the sun goddess.

During the Tokugawa period in Japan (1600–1868), thinkers made another effort to define the "native" Japanese religion, as opposed to foreign incursions, by collating various texts, popular practices, and myths.

Then, in 1868, the Meiji Restoration brought Emperor Meiji and an imperial state apparatus into power. To confront subjugation by Western colonial powers, the Meiji regime turned to conservatism and nationalism, with emphasis on worship of the emperor. The extreme nationalism fostered by this trend, supported by religious veneration of the emperor, came to an end with World War II, with the victors forcing Japan to separate religion and politics.

Now the authorities who run the many shrines in Japan are again promoting the idea that Shinto is a religion unto itself, native to Japan. In this chapter we will examine the characteristics of Japanese culture that are attributed by the priestly establishment to Shinto religion. Retired Grand Master Motohisa Yamakage describes Shinto as "Japan's spiritual heart."[3]

Kinship with nature

Despite industrial pollution and urbanization, Japan is still a country of exquisite natural beauty. The islands marry mountains to sea, and mountainous areas that have not yet been subjected to urban development are laced with streams, waterfalls, and lush forests. Even the agriculture is beautiful, with flowering fruit trees and terraced fields. The Japanese people lived intimately with this environment until they began importing modern Western ideas late in the nineteenth century. Living close to nature, they organized their lives around the turn of the seasons, honoring the roles of the sun, moon, and lightning in their rice farming. Mount Fuji, with its perfect volcanic cone rising dramatically from the surrounding plains, was honored as the sacred embodiment of the divine creativity that had thrust the land up from the sea. The sparkling ocean and rising sun, so visible along the extensive coastlines, were revered as earthly expressions of the sacred purity, brightness, and awesome power at the heart of life.

The Japanese people have traditionally honored the natural beauty of their land and have considered Mount Fuji to be its most sacred peak. Pilgrims have long made the arduous climb up Fuji seeking purification and good fortune.

To be fully alive is to have an aesthetic perception of life because a major part of the world's goodness lies in its often unspeakable beauty.

Rev. Yukitaka Yamamoto, Shinto priest[4]

Industrialization and urbanization have blighted much of the natural landscape. There is said to be more concrete per square kilometer in Japan than in any other country in the world. However, the sensitivity to natural beauty survives in small-scale arts. In rock gardening, flower arranging, the tea ceremony, and poetry, Japanese artists honor the simple and natural. If a rock is placed "just right" in a garden, it seems alive, radiating its natural essence. In a tea ceremony, great attention is paid to each natural sensual delight, from the purity of water poured from a wooden ladle to the genuineness of the clay vessels. These arts are often linked with Zen Buddhism, but the sensitivities seem to derive from more ancient Japanese ways.

Relationships with the kami

The most ancient forms of spirituality in Japan were probably linked to the spirits perceived in the natural world—the **kami**. This continues to be the main feature defining what is now called Shinto. Although the word "kami" is usually translated as "god" or "spirit," these translations are not exact. Kami can be either singular or plural, for the word refers to a single essence manifesting in many places. Rather than evoking an image, like the Hindu or Mahayana Buddhist deities, kami refers to a quality. It means, literally, "that which is above," and also refers to that which evokes wonder and awe. The kami harmonize heaven and earth and also guide the solar system and the cosmos. They tend to reside in beautiful or powerful places, such as mountains, certain trees, unusual rocks, waterfalls, whirlpools, and animals. In addition, they manifest as wind, rain, and fearsome forces such as thunder, lightning, tsunamis, and earthquakes. Kami also appear in abstract forms, such as the creativity of growth and reproduction. In general, explains Sakamiki Shunzo, kami include:

> *all things whatsoever which deserve to be dreaded and revered for the extraordinary and preeminent powers which they possess. ... [Kami] need not be eminent for surpassing nobleness, goodness, or serviceableness alone. Malignant and uncanny beings are also called kami, if only they are the objects of general dread.*[5]

The earliest ways of kami worship probably resembled indigenous religious ways in other parts of the world—carried on in open-air sites without buildings, but perhaps with efforts to propitiate the kami by specialists in communicating with them. Such local traditions may have been eventually institutionalized in the building of shrines in which the kami could be contacted, with priests and rituals for negotiating with them for agricultural development and evolving political structures. This process is suggested in an eighth-century CE account of a sixth-century CE man named Matachi who came into contact with the local kami when the people were trying to clear natural reed plains and turn them into rice fields:

> *Then,* yato-no-kami *flocked together and appeared in great numbers, stopping people from entering and cultivating the fields. According to local people,* yato-no-kami *have the bodies of snakes, carrying horns on their heads. If one looks back at them while fleeing, one's house and kin will be wiped out and one will have no descendants. Matachi was greatly angered by this. Wearing armor and carrying a spear in his hand, he slew them and chased them away. At the mountain entrance he planted a stick in a ditch as a mark, and he announced to the* yato-no-kami: *"We shall give the land above this stick to you, as the domain*

of the kami, *but the land below it will be turned into rice fields for the people.
I shall become a priest of the* kami, *and I shall revere and worship you in all
eternity. I pray, do not strike us; do not bear a grudge against us!" He set up a*
yashiro *[temporary shelter] and did worship there for the first time. He cleared
ten* tokoro *of rice fields, and Matachi's descendants have performed worship here
until this day.*[6]

With time, local control of kami worship seems to have been partially subsumed by the evolving Japanese state, with the emperor assuming the central
role since the seventh century CE as the divinely descended ruler upon whom
the well-being of the country depended. The *Kojiki* and *Nihongi* appear to have
been compiled from various myths with the intention of linking the imperial
hierarchy with the kami. According to the *Nihongi*'s account of creation:

*In primeval ages, before the earth was formed, amorphous matter floated freely
about like oil upon water. In time there arose in its midst a thing like a sprouting
reedshoot, and from this a deity came forth of its own.*[7]

This deity gave birth to many kami, two of which—the Amatsu (heavenly)
kami—were told to organize the material world. Standing on the Floating Bridge
of Heaven, they stirred the ocean with a jeweled spear. When they pulled it out

Amaterasu Comes Out of the Cave

The goddess of the sun, Amaterasu, was born from
the left eye of the god Izanagi. The god of the wind,
Susanoo, was born from his nose, and the god
Tsukiyomi was born from his right eye. Izanagi gave
Amaterasu charge of Heaven, Susanoo of the sea, and
Tsukyomi of the night.

Of these three "august children," Susanoo was
known as a wild child. He wanted to see their mother,
who had died and was in the land of the dead. Izanagi
agreed, but when Susanoo went to Heaven on the way
to visit his older sister Amaterasu she was suspicious of
what mischief he might cause. To check his sincerity,
she challenged him to a jewel-spitting contest in which
each would spit jewels from the other's collection.
Since jewels were associated with fetuses, each jewel
they spat out became a child: three daughters from
Amaterasu's mouth via Susanoo's sword and five sons
from the mouth of Susanoo via Amaterasu's jewelry.
Amaterasu declared that the sons born from her
jewelry were hers and the daughters from Susanoo's
sword were his. Susanoo pointed out that since "gentle
females" had been born from his jewels, his sincerity
was proved. Amaterasu accepted his point, and allowed
him to stay in Heaven for a while. However, Susanoo
proved such a wild visitor that he caused great havoc,
which made it impossible for Amaterasu to carry out
her sacred duty: dedicating the first harvest of rice
at the sacred altar, wearing a new robe—the chief
symbolic duty of the emperor, up to today.

Susanoo's wild actions led to the death of the
maidservant of Amaterasu. The goddess was so appalled
that she hid in a cavern. The earth became perpetually
dark. To lure her out and bring back the sun, the
kami decided to hold a festival outside her cave. They
transplanted a sacred evergreen *sakaki* tree there,
hung from its branches sacred jewels, placed a thick
straw rope near the mouth of the cave, and prepared
a sacred mirror. One of the goddesses began dancing
on a wooden tub, making such a loud thumping sound
that she went into ecstasy and bared her private parts
(symbolic of Mother Earth's fertility). The gods and
goddesses began laughing and clapping so hard that
Amaterasu peeped out of the cave to see what was
happening. One of the deities immediately placed the
mirror in front of her face. She was confused to see her
own great beauty reflected in it. In her confusion, she
was brought out of the cave by one strong god; another
barred the entrance with the braided rope. Light
returned to the world.

After more adventures on the part of Susanoo,
Amaterasu sent her grandson to rule over his land. She
sent with him the "three regalia"—the divine mirror,
the divine jewel that had been hung in the *sakaki* tree,
and the sword that Susanoo had discovered in the tail
of an eight-headed serpent, whom he had heroically
killed. He had sent the sword to Amaterasu as a peace
offering. Her grandson's grandson, Jinmu, became the
legendary first emperor of Japan in 660 BCE, and the
imperial family has kept the three regalia as revered
symbols of its spiritual inheritance up to the present,
126 generations later.

of the water, it dripped brine back into the ocean, which coagulated into eight islands (interpreted as either Japan or the whole world). To rule this earthly kingdom they created the kami Amaterasu, literally "the one who illuminates the sky," or goddess of the sun. The Amatsu kami also gave birth to the ancestors of the Japanese. All of the natural world—land, trees, mountains, waters, animals, people—is thus joined in kinship as the spiritual creation of the kami.

In the primeval sense, *kannagara*, following the way or nature of the kami, may be referred to as "natural religion," as in this statement by Yukitaka Yamamoto, ninety-sixth Chief Priest of the Tsubaki Grand Shrine:

> *Natural Religion is the spontaneous awareness of the Divine that can be found in any culture. … The Spirit of Great Nature may be a flower, may be the beauty of the mountains, the pure snow, the soft rains or the gentle breeze. Kannagara means being in communion with these forms of beauty and so with the highest level of experiences of life. When people respond to the silent and provocative beauty of the natural order, they are aware of* kannagara. *When they respond in life in a similar way, by following ways "according to the* kami, *" they are expressing* kannagara *in their lives. They are living according to the natural flow of the universe and will benefit and develop by so doing.*[8]

Shrines

It is thought that there were no shrines in early Shinto; rather, these may have developed after the sixth-century CE introduction of Buddhist influences in Japan. At present, there are more than 100,000 shrines in Japan, built to honor the kami. Shrines may be as small as beehives or elaborate temple complexes covering thousands of acres. Some honor kami protecting the local area; others honor kami with special responsibilities, such as healing or protecting crops from insects. The local shrines are situated on sites thought to have been chosen by the kami for their sacred atmosphere. At one time, every community had its own guardian kami. Organizations may also invite the kami to a place they have built for them. In Kyoto, home of many shrines and temples and also famous cakes, the cake makers have created a shrine to the kami of cakes.

The greatest number of shrines is dedicated to Inari, the god of rice. His messengers are foxes, so these shrines are distinguished by statues of foxes, rather than the statues of dogs or lions that are often placed to guard shrine entrances. Inari shrines are traditionally associated with good harvests but are now frequented by people seeking success in business of any sort. Other shrines include imperial shrines previously funded and administered by the government, shrines dedicated to Hachiman, the kami of war (previously popular among military clans), Tenjin shrines dedicated to the kami of a ninth-century CE scholar (popular among students getting ready for exams), Sengen shrines dedicated to the princess who is considered the guardian deity of Mount Fuji, and shrines dedicated to clan founders.

Most important of all these is Ise Shrine, which is actually a complex of more than 100 shrines. Historians think they were first constructed in their current form in 690 CE. The main shrine is the place of worship of the kami Amaterasu, and its secret inner sanctum, entered only by selected priests, is thought to hold the Sacred Mirror, which is believed to have been given to the first emperor by the gods. This imperial shrine is considered so sacred that the general public is kept at a distance by fences, beyond which they can see only the thatched roofs of the main structures. To always offer the kami a clean and fresh place, all the buildings are dismantled every twenty years and then replaced with new buildings constructed in exactly the same ancient way, with massive wooden frames and thick thatched roofs. The 130,000 Japanese cypresses required for each rebuilding must be more than 200 years old and in excellent condition, so new trees are carefully planted in a sacred forest for buildings that will be constructed long after the lives of their caretakers. Since the seventh century CE, the

An Interview with a Japanese Businessman

Shinto priest performing ritual worship for a client at Fushimi Inari shrine, Kyoto.

Although many Japanese visit Shinto shrines, very few identify themselves as Shinto. This anomaly is illustrated by the feelings of an international life-insurance company representative who lives near Mount Fuji. He often visits shrines wherever he goes but does not consider himself a Shintoist. And even though he kindly agreed to be interviewed about his experiences, he requested that neither his name nor his picture be given. He was interviewed after he had finished praying at the Fushimi Inari Shrine in Kyoto.

I know this shrine is associated with business success. Whenever I visit Kyoto for business, I come here to pray. Many of my friends who run their own businesses come to this shrine. One of my co-workers donated a torii gate to this Inari shrine; he believes in the Inari shrine. I am personally thinking that I want to donate torii in the future. But it is expensive to do so. When I visited this shrine last year, when it was celebrating its 1,300th anniversary, I donated some money to the shrine, as much as I could afford. Two weeks ago, I received a thankyou letter from the shrine. So I came here to thank it today.

I am not a follower of Shinto. I go to Buddhist temples for memorial services and for visiting my ancestral grave. But I naturally came to pray at shrines because my grandparents and parents were praying at shrines, putting their hands together. Recently I heard a story that one of my ancestors built the Ontake Shrine in Nagano, so it seems that my family lineage had deep faith in the Shinto kami. But I do not actually know whether my family has faith in kami. I have a small kami shelf in my house. My parents who live separately from us have a Buddhist altar in their house. They do not talk to me about Inari kami. But I know they pray at the shrine because they have their own business, which is different from my business.

Since I have my own business, I pray at Inari shrine, whose kami is the deity of business, as part of my business. I believe that kami are real, but I do not think that their power helped me. When I go to a shrine, I do not pray for fulfillment of my wishes. I go to a shrine to express my gratitude. When my business does not go well, that's my fault. When my business goes well, I thank my clients, colleagues, and kami.

Although I started to pray to Inari kami for business in the beginning, now I often visit various shrines in my town to pray. I have begun to pray to various kami to wish my family and friends, etc., good health and happiness. Praying is not only for my own business any more.

Whenever I visit Kyoto, I go to pray at Fushimi Inari Shrine, but I also go to other shrines and temples. If I go to Tokyo, I go to Meiji Shrine and Asakusa Sensoji temple. Wherever I go, I visit shrines and temples.

Whenever I visit Mount Fuji, I get new energy and feel like I have to hang in there. People who live in that area can look at Mount Fuji any time, but people who live elsewhere feel that Mount Fuji is a special mountain.

For me, religion and belief are my individual matter, so I do not care what other people believe. I myself do not know my family's religion. I used to be suspicious of religions. But nowadays, I feel that life without religious faith is a little bit sad. What changed my mind? Perhaps I am getting old. Joking aside, I am working for a foreign insurance company which places great responsibility on the employee. So I may need some spiritual help to maintain my normal condition.[9]

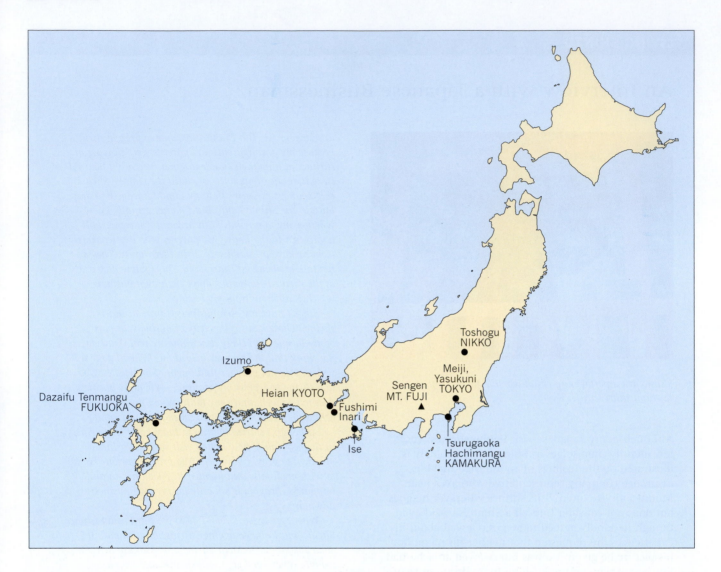

There are tens of thousands of Shinto shrines in Japan. Some of the major ones are shown above.

emperor was responsible both for political administration and for religious duties; in time, one of the imperial princesses was given the important task of properly worshiping the kami at Ise Shrine on behalf of the nation. She was sequestered and purified for this duty. Ise Shrine itself was established by Princess Yamamoto when the emperor decided that Amaterasu could not be properly worshiped within the imperial compound. Allegedly having shamanic powers, Princess Yamamoto was instructed in a vision by Amaterasu that her shrine was to be constructed at Ise on the southern coast. According to the *Nihongi*, the goddess told Princess Yamamoto:

> *The province of Ise, of the divine wind, is the land whither repair the waves from the eternal world, the successive waves. It is a secluded and pleasant land. In this land I wish to dwell.*[10]

The word "kamikaze," meaning "divine wind," became one of the aspects of Amaterasu and later, a symbol of divine protection of Japan by the kami.

The earliest places of worship were probably sacred trees or groves, perhaps with some enclosure to demarcate the sacred area. Shrine complexes that developed later also have some way of indicating where sacred space begins: tall gate-frames, known as *torii*; walls; or streams with bridges, which must be crossed to enter the holy precinct of the kami. Water is a purifying influence, and stone water troughs with bamboo dippers are also provided for washing one's mouth and hands before passing through the *torii*. Statues of guardian animals may further protect the area from evil intrusions, as do ropes with pendants hanging down.

Toriis *at an open-air shrine in* Fushimi Inari Complex, Kyoto, *with engraved stones honoring many* kami *(the central and largest being for Amaterasu), and small* toriis *offered by pilgrims. On the left is a rope with a clanging device, which can be pulled to draw the attention of the* kami *and frighten away evil spirits.*

Inside the shrine compound, there may be an area for public worship. Visitors may throw coins into an offering box, stand praying with bowed head, clap their hands twice, and pull a rope attached to a suspended metal gourd that clatters to set up vibrations in the air, attracting the kami so that one can communicate with them and also perhaps chasing away evil spirits. Beyond the public space may be a roofed structure where priests conduct rites. Beyond that is the sacred sanctuary, which is entered only by the high priest. Here the spirit of the kami is invited to dwell within a special natural object or perhaps a mirror, which reflects the revered light of brightness and purity, considered the natural order of the universe. If there is a spiritually powerful site already present—a waterfall, a crevice in a rock, a hot spring, a sacred tree—the spirit of the kami may dwell there. Some shrines are completely empty at the center. In any case, the worshipers do not see the holy of holies; their worship is imageless. As Kishimoto Hideo explains:

Modern Japanese visit Shinto shrines for many purposes, asking the blessing of kami *on the patterns of their lives. Most Shinto shrines are built with an appreciation for simple natural materials, and the larger ones are periodically rebuilt with great ceremony.*

> *A faithful believer would come to the simple hall of a Shinto sanctuary, which is located in a grove with a quiet and holy atmosphere. He may stand quite a while in front of the sanctuary, clap his hands, bow deeply, and try to feel the deity in his heart.*[11]

At times Shinto has been strongly **iconoclastic** (opposed to images of the divine). In the eighteenth century, for instance, a famous Shinto scholar wrote:

> *Never make an image in order to represent the Deity. To worship a deity is directly to establish a felt relation of our heart to the living Divinity through sincerity or truthfulness on our part. If we, however, try to establish a relation between Deity and man indirectly by means of an image, the image will itself stand in the way and prevent us from realizing our religious purpose to accomplish direct communion with the Deity. So an image made by mortal hands is of no use in Shinto worship.*[12]

Ceremonies and festivals

To properly encourage the spirit of the kami to dwell in a shrine, long and complex ceremonies are needed. In some shrines, it takes ten years for the priests to learn them. The priesthood was traditionally hereditary. One shrine claims to have drawn its priests from the same four families for more than a hundred generations. Not uncommonly, the clergy may be priestesses. The priests may be assisted by *miko*, young unmarried women—often daughters of the priests—dressed in white kimonos. Neither priests nor priestesses live as ascetics; it is common for them to be married, and they are not traditionally expected to meditate. Rather, they are considered specialists in the arts of maintaining the connection between the kami and the people.

Everything has symbolic importance, so rites are conducted with great care. The correct materials in temple furnishings, the bowing, the sharp clapping of hands, beating of drums, the waving of a stick with paper strips for purification—everything is established by tradition and performed with precision. When people have made a pilgrimage to a special shrine, they often take back spiritual mementos of their communion with the kami, such as a paper symbol of the temple encased within a brocade bag. The sale of such amulets is a major source of shrine income, along with payments for the performance of special prayers and rites.

Japanese people may also make daily offerings to the kami in their home. Their place of worship usually consists of a high shelf on which rests a miniature shrine, with only a mirror inside. The daily home ritual may begin by greeting the sun in the east with clapping and a prayer for protection for the household. Then offerings are placed before the shrine: rice for health, water for cleansing and preservation of life, and salt for purification and the harmonious seasoning of life. When a new house is to be built, the blessings of the kami are ceremonially requested.

Another common feature of Japanese popular culture that is associated with shrine worship is festivals, which are held throughout the year and throughout a person's life. They begin four months before the birth of a baby, when the soul is thought to enter the fetus. Then, thirty-two or thirty-three days after the infant's birth, its parents take it to the family's shrine for initiation by the deity. In a traditional family, many milestones—such as coming of age at thirteen, or first arranging one's hair as a woman at age sixteen, marriage, turning sixty-one, seventy-seven, or eighty-eight—are also celebrated with a certain spiritual awareness and ritualism.

There are also seasonal festivals, exuberant affairs in which the people and the kami join in celebrating life. Many have an agricultural basis, ensuring good crops and then giving thanks for them.

All local shrines celebrate their own kami with a festival that usually includes a great parade in which the local kami is thought to be taken out of the shrine where it lives and carried through the streets in a portable shrine in order to show it the world outside. The kami may be accompanied by elaborate floats and music-makers. During the festivals, offerings of rice, fish, and vegetables may be presented to the kami, as well as offerings of music, dance, and praises. Everyone present is blessed by the priests with water flung from *sakaki* tree branches dipped into sanctified water.

The biggest annual festival celebrates New Year. It begins in December with ceremonial house-cleaning, the placing of bamboo and pine "trees" at doorways of everything from homes to offices and bars to welcome the kami, and dressing in traditional kimonos. On 31 December, there is a national day of purification. On New Year's Day, people watch the first sunrise of the year and will try to visit a shrine as well as friends and relatives. More than three million people visit the large Meiji Shrine in Tokyo for New Year to pray for good luck in the year to come. This ritual is one of many popular rites that were created at Shinto shrines during the twentieth century. Other new rites include drawing paper lots to tell one's fortune and tying them to tree branches, and engaging shrine priests to purify new cars or building plots.

There are also many ceremonies honoring those who have reached a certain age. For instance, on 15 January, those who are twenty years old are recognized as full-fledged adults, and on 15 November, children who are three, five, or seven years old (considered delicate ages) are taken to a shrine to ask for the protection of the kami.

In addition, on 3 February, the end of winter, people throw beans to toss out bad fortune and invite good, and at shrines the priests shoot arrows to break the power of misfortune. A month-long spring festival is held from March to April, with purification rites and prayers for a successful planting season. The month of June is devoted to rites to protect crops from insects, blights, and bad weather. Fall brings thanksgiving rites for the harvest, with the first fruits offered to the kami and then great celebrating in the streets.

This is not to say that the majority of Japanese people commonly visit shrines or understand what goes on there. According to a 2007 survey by the National Association of Shrines, some thirty-five percent of Japanese have no knowledge of their local shrine.[13] However, some who visit shrines do so secretly, going to a particular shrine for special help—such as problems with work or love—in the dead of night when no one will see them. Husbands and wives may not even tell each other of their visits. If asked by researchers, they may deny knowing anything about shrines.

Purification

In the traditions collectively referred to as Shinto or *kannagara*, the world is beautiful and full of helpful spirits. Sexuality per se is not evil; the world was created by mating deities, and people have traditionally bathed together communally in Japan. However, ritual impurity is a serious problem that obscures our originally pristine nature; it may offend the kami and bring about calamities, such as drought, famine, or war.

The quality of impurity or misfortune is called *tsumi* or *kegare*. It can arise through contact with low-level spirits, negative energy from corpses, negative vibrations from wicked minds, hostility toward others or the environment, or natural catastrophes. In contrast to repentance required by religions that emphasize the idea of human sinfulness, *tsumi* requires purification. The body and mind must be purified so that the person can be connected with kami that are clean, bright, right, and straight. One way of removing *tsumi* is paying attention to problems as they arise:

> *To live free of obstructing mists, problems of the morning should be solved in the morning and those of the evening should be solved by evening. Wisdom and knowledge should be applied like the sharpness of an axe to the blinding effect of the mists of obstruction. Then may the* kami *purify the world and free it of* tsumi.[14]
>
> *After this has been completed, the heavenly* kami, *the earthly* kami *and the myriad of* kami *can recognize man as purified and everything can return to its original brightness, beauty and purity as before since all* tsumi *has wholly vanished from the world.*[15]

People may also be purified in a kind of spontaneous movement that washes over them, often in nature, bringing them into awareness of unity with the universe. Hitoshi Iwasaki, a Shinto priest, says that he likes to look at the stars at night in the mountains where the air is clear:

> *When I am watching the thoroughly clear light of the stars, I get a pure feeling, like my mind being washed. I rejoice to think this is a spiritual* misogi *[purification ritual].*[16]

Purification by Waterfall

The cleansing power of water, plentiful in natural Japan, is often used for spiritual purification in Shinto, a practice generally known as *misogi*. One may take a ritual bath in the ocean, source of life. Or, in a lengthy ritual also called *misogi*, a believer may stand beneath a waterfall, letting its force hit his or her shoulders and carry impurities and tensions away. Before even entering the waterfall, those seeking purification must undergo preliminary purification practices because the waterfall itself is kami. The women put on white kimonos and headbands, the men white loincloths and headbands.

The *misogi* ritual proceeds with shaking the soul by bouncing the hands up and down in front of the stomach, to help the person become aware of the soul's presence. Next comes a form of warm-up calisthenics called "bird rowing." Following a leader, the participants then shout invocations that activate the soul, affirm the potential for realizing the infinite in their own souls, and unify them with the kami of earth, guidance, water, life, and the ki energy (which the Chinese know as qi).

Before entering the waterfall, the participants raise their metabolism and absorb as much ki as possible by practicing a form of deep breathing. They are sprinkled with purifying salt and are given sake (rice wine) to spray into the stream in three mouthfuls. The leader counts from one to nine, to symbolize the impurity of the mundane world, and then cuts the air and shouts "*Yei!*" to dispel this impurity. With ritual claps and shouts the participants then enter the waterfall, continually chanting "*Harae-tamae-Kiyome-tamae-ro-kon-sho-jo!*" This phrase requests the kami to wash away all *tsumi* from the six elements that form the human being, from the senses, and from the mind. This part of the ritual has been scientifically proven to lower blood pressure.

After this powerful practice, participants dry off, spend time in meditation to calm the soul, and share a ceremonial drink to unify themselves with the kami and with each other. The whole ceremony is designed to restore one's natural purity and sense of mission in life. As Yukitaka Yamamoto explains:

> As imperfect beings, we often fail to recognize our mission. These failures come about because we have lost something of our natural purity. This is why purification, or misogi, is so central to Shinto. It enables man to cultivate spirituality and to restore his or her natural greatness.[17]

Misogi, *or ritual purification by standing beneath a waterfall.*

In addition to these personal ways of cleansing, there are ritual forms of purification. One is *oharai*, a ceremony commonly performed by Shinto priests, which includes the waving of a branch from a sacred *sakaki* tree, to which white streamers are attached (the Japanese version of the shaman's medicine fan of feathers or the Hindu yak-tail whisk, all used to sweep through the air and thus purify an area). This ceremony is today performed on cars and new buildings. A version used to soothe a kami that is upset by an impurity was called for in 1978 when there was a rash of suicides by residents jumping off roofs in a Tokyo housing complex.

Before people enter a Shinto shrine, they will splash water on their hands and face and rinse their mouth to purify themselves in order to approach the kami. Water is also used for purification in powerful ascetic practices, such as standing under a waterfall (see Box, facing page). Sprinkling salt on the ground or on ritual participants is also regarded as purifying.

Buddhist, Daoist, and Confucian influences

What elements of Confucianism and Buddhism have influenced Shinto?

Over time, the ways of the kami that have been labeled "Shinto" have blended with other religions imported into Japan, particularly Buddhism, first introduced into Japan in the sixth century CE, and Daoist and Confucian influences, which have been part of Japanese culture since its earliest contact with China.

Confucian ideals became embedded in Japanese ethics, particularly with reference to comfortable human relationships. The striking politeness and respectful and helpful behavior of many contemporary Japanese people may be traced back to those Confucian ideals. But Confucian ideals were also used by the government to control and pacify the people, especially during the Edo period (1603–1868). Since the Confucian model was regarded as the best way to stabilize the country, Confucian scholars were sponsored.

Buddhism has become an integral part of Japan's religious landscape. Buddhist monks of medieval times tried to convince the Japanese that the kami were protectors of Buddhist temples, and then that they were actually manifestations of the Buddha essence. During the Heian period (794–1192) Buddhism and reverence for the kami merged to a considerable extent. During the Kamakura period (1192–1333), Shinto became more self-conscious and systematic, and the idea was promoted that the kami were the original essence and the Buddhas and bodhisattvas their manifestations. The two religions continued to be closely interwoven in many ways until the nineteenth century, when the Meiji government promoted its version of Shinto as part of its program of nationalistic revival. In the Meiji Restoration, Shinto was distinguished from Buddhism, which was denounced for its foreign origins.

Today Buddhism is practiced side by side with the ways called Shinto. The Japanese may go to Shinto shrines for life-affirming events, such as conception, birth, and marriage, and to Buddhist temples for death rites. Since a Shinto shrine is maintained as a clean place for kami, dead bodies would defile the shrine, so Buddhist temples have long managed funerals. Some villages have stone monuments to the kami and statues of Nichiren placed next to each other.

Reverence toward the kami is mixed with Buddhist practices in traditions such as ritual ascent of sacred mountains in search of enlightenment. Mountain caves are considered to have special powers in Japan because of the spiritual power of the mountains plus that of the kami who are thought to spend the winters there. To reach the cave of Omine-san, a sacred mountain in Nara Prefecture, pilgrims and ascetics climb up a steep trail to the cave mouth while chanting the Buddhist *Heart Sutra*. Small shrines dedicated to various kami and also Buddhist figures are encountered on the mountainside. Crawling into the cave and then into an upper chamber, pilgrims find themselves in a dark, wet, womb-like world with secretions dripping from the rocks. This sacred natural space in the deep recesses of the mountain is considered an excellent place for progressing toward full realization of the truth by Buddhist practices such as chanting of the *Heart Sutra*.

Inoue Nobutaka of the Faculty of Shinto Studies at Tokyo's Kokugakuin University suggests that Chinese folk religion (practices including worship of spirits, spirit possession, divination, and oracles), Chinese yin–yang theories, and elements of Daoism and Confucianism have also become blended with whatever kami practices might have existed since prehistory in Japan, to the extent that "The influence of Chinese religion in East Asia is so prominent that the whole region may well be regarded as a single 'Chinese religio-cultural sphere.'"[18]

In the seventeenth century, Japanese Confucian scholars attempted to free themselves from Buddhism and to tie the Chinese beliefs they were importing to the kami traditions. One scholar, for instance, likened *li* to the way of the kami as a means of social cohesion. Another stressed reverence as the common ground of the two paths and was himself revered as a living kami. The Neo-Confucianists' alliance with the ways of the kami to throw off the yoke of Buddhism made the somewhat formless Japanese traditions more self-conscious. Scholars began to study and interpret them. The combination of Confucian emphasis on hierarchy and devotion to the kami helped to pave the way for the establishment in 1868 of the powerful Meiji monarchy.

State Shinto

Why has Shinto been so closely tied to Japanese nationalism?

The Meiji regime took steps to promote Shinto as the spiritual basis for the government. The state cult, amplifying the Japanese traditions of ancestor veneration, had taught since the seventh century CE that the emperor was the offspring of Amaterasu, the sun goddess. *Naobi no Mitama* (Divine Spirit of Rectification), written in the eighteenth century, expressed this ideal:

> *This great imperial land, Japan, is the august country where the divine ancestral goddess Amaterasu Omikami was born, a superb country. … Amaterasu deigned to entrust the country with the words, "So long as time endures, for ten thousand autumns, this land shall be ruled by my descendants."*
>
> *According to her divine pleasure, this land was decreed to be the country of the imperial descendants … so that even now, without deviation from the divine age, the land might continue in tranquility and in accord with the will of the* kami, *a country ruled in peace.*[19]

It had been customary for members of the imperial family to visit the great shrine to the sun goddess at Ise to consult the supreme kami on matters of importance. But Emperor Meiji was the first emperor ever to go there. He decreed that the way of the kami should govern the nation. This way, now referred to as "State Shinto," was administered by government officials rather than Shinto priests, whose objections were silenced, and many of the old rituals were suppressed. State Shinto became the tool of militaristic nationalists as a way to enlist popular support for the throne and the expanding empire.

In the profound changes that occurred, nationalists idealized Japan's ancient "Shinto" past, using Confucian-style ancestor worship to promote reverence for historical emperors and people who had died for their country. Japan was projected as a large family with the emperor as its benevolent father, ruling under the protection of the kami. Teachers and schoolchildren were ordered to honor special festival days by assembling and bowing deeply to an image of the emperor and empress. Great pageants promoting these ideals were celebrated in the cities. As "ancient traditions" were invented, hereditary lineages of shrine priests were disbanded and replaced by state-appointed priests who would perform standardized rituals on behalf of the emperor. Buddhist authorities insisted that "Shinto" was not a real religion; shrines were only places for the performance of rituals. Thus, in 1882, shrine priests were barred from carrying on any "religious" activities, including preaching and holding funerals. And in 1906, thousands of local shrines were consolidated, with the goal—not fully implemented—of having only one shrine in each area as a platform for conducting national imperial ceremonies. After Emperor Meiji died in 1912, a huge plot in central Tokyo was set aside for a shrine honoring his spirit: this is now the lavish Meiji Shrine. Although traditional shrines for worship of kami were constructed in natural forests, there was no forest in urban Tokyo, so people came from all over Japan to plant a forest there.

Ultimately, Emperor Hirohito (1901–1989), Meiji's grandson, was held up as a god, not to be seen or touched by ordinary people. But after Japan's surrender in World War II, the emperor officially renounced his hereditary claim to being divine in order to protect the monarchy from being totally disbanded by the occupying powers.

"Sect Shinto"

What is "Sect Shinto"?

With modern industrialization and urbanization, worship for generations at the same village shrines further declined. And the designation of shrines as "non-religious" lingered, with spiritual practices such as divination, healing, and communication with ancestors looked down on as superstitions. Nevertheless, such practices never totally died out, and during the nineteenth and twentieth centuries, many new religious sects appeared that had their roots in practices of communicating with the kami. In rural areas, certain women had long been acting as shamans by falling into trances, in which the kami would speak through them. Some of these shamanistic women developed a following of their own, leading to movements that were labeled "Sect Shinto" by the Meiji regime. Some of these movements are still popular today. For example, a new movement called Oomoto developed from revelations given to Nao Deguchi, an illiterate widow, when she was reportedly possessed by the previously little-known kami Ushitora no Konjin in 1892. Some 200,000 pages of revelations, which Madame Deguchi received by automatic writing, criticized the "beastly" state of humanity, with:

> the stronger preying on the weaker. … If allowed to go on in this way, society will soon lose the last vestiges of harmony and order. Therefore, by a manifestation of Divine Power, the Greater World shall undergo reconstruction, and change into an entirely new creation. … The Greater World shall burst into bloom as plum blossoms at winter's end.[20]

The movement attracted some nine million supporters and survived two periods of severe persecution during the Meiji regime. Its followers study traditional Japanese arts, such as calligraphy, ceramics, and Noh drama, with the idea that artistic creation can be a way of cleaning mind and heart. Spiritual leadership of the organization is always passed down through women of Madame Deguchi's lineage, because of her assertion that women are more spiritually open. The followers feel that they are living according to ancient Shinto traditions, except that they worship together and see the many kami as manifestations of one god, Oomoto, the "Great Source." The movement now has a universalist approach, recognizing founders of other religions as kami.

An Oomoto priest purifies a devotee by waving a sakaki branch with paper streamers in his direction.

Shinto today

What rituals and ceremonies are practiced in contemporary Shinto?

In general, the ways attributed to Shinto remain indigenous to Japan. Outside Japan, Shinto beliefs and practices are common only in Hawai'i and Brazil, because many Japanese have settled there. Most Japanese people who visit shrines and pray to the kami do not even think of themselves as Shinto adherents. This label is applied mostly by the priestly establishment.

Within Japan, reaction to the horrors of World War II, the elimination of the imperial mythology of State Shinto, and a desire for modernization threatened institutionalized Shinto. After the war, the Japanese Teachers Association began teaching rejection of the imperial family, of Japanese history, and also of the beliefs and practices that had become associated with Shinto. The Japanese national flag—a red circle on a white background—became a symbol of the past, although its symbolism transcends history. The red circle signifies the rising sun and the white background purity, righteousness, and national loyalty. For a time it was difficult for young people to learn about the ways of the kami. But the shrines remain and are visited by more than eighty million Japanese at New Year. People often visit more as tourists than as believers, but many say they experience a sense of spiritual renewal when they visit a shrine. Long-established households still have their kami shelf, often next to the Buddhist family altar, which combines tablets memorializing the dead with scrolls or statues dedicated to a manifestation of the Buddha.

Shinto priest Hitoshi Iwasaki explains this eclectic approach:

People come to the shrines. They gather there because these are sacred places from ancient times where people have come to pray. And other people want to go where people are gathered, so some of the shrines become vacation places, surrounded by souvenir shops. Many come to Shinto shrines and pray Buddhist prayers. Why not? Buddha is one of the kami. Everything has kami.[21]

It is certainly the case that in contemporary life, visits to shrines often resemble tourism more than spirituality. The large Yasaka shrine in Kyoto is a passageway between a popular garden and the urban area, though ostensibly demarcated as a sacred space by *torii* at either end, and most people simply stroll among the shrine buildings, souvenir shops, and stalls selling food without washing

Yamada Hachiman Shrine's festival was organized by priests and young people in the fishing town of Yamada soon after the catastrophic tsunami. Carrying a palanquin for the kami from the local shrine, which had remained unharmed, and doing the traditional performances brought a sense of renewal and joy to the devastated area.

their hands and mouth or giving much thought to the kami. The entertainment dimension of shrine visits is prominent in such new practices as the "thousand-shrine pilgrimage" and tours of shrines and temples venerating deities of good fortune. Nevertheless, despite the fact that Japan is now one of the most technologically advanced countries in the world, with business its primary focus, there still seems to be a place for ritual—and in some cases, heartfelt—communion with the intangible kami that, in traditional belief, permeate all of life.

Rapid and extreme urbanization, industrial pollution, and despoliation of the natural environment—including the nuclear disaster following the terrible earthquake and tsunami of 2011—have resulted in a backlash from concerned citizens urging more respect for the earth. The Shinto establishment offered rites in their Tokyo headquarters seeking the kami's help in quickly restoring the devastated areas, as well as sending young shrine priests out to gather funds for disaster relief. In the chaos and distress following the disaster, many people took refuge in shrines that survived. Many devastated towns and villages revived old festivals for dealing with seasonal damage by winds and floods. Ritual performances known as *kagura* mirrored the festivities said to have been used to lure Amaterasu out of the cave. Participating in such shrine festivals helped to rebuild community bonds, comfort the mourners, and develop the feeling that the cosmos was being restored in the wake of chaos.

Sumo wrestling is still imbued with Shinto rituals traditionally performed for the sake of abundant harvests and homage to the kami. The canopy hung over the ring represents a Shinto shrine. The officials wear robes and hats similar to those of Shinto priests and perform a ceremony with salt to purify the area before the match starts. The wrestlers also perform solemn Shinto-like ceremonies, including hand-clapping to draw the attention of the kami.

A great controversy has developed around one of the new shrines in Tokyo, now called the "Yasukuni Shrine." It was dedicated during the Meiji Restoration in honor of those who have given their lives in war for the sake of Japan, with the idea that they died to preserve peace in Japan. *Yasukuni* means "peaceful country." Written records of some 2.5 million people who died in various conflicts are enshrined therein. The political controversy concerns the 1978 inclusion of fourteen Japanese leaders from World War II who had been classified as Class A war criminals by an Allied tribunal. When highly visible political figures—including Japanese prime ministers—have paid their respects at the shrine, there has been strong criticism from abroad. Critics from countries

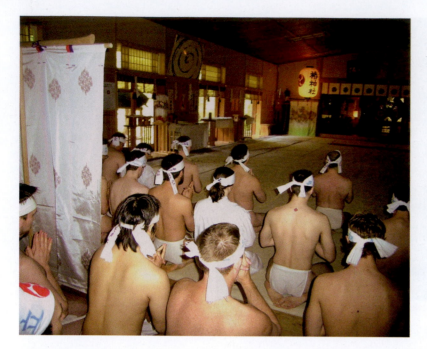

Participants in a misogi *ceremony at Tsubaki Shrine in the United States ritually prepare themselves for the purification.*

who suffered in the past from Japanese imperialist violence, including China and Korea, regard the shrine as a symbol of militarism and ultranationalism, and the prime ministers' visits as disregard for the principle of separation of religion from the state. Yasukuni Shrine officials have thus far refused to remove the war criminals from the list of those being honored at the shrine.

Some Shinto adherents now explain their path as a universal natural religion, rather than an exclusively Japanese phenomenon, and try to explain the way of harmony with the kami to interested non-Japanese, without striving for conversions. Accordingly, there are now Shinto shrines in Brazil, Canada, France, North and South Korea, the Netherlands, Taiwan, and the United States. In Washington state, the American branch of Tsubaki Grand Shrine offers a variety of ceremonies, including *misogi* in a clear river. The universal application and contemporary relevance of this traditional purification ceremony can be inferred from the shrine's description of it as "a sacred activity meant to teach us how to live every day fully, how to pray sincerely to fulfill your wishes, how to chose the most correct life path, how to work for the benefit of humanity and the world, how to assist in purifying *tsumi/ kegare*, how to pray for health of our family, how to find right livelihood, how to pass through critical junctures, how to solve problems."[22]

Within Japan, especially after the 2011 disasters, there are signs of a return to the central theme of Shinto as harmony with nature. There are new attempts to teach children the thousands-of-years-old rice-cultivation ceremony, and with it, values such as co-existence and "co-prosperity" with the natural environment and with each other. The Association of Shinto Shrines feels that it can play a role in helping people to remember the natural world. The association has stated:

> [Traditionally] the Japanese viewed nature not as an adversary to be subdued, but rather as a sacred space overflowing with the blessings of the kami, and toward which they were to act with restraint. … While the Japanese have loathed environmental destruction, the advance of civilization centered on science and technology, and the rush toward economic prosperity have created a tidal wave of modernization that has frequently resulted in the loss of that traditional attitude handed down from ancestors. … By reconsidering the role of the sacred groves possessed by the eighty thousand or so shrines in Japan, we hope to heighten Japanese consciousness, and expand the circle of active involvement in environmental preservation.[23]

Key terms

kami The invisible sacred quality that evokes wonder and awe; the invisible spirits throughout nature that are born of this essence.

kannagara Harmony with the way of the kami.

misogi The Shinto waterfall purification ritual.

oharai Shinto purification ceremony.

tsumi Impurity or misfortune, a quality that Shinto purification practices are designed to remove.

Suggested reading

Bocking, Brian, *A Popular Dictionary of Shinto*, Richmond, Surrey: Curzon Press, 1996. Thorough discussions of ancient and contemporary facets of Shinto, including shrines, festivals, kami, new religious movements, historical events, and key figures.

Breen, John and Mark Teeuwen, *A New History of Shinto*, Oxford: Wiley-Blackwell, 2010. Significant reconsideration of scholarship regarding the nature of Shintoism, with the conclusion that it is best seen as a group of institutions and practices that are still evolving, rather than the remains of a pristine indigenous tradition.

Breen, John and Mark Teeuwen, eds, *Shinto in History: Ways of the Kami*, Honolulu: University of Hawai'i Press, 2000. Scholarly essays distinguishing between unnamed shrine cults and establishment Shinto in historical context.

Carter, Robert E., *The Japanese Arts and Self-Cultivation*, Albany, New York: State University of New York Press, 2008. Examination of aikido, gardening, tea ceremony, flower arrangement, and ceramics as experiential the spiritual paths based in ancient Japanese traditions.

Hardacre, Helen, *Shinto and the State, 1868–1988*, Princeton, New Jersey: Princeton University Press, 1991. Detailed analysis of state involvement with Shinto from the Meiji Restoration onward, plus Hardacre's theory that the idea of Shinto has also been used to benefit popular religious movements, individual political ambitions, and local government administrations.

Hori, Ichiro, *Folk Religion in Japan*, Chicago and London: University of Chicago Press, 1968. A lively study of Japanese folk traditions, such as shamanism and mountain worship, which contributed to Shinto.

Kitagawa, Joseph M., *On Understanding Japanese Religion*, Princeton, New Jersey and Guildford, Surrey: Princeton University Press, 1987. A scholarly history including Shinto and "new religions," making distinctions between shrine Shinto, folk Shinto, and Sect Shinto.

Nelson, John K., *A Year in the Life of a Shinto Shrine*, Seattle: University of Washington Press, 1995. Both an in-depth description of the ritual cycle at a major Shinto shrine and an accessible introduction to Shinto.

Picken, Stuart D. B., *Essentials of Shinto: An Analytical Guide to Principal Teachings*, Westport, Connecticut and London: Greenwood Press, 1994. A clear introduction by a minister of the Church of Scotland who is also a *misogi* practitioner.

Swanson, Paul L. and Clark Chilson, *Nanzan Guide to Japanese Religions*, Honolulu: University of Hawai'i Press, 2006. A collection of articles about the various religious traditions of Japan, including themes that are common to them all.

Yamakage, Motohisa, *The Essence of Shinto: Japan's Spiritual Heart*, Tokyo and New York: Kodansha International, 2006. A Shinto master from a long lineage of masters explains the inner meanings of Shinto practices.

7.1 *Explain the importance of the natural world in the roots of "Shinto"*

Living so close to nature—the sea and mountains, the waterfalls and lush forests—Japanese people organized their lives around the turn of the seasons, honoring the roles of the sun, moon, and lightning in their rice farming. Mount Fuji, greatest of the volcanic peaks, was honored as the sacred embodiment of the divine creativity that had thrust the land up from the sea. The most ancient forms of spirituality in Japan were probably linked to the spirits perceived in the natural world—the kami. This continues to be the main feature defining what is now called Shinto.

The earliest ways of kami worship were carried out in open-air sites without buildings, but with the introduction of Buddhist influences in the sixth century CE shrines were built to honor the kami, such as Inari (the god of rice). Most important of these shrines was Ise Shrine, a complex of 100 shrines with the main shrine a place of worship of the kami Amaterasu (sun goddess). Kami were also worshiped with daily offerings at shrines in homes and at seasonal festivals to ensure good crops and to celebrate life.

7.2   Outline the elements of Confucianism and Buddhism that have been blended with Shinto

Daoist and Confucian influences have been part of Japanese culture since its earliest contact with China in the first centuries CE. Confucian ideals became embedded in Japanese ethics, particularly with reference to comfortable human relationships. The striking politeness and respectful and helpful behavior of many contemporary Japanese people may be traced back to those Confucian ideals. But Confucian ideals were also used by the government to control and pacify the people, particularly during the Edo period (1603–1868).

Buddhism was first introduced into Japan in the sixth century CE and Buddhist monks tried to convince the Japanese that the kami were manifestations of the Buddha essence. During the Heian period (794–1192) Buddhism and reverence for the kami merged to a considerable extent and during the following Kamakura period (1193–1333), the idea was promoted that the kami were the original essence and the Buddhas and bodhisattvas their manifestations. Today, reverence toward the kami is mixed with Buddhist practices in traditions such as ritual ascent of sacred mountains in search of enlightenment. Buddhism is practiced side by side with the ways called Shinto. Japanese may go to Shinto shrines for life-affirming events, such as conception, birth, and marriage, and to Buddhist temples for death rites.

7.3   Discuss the reasons why Shinto has been so closely tied to Japanese nationalism

The Meiji regime (which began with the Meiji Restoration in 1868) took steps to promote Shinto as the spiritual basis for the government. Emperor Meiji decreed that the way of the kami should govern the nation. This way, now referred to as "State Shinto," was administered by government officials rather than Shinto priests, whose objections were silenced, and many of the old rituals were suppressed. State Shinto became the tool of militaristic nationalists as a way to enlist popular support for the throne and expanding empire.

Nationalists idealized Japan's ancient "Shinto" past, using Confucian-style ancestor worship to promote reverence for historical emperors and people who had died for their country. Teachers and schoolchildren were ordered to honor special festival days by assembling and bowing deeply to an image of the emperor and empress. Great pageants promoting these ideals were celebrated in the cities. Hereditary lineages of shrine priests were disbanded and replaced by state-appointed priests who would perform standardized rituals on behalf of the emperor. Buddhist authorities insisted that "Shinto" was not a real religion; shrines were only places for the performance of rituals. After Japan's surrender in World War II, and with Emperor Hirohito officially renouncing his hereditary claim to being divine, State Shinto came to an end.

7.4   Define what is meant by "Sect Shinto" and give an example

Despite the designation of shrines as "nonreligious" during the Meiji regime, practices such as divination, healing, and communication with ancestors never totally died out. During the nineteenth and twentieth centuries many new religious sects appeared that had their roots in practices of communicating with the kami. In rural areas, certain women had long been acting as shamans and some of them developed a following of their own, leading to movements that were labeled "Sect Shinto" by the Meiji regime.

Some of these movements are still popular today. An example is Oomoto, which developed from the revelations given to Madame Nao Deguchi, an illiterate widow, in 1892. The movement attracted some nine million supporters and survived two periods of severe prosecution. Its followers study traditional Japanese arts, such as calligraphy, ceramics, and Noh drama, believing that artistic creation can be a way of cleaning mind and heart.

7.5 *Summarize the main aspects of contemporary Shinto*

Reaction to the horrors of World War II, the elimination of the imperial mythology of State Shinto, and a desire for modernization threatened institutionalized Shinto. After the war, the Japanese Teachers Association began teaching a rejection of the imperial family, of Japanese history, and also of the beliefs and practices that had become associated with Shinto. However, the shrines remain and are still visited by millions of Japanese, particularly at New Year. These visits often resemble tourism more than spirituality. Nevertheless, long-established households still have their kami shelf, often next to the Buddhist family altar. Some Shinto adherents now explain their path as a universal natural religion, rather than an exclusively Japanese phenomenon.

Rapid and extreme urbanization, industrial pollution, and despoliation of the natural environment—including the nuclear disaster following the terrible earthquake and tsunami of 2011—have resulted in a backlash from concerned citizens urging more respect for the earth. There are signs now of a return to the central theme of Shinto as harmony with nature and new attempts to teach children about ancient ceremonies, such as the rice cultivation ceremony.

ZOROASTRIANISM

A bridge between Asia and the West

1. *Describe the life and teachings of Zarathushtra*
2. *Identify the key texts of Zoroastrianism*
3. *Summarize the main Zoroastrian rituals*
4. *Discuss Zoroastrianism in the modern world*

Zoroastrianism, a religion from ancient Iran, at present has perhaps only 124,000 to 190,000 remaining practitioners, but for more than 1,000 years it may have been the official religion of the vast Iranian Empire that extended from Iraq or Turkey to India. It is in some ways a bridge between Asian and Western religions. Its origins are synchronous with, and similar to, Hinduism, it is thought to have influenced Buddhism, and it introduced beliefs that are similar to those later found in Jewish, Christian, and Muslim religions. Supplanting polytheism, it brought an early form of monotheism, which was subsequently central to those "Western" faiths, as well as to Sikhism, which was born on Indian soil.

However, the extent of Zoroastrianism's direct influence on later faiths is not clear. The theology of ancient Zoroastrianism itself is subject to debate, for over the centuries a large portion of its sacred scriptures was destroyed or forgotten and the meanings of the old language were lost.

In the early faith, people worshiped a pantheon of gods representing the elements, aspects of nature, and abstract principles such as justice and obedience. These gods often corresponded with those worshiped by Vedic Indians and were similarly named *daevas*, like the Indian devas, meaning "Shining Ones," with the highest gods called *Ahuras* (Lords). The ritual worship conducted by the priests was designed, as in India, to maintain the natural order, truth, and righteousness of the universe by re-enacting the original sacrifice that led to its creation.

ZARATHUSHTRA'S MISSION

Who was Zarathushtra?

Whereas the faith is known in Iran as Mazdayasna—"the worship of the Wise Lord, Ahura Mazda"—Western scholars refer to the tradition by the name of one of its great reformers, the prophet Zarathushtra (Greek: Zoroaster), who may have lived some time between 1800 and 1500 BCE in Central Asia. The Greeks in the time of Plato mentioned him as an ancient prophet.

It is thought that Zarathushtra was trained as a priest in the Indo-Iranian tradition. He was also apparently a mystical seeker who spent many years in spiritual retreat. At the age of thirty, he is said to have had a stunning vision of a great shining being, Vohu Manah, the embodiment of the good mind. Vohu Manah led him into the presence of Ahura Mazda, the creator god. Ahura Mazda was surrounded by angelic presences manifesting six attributes of the divine. Scholars suggest that these attributes represent earlier Indo-Iranian deities, transformed by Zarathushtra to suit his monotheistic belief but still retaining their association with forces of nature—the earth, the arch of the sky, water, plants, cattle, and fire.

Zarathushtra said he experienced communion with Ahura Mazda and his attributes on many occasions. From these direct contacts with the divine, Zarathushtra reportedly determined that in contrast to the multiplicity of gods worshiped by the Indo-Iranians, Ahura Mazda was the wise Lord, from whom all good things flowed. Zarathushtra denounced all cruelty, selfishness, distortion, and hypocrisy in the name of religion. He insisted that Ahura Mazda creates only goodness and should be worshiped by good thoughts, words, and deeds. There is a cosmic battle between sustaining and destroying forces, and to assure the victory of good over evil, humans must dedicate themselves as spiritual warriors for goodness.

Zoroastrian priests conduct a ceremony around a sacred fire.

Zarathushtra poured forth his adoration for the Supreme in metric verses called **Gathas**. These hymns are the only words of the prophet that have been retained over centuries of vicissitudes. "Speak to me as friend to friend," he implores Ahura Mazda. "Grant us the support which friend would give to friend."[1] The Gathas are the major existing source of information about Zarathushtra's life and theology, but they are written in an ancient language whose meanings are now obscure. Scholars see linguistic and thematic links between the Gathas and the earliest Vedas.

Zarathushtra was long unable to convince anyone else to follow him in honoring Ahura Mazda above all other gods. At last he journeyed to another kingdom and convinced its king, Vishtapa, of the truth of his understanding. King Vishtapa adopted Zarathushtra's creed and proclaimed it the state religion. Zarathushtra is said to have preached for almost fifty years until his death by assassination at a fire temple at the age of seventy-seven.

SPREAD OF ZOROASTRIAN BELIEFS

What are the key texts of Zoroastrianism?

It is very difficult to trace the later spread of Zarathushtra's teachings. The Magi—a tribe of priestly specialists in western Iran whose practices included magic and astrology—seem to have become involved with transmission of Zoroastrianism some time after Zarathushtra died, but they may have altered it significantly. They are mentioned in the Book of Matthew in the Christian Bible, in which some Magi reportedly followed a star to present gifts to the infant Jesus, but this may have been a legend written to interest the Magi in converting to Christianity.

Ahura Mazda was apparently revered by the Achaemenid kings of the great Persian Empire. This was set up in the mid-sixth century BCE by King Cyrus, who seems to have been a follower of Ahura Mazda. However, he and the succeeding Achaemenid kings left no written mention of the prophet Zarathushtra. Cyrus's reign was noted for its religious tolerance as well as its power and wealth. The empire Cyrus created by far-reaching conquests stretched from the Indus Valley to what is now Greece. The Jews within this territory were allowed to practice their own religion but may have adopted certain Zoroastrian beliefs, such as the belief that there is an evil aspect in life, an immortal soul, reward or punishment in an afterlife, and final resurrection of the body at the apocalyptic end of the present age—for these beliefs were absent from earlier Judaic religion. From Judaism, they may have passed indirectly into Christianity and Islam.

The spiritual tradition of devotion to Ahura Mazda was severely threatened by the 331 BCE invasion of Alexander, known as "the Great" in the West but "the Accursed" in Iran. According to Zoroastrian belief, he ransacked the beautiful capital of Persepolis, destroying fire temples, burning the library containing the holy scriptures of Zarathushtra, and killing so many Zoroastrian priests that oral transmission of many scriptures was also lost. It is thought that the Gathas of Zarathushtra survived because many people knew them by heart, as they did the most commonly used ritual prayers.

Two centuries later, Zoroastrianism was re-established in a shrunken Iranian Empire by the Parthians, who ruled for almost 500 years to 224 CE. Under the Parthians the surviving revealed teachings of Zoroastrianism were reassembled as the **Avesta**, or "holy texts." Then under the Sassanids of the third to mid-seventh centuries CE, Zoroastrianism came to the fore as the state religion, serving the aristocracy of Iran, and was thus one of the major religions of the ancient world.

However, a major threat to Zoroastrianism came from the spread of Islam after the death of Muhammad in 632 CE. Arabic Muslims defeated the Zoroastrian Iranian forces, and when Mongols invaded from the east they were gradually converted to Islam rather than Zoroastrianism. A number of Persian Zoroastrians avoided conversion to Islam by migrating to western India, whose spiritual origins were similar to their own. In India they were called **Parsis** (Persians). The sacred fire they consecrated on reaching India is said to have been kept burning continuously ever since. Some Parsis also migrated to what is now Pakistan.

The numbers of Zoroastrians remaining in Iran dwindled over the centuries under Muslim dominance. Even when Zoroastrians had become a minority in Iran, detailed instructions about the rituals and customs of the faith were preserved in a vast new literature, the **Pahlavi texts**, written or translated in Middle Persian from about the ninth century CE. A small community of believers still survives in Iran.

Today, India—particularly the Mumbai area—is the major center of Zoroastrian population, but whether it is also the repository of the purest surviving Zoroastrian teachings is a matter of debate. Zoroastrianism in India seems to have been affected by surrounding religious traditions—such as Hinduism, Buddhism, and Christianity—and, from the nineteenth century onward, by modern spiritual movements such as Theosophy. In its Indian setting, it has nonetheless remained vibrant and meaningful.

ZOROASTRIAN TEACHINGS

What are the important rituals in Zoroastrianism?

After Zarathushtra's death, his teachings seem to have been merged with earlier polytheistic trends. Today there is uncertainty about exactly what he taught, but enough is known for his theology to be sketched, along with its later transformations.

The primacy of Ahura Mazda

Zarathushtra is considered the first of the monotheists of the Western traditions, in the sense that he elevated one god above all others worshiped by the earlier Iranians. His mystical visions convinced him that there is only one divine being who creates and orders the universe. He refers to this god, Ahura Mazda, by the masculine gender. In the Gathas Zarathushtra makes impassioned pleas to Ahura Mazda to make him a more fit spiritual vehicle, so that he can "dedicate to Mazda the life-breath of his whole being."[2] He asks for guidance in the mission of protecting "the poor in spirit, the meek and lowly of heart, who are

Thine." He emphasizes the need for clear thought in this mission:

O Lord of Life, we long for Thy mighty Fire of Thought which is an enduring, blazing Flame bringing clear guidance and joy to the true believer, but as for the destruction-loving, this quickening Flame overcomes his evil in a flash.[3]

Although Zarathushtra perceived Ahura Mazda as the one Eternal Being, he also described six divine powers that radiate from the godhead: The Good Mind, Righteousness, Absolute Power, Devotion, Perfection, and Immortality. After the prophet's death, these six attributes were personified and worshiped as beings, and uttering their names was thought to bring great power. These Holy Immortals, the **Ameshta Spenta**, were described as luminous deities with shining eyes and beautiful forms, guardians of Ahura Mazda's creation who held celestial councils in the heavens and descended to earth on radiant paths. They are chief among the angels, who also include many of the deities worshiped by the earlier Iranians. One of these is the popular Mithra, guardian of the light, protector of the truth, and bestower of wealth. Mithra was worshiped in Hinduism, Manicheanism, and Mithraism, as well as in Zoroastrianism.

The choice between good and evil

Zarathushtra wrestled with the problem of the existence of evil. Many Western scholars describe Zarathushtra's theology as cosmic dualism, with Ahura Mazda opposed by a dark force of equal power. Others feel that this is a later development in Zoroastrianism and that the original teaching was that although there were two opposing forces in the universe, Ahura Mazda was much the stronger. In any case, in Zoroastrian belief Ahura Mazda is a good creator who creates only perfection and purity.

Zarathushtra did speak of two opposing powers: Spenta Mainyu, the good spirit, and Angra Mainyu, the evil spirit. Spenta Mainyu is life, order, perfection, health, happiness, increase. Angra Mainyu is not-life, chaos, imperfection, disease, sorrow, destruction. The two principles will always actively oppose each other in humans and in creation as a whole until the good spirit is at last victorious. Evil, Zarathushtra asserts, is not all-powerful or eternal, but to assure the victory of good over evil humans must dedicate themselves as spiritual warriors on the side of Spenta Mainyu. Human beings are given the free will and mental capacity to choose between the two powers. In their thoughts, words, and deeds, they can grow in love, devotion, and service, or they can contribute to evil.

Zarathushtra felt that nonloving acts in the name of religion aided the cause of evil. He railed against selfish ritualism and worship of the *daevas*, using the old word for the "shining deities" for what he considered dark forces and magic.

Heaven, hell, and resurrection

At death, Zoroastrians believe, each of us is judged according to the total goodness or evilness of our thoughts, words, and deeds. The greater the goodness, the wider the bridge to heaven, the Kingdom of Light where the souls of the righteous reside. The greater the accumulated evil, the narrower the bridge, until it is so narrow that souls cannot cross. They fall into hell, the House of the Lie, a murky, woeful place.

It is not Ahura Mazda who judges and metes out reward or punishment. By natural law, good deeds bring their own reward and evil deeds their just punishment. Zoroastrians feel that the effects of our actions will be felt both in the present and in an afterlife. Tehmurasp Rustamji Sethna explains:

When a man's actions are good he has self-confidence and usually people say he has nothing to worry about, his road is clear. On the other hand, if a man's actions are bad, it is usually said he is following a precarious path and any moment he will fall.[4]

There is no eternal hell in Zoroastrianism, for good is ultimately victorious. With the help of all individuals who choose goodness over evil, the world will gradually reach a state of perfection in which all souls, living or dead, are liberated forever from evil. This time is the Frashokereti, the "refreshment" of the world in which all of creation is resurrected into perfected immortality. Thenceforth the world will never grow old and never die. This refreshment requires the contributions of many people. Zoroastrianism therefore places great emphasis on the moral responsibility of each person, for the good of the whole.

Religious practices

Rituals are major elements of Zoroastrian practice. One that is particularly important is the act of tying the sacred cord (kusti) around one's mid-section, traditionally performed at least five times a day. Symbolically, the faithful are girding themselves as soldiers for Ahura Mazda, strengthening their resolve to follow the spiritual path. The kusti is worn by both males and females, in contrast with the male-only Hindu tradition of the sacred thread, for women and men are treated equally in many ways within Zoroastrianism. While tying the kusti, the faithful recite a prayer to keep evil at bay.

Zoroastrian rituals also emphasize purification. Water is venerated as a means or symbol of purification. The devout will often dip their fingers into water, apply it to their eyes and forehead, and raise their hands in prayer to Ahura Mazda. It is a great sin to pollute water or to place anything dead in it. Zoroastrians regard the natural world with profound reverence and are taught from childhood to avoid defiling it.

As of old, the other element emphasized in Zoroastrian rituals is fire, long used in Indo-Iranian tradition for its purifying, transformative power. Only Zoroastrians can enter a fire temple, and within the temple certain areas are accessible only by priests in a highly elevated state of purity. However, lay Zoroastrians also worship in their homes or in an open area, facing a light source.

When the physical body dies, Zoroastrians carry it to a Tower of Silence, a special circular building open at the top so that vultures can alight on the corpse to pick the bones clean. This is done to avoid polluting the earth with decaying flesh, which the birds dispose of within an hour or two. The recent near-extinction of vultures in India, perhaps due to their eating the carcasses of animals that had been fed certain medicines, has posed a crisis for this tradition, with some Parsis choosing cremation. Mumbai Parsis have proposed building aviaries to allow the vulture population to recover.

The survivors continue to pray for the departed and continue to observe death anniversaries at which the *fravashi*, or eternal principle and guide, of the deceased person is invoked. The *fravashi* is thought to continually evolve toward perfection and to help the living in their good works.

ZOROASTRIANISM TODAY

Where is Zoroastrianism still practiced today?

Few followers remain of this ancient way of combating evil with personal goodness. The number of Zoroastrians is falling toward possible extinction. In Yazd, the central area where Zoroastrianism is still practiced in Iran, a holy flame has been burning continuously for 1,500 years, but there are not enough devotees to keep a Tower of Silence open. If a Zoroastrian living in Iran wants traditional burial rites, the body must be shipped to Mumbai in India, where the last Tower of Silence is still operating. But Zoroastrian pilgrims from around the world still visit sacred shrines in Yazd.

Conversion to the faith is not emphasized, partly because of a desire not to dilute the teachings or the identity as a distinct faith community. In contemporary Iran, there is little incentive to convert, since Zoroastrians, like Jews

Thousands of Zoroastrian pilgrims travel to the sacred mountain shrine of Chak Chak near Yazd in Iran every June, where they pray around a sacred fire at the base of a cliff in the desert.

and Christians, are tolerated but limited in their privileges under Muslim rule. Historically, however, many Muslims converted to Zoroastrianism during the last years of the Pahlavi dynasty (1925–79). Some Zoroastrians in North America favor active conversion of non-Zoroastrians to the faith; others are opposed to proselytizing but favor the acceptance of those who are truly moved by personal religious experience. In India, the high priests of the Mumbai Zoroastrian community declared in 2003 that anyone marrying outside the religion would be excommunicated, but this brought such an outcry that they clarified that their statement was only a "guideline" to assure the survival of the Parsi faith. However, late marriage, low birth rates, and divorce remain concerns as the Parsi population continues to decline.

When the Parsis were influenced by Westernization and Protestant missionary activity, they became somewhat embarrassed about the mystical aspects of their faith. Some began reciting their prayers in English rather than the ancient Avestan language, and interpreting what they were doing as talking to God rather than uttering powerful sacred mantras. They tended to de-emphasize rituals and beliefs in an evil spirit and the end of the temporal world in favor of the more abstract philosophy and ethical standards of the Gathas.

The pendulum now seems to be swinging in the other direction. Training is still available in Iran and India for the hereditary lineage of Zoroastrian priests, and there is now considerable interest in preserving and understanding the tradition. Religious historians, metaphysicians, and linguists have attempted to translate the ancient language, uncover the deep significance behind the rituals, and sift out the origins of the tradition from the thousands of years of later accretions. A program called "Return to Roots" seeks to strengthen Zoroastrian youth identity around the world, sponsoring visits to important sites in India. Such efforts have brought a renewed sense of pride and appreciation within Zoroastrianism.[5]

Key terms

Avesta Holy text of teaching and liturgy, only fragments of which have survived.
Ameshta Spenta Six divine powers (the Good Mind, Righteousness, Absolute Power, Devotion, Perfection, and Immortality), personified and worshiped as deities after Zarathushtra's death.
Gathas Metric verses or hymns that were the words of the prophet Zarathushtra.

Pahlavi texts Texts written or translated in Middle Persian from about the ninth century CE with detailed instructions and customs of the Zoroastrians in Iran.

Parsis Persian Zoroastrians who avoided conversion to Islam by migrating to western India.

Suggested reading

Bode, Dastur Framroze Ardeshir and Nanavutty, Piloo, *Songs of Zarathushtra: The Gathas*, translated from the *Avesta*, London: George Allen and Unwin, 1952. A theosophically oriented translation of the Gathas into English.

Boyce, Mary, *Zoroastrians: Their Religious Beliefs and Practices*, London: Routledge and Kegan Paul, 1985. Detailed historical information, beginning with the pre-Zarathushtran roots of the tradition.

Boyce, Mary, ed. and trans., *Textual Sources for the Study of Zoroastrianism*, Manchester, UK: Manchester University Press, 1984. Useful extracts from many sources, with a concise general introduction and interpretative material for each text.

Choksy, Jamsheed K., *Purity and Pollution in Zoroastrianism: Triumph over Evil*, Austin: University of Texas Press, 1989. A very readable analysis of purifying rituals as a key to the Zoroastrian view of life.

Hinnells, John R., *Zoroastrianism and the Parsis*, London: Ward Lock International, 1981. A readable, straightforward portrayal of Zoroastrian history, beliefs, and practices, with illustrations.

Hinnells, John R., *Zoroastrians in Britain*, Oxford: Oxford University Press, 1996. A study of the Zoroastrian community in Britain, which dates to the early eighteenth century.

Insler, Stanley, *The Gathas of Zarathushtra*, Leiden: E. J. Brill, 1975. An English translation approved by many current scholars.

Luhrmann, Tanya M., *The Good Parsi: The Fate of a Colonial Elite in a Postcolonial Society*, Cambridge, Massachusetts: Harvard University Press, 1996. A study of how India's independence from Britain has affected the Indian Parsi community.

Malandra, William W., trans. and ed., *An Introduction to Ancient Iranian Religion: Readings from the Avesta and the Achaemenid Inscriptions*, Minneapolis: University of Minnesota Press, 1983. A selection of key Parsi texts with an introductory essay.

Mehr, Farhang, *The Zoroastrian Tradition: An Introduction to the Ancient Wisdom of Zarathushtra*, New York: Amity House, 1989. Good discussion of the principles of the Gathic and Pahlavi texts by an Iranian economist living in the United States.

Mirza, Dastur Hormazdyar Kayoji, *Outlines of Parsi History*, Bombay: Dastur Hormazdyar Mirza, 1987. A scholarly summary of Zoroastrian religion, literature, ritual, and art from the Indian Parsi perspective.

Taraporewala, I. J. S., *The Religion of Zarathushtra*, Madras, India: Theosophical Publishing House, 1926. A mystical interpretation of Zoroastrian spirituality.

1. Describe the life and teachings of Zarathushtra

The prophet Zarathushtra may have lived in Central Asia sometime between 1800 and 1500 CE. It is thought that he was trained as priest in the Indo-Iranian tradition and was also a mystical seeker. At the age of thirty he experienced communion with Ahura Mazda, the creator god. He insisted that Ahura Mazda (the one Eternal Being) created only goodness and should be worshiped by good thoughts, words, and deeds.

2. Identify the key texts of Zoroastrianism

Zarathushtra poured forth his adoration for Ahura Mazda in metric verses or hymns called Gathas. Under the Parthians, who ruled Iran for almost 500 years to 224 CE, the surviving revealed teachings of Zoroastrianism were reassembled as the Avesta ("holy texts"). Under Muslim dominance, the number of Zoroastrians remaining in Iran dwindled, but detailed instructions about the rituals and customs of the faith were preserved in a vast new literature, the Pahlavi texts, which were written or translated in Middle Persian from about the ninth century CE.

3.   *Summarize the main Zoroastrian rituals*

Tying the sacred cord (kusti) around the mid-section at least five times a day is one of the most important rituals. Symbolically the faithful are girding themselves as soldiers for Ahura Mazda. Water is venerated as a means or symbol of purification. The devout will often dip their fingers into water, apply it to their eyes and forehead, and raise their hands in prayer to Ahura Mazda. Fire is the other element emphasized in Zoroastrian rituals, used for its purifying and transformative power. Practitioners worship at fire temples or at home in pen areas, facing a light source. When the physical body dies, it is carried to a Tower of Silence, where vultures can pick the bones clean, thus avoiding polluting the earth with decaying flesh.

4.   *Discuss Zoroastrianism in the modern world*

Few followers remain of this ancient way of combating evil with personal goodness. There is a community in Mumbai, India (called Parsis) and a small community survives in Yazd in Iran. Conversion to the faith is not emphasized, although some Zoroastrians in North America favor active conversion. Training is still available in Iran and India for the hereditary lineage of Zoroastrian priests, and there is now considerable interest in preserving and understanding the tradition. A program called "Return to Roots" seeks to strengthen Zoroastrian youth identity around the world, sponsoring visits to important sites in India.

CHAPTER 8

JUDAISM

"God wants us to effectively be his partner in helping the world, in repairing the world, and in improving the condition of people and civilization around us." Eli Epstein[1]

8.1 Contrast biblical Judaism with rabbinic Judaism

8.2 Examine the role the European Enlightenment played in the development of Judaism

8.3 Identify the key tenets of the Jewish faith

8.4 Summarize the main sacred practices

8.5 Describe the High Holy Days and key festivals in the Jewish calendar

8.6 Differentiate between the major branches of contemporary Judaism

Judaism, which has no central leader or group making theological decisions, encompasses the diverse ethnic and religious traditions of the Jewish people, from a shared heritage of law and narrative they see as dating back to earliest human times.

In religious terms, Jews are those who experience their long and often difficult history as a continuing dialogue with God. In a religious sense, "Israel" refers to all those who struggle to answer the call of God and who acknowledge and strive to obey the one God, through the **Torah**, or "teaching," given to the patriarchs, Moses, and the prophets.

As a nation, the Jews preserved memories of both a homeland in the land of Israel and their own exile from that land. Both memories contributed to their survival through millennia of dispersion and oppression. After the horrors of the Holocaust in the twentieth century, some Jews successfully promoted the idea of a state for a concentration of Jews in the land of Israel as the only safe way for Jews to resist **anti-Semitism** and to survive. Other Jews continued to believe that they could seek safety in communities around the world. Many who consider themselves Jews have been born into a Jewish ethnic identity but do not feel a strong connection to the practice of Jewish religious traditions.

Given the persecution, dispersion, and even lack of religiosity among many Jews, how have they not dissolved as a people? Their survival, and that of Judaism as a whole, has required constant accommodation to changing circumstances. Nonetheless, they have managed to sustain a remarkable degree of cohesiveness and similar practices and beliefs.

TIMELINE

Judaism

BCE *c.* 1900–1700	Abraham, the first patriarch
c. 1300–1200	Moses leads the Israelites out of bondage in Egypt
1207	Israelites present in Canaan
c. 1010–970	David, king of Judah and Israel
961–931	King Solomon builds the First Temple of Jerusalem
722	Fall of northern kingdom of Israel to Assyria
586	Fall of Judah to Babylon; First Temple destroyed; Jews exiled to Babylon, some flee to Egypt.
c. 535	Jews return to Jerusalem and Judaea
515	Second Temple of Jerusalem built
c. 430	Torah read to the public by Ezra the Scribe
c. 333	Alexander's conquest; beginning of Hellenization of the East.
167	Maccabean Revolt
30 BCE–10 CE	Hillel the Elder
CE 70	Jerusalem falls to the Romans and Second Temple destroyed
c. 90	Jewish canon of Tanakh set, under Rabbi Akiva's leadership
132–135	Bar Kokhba revolt
c. 200	Mishnah compiled; diaspora extends through Mesopotamia and North Africa
c. 500	Babylonian Talmud completed
1095	Crusaders begin massacring Jews in Europe en route to the Holy Land
1135–1204	Life of Maimonides
1478	The Spanish Inquisition begins
1492	Mass expulsion of Jews from Spain
1555 onward	Ghettos of Italy and Germany
1654	Jews begin to settle in North America
c. 1700–1760	The Baal Shem Tov begins Hasidism
c. 1770–1880	Haskalah, the Jewish Enlightenment
1881	Large-scale Jewish migrations to North America begin
1933–1945	The Holocaust, reaching its climax in World War II
1947	Discovery of the Dead Sea Scrolls
1948	Israel declared an independent state
1950	Law of Return
1967	Six-Day War; acquisition of territories transforms Israeli–Palestinian relationships
1972	First woman rabbi ordained
1982	United Nations supports independent Palestinian state
1990 onward	Israeli–Palestinian conflicts and peace initiatives
2013	Women's rights to wear prayer shawls and *tefillin* and read Torah at Western Wall supported by court order

In this chapter we will focus on Judaism as an evolving tradition, first by taking an overview of the history of the Jewish people and then by examining the religious concepts and practices that characterize followers of the Torah today.

Biblical and rabbinic Judaism
What is the difference between biblical and rabbinic Judaism?

The Jewish sense of history begins with the stories recounted in the Hebrew Bible, or **Tanakh**. Biblical history begins with the creation of the world by a supreme deity, or God, and progresses through the patriarchs, matriarchs, and Moses who spoke with God and led the people according to God's commandments, and the prophets who heard God's warnings to those who strayed from the commandments. But Jewish history does not end where the stories of the Tanakh end, about the second century BCE. After the holy center of Judaism, the Temple of Jerusalem, was conquered and destroyed by the Romans in 70 CE, Jewish history is that of a dispersed people, finding unity in their evolving teachings and traditional practices. These were eventually codified in the great compendium of Jewish law and lore, the **Talmud**.

Biblical stories

Although knowledge of the early history of the Children of Israel is based largely on the narratives of the Tanakh, scholars see different degrees of historical authenticity in the varied textual accounts. Some of the people, events, and genealogies set forth cannot be verified by other evidence. It may be that the Israelites were too small and loosely organized a group to be noted by historians of other cultures. No mention of Israel appears in other sources until about 1230 BCE, but biblical narratives and genealogies place Abraham, said to be the first patriarch of the Israelites, at about 1700 to 1900 BCE.

The Jewish scriptures consist of the Torah (or Pentateuch), the Prophets, and the Writings. These books date roughly from the 10th to the 2nd century BCE, and were written mostly in classical Hebrew. They are often referred to as Tanakh, an acronym from the first letters of each division— Torah, Nevi'im, Kethuvim.

TORAH	The Five Books of Moses	NEVI'IM	The Prophets
בראשית	GENESIS	יהושע	JOSHUA
שמות	EXODUS	שופטים	JUDGES
ויקרא	LEVITICUS	שמואל א	I SAMUEL
במדבר	NUMBERS	שמואל ב	II SAMUEL
דברים	DEUTERONOMY	מלכים א	I KINGS
		מלכים ב	II KINGS
		ישעיה	ISAIAH
		ירמיה	JEREMIAH
		יחזקאל	EZEKIEL

KETHUVIM	The Writings		The Twelve Minor Prophets
תהילים	PSALMS		
משלי	PROVERBS	הושע	HOSEA
איוב	JOB	יואל	JOEL
שיר השירים	THE SONG OF SONGS	עמוס	AMOS
רות	RUTH	עבדיה	OBADIAH
איכה	LAMENTATIONS	יונה	JONAH
קהלת	ECCLESIASTES	מיכה	MICAH
אסתר	ESTHER	נחום	NAHUM
דניאל	DANIEL	חבקוק	HABAKKUK
עזרא	EZRA	צפניה	ZEPHANIAH
נחמיה	NEHEMIAH	חגי	HAGGAI
דברי הימים א	I CHRONICLES	זכריה	ZECHARIAH
דברי הימים ב	II CHRONICLES	מלאכי	MALACHI

Jews hold the **Pentateuch**, the "five books of Moses" that appear at the beginning of the Tanakh, as the most sacred part of the scriptures. Traditionalists believe that these books were divinely revealed to Moses in a covenantal event at Mt. Sinai and were written down by him as a single document. Contemporary biblical scholars view the texts in a different light, utilizing clues such as duplicated narratives and variant names of God to identify a series of sources within the texts of the Torah. They argue that distinct oral and then written traditions were brought together in an editorial process with the intent of interpreting the formation of Israel from a religious point of view, as the results of God's actions in human history. The Pentateuch seems to have assumed its final form in the days of Ezra the Scribe (fifth century BCE).

Some stories in the Pentateuch, such as the Creation, the Garden of Eden, the Great Flood, and the Tower of Babel, are similar to earlier Mesopotamian legends. The biblical legal material also reflects the ancient Near Eastern legal tradition, albeit with many innovations. Only in the latest books of Israelite history and the contemporaneous prophetic books do we begin to see references to events and figures whose existence can be confirmed by external literary and archaeological evidence. The significance of biblical history is thus better understood not in terms of an emphasis on historicity but rather as narratives of peoplehood and as a backdrop for the communal traditions that follow.

From creation to the God of Abraham The Hebrew scriptures begin with a sweeping poetic account of the creation of Heaven and Earth by God in six days, from the time of "the earth being unformed and void, with darkness over the surface of the deep and a wind from (or: the spirit of) God sweeping over the water."[2] After creating the material universe, God created man and woman in the divine "image" or "likeness," establishing them as masters of the earth, rulers of "the fish of the sea, the birds of the sky, and all the living things that creep on the earth."[3] In this account, God is portrayed as a transcendent Creator, without origins, gender, or form, a being utterly different from what has been created. Since Hebrew has no gender-neutral pronouns, God is generally—though not always—described in male singular terms. This creation story (in Genesis 1 and 2:1–4) is attributed by scholars to the "priestly source," thought to be editors writing immediately before or after the exile of the Jews to Babylon in 586 BCE.

A second, probably earlier, version of the creation story follows, beginning in Genesis 2:4. It is thought to be a contribution to the scriptures from the "Yahwist source," which called the supreme deity by the name "Yahweh." Instead of presenting woman as the equal of man, the second account of creation portrays her as an offshoot of Adam, the first man, formed to be his partner and helpmeet. The story that follows has commonly been interpreted as blaming woman for the troubles of humanity, although this reading is not supported in the story itself. According to the legend of Adam and Eve, originally God placed the first two humans in a garden paradise. The woman, Eve ("mother of all the living"), was promised wisdom by a serpent (often interpreted by Christians as a symbol of Satan) to encourage her to taste the fruit of the tree of knowledge of good and evil, against God's command. She gave some to Adam as well. According to the legend, this ended their innocence. God cursed the serpent and the land, and banished Adam and Eve

After eating the fruit of knowledge, Adam and Eve are exiled from paradise. (The Wandering of Adam and Eve, Abel Pann, c. 1925, Jerusalem. Colored lithograph.)

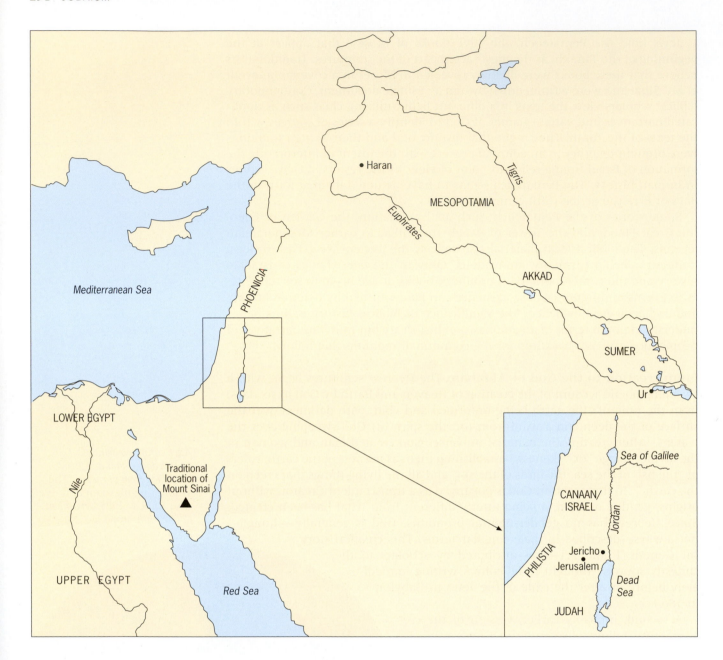

The Israelites identified themselves as a people whose ancestors, Abraham and Sarah, moved from Ur and Haran in Mesopotamia to Canaan; Abraham's grandson, Jacob, called "Israel," resettled his large family in Egypt, where the Israelites were eventually treated as slaves.

from their garden. Their lives were no longer paradisical, and nor were they immortal, for they no longer had access to the "tree of life."

The theme of exile reappears continually in the Hebrew Bible, and in later Jewish history the people are rendered homeless again and again. The biblical narratives emphasize that the people risk God's displeasure every time they stray from God's commands. They are repeatedly exiled from their spiritual home because of these transgressions and continually seek a return to it.

Some Jews developed a more optimistic interpretation of exile. This was the feeling that the Jewish people were spread throughout the world by God's will, for a sacred purpose: to be good citizens of whatever land they reside in, and to help raise the imperfect world again to the condition of perfection in which God had created it. The rabbinic tradition, which began in the first century CE and has shaped Jewish theology into the modern period, emphasized that the way out of exile was through study and righteous living. Commandments have their origin in God and, if followed, will lead humanity back to a life in harmony with God.

Covenant A unique belief introduced by Jewish theology was the idea of a special covenantal relationship between the Jewish people and God. In the ancient

Near East, every nation had a god, with whom it had a reciprocal contract in which both were accountable. On the people's side, obedience to their god was expected. On the divine side, the god granted special favors and was also bound by his own ethical agreements to the people. In Jewish **monotheism**—the belief that only one God is real, and all other gods are false—Israel's covenant with its God came to be seen as unique in the world, with Israel viewed as the one God's only "chosen" people. The paradigm for this special relationship was the covenant between God and Abraham on behalf of the Jewish people.

A more universal covenant with humanity as a whole is portrayed in the story of Noah, who was said to be the sole righteous man of his time. According to the biblical narrator, who attributes thoughts and emotions to God, God despairs of the general wickedness of humans, regrets having created them, and sends a great flood "to destroy all flesh under the sky."[4] Ancient Near Eastern traditions include stories of great floods, which emphasize the power of the gods and the finiteness of human life. In the biblical story, God establishes a covenant with Noah and gives directions for the building of an ark, which saves Noah's family and two of each of God's creatures. God promises never again to destroy the created world or to interfere with the established natural order, with the rainbow as a sign of this covenant "between me and all flesh that is on earth."[5]

God does, however, continue to intervene in history, according to the narrators. Ten generations after the legend of Noah, the narrative focuses on Abraham, Isaac, and Jacob (the "patriarchs"), and their wives, Sarah, Rebecca, Leah, and Rachel (the "matriarchs"). According to the biblical narratives, Abraham was born in Ur (now in Iraq), migrated to Haran (now in Turkey), and then was called by God to journey to Canaan. With his wife Sarah and his household, he left the land of his father and also the religion of his father, a worshiper of the old gods.

Abraham's descendants are said to have given birth to the twelve tribes of Israel. They are symbolically depicted here as sitting in the patriarch's lap. (Souvigny Bible, 12th century, France.)

TEACHING STORY

Abraham's Willingness to Sacrifice Isaac

God put Abraham to the test. He said to him, "Abraham," and he answered, "Here I am." And He said, "Take your son, your favored one, Isaac, whom you love, and go to the land of Moriah, and offer him there as a burnt offering on one of the heights that I will point out to you." So early next morning, Abraham saddled his ass and took with him two of his servants and his son Isaac. He split the wood for the burnt offering, and he set out for the place of which God had told him. On the third day Abraham looked up and saw the place from afar. Then Abraham said to his servants, "You stay here with the ass. The boy and I will go up there; we will worship and we will return to you."

Abraham took the wood for the burnt offering and put it on his son Isaac. He himself took the firestone and the knife; and the two walked off together. Then Isaac said to his father Abraham, "Father!" And he answered, "Yes, my son." And he said, "Here are the firestone and the wood, but where is the sheep for the burnt offering?" And Abraham said, "God will see to the sheep for His burnt offering, my son." And the two of them walked on together.

They arrived at the place of which God had told

him. Abraham built an altar there; he laid out the wood; he bound his son Isaac; he laid him on the altar, on top of the wood. And Abraham picked up the knife to slay his son. Then an angel of the LORD called to him from heaven: "Abraham! Abraham!" And he answered, "Here I am." And he said, "Do not raise your hand against the boy, or do anything to him. For now I know that you fear God, since you have not withheld your son, your favored one, from Me." When Abraham looked up, his eye fell upon a ram, caught in the thicket by its horns. So Abraham went and took the ram and offered it up as a burnt offering in place of his son. …

The angel of the LORD called to Abraham a second time from heaven, and said, "By Myself I swear, the LORD declares: Because you have done this and have not withheld your son, your favored one, I will bestow My blessing upon you and make your descendants as numerous as the stars of heaven and the sands on the seashore; and your descendants shall seize the gates of their foes. All the nations of the earth shall bless themselves by your descendants, because you have obeyed My command."

Genesis 22:1–18

Abraham is held up as an example of obedience to God's commands. Without hesitation, he is said to undergo circumcision (cutting away of the foreskin of the penis) as an initiatory rite, a sign of the covenant in which God agrees to be the divine protector of Abraham and his descendants, with all males to be likewise circumcised on the eighth day after birth.

Abraham and his wife Sarah were childless for many years. Sarah offered her servant, the Egyptian woman Hagar, as Abraham's concubine. According to social tradition, any child who was born of this relationship was considered to be the offspring of Abraham and Sarah, but if Sarah herself were to give birth to a child, it would carry the inheritance rights of the firstborn. After Hagar conceived a son by Abraham—Ishmael—God blessed Sarah at the age of ninety, saying that she would become the "mother of nations: the kings of many people shall spring from her" (Genesis 17:16). According to the biblical account, Sarah does indeed give birth to a son, Isaac, and then insists that Ishmael and Hagar be banished to the wilderness. God supports this demand, assuring Abraham that he will be father of two nations—one line through Isaac (to become the Israelites) and one through Ishmael (whom Arabs consider their ancestor).

According to the biblical narrative, God tested Abraham by demanding that he sacrifice his most precious possession, which was his beloved son Isaac (see Box, p. 255). Thinkers have struggled to explain this demand, for human sacrifice was deemed to be very loathsome, but the point of the story seems to be the merit of Abraham's great obedience to God. When Abraham prepares to sacrifice Isaac, the Lord stops him, satisfied that "now I know that you fear God."[6] The Hebrew word *yirah*, usually translated as "fear" of God, also implies "awe of God's greatness," or what Rabbi Lawrence Kushner calls "trembling in the presence of ultimate holiness."[7]

Early monotheism Scholars disagree on whether pure monotheism—the worship of a single God of the universe, exclusive of any other divine beings—was practiced by the early patriarchs. Many names for divinity are used in the early scriptures, and some researchers consider them names of separate gods. It is known that the religion of the Canaanites had some influence on that of the Israelites. The Canaanites were polytheistic, with highly developed mythology and ritual directed largely to agricultural fertility. They were settled agricultural peoples who paid homage to a high male god called El, and a Great Mother Goddess named Asherah, whose worship may be more ancient. The goddess, associated with vegetation, agricultural knowledge, and abundance, was worshiped at *asherahs* (sacred poles or trees).

Although the Israelites destroyed the *asherahs*, they apparently incorporated or adapted elements of the older faiths of the area into their own. The hymns recorded in the biblical book of Psalms, for example, may have roots in Canaanite traditions. In any case, Judaism ultimately rejected the gods of surrounding peoples. The Israelites came to see themselves as having been chosen by a single divine patron. In their patriarchal culture, this God was perceived as a ruler in a close relationship to the people, like a parent to children, or a sovereign to vassals. At first Israel's God may have been perceived as a private tribal god, later known as the supreme and only deity of the universe.

Israel's birth in struggle It is also unclear who the people of the biblical narratives were. Some scholars think the word "Hebrew" is derived from the generic term *habiru*, used for the low-class, landless people who lived as outlaws and were often hired as mercenaries. Another derivation may relate to the Hebrew word *ivrim*, which means nomads or wanderers. Others point to '*ibri* as the biblical word for Hebrew, meaning "children of Eber," an ethnic term. But because of frequent moving and intermarrying, the Israelites were actually of mixed ethnic stock, including Hebrew, Aramaean, and Canaanite. The word "**Semite**" is a modern linguistic term applied to Jews, Arabs, and others of

Statue of the Canaanite high god El, 13th century BCE.

eastern Mediterranean origin whose languages are classified as Semitic; it is often inaccurately used as an ethnic designation.

According to the genealogies set forth in the Pentateuch, the people who became known as Israelites were the offspring of Jacob, grandson of Abraham. Jacob received a new name, Israel, after wrestling all night with a being who turned out to be an **angel** of God ("Israel" means "the one who struggled with God").

This story in which a human being struggles and finally is reborn at a higher level of spirituality has been taken as a metaphor for the spiritual evolution of the people of Israel. As a result of the struggle, Israel the patriarch receives the promise that many nations will be born from him. The nation Israel—"the smallest of peoples"[8]—is perceived as the spiritual center for the world to grow toward God.

Egypt: bondage and exodus Jacob/Israel is said to have had one daughter and twelve sons by his two wives and their two maidservants. The twelve sons became the progenitors of the twelve tribes of Israel. The whole group left Canaan for Goshen in Egypt during a famine. Exodus, the second book of the Tanakh, opens about four centuries later with a statement that the descendants of Israel had become numerous. To keep them from becoming too powerful, the reigning pharaoh ordered that they be turned into slaves for massive construction projects. To further curb the population, the pharaoh ordered midwives to kill all boy babies born to the Israelite women.

One who escaped this fate was Moses, an Israelite of the tribe of Levi, who was raised in the palace by the pharaoh's own daughter. He is said to have fled the country after killing an Egyptian overseer who was beating an Israelite worker. According to the scriptural Book of Exodus, Moses was chosen by God to defy the pharaoh and lead the people out of bondage, out of Egypt. On a mountain, an angel of God appeared to him from within a bush blazing with fire but not consumed by it. God called to him out of the bush and yet cautioned, "Do not come closer. Remove your sandals from your feet, for the place on which you stand is holy ground."[9] When God told Moses to go and rescue "My people, the Israelites, from Egypt,"[10] Moses demurred, but God insisted:

> I will be with you … Thus you shall say to the Israelites, "Ehyeh [I Am] sent me to you. … The LORD, the God of your fathers, the God of Abraham, the God of Isaac, and the God of Jacob, has sent me to you."[11]

The word given in this biblical translation as "LORD" is considered too sacred to be pronounced. In the Hebrew scriptures it is rendered only in consonants as YHWH or YHVH; the pronunciation of the vowels is not known.

With his brother Aaron to act as spokesperson, Moses did indeed return to Egypt. Many chapters of Exodus recount miracles used to convince the pharaoh to let the people go into the wilderness to worship their God. These signs included a rod that turned into a serpent, plagues of locusts, flies, and frogs, animal diseases, a terrible storm, lasting darkness, and finally the killing by the Lord of all firstborn children and creatures. The Israelites were spared this fate, marking their doors with the blood of a slaughtered lamb so that the Lord would pass over them. (The holiday Passover commemorates this story.) At this, the pharaoh at last let the Israelites go. The redemption from bondage by the special protection of the Lord has served ever since as a central theme in Judaism.

According to the scriptural account, the Lord's presence led the Israelites, manifesting as a pillar of cloud by day and a pillar of fire by night. The armies of the deceitful pharaoh pursued them until the famous scene in which Moses stretched his staff toward the sea and God caused an east wind to blow all night, dividing the waters so that the Israelites could pass through safely on a dry seabed. As the Egyptians

God speaks to Moses from a burning bush, as depicted by Marc Chagall (1887–1985). (Detail of stained-glass window, Cathedral of St. Etienne, Metz, France.)

According to the biblical narrative, Miriam the prophetess danced triumphantly with a timbrel after the Israelites safely crossed the seabed, with the returning waters drowning the Egyptians. (Anna Kocherovsky, Miriam Dancing, *tapestry.)*

tried to follow, God told Moses again to hold out his arm over the sea, and the walls of water came crashing down on them, drowning every one. Miriam the prophetess, sister of Moses and Aaron, took a timbrel and danced in triumph, and all the women joined her.

From the wilderness to Canaan According to the Pentateuch, God told Moses that he would lead the people back to Canaan. First, however, it was necessary to travel to the holy Mount Sinai to re-establish the covenant between God and the people. The Lord is said to have descended to its summit in a terrifying show of lightning, thunder, fire, smoke, and trumpeting. God is said to have then given the people through Moses a set of rules for righteous living, later called the Torah. Among them were the utterances that Christians call "the Ten Commandments" (see Box, facing page), on stone tablets. God also gave a set of social norms, prescribed religious feasts, and detailed instructions for the construction of a portable tabernacle with a holy ark, the **Ark of the Covenant**, in which to keep the stone tablets on which God inscribed the commandments.

During the forty days that Moses was on the mountain receiving these instructions, the people who had just agreed to a holy covenant with God became disturbed and impatient. The biblical account says that under Aaron's reluctant supervision they melted down their gold jewelry and cast it into the form of a golden calf, practicing what the authors of the biblical narratives considered idol-worship, which had been explicitly forbidden by God. Moses is said to have been so outraged by their idolatry that he smashed the stone tablets and destroyed the idol. He ordered the only people still siding with YHWH, the Levites, to slay 3,000 of those who had strayed.

After another forty-day meeting with God on the summit of Mount Sinai, Moses again returned with stone tablets on which God had inscribed the commandments. Moses' face was said to be so radiant from his encounter with God that he had to veil it. Aaron and his sons were invested as priests, the tabernacle was constructed as directed, and the people set off for the land of Canaan, with the Presence of the Lord filling the tabernacle.

Acceptance of the laws given to Moses at Mount Sinai brought a new dimension to the covenant between God and Israel. God had freed the Jews from slavery and extinction at the hands of the Egyptians, and now the Jews freely agreed to accept the Torah. As Rabbi Irving Greenberg explains:

In faithfulness to that commitment, the people of Israel pledge to teach the way of justice and righteousness as best they can, to remain distinctive and unassimilated in the world and thus hold up the message for all people to see, to create a model community showing how the world can go about realizing the dream, and to work alongside others to move society toward the end goal of redemption. Thus, the Jewish covenantal mission will be a blessing for all families of the earth.

For its part, the Divine is pledged never to abandon Israel, to protect and safeguard the people, to help in the realization of the dream.[12]

Carrying the ark representing this covenant, the Israelites headed for the land of Canaan. An initial foray into that land was unsuccessful, owing to the people's fearfulness, and they then had to wander for forty years through the desert before they could re-enter the promised land, fertile Canaan, which at that time belonged to other peoples. The long sojourn in the wilderness is a familiar metaphor in the spiritual search. Faith is continually tested by difficulties. But even in the wilderness, the Israelites' God did not forsake them. Every day they found their daily bread scattered on the ground, in the form of an unknown food, which they named manna.

The entry into the promised land of Israel is remembered differently in two biblical books. While the book of Joshua tells of an organized assault and full conquest, Judges portrays a more stop-and-start campaign, a picture that is supported by archaeological evidence of major military conflicts in the thirteenth to eleventh centuries BCE. In any case, the people of Israel were certainly present in the land by 1207 BCE, when the Egyptian pharaoh Merneptah set up a stone inscription claiming to have conquered them and the Canaanites. At Sinai, God had vowed to oust the inhabitants of the lands into which the Israelites advanced, and warned them against adopting the local spiritual practices: "You

The Ten Commandments

I am the LORD your God who brought you out of the land of Egypt, the house of bondage:

You shall have no other gods before Me.

You shall not make for yourself a sculptured image, or any likeness of what is in the heavens above, or on the earth below, or in the waters under the earth. You shall not bow down to them or serve them. For I the LORD your God am an impassioned God, visiting the guilt of the parents upon the children, upon the third and upon the fourth generations of those who reject Me. But showing kindness to the thousandth generation of those who love Me and keep My commandments.

You shall not swear falsely by the name of the LORD your God; for the LORD will not clear one who swears falsely by His name.

Remember the Sabbath day and keep it holy. Six days you shall labor and do all your work, but the seventh day is a Sabbath of the LORD your God: you shall not do any work. … For in six days the LORD made heaven and earth and sea, and all that is in them, and He rested on the seventh day; therefore the LORD blessed the Sabbath day and hallowed it.

Honor your father and your mother, that you may long endure on the land that the LORD your God is assigning to you.

You shall not murder.

You shall not commit adultery.

You shall not steal.

You shall not bear false witness against your neighbor.

You shall not covet your neighbor's house: you shall not covet your neighbor's wife, or his male or female slave, or his ox or his ass, or anything that is your neighbor's.

Exodus 20:2–14

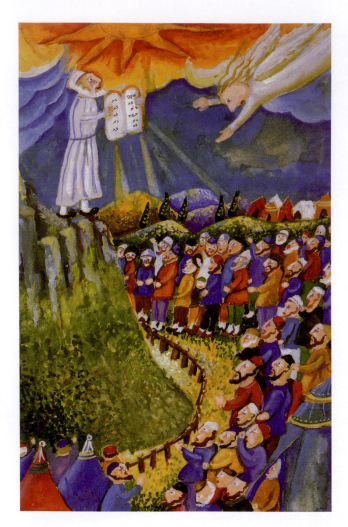

Moses presents the Ten Commandments of God to his people. (Detail of Michal Meron, The Ten Commandments.)

must tear down their altars, smash their pillars, and cut down their sacred posts."[13] The editors of the scriptures clearly considered the Canaanite religion spiritually invalid and morally inferior to their own.

The First Temple of Jerusalem David, the second king of Israel, is remembered as Israel's greatest king. An obscure shepherd, David was chosen by the prophet Samuel to be anointed on the head with oil, for thus were future kings found and divinely acknowledged in those times. Composer and singer of psalms, David was summoned to the court of the first Israelite king, Saul, to play soothing music whenever an evil spirit seized the king. When Saul and his son were killed in battle, David was made king. By defeating or making allegiances with surrounding nations, David created the beginnings of a secure, prosperous Israelite empire. He made the captured city of Jerusalem its capital and brought the Ark of the Covenant there.

Under the reign of David's son King Solomon, a great temple was built in Jerusalem. It was to be a permanent home for the Ark of the Covenant, which was housed in the innermost sanctum, with an altar outside for making the burned offerings of animals, grain, and oil to the divine. There already existed an ancient practice among pre-Israelite peoples of using high places for altars where sacrifices were made to the gods. After centuries of wandering worship, the Israelites now had a central, stationary place where God would be most present to them. God is said to have appeared to Solomon after the fourteen-day Temple dedication ceremony and pledged: "My eyes and My heart shall ever be there."[14]

The Temple became the central place for sacrifice in Judaism. But its builder, Solomon, also accumulated great personal wealth, at the expense of the people, and built altars to the gods of his wives, who came from other nations. This so angered the Lord, according to the scriptures, that he divided the kingdom after Solomon's death. An internal revolt of the ten northern tribes established a new kingdom of Israel, which was independent of Jerusalem and the dynasty of David. The southern kingdom, continuing in its allegiance to the house of David and retaining Jerusalem as its capital, renamed itself Judah, after David's tribe.

Prophets such as Elijah warned the people against worshiping gods other than the Lord, and exhorted them to end their evil ways. Over the centuries, these prophets were men and women who had undergone transformational ordeals that made them instruments for the word of God. The "early prophets," including Elijah, focused on the sin of idolatry; the "later prophets" warned that social injustice and moral corruption would be the ruin of the Jewish state.

By the reign of King Hoshea of Israel, the kingdom was so corrupt and idolatrous, at least according to the interpretation of the Judean biblical writers, that God permitted the kingdom of Assyria to overtake what was left of the small country in 722 BCE. Assyria carried off most of the Israelites to exile among the **Gentiles** (non-Jewish people). Most of the Israelites became dispersed within Assyria; these people who thenceforth lost a distinct ethnic identity are known as the "Ten Lost Tribes of Israel."

Judah maintained its independence, declining and continually warned of impending doom by its prophets. Indeed, King Nebuchadnezzar of Babylonia (which had taken over the Assyrian Empire) captured Jerusalem. In 586 BCE the great walls of Jerusalem were battered down and its buildings put to the torch by the Babylonians. The great Temple was emptied of its sacred treasures, the altar dismantled, and the building destroyed. Many Judaeans, especially from the elite upper classes, were taken to exile in Babylonia, where they were thenceforth known as "Jews," since they were from Judah. The psalmist describes the feeling of exile from **Zion**, God's chosen place:

> By the waters of Babylon there we sat, sat and wept, as we thought of Zion.
> There on the poplars we hung up our lyres,
> for our captors asked us there for songs, our tormenters, for amusement,
> "Sing us one of the songs of Zion."
> How can we sing a song of the Lord on alien soil?

Psalms 137:1–4

In exile among foreigners, the Jews nonetheless remained loyal to their God. They transformed the taunt of their captors into a spiritual challenge. This faithfulness in the midst of difficulties, without the security and support for community provided by territory, was an important development in the history of Western religions. Remembering the terrestrial Zion, maintaining communities of Jews in the land of Israel, and turning in the direction of Zion three times a day in prayer helped preserve the Jews as a scattered people through what they experienced as their thousands of years of exile.

> I never could forget you.
> See, I have engraved you
> On the palms of My hands ...

Isaiah 49:15–16

Return to Jerusalem

After fifty years of exile in Babylon, a small group of devoted Jews, probably fewer than 50,000, returned to their holy city and land, now called Judaea. They were allowed to return by the Persian king, Cyrus. But many Jews did not return to Jerusalem from Babylon, which was now their home. They were thenceforth said to be living in the **diaspora**, from the Greek word for dispersion. They always remembered Zion as a central part of their faith, but also learned to establish their creative lives in the diaspora.

King Cyrus authorized the rebuilding of the Temple of Jerusalem, which was completed in 515 BCE. The Second Temple became the central symbol to a scattered Jewish nation. A new emphasis on temple rites developed, with an hereditary priesthood tracing its ancestry to Aaron.

The priestly class, under the leadership of Ezra (a priest and scribe), also undertook to organize the stories of the people, editing the Pentateuch to reveal the hand of God. Some scholars think that it was these priestly editors who wrote the creation account in Genesis 1, glorifying their God as creator of the universe.

The Torah was now established as the spiritual and secular foundation of the dispersed nation. In approximately 430 BCE, Ezra the scribe set the precedent of reading for hours from the Torah scrolls in a public square. These "five books of Moses" were accepted as a sacred covenant.

As the Jews lived under foreign rule—Persian, Greek, Parthian, and then Roman—they were exposed to cross-cultural religious traditions, many of which they wove into their own worldviews and practices. Concepts of Satan, the hierarchy of angels, reward or punishment in an afterlife, and the final resurrection of the body on the Day of Judgment are thought by some scholars to have made their way into Jewish belief from the Zoroastrianism of the Persian Empire, for these beliefs were absent from earlier Judaic religion. However, they were not uniformly accepted. Greek lifestyle and thought were introduced into the

Middle East by Alexander the Great in the fourth century BCE. The rationalistic, humanistic influences of Hellenism led many wealthy and intellectual Jews, including the priests in Jerusalem, to adopt a Hellenistic attitude of scepticism rather than unquestioning belief.

Tension between traditionalists and those embracing Greek ways came to a head during the reign of Antiochus IV Epiphanes, a Hellenistic ruler of Syria (175–164 BCE), the nation that then held political sovereignty over the land of Israel. Antiochus seems to have tried to achieve political unity by forcing a single Hellenistic culture on all his subjects, abolishing the Torah as the Jewish constitution, burning copies of the Torah, killing families who circumcised their sons, building an altar to Zeus in the Temple of Jerusalem, and sacrificing a hog on it (in defiance of the Mosaic law against eating or touching dead pigs as unclean). The Maccabean rebellion, a revolt led by the Hasmon family of priests, called in Hebrew the Maccabees (Hammers), won a degree of independence for Judaea in 164 BCE. The successful rebellion established a new and independent kingdom, once again called Israel, once again centered around Jerusalem, and ruled by the Hasmonean family.

At the time of the Hasmonean kings, three sects of Jews formed in Judaea. One was the **Sadducees**, priests and wealthy businesspeople, conservatives intent on preserving the letter of the law. The **Pharisees** were more liberal citizens from all classes who sought to study the applications of the Torah to everyday life. A third general movement was uncompromising in its piety and its disgust with what it considered a corrupted priesthood. The Jewish historian Josephus describes one of these groups: the **Essenes**. Its initiated members were males who dressed in white, shared their property communally, avoided luxury, and placed great emphasis on ritual purity. What may have been a similar or related group retreated to the desert soon after the Hasmonean takeover of the high priesthood in 152 BCE, and there developed a communal habitation at Qumran, near the Dead Sea. Their leader was the "Teacher of Righteousness," a priest, reformer, and mystic. The library of this community, now known as the Dead Sea Scrolls, was discovered near Qumran in 1947 and is yielding precious clues about that period. It is possible that members of the dissident sect that collected and wrote the scrolls were scattered throughout Palestine, with Qumran as their center for study and initiation. They apparently were preparing themselves for a cosmic battle in which the "Sons of Light" would be victorious over the "Sons of Darkness" and establish a reign of utmost purity centered in Jerusalem.

Ruins of the Qumran settlement.

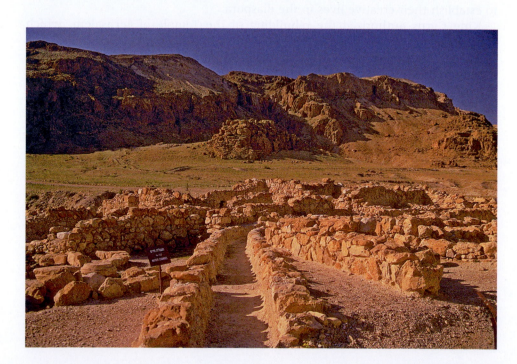

Eventually the conflicts among the Hasmoneans erupted into civil war. The Roman general Pompey was called in from Syria in 63 BCE to choose between contenders to the Hasmonean throne, but he took over the country instead. There followed four centuries of oppressive Roman rule of Judaea.

Under Roman rule, belief grew among Jews about a messianic age in which the people would at last be rescued from their sufferings and Jews would return to their homeland. This belief had been voiced by earlier prophets. For instance, the prophet Ezekiel received a vision in which God showed him a valley of scattered, dry human bones, which God then reunited and brought back to life, explaining:

> *O mortal, these bones are the whole House of Israel. … I am going to take the Israelite people from among the nations they have gone to, and gather them from every quarter, and bring them to their own land. … They shall follow My rules and faithfully obey My laws. Thus they shall remain in the land which I gave to My servant Jacob and in which your fathers dwelt; they and their children and their children's children shall dwell there forever, with My servant David as their prince for all time.*

> *Ezekiel 37:11–28*

In addition to anticipating the ingathering of the Jewish people back to the land of Israel, the classical prophets had foreseen a universal destiny for Israel. Combining the particular and universal orientations of Judaism, they had prophesied a coming "End of Days" in which disaster would be followed by universal redemption, when all nations would recognize the one God. In the books of both Isaiah and Micah appears a famous passage about the coming reign of world peace:

> *Instruction shall come forth from Zion,*
> *The word of the Lord from Jerusalem.*
> *Thus He will judge among the many peoples,*
> *And arbitrate for the multitude of nations,*
> *However distant;*
> *And they shall beat their swords into plowshares*
> *And their spears into pruning hooks.*
> *Nation shall not take up*
> *Sword against nation;*
> *They shall never again know war;*
> *But every man shall sit*
> *Under his grapevine or fig tree*
> *With no one to disturb him.*

> *Micah 4:2–4*

Under oppressive Seleucid Greek rule, **apocalyptic** literature became very popular. Such literature sees the world in stark terms of good and evil, predicts the coming of God's victory over evil, asserts that God will then reward good people and punish evil people, and thus urges people to live righteous lives now in preparation for that time. Among some Jews, the belief grew that there would be a **Messiah**, who would come to bring evil times to an end and establish the reign of peace. In the biblical book of Daniel, probably written while Jews were being persecuted by the Seleucid emperor Antiochus IV, the chief character Daniel describes a symbolic vision of "one like a human being" who would come on heavenly clouds, and on him the white-haired, fiery-throned "Ancient of Days" would confer "everlasting dominion" over all people, a kingship "that shall not be destroyed."[15] By the first century CE, expectations had developed that through this Messiah, God would gather the chosen people and not only free them from oppression but also reinstate Jewish political sovereignty in the land of Israel. The messianic end of the age, or end of the world, would be

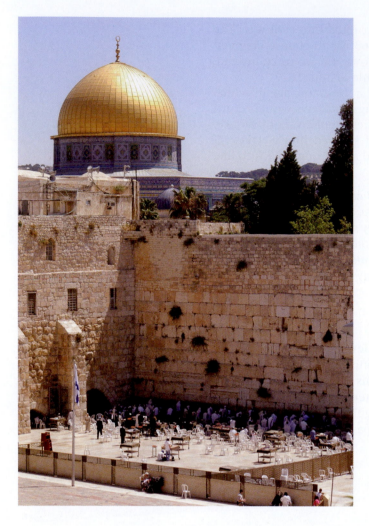

Although the Second Temple of Jerusalem was largely destroyed in 70 CE, a section of its western supporting wall remains intact. It is considered the most sacred place in Judaism because of its proximity to the Holy of Holies in the former Temple. The Muslim Dome of the Rock is seen behind, on the site of the Temple Mount itself.

heralded by a period of great oppression and wickedness. Many felt that this time was surely at hand. There were some Jews who felt that Jesus was the long-awaited Messiah.

Spurred by anti-Roman militants called **Zealots**, some Jews rose up in armed rebellion against Rome in 66 CE. The rebellion was suppressed, and after heroic resistance, the Jewish defenders were slaughtered in the holy walled city of Jerusalem in 70 CE. The Roman legions destroyed the Jewish Temple in Jerusalem, leaving only a course of foundation stones still standing. The Temple has never been rebuilt. A remaining portion of the Temple's retaining wall, known as the Western Wall, has been a place of Jewish pilgrimage and prayer for twenty centuries.

A second ultimately disastrous revolt followed in 132 CE. Its leader was Simon bar Kokhba. His initial success against the Romans brought short-lived excitement over what some considered the long-awaited Messianic Age. Bar Kokhba's rule over the independent state lasted only three years, however, for the Romans committed up to one-half of their entire army to reconquer the area. A Roman historian of the time reported that 580,000 Jews were killed. Jerusalem was reduced to ruins, along with all Judaean towns. Those remaining Jews who had not been executed were forbidden to read the Torah, observe the Sabbath, or circumcise their sons. None was allowed to enter Jerusalem when it was rebuilt as the Roman city Aelia Capitolina, except on the anniversary of the destruction of the Temple, when they could pay to lean against all that remained of it—the Western Wall—and lament the loss of their sacred home. Judaea was renamed Palestine after the ancient Philistines. Judaism no longer had a physical heart or a geographic center.

Rabbinic Judaism

Judaism could have died then, as its people scattered throughout the Mediterranean countries and western Asia. However, one of the groups who survived the destruction of Judaea were the **rabbis**, inheritors of the Pharisaic tradition. They are the founders of rabbinic Judaism, which has defined the major forms of Jewish practice over the last 2,000 years. Another was the messianic movement that had formed around Jesus of Nazareth, which later developed into the separate religious tradition known as Christianity.

Contemporary scholars think that Jesus, a Jew who can be seen within the context of the Jewish movements of the first century CE, including the apocalyptic expectations of the Essenes and roaming preachers advocating repentance, was also closely related to the Pharisees and the school of Hillel the Elder, who taught from about 30 BCE to 10 CE, probably overlapping with the life of Jesus. Jesus emphasized holiness in worldly life and, like the Jewish prophets, observance of the spirit and the full and often complex ethical implications of the law, not merely fulfillment of the letter of the law. The early **apostles** of Jesus emphasized traditions shared by the rabbis, that, with the arrival of the Messiah and the age of messianic redemption, observance of the ritual laws would be abrogated. The apostle Paul, who became the major missionary of the Christian sect, preached to both Jews and Gentiles in the diaspora that with the advent of Jesus, God would accept them without their practicing circumcision and Mosaic laws governing many aspects of daily life and hygiene. Judaism and Christianity are both monotheistic and from common stock. Between them, in their different ways, they have kept the teachings of the Tanakh vibrantly alive. Both the Jesus movement and rabbinic Judaism used the Hebrew Bible as a foundation document, but from it they have developed in their own paths.

The rabbis were teachers, religious decision-makers, and creators of liturgical prayer. No longer were there priests or a Temple for offering sacrifices. The substitute for animal sacrifice was liturgical prayer and ethical behavior. The people met in **synagogues**, which simply means "meeting places," to read the Torah and to worship communally, praying simply and directly to God. A **minyan**—a quorum of ten adult males—had to be present for community worship.

Everyone was taught the basics of the Torah as a matter of course, but, from the age of five or six, many men also occupied themselves with deep study of the scriptures. Women were excluded or exempted from formal Torah study, for their family responsibilities at home were considered primary for them. They were responsible for keeping the dietary laws, preparing for the Sabbath and other home-centered aspects of Jewish religious life, lighting the Sabbath candles, caring for young children, teaching their daughters the commandments they would be expected to fulfill as women, and regulating sexual expression in the marriage according to rabbinic laws in order to maintain ritual purity in their homes. Although they were under sacred obligation to pray, they were obligated neither to a particular **liturgy** nor to a particular time of prayer. By contrast, men's prayer and study assumed the significant value of textual and religious literacy. It is said that in the afterlife one can see the Jewish sages still bent over their books studying. This is Paradise.

The revealed scriptures were closed; what remained was to interpret them as indications of God's word and will in history. This process continues to the present, giving Judaism a continually evolving quality in tandem with unalterable roots in the ancient books of Moses. Centering the religion in books and teachings rather than in a geographical location or a politically vulnerable priesthood has enabled the dispersed community to retain a sense of unity across time and space, as well as a common heritage of law, language, and practice.

The rabbis set themselves the task of thoroughly interpreting the Hebrew scriptures. Their process of study yielded two types of interpretation: legal decisions, called *halakhah* (proper conduct), and non-legal teachings, called *haggadah* (folklore, sociological and historical knowledge, theological arguments, ritual traditions, sermons, and mystical teachings).

In addition to delving into the meanings of the written Torah, the rabbis undertook to apply the biblical teachings to their contemporary lives, in very different cultural circumstances from those of the ancients, and to interpret scripture in ways acceptable to contemporary values. The model for this delicate task of living interpretation had been set by Hillel the Elder. He was known as a humble and pious scholar, who stressed loving relationships, good deeds, and charity toward the less advantaged. His most famous disciple, Yochanan ben Zakkai, was a pacifist who managed to get himself smuggled out of Jerusalem in a coffin while the city was held by the Zealots. He was taken to the Roman general Vespasian, who permitted him to set up a school in Yavne where scholars could continue to study the Torah in peace. When Jerusalem fell to the Romans in 70 CE, ben Zakkai's school became for some time the center of Jewish learning, assuring continuation of rabbinic tradition.

What is hateful to you, do not do to your neighbor:
that is the entire Torah;
the rest is commentary;
go and learn it.

Hillel the Elder[16]

The rabbis' biblical interpretations, referred to as **Midrash** ("seeking," "searching"), yielded a vast body of legal and spiritual literature, known in Jewish tradition as the **oral Torah**. According to rabbinical tradition, God gave Moses two versions of the Torah at Sinai: the written Torah, which appears in the five books of Moses, and the oral Torah, a larger set of teachings, which was memorized and passed down through the generations all the way to the early rabbis. After the fixing of the Jewish canon—the scriptures admitted to the Tanakh—in about 90 CE, the rabbinical schools set out to systematize all the commentaries and the oral tradition, which was continually evolving on the basis of expanded and updated understandings of the original oral Torah.

In about 200 CE, Judah the Patriarch completed a terse edition of legal teachings of the oral Torah, which was thenceforth known as the **Mishnah**. The Mishnah's method of deriving legal principles for social order is based on logical analysis of how things are and why they are so. It systematically sets up hierarchical classifications, such as levels of women's status and domestic responsibilities. Despite the subordination of women to men in traditional Jewish legal codes, a woman enjoys rights and protection from her husband and benefits from the expectations that she be creative and a moral beacon. There are also directives in the Mishnah regarding men's responsibility to women—such as a husband's obligation to give sexual pleasure to his wife—and, in general, the responsibility of rulers and privileged members of society to insure legal justice for people of all classes and to provide for the material well-being of the lower classes, widows, orphans, and resident aliens. Accordingly, Jews have often been prominent in movements for social justice.

The Mishnah became the basic study text for rabbinic academies in Judaea and Babylonia, and after several centuries, the Mishnah and the rabbis' commentaries on it were organized into the Talmud. This is a vast compendium of law, Midrash, and argument. It does not have a beginning, middle, and end in any traditional sense. It records disagreements among rabbis and sometimes leaves them standing. Drawing on "prooftexts" from the Torah, the rabbis came to different and often inventive conclusions.

There are actually two authorized Talmuds. Both have the same Mishnah; what differs is the additional commentaries, or **Gemara**. The Jerusalem Talmud is the earlier one, written down about 400 CE. It emphasizes continual study of the Torah as a spiritual practice, a primary way of coming to know the will and ways of God. Talmudic scholar Adin Steinsaltz refers to the Talmud as "a book of holy intellectualism."[17]

The Babylonian Talmud grew out of the other major center of rabbinical study: Babylonia. Completed about 500 CE, it is more developed as an encyclopedia of the Torah, for Jewish life in Babylonia was less precarious. The Babylonian Talmud was also better preserved than the Jerusalem Talmud, and it has thus

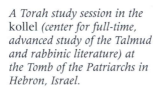

A Torah study session in the kollel *(center for full-time, advanced study of the Talmud and rabbinic literature) at the Tomb of the Patriarchs in Hebron, Israel.*

become the dominant version in Jewish theology and law. It, too, describes study of the Torah as essential to Israel's destiny as a nation upholding God's laws.

Midrash is still open-ended, for significant commentaries and commentaries on commentaries have continued to arise over the centuries. No single voice has dominated this continual study of the Torah and its interpretations. Rabbis have often disagreed in their interpretations, and these disagreements, sometimes between rabbis from different centuries, are presented together. This continual interweaving of historical commentaries, as if all Jewry were present at a single marathon Torah-study event, has been a significant unifying factor for the far-flung, often persecuted Jewish population of the world.

In the process of **exegesis**, the rabbis have actually introduced new ideas into Judaism, while claiming that they were merely revealing what already existed in the scriptures. Notions of the soul are not found in the Tanakh, but they do appear in the Talmud and in Midrash. The ways in which God is referred to and perceived also change. In the early biblical narratives, the Lord appears to the patriarchs and Moses in dramatic forms, such as the burning bush and the smoking mountain. Later, the prophets are visited by angelic messengers, and they sometimes hear a divine inner voice speaking to them. In the rabbinical mystical literature, God is presented in even more transcendent, less anthropomorphic ways. God's presence in the world, in relationship to the people, is called the **Shekhinah**, a feminine noun that often represents the nurturing aspect of God. Sometimes the loving protection of the Shekhinah is depicted as a radiant, winged presence.

The Throne of the Shekhinah, as depicted by contemporary artist Hannah Omer and cyber-architect Yitzhak Hayut-Man.

The rabbis also developed prayers that over time replaced the animal sacrifices of the Temple. These are still used in contemporary Jewish liturgy. For instance, the *Kaddish*, exaltation of God's name recited repeatedly in Jewish prayer services, is preserved in Aramaic, the language of Babylonia.

> *May His great name be praised to all eternity.*
> *Hallowed and honored, extolled and exalted, adored and acclaimed be the name of the Holy One, though He is above all the praises, hymns, and songs of adoration which men can utter.*
>
> *Excerpt from the* Kaddish[18]

Evolving Judaism

What role did the European Enlightenment play in the development of Judaism?

In the early centuries of the Common Era, the Jewish population of the land of Israel declined, though it never disappeared, nor did the land of Israel ever lose its spiritual centrality in Jewish consciousness. Some Jews settled in other regions of the Roman Empire, and larger numbers established themselves among the Zoroastrian Persians in Mesopotamia. The city of Babylon became the major center of Jewish intellectual activity, a position it would hold well into the tenth century.

Even when the Babylonian Talmud was completed in the sixth century CE, the rabbinic enterprise continued. The two great Babylonian rabbinic academies were often appealed to with difficult questions from far-flung Jewish communities. Their answers, which were considered binding on all Jews, and the questions themselves, became a new and enduring form of legal writing, *Responsa* literature, which continues to the present.

When Baghdad became the capital city of the great Abbasid Empire in the eighth century, Jewish life concentrated around that city as well. Jews were treated relatively well under Islamic rule. Like Christians, they were recognized as a "People of the Book," and were allowed to maintain their religious traditions and run their communities autonomously as long as they paid a substantial head tax. In Baghdad, as throughout the Islamic Middle East, many Jews were prosperous merchants, professionals, and craftsmen. In the early Middle Ages, in fact, Jews played a significant role in international trade because of their facility with languages and their ability to find supportive co-religionists in virtually any community.

Life under Islamic rule was also intellectually exciting for the Jewish community, which had rapidly adopted Arabic as its spoken language. During its early centuries, the world of Islam was far advanced beyond Christian Europe in its explorations of science, medicine, philosophy, poetry, and the fine arts. Jews living in Muslim countries benefited from an atmosphere of cultural creativity and tolerance. Many Jews were well-known physicians. Muslim Spain, in particular, where some Jews rose to high political position in Muslim courts, was renowned for its outstanding Hebrew poets and major philosophical and scientific Jewish writers.

From time to time, however, Jews were threatened by intolerant Muslim rulers and were forced to flee to other territories. The great scholar and physician Maimonides (1135–1204) was forced to leave his ancestral home of Córdoba, Spain, in the mid-twelfth century; he and his family eventually settled in Egypt. Considered one of the greatest of all Jewish intellectuals, Maimonides is particularly famous for his synthesis between reason and faith. In writings such as *The Guide for the Perplexed* he spoke on behalf of the rationality that he saw as characterizing Judaism since the dawning of the rabbinic age:

> *What is man's singular function here on earth? It is, simply, to contemplate abstract intellectual matters and to discover truth. … And the highest intellectual contemplation that man can develop is the knowledge of God and his unity.*[19]

Jews who lived in Christian countries were less exposed to the vibrant intellectual energy of the Islamic world between the seventh and twelfth centuries. Christian Europe in those centuries was primarily a feudal agricultural society in which literacy mainly belonged to the Church. Jews, who were primarily merchants, became expendable, and throughout the later Middle Ages there was a steady pattern of expulsions of Jews from countries in which they had long lived.

Prejudice against Jews had long been simmering among Christians. While Jews and Christians, like all humans, suffered from hatred and unwarranted attacks and often directed their vitriol against each other, Christians had particular reasons for their hatred of Jews: Jesus was a Jew, and his own people had not accepted Christian claims that he was the Messiah. Moreover, Jews were blamed for his murder and for preventing his messianic successes ever after by refusing to believe in him.

Beginning in 1095, Jews became victims of mobs of Christian **crusaders** traveling through Europe with the intention to defend the Holy Land. They had been provoked by rumors that Christians were being harmed there by Muslims, with Jews as their accomplices. Believing in the holiness of their mission, crusaders and orders of knights also attacked Jews as nonconformists who did not agree with the doctrines of the Christian Church. They massacred so many Jews that many formerly prosperous Jewish communities in Germany were wiped out.

In the twelfth century, superstitious rumors were spread in England that Jews were engaged in ritual murders of Christians, and many Jews were subsequently slaughtered. Then, in thirteenth-century Germany, Jews were accused of stealing the consecrated bread used by Christians for communion with Jesus, and then torturing it. Such strange rumors were never verified, but they spread rapidly, and with them, killings of Jews. In the fourteenth century, Jews were blamed for the plague and thus were either killed or forced out of many countries. In 1492, tens of thousands of Jews were forced to leave Spain, where they had lived for more than a thousand years. Others chose to convert to Christianity rather than to leave their homeland even though staying in Spain as *conversos* (converted Jews) would expose them to the dreaded Inquisition, which had been established in Spain in 1478. The Inquisition represented the Roman Catholic Church, and its mission was to discover perceived **heretics** within the Christian community. It had no power over Jews, but it did have jurisdiction over the large numbers of Jews who had converted to Christianity, whether voluntarily or by force, and who might be practicing their former religion in secret. The Inquisition, which had the power to torture the accused and to execute the convicted, continued to function in Spain and in Spanish territories well into the eighteenth century.

There was further deterioration of Jewish life in western Europe in the sixteenth and seventeenth centuries. After 1555, those Jews who remained in some cities of Italy and Germany were forced to live in **ghettos**, special Jewish-only quarters, which were often walled in and locked at night and during Christian holy days, to limit mixing between Christians and Jews.

During the later Middle Ages, Poland became a haven for the expelled Jews of western Europe. Jews were welcomed by Poland's feudal leaders, who needed a middle class for the economic development of their agricultural country. Jews were allowed freedom of residence and occupation, and they rapidly grew in numbers, finding in their new home an enclave of peace and prosperity. Jews lived an intensely religious life in villages and towns that were almost completely Jewish, speaking Yiddish, a distinctive Jewish language that was based on the medieval German they had spoken in western Europe.

In 1648, the flourishing of the Ashkenazi Jewish communities of central and eastern Europe suffered a great setback when the Cossack peasants of the Ukraine revolted against Polish rule. Associating Jewry with their Roman Catholic Polish oppressors, Greek Orthodox Cossacks led terrible **pogroms** (massacres) against the Jews, which were followed by even more killing as Poland collapsed.

In this time of despair in both eastern and western Europe, Jews were heavily taxed and ill-treated. Their longing for deliverance from danger, poverty, and oppression fueled the old messianic dream. Among the "pseudo-Messiahs" who rose to the occasion, the most famous was Shabbatai Tzevi (1626–1676) of Smyrna, a Turkish port. A rather unstable personality, he became convinced that it was his calling to be the Messiah. A young man named Nathan, who became his enthusiastic prophet, sent letters to Jews throughout Europe, Asia, and Africa announcing that the Messiah had at last appeared in his master. Many believed him and prepared for their return to the Holy Land. However, when Tzevi entered the Ottoman Empire he was arrested and put in jail. Given the choice of converting to Islam or being executed, he chose conversion and was given a government position. The shock to his supporters was terrible.

Kabbalah and Hasidism

Mystical yearning has been a part of Jewish tradition since biblical times. The fervent experience of, and love for, God is an undercurrent in several writings of the biblical prophets, and is incorporated into the Talmud as well. The Merkabah (chariot) mystical traditions from the late Hellenistic period are based on the account attributed to the prophet Ezekiel of a vision of "the semblance

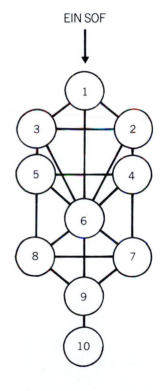

A central Kabbalistic image is the Tree of God, a representation of the emanation of the qualities of the infinite Ein Sof *into revealed aspects, the* sephiroth. *The topmost circle represents Will; the tenth represents the Shekhinah—the presence of God.*

of the Presence of the LORD" (Ezekiel 1:26–28). Some mystical writings are found in the extra-biblical collections of texts known as the Apocrypha and the Pseudepigrapha. The apocryphal Book of Enoch describes the ascent to God as a journey through seven heavenly spheres to an audience with the King of the celestial court. Some texts from the Qumran settlement also seem to concern mystical experiences.

In the Middle Ages, esoteric teachings developed known as **Kabbalah**. The most important book in this genre is the Zohar (Way of Splendor). The Zohar is a massive and complex offering of stories, explanations of the esoteric levels of the Torah, and descriptions of visionary practice and experiences. It depicts many unseen spiritual dimensions interacting with the physical world in which we live.

During the sixteenth century Kabbalah's most influential leader was Isaac Luria (1534–1572). He explained creation as the beaming of the divine light into ten special vessels, some of which were shattered by the impact because they contained lower forces that could not bear the intensity of the light. The breaking of the vessels spewed forth particles of evil as well as fragments of light into the world. Humans have a great responsibility to help end chaos and evil in the world by regathering the "sparks of holiness" in the unclean realms to repair the holy vessels. This concept of *tikkun olam* (repairing the world) has continued to be very important in Jewish thought, emphasizing the relationship between God and humans as a covenantal one with reciprocal responsibilities in which both are working together to uplift the world, and where every human act, both good and bad, has ultimate significance. To this end, Luria asked his followers to follow strict ascetic purification practices, prayer, and observance of the commandments of the Torah, and to chant sacred formulas.

Lurianic Kabbalism resurfaced in a very different form in the eighteenth century as **Hasidism**, the path of ecstatic piety. It developed in Ukraine and Poland, where Jews had become legally oppressed, poverty-stricken, and fearful for their lives from riots and murders. The rabbis had little to offer them, retreating into academic debates about legal aspects of the Torah.

Into this grim setting came the Baal Shem Tov (1700–1760), a beloved healer and Hasidic teacher, who offered a joyful version of Jewish holiness. He believed that Torah study and obedience to the letter of the law were not superior to deep-felt, pure-hearted prayer; everyone is capable of the highest enlightenment. He asserted that the divine could be found everywhere, in the present, thereby de-emphasizing the perennial waiting for a future Messiah. "Leave sorrow and sadness," he cried, "man must live in joy and contentment, always rejoicing in his lot."[20] Followers of the Baal Shem Tov worshiped through joyous songs and ecstatic, swaying prayer, and found God in the midst of oppression.

> *As the hand held before the eye conceals the greatest mountain, so the little earthly life hides from the glance the enormous lights and mysteries of which the world is full, and he who can draw it away from before his eyes, as one draws away a hand, beholds the great shining of the inner worlds.*
>
> *Attributed to Reb Nachman of Bratislava*

The spread of Hasidism was swift. Soon an estimated half of all eastern European Jews were followers of the Hasidic path. Spread of the teachings is credited to Dov Ber, who emphasized the importance of the *tzaddik*, or enlightened saint and teacher, called *rebbe* (or Reb) when ordained as a Hasidic spiritual guide. Dov Ber urged Hasidim to take spiritual shelter with a *tzaddik*, whose prayers and wisdom would be more powerful than their own because of the *tzaddik*'s personal relationship with God. This idea stirred enormous opposition from non-Hasidic leaders, who believed that each Jew should be his or her own *tzaddik*. While the position of *tzaddik* became hereditary and was sometimes subject to exploitation by less-than-holy lineage carriers, such charismatic leadership remains a central element and perhaps one of the enduring attractions of modern Hasidism.

Judaism and modernity

In the late eighteenth and nineteenth centuries, the great majority of Jews lived in eastern European countries such as Poland and Russia, which were little affected by the eighteenth-century European Enlightenment. The Enlightenment, however, provided new opportunities and better conditions for the Jews in western Europe. In such a rational atmosphere of tolerance, reason, and material progress, restrictions on Jews began to decrease. The French Revolution (1789–1799) brought equality for the masses, including Jews living in France, and in the nineteenth century this trend spread to other European nations. Ghettos were torn down, and some Jews ascended to positions of prominence in western European society. The Rothschild family, for instance, became international financiers, benefactors, and patrons of the arts.

Inspired by Enlightenment views and liberated from the social restrictions that had kept them isolated as a religious community, some European Jews also embarked on a path of secularization and acculturation that has brought a sea change in Judaism in the modern world. This path was called the Jewish Enlightenment, or Haskalah, from a Hebrew word for "reason." Moses Mendelssohn (1729–1786) was considered the father of the Haskalah. He urged his fellow Jews to learn German, the language of scholars, and to be open to change and modern secular education. Talmud study was de-emphasized, in favor of secular knowledge and practical training that would help integrate Jews into their surrounding cultures. Opponents of these trends warned that in the name of Enlightenment, Judaism could lose its distinctive position at the center of Jewish life, and that in adapting to the surrounding culture, Jews would inevitably cease to observe their traditional rituals. In the face of this threat to the integrity of their received religious traditions, some scholars and rabbis encouraged Jews not only to live by *halakhah* but also to segregate themselves from non-Jewish secular culture. This position led to what came to be called **Orthodox Judaism**. One of its staunchest advocates was Moses Sofer (1762–1839), the leader of central European traditional Judaism. His testament is still read by today's ultra-Orthodox Jews. In part:

> *Be warned not to change your Jewish names, speech, and clothing—God forbid. … Never say: "Times have changed!" We have an old Father—praised be His name—who has never changed and never will change.*[21]

Meanwhile, the movements to reform Jewish religious practice—which would eventually coalesce as **Reform Judaism**—were moving farther and farther away from their traditional moorings. They adopted changes such as hymns and sermons in the vernacular instead of Hebrew, a shorter version of the liturgy, emphasis on the weekly Saturday service rather than the traditional prayers three times every weekday, choirs and organ music as in Christian Churches, and a new prayerbook omitting references to Jews' longing for a personal Messiah and return to Zion.

Judaism was also evolving in the Americas. In 1654 a small group of Sephardic Jews who had emigrated to Brazil sought to enter the colony of New Amsterdam as refugees. In Brazil the emigrants had enjoyed a period of legal equality and economic freedom. In the New Amsterdam colony as well, they were protected by a directive from the Dutch West India Company that the colony should allow people to pursue their own religions, so long as they did not cause any trouble.

With the independence of the United States and the framing of its Constitution, Jews as well as other minorities were automatically granted equal rights, under the ideals of equality of all humans and separation of Church and state. George

Washington wrote a famous letter to the Touro Synagogue of Newport, Rhode Island, affirming the ideal of freedom of religion with the words:

> *The Government of the United States, which gives to bigotry no sanction, to persecution no assistance, requires only that they who live under its protection should demean themselves as good citizens in giving it on all occasions their effectual support.*[22]

As the new country became a haven for persecuted minorities and was perceived as a land of economic opportunity as well as religious freedom, substantial Jewish immigration to the United States began in the mid-nineteenth century. Today, the United States, with approximately six million Jews, has the largest Jewish population in the world.

The Holocaust

For many Jews the defining event of the twentieth century and the overwhelmingly tragic event of Jewish history was the **Holocaust**, the murder of almost six million European Jews by the Nazi leadership of Germany during World War II. These Jews constituted more than a third of the Jewish people in the world and half of all Jews in Europe.

Anti-Judaism had been part of Greco–Roman culture, and had been present in Europe since the Roman Empire adopted Christianity as its state religion in the fourth century CE. Anti-Judaism re-emerged in western Europe at the end of the nineteenth century as anti-Semitism, with the idea that there is a racial, ethnic, genetic component of Judaism. Racist theories spread that those of "pure" Nordic blood were genetically ideal, while Jews were a dangerous "mongrel" race.

Reactionary anti-Jewish feelings also resurfaced late in the nineteenth century in Russia and in eastern Europe, where Jews formed a sizable minority of the population and where they were accumulating wealth and establishing a presence in higher educational circles. Jews were increasingly associated with left-wing movements pushing for social change, even though many Jewish socialists such as Leon Trotsky were nonobservant Jews. Trotsky's leadership in the violent Bolshevik Revolution and the Red Army brought terrible reprisals against Jewish communities by White Russians in the civil war. Up to 70,000 Jews were killed by unrestrained rioting mobs.

Many Jewish families left their homes in Europe and Russia as anti-Jewish violence increased (Maurycy Minkowski, After the Pogrom, *1910.)*

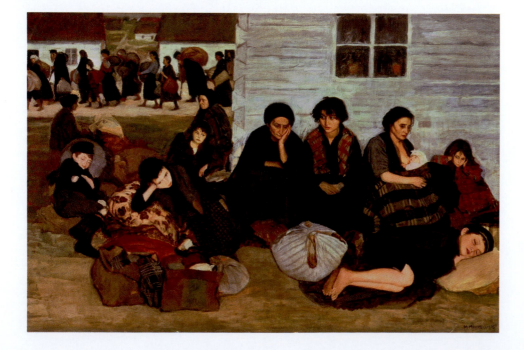

In the aftermath of Germany's defeat in World War I and the desperate economic conditions that followed, Adolf Hitler's Nazi Party bolstered its popular support by blaming the Jews for all of Germany's problems. Germany, the Nazis claimed, could not regain its health until all Jews were stripped of their positions in German life or driven out of the country. Demands to eliminate the Jews for the sake of "racial hygiene" were openly circulated. Seeing the writing on the wall, many Jews, including eminent professionals, managed to emigrate, leaving their homes, their livelihoods, and most of their possessions behind. Others stayed, hoping that the terrifying signs would prove to be short-lived.

As Hitler rose to power, the Nazis instigated acts of violence against Jews in Germany and passed laws that separated Jews from the rest of the population and deprived them of their legal and economic rights. When Hitler annexed Austria in 1938 and then invaded Poland, Denmark, Norway, Belgium, Holland, and France, several million more Jews fell under Nazi control.

Systematic oppression started, with orders to all Polish Jews to move into the towns, where walled ghettos were created to confine them. Jews were made to wear a badge with the Star of David on it to reveal their stigmatized status, and since all other jobs were taken away from them, they could do only menial labor.

Along the Russian front, special "action groups" were assigned to slaughter Jews, Gypsies, and heads of government departments as the German troops advanced, and to incite the local militias to do the same. One cannot comprehend the numbers of men, women, and children killed in these mass murders—34,000 at Babi Yar, 26,000 at Odessa, 32,000 at Vilna—probably totaling hundreds of thousands.

By 1942, large-scale death camps had been set up by the Nazis to facilitate the "final solution"—the total extermination of all Jews in Europe. From the ghettos Jews were transported by cattle cars (in which many died) from all over Europe to concentration camps. There they were starved, worked to death as slaves, tortured, and "experimented" on. Many were then shipped to extermination camps, where industrial-scale gas chambers were used as the most efficient means of killing.

The governments of some countries tried to protect their Jews; also some individuals, at great personal risk, hid Jews or tried to help them escape. For example, Chiune Sugihara, a Japanese diplomat, managed to issue Japanese transit

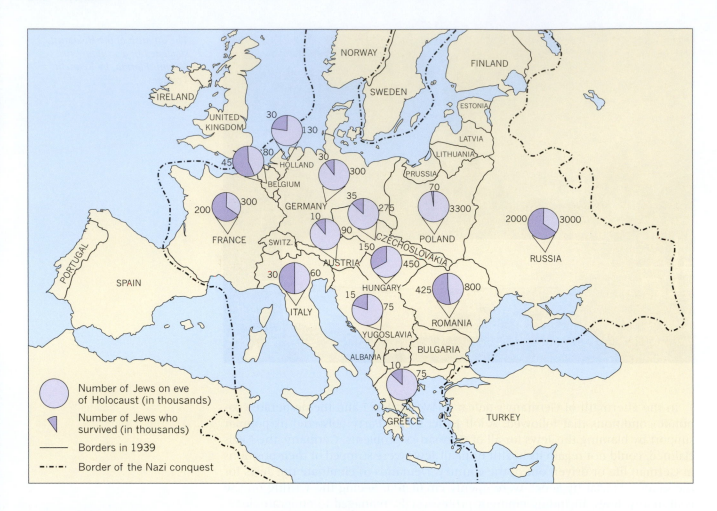

Number of Jews on eve of Holocaust (in thousands)

Number of Jews who survived (in thousands)

Borders in 1939

Border of the Nazi conquest

Hitler's final solution was to herd Jews into concentration camps throughout Nazi-occupied Europe and then ship the survivors east into extermination camps in Poland. The pie charts show the number of Jews in each country who were left after the Holocaust, compared to their previous populations.

visas to some 10,000 Jews, ignoring all risks to himself in order to help them quickly escape from danger. But there was little outcry from the outside world. In hindsight, many historians have concluded that Hitler's genocidal actions could have been slowed by determined resistance from free Allied countries.

No modern Jewish thinker can ignore the challenge that the Holocaust poses to traditional Jewish beliefs of an omnipotent and caring God. Elie Wiesel (b. 1928), who as a boy survived a Nazi death camp in Poland but lost all his other family members and suffered great atrocities, writes of a bitterness so deep that it could prevent him from uttering the traditional prayers to God:

> *Why, but why would I bless Him? Every fiber in me rebelled. Because He caused thousands of children to burn in His mass graves? Because He kept six crematoria working day and night, including Sabbath and the Holy Days? Because in His great might He had created Auschwitz, Birkenau, Buna, and so many other factories of death? How could I say to Him: "Blessed be Thou, Almighty, Master of the Universe, who chose us among all nations to be tortured day and night, to watch as our fathers, our mothers, our brothers, end up in the furnaces?"[23]*

Wiesel says that we cannot turn away from the questions about how it could happen, for genocidal actions are being undertaken against other minority groups in our times as well.

Zionism and contemporary Israel

The horrors of the Holocaust brought increased attention to the cause of **Zionism**, the Jewish movement dedicated to the establishment of a political-ly viable, internationally recognized Jewish state in the biblical land of Israel. While political Zionism was a reaction to increasing anti-Semitism in Europe in the late nineteenth century, it is a movement with deep roots in Judaism and

Jewish culture. The desire to end the centuries-long exile from Zion (the site of the Jerusalem Temples) was a central theme in all Jewish prayer and in many religious customs. Jewish messianism is focused around a descendant of King David who will return his united people to the land of Israel, where Jewish sovereignty will be eternally re-established in an atmosphere of universal peace. Professor Aviezer Ravitzky describes the Zionist ideal:

It was a dream of utter perfection: the day would come when the entire Jewish people, the whole Congregation of Israel, would reassemble as one in an undivided Land of Israel, reconstituting its life there according to the Torah in all its aspects. The Jewish people would free itself completely from its subjugation to the great powers. It would then be a source of blessing for all nations, for its redemption would bring about the redemption of the world as a whole.[24]

Zionism became an organized international political movement under the leadership of the journalist Theodor Herzl (1860–1904), who believed that the Jews could never defend themselves against anti-Semitism until they had their own nation. Herzl worked to provide political guarantees for the Jewish settlement that existed in Palestine through the nearly 2,000 years of exile and to offer institutional support to encourage Jews from around the world to immigrate to Palestine. Simultaneously, pioneers, mainly secular Jews from eastern Europe, began increasing the Jewish presence on the land. In 1917, as the Allies prepared to carve up the former Ottoman Empire at the end of World War I, Great Britain's foreign secretary, Lord Balfour, sent a letter to Lord Rothschild, a leader of the British Jewish community, advising him that the British government would support the creation in Palestine of a "national home for the Jewish people…, it being clearly understood that nothing shall be done which may prejudice the civil and religious rights of existing non-Jewish communities in Palestine." The existing non-Jewish communities in Palestine at the time were primarily Muslims, plus some Christians. Out of Palestine's total estimated population of 600,000, some 85,000 to 100,000 were Jews living there[25] when Lord Balfour wrote this brief note, which ultimately had a tremendous impact on the history of West Asia. It became known as the Balfour Declaration. Its language was replicated in a 1922 League of Nations mandate giving the United Kingdom administrative control of Palestine. Neither document offered any clarity about how the rights of Arabs living in Palestine were to be protected.

Zionist leader Henrietta Szold discusses plans with pioneers of the kibbutz system in about 1940.

In the period before the Holocaust, not all Jews supported the Zionist movement. Most Reform Jews of that time believed the destiny of Jews was to be lived out among the Gentiles, where the Enlightenment had fueled hopes of a freer future. Some support for Zionism came from traditional Orthodox Jews, but not all of the traditional community embraced the idea. Many felt it was God who had punished the people for their unfaithfulness by sending them away from the promised land and that only God would end the exile.

Nonetheless, by a United Nations decision in 1947 after World War II, Palestine was partitioned into two areas, one to be governed by Jews and the other by Arabs, with Jerusalem an international zone. The Jews accepted the plan, and in 1948 declared Israel an independent Jewish state with full rights for minorities. However, the Arabs did not accept the partition and as soon as British troops moved out, Israel was attacked by its Arab neighbors—Jordan, Iraq, Syria, Lebanon, and Egypt. Outnumbered, Israel nonetheless managed to gain control of a larger area than was allotted to it in the partition plan, thus bringing many Arabs under its rule. Those Arabs who fled to avoid violence were not allowed into the surrounding countries; they were instead kept in refugee camps, in which for generations people have continued to live in distress and with growing hatred for Israel. Egypt and Jordan kept sending guerrilla troops, known as "*fedayeen*," to attack the Israelis, whose sovereignty they refused to recognize.

When an attack by Arab neighbors and Palestinians seemed imminent in 1967, Israel launched a stunningly successful pre-emptive strike—the Six-Day War. Nevertheless, the Arab countries still refused to recognize Israel's nationhood and Palestinian resistance grew. Despair over attaining any lasting peace with the surrounding Arabs brought hardliners to the fore in Israeli politics. They saw in expanded settlements a fulfilment of biblical prophecy and a defense against Palestinian terrorism.

From time to time, a negotiated peace has seemed almost possible, but it has not yet happened. Frameworks for Palestinian–Israeli settlement have offered some hope of decreasing hostilities in the region by creating two independent states of Palestine and Israel, but they have not satisfactorily dealt with major sticking points. One of these is the "right of return" sought by Palestinian refugees from the 1948–1949 war and their descendants. Countering this demand, some Jews point out that more than one million Jews had to flee Arab lands before and after the creation of Israel because of severe persecution. There is also Palestinian concern that the new state of Palestine would consist only of isolated, dependent enclaves under Israeli control. Yet another problem is control of, and access to, sites that are holy to both Muslims and Jews, such as the Temple Mount in Jerusalem, known to Muslims as the place from which the Prophet Muhammad began his Night Journey to the seven heavens but also the most sacred place in Judaism, as the site of the former Temples.

One attempt of Jews to protect themselves from Palestinian terrorist attacks has been the building of massive security fences and walls up to 25 feet (7.6 meters) high that impede the mixing of the two communities in some particularly sensitive areas, such as the West Bank, where colonies of Israeli settlers are occupying areas of Jordan taken over by Israel during the Six-Day War. Palestinian communities in those areas may thus live in isolated cages in which farmers are cut off from their own land and water, and in some cases, even from the other side of their now-divided villages. However, efforts persist to keep person-to-person contacts open between Israeli Jews and those who have been historically pitted as their opponents. Joint Arab–Jewish initiatives are proliferating, as citizens from both communities attempt to meet, understand, and co-operate with each other on a local basis. More than 150 organizations are now involved in this work. For instance, the International Center for Conciliation and Ossim Shalom (Social Workers for Peace and Social Welfare) have organized many workshops that are designed to help participants understand and relate to the others' fears and concerns by developing empathy toward others' "pained memories" stretching back several generations.

Arab and Jewish parents and board members of an ethnically mixed school in Beersheva after collectively exploring their pains, fears, needs, and hopes at an intensive weekend retreat sponsored by the International Center for Conciliation and Ossim Shalom.

Rabbi Hillel Levine, president of the International Center for Conciliation, observes that throughout the centuries there were some Jews living in the historic Land of Israel but even more Jews remembering why they were no longer actual residents of their homeland. In their yearning to return, he says, they saw it as their task to repent for violations of their covenant with God:

We are custodians of the land. … Essentially, the Lord provides the earth to humanity on a long-term lease, full of contingencies but the earth is the Lord's. Jews, in their attachment to the Land of Israel, lived with this sense of contingency and responsibility. They knew that it was not a one-time grant based on the merit of their Father Abraham. … He left his homeland, with all of its comforts, with little more than God's assurance of "the place that I shall show you." That place was a very special rim that rises out of the Mediterranean and the West reaching to Mount Zion and Jerusalem and then slopes down to the deserts of the East. It is at the center of the world and provided the Jewish people with special opportunities. It is also a place that other nations so often sought. The biblical covenant making it the land of the Jews makes all entitlements contingent upon behavior. It's not a free gift by any means. To keep the land we have to behave in a certain way. … Security, particularly after the Holocaust, is of paramount value. But that security must include spiritual security, moral security, and that which secures our identity as a people who strive for holiness and justice.[26]

Rabbi Jeremy Milgrom, a leader in many Israeli peace initiatives, points out that in the first century CE Hillel the Elder summarized the Torah's central message thus:

"That which is hateful unto you, do not do to your comrade … I am YHWH: Let your love for Me overcome your hatred for him, and keep you from taking revenge; in this way love vanquishes hatred, and peace will come between you." This is the way of the Torah, "whose ways are pleasant, and all of whose paths are peace" (Proverbs 3:17).[27]

In addition to Israeli-Palestinian political tensions, tensions also exist within the Jewish community in Israel. Jews have come to Israel from many divergent backgrounds. Those who are of eastern European origin—the Ashkenazi who founded the state—tend to regard themselves as superior to Jewish Israelis from

RELIGION IN PUBLIC LIFE

Rabbi Michael Melchior

 Rabbi Michael Melchior was born in 1954 into a Danish family that had served as chief rabbis of Denmark for seven generations. After his ordination as a rabbi, he became the Chief Rabbi of Norway, and then moved to Israel. There he has held many political positions as leader of the left-wing religious party Meimad, including ten years as a Knesset member and minister holding various posts. He is deeply committed to the peace process and helped to found the Mosaica Center, which is promoting Jewish–Muslim dialogue in West Asia.

Of the importance of Jerusalem in his life, Rabbi Melchior says:

I grew up in Denmark in a family with deep Jewish traditions and deep Danish traditions. As a young teenager, I had my first visit to Jerusalem—I was at that time just turned fifteen. Three times a day we had turned to Jerusalem in prayer and talked about its holiness, but I didn't have a clue what it was.

Three years later I moved to Jerusalem, where I studied in a yeshiva—institute of Jewish learning—in the Old City. It was a short time after the Six-Day War, when Jerusalem had become unified and open for the first time to all peoples and all religions. For me, the Old City was a very, very special place to live—among the different Jewish populations, who were just as much at strife as are ... the Jewish and non-Jewish, Christians and Armenians and Muslims.

In the very first lecture which I heard in my yeshiva the head rabbi said something which stayed with me a long time. He said, "This place where we are now: It's a square kilometer, not even a square mile. They will be able to solve everything, all the conflicts of the world, but this square kilometer they will never be able to solve." I decided to devote my life to prove him wrong, because I feel that cannot be true. It is the most holy place for the Jewish religion, maybe the only holy place where there is a permanent holiness. It cannot be that that sanctification of that place should only result in people's fearing each other, despising each other, hating each other, and crushing the image of each other.[28]

In a statement made to a conference against racism and intolerance in 2001, Rabbi Melchior explains the aspirations of the State of Israel in terms of equality and freedom:

The twentieth century which witnessed the atrocities of the Holocaust also witnessed the fulfillment of the Zionist dream, the reestablishment of a Jewish state in Israel's historic land. For Zionism is quite simply that— the national movement of the Jewish people, based on an unbroken connection, going back from 4,000 years, between the People of the Book and the Land of the Bible. It has strived continually to establish a society which reflects highest ideals of democracy and justice for all its inhabitants, in which Jew and Arab can live together, in which women and men have equal rights, in which there is freedom of thought and of expression, and in which all have access to the judicial process to ensure these rights are protected. The aspiration to build such a society was enshrined from the outset in Israel's Declaration of Independence: "The State of Israel ... will foster the development of the country for the benefit of all its inhabitants; it will ensure complete equality of social and political rights to all its inhabitants, irrespective of creed, race or gender; it will guarantee freedom of religion, conscience, language, education and culture."

It is a tall task. It is a constant struggle, and we do not always succeed. But even in the face of the open hostility of its neighbors and continued threats to its existence, there are few countries that have made such efforts to realize such a vision.[29]

For the peace process in the Middle East to succeed, Rabbi Melchior believes that the role of religion should not be ignored. He states:

When we look at the successes and failures in the pursuit of peace in the Middle East, we can see that there has been a failure to integrate religion and interreligious dialogue. The repeated attempts to ignore religion's critical role in the search for peace have been wrong. This is the century of religion, with both its positive and negative consequences.

There is a dominant view among left-wing Israeli and Palestinian policy-makers that peace is a vehicle to secularizing society and that if there were no conflict, people wouldn't need religion. This attitude has emptied the peace process of its soul. Although there are religious components to the conflict, it is a national conflict between two peoples claiming the same piece of land. However, because religion was excluded from the solution, it became an ever-growing part of the problem. It was filled by extremist elements who tried to turn the conflict into a religious one—a conflict between "my God" and "your God" where there can be no compromise and no solution.

If it can be proven that religion can facilitate cooperation and peacemaking, that Islam is willing to live with the State of Israel in the midst of the Islamic world, Israelis would be much more open to the peace process, and it would restore hope for real progress. Likewise if the Palestinians would see that Israelis are not here to spearhead the clash of civilizations or to wipe out their national-religious aspiration, the Muslim world would be much more open to creating a different future together with Israelis. We who look toward religion as our main source of identity can find a world not only of common interests but also of common values.[30]

other areas. Ultra-Orthodox religious authorities insist on strict observance of religious rituals, assert considerable control over education and politics in the nation, and claim that converts consecrated by Reform and Conservative rabbis in the United States are not really Jews. The Orthodox rabbis generally favor hardline political policies in Israel, and yet Ultra-Orthodox Jews who claimed to be studying "day and night" in *yeshiva* (traditional schools devoted mostly to study of rabbinic literature and Talmud) were exempted from military service until 2014, when a controversial law was passed ordering gradual conscription of Ultra-Orthodox Jewish men. The Orthodox rabbis do not represent the majority of Israeli citizens in religious terms either, for only an estimated fifteen percent of Israelis claim to live completely according to religious laws. The majority are non-Orthodox or not religiously observant. Nevertheless, Israel is a country in which businesses close and buses stop running on the Jewish Sabbath, Jewish holidays are national holidays, and most people celebrate Passover, marry other Jews, and light the Hanukkah menorah if not the Sabbath candles. There is also internal dissension over relationships with the Palestinians. Many Israeli Jews sympathize with the Palestinians' situation, even as Religious Zionists believe that the land has been promised to them by God for the redemption of the Jewish people and eventually the entire world.

Although the dream of a sovereign Torah-based nation or a peaceful two-state solution is still elusive, Israel is nonetheless a unique home or place of pilgrimage for Jews, and many immigrants are still arriving from countries such as India, Yemen, Morocco, Ethiopia, and the former Soviet Union. According to the Law of Return passed in 1950, any Jew is granted automatic citizenship in Israel. Some new immigrants from West Asia and North Africa are Jews from Arabic cultures and thus have mixed cultural identities. From Israel, where they are known as "Mizrahi" Jews, a group of these young second- and third-generation Arabic Jewish immigrants have stated their desire to be peacemakers in the troubled region:

> We now express the hope that our generation—throughout the Arab, Muslim, and Jewish world—will be a generation of renewed bridges that will leap over the walls and hostility created by previous generations.[31]

Torah

What are the key tenets of the Jewish faith?

It is difficult to outline the tenets of the Jewish faith. As we have seen, Jewish spiritual understanding has changed repeatedly through history. Rationalists and mystics have often differed. Since the nineteenth century, there has been disagreement between liberal and traditional Jews, to be discussed later.

Nevertheless, there are certain major themes that can be extricated from the vast history and literature of Judaism. Jewish teachings are known as the Torah. In its narrowest sense, the Torah refers to the "five books of Moses." On the next level, it means the entire Hebrew Bible and the Talmud, the written and the oral law. For some, "Torah" can refer to all sacred Jewish literature and observance. At the highest level, Torah is God's will, God's wisdom.

The one God

The central Jewish belief is monotheism. It has been stated in different ways in response to different cultural settings (emphasizing the divine unity when Christians developed the concept of the Holy Trinity, for instance, and emphasizing that God is formless and ultimate holiness in opposition to the earthly local gods). But the central theme is that there is one Creator God, the "cause of all existent things."[32]

God is everywhere, even in the darkness, as David sings in Psalms:

Where can I escape from Your spirit?
Where can I flee from Your presence?
If I ascend to Heaven, You are there:
if I descend to Sheol [the underworld],
You are there too.

If I take wing with the dawn
to come to rest on the western horizon,
even there Your hand will be guiding me,
Your right hand will be holding me fast.

Psalm 139:7–14

This metaphysical understanding of God's oneness is difficult to explain in linear language, which refers to the individual objects perceived by the senses. As the eleventh-century Spanish poet and mystical philosopher Ibn Gabirol put it, "None can penetrate ... the mystery of Thy unfathomable unity."[33]

One of the most elegant attempts to "explain" God's oneness has been offered by the great twentieth-century thinker Abraham Joshua Heschel (1907–1972). He linked the idea of unity to eternity, explaining that in eternity, "past and future are not apart; here is everywhere, and now goes on forever." Time as we know it is only a fragment, "eternity broken in space." According to Heschel:

The craving for unity and coherence is the predominant feature of a mature mind. All science, all philosophy, all art are a search after it. But unity is a task, not a condition. The world lies in strife, in discord, in divergence. Unity is beyond, not within, reality. … The world is not one with God, and this is why his power does not surge unhampered throughout all stages of being. Creature is detached from the Creator, and the universe is in a state of spiritual disorder. Yet God has not withdrawn entirely from this world. The spirit of this unity hovers over the face of all plurality, and the major trend of all our thinking and striving is its mighty intimation. The goal of all efforts is to bring about the restitution of the unity of God and world.[34]

Plurality is incompatible with the sense of the ineffable. You cannot ask in regard to the divine: Which one? There is only one synonym for God: One.

Abraham Joshua Heschel[35]

In traditional Judaism, God is often perceived as a loving Father who is nonetheless infinitely majestic, sometimes revealing divine power when the children need chastising.

Love for God

The essential commandment to humans is to love God. The central recitation in a Jewish religious service and the inscription on the *mezuza* at the doorpost of every traditional Jewish home is the *Shema Israel*:

Hear, O Israel! The Lord is our God, the Lord alone. You shall love the Lord your God with all your heart and with all your soul and with all your might. Take to heart these instructions with which I charge you this day. Impress them upon your children. Recite them when you stay at home and when you are away, when you lie down and when you get up. Bind them as a sign on your hand and let them serve as a symbol on your forehead; inscribe them on the doorposts of your house and on your gates.

Deuteronomy 6:4–9

Even Maimonides, the great proponent of reason and study, asserted the primacy of love for God. He emphasized that one should not love God from selfish or fearful motivations, such as receiving earthly blessings or avoiding problems in the life after death. One should study the Torah and fulfill the commandments out of sheer love of God.

The sacredness of human life

Humans are the pinnacle of creation, created in the "image" of God, according to the account of Creation in Genesis 1. Jews do not take this passage to mean that God literally looks like a human. It is often interpreted in an ethical sense: That humans are so wonderfully endowed that they can mirror God's qualities, such as justice, wisdom, righteousness, and love.

All people are potentially equal; they are said to be common descendants of the first man and woman. But they are also potentially perfectible, and in raising themselves they uplift the world. God limited the divine power by giving humans free will, involving them in the responsibility for the world's condition, and their own.

The German scholar Martin Buber (1878–1965) described the relationship between God and humans as reciprocal:

> *You know always in your heart that you need God more than everything; but do you not know too that God needs you—in the fulness of His eternity needs you? How would man exist, how would you exist, if God did not need him, did not need you? You need God, in order to be—and God needs you, for the very meaning of your life. … We take part in creation, meet the Creator, reach out to him, helpers and companions.*[36]

Human life is sacred, rather than lowly and loathsome; Judaism celebrates the body. Sexuality within marriage is holy, and the body is honored as the instrument through which the soul is manifested on earth. Indeed, according to some thinkers, body and soul are an inseparable totality.

> *I praise You, for I am awesomely, wondrously made.*
>
> Psalm 139:14

Jewish theology has been shaped by the most compelling thinkers of each era. In the 20th century, Martin Buber described the cherished human–divine encounter as an I–Thou relationship, in which the self experiences its wholeness.

Law

Because of the great responsibility of humankind, traditional Jews give thanks that God has revealed in the written and oral Torah the laws by which they can be faithful to the divine will and fulfill the purposes of Creation by establishing a Kingdom of God here on earth, in which all creatures can live in peace and fellowship. In the words of the biblical prophet Isaiah, speaking for God:

> *The wolf and the lamb shall graze together,*
> *And the lion shall eat straw like the ox,*
> *And the serpent's food shall be earth.*
> *In all my sacred mount*
> *Nothing evil or vile shall be done.*[37]

To the extent that traditional Jews act according to the Torah, they feel they are upholding their part of the ancient covenant with God.

The Torah, as indicated through rabbinic literature, is said to contain 613 commandments, or **mitzvot** (singular: **mitzvah**). Jewish law does not differentiate between sacred and secular life, so these include general ethical guidelines such as the Ten Commandments and the famous saying in Leviticus 19:18—"Love your fellow as yourself"—plus detailed laws concerning all aspects of life, such as land ownership, civil and criminal procedure, family law, sacred observances,

An Interview with Eli Epstein

 Eli Epstein, an Orthodox Jew, is a successful international businessman living in New York. In accordance with the teaching of his ancestors, he is also a philanthropist. His particular interest is in promoting interfaith understanding, having noted surprising similarities between Judaism and Islam during his many trips to West Asia. One of the projects he has initiated and supported is "Children of Abraham," which he co-directs with a Muslim philanthropist, to develop dialogue between Jewish and Muslim teenagers through the Internet. He explains the attitude toward giving that he has been taught:

Jewish philanthropy has its antecedents in scripture. The Torah speaks about the fact that the farmers, for example, have to leave some of their crop for the poor to be able to take the droppings and the things that are extra. It has been inculcated into our tradition, to every home and every family. It gives us firstly the sense that what we have is not necessarily our own. And if we are blessed with things that are beyond our own needs, it is because God wants us to effectively be his partner in helping the world, in repairing the world, and in improving the condition of people and civilization around us, Jewish and non-Jewish.

Jewish people who believe in the giving of charity, which is called tzedakah, *know that it is based on the word meaning "justice." So it's not something we do out of the amazing ability of our hearts. It's because God says it's a form of justice, to equal out to people around us that which they can't do for themselves, for reasons which we never really understand. We don't have to ask why God gave us more than we need. But when we do have it, we shouldn't be attached to it. We should feel like it's an important thing to do, just to give. In fact, the sages say that the more you give, the more you will be blessed with being able to give more afterwards.*

We want to be able to give with an open heart, to everyone who comes and asks. Sometimes you do more, sometimes you do less. But the notion of giving is very much part of our lives and in fact, almost all Jewish homes will have something which is called a "charity box" in English. We will use it even for small coins. So we show our young children that giving is very much part of our lives.

[In our family life], there was almost no occasion in which you wouldn't give. Even in families such as mine which comes from eastern Poland, which was very poor and impoverished, the poor people themselves gave. It's almost as if nobody was excused from giving. The truth is that beggars have the responsibility to give as well. These people who were asking for money because they don't have enough to even feed themselves are responsible to give. It's not always in the form of money. You can give of your time and your efforts. You should give all different kinds and forms. The highest form is when you give a person a job, so you're not giving him anything but his own dignity. And the most perfect form of charity is when you clean a body before burial. It's called in Hebrew "chesed shel emet." Chesed *means "kindness,"* emet *being "of truth." It is the most pristine form of giving, because there is no one who will say, "Thank you." So when you are cleaning the body of nobody you will ever see again, you wash it, you purify it, you dress it in shrouds. Even when you finish that act of ultimate kindness, you can't even tell people you did it, because in the acknowledgment that you did it, they will see you as a higher person, and you can't even have that. The family can't pay you, the family can't thank you. You just walk away. You don't even say "Good night" to the person you worked with, because "Good night" is a blessing. So you say, "You should be worthy of doing more acts of kindness," and you walk away."*[38]

diet, and ritual slaughter. The biblical Book of Genesis also sets forth what is called the Noahide Code of seven universal principles for a moral and spiritual life, prohibiting idolatry (worshiping many gods or images of God), blasphemy against God, murder, theft, sexual behaviors outside of marriage, and cruelty to animals, and affirming the rule of law and justice in society. From the time of its final editing in Babylonia in the mid-sixth century CE, the Talmud, together with its later commentaries, has served as a blueprint for Jewish social, communal, and religious life. Through the rabbinic tradition, law became the main category of Orthodox Jewish thought and practice, and learned study of God's commandments one of the central expressions of faith.

From a contemporary point of view, Ismar Schorsch notes that many of the ancient commandments are ecologically useful, for they restrain humanity's ways of using the natural environment. They are addressed to humans not as wise masters of the earth, as envisioned in the first account of Creation in Genesis, but as the Adam and Eve of the second Creation story, who are disobedient and must be saved from themselves lest they destroy the planet, "for as the Bible so often avers: the land ultimately belongs to its Creator and we mortals are but His tenants."[39]

A Sabbath prayer, *Ahavat Olam*, expresses Jews' profound gratitude for God's laws:

> *With everlasting love You have loved Your people Israel. You have taught us the Torah and its* Mitzvot. *You have instructed us in its laws and judgments.*
>
> *Therefore, O Lord our God, when we lie down and when we rise up we shall speak of Your commandments and rejoice in Your Torah and* Mitzvot.
>
> *For they are our life and the length of our days; on them we will meditate day and night.*[40]

Suffering and faith

Jewish tradition depicts the universe as being governed by an all-powerful, personal God who intervenes in history to reward the righteous and punish the unjust. Within this context, Jews have had considerable difficulty in answering the eternal question: Why must the innocent suffer? This question has been particularly poignant since the Holocaust.

The Hebrew Bible itself brings up the issue with the challenging parable of Job, a blameless, God-fearing, and wealthy man. The story includes the only mention of Satan as a personified character in the Tanakh. Here he is a participant in God's court, who, in a conversation with God, predicts that Job will surely drop his faith and blaspheme the Lord if he is stripped of all his possessions. With God's assent, Satan tests Job by destroying all that Job has, including his children and his health. On hearing the news of his children's deaths:

> *Job arose, tore his robe, cut off his hair, and threw himself on the ground and worshiped. He said, "Naked came I out of my mother's womb, and naked shall I return there; the Lord has given, and the Lord has taken away, blessed be the name of the Lord."*[41]

Later, however, with an itchy skin affliction covering him from head to foot, Job begins to curse his life and to question God's justice. In the end, Job acknowledges not only God's power to control the world but also his inscrutable wisdom, which is beyond human understanding. God then rewards him with long life and even greater riches than he had before the test.

Debate over the meanings of this ancient story has continued over the centuries. One rabbinical interpretation is that Satan was co-operating with God in helping Job grow from fear of God to love of God. Another is that faith in God will finally be rewarded in this life, no matter how severe the temporary trials. Another is that those who truly desire to grow toward God will be asked to suffer more, that their sins will be expiated in this life so that they can enjoy the divine bliss in the life to come. Such interpretations assume a personal, all-powerful, loving God doing what is best for the people, even when they cannot understand God's ways. In such belief, God is seen as always available, like a shepherd caring for his sheep, no matter how dark the outer circumstances.

> *Though I walk through a valley of deepest darkness,*
> *I fear no harm, for You are with me;*
> *Your rod and Your staff—they comfort me.*
>
> *Psalm 23:4*

On the other hand, oppression and then the Holocaust have led some Jews to cry out to God in anguish. They, too, feel close to God, but in a way that allows them to scream at God, as it were. In questioning the justice of history, they hold God responsible for what is inexplicably monstrous. But even in the Holocaust, there were those who held fast to hope for better times. As they walked to their death in Nazi gas chambers, some were reciting the hymn *Ani maamin*: "I believe with complete faith in the coming of the Messiah, and even though he may delay, nevertheless I anticipate every day that he will come."[42]

Sacred practices
Which sacred practices do traditional Jews observe?

Since the rabbinic period began, a major Jewish spiritual practice has been daily scriptural study. Boys were traditionally taught how to read and write ancient Hebrew and how to interpret scripture through the process of exegesis, by means of the oral Torah. This required extensive knowledge of the scriptures and concentrated intellectual effort. This classical pattern continues today even in the diaspora, where some children continue to attend yeshivot, or Jewish day schools, where they are trained in the study of Torah and encouraged to learn and obey the commandments but also through rational analysis to delve into deeper understanding of truth.

In addition to study, a Jew is urged to remember God in all aspects of life, through prayer and observance of the commandments. These commandments are not otherworldly. Many are rooted in the body, and spiritual practices often engage all the senses in awareness of God.

Boys are ritually circumcised in the *brit milah* ceremony when they are eight days old, to honor the seal of God's commandment to Abraham. Orthodox Jews consider women ritually impure during their menstrual periods and for seven blood-free days afterwards, during which time they and their husbands are prohibited from having sexual intercourse with each other. At the end of this forbidden period Orthodox Jewish women undertake complete immersion in a *mikveh*, a special deep bath structure, symbolizing their altered state. Marital sex is sacred, with the Sabbath night the holiest time for making love. By contrast, adultery is strictly forbidden as one of the worst sins against God, for Jewish tradition is extremely concerned with maintaining pure lines of descent.

What one eats is also of cosmic significance, for according to the Torah some foods are definitely unclean. For example, the only **kosher** (ritually acceptable) meats are those from warmblooded animals with cloven hoofs that chew their cuds—such as cows, goats, and sheep—and poultry. Pork is not kosher, nor is shellfish. Meat is kosher only if it has been butchered in the traditional way, with an extremely sharp, smooth knife by an authorized Jewish slaughterer. Great pains are taken to avoid eating blood; meat must be soaked in water and then drained on a salted board before cooking. Meat and milk cannot be eaten together, and separate dishes are maintained for their preparation and serving.

The rudiments of these dietary instructions are laid out in the biblical Book of

Leviticus, which quotes God as saying to Moses and Aaron, "For I the Lord am He who brought you up from the land of Egypt to be your God: you shall be holy, for I am holy."[43] The rules of diet, if strictly followed, give Jews a feeling of sacred identity and community and link them to the eternal authority of the Torah.

Some contemporary Jews feel that consciousness about what they eat should be extended to environmental considerations. To them, the styrofoam box in which a cheeseburger is sold at fast-food places is as much a problem as the mixing of meat and milk. Nuclear-generated electricity used for cooking might itself be non-kosher, if there is no safe provision for disposing of nuclear waste.

For traditional observant Jews, the morning begins with a prayer before they open their eyes to thank God for restoring the soul. The hands must then be washed before reciting blessings and, for all traditional male Jews, putting on a special fringed garment, a rectangle of cloth called a *tallit katan*. It is usually worn under a man's shirt as a reminder of the privilege of being given divine commandments. During weekday morning prayers men also put *tefillin*, or phylacteries, small leather boxes containing biblical verses about the covenant with God, on the forehead and the upper arm, held against the heart, in fulfillment of the Shema commandment, as literally understood: "Bind them [the Shema's words about the primacy of love for God] as a sign on your hand and let them serve as a symbol on your forehead." Traditional Jewish men also keep their heads covered at all times, if possible.

In addition to prayers recited on waking and at bedtime, three prayer services are chanted daily in a synagogue by men if there is a minyan (quorum of ten). Women can say them also, but they are excused from rigid schedules partly because of their household responsibilities, and partly because of the belief that women have a more intuitive sense of spirituality.

Jews are also expected to give thanks continually. Tradition holds that one should recite a hundred benedictions to God every day. To this end, there is a blessing to be said every time one takes a drink of water. There is even a blessing to be recited after using the toilet:

Blessed art thou, our God, Ruler of the universe, who hast formed (human) beings in wisdom, and created in them a system of ducts and tubes. It is well known before thy glorious throne that if but one of these be opened, or if one of those be closed, it would be impossible to exist in thy presence. Blessed art thou, O God, who healest all creatures and doest wonders.[44]

During morning prayers, traditional Jewish men bind tefillin *to their arms and foreheads in remembrance of their covenant with God. Here a father is training his son in their use as part of his Bar Mitzvah ceremony: They are also wearing traditional prayer shawls.*

The Jewish **Sabbath** is observed as an eternal sign of the covenant between the Jews and God. The Sabbath runs from sunset Friday night to sunset Saturday night, because the Jewish "day" begins with nightfall. The Friday night service welcomes the Sabbath as a bride and is often considered an opportunity to drop away the cares of the previous week so as to be in a peaceful state for the day of rest. Just as God is said to have created the world in six days and then rested on the seventh, all work is to cease when the Sabbath begins. Rabbi Nina Beth Cardin explains Sabbath as:

> a magical, holy place that opens its doors to us once a week. ... Shabbat is a weekly dose, a megadose, of holiness. For on Shabbat, we are invited to enter God's dream for our world, a place of wholeness and fullness, a place of caring and peace. We wish each other Shabbat shalom, a day full of the peace we hope one day to find.[45]

Ruth Gan Kagan describes the Sabbath experience:

> I am aware of a wave of peace flooding my heart and that transparent veils of tranquility are covering the World around me. A moment before I would probably be rushing around trying to finish all the preparations, ... but all this tension and rush vanishes when the fixed moment arrives. ... The moment I light the Sabbath candles and usher in the Sabbath spirit everything undergoes a magical transformation.
>
> The Queen has arrived. In Her presence there are not even talks of weekday matters. The mind quiets down leaving business, plans and worries behind as one quietly walks to the synagogue for services; the sky is aglow with the colours of sunset; the bird-song is suddenly more present; the people of the congregation gather to welcome in the Sabbath in song, prayer and silence.
>
> Coming home, the stars are out; in a religious neighborhood, no traveling cars break the descended peace; children are holding their parents' hands, walking in the middle of the road without fear of death.[46]

The Saturday morning service incorporates public and private prayers, singing, and the reading of passages from the Torah scrolls, which are kept in a curtained ark on the wall facing Jerusalem. These are treated with great reverence, and it is a great honor to be "called up" to read from or recite blessings over them.

More liberal congregations may place emphasis on an in-depth discussion of the passage read. Often it is examined not only from an abstract philosophical perspective but also from the point of view of its relevance to political events and everyday attempts to live a just and humane life. Torah and Talmud study is highly valued as a form of prayer in itself, and synagogues usually have libraries for this purpose.

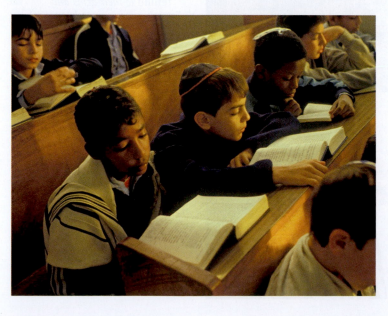

Boys praying in a synagogue in Neve Michael, Israel.

In Hasidic congregations, the emphasis falls on the intensity of praying, or **davening**, even in saying fixed prayers from the prayer book. Some sway their bodies to induce the self-forgetful state of ecstatic communion with the Loved One. The rabbinical tradition states the ideal in prayer: "A person should always see himself as if the Shekhinah is confronting him."[47]

In addition to, or instead of, going to a service welcoming the Sabbath, observant families usually begin the Sabbath eve with a special Friday-night dinner. The mother lights candles to bring in the Sabbath light; the father recites a blessing over the wine. Special braided bread, challah, is shared as a symbol of the double portions of manna in the desert. The rituals help to set a different tone for the day of rest, as do commandments against working, handling money, traveling except by foot, lighting a fire, cooking, and the like. The Sabbath day is set aside for public prayer, study, thought, friendship, and family closeness, with the hope that this renewed life of the spirit will then carry through the week to come.

It is customary to recognize coming of age in the ceremony of **Bar Mitzvah** (for Jewish boys at the age of thirteen) and **Bat Mitzvah** (for girls at the age of twelve, in non-Orthodox and even some Orthodox Jewish communities). The boy or girl celebrating the Bar or Bat Mitzvah has usually undertaken some religious instruction, including learning to pronounce Hebrew, if not always to understand it. He or she is called up to read a portion from the Torah scroll and recite a passage from one of the books of the Prophets, in Hebrew, and then perhaps to give a short teaching about a topic from the reading. Afterwards there may be a simple celebration with blessing of wine and sweet bread or cake, though a big party is more likely.

An American Jewish family reciting the blessing over the challah before the Sabbath meal.

Holy days

How are the High Holy Days and festivals celebrated?

Judaism follows an ancient lunar calendar of annual holidays and memorials linked to special events in history. The spiritual year begins with the High Holy Days of Rosh Hashanah and Yom Kippur. Rosh Hashanah (New Year's Day) is a time of spiritual renewal in remembrance of the original creation of the world. It is celebrated on the first two days of the seventh month (around the fall equinox). For thirty days prior to Rosh Hashanah, each morning synagogue service brings the blowing of the shofar (a ram's horn that produces an eerie, unearthly

Rosh Hashanah includes the blowing of the shofar in a note of alarm, three wails, and nine sobbing blasts of contrition.

blast) to remind the people that they stand before God. At the service on the eve of Rosh Hashanah, a prayer is recited asking that all humanity will remember what God has done, that there will be honor and joy for God's people, and that righteousness will triumph while "all wickedness vanishes like smoke."[48]

The ten Days of Awe follow Rosh Hashanah. People are encouraged to change inwardly, by looking at their mistakes of the past year. It is said that during this period God makes it easier for a person to be repentant, and is also more likely to accept repentance.

Yom Kippur completes the High Holy Days, renewing the sacred covenant with God in a spirit of atonement and cleansing. Historically, this was the only time when the high priest entered the Holy of Holies in the Temple of Jerusalem, and the only time that he would pronounce the sacred name of the Lord, YHWH, in order to ask for forgiveness of the people's sins. Today, there is an attempt at personal inner cleansing, and individuals must ask pardon from everyone they may have wronged during the past year. If necessary, restitution for damages should be made. Congregations also confess their sins communally, ask that their negligence be forgiven, and pray for their reconciliation to God in a new year of divine pardon and grace.

Sukkot is a Fall harvest festival. A simple outdoor booth (a sukkah) is built and decorated as a dwelling place of sorts for seven days. Usually this is done as a ritual act, but, seeking a deeper experience of the meaning of Sukkot, some contemporary Jews are actually attempting to live in the sukkah they construct. The fragile home reminds the faithful that their real home is in God, who sheltered their ancestors on the way from Egypt to the promised land of Canaan. Participants hold the *lulav* (a bundle made of a palm branch, myrtle twigs, and willow twigs) in one hand and the *etrog* (a citrus fruit) in the other and wave them together toward the four compass directions and to earth and sky, praising God and acknowledging him as the unmoving center of creation. Traditionally there was an offering of water, precious in the desert lands of the patriarchs, and great merrymaking. During the Second Temple days, later rabbis claimed, the ecstatic celebration even included burning of the priests' old underclothes. The day after the seven-day Sukkot festival is Simhat Torah (Joy in Torah), ending the yearly cycle of Torah readings, from Creation to the death of Moses, and beginning again.

Near the winter solstice, the darkest time of the year, comes Hanukkah, the Feast of Dedication. Each night for eight nights, another candle is lit on a

Simhat Torah is a joyous celebration of the Torah, with dancing and singing. Here the Torah scrolls are being carried in a celebration in Tel Aviv.

Some of the 80 women who gathered in Dati-Leumi Synagogue in Jerusalem to celebrate Purim by reading the Book of Esther aloud together. The funny hats are part of the celebration.

Hanukkah menorah (candle stand). The amount of light gradually increases like the lengthening of sunlight. Historically, Hanukkah was a celebration of the victory of the Maccabean rebellion against the attempt by Antiochus to force non-Jewish practices on the Jewish people. According to legend, when the Jews regained access to the Temple, they found only one jar of oil left undefiled, still sealed by the high priest. It was enough to stay alight for only one day, but by a miracle the oil stayed burning for eight days. Many Jewish families also observe the time by nightly gift-giving. The children have their own special Hanukkah pastimes, such as spinning the *dreidel*, a top with four letters on its sides as an abbreviation of the sentence "A great miracle happened there."

As the winter rainy season begins to diminish in Israel, some Jews celebrate the reawakening of nature on Tu B'shvat. Observances lavish appreciation on a variety of fruits and plants. In Israel, eco-minded Jewish communities now mark the time by planting trees to help restore life to the desert.

On the full moon of the month before spring comes Purim. It commemorates the legend of Esther, queen of Persia, and Mordecai, who saved their fellow Jews from destruction by the evil viceroy Haman. It has been linked to Mesopotamian mythology about the goddess Ishtar, whose spring return brings joy and fertility. Purim is a bawdy time of dressing in costumes and mocking life's seriousness, and the jokes frequently poke fun at sacred Jewish practices. As the story of Esther is read from an ornate scroll, the congregation responds with noisy stomping, rattles, horns, and whistles whenever Haman's name is read. Purim is also celebrated with gifts of money to the poor and gifts of food to friends and family.

The next major festival is Pesach, or Passover, celebrated by more Jews than any other ritual. This much-loved celebration honors the liberation from bondage in Egypt and the springtime advent of new life. At the time of the tenth plague, death to all firstborn sons of the Egyptians, the Israelites were warned to slaughter a lamb for each family and mark their doors with its blood so that the angel of death would pass over them. They were to roast the lamb and eat it with unleavened bread and bitter herbs. So quickly did they depart that they did not even have time to bake the bread, which is said to have baked in the sun as they carried it. The beginning of Pesach is marked by a **Seder** dinner, with the eating of unleavened bread (matzah) to remember the urgency of the departure, and bitter herbs as a reminder of slavery, so that they would never

Family Seders involve people of all generations in reading scripts explaining the symbolic significance of the special foods.

impose it on other peoples. Also on the table are *charoset* (a sweet fruit and nut mixture, a reminder of the mortar that the enslaved Israelites molded into bricks) and salt water (a reminder of the tears of the slaves) into which parsley or some other plant (a reminder of spring life) is dipped and eaten. Children ask ritual questions about why these things are done, as basic religious instruction. A movement for contemporary liturgical renewal has yielded countless new **Haggadahs**, scripts for the Seder—such as special Haggadahs for children, feminists, LGBT (lesbian, gay, bisexual, and transgender) Jews, secular Zionists, secular humanists, victims of domestic violence, and co-celebration of Pesach with Muslims. Since the Seder is often celebrated at home, people are free to choose or put together their own Haggadah liturgy and post it on the Internet to share with others.

A new holy day may be observed in April or May: Holocaust Remembrance Day. Observances often include the singing in Yiddish of a song from the Jewish Resistance Movement. In part:

> Never say that you are
> going your last way,
> though leaden skies
> blot out the blue of day.
> The hour for which we
> long will certainly appear.[49]

In Israel, Holocaust Remembrance Day is observed with a countrywide minute of silence, in which all traffic, speaking, and movement stop entirely. This is a powerful secular ritual that enables secular and religious Jews to remember the Holocaust together.

Early summer brings Shavuot, traditionally identified with the giving of the Torah to Moses on Mount Sinai and the people hearing the voice of God. It is likely that Shavuot was initially a summer harvest festival that later was linked with the revelation of the Torah. In Israeli kibbutzim, the old practice of bringing the first fruits to God has been revived. Elsewhere, the focus is on reading the Ten Commandments and on presenting the Torah as a marriage contract between God and Israel.

Then come three weeks of mourning for the Temples of Jerusalem, both of which were destroyed on the ninth day of the month of Av (July or August), Tisha Be-av. This is traditionally a time of fasting and avoidance of joyous activities. Some feel that there is no longer cause for mourning because even though the Temples have not been rebuilt, the old city of Jerusalem has been recaptured. Others feel that they are all still in exile from the state of perfection.

Contemporary Judaism

How do the major branches of contemporary Judaism differ?

Within the extended family of Judaism, there are many groups, many different focuses, and many areas of disagreement. Currently disputed issues include the degree of adherence to the Torah and Talmud, requirements for conversion to Judaism, the extent of the use of Hebrew in prayer, and the full participation of women.

Major branches today

To a certain extent, contemporary Jews may be divided along historic ethnic lines. The majority—at least sixty-five percent—are descendants of the **Ashkenazim**, who originally migrated to Italy from West Asia during the first and second centuries CE, and then spread through central and eastern Europe, and thence to the Americas. The second largest grouping is the **Sephardim**, descendants of those who migrated to Spain from West Asia in the eighth and ninth centuries, and thence to North Africa, the Americas, and back to West Asia. As indicated earlier, **Mizrahi** Jews from Arab lands comprise a third category.

Other distinctions among Jews who are religiously observant have developed as Judaism has encountered the modern world. Judaism, like all modern religions, has struggled to meet the challenge of secularization: the idealization of science, rationalism, industrialization, and materialism. The response of the Orthodox has been to stand by the Torah as the revealed word of God and the Talmud as the legitimate oral law. Orthodox Jews feel that they are bound by the traditional rabbinical *halakhah*, as a way of achieving closeness to God. But within this framework there are great individual differences, with no central authority figure or governing body. Orthodoxy includes mystics and rationalists, Zionists and anti-Zionists. The Orthodox also differ greatly in their tolerance for other Jewish groups and in their degree of accommodation of the surrounding

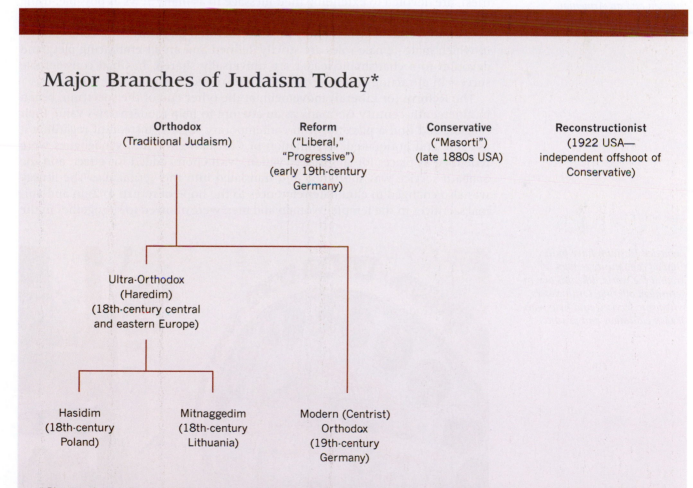

Major Branches of Judaism Today*

Orthodox (Traditional Judaism)

Reform ("Liberal," "Progressive") (early 19th-century Germany)

Conservative ("Masorti") (late 1880s USA)

Reconstructionist (1922 USA—independent offshoot of Conservative)

Ultra-Orthodox (Haredim) (18th-century central and eastern Europe)

Hasidim (18th-century Poland)

Mitnaggedim (18th-century Lithuania)

Modern (Centrist) Orthodox (19th-century Germany)

* Places and approximate dates of origin are indicated. In Israel, most of the fifteen percent who consider themselves religiously observant are either the equivalent of Modern Orthodox or identify themselves as Haredim. The Haredim (Strict or Ultra-Orthodox) remain divided over worship, with the Hasidim following Isaac Luria's mostly Sephardi prayerbook, and the Mitnaggedim using the traditional Ashkenazi Polish rites. The Masorti (traditional) movement in Israel is most closely related to the American Conservative movement. The Progressive movement in Israel is related to the American Reform movement.

Orthodox men wearing their traditional dress in the Jewish Quarter of the Old City of Jerusalem, which also has a Christian Quarter, a Muslim Quarter, and an Armenian Quarter, plus the Temple Mount.

secular environment. **Modern Orthodoxy** values secular knowledge and integration with non-Jewish society so that its members can interact with the modern world and also help to uplift it. At the same time, Modern Orthodoxy, which first developed in nineteenth-century western Europe, is dedicated to the national and religious significance of Israel and to Jewish law as divinely given. **Religious Zionism**, which is based on the teachings of Rabbi Abraham Isaac Kook (1864–1935), places central emphasis on resettlement of the Jewish people in Israel as the working out of a divine plan for the salvation not only of Jews but also for the whole world. Involvement with secular society is permissible only when such involvement is beneficial for the state of Israel. **Haredi** (Ultra-Orthodox) Judaism—which may overlap with Religious Zionism, especially in Israel—is generally in favor of a degree of detachment from non-Jewish culture, so that the community can focus on study of the Torah. Some Haredi groups practice complete withdrawal from the secular world and the rest of the Jewish community, while others, such as the **Lubavich Hasidim** (originally from Lithuania, with strong communities in many countries), are devoted to extending their message to as many Jews as possible, using all the tools of modern technology for their sacred purpose. The Lubavich or Chabad movement, which offers highly structured and nurturing communities in which male–female roles are strictly defined and an all-embracing piety and devotion to a charismatic leader are universally shared, has had considerable success in attracting young Jews to this way of life.

The **Reform** (or **Liberal**) movement, at the other end of the spectrum, began in nineteenth-century Germany as an attempt to help modern Jews value their religion and find a place for it in contemporary society, instead of regarding it as static and antiquated. In imitation of Christian churches, synagogues were redefined as places for spiritual elevation, with choirs added for effect, and the Sabbath service was shortened and translated into the vernacular. The liturgy was also changed to eliminate references to the hope of return to Zion and animal sacrifices in the temple. Women and men were allowed to sit together in the

Lubavich Hasidim have built Chabad community centers around the world, like this one in Jerusalem offering Torah classes, synagogue services, and help with Jewish education and practice.

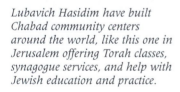

synagogue, in contrast to their traditional separation. *Halakhic* observances were re-evaluated for their relevance to modern needs, and Judaism was understood as an evolving, open-ended religion rather than one fixed forever by the Torah. Reform congregations are numerous in North America, where they are continually engaged in a "creative confrontation with modernity." Rather than exclusivism, Reform rabbis cultivate a sense of the universalism of Jewish values.

Given this approach, it is not surprising that Reform Judaism, particularly in North America, has been at the forefront in the establishment of **interfaith dialogue** and faith-based social activism, in co-operation with non-Jewish groups. Rabbi Maria Feldman of the Religious Action Center of Reform Judaism affirms:

> To be a Reform Jew is to hear the voice of the prophets in our head; to be engaged in the ongoing work of tikkun olam; to strive to improve the world in which we live. The passion for social justice is reflected in the ancient words of our prophets and sages and in the declarations of our Movement's leaders throughout its history. The ancient command "Tzedek, Tzedek Tirdof! *Justice, justice shall you seek!*" constantly reverberates in our ears.[47]

Reform Judaism is not fully accepted in Israel, where the Israeli rabbinate does not recognize the authority of non-Orthodox rabbis.

The liberalization process has also given birth to other groups with intermediate positions. With roots in mid-nineteenth-century Germany, **Conservative Judaism** seeks to maintain, or conserve, traditional Jewish laws and practices while also using modern means of historical scholarship, sponsoring critical studies of Jewish texts from all periods. In the United States, Conservative Judaism received a great boost in 1902 when the famous scholar Solomon Schechter became President of the Jewish Theological Seminary, which thenceforth became one of the major centers of Jewish scholarship. Conservative Jews believe that Jews have always searched and added to their laws, liturgy, Midrash, and beliefs to keep them relevant and meaningful in changing times. Conservative women have long served as cantors and have been ordained as rabbis since 1985.

Rabbi Mordecai Kaplan, an influential American thinker who died in 1983, branched off from Conservatism and founded a movement called **Reconstructionism**. Kaplan held that the Enlightenment had changed everything and that strong measures were needed to preserve Judaism in the face of rationalism. Kaplan asserted that "as long as Jews adhered to the traditional conception of the Torah as supernaturally revealed, they would not be amenable to any constructive adjustment of Judaism that was needed to render it viable in a non-Jewish environment."[51] He defined Judaism as an "evolving religious civilization," both cultural and spiritual, and asserted that the Jewish people are the heart of Judaism. The traditions exist for the people, and not vice versa, he said. Kaplan rejected the idea that the Jewish people were specially chosen by God, an exclusivist idea. Rather, they had chosen to try to become a people of God. Kaplan created a new prayer book, deleting traditional portions he and others found offensive, such as derogatory references to women and Gentiles, references to physical resurrection of the body, and passages describing God as rewarding or punishing Israel by manipulating natural phenomena. Two of Kaplan's ideals became common in American Jewish life: promotion of Jewish culture (dance, food, music, arts) and of synagogues as multipurpose community centers with recreational, educational, and cultural as well as religious activities.

In addition to those who are affiliated with a religious movement, there are many Jews who identify themselves as secular Jews, affirming their Jewish origins and maintaining various Jewish cultural traditions while eschewing religious practice. There are also significant numbers of people of Jewish birth, particularly in North America and western Europe, whose Jewish identity is vestigial at best, and unlikely to survive in future generations. The possibilities for total assimilation into Western culture are evident in statistics indicating that more than fifty percent of Western Jews marry non-Jews. In most cases,

Rebbe Menachem Mendel Schneerson (1902–1994) developed a worldwide mission to bring Jews back to Jewish traditions, radiating from his Lubavich Hasidic headquarters in Brooklyn, New York.

neither spouse in such a marriage converts, and research indicates that it is highly unlikely that their children will identify as Jews. Thus, one of the great ironies of the liberty offered to the Jewish people by democratic secular societies is the freedom to leave Judaism as well as to affirm it.

Jewish feminism

In contrast to the option of leaving Judaism, some feminists are coming back to religious observance, but not in the traditional mold, which they regard as patriarchal and sexist. Since the mid-twentieth century, women have taken an active role in claiming their rights to full religious participation. They are also redefining Judaism from a feminist perspective. Part of this effort involves trying to reconstruct the history of significant biblical women, for the Torah was written down by men who devoted far more space to the doings of men than of women. There are hints, for instance, that there were powerful prophetesses, such as Miriam and Huldah, but little information is given about them. There have also been post-biblical women scholars, writers, and teachers, women who supported synagogues and Jewish publications from their earnings as business-women, and women who were active in social reform, and their stories and names are being uncovered.

In the past half-century, Jewish feminists have also tackled liturgical issues, changing language to gender-neutral and gender-inclusive terms for worshipers and for God. The Hebrew scriptures describe God in both masculine and feminine terms, validating translations from the Hebrew that use gender-neutral language. There was initial resistance and even shock over feminists' attempts to replace references to God as "He" or "King." But decades after these initial attempts, Rabbi Karyn D. Kedar proposes:

> As Jewish feminists, the greatest service we can give is to call upon the poets of our generation to teach us once again that metaphor is symbolic, that God is beyond reach and can only be understood in whispers of meaning through images, and in pictures that are diverse and rich. God is "like" father and "like" mother. God is "like" king and "like" the womb. Above all, God is none of these. And beyond the metaphor of gender, God is my light, Adonai ori (Psalms 27:1), and God is wind, ruach Elohim merachefet (Genesis 1:2), and God is a silent whisper, kol damma daka (1 Kings 19:12), and God is the shadow beneath the wings, b'tzel kanfefecha (Psalms 63:8).[52]

As a result of feminist efforts, gender-neutral liturgy and women's participation in synagogue worship have become quite common in contemporary Judaism. In Reform, Conservative, and Reconstructionist synagogues, women are counted in the minyan and called up to recite blessings and read from the Torah. Women make up large proportions of the student populations in rabbinical seminaries; women rabbis are no longer the exception to the rule in most Jewish settings. Women have also been invested as cantors who lead the prayer service, and installed as presidents of synagogues as well as heads of philanthropical organizations. Many liberal congregations use prayer books with gender-neutral language. Many couples are making egalitarian commitments to each other in their wedding vows, as in this contemporary sample:

> In the spirit of Jewish tradition, I will be your loving friend as you are mine. …
> I will respect you and the divine image within you. May our hearts be united
> forever in faith and hope. Let our home be built on Torah and loving-kindness,
> rich in wisdom and reverence. May we always keep these words in our hearts
> as a symbol of our eternal commitment to each other: I am my beloved's and my
> beloved is mine.[53]

Reform and Conservative denominations in the United States now allow their rabbis to officiate at same-sex weddings. Even in Orthodox congregations, the Jewish Orthodox Feminist Alliance is serving as a resource "for a community constantly balancing tradition and modernity, … guided by the principle that *halakhic* Judaism offers many opportunities for observant Jewish women to enhance their ritual observance and to increase their participation in communal leadership."[54] Yeshivat Maharat in New York is now training Orthodox women in Jewish law and spirituality so that they can serve as legal and spiritual authorities.

Having achieved considerable success in bringing about these changes, Jewish feminists are now expanding their perspective to consider global problems such as the threats of terrorist violence and ecological disaster. Since solutions to such problems will require a change in human thinking, some Jewish feminists have turned to the ongoing process of Midrash—interpretation of the deeper meanings of traditional texts. Rabbi Tirzah Firestone reports:

Worship at the Western Wall in Jerusalem is divided by gender, and only on the men's side are groups permitted to gather in worship, using ritual Torah scrolls. The activist group Women of the Wall protests this inequity by holding services in the women's section each month to celebrate Rosh Hodesh, a holiday traditionally associated with women's religious devotion.

> *I am a teacher of Jewish texts—Tanach, Chasidut, Zohar—that have a unique power to engage and call us into discovery and wisdom. Rarely have I witnessed more eagerness and excitement than when I invite women to enter the text itself. … With more aplomb than ever before, today's women are entering the stories and changing them, breaking them open to reveal the places of both wounds and opportunity. They are seizing the chance to transform the stories that guide our lives, and in so doing, they are rewriting the maps that determine the paths we will travel.[55]*

An example of new feminist Midrash revolves around the inter-woven stories of Sarah and Hagar, the mothers of the sons of Abraham who are said to be the founders of Judaism and Islam respectively. Rabbi Firestone explains:

> *The story of Hagar and Sarah and their sons lies deep in our collective unconscious and affects our beliefs about the entrenched relationship with our Arab cousins. To change the rigid story lines requires that we first collectively re-vision and humanize the story of these two women. Many female midrashists have taken up the task of plumbing their relationship. … [In a musical exploration by Linda Hirschhorn] they understand that to survive they must finally speak each other's name, hear each other's prayers, share each other's dream of a homeland. I have witnessed hundreds of people weeping as they hear this musical midrash, the reaching out in longing and regret of Sarah and Hagar becoming their own, the pain of the centuries and the possibility for healing alive, palpable, urgent.[56]*

There is also a feminist critique of women's position in the state of Israel. Feminists among the early Zionist settlers envisioned a society in which men and women would work side by side and each apply their full capabilities to the creation of a new society. Nevertheless, traditional sexual divisions of labor were perpetuated, especially once the Orthodox parties took a major role in the formation and governance of the state. However, some progress toward women's equality and empowerment is occurring within all denominations in Israel, including Orthodoxy. In 2013, the Jerusalem District Court upheld the right of Women of the Wall to wear prayer shawls and *tefillin* and read from the Torah at the Western Wall, despite great protests from Ultra-Orthodox Jews.

LGBT Jews

In all cultures and religions, same-sex orientations have always existed. But biblical teachings restrict sexual expression to heterosexual marriage, with emphasis on procreation. Many modern Jews ignored most of the traditional

Inclusiveness

Judaism has developed in many directions, all still linked to its ancient origins. Contemporary practice of Judaism ranges from Ultra-Orthodox to liberal manifestations. Many of these adaptations have developed to include modern understandings of human rights, such as welcoming people of various sexual orientations. Sarah Meytin was ordained as a rabbi in 2004, has worked as Assistant Director of the Jewish Community Relations Council of Greater Washington and Assistant Director of a Jewish preschool program, leads workshops for preschool teachers on welcoming gender non-conforming children, and founded Rockville Open House in 2009 as a safe space for LGBTQ* Jewish teenagers and their allies. In 2003 she and Rachel Meytin married each other in a Jewish wedding ceremony, complete with all their friends and family. Rachel works with Jewish teenagers and professionals through BBYO, an international youth movement which for almost one hundred years has been offering meaningful Jewish experiences for hundreds of thousands of Jewish teenagers. They have two children, Coby and Ruthie.

Sarah explains the process by which she became so active in the Jewish community:

I grew up in a family that belonged to a Reform synagogue and sent me to "Sunday school" from the time I was in kindergarten. I hated it. My family observed Passover and the High Holy Days as family gathering days; they were not otherwise particularly religious. I had no interest in Judaism or being part of the Jewish community. When I was in ninth grade, I agreed to go to a Jewish youth group sleepover with a friend. I went to support her, not because I was interested. But I had so much fun that I immediately

got more involved. A year later, I had a love of Judaism and Jewish community, and knew I wanted Judaism to be central in whatever work I did later in life. I was pretty sure I didn't want to be a congregational rabbi, so I went to graduate school in Social Work while I figured out what would come next. The intersection of Judaism and social justice was what turned me on, and that led me to rabbinic school.

I have always felt very blessed to have a wonderful, supportive, loving family, but witnessed friends when I was growing up who were not so lucky. I always knew I wanted to help children to feel that same love, support, and affirmation that I had. Starting Rockville Open House was part of trying to 'give back' and give other kids this kind of acceptance and affirmation. As a rabbi, and a queer-identified adult, I am very aware of how religion has been, and continues to be, one of the major sources of intolerance and pain inflicted on queer kids. It is important to me that these teens know there is a space for them in the Jewish community—and a way for them to affirm both their queer and their Jewish identities without their feeling that they have to be in conflict.

The Jewish roots of this work are plentiful: 1) All people are made in God's image. 2) God made humankind male and female in one. 3) Another's dignity should be as precious to us as our own. 4) Sexuality existed, according to Judaism, in the Garden of Eden. Sex is not the result of a "fall" or "sin," and is a natural, healthy part of who we are as adults/in adult relationships. 5) There are at least six "gender" categories mentioned in the Talmud. 6) Loving others as we love ourselves. 7) Human dignity is so important that it can even supersede a negative biblical commandment. I could go on listing all of the "justice"

---

*"Q" is for "queer," a previously pejorative term reappropriated by some as a positive label for unspecified non-heterosexual gender identity.

texts and the Rabbinic "fixes" over the millennia that prove that when there is a Rabbinic will, there is always a halakhic *way. It's important to me that these kids know the tradition can and does see them, and affirms them, even if there will always remain pockets of the community that may never accept them. For the preschoolers, it's about wanting to give the young kids everything they need to grow up to be the best themselves they can be, for all the same reasons.*[57]

Rachel also speaks of the importance of helping teenagers find and live by their truths:

The teen years are full of mixed signals, testing out different roles, discarding all sorts of identities, and seeing how the different parts of ourselves—the inside ones and the outside ones—might fit together. … Then when teens are ready to tackle their community's largest issues, we can help them focus on issues that align most closely with their understanding of Judaism's commitment to social justice. We can make explicit to teens the increased power that their individual selves have when they come together in community, to serve and support each other.[58]

Rachel grew up in a family that quietly embraced Judaism in a small town, and she recalls even liking attending Hebrew school. Still, she didn't anticipate a professional career as a Jewish educator, but stumbled upon it accidentally.

I was a substitute Sunday school teacher for a few weeks and realized I really enjoyed both teaching and showing my students the positive challenges that Judaism offers. Judaism isn't passive; you can't just believe, you have to do. You have to argue and debate the text to really understand it. You have to take responsibility. I appreciate those aspects of Judaism and love sharing them with others.

Sarah and Rachel have created a home life that is infused with Judaism and Jewish values. They frame family decisions and rules in Jewish language and are trying to make sure their children have a positive relationship with Judaism. By weaving Judaism and its social action values into daily life, they're hoping to set up Coby and Ruthie to be social-change agents with strong Jewish values.

Rachel (left) and Sarah (right) Meytin with their children.

restrictions on sexuality outside of marriage, but same-sex relationships were nonetheless usually hidden to avoid social ostracism. Heterosexuality was the assumed norm. Other orientations remained largely invisible. During the twentieth century, this situation began to change in many Jewish communities in the United States as the feminist movement, gay liberation movement, and Jewish renewal developed and began to converge. LGBT Jews found social support groups and courage to come out about their sexual orientations. Orthodoxy has been the last bastion of traditional sexual norms. Media portrayals such as the award-winning 2001 documentary "Trembling Before G-d" poignantly brought to public awareness the dilemmas of Orthodox LGBT Jews who were struggling to reconcile their sexual and religious identities. Jewish communities across the board have now become more inclusive and welcoming of LGBT Jews. The Reconstructionist movement had welcomed LGBT Jews even earlier. Gay marriage is now accepted in Reconstructionist, Reform, and Conservative Judaism (with some limitations), and gay rabbis are found in all the denominations, though rare and not accepted in many Orthodox circles.

Many new inclusive rituals and liturgies have been created for lesbian, gay, and transgender Jews. Feminist scholar Susannah Heschel, for instance, has added an orange to the Passover Seder plate to signify solidarity with all those who felt marginalized by traditional Judaism, including widows as well as lesbians and gay men. She explains that it symbolizes:

> the fruitfulness for all Jews when lesbians and gay men are contributing and active members of Jewish life. In addition, each orange segment had a few seeds that had to be spit out—a gesture of spitting out, repudiating the homophobia that poisons too many Jews.[59]

Jewish renewal

Both men and women from varied backgrounds are being attracted to newly revitalized expressions of Jewish spirituality, and conversions to Judaism seem to be increasing. Many young adults whose parents were nonobservant Jews are now coming back to their roots and taking great interest in the traditions. Many Jewish people have become *baal teshuvah*—that is, taking on *halakhic* responsibilities with regard to dietary practice, Sabbaths, holidays, and other aspects of daily life.

In Russia, where under Stalin Jews had been so persecuted that only a few rabbis remained in all of Russia, there are now Jewish seminaries and universities, schools, and kindergartens. In 2011, eighty Jewish and Muslim leaders from throughout Russia and Ukraine held a conference entitled "Muslims and Jews United Against Hatred and Extremism" to jointly counteract extremism, discrimination, and abuse, whether in the form of anti-Semitism or Islamophobia.

Contemporary Jewish renewal is an active search for personal meaning in the ancient rituals and scriptures, and the creation of new rituals for our times. The Jewish Renewal Movement provides many Jewish people with hands-on engagement with their tradition, often in an egalitarian and ecologically sensitive setting. Many organizations are welcoming Jews to creative, fun, and meaningful ways of learning about Jewish traditions, including special workshops and retreats for post-Bar and Bat Mitzvah teenagers and college students. Even the ritual bath for women—*mikveh*—is now carried on in pleasant spaces, surrounded by community-building and celebratory activities.

In addition to outreach by Reform and Conservative congregations to formerly secular Jews, Lubavich Hasidism and the newer Aish HaTorah movement have had great impacts on Jewish return to *halakhic* observance. Aish HaTorah is an Orthodox organization that encourages Jewish people to visit Israel and become connected to the land and its history. Its *yeshiva* in Jerusalem teaches the Torah as wisdom to live by, for a more successful and happy life. Jerusalem is also home to organizations that are pushing the boundaries of Orthodox

Celebrations of life-cycle events, such as this naming ceremony for a girl child, are bringing many Jews back to Jewish practice.

religious observance, such as Shira Hadasha ("a new song"), which offers egalitarian worship jointly conducted by women and men without a rabbi. There are also numerous small *havurot*, communities of "post-denominational" Jews who are not affiliated with any formal group but get together on a regular basis to worship and celebrate the traditions. They favor a democratic organization and personal experience, choosing what parts of the traditions to use and how. Some incorporate study groups, continuing the ancient intellectual tradition of grappling with the ethical, philosophical, and spiritual meanings of the texts. Some are bringing fresh ideas to traditional celebrations, so that they are actively transformational rather than simply matters of habit.

From highly conservative to highly liberal quarters, there are now many attempts to renew the ancient messianic ideal of Judaism, that by its practice the world might be healed.

> *From a Jewish point of view, we are living in the worst of all possible worlds, in which there is still hope.*
>
> *Rabbi Adin Steinsaltz*[60]

Key terms

anti-Semitism A nineteenth-century term referring to expressions of hatred toward and fear of Jews, not to "Semites" (including Arabs and other people) more generally.

apocalypse A narrative account of the predetermined history of humanity, often with emphasis on its dramatic final end in the present day.

Ashkenazim An ethnic grouping of the Jews with origins in Italy, France, and Germany.

diaspora The dispersal of the Jews after the Babylonian exile.

ghetto An urban area occupied by those rejected by a society, such as quarters for Jews in some European cities.

haggadah The nonlegal part of the Talmud and Midrash; **Haggadah**, the Seder text.

halakhah Jewish legal decision and the parts of the Talmud dealing with laws.

Hasidism Ecstatic Jewish piety, dating from eighteenth-century Poland.

Kabbalah The Jewish mystical tradition.

kosher Ritually acceptable according to Jewish tradition. Applied predominantly to food, but also to ritual objects and practices.

Messiah The "anointed," the expected king and deliverer of the Jews; a term later applied by Christians to Jesus.

Midrash "Seeking," "searching," a reference to rabbinic biblical interpretation and the larger rabbinic attitude toward scriptural tradition.

minyan The quorum of ten adult Jews (traditionally, adult men) required for the recitation of certain communal prayers.

mitzvah (plural: **mitzvot**) In Judaism, a divine commandment or sacred deed in fulfillment of a commandment.

oral Torah The rabbinic tradition, including the Mishnan, Talmud, and other texts, whose origins the rabbis assign to the covenant at Mount Sinai.

Orthodox Judaism A modern Jewish movement that emphasizes traditional rabbinic authority and *halakhah*.

Pentateuch The five books of Moses; the first section of the three-part Jewish Bible.

rabbi Teacher; an ordained religious authority, who may serve as a teacher, a legal decision-maker, or the spiritual leader of a Jewish congregation.

Reform or **Liberal Judaism** A modern Jewish movement whose emphasis is on the relevance of Judaism for present and future Jews, rather than the *halakhic* tradition.

Sabbath The day of the week set aside for rest and worship; in Judaism running from sunset Friday night to sunset Saturday night.

Sephardim An ethnic grouping of the Jews with origins in Spain and North Africa.

Shekhinah The presence of God in the world, especially emphasized in Jewish mystical circles.

synagogue Meeting place for Jewish study and worship.

Talmud One of two collections of Jewish law and tradition, compiled in the fifth century CE in Palestine and the sixth century CE in Babylonia.

Tanakh The Jewish Bible, made up of the Torah, Nevi'im (Prophets), and Kethuvim (Writings).

Torah "Law" or "teaching." The first five books of the Jewish Bible. Can also refer to Jewish teaching or tradition more generally.

Zionism Movement dedicated to the establishment of a politically viable, internationally recognized Jewish state in the biblical land of Israel.

Suggested reading

Baskin, Judith R., ed., *Jewish Women in Historical Perspective*, Detroit: Wayne State University Press, second edition, 1998. Fifteen pioneering essays by modern scholars explore Jewish women and their activities in a variety of times and places.

Berger, Alan L., ed., *Judaism in the Modern World*, New York: New York University Press, 1994. Articles by leading contemporary Jewish scholars on facets of the changing identities and paradoxes of modern Jewry.

Berlin, Adele, with Maxine Grossman, eds, The Oxford Dictionary of the Jewish Religion, New York: Oxford University Press, 2011. Concise discussion of major events, personalities, practices, and cultural formations within Jewish religious history.

Cardin, Rabbi Nina Beth, *The Tapestry of Jewish Time*, Springfield, New Jersey: Behrman House, 2000. Material about Jewish festivals and life-cycle celebrations.

Encyclopedia Judaica, New York: Macmillan Press, 2006. The authoritative, multivolume reference on all aspects of Judaism, as seen from a broad spectrum of points of view.

Freedman, Samuel G., *Jew vs. Jew: The Struggle for the Soul of American Jewry*, New York: Simon and Schuster, 2000. An exploration of religious tensions in contemporary American Jewish communities, with important speculation on the future of American Judaism.

Goldstein, Rabbi Elyse, ed., *New Jewish Feminism: Probing the Past, Forging the Future*, Woodstock, Vermont: Jewish Lights Publishing, 2009. An anthology of contemporary feminist writings from many different denominations, assessing the past and future of Jewish feminist theology, rituals, Torah interpretation, religious leadership, and gender, age, and social justice issues.

Goldstein, Rabbi Elyse, ed., *The Women's Torah Commentary: New Insights from Women Rabbis on the 54 Weekly Torah Portions*, Woodstock, Vermont: Jewish Lights Publishing, 2000. Scholarship and Midrash about portions of the Five Books of Moses drawing on women's personal perspectives.

Greenburg, Blu, *On Women and Judaism: A View from Tradition*, Philadelphia: The Jewish Publication Society of America, 1998. An intimate personal attempt to reconcile Jewish feminism and the practice of Orthodox Judaism.

Grossman, Susan and Rivka Haut, eds, *Daughters of the King: Women and the Synagogue*, Philadelphia: Jewish Publication Society, 1992. An excellent anthology of history, *halakhah*, and contemporary testimonies concerning women and synagogue participation.

Henry, Sondra and Emily Taitz, *Written out of History: Our Jewish Foremothers*, New York: Biblio Press, 1990. The stories of significant Jewish women rediscovered and placed within their historical context.

Heschel, Abraham J., compiled by Fritz A. Rothschild, *Between God and Man: An Interpretation of Judaism*, New York: The Free Press, 1959. An intimate exploration of the relevance of traditional Judaism for today's world, by a great twentieth-century theologian.

Holtz, Barry, *Back to the Sources*, New York: Schocken Books, 1984. Excellent introduction to classical Jewish religious texts. Each chapter takes the reader through a step-by-step approach on how to read representative selections of the Bible, Talmud, Midrash, the Zohar, liturgical texts, and others.

Jacobs, Jill, *Where Justice Dwells: A Hands-On Guide to Doing Social Justice in Your Jewish Community*, Woodstock, Vermont: Jewish Lights Publishing, 2011. Philosophical engagement with Jewish theology and pragmatic attention to the practice of working for social justice in contemporary American Jewish communities.

Kamenetz, Rodger, *The Jew in the Lotus: A Poet's Rediscovery of Jewish Identity in Buddhist India*, San Francisco: HarperSanFrancisco, 1994. The visit of a diverse group of Jewish leaders to the Dalai Lama provides the opportunity to explore fundamental questions of contemporary Jewish identity and community.

Lerner, Michael, *Jewish Renewal: A Path to Healing and Transformation*, New York: HarperCollins, 1994. Profound and moving analyses of why Jews left Judaism and the revitalization that is drawing them back to faith.

Levine, Hillel, *Economic Origins of Antisemitism: Poland and its Jews in the Early Modern Period*, New Haven: Yale University Press, 1991. Brilliant insights into the relationships between anti-Semitic trends and failed modernization in Poland when it was home to half of the world's Jews.

Liebman, Charles S., *Religion, Democracy and Israeli Society*, The Netherlands: Harwood Academic Publishers, 1997. A case study of Israel with reference to the problems of trying to manifest the vision of a religious state, and the problems raised by religious fundamentalism in a democratic society.

Mendes-Flohr, Paul and Jehuda Reinharz, *The Jew in the Modern World: A Documentary History*, second edition, New York and Oxford: Oxford University Press, 1995. A wealth of historical documents from the seventeenth to the twentieth centuries tracing the many facets of Judaism as it encountered modernity.

Ochs, Vanessa L., *Inventing Jewish Ritual*, Philadelphia: Jewish Publication Society, 2007. Exploration of new forms of ritual appearing in popular culture in twenty-first century America.

Plaskow, Judith, *Standing Again at Sinai: Judaism from a Feminist Perspective*, San Francisco: HarperSanFrancisco, 1991. Studies of all aspects of Jewish feminism, including the reconstruction of women's history, women in Israel, gender-equal God-language, sexuality in feminist religious context, and women's role in the repair of the world.

Ravitzky, Aviezer, *Messianism, Zionism, and Jewish Religious Radicalism*, Chicago: University of Chicago Press, 1996. Extensive analysis of varying Orthodox religious responses to Jewish statehood in Israel.

Robinson, George, *Essential Judaism*, New York: Pocket Books, 2000. Concise guide to Jewish beliefs, customs, and rituals.

Sarna, Jonathan D., *American Judaism*, New Haven: Yale University Press, 2004. Detailed history of the development of Judaism in the United States as the largest Jewish community in the world.

Schachter-Shalomi, Zalman, with Donald Gropman, *The First Step: A Guide for the New Jewish Spirit*, New York: Bantam Books, 1983. A modern explanation of the essence of Judaism, of special interest to nonobservant Jews who want to find their way back into the faith.

Schiffman, Lawrence H., *Reclaiming the Dead Sea Scrolls: Their True Meaning for Judaism and Christianity*, New York: Doubleday, 1995. Re-examination of the Dead Sea Scrolls as clues to Jewish history.

Scholem, Gershom G., *Major Trends in Jewish Mysticism*, New York: Schocken Books, 1974.The classic scholarly work on the development of mystical Judaism.

Shneer, David and Caryn Aviv, eds, *Queer Jews*, New York: Routledge, 2002. First-person discussions of Jewish identity across a spectrum of LGBT perspectives.

Strassfeld, Michael, *A Book of life: Embracing Judaism as a Spiritual Practice*, Woodstock, Vermont: Jewish Lights Publishing, 2002. Jewish life presented as everyday possibilities for connecting with the sacred.

Tanakh: The Holy Scriptures, The New JPS Translation according to the Traditional Hebrew Text, Philadelphia: The Jewish Publication Society, 1988. The preferred translation of the Hebrew scriptures, in graceful and spiritually sensitive modern English.

Umansky, Ellen M. and Dianne Ashton, *Four Centuries of Jewish Women's Spirituality: A Sourcebook*, Boston: Beacon Press, 1992. Firsthand accounts of the spiritual lives of a great variety of Jewish women.

Wiesel, Elie, *Night*, New York: Bantam, 1960. Short, searing memoir of a teenage boy's Holocaust experience.

8.1   Contrast biblical Judaism with rabbinic Judaism

Jewish sense of religious history begins with the stories recounted in the Hebrew Bible or Tanakh, starting with the creation of the world by a supreme deity, or God, and progressing through the patriarchs and matriarchs, Moses, and the prophets, who spoke with God and instructed the people according to God's commandments. Jews were taught that they had a special covenantal relationship with God, tested through many times of trial.

Jewish history does not end where the stories of the Tanakh end, about the second century BCE. After the holy center of Judaism, the Temple of Jerusalem, was conquered and destroyed by the Romans in 70 CE, new forms of Judaism developed under the leadership of the rabbinic movement. Centers of rabbinic Judaism were found in synagogues and study houses, where people worshiped communally, prayed directly to God, and studied the Torah. The rabbis interpreted the Hebrew Scriptures through a process of study known as Midrash, and they formulated an oral law, which was compiled in the Talmud by the sixth century CE.

8.2   Examine the role the European Enlightenment played in the development of Judaism

In the late eighteenth and nineteenth centuries the Enlightenment provided new opportunities and better conditions for the Jews in western Europe. Here restrictions on Jews began to decrease thanks to the more rational atmosphere of tolerance, reason, and material progress. The French Revolution (1789–99) brought equality for the masses, including Jews living in France, and this trend spread to other European nations.

Inspired by Enlightenment views and liberated from the social restrictions that had kept them isolated as a religious community, some European Jews also embarked on a path of secularization and acculturation—called the Jewish Enlightenment (or Haskalah)—that has brought a sea change in Judaism in the modern world. Talmud study was de-emphasized in favor of secular knowledge and practical training that would help integrate Jews into their surrounding cultures. Opponents of these trends warned that in adapting to the surrounding culture, Jews would inevitably cease to observe their traditional rituals. In the face of this threat to the integrity of their received religious traditions, some scholars and rabbis encouraged Jews not only to live by *halakhah* (Jewish legal decision) but also to segregate themselves from non-Jewish secular culture. This position led to what came to be called Orthodox Judaism.

8.3   Identify the key tenets of the Jewish faith

Jewish spiritual understanding has changed repeatedly throughout history and it is difficult to outline the tenets of the Jewish faith. There are, however, certain major themes that can be extracted from the vast history and literature of Judaism.

The central Jewish belief is monotheism—the belief that only one God is real, and all other gods are false—and the essential commandment to humans is to love God. Jews also believe that God gave humans free will, involving them in the responsibility for the world's condition and their own. Traditional Jews give thanks that in the written and oral Torah God has revealed the laws (commandments, or mitzvot) by which they can be faithful to the divine will and establish a Kingdom of God on earth, in which all creatures can live in peace and fellowship.

8.4   Summarize the main sacred practices

In addition to daily scriptural study, Jews are urged to remember God in all aspects of life, through prayer and observance of the commandments, and to give thanks continually. For traditional observant Jews, prayers are recited on waking and at bedtime. Three prayer services are chanted daily in a synagogue by men if there is a minyan (quorum of ten).

Boys are ritually circumcised in the *brit milah* ceremony when they are eight days old. It is customary to recognize coming of age in the ceremony of Bar Mitzvah (at the age of thirteen for Jewish boys) and Bat Mitzvah (at the age of twelve for girls, in non-Orthodox and even some Orthodox Jewish communities).

What Jews eat is of cosmic significance, and the only kosher (ritually acceptable) meats are those from warmblooded animals with cloven hoofs that chew their cud. Meat is kosher only if it has been butchered in the traditional way. Meat and milk cannot be eaten together.

The Jewish Sabbath is observed as an eternal sign of the covenant between the Jews and God. The Sabbath runs from sunset Friday night to sunset Saturday night. A special Friday-night dinner may be served in addition to, or instead of, going to a service. The Saturday morning service incorporates public and private prayers, singing, and the reading of passages from the Torah scrolls.

8.5   Describe the High Holy Days and key festivals in the Jewish calendar

Judaism follows an ancient lunar calendar of annual holidays and memorials linked to special events in history. The spiritual year begins with the High Holy Days of Rosh Hashanah (New Year's Day), a time of spiritual renewal in remembrance of the original creation of the world, and Yom Kippur, in which the sacred covenant with God is renewed in a spirit of atonement and cleansing.

Sukkot is a harvest festival in fall and the day after it is Simhat Torah, ending the yearly cycle of Torah readings. Near the winter solstice comes Hanukkah, the Feast of Dedication. Each night for eight nights, another candle is lit on a special candle holder. On the full moon of the month before spring comes Purim which commemorates the legend of Esther. Purim is a boisterous reading of the book of Esther and is also celebrated with gifts of money to the poor and gifts of food to friends and family. The next major festival is Pesach, or Passover, which celebrates the liberation from bondage in Egypt and the springtime advent of new life. The beginning of Pesach is still marked by a Seder dinner, with the eating of unleavened bread to remember the urgency of the departure.

8.6 Differentiate between the major branches of contemporary Judaism

Orthodox Jews stand by the Torah as the revealed word of God and the Talmud as the legitimate oral law. They feel that they are bound by the traditional rabbinical *halakhah* as a way of achieving closeness to God. However, within this framework there are great individual differences, with no central authority figure or governing body. The Orthodox branches also differ greatly in their tolerance for other Jewish groups and in their degree of accommodation of the surrounding secular environment.

The Reform (or Liberal) movement began in the nineteenth-century as a way of modernizing the religion and making it an evolving, open-ended religion rather than one fixed forever by the Torah. In addition to changes to the Sabbath service and the liturgy, men and women were also allowed to sit together in the synagogue. *Halakhic* observances were re-evaluated for their relevance to modern needs. Rather than exclusivism, Reform rabbis cultivate a sense of the universalism of Jewish values.

Conservative Judaism, which has its roots in mid-nineteenth century Germany, seeks to conserve traditional Jewish laws and practices while also using modern means of historical scholarship, sponsoring critical studies of Jewish texts from all periods. Conservative Jews believe that Jews have always searched and added to their laws, liturgy, Midrash, and beliefs to keep them relevant and meaningful in changing times. Conservative women have long served as cantors and have been ordained as rabbis since 1985.

Reconstructionism was founded in the twentieth century by Rabbi Mordecai Kaplan, an influential American thinker. He held that the Enlightenment had changed everything and that strong measures were needed to preserve Judaism in the face of rationalism. He defined Judaism as an "evolving religious civilization."

In addition to those who are affiliated with a religious movement, there are many Jews who identify themselves as secular Jews, affirming their Jewish origins and maintaining various Jewish cultural traditions while eschewing religious practice.

CHAPTER 9

CHRISTIANITY

"What did it mean to 'love my neighbor as myself'?" David Vandiver[1]

9.1 Discuss the four gospels on which Christian beliefs about the life and teachings of Jesus are founded

9.2 Outline the major events in the life of Jesus as described in the gospels

9.3 Discuss the significance of Paul in the early Christian Church

9.4 Summarize the division between the Eastern and Western Churches in the Middle Ages

9.5 Identify the major reforms of the Protestant and Roman Catholic Reformations

9.6 Describe the distinctive features of Orthodox spirituality

9.7 Summarize the central beliefs in contemporary Christianity

9.8 Define "sacrament" and outline the seven sacraments observed by the Roman Catholic and Eastern Orthodox Churches

9.9 Differentiate between evangelicalism and Spirit-oriented movements

Christianity is a religion based on the life, teachings, death, and resurrection of Jesus. He was born as a Jew about 2,000 years ago in Roman-occupied Palestine. He taught for fewer than three years and was executed by the Roman government on charges of sedition. Nothing was written about him at the time although some years after his death, attempts were made to record what he had said and done. Yet his birth is now celebrated around the world and since the sixth century has been used as the major point from which public time is measured, even by non-Christians. The religion centered around him has more followers than any other.

In studying Christianity we will first examine what is known or inferred about the life and teachings of Jesus. We will then follow the evolution of the religion as it spread to all continents and became theologically and liturgically more complex. This process continues in the present, in which there are not one but many different versions of Christianity.

We do not know what Jesus, the founder of the world's largest religion, looked like. Rembrandt used a young European Jewish man as his model for this sensitive "portrait" of Jesus.

The Christian Bible

On which four gospels are Christian beliefs about the life and teachings of Jesus founded?

There is very little historical proof of the life of Jesus. More is known about the milieu in which he lived. He was born as a Jew in the land of Israel, where the king of the Judaeans, Herod "the Great," was a half-Jew who had been installed with Roman backing. Matters of Torah interpretation were under dispute between the Sadducees and Pharisees, while a third party, the Essenes, seem to have rejected the priesthood as corrupt and engaged in ascetic practices while awaiting divine intervention. Expectations of a messiah who would save the people from foreign oppression were running high. Many **apocalyptic** texts were circulating that announced the imminent end of the present age, with evil giving way to a reign of righteousness. Unrest over increased taxes and economic difficulties under Roman rule was also brewing, and would eventually spawn various urban terrorist movements and armed resistance in the countryside. By contrast, the Jesus movement did not advocate violence or political activism.

Many Christians feel that the true story of Jesus can be found in the Bible. Traditionally, the holy scriptures have been reverently regarded as the divinely inspired Word of God. Furthermore, in Eastern Orthodox Christianity, "the Gospel is not just Holy Scripture but also a symbol of Divine Wisdom and an image of Christ Himself."[2] Bibles used by various Christian groups are not uniform. All use a version of the Hebrew Bible called the **Old Testament**, which is organized differently from the Bible of the Jews, plus the twenty-seven books of the **New Testament** written after Jesus' earthly mission. Some Bibles also include noncanonical Jewish texts called the Apocrypha or Deuterocanonical books, such as "The Wisdom of Solomon," from the long-standing "wisdom tradition" in which a sage imparts wise teachings about life.

Given the textual complexity of the Bible, Christians have attempted to clarify what Jesus taught and how he lived, so that people might truly follow him. Differing concepts of Jesus have led to vast diversity within Christianity.

The field of theological study that attempts to interpret scripture is called **hermeneutics**. In the late second and early third centuries CE, Christian thinkers developed two highly different approaches to biblical hermeneutics. One of these stressed the literal meanings of the texts; the other looked for allegorical rather than literal meanings. Origen, an Egyptian theologian (*c.* 185–254 CE) who was a major proponent of the allegorical method, gave this example from the Book of Genesis:

> *When God is said to "walk in the paradise in the cool of the day" and Adam to hide himself behind a tree, I do not think anyone will doubt that these are figurative expressions which indicate certain mysteries through a semblance of history and not through actual events (Gen. 3:8).*[3]

During the eighteenth century, critical study of the Bible from a strictly historical point of view began in western Europe. This approach, now accepted by many Protestants, Catholics, and some Orthodox, is based on the literary method of interpreting ancient writings in their historical context, with their intended audience and desired effect taken into account. In the nineteenth and twentieth centuries, emphasis shifted to the history of the biblical texts and to questions such as how the biblical message is conveyed through the medium of language.

Christian beliefs about the life and teachings of Jesus are especially founded on biblical texts, particularly the first four books of the New Testament, which are called the **gospels** ("good news"). On the whole, they seem to have been originally written about forty to sixty years after Jesus' death. They are based on the oral transmission of the stories and discourses, which may have been influenced by the growing split between Christians and Jews. The documents, thought to be pseudonymous, are given the names of Jesus' followers Matthew and John, and of the apostle Paul's companions Mark and Luke. The gospels were first written down in Greek and perhaps Aramaic, the everyday language that Jesus spoke, and then copied and translated in many different ways over the centuries. They offer a composite picture of Jesus as seen through the eyes of the Christian community.

Three of the gospels, Matthew, Mark, and Luke, are so similar that they are called the **synoptic** gospels, referring to the fact that they can be "seen together" as presenting rather similar views of Jesus' career, though they are organized somewhat differently. The Gospel of John, traditionally attributed to "the disciple Jesus loved," is of a very different nature from the other three. It concerns itself less with following the life of Jesus than with confirming Jesus' Messiahship. It is also more mystical and devotional in nature than the synoptic gospels.

> *The light shines on in the dark, and the darkness has never mastered it.*
>
> *The Gospel of John 1:5*

Other gospels circulating in the early Christian Church were not included in the canon of the New Testament. They include magical stories of Jesus' infancy, such as an account of his making clay birds and then bringing them to life. The Gospel of Thomas, one of the long-hidden manuscripts discovered in 1945 in a grave near Nag Hammadi, Egypt, is of particular interest. It contains many wise sayings of Jesus in common with the other gospels but also others that were unknown until the Nag Hammadi discovery, such as this mystical statement:

> *Jesus said:*
> *I am the Light that is above them all.*
> *I am the All,*
> *The All came forth from me*
> *And the All attained to me.*
> *Cleave a (piece of) wood, I am there.*
> *Lift up the stone and you will find Me there.[4]*

The life and teachings of Jesus

What are the major events in the life of Jesus, as described in the gospels?

It is not possible to reconstruct from the gospels a single chronology of Jesus' life nor to account for much of what happened before he began his ministry. Nevertheless, the stories of the New Testament are important to Christians as the foundation of their faith. And after extensive analysis most scholars have concluded on grounds of linguistics and regional history that many of the sayings attributed to Jesus by the gospels may be authentic.

Birth

According to the Christian doctrine of the **incarnation**, Jesus is the divine Son of God who "became flesh" by being conceived and born as a human being. The biblical Book of Colossians states, "In him the whole fullness of deity dwells bodily" (Colossians 2:9).

Most historians think Jesus was probably born a few years before the first year of what is now called the **Common Era**. When sixth-century Christian monks began figuring time in relationship to the life of Jesus, they may have miscalculated slightly. Traditionally, Christians have believed that Jesus was born in Bethlehem. This detail fulfills the rabbinic interpretation of the Old Testament prophecies that the Messiah would be born in Bethlehem, the home of David

Jesus is often pictured as a divine child, born in a humble stable, and forced to flee on a donkey with his parents. (Monastère Bénédictin de Keur Moussa, Senegal, Fuite en Egypte.)

"The Nativity," Jesus' humble birth depicted in a 14th-century fresco by Giotto. (Scrovegni Chapel, Padua, Italy.)

the great king, and in the lineage of David. However, some scholars suggest that Jesus was actually born in or near Nazareth, his own home town in Galilee. This region, whose name meant "Ring of the Gentiles," was not fully Jewish; it was also scorned as somewhat countrified by the rabbinic orthodoxy of Judaea.

According to the gospels, Jesus' mother was Mary, who was a virgin when she conceived him by the Holy Spirit; her husband was Joseph, a carpenter from Bethlehem. Luke states that they had to go to Bethlehem to satisfy a Roman ruling that everyone should travel to their ancestral cities for a census. When they had made the difficult journey there was no room for them in the inn, so the baby was born in a stable among the animals. He was named Jesus, which means "God saves." This well-loved birth legend exemplifies the humility that Jesus taught. According to Luke, those who came to pay their respects were poor shepherds. Matthew tells instead of Magi, sages from "the east," who may have been Zoroastrians, and who brought the Christ child symbolic gifts of gold and frankincense and myrrh, confirming his divine kingship and his adoration by **Gentiles** (non-Jews). Matthew also describes Joseph and Mary's taking the baby Jesus to Egypt for safety, returning to live in Nazareth only after King Herod died.

Preparation

No other stories are told about Jesus' childhood in Nazareth until he was twelve years old, when, according to the Gospel of Luke, he accompanied his parents on their yearly trip to Jerusalem for Passover. Left behind by mistake, he was said to have been discovered by his parents in the Temple discussing the Torah with the rabbis; "all who heard him were amazed at his understanding and his answers." When scolded, he reportedly replied, "Did you not know that I must be in my Father's house?"[5] This story is used to demonstrate his sense of mission even as a boy, his knowledge of Jewish tradition, and the close personal connection between Jesus and God. In later accounts of his prayers, he spoke to God as "Abba," a very familiar Aramaic and Hebrew word for father.

The New Testament is also silent about the years of Jesus' young manhood. What is described, however, is the ministry of John the Baptist, a prophet citing Isaiah's apocalyptic prophecies of the coming Kingdom of God. He was conducting baptism in the Jordan River in preparation for the Kingdom of God.

According to all four gospels, at the age of about thirty Jesus appeared before John to be baptized. John was calling people to repent of their sins and then be spiritually purified and sanctified by immersion in the river. He felt it improper to perform this ceremony for Jesus, whom Christians consider sinless, but Jesus insisted. How can this be interpreted? One explanation is that, for Jesus, this became a ceremony of his consecration to God as the Messiah. The gospel writer reports:

When he came up out of the water, immediately he saw the heavens opened and the Spirit descending upon him like a dove; and a voice came from heaven. "Thou art my beloved Son; with thee I am well pleased."[6]

John the Baptist is said to have baptized Jesus only reluctantly, saying he was unworthy even to fasten Jesus' shoes. When he did so, the Spirit allegedly descended upon Jesus as a dove. (Painting by Esperanza Guevara, Solentiname, Nicaragua.)

Another interpretation is that Jesus' baptism was the occasion for John to announce publicly that the Messiah had arrived, beginning his ministry. A third interpretation is that by requesting baptism Jesus identified himself with sinful humanity. Even though he had no need for repentance and purification, he accepted baptism on behalf of all humans.

After being baptized, Jesus reportedly undertook a forty-day retreat in the desert wilderness, fasting. During his retreat, the gospel writers say he was tempted by Satan to use his spiritual power for secular ends, but he refused.

Ministry

In John's gospel, Jesus' baptism and wilderness sojourn were followed by his gathering of the first disciples, the fisherman Simon (called Peter), Andrew (Peter's brother), James, and John (brother of James), who recognized him as the Messiah. Jesus warned his disciples that they would have to leave all their possessions and human attachments to follow him—to pay more attention to the life of the spirit than to physical comfort and wealth. This call to discipleship continues to be experienced by Christians today. The great German theologian Dietrich Bonhoeffer (1906–1945), who, opposing the Nazis, ultimately gave his life for his beliefs, wrote that to follow Jesus one must leave worldly ties and self-centered thinking behind: "Only the man who is dead to his own will can follow Christ."[7]

Jesus said that it was extremely difficult for the wealthy to enter the kingdom of Heaven. God, the Protector, takes care of physical needs, which are relatively unimportant anyway:

> *Is not life more than food, and the body more than clothing? Look at the birds of the air; they neither sow nor reap nor gather into barns, and yet your heavenly Father feeds them. Are you not of more value than they? And which of you by being anxious can add one cubit to his span of life?*[8]

Jesus taught that his followers should concentrate on laying up spiritual treasures in Heaven, rather than material treasures on earth, which are short-lived. Because God is like a generous parent, those who love God and want to follow the path of righteousness should pray for help, in private: "Ask, and it will be given you; seek, and you will find; knock, and it will be opened to you."[9]

From north to south, the area covered by Jesus during his ministry was no more than 100 miles (160 kilometers). Yet his mission is now worldwide, with more followers than any other religion.

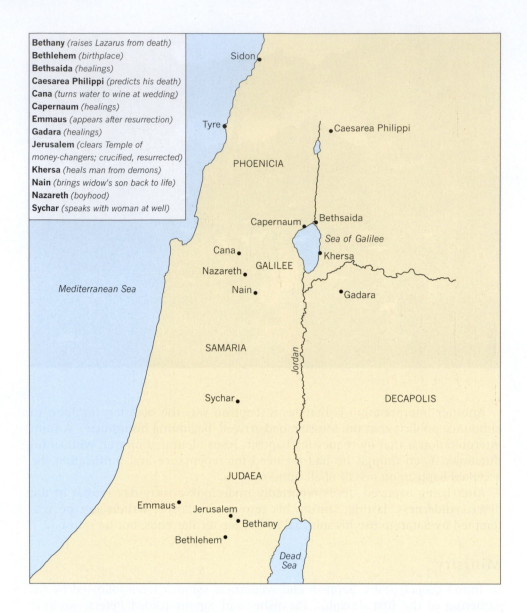

Bethany (raises Lazarus from death)
Bethlehem (birthplace)
Bethsaida (healings)
Caesarea Philippi (predicts his death)
Cana (turns water to wine at wedding)
Capernaum (healings)
Emmaus (appears after resurrection)
Gadara (healings)
Jerusalem (clears Temple of money-changers; crucified, resurrected)
Khersa (heals man from demons)
Nain (brings widow's son back to life)
Nazareth (boyhood)
Sychar (speaks with woman at well)

As Jesus traveled, speaking, he is said to have performed many miracles, such as turning water into wine, healing the sick, restoring the dead to life, walking on water, casting devils out of the possessed, and turning a few loaves and fish into enough food to feed a crowd of thousands, with copious leftovers. Jesus reportedly performed these miracles quietly and compassionately; the gospels interpreted them as signs of the coming Kingdom of God.

The stories of the miracles performed by Jesus have symbolic meanings taken from the entire Jewish and early Christian traditions. In the sharing of the loaves and fishes, for instance, it may have been more than physical bread that Luke was talking about when he said, "and all ate and were satisfied."[10] The people came to Jesus out of spiritual hunger, and he fed them all, profligate with his love. Bread often signified life-giving sustenance. Jesus was later to offer himself as "the bread of life."[11] On another level of interpretation, the story may prefigure the Last Supper of Jesus with his disciples, with both stories alluding to the Jewish tradition of the Great Banquet, the heavenly feast of God, as a symbol of the messianic age. The fish were a symbol of Christ to the early Christians; what he fed them was the indiscriminate gift of himself.

Jesus preached and lived by truly radical ethics. In contrast to the prevailing patriarchal society and extensive proscriptions against impurity, lepers and a bleeding woman touched him and were healed. In his inclusive "table fellowship," he ate with people of all sorts, including those designated as impure by Jewish law in order to preserve Temple purity. These marginalized people

Jesus is said to have brought Lazarus back to life four days after he died and was laid in a tomb. (Fresco by Giotto, Scrovegni Chapel, Padua, Italy.)

included all women because of menstruation and childbirth; most poor and uneducated people because they could not understand or observe the laws of purity; the sick, blind, deformed, and lame; people with skin diseases and secretions; people who earned their living in ways that were regarded as sinful or polluting; and Gentiles, for they were not worshipers of the God of Israel. Feminist scholar Rosemary Radford Ruether explains, "All these would be collectively referred to by the Jesus movement simply as 'the poor,' a group whose deprivation was of many kinds, but united in their 'unholy' status vis-à-vis 'the righteous.'"[12]

In a culture in which the woman's role was strictly circumscribed, Jesus welcomed women as his disciples. Mary Magdalene, Mary the mother of James the younger and Joses, Salome the mother of the disciples James and John, Mary of Bethany, Martha, Susanna, and Joanna are among those mentioned in the gospels. Some of them traveled with Jesus and even helped to support him and his disciples financially, a great departure from orthodox Jewish tradition. In addition, wives of some of the married men among Jesus' first disciples apparently accompanied them as they traveled with Jesus (1 Corinthians 9:5). His was a radically egalitarian vision.

He also extended the application of Jewish laws: "You have heard that it was said to the men of old, 'You shall not kill; and whoever kills shall be liable to judgment.' But I say to you that every one who is angry with his brother shall be liable to judgment."[13] Not only should a man not commit adultery, it is wrong even to look at a woman lustfully. Rather than taking revenge with an eye for an eye, a tooth for a tooth, respond with love. If a person strikes you on one cheek, turn the other cheek to be struck also. If anyone tries to rob you of your coat, give him your cloak as well. And not only should you love your neighbor:

Love your enemies and pray for those who persecute you, so that you may be sons of your Father who is in heaven; for he makes his sun rise on the evil and on the good, and sends rain on the just and on the unjust.[14]

An Interview with David Vandiver

 Born into a devout small-town Southern Baptist family, David Vandiver became the manager of a wilderness camp in the Appalachian Mountains near Washington, D.C., for inner-city African American children whose backgrounds were very different from his own. Now he and his wife and daughters are living in voluntary simplicity in rural Maine, trying to maximize their family time and minimize their impact on the environment. Here he describes the evolution of his understanding and practice of Christianity, and his hope for its future:

The primary values as I grew up were ones of honesty, fairness, and caring for others. The great sins were the ones most affecting families—divorce, adultery, and irresponsible parenting. It was not until much later in my life that the vast scope of values held by Christians in differing places in the world came to my attention. I was not aware, for example, that there were Christians who believed God wanted them to influence politics for justice, work for equal rights for all people, protect the natural environment, or make peace with other nations and peoples of differing faiths. We had no cause to practice tolerance because we were all so similar, except for the African Americans in our town—about twenty percent of the population—who were already Christian and from whom we, as Anglo-Americans, wished to stay separated. I grew up with racism all around me.

Nonetheless, as a high school youth in the early 1970s, I joined my friends in dragging my church into the foray of the U.S. Civil Rights Movement because I couldn't see Jesus as one who would keep any group of people powerless and poor. Christianity was a voice for the downtrodden and oppressed of the world, and if I was to follow Jesus, I would have to take up their cause for justice in some way.

The most accessible way for me to take up this cause was to enter an educational path that would lead to a paid vocation as a Christian minister. In my studies I began to consider the teachings of Jesus the Christ more deeply. What did it mean to "love my neighbor as myself"? In practical terms, it came to mean that I could not simply spend the rest of my life pursuing a comfortable living while ignoring the fact that millions are living in poverty and oppression. I saw that

following Jesus would take me out of the mainstream of the world in order to love it fully. On the other hand, I was painfully aware of the impossibility of loving others unconditionally.

Vocationally and geographically, I found a home as the manager of a wilderness camp for inner-city children from Washington. Many of the children who came to our camp had never been out of the city. As I watched and listened to them entering this environment that was foreign to them, they became my teachers, helping me to understand the fears with which they faced the wilderness, and the fears they confronted at home in the city. I was reminded of how I grew up, unaware of the larger world around me. I worked to help them find the tools that would assist them in loving their enemies, abusers, oppressors, and those who ignore them.

Now I have become a minister due to a growing sense of historical urgency. Evidence has accumulated that our planet is reaching carrying capacities for population, atmospheric carbon, and extraction of certain resources such as petroleum. As Rob McCall, our local Congregational minister, says, "If we ignore the laws of Mother Nature, she will sweep up our species, hair and bone, with neither malice nor discrimination, and we will inhabit this world no more." The suffering resulting from our greed-based decision-making is already real, both for the rich and the poor.

I am turning my energies toward the contributions that could be made by a healthy faith. Since the Protestant Reformation, Western Christianity has become increasingly focused on the individual. We have an underdeveloped ability to make life-affirming decisions as a group. In the North American context of gross overconsumption, the time has come for a new Reformation that would recover—among other things— widespread respect for the laws of nature. Christianity can make a great contribution, but alone could never bring the changes necessary to change life. An unprecedented level of mutual understanding between all faiths, each one enriching respect for life, is being called forth.

As for my civil rights experiences, I now see them as an example of how the whole world needs to operate, judging all species as worthy of dignity and respect. My faith supports that.[15]

The extremely high ethical standards of the Sermon on the Mount (Matthew 5–7) may seem impossibly challenging. And Jesus said these things to people who had been brought up with the understanding that to fulfill incompletely even one divine commandment is a violation of the Law. But when people recognize their helplessness to fulfill such commandments, they are ready to turn to the divine for help. Jesus pointed out, "With man this is impossible, but not with God; all things are possible with God."[16]

The main thing Jesus taught was love. He stated that to love God and to "love your neighbor as yourself"[17] were the two great commandments in Judaism, upon which everything else rested. To love God means placing God first in one's life, rather than concentrating on the things of the earth. To love one's neighbor means selfless service to everyone, even to those despised by the rest of society. Jesus often horrified the religious authorities by talking to sinful prostitutes and tax-collectors, and the poorest and lowliest of people. He set an example of loving service by washing his disciples' feet. This kind of love, he said, should be the mark of his followers, and at the Last Judgment, when the Son of Man judges the people of all time, he will grant eternal life in the kingdom to the humble "sheep" who loved and served him in all:

> Then the righteous will answer him, "Lord, when did we see thee hungry and feed thee, or thirsty and give thee drink? And when did we see thee a stranger and welcome thee, or naked and clothe thee? And when did we see thee sick or in prison and visit thee?" And the King will answer them, "Truly, I say to you, as you did it to one of the least of these my brethren, you did it to me."[18]

Jesus preached that God is forgiving to those who repent. He told a story likening God to the father who welcomed with gifts and celebration his "prodigal son" who had squandered his inheritance and then humbly returned home. He told story after story suggesting that those who considered themselves superior were more at odds with God than those who were aware of their sins. Those who sincerely repent—even if they are the hated toll-collectors, prostitutes, or ignorant common people—are more likely to receive God's forgiveness than are the learned and self-righteous. Indeed, Jesus said, it was only in childlikeness that people could enter the kingdom of Heaven. In a famous series of statements

TEACHING STORY

The Good Samaritan

On one occasion a lawyer came forward to put this test question to Jesus: "Master, what must I do to inherit eternal life?" Jesus said, "What is written in the Law? What is your reading of it?" He replied, "Love the Lord your God with all your heart, with all your soul, with all your strength, and with all your mind; and your neighbor as yourself." "That is the right answer," said Jesus; "do that and you will live."

But he wanted to vindicate himself, so he said to Jesus, "And who is my neighbor?" Jesus replied, "A man was on his way from Jerusalem down to Jericho when he fell in with robbers, who stripped him, beat him, and went off leaving him half dead. It so happened that a priest was going down by the same road; but when he saw him, he went past on the other side. So too a Levite came to the place, and when he saw him went past on the other side. But a Samaritan (a person from a region against whom the Jews of Judaea had developed religious and racial prejudice) who was making the journey came upon him, and when he saw him was moved to pity. He went up and bandaged his wounds, bathing them with oil and wine. Then he lifted him on to his own beast, brought him to an inn, and looked after him there. Next day he produced two silver pieces and gave them to the innkeeper, and said, 'Look after him; and if you spend any more, I will repay you on my way back.' Which of these three do you think was neighbor to the man who fell into the hands of the robbers?" He answered, "The one who showed him kindness." Jesus said, "Go and do as he did."[19]

about supreme happiness called the **Beatitudes**, Jesus is quoted as promising blessings for the "poor in spirit,"[19] the mourners, the meek, the seekers of righteousness, the pure in heart, the merciful, the peacemakers, and those who are persecuted for the sake of righteousness and of spreading the gospel.

Jesus' stories were typically presented as **parables**, in which earthly situations familiar to people of his time and place were used to make a spiritual point. He spoke of parents and children, of masters and servants, of sowing seeds, of fishing. But even though the subject matter was familiar, the outcomes often contained paradoxes that turned conventional thinking upside-down. For example:

> *The kingdom of heaven is like treasure hidden in a field, which someone found and hid; then in his joy he goes and sells all that he has and buys that field.*[21]

Messianic expectations were running very high among Jews of that time, oppressed as they were by Roman rule. They looked to a time when the people of Israel would be freed and the authority of Israel's God would be recognized throughout the world. Jesus reportedly spoke to them again and again about the fulfillment of these expectations: "The time is fulfilled, and the kingdom of God is at hand; repent, and believe in the gospel."[22] He taught them to pray for the advent of this kingdom: "Thy kingdom come, Thy will be done on earth as it is in heaven."[23] However, in contrast to expectations of secular deliverance from the Romans, Jesus seems to refer to the kingdom as a manifestation of God's full glory, the consummation of the world.

> *Every one who drinks of this water will thirst again, but whoever drinks of the water that I shall give him will never thirst; the water that I shall give him will become in him a spring of water welling up to eternal life.*
>
> Jesus, as quoted in the Gospel of John 4:13–14

Jesus' references to the kingdom, as reported in the gospels, indicate two seemingly different emphases: one that the kingdom is expected in the future, and the other that the kingdom is already here. In his future references, as in the apocalyptic Jewish writings of the time, Jesus said that things would get much worse right before the end. He seemed to foretell the destruction of Jerusalem by the Romans that began in 70 CE. But:

> *then will appear the sign of the Son of man in heaven, and then all the tribes of the earth will mourn, and they will see the Son of man coming on the clouds of heaven with power and great glory; and he will send out his angels with a loud trumpet call, and they will gather his elect from the four winds, from one end of heaven to the other.*[24]

It was his mission, he said, to gather together everyone who could be saved.

Challenges to the authorities

As Jesus traveled through Galilee, many people gathered around him to be healed. Herod Antipas, a Jew who had been appointed by the Romans as ruler of Galilee, had already executed John the Baptist and may have been concerned that Jesus might be a troublemaker, perhaps one of the Zealots of Galilee who were stirring up support for a political uprising against the Romans. Jesus therefore moved outside Herod's jurisdiction for a while, to carry on his work in Tyre and Sidon (now in Lebanon).

According to the gospels, Jesus was also regarded with suspicion by prominent Jewish groups of his time—the emerging **Pharisees** (the shapers of rabbinic Judaism), **Sadducees** (the temple priests and upper class), and the scribes (specially trained laymen who copied the written law and formulated the oral law of Judaism). Jesus seems not to have challenged Mosaic law but, rather, its

TIMELINE

Christianity

c. 4 BCE–1 CE	Jesus born
c. 27–33 CE	Jesus crucified
c. 50–60	Paul organizes early Christians
c. 70–95	Gospels written down
c. 150	Last of New Testament writings
c. 185–254	Life of Origen, who supports allegorical interpretation of Bible
306–337	Constantine emperor of Roman Empire
325	Nicene Creed; Council of Nicaea affirms divinity of Jesus
354–430	Life of St. Augustine, influential formulator of Christian doctrines
379–395	Christianity becomes state religion under rule of Emperor Theodosius
c. 480–542	Life of St. Benedict and creation of his monastic rule
800–1300	Middle Ages in Europe; centralization of papal power
1054	Split between Western and Eastern Orthodox Church
1182–1226	Life of St. Francis of Assisi
1225–1274	Thomas Aquinas
1232	The Inquisitions begin suppressing and punishing heretics
1300s	Proliferation of monastic orders
1453	Gutenberg Bible published
1478	Spanish Inquisition set up
1509–1564	Life of John Calvin
1517	Martin Luther posts ninety-five theses; Protestantism begins
1534	Church of England separates from Rome
1545–1563	The Council of Trent; Roman Catholic Reformation
1624–1691	Life of George Fox, English founder of Quakers
1703–1791	Life of John Wesley, founder of Methodist Church
c. 1720–1780	The Enlightenment in Europe
1859	Charles Darwin's *On the Origin of Species* challenges beliefs in creation by God
1906–1909	Asuza Street Revival
1945	Discovery of the Nag Hammadi manuscripts
1947	First Dead Sea Scrolls discovered
1948	World Council of Churches formed
1962–1965	The Second Vatican Council
1988	Churches reopened in Soviet Union
2000	Pope John Paul II asks forgiveness for sins of the Roman Catholic Church
2002	Boston's Roman Catholic bishop resigns in growing scandal over sexual abuse by priests
2013	Pope Benedict XVI resigns; Pope Francis chosen as first Latin American pope

interpretations in the evolving rabbinic traditions and the hypocrisy of some of those who claimed to be living by the law. It is written in the Gospel of Matthew that the Pharisees and scribes challenged Jesus' disciples for not washing their hands before eating. Jesus responded:

"What goes into the mouth does not make a man unclean; it is what comes out of the mouth that makes him unclean. ..."[25]

"Alas for you, scribes and Pharisees, you hypocrites! You who are like whitewashed tombs that look handsome on the outside, but inside are full of dead men's bones and every kind of corruption. In the same way you appear to people from the outside like good honest men, but inside you are full of hypocrisy and lawlessness."[26]

Despite such critical remarks about the Pharisees appearing in the New Testament, scholars have noted many similarities between Pharisees and the beliefs of early Christians. For instance, the Pharisees did not see God as belonging only to Israel, but rather as the parent watching over, and taking care of, every individual. They addressed God by new names, such as *Abinu she-Basha-mayim* (Our Father Who art in Heaven), the same form of address by which Jesus reportedly taught his followers to pray to God (Matthew 6:9).

Many seemingly anti-Jewish statements in the New Testament are suspected by some modern scholars to be additions or interpretations dating from the period after Jesus' death, when rabbinic Judaism and early Christianity were competing for followers. Nevertheless, more universal teachings are apparent in such stories attributed to Jesus. For instance, in all times and all religions there have been those who do not practice what they preach when claiming to speak with spiritual authority.

Jesus is said to have also confronted the commercial interests in the Temple of Jerusalem, those who were making a living by charging a profit when exchanging money for Temple currency and selling animals for sacrificial offerings:

So they reached Jerusalem and he went into the Temple and began driving out those who were selling and buying there; he upset the tables of the money changers and the chairs of those who were selling pigeons. Nor would he allow anyone to carry anything through the Temple. And he taught them and said, "Does not scripture say; 'My house will be called a house of prayer for all the peoples?'[27] *But you have turned it into a robbers' den."*[28] *This came to the ears of the chief priests and the scribes, and they tried to find some way of doing away with him; they were afraid of him because the people were carried away by his teaching.*[29]

According to the gospel accounts, Jesus appropriated to himself the messianic prophecies of Second Isaiah. It is written that he privately asked his disciples, "Who do you say that I am?" Peter answered, "You are the **Christ**."[30] "Christ" is Greek for "anointed one," a translation of the Aramaic word *M'shekha* or **Messiah**, which also means "perfected" or "enlightened one." His faithful follower Martha, sister of Lazarus whom Jesus reportedly raised from the dead, is quoted as having said to Jesus, "I now believe that you are the Messiah, the Son of God who was to come into the world."[31] His other disciples spoke of him as the Messiah after he died and was resurrected. Some contemporary biblical scholars have concluded, however, that Jesus rejected the title of Messiah, for it might have been misunderstood.

According to the gospel tradition, a transcendental phenomenon, the **"Transfiguration,"** was witnessed by three disciples. Jesus had climbed a mountain to pray, and as he did:

He was transfigured before them, and his face shone like the sun, and his garments became white as light. And behold, there appeared to them Moses and Elijah, talking with him. ... When lo, a bright cloud overshadowed them, and a voice from the cloud said, "This is my beloved Son, with whom I am well pleased; listen to him."[32]

The presence of Moses and Elijah (who in Jewish apocalyptic tradition were expected to return at the end of the world) placed Jewish law and prophecy behind the claim that Jesus is the Christ. They were representatives of the old covenant with God, by which the Jewish people agreed to obey the laws of God and to regard God as their sole ruler. Jesus brought a new dispensation of grace.

Jesus claimed that John the Baptist was Elijah come again. The authorities had killed John the Baptist, and, Jesus prophesied, they would attack him, too, not recognizing who he was. John quotes Jesus as saying such things as "My teaching is not mine, but his who sent me"; "I am the light of the world"; "You are from below, I am from above; you are of this world, I am not of this world"; and "Before Abraham was, I am."[33] Jesus characterized himself as a good shepherd who is willing to lay down his life for his sheep. Foreshadowing the **Crucifixion**, he said he would offer his own flesh and blood as a sacrifice for the sake of humanity. His coming death would mark a "new covenant" in which his blood would be "poured out for many for the forgiveness of sins."[34]

It is possible that such passages defining Jesus' role were later interpolations by the early Christians as they tried to explain the meaning of their Master's life and death in new terms during the decades when the New Testament was in the process of formation.

Crucifixion

The anti-institutional tenor of Jesus' teachings did not endear him to those in power, who were wary of incipient revolts. Jesus knew that to return to Jerusalem would be politically dangerous. But eventually he did so, at Passover. He reportedly entered the town in a humble way, riding on a donkey and accompanied by supporters who waved palm branches and announced him as the Messiah, crying:

> *"Hosanna! Blessed be he who comes in the name of the Lord! Blessed be the kingdom of our father David that is coming! Hosanna in the highest!"*[35]

However, Jesus warned his disciples that his end was near. At the Last Supper, a Jewish Seder meal during the Passover season, he is said to have given them instructions for a ceremony with bread and wine to be performed thenceforth to maintain an ongoing communion with him. One of the disciples would betray him, he said. This one, Judas, had already done so, selling information leading to Jesus' arrest for thirty pieces of silver.

Jesus took three of his followers to a garden called Gethsemane, on the Mount of Olives, where he is said to have prayed intensely that the cup of suffering would pass away from him, if it be God's will, "yet not what I will, but what thou wilt."[36] The gospels often speak of Jesus' spending long periods in spontaneous prayer addressing God very personally as "Abba." It is possible to interpret Jesus' prayer at Gethsemane as a confirmation of his great faith in God's mercy and power. In the words of New Testament theologian Joachim Jeremias:

> *Jesus takes into account the possibility that God may rescind his own holy will … The Father of Jesus is not the immovable, unchangeable God who in the end can only be described in negations. He is not a God to whom it is pointless to pray. He is a gracious God, who hears prayers and intercessions, and is capable in his mercy of rescinding his own holy will.*[37]

Nevertheless, after this period of prayer Jesus said, according to Mark's gospel, "It is all over. The hour has come."[38] A crowd including Judas approached with swords and clubs; they led Jesus away to be questioned by the chief priest, elders, and scribes.

Before the Last Supper, Jesus humbly served his disciples by washing their feet and told them to serve each other likewise.

Ancient olive trees—some thought to be at least 1,000 years old—in the garden of Gethsemane.

All four gospels include **"passion narratives"** describing Jesus' sufferings during his betrayal, trial, and execution by crucifixion. Matthew and Mark report a hearing before the high priest, Joseph Caiaphas. According to the Gospel of Matthew, the high priest asked Jesus if he was the Messiah, the Son of God. Jesus reportedly answered:

> *You have said so. But I tell you, hereafter you will see the Son of man seated at the right hand of Power, and coming on the clouds of heaven.*[39]

Caiaphas pronounced this statement blasphemy, meaning attributing divinity to oneself and thus showing a lack of reverence for God, a crime punishable by death according to Jewish law. However, under Roman occupation the Sanhedrin (supreme Jewish court made up of chief priests, elders, and law teachers) was forbidden to pass the death sentence. Therefore Jesus was taken to Pontius Pilate, the Roman governor, for sentencing. To Pilate's leading question, "Are you King of the Jews?" Jesus is said to have replied, "You have said so."[40] According to the biblical accounts, Pilate seemed to prefer to let Jesus off with a flogging, for he saw no reason to sentence him to death. Nevertheless, the crowd demanded that he be killed on the grounds that he was a challenger to the earthly king, Caesar. The Gospel of John reports extraordinary dialogues between Pilate and Jesus as the crowd clamors for his execution. For instance, Pilate asks Jesus, "What have you done?" and Jesus reportedly replies:

> *"My kingdom does not belong to this world. My kingly authority comes from elsewhere." "You are a king then?" said Pilate. Jesus answered, "King is your word. My task is to bear witness to the truth. For this was I born; for this I came into the world, and all who are not deaf to truth listen to my voice." Pilate said, "What is truth?" and with those words went out again to the Jews.*[41]

At last, unable to pacify Jesus' critics, Pilate turned him over to his military guard for execution by crucifixion, a form of death by torture widely used within the Roman Empire. In this method, the victim was typically tortured or beaten brutally with whips and then hung or nailed onto a wooden cross to die as a hideous example to intimidate the public. The guards put a crown made of thorns on Jesus' head and paraded him and his cross to the hill called Golgotha (Place of the Skull). It was probably used frequently for such executions. The

Jesus' crucifixion was interpreted by many later Christians as the sacrifice of an innocent lamb as atonement for the sins of humanity. Another interpretation was that God gave "himself or herself" in love, drawing the world into a loving relationship with the divine. (Rembrandt, The Three Crosses, 1653.)

accusation—"This is Jesus, King of the Jews"—was set over his head, and two robbers were crucified alongside him. The authorities, the people, and even the robbers mocked him for saying that he could save others when he could not even save himself.

Jesus hung there for hours nailed to the cross until he died. This event is thought to have happened on a Friday sometime between 27 and 33 CE. A wealthy Jewish disciple named Joseph of Arimathea asked Pilate for Jesus' body, which Joseph wrapped in a linen shroud and placed in his own tomb, with a large stone against the door. A guard was placed at the tomb to make sure that no followers would steal the body and claim that Jesus had risen from the dead.

Resurrection and Ascension

That seemed to be the end of it. Jesus' disciples were terrified, so some of them hid, mourning and disheartened. The whole religious movement could have died out, as did other messianic cults. However, what is reported next in varying gospel accounts seemed to change everything. Some of the women who had been close to Jesus and had traveled with him from Galilee—Mary Magdalene, plus, according to different gospels, Mary mother of James, Joanna, Salome, and perhaps others—visited the tomb on Sunday to prepare the body for a proper burial, a rite that had been postponed because of the Sabbath. Instead, they found the tomb empty, with the stone rolled away. Angels then appeared and told them that Jesus had risen from death. The women ran and brought two of the male disciples, who witnessed the empty tomb with the shroud folded.

Then followed numerous reports of appearances of the risen Christ to various disciples. He dispelled their doubts about his **Resurrection**, having them touch his wounds and even eating a fish with them. He said to them, as recounted in the Gospel of Matthew:

> *All authority in heaven and on earth has been given to me. Go therefore and make disciples of all nations, baptizing them in the name of the Father and of the Son and of the Holy Spirit, teaching them to observe all that I have commanded you; and lo, I am with you always, to the close of the age.*[42]

The Church of the Holy Sepulchre in Jerusalem encompasses many rock slabs, each of which is revered as having possibly been part of the tomb where the body of Jesus was laid.

The details of the appearances of the resurrected Jesus differ considerably from gospel to gospel. However, some scholars think that to have women as the first witnesses to the empty tomb suggests that there must be some historical truth in the claims of Jesus' Resurrection, for no one trying to build a case would have rested it on the testimony of women, who had little status in a patriarchal society. Feminist scholar Elisabeth Schüssler Fiorenza finds deep meaning in the presence of women disciples at the time of Jesus' death and resurrection:

> *Whereas according to Mark the leading male disciples do not understand this suffering messiahship of Jesus, reject it, and finally abandon him, the women disciples who have followed Jesus from Galilee to Jerusalem suddenly emerge as the true disciples in the passion narrative. They are Jesus' true followers who have understood that his ministry was not rule and kingly glory but* diakonia, *"service" (Mark 15:41). Thus the women emerge as the true Christian ministers and witnesses.*[43]

It was the Resurrection that turned defeat into victory for Jesus, and discouragement into hope for his followers. As the impact of all they had seen set in, the followers came to believe that Jesus had been God present in a human life, walking among them. Jesus was no longer seen as a victim but a victor. The Resurrection became the basis for the Christian hope of salvation through belief in Jesus. Peter proclaimed:

> *This Jesus is the stone that was rejected by you, the builders;*
> *It has become the cornerstone.*
> *There is salvation in no one else.*[44]

According to two gospel accounts, after the resurrected Jesus appeared to his disciples, encouraging them to carry the gospel to the whole world, he ascended into Heaven. The end of the Gospel of Mark, which is thought to be a later addition to the chapter, adds, "and sat down at the right hand of God" (Mark 16:19). Some Christians believe that Jesus miraculously ascended bodily into the highest heaven, an invisible realm in the sky where God is sitting with Jesus beside him, as an advocate for his faithful followers. Whether understood metaphorically or literally, the **Ascension** is an article of Christian faith. It is further extended in the Acts of the Apostles into belief that Jesus will return bodily to the earth in the future:

As they were watching, he was lifted up, and a cloud took him out of their sight. While he was going and they were gazing up toward heaven, suddenly two men in white robes stood by them. They said, "Men of Galilee, why do you stand looking up toward heaven? This Jesus, who has been taken up from you into heaven, will come in the same way as you saw him go into heaven."[45]

Jesus' Resurrection and Ascension give rise to the Christian belief in eternal life for those who believe in God. Greek Orthodox Professor Christos Yannaras explains:

Many religions and philosophies proclaim the "immortality of the soul," but the Church is differentiated from all these, because she understands immortality, not as an uninterpreted form of "survival" after death, but as a transcendence of death by means of the relationship with God. Death is, for the Church, separation from God, the denial of the relationship with Him, the refusal of life as love and intimate communion. … Faith in eternity is the trust that this love will not stop but will always constitute my life whether my psychosomatic capacities function or do not function.[46]

The early Church

How important was Paul's role in the development of the early Christian Church?

Testing their faith, persecution at times became the lot of Jesus' followers. But by 380 CE, despite strong opposition, Christianity became the official religion of the vast Roman Empire. As it became the establishment, rather than a tiny, scattered band of dissidents within Judaism, Christianity continued to define and organize itself.

From persecution to empire

The earliest years of what became the mainstream of Christianity are described in the New Testament books that follow the gospel accounts of the life of Jesus. "The Acts of the Apostles" was presumably written by the same person who wrote the Gospel of Luke, and Acts refers back to the Gospel of Luke as an earlier part of a single history of the rise of Christianity. Acts is followed by letters to some of the early groups of Christians, many of them written by Paul, a major organizer and **apostle** (missionary), in about 50 to 60 CE.

Like the gospel accounts, the stories in these biblical books are examined by many contemporary scholars as possibly romanticized, idealized documents, used to convert, to increase faith, to teach principles, and to establish Christian theology, rather than to accurately record historical facts.

According to Acts, an event called **Pentecost** galvanized the early Christians into action. At a meeting of the disciples, something that sounded like a great wind came down from the sky, and what looked like tongues of fire swirled around to touch each one's head. The narrative states that they all began speaking in different languages, so that all who listened could understand in their own language. Peter declared that they had been filled with the Spirit of God, as the Old Testament prophet Joel had prophesied would happen in the last days before the onset of the Kingdom of God. He testified that the Jesus whom the people had crucified had been raised up by God, who had made him "both Lord

Books of the New Testament

Gospels
Matthew
Mark
Luke
John

The Acts of the Apostles

Epistles
Romans*
1 and 2 Corinthians*
Galatians*
Ephesians
Philippians*
Colossians
1* and 2 Thessalonians
1 and 2 Timothy
Titus
Philemon*

Hebrews
James
1 and 2 Peter
1, 2, and 3 John
Jude

Revelation

*These are the undisputed letters of Paul. Of other epistles, some are attributed to Paul, but most scholars agree they were written by others using his name as a pseudonym, in the custom of the times.

Depiction of Pentecost by modern Chinese artist He Qi.

and Christ."[47] Reportedly, 3,000 people were so convinced that they were baptized that day.

One of the persecutors of Christians was Saul. He was a Pharisee tentmaker who lived during the time of Jesus but never met him. Instead, after Jesus died, he helped to throw many of his followers into prison. Acts relates that on the way to Damascus in search of more heretics, he saw a light brighter than the sun and heard the voice of Jesus asking why Saul was persecuting him. This resistance was useless, said the vision of Jesus, who then appointed him to do the opposite—to go to both Jews and Gentiles:

to open their eyes, that they may turn from darkness to light and from the power of Satan to God, that they may receive forgiveness of sins and a place among those who are sanctified by faith in me.[48]

This meeting with the risen Christ, and through him, God, was an utterly transformational experience for Saul. He was baptized and immediately began promoting the Christian message under his new name, Paul. His indefatigable work in traveling around the Mediterranean was of great importance in shaping and expanding the early Christian Church. He was shipwrecked, stoned, imprisoned, and beaten, and probably died as a martyr in Rome, but nothing short of death deterred him from his new mission. He also fought against other followers about interpretations of Jesus; ultimately, Paul's version prevailed and has shaped Christianity ever since.

As described in the Acts of the Apostles, Paul tried to convince Jews that Jesus' birth, death, and Resurrection had been predicted by the Old Testament prophets. This was the Messiah they had been waiting for, and now, risen from death, he presided as the cosmic Christ, offering God's forgiveness and grace to those who repented and trusted in God rather than in themselves. This forgiveness and grace was mediated through God's sacrifice of Jesus and not dependent on Jewish Temple sacrifice, an important point especially after the destruction of the Second Temple in 70 CE. Some Jews were converted to this belief, and the Jewish authorities repeatedly accused Paul of leading people away from Jewish law and tradition. There was a major difference between Jews and Christians over the central importance given to Jesus. It is possible that Jesus himself may not have claimed that he was the Messiah, and that it was Paul who developed this claim. To this day, Jews tend to feel that to put heavy emphasis on the person of Jesus takes attention away from Jesus' message and from God.

The New Testament writings reflect the criticisms of the early Christians against the large Jewish majority who did not accept Jesus as their Messiah. Opposition in Israel led to Christian apostles' spreading out to carry the gospel elsewhere, thus helping to expand their mission, but Christian animosity toward Jews lingered, to resurface in virulent forms from time to time.

Paul also tried to sway Gentiles: worshipers of the old gods whose religion was in decline, supporters of the emperor as deity, ecstatic initiates of mystery cults, and followers of dualistic Greco-Roman philosophers who regarded matter as evil and tried to emancipate the soul from its corrupting influence. He taught them that God did not reside in any idol but yet was not far from them, "For in him we live and move and have our being."[49] For Gentiles embracing Christianity, Paul and others argued that the Jewish tradition of circumcision should not be required of them. As Paul interpreted the gospel, salvation came by repentant faith in the grace of Christ, rather than by observance of a traditional law. He argued that even Abraham was **justified**, or accepted by God in spite of sin, because of his great faith in God rather than by his circumcision. Greco-Romans had idealized the male human body, with great athletic spectacles performed by nude men, so the necessity of altering the human form would have been a barrier to their acceptance of Paul's teachings. Shifting away from circumcision as a traditional requirement was a significant example of the enculturation of Christianity as it evolved in various contexts and began to distinguish itself from Judaism.

Christianity spread rapidly through the efforts of the apostles and soon became largely non-Jewish in membership. By 200 CE, it had spread throughout the Roman Empire and into Mesopotamia, despite fierce opposition. Many Christians were subjected to imprisonment, torture, and confiscation of property, because they rejected polytheistic beliefs, idols, and emperor worship in the Roman Empire. They were suspected of being revolutionaries, with their talk of a Messiah, and of strange cultic behaviors, such as their secret rituals of symbolically drinking Jesus' blood and eating his flesh. Persecution did not deter the most ardent of Christians; it united them intimately to the passion and death of Christ. In addition to martyrdom, many early Christians embraced a life of ascetic self-denial by fasting, wearing coarse clothes, renouncing sexuality, spending hours in prayer and contemplation, and serving others. With the rise of Constantine to imperial rule early in the fourth century CE, opposition turned to the official embracing of Christianity. Constantine said that in 312 CE God showed him a vision of a cross to be used as a standard in battle. After he used it and won a major victory, he instituted tolerance of Christianity alongside the state cult, of which he was the chief priest. Just before his death, Constantine was baptized as a Christian.

Places visited by the apostle Paul during his far-reaching missionary journeys, 46–60 CE.

By the end of the fourth century CE, people of other religions were stripped of all rights, and ordered into Christian churches to be baptized. Some paid outward service to Christianity but remained inwardly faithful to their old traditions. As Christianity became the favored religion, many converted for secular reasons, but missionary activities also convinced people to convert for spiritual reasons.

By the end of the fifth century CE, Christianity was the faith claimed by the majority of people in the vast former Roman Empire. It also spread beyond the empire, from Ireland in the west to India and Ceylon (Sri Lanka) in the east.

Evolving organization and theology

During its phenomenal growth from persecuted sect to state religion throughout much of the ancient world, Christianity was developing organizationally and theologically. By the end of the first century CE, it had bureaucracies that carried on the rites of the Church and attempted to define mainstream Christianity, denigrating trends judged heretical.

One form that was judged to be outside the mainstream was Gnostic Christianity, which appeared as a movement in the second century CE. **Gnosticism** is based on the mystical perception of knowledge. The Nag Hammadi library found in Egypt presents Jesus as a great Gnostic teacher. His words are interpreted as the secret teachings given only to initiates. When New Testament texts were translated into Latin in the fourth century, the Gnostic gospels were not included. Instead, the Church treated possession of Gnostic texts as a crime against Church law because the Christian faith community felt that Jesus had not taught an elitist view of salvation.

What became mainstream Christianity is based not only on the life and teachings of Jesus, as set forth in the gospels selected for the New Testament, but also on the ways that they have been interpreted over the centuries. One of the first and most important interpreters was Paul. His central contribution—which was as influential as the four gospels in shaping Christianity—was his interpretation of Jesus' death and Resurrection.

Paul spoke of *agape*—altruistic, self-giving love—as the center of Christian concern. Love was applied not only to one's neighbors but also to one's relationship with the divine. It was love plus knowledge of God, permeated with love, that became the basis of contemplative Christianity, as it was shaped by the "Fathers" of the first centuries.

> *Let all that you do be done in love.*
>
> *1 Corinthians 16:14*

The cross, with or without an image of Jesus crucified on it, became a central symbol of Christianity. It marked the path of suffering service, rather than political domination, as the way of conquering evil and experiencing union with a compassionate God. To participate in Jesus' sacrifice, people could repent of their sins, be baptized, and be reborn to new life in Christ.

The expectation of the coming of God's kingdom and final judgment of who would go to Heaven and who to hell, so fervent in the earliest Christianity, began to wane as time went by and the anticipated events did not happen. The notion of the Kingdom of God began to shift to the indefinite future, with emphasis placed on a preliminary judgment at one's death. There was nevertheless the continuing expectation that Christ would return in glory to judge the living and the dead and bring to fulfillment the "new creation." This belief in the "Second Coming" of Christ is still a literal article of faith today for some Christians; others regard it as pointing to the certainty of God's coming rule of love and peace.

Reflecting on the life of Jesus and their experience of the risen Christ, Christians believed that the transcendent and invisible God had become immanent and visible in Jesus. This led to the early development of the doctrine of the **Holy Trinity**, which speaks of three equal "persons" within one divine being: Father, Son, and Holy Spirit. The Father is the one who sends the Son to become incarnate in Jesus with the mission to reveal God's love to the world. The Son or Word manifests God in the world in many ways, but the incarnation in Jesus is a culmination of that revelation. The Holy Spirit, or Holy Ghost, who Jesus promises will be sent after his death, is the power and presence of God, actively guiding and sustaining the faithful.

Although Jesus had spoken in parables, the evolving Church found it necessary to articulate some of its beliefs more openly and systematically. A number of **creeds**, or professions of faith, were composed for use in religious instruction and baptism, to define who Jesus was and his relationship to God, and to provide clear stands in the face of various controversies. One major controversy concerned the teachings of Arius, a leader of the congregation in Alexandria. The issue was the relationship between God and Jesus. The Christians worshiped Jesus, but at the same time came from monotheistic Jewish tradition, in which God alone is worshiped. Was Jesus therefore somehow the same as God? To Arius, God the Father pre-existed God the Son, whereas opponents of this belief insisted that the Son of God was equally eternal with God the Father.

Constantine convened a general council of the bishops of all area churches in Nicaea in 325 CE to settle this critical issue. Arius's beliefs were rejected at the Council of Nicaea and again at the Council of Constantinople in 381 CE. The **Nicene Creed**, as it is known today, is a compilation of the statements of faith from both of these councils. It is still the basic profession of faith for many Christian denominations and has been proposed as a basis for unifying all Christians:

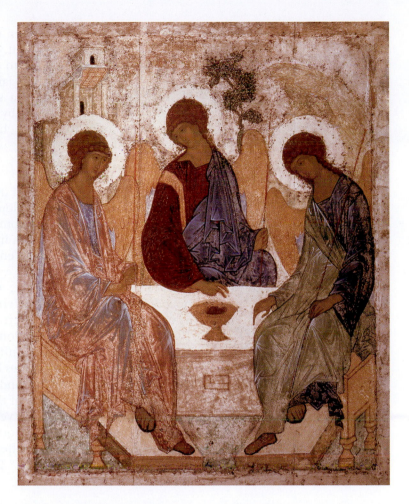

The Holy Trinity is a distinctively Christian view of God. God is One as a communal plurality, an endless circle sharing the love intrinsic to the Godhead, inviting all to be healed and saved by this love.

We believe in one God, the Father, the almighty, maker of heaven and earth, of all that is, seen and unseen. We believe in one Lord, Jesus Christ, the only Son of God, eternally begotten of the Father, God from God, Light from Light, true God from true God, begotten not made, of one Being with the Father. Through him all things were made. For us men and for our salvation he came down from heaven; by the power of the Holy Spirit he became incarnate of the Virgin Mary, and was made man. For our sake he was crucified under Pontius Pilate; he suffered death and was buried. On the third day he rose again in accordance with the Scriptures; he ascended into heaven and is seated at the right hand of the Father. He will come again in glory to judge the living and the dead, and his kingdom will have no end. We believe in the Holy Spirit, the Lord, the giver of life, who proceeds from the Father [and from the Son]. With the Father and the Son he is worshiped and glorified. He has spoken through the Prophets. We believe in one holy, catholic, and apostolic Church. We acknowledge one baptism for the forgiveness of sins. We look for the resurrection of the dead, and the life of the world to come. Amen.

As we will see later, the small phrase "and from the Son" was added to the creed by the Western part of the Church in the early Middle Ages and became a major point of disagreement between the Western Church and the Eastern Christian Churches, which did not add it.

Christology—the attempt to define the nature of Jesus and his relationship to God—received further official clarification during the Council of Chalcedon in 451. This council issued a statement that allows considerable leeway in Christological interpretations by declaring that Jesus is of "two natures"—perfectly divine and also perfectly human.

Early monasticism

Alongside the development of doctrine and the consolidation of Church structure, another trend was developing. Some Christians were turning away from the world to live in solitary communion with God, as ascetics. There had been a certain amount of asceticism in Paul's writings. He himself was celibate, as he believed that avoiding family entanglements helped one to concentrate on the Lord.

By the fourth century CE, Christian monks—and apparently also some remarkable ascetic women referred to as *ammas* (mothers)—were living simply in caves in the Egyptian desert with little regard for the things of the world. They had no central organization but tended to learn from the examples of other ascetics. Avoiding emphasis on the supernatural powers that often accompany the ascetic life, they told stories demonstrating the virtues they valued, such as submission, sharing of food, and humility. For example, an earnest young man was said to have visited one of the desert fathers and asked how he was faring. The old man sighed and said, "Very badly, my child." Asked why, he said, "I have been here forty years doing nothing other than cursing my own self each day, inasmuch as in the prayers I offer, I say to God, 'Accursed are those who deviate from Your commandments.'"[50] The young seeker was moved by such humility and made it his model.

> *The carefree man, who has tested the sweetness of having no personal possessions, feels that even the cassock which he wears and the jug of water in his cell are a useless burden, because these things, too, sometimes distract his mind.*
>
> *A Desert Father*[51]

The desert fathers and mothers were left to their own devices at first. In Christian humility, they avoided judging or trying to teach each other and attempted to be, at best, harmless. But by the fifth century CE, the monastic life shifted from solitary, unguided practice to formal spiritual supervision. Group monasteries and structures for encouraging obedience to God through an abbot or abbess were set up, and rules devised to help monks persevere in their calling. The Rule of St. Benedict became a model for all later monastic orders in the West. It emphasized poverty, chastity, and obedience to the abbot, and insisted that each monastery be economically self-sufficient through the labor of the monastics. Humility was enforced by the rule of obedience:

> *The first degree of humility is obedience without delay.*
> *This is the virtue of those*
> *who hold nothing dearer to them than Christ;*
> *who, because of the holy service they have professed,*
> *and the fear of hell,*
> *and the glory of life everlasting,*
> *as soon as anything has been ordered by the Superior,*
> *receive it as a divine command*
> *and cannot suffer any delay in executing it.*[52]

Church administration

Why did divisions between the Eastern and Western Churches worsen in the Middle Ages?

During the late first and early second centuries CE, some men and women had followed a charismatic Christian life, leaving home to preach, baptize, prophesy, and perhaps die as martyrs; others had moved toward an institutionalized patriarchal Church. By the beginning of the second century CE, a consolidation of spiritual power had begun with the designation of specific people to serve as clergy and bishops (superintendents) to administer the Church affairs of each city or region. While some women served as deacons ministering to women, the clergy and bishops had to be male. The bishops of the chief cities of the Roman Empire had the greatest responsibilities and authority, with the greatest prestige being held by the Bishop of Rome, eventually known as the **pope.**

Politically, late in the third century CE, the Roman Empire had been divided into two: an eastern section and a western section. In the fourth century CE, Constantine established a second imperial seat in the east, in Constantinople (now Istanbul, Turkey). It was considered a "second Rome," especially after the sack of Rome by the Goths in 410 CE. The two halves of the Christian world grew apart from each other, divided by language (Latin in the west, Greek in the east), culture, and religious differences.

In terms of religious organization, the Christian world was divided into a number of **sees.** The five major sees were those of Rome, Constantinople, Alexandria, Antioch, and Jerusalem. While religious power in the west became more and more centralized in the Roman pope, the eastern sees had no equivalent centralization, nor did they recognize the Roman pope's claim to universal authority over the Church.

By the fifth century CE, Pope Leo I argued that all popes were apostolic successors to Peter, the "rock" on which Jesus in Matthew's gospel said he would found his Church. The Roman emperor passed an edict that all Christians were to recognize the authority of the Bishop of Rome.

The strongest of Church administrators during these early centuries was Gregory I ("the Great"), who died in 604 CE. Wealthy by birth but ascetic by choice, he devoted his personal fortune to founding monasteries and feeding the poor. At a time of pestilence, floods, and military invasions, he promoted the discipline of the clergy, including the Western ideal that priests should be celibate in order to concentrate on piety and ministry without family obligations. He revamped the liturgy (Gregorian chanting is named after him), and re-established the Church as a decent, just institution carrying high spiritual values.

Pope Gregory also sent missionaries to convert England to Christianity. They were ultimately successful in gradually turning the people from worship of indigenous deities to worship of Jesus and the saints of the Church, partly because of the royal protection the missionaries and converts won and partly because rather than destroying the old religious shrines, Gregory instructed the missionaries to replace the old idols with relics of martyrs and saints, which they carried to England. Worship of goddesses of the area was thus deflected to devotion to holy women from far away, whose deep spirituality was thought to be so strong that it was present in their relics.

Worship of relics was a major feature of popular Christian faith. Pieces of the clothing, bones, and even dirt from the burial areas of saints were considered powerful sources of spiritual energy and healing. Great claims were made for their magical powers, so trade in relics—even reputed pieces of the cross of Jesus—became quite lively. Ultimately, almost every church in the West had something alleged to be a relic on its altar. Another lucrative trade grew up around pilgrimages by the devout to places considered particularly holy, such as Jerusalem, Rome, or Compostela in northern Spain, where the remains of the martyred St. James were thought to have landed by ship. Months-long pilgrimages on foot to such places were undertaken out of penance or for forgiveness of sins and increase in righteousness.

The papacy began to wield tremendous secular power in the west. Beginning in the eighth century, the approval of the papacy was sought as conferring divine sanction on feudal kings. In the ninth century the Church produced documents old and new believed to legitimate the hierarchical authority of the papacy over the Church, and the Church over society, as the proper means of transmitting inspiration from the divine to humanity. Those who disagreed could be threatened with **excommunication**. This exclusion from participation in the sacraments was a dread ban, cutting a person off from the redemption of the Church (blocking one's entrance to Heaven in the afterlife), as well as from the benefits of the Church's secular power.

Late in the eleventh century, Pope Gregory VII set forth unprecedented claims for the papacy. The pope, he asserted, was divinely appointed and therefore could be ruled by no human. The pope had the right to depose emperors; the princes of the world should kiss his feet.

East–West division

The eastern part of Christendom did not accept the absolute claims of the papacy. By the early Middle Ages, there were also doctrinal disagreements. In its version of the Nicene Creed, for example, the Western Church added the *filioque*, a formula professing that the Holy Spirit came from the Father *"and from the Son"*; the Eastern Church retained what is considered the more original text, professing that the Holy Spirit proceeds only from the Father.

In 1054, leaders of the eastern and western factions excommunicated each other over the disagreement about the Holy Spirit, the papal claim, and whether the eucharistic bread should be leavened or unleavened. To the Eastern Church, the last straw was its treatment by crusaders.

From 1095 to about 1290, loosely organized waves of Christians poured out of Europe in what were presented as "holy **crusades**" to recapture the holy land of

After Jerusalem fell in 1077 to Turkish forces, who then denied Christian pilgrims access to the city, Western popes launched a series of crusades to recover what Christians considered their holy land, where Jesus had walked. These military expeditions were considered holy missions, and crusaders carried the cross and the Bible.

Priests chant and beat drums in the Ethiopian Orthodox Church of St. George, carved out of rock in Lalibela, Ethiopia, in the 12th century.

Palestine from Muslims, and in general to wipe out the enemies of Christianity. When crusaders entered Constantinople in 1204, they destroyed the altar and sacred icons in Hagia Sophia, the awesome Church of the Holy Wisdom, and placed prostitutes on the throne reserved for the patriarch. Horrified by such profanity, the Orthodox Church ended its dialogue with Rome and proceeded on its own path, claiming to be the true descendant of the apostolic Church. Despite periodic attempts at reconciliation, the Eastern and Western Churches are still separate.

The Eastern Church itself also became divided over doctrinal and political issues at the time of the Council of Chalcedon in 451 CE. Bishops who refused to accept the dogma established by the council that Jesus is of two natures—one divine and one human—were declared to be "out of communion" with the bishops both of Rome and of Constantinople, and were thus excommunicated. These Non-Chalcedonian Churches or Oriental Orthodox Churches remain distinct from the Eastern Orthodox Church in general. They include Syriac Orthodox, Coptic Orthodox, Ethiopian Orthodox, Eritrean Orthodox, Malankara Orthodox Syrian Church (India), and Armenian Apostolic Churches. The Ethiopian Orthodox Church is the largest of these.

Social chaos and the papacy

In the Western Church, centralization of power under the pope became a major unifying element in the Europe of the Middle Ages. Kingdoms broke up between 800 and 1100 as Vikings invaded from the north and Magyars from the east, and feudal lords waged war against each other. In the midst of the ensuing chaos, people looked to the pope as an orderly wielder of power.

Church and states were at times locked in a mutual struggle for dominance, with popes alternately supporting, dominating, and being deposed by secular rulers. The power of the papacy was also somewhat limited by the requirement that the pope be elected by a council of cardinals. The position was nonetheless open to intrigue, scandal, and power-mongering.

The thirteenth century saw the power of the papacy placed behind the **Inquisition**, an ecclesiastical court set up during the 1230s to investigate and suppress heresy. This court was based on the concept that heretics should be controlled for the sake of their own eternal salvation. In some cases the medieval inquisitors had them tortured and burned to deter others from dangerous views. For example, in northern Italy and southern France a sect arose that was later called Cathari (the pure), for its members lived ascetically, emphasizing poverty and mutual aid. Though similar to established Christianity in organization and worship, the movement denied that Jesus was the incarnation of God, and saw spirit as good but matter as bad. Such beliefs were proclaimed heretical by the papacy; the Cathars, attacked by the Inquisition, disappeared.

Though strong, the papacy was often embroiled in its own political strife. During the fourteenth century, the popes left their traditional seat in turbulent Rome for the more peaceful climate of Avignon, France. There they built up an elaborate administrative structure, increasingly involved in worldly affairs. After the papacy was persuaded to return to Rome, a would-be reformer, Pope Urban VI, got so embroiled in power politics that at one point he had five cardinals tortured and killed. Several rival lines of "anti-popes" began, including one sitting in Avignon, creating divisions that lasted for decades.

Reform efforts

What were the major reforms of the Protestant and Roman Catholic Reformations?

Although the papacy was subject to abuses, mirrored on a lesser scale by the clergy, Christian spirituality was vigorously revived in other quarters of medieval society. During the twelfth and thirteenth centuries great universities developed in Europe, often from cathedral schools. Theology was considered the greatest of the sciences, with Church ideals permeating the study of all areas of life. Soaring Gothic cathedrals were built to uplift the soul to heavenly heights, for God was perceived as being enthroned in the heavens, far above the workaday world.

The yearning for spiritual purity was particularly pronounced in monasticism. It was largely through monks and nuns that Christian spirituality survived and spread. Monasteries also became bulwarks of Western civilization. In Ireland, particularly, they were the centers of larger communities of laypeople and places of learning within illiterate warring societies.

During the twelfth century many new monastic orders appeared in the midst of a massive popular reinvigoration of spiritual activity. A major influence was a community in Cluny, France. Its monks specialized in liturgical elaborations and prayer, leaving agricultural work to serfs. An alternative direction was taken by the Cistercians, Gregorians, and Carthusians. They returned to St. Benedict's rule of combining manual work and prayer; "to labor is to pray," said the monks. The Carthusians lived cloistered lives as hermits, meeting each other only for worship and business matters. Despite such austere practices, people of all classes flocked to monastic life as a pious refuge from decadent society.

> It is not only prayer that gives God glory but work. … He is so great that all things give Him glory if you mean they should.
>
> Gerard Manley Hopkins[53]

In contrast to monks and nuns living cloistered lives, mendicant friars, or brothers, worked among the people. In 1215, the Dominican Order was instituted primarily to teach the faith and refute heresies. A famous Dominican scholar, Thomas Aquinas, created a monumental work, *Summa Theologiae*, in which rational sciences and spiritual revelations were joined in an immense, consistent theological system. Aquinas was much influenced by the recovery of the classical writings of Aristotle that had been preserved by Muslims and returned to Europe through Spain.

Franciscans, following the lead of the beloved St. Francis of Assisi (see below), wandered about without personal property or established buildings, telling people about God's love and accepting charity for their meager needs. The mendicant Dominicans and Franciscans, still noted as missionaries today, became one of the major features of medieval Christianity.

In addition to organized orders of nuns, there was a grassroots movement among thirteenth-century German and Flemish women to take private vows of chastity and simplicity. These women, who were called "beguines," lived frugally by their own work. Because they were not organized into a religious order, they chose their own lifestyles, intending simply to live "religiously." At times persecuted because it did not fit into any traditionally sanctioned pattern, the movement persisted, drawing tens of thousands of women. Eventually they built small convents for themselves; by the end of the fourteenth century, there were 169 beguine convents in Cologne, the heart of the movement.

Medieval mysticism

Mysticism also flowered during the Middle Ages, renewing the spiritual heart of the Church. Especially in cloistered settings, monks and nuns sat in contemplation of the meanings of the scriptures for the soul. Biblical stories of battles between heroes and their enemies were, for instance, interpreted as the struggle between the soul and one's baser desires. Beyond this rational thought, some engaged in quiet nonconceptual prayer, simply resting receptively in the presence of God.

One remarkable mystic was the German abbess Hildegard of Bingen (1098–1179). Founder of two monasteries on the Rhine, from a young age she experienced frequent visions, which she recorded in several books of revelations. She wrote treatises on medical and scientific matters as well as much fine spiritual poetry, and achieved considerable fame as a composer. Corresponding with popes, emperors, and kings, she remained privately devoted to mystical thought and to prophecy.

In thirteenth-century Italy, there was the endearing figure of St. Francis of Assisi (1182–1226). The carefree, dashing son of a merchant, he underwent a radical spiritual transformation. He traded his fine clothes for simple garb and "left the world"[54] for a life of total poverty, caring for lepers and rebuilding dilapidated churches, since in a vision Jesus spoke to him from the cross, saying: "Repair my Church." Eventually Francis understood that his real mission was to rebuild the Church by re-emphasizing the gospel and its commands of love and poverty. A band of brothers, and then of sisters led by the saintly Clare, gathered around him. The friars preached, worked, begged, tended lepers, and lived a simple life of penance and prayer while wandering from town to town. This ascetic life was permeated with mystical joy, one of St. Francis's hallmarks. He was also known for his rapport with wild animals and is often pictured with birds resting lovingly on his shoulders. Two years before his death, Francis received the "stigmata," replicas on his own body of the crucifixion wounds of Jesus. This miracle was interpreted as a sign of the saint's union with Christ by suffering, prayer, holiness, and love.

An anonymous fourteenth-century English writer contributed a volume entitled *The Cloud of Unknowing.* Christianity then and now largely follows what is called the affirmative way, with art, liturgy, scriptures, and imagery to aid devotion. But the author of *The Cloud* spoke to those who were prepared to undertake the negative way of abiding in sheer love for God, with no thoughts. God cannot be known through ideas or physical images; "a naked intent toward God, a desire for him alone, is enough."[55]

In memory of St. Francis, many churches, such as this one in Miami Beach, Florida, now hold ceremonies in which congregants bring all kinds of animals to be blessed.

Russian Orthodox Kenoticism

A great mystical spiritual tradition emerged on Russian soil. The **kenotic** pattern of loving and world-directed monastic work was set by the eleventh-century saint Theodosius, who attempted to imitate the poverty and self-sacrificing humility of Jesus. He ate nothing but dry bread and herbs, spent his nights in prayer and his days in work. He dressed in the rough clothes of a peasant, patiently bore insults, worked with his own hands—chopping wood, spinning thread, baking bread, comforting the sick—and refused to present himself as an authority, even though he became the revered leader of this monastic community.

It is recorded that once, after Theodosius had visited a distant prince, the prince sent his own coach to take the saint home in comfort. The coachman, seeing Theodosius' crude clothing, assumed he was a beggar, and asked him to mount the horse so that the coachman could sleep. The saint humbly did so and thus drove the coach all night, with the coachman sleeping inside. When St. Theodosius became too sleepy to drive, he dismounted and walked; when he became weary of walking, he rode again. As the morning sun rose, the noblemen of his area recognized him, dismounted, and bowed to him, whereupon the saint gently said to the coachman, "My child, it is light. Mount your horse." The coachman was amazed and terrified as he saw the great reverence paid to the saint as they proceeded. Rather than chastizing him, Theodosius led him by the hand to the refectory, ordered that he should be given all the food and drink that he wanted, and paid him for the journey.

In the thirteenth century, Russia suffered from Mongolian invasions. Even though the Tartar Mongol khans nominally protected the Christians' freedom of religious practice when they themselves adopted Islam, spiritual and social life were in disarray. Monasticism shifted from urban settlements to the wilderness of the great forests of northern Russia. Hermit monks lived there in silence and solitary prayer until so many of the faithful gathered that thriving communities developed around them.

One of the most celebrated of the forest monks was St. Sergius. As a boy, Sergius retreated to the forest and built a small chapel for his intense devotions. Despite his noble lineage, he dressed like a peasant and did manual work. Even when he was abbot of the community that grew up around him, he was asked by one of his monks to build a cell, for which labor he was given a bit of moldy bread. In his contemplations, Sergius was said to be graced with visions of Mary, Mother of Christ, and of angels, fire, and light. He was nonetheless socially engaged with the national effort to resist foreign rule, and his blessing of the first victorious battle of Russians against Tartars set the precedent for the future close links between church and state in Russia. The relics of St. Sergius's body still lie undecayed in the huge and ornate Holy Trinity Lavra near Moscow, in Zagorsk where once he had built his simple chapel. Among his followers were seventy famous saints of Russia.

St. Sergius and the bear. (Mikhail Nesterov, The Youth of St Sergius, *1897.)*

In the silence of wordless prayer, the light of God may pierce the cloud of human unknowing that obscures the divine from the seeker.

Fourteenth-century Italy witnessed a period of unprecedented degradation among the clergy, while the papacy occupied itself with organizational matters in Avignon. In this spiritual vacuum, laypeople gathered around saintly individuals to imbibe their atmosphere of genuine devotion. One of the most celebrated of these was the young Catherine of Siena. In her persistent efforts to restore spiritual purity and religious discipline to the Church, she gained the ear of Pope Gregory XI, helping to convince him to return to Rome. She was called "mother of thousands of souls," and people were said to be converted just by seeing her face.

The Protestant Reformation

Despite the genuine piety of individuals within the Catholic Church, some who clashed with its authority claimed that those in power seemed often to have lost touch with their own spiritual tradition. With the rise of literacy and printing in the late fifteenth century, many Christians were rediscovering early Christianity and comparing it unfavorably with what the Roman Catholic Church had made of it. Roman Catholic fundraising or church-building financial activities were particularly criticized. These included **indulgences** (clergical remission of the punishment for sin in return for services or payments), the sale of relics, purchases of masses for the dead, spiritual pilgrimages, and the earning of spiritual "merit" by donating to the Church.

Most significant among the reformists was Martin Luther (1483–1546). Luther was a monk, priest, and Professor of Biblical Studies at the University of Wittenberg. He struggled personally with the question of how one could ever do enough good to merit eternal salvation. Luther was also disturbed by the moral corruption of his parishioners from the selling of indulgences, through which people could gain the merit accumulated in the church to decrease time in **Purgatory** (the intermediate place of purifying suffering for those who were not yet sufficiently stainless to enter heaven). The Castle Church at Wittenberg housed an immense collection of relics, including what were believed to be hairs from the Virgin Mary and a thorn from the "crown" of thorns placed on Jesus' head before he was crucified. This relic collection was deemed so powerful that those who viewed them on the proper day and contributed sufficiently to the Church could receive indulgences from the pope freeing themselves or their loved ones from almost two million years in Purgatory.

By intense study of the Bible, Luther began to emphasize a different approach. Both Paul and St. Augustine could be interpreted as saying that God, through Jesus, offered salvation to sinners in spite of their sins. This salvation was offered by God's grace alone and received solely by repentant faith. The good works and created graces prescribed by Catholics to earn merit in heaven were not part of original Christianity, Luther argued. Salvation from sin comes from faith in God, which itself comes from God, by grace. This gift of faith brings **justification** (being found righteous in God's sight) and then flowers as unselfish good works, which characterize the true Christian:

The young Catherine of Siena, "mother of thousands of souls," had a vision in which Christ, in the company of the Virgin Mary and other saints, gave her a wedding ring, the sign of the mystical marriage. (Domenico Beccafumi, The Marriage of Catherine of Siena, *1528.)*

Martin Luther's political influence and prolific writings led to a deep split in the Western Church, severing Protestant reformers from the Roman Catholic Church. (Lucas Cranach the Elder, Martin Luther, *1533.)*

From faith flows love and joy in the Lord, and from love a joyful, willing and free mind that serves one's neighbor willingly and takes no account of gratitude or ingratitude, of praise or blame, of gain or loss. ... As our heavenly father has in Christ freely come to our help, we also ought freely to help our neighbor through our body and its works, and each should become as it were a Christ to the other.[56]

In 1517 Luther invited the university community to debate this issue with him, by the established custom of nailing his theses to the door of the church. He apparently had no intention of splitting with the Church. Nevertheless, he refused to recant passages from his theses when threatened with excommunication. He was thenceforth excommunicated by a papal bull (decree) in 1521.

Luther's evolving theology took him farther and farther from the institutions of the Roman Catholic Church. He did not think that the Bible supported the Catholic teaching on the importance of pope, bishops, priests, and monks to mediate between God and laypeople. Instead, he emphasized that there is "a priesthood of all believers." He also felt that the sacred rites, or **sacraments**, of the Church were ways of nourishing faith instituted by Jesus and that they included only **baptism** and the **Eucharist** (also known as the Lord's Supper, **Holy Communion**, or **Mass**).

Another major reformer who eventually broke with Rome was the Swiss priest Ulrich Zwingli (1484–1531). He rejected practices not mentioned in the Bible, such as abstaining from meat during Lent, veneration of relics and saints, religious pilgrimages, and celibacy for monks and priests. Zwingli asserted that the Lord's Supper should be celebrated only as a memorial of Jesus' sacrifice; he did not believe in the mysterious presence of Jesus' blood and body in the consecrated wine and bread. He even questioned the spiritual efficacy of rituals such as masses for the dead and confession of one's sins to a priest:

It is God alone who remits sins and puts the heart at rest, so to Him alone ought we to ascribe the healing of our wounds, to Him alone display them to be healed.[57]

The ideals of these reformists were adopted by many Christians. The freedom of scriptural interpretation opened numerous options. **Protestantism**, as the new branch of Christianity came to be called, was never as monolithic as the Roman Catholic Church had been. Reform movements branched out in many directions, leading over time to a great proliferation of Protestant **denominations** (organized groups of congregations).

A major seat of Protestantism developed in Geneva, under John Calvin (1509–1564). He shared the reform principles of salvation by faith alone, the exclusive authority of the Bible, and "the priesthood of all believers." But Calvin carried the doctrine of salvation by faith to a new conclusion. To him, the appropriate response to God is a zealous piety and awe-struck reverence in which one "dreads to offend him more than to die."[58] Human actions are of no eternal significance because God has already decided the destiny of each person. By grace, some are to be saved; for God's own reasons, others are predestined to be damned eternally.

Although only God absolutely knew who was saved, there are three signs that humans could recognize: profession of faith, an upright life, and participation in the sacraments. Calvin felt that the Church has the right to chastise and, in some extreme situations, excommunicate those who seemed to violate the sanctity of the Church. Calvin envisioned a holy commonwealth in which the Church, government, and citizens all co-operate to create a society dedicated to the glory and mission of God.

Calvin's version of Christianity made its followers feel that they should fear no one except God, so they were impervious to worldly obstacles to the spread of their faith. **Calvinism** became the state religion of Scotland and also had a following in England.

Concurrently, the Church of England separated from the Church of Rome when Henry VIII declared the English Church's independence from the Church

Major Divisions of Christianity Today*

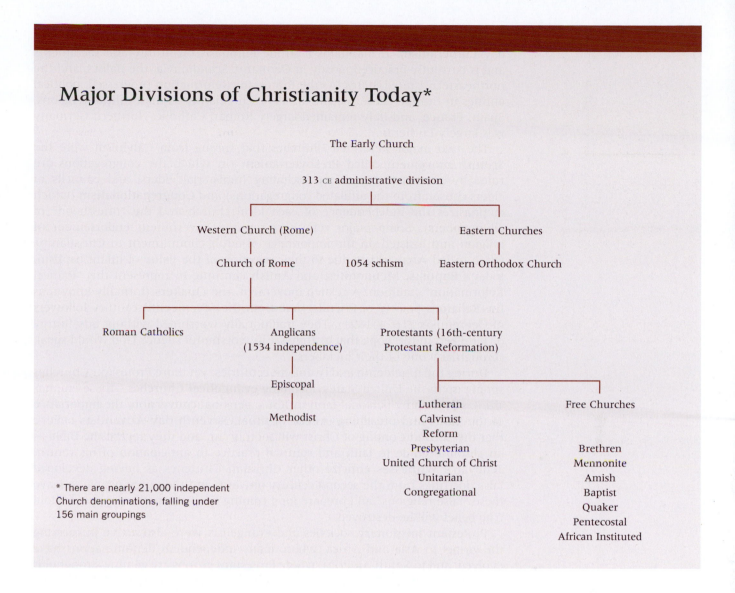

The Early Church

313 CE administrative division

Western Church (Rome) — 1054 schism — Eastern Churches

Church of Rome — Eastern Orthodox Church

Roman Catholics

Anglicans
(1534 independence)

Episcopal

Methodist

Protestants (16th-century
Protestant Reformation)

Lutheran
Calvinist
Reform
Presbyterian
United Church of Christ
Unitarian
Congregational

Free Churches

Brethren
Mennonite
Amish
Baptist
Quaker
Pentecostal
African Instituted

* There are nearly 21,000 independent Church denominations, falling under 156 main groupings

---

of Rome. His daughter Elizabeth I finalized the breach with Rome in 1559. Now called **Anglicanism**, this form of Christianity is in communion with Old Catholics and also shares some similarities with the Protestant Churches, but it is now generally considered a separate, independent Church. The Anglican Church retains many of the Roman Catholic rituals but rejects the authority of the Roman Catholic pope (referring instead to the Archbishop of Canterbury as its spiritual leader) and allows priests to marry. One of its thirty-seven autonomous Churches is the Episcopal Church in the United States, a name referring to its being a Church with bishops.

Another offshoot of the Church of England is **Methodism**. It originated with the **evangelist** John Wesley (1703–1791), who emphasized personal holiness and methodical devotions. He traveled an average of 8,000 miles a year by horseback to urgently call people to wake up to a life of repentance and faith in Jesus' intercession:

Repentance frequently means an inward change, a change of mind from sin to holiness. But we now speak of it in a quite different sense, as it is one kind of self-knowledge, the knowing ourselves sinners, yea, guilty, helpless sinners, even though we know we are children of God. … "I sin in every breath I draw, Nor do Thy will, nor keep Thy law on earth, as angels do above: But still the fountain open stands, Washes my feet, my heart, my hands, Till I am perfected in love."[59]

John Wesley, founder of Methodism, rode thousands of miles every year on horseback as an evangelist.

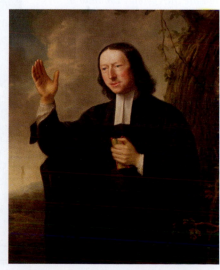

Martin Luther's reformation of the German Church led directly to present-day **Lutheranism**. It maintains a strong emphasis on liturgy and sacraments and is currently practiced mostly in Germany, Scandinavia, the Baltics, and the northeastern United States. As the Protestant Reformation progressed, political entities in Europe chose specific forms of Christianity as their official religions. Spain, France, and Italy remained largely Roman Catholic. Northern Germany was largely Lutheran.

The two major Reformed Churches that sprang from Calvinism were the Scottish movement called **Presbyterianism** (in which the congregations are ruled by presbyters, or elders, including ministerial elders, and councils of elders chosen from the affiliated congregations) and **Congregationalism** (which emphasizes the independence of each local church and the "priesthood" of all members). Some major reformers rejected government endorsement of religion and insisted on the importance of adult commitment to Christianity. Often called **Anabaptists** due to their rejection of the value of infant baptism, today's **Baptists**, **Mennonites**, and **Amish** continue to represent this "Radical Reformation" tradition. A related movement, the **Quakers** (formally known as the Religious Society of Friends) date from the seventeenth-century followers of George Fox (1624–1691). They traditionally worshiped without any liturgy or minister, in the hope that as they sat in worshipful silence God would speak through any one of their members.

During the nineteenth and twentieth centuries, yet more Protestant Churches sprang up in the United States, including **evangelical** Churches—those emphasizing salvation by personal faith in Jesus, personal conversion, the importance of the Bible, and preaching instead of ritual. **Seventh-day Adventists** believe that the Second Coming of Christ will soon occur, and they regard the Bible as an absolute guide to faith and spiritual practice in anticipation of his return. **Jehovah's Witnesses** criticize other Christian Churches as having developed false doctrines from the second century onward, and they urge people to leave these "false religions" and prepare for a coming time when all who do not hold true belief will be destroyed.

Protestant missionary societies and evangelists were also active in carrying the gospel to Asia and Africa, where many independent denominations have evolved, and to South America, where Protestant groups are gaining strongholds

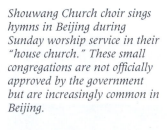

Shouwang Church choir sings hymns in Beijing during Sunday worship service in their "house church." These small congregations are not officially approved by the government but are increasingly common in Beijing.

in areas that had formerly been largely Roman Catholic since the Spanish conquests of these countries. This multiculturalism and contemporary evangelism will be examined in detail at the end of this chapter.

Despite the great diversity among Protestant denominations, most share several characteristics that distinguish them somewhat from Orthodoxy and Roman Catholicism, though the Catholic Church's positions are now much closer to those of Protestants as a result of the profound changes introduced in 1962 by the Second Vatican Council. Both take the Bible as their foundation, but differ on how it is to be interpreted. Protestants tend to follow Martin Luther in believing that the individual's conscience and reason are the ultimate guides to understanding the scripture. This is in contrast to Roman Catholics, who assert the authority of Church tradition and the infallibility of the Vatican's pronouncements about essentials of the faith. A second point that has divided Protestants and Roman Catholics is the Protestant belief that people can achieve salvation only by God's grace, through repentance and faith; Roman Catholics support the doctrine of salvation by God's grace, received through repentance, faith, and good works. A third divisive issue is that of spiritual authority. Protestantism asserts the "priesthood of all believers" and the individual's direct relationship to God and Jesus, in contrast to Roman Catholicism, which stands on mediation of God's grace through the officials of the Church. The officials themselves differ in many respects, such as the provision that Protestant ministers can be married, unlike Catholic priests, who are expected to remain celibate in the belief that restraint of physical desires enhances spirituality. Fourth, some Protestants have radically redefined the Roman Catholic and Orthodox concept of sacraments; Zwingli, for example, insisted that the only holy sacraments are those instituted by Jesus and regarded even those as instructive or commemorative rather than as mystical vehicles for God's grace. The sacraments and their meanings for Protestants, Roman Catholics, and Orthodox believers will be examined in depth later in this chapter.

The Roman Catholic Reformation

As the Protestant reformers were defining their positions, so was the Roman Catholic Church. Because reform pressures were under way in Catholicism before Luther, Catholics refer to the movement as the Catholic Reformation, rather than the "Counter-Reformation," as Protestants call it. However, the Protestant phenomena provoked the Roman Catholic Church to clarify its own position through councils of bishops, especially the Council of Trent (1545–1563). It attempted to legislate moral reform among the clergy, to tighten the Church administration, and to recognize officially the absolute authority of the pope as the earthly vicar of God and Jesus Christ. The council also took historic stands on a number of issues, emphasizing that its positions were **dogmas**, or authoritative truths.

The Council of Trent reiterated that salvation requires "good works" as well as faith. These works include acts of mercy, veneration of the saints, relics, and sacred images, and participation in the sacraments. In the sacrament of the Eucharist, the Council reiterated the doctrine of **transubstantiation**: what appear to be ordinary bread and wine are mysteriously transformed into the body and blood of Christ.

In addition to the actions of the Council of Trent, the Roman Catholic Church gradually chose popes who were more virtuous than some in the past, and several new monastic orders grew out of the desires for reform. The Jesuits offered themselves as an army for God at the service of the pope. The Society of Jesus, as the order was formally called, was begun by Ignatius Loyola (1491–1556) in the sixteenth century. His *Spiritual Exercises* is still regarded as an excellent guide to meditation and spiritual discernment. However, it was as activists and educators in the everyday world that Jesuits were highly influential in the Reformation, and they were among the first to carry Roman Catholicism to Asia.

Another Teresa, St. Thérèse of Lisieux (1873–1897), the "Little Flower," lived as a cloistered Carmelite nun for ten years of her short life. Her journal is full of small, secret sacrifices. Published posthumously as Story of a Soul, *it brought so much fame to this "little one" that she was soon declared a saint.*

Spain was host to a number of outstanding mystics during the sixteenth and seventeenth centuries. St. Teresa of Avila (1515–1582), a Carmelite nun, became at mid-life a dynamo of spiritual activity, in an order of ascetic discalced (bare-footed) Carmelite nuns and monks. The order continues its deep spiritual practices today, with two hours of silent prayer daily as well as observance of the full Liturgy of the Hours—daily prayer services of hymns and scriptural readings that punctuate the day and night. Despite her organizational activity, St. Teresa was able to maintain a calm sense of deep inner communion with God. In her masterpiece entitled *The Interior Castle*, she described the state of "spiritual marriage":

> *Here it is like rain falling from the heavens into a river or a spring; there is nothing but water there and it is impossible to divide or separate the water belonging to the river from that which fell from the heavens.*[60]

St. Teresa's great influence fell onto a young friend, now known as St. John of the Cross. He became a member of one of the Carmelite houses for men; when imprisoned by other Carmelites who opposed the reforms, he experienced visions and wrote profound spiritual poetry. For John, the most important step for the soul longing to be filled with God is to surrender all vestiges of the self. This state he called the "dark night of the soul," a relinquishing of human reasoning into a state of not-knowing into which the pure light of God may enter without resistance. He is still considered one of the great masters of the spiritual life.

The missionary enterprise

As European countries spread their influence through colonization, they sent the cross along with the sword to justify conquering people by converting them to Christianity, thus "saving" them from their "pagan" practices. Spanish and Portuguese conquistadores were joined by Franciscan and Dominican missionaries in the conquest of Latin America in the sixteenth century. The missionaries were involved in suppression of the indigenous religions to the extent that Latin American culture is still largely colored by Roman Catholic traditions, such as celebrating feast days of the saints.

French missionaries carried Christianity to Vietnam, with significant proselytizing efforts beginning in the sixteenth century. From Vietnam, missionaries took Christianity to Laos, Myanmar (Burma), Cambodia, and ultimately Indochina. Roman Catholic missionaries likewise went to the Philippines along with Spanish explorers. After the United States won the Spanish–American war, its Protestant missionaries began proselytizing in the Philippines as well, particularly among ethnic minorities.

In Africa, 500 years of European colonialism was accompanied by Christian missionaries who thought they were bringing light into the darkness. But there, as elsewhere, indigenous people found ways of mixing their old traditions with the imported faith, giving it many different local variations around the world.

Liberal trends

As missionaries were spreading Christian faith far and wide, during the eighteenth-century Enlightenment in Europe, intellectual circles exalted human reason and on this basis rejected faith in biblical miracles and revelations. As discussed in Chapter 1, some people felt that nineteenth-century scientific advances undermined the biblical story of the creation of the world. However, many nineteenth-century scientists were devout Christians who viewed the truth of science as supporting the truth of faith.

Undaunted, and in some cases invigorated, by rationalist challenges to traditional faith, Protestantism developed a strong missionary spirit, joining Roman Catholic efforts to spread Christianity to every country along with colonialism. As John Wesley, the founder of Methodism, had explained:

I looked upon all the world as my parish; … that in whatever part of it I am, I judge it meet, right, and my bounden duty to declare unto all that are willing to hear, the glad tidings of salvation.[61]

Challenges to traditional theologies had also taken the form of **Unitarianism** in sixteenth- and seventeenth-century Europe and eighteenth-century North America. This Protestant movement refused the doctrine of the Trinity and the divinity of Jesus in favor of a simple theism, imitation of Jesus, and seeking truths found in human experience.

In the late nineteenth and early twentieth centuries, Protestant Churches came to the forefront of efforts at social and moral reform. Women, long excluded from important positions in the Church, played major roles in Church-related missionary and reform efforts, such as the abolition of slavery; they cited certain biblical passages as supporting equality of the sexes. When Sarah Grimke (1792–1873) and other women were criticized by their Congregational Church for speaking publicly against slavery, Grimke asserted, "All I ask of my brethren is that they will take their feet off our necks and permit us to stand upright on that ground which God has designed us to occupy."[62]

Liberal trends in Protestant theology led to efforts to analyze the Bible as literature. What, for instance, were the earliest texts? Who wrote them? How did they relate to each other? Who was the historical Jesus? Such questions were unthinkable in earlier generations.

The Second Vatican Council

In the meantime, the Roman Catholic and Eastern Orthodox Churches had continued to defend tradition against the changes of modern life. A general council of the Roman Catholic hierarchs was held in 1869–1870. It found itself embroiled chiefly in the question of papal infallibility, a doctrine it ultimately upheld. The pope, proclaimed the bishops of the council, can never err when he speaks from the seat of his authority (*ex cathedra*), on matters of faith and morals.

In 1962, Pope John XXIII, known for his holiness and friendliness, convened the Second Vatican Council (also known as Vatican II) for the express purposes of updating and energizing the Church and making it serve the people better as a living force in the modern world rather than being an old, embattled citadel. When questioned about his intentions, he demonstrated them by opening a window to let in fresh air. With progressives and traditionalists in the Council often at odds, the majority nevertheless voted for major shifts in the Church's mission.

Many of the changes involved the liturgy of the mass, or the Eucharist. Rather than celebrate it in Latin, which most people did not understand, the liturgy was to be translated into the local languages. Rites were to be simplified. Greater use of sacred music was encouraged, and not just formal, traditional organ and choir offerings.

For the first time in centuries the laity were to be invited to participate actively. After Vatican II thus unleashed creativity and simplicity in public worship, entirely new forms appeared, such as informal folk masses—with spiritual folk songs sung to guitar accompaniment.

Another major change was the new emphasis on **ecumenism**, in the sense of rapprochement among all branches of Christianity. The Roman Catholic Church acknowledged that the Holy Spirit is active in all Christian Churches, including Protestant denominations and the Eastern Orthodox Churches. It pressed for a restoration of unity among all Christians, proclaiming that each could preserve its traditions intact. It also extended the concept of revelation, increasing the hope of dialogue with Jews, with whom Christians share "spiritual patrimony,"[63] and with Muslims, upon whom the Church "looks with esteem," for they "adore one God" and honor Jesus as a prophet. Appreciative mention was also made of other world religions as ways of approaching the same One whom Christians call God.

Vatican II clearly marked major new directions in Catholicism. Its relatively liberal, pacifist characteristics are still meeting with some opposition within the Church decades later. In the late twentieth century, conservative elements in the Vatican began to reverse the direction taken by Vatican II to some extent, to the dismay of liberal Catholics.

The Orthodox world today

What are the distinctive features of Orthodox spirituality?

After its 1054 split with the Western Church, the Eastern Orthodox Church had spread throughout the Slavic and eastern Mediterranean countries. After the Muslim Ottoman Turks took Constantinople in the fifteenth century, Russia became prominent in the Orthodox Church, calling itself the "third Rome."

There are now fifteen self-governing Orthodox Churches worldwide, each having its own leader, known as patriarch, metropolitan, or archbishop. The majority of Orthodox Christians now live in Russia, the Balkan states, and eastern Europe, in formerly communist countries where the teaching and propagation of Christianity had been severely restricted. Autocephalous (independent) Churches there include the large Church of Russia, which is dominated by the Patriarchate of Moscow, plus the Churches of Serbia, Bulgaria, Romania, Albania, Poland, and the Czech Republic. The original and still central Patriarchate of Constantinople is based within Turkey, as a small minority within a Muslim country, which now has no Orthodox seminaries. The Patriarchate of Constantinople nonetheless tries to play a central role in maintaining Orthodox

The Holy Trinity Lavra, one of the greatest monasteries of the Russian Orthodox Church, grew up in Sergeyev Posad near Moscow, where St. Sergius used to live as an ascetic in the forest. It is now a popular tourist attraction.

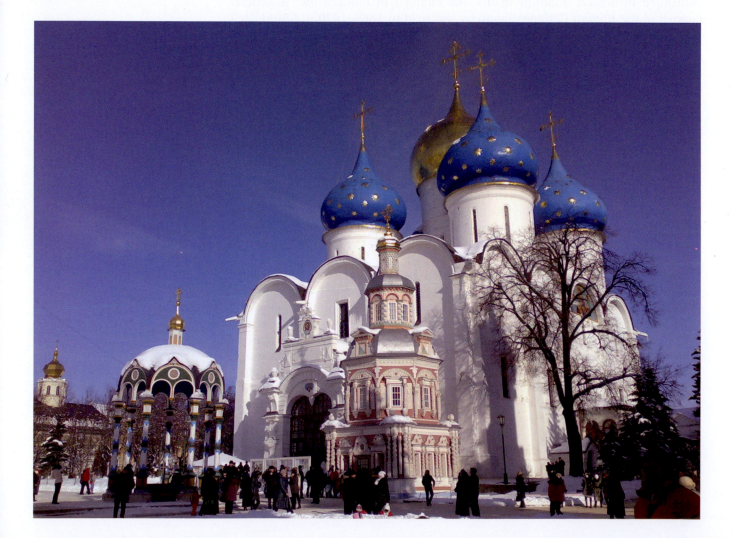

Eastern Orthodox Church

- Patriarchate of Constantinople (Turkey, Mount Athos)
- Patriarchate of Alexandria (Egypt, Africa)
- Patriarchate of Antioch (Syria, Lebanon)
- Patriarchate of Jerusalem
- Self-governing local Churches (Russia, Serbia, Romania, Bulgaria, Georgia, Cyprus, Greece, Poland, Albania, Czech lands and Slovakia)
- Plus archbishops or metropolitans in the Americas, Australia, India, and European countries

unity and the historical continuity of Orthodox sacred practices, dating back to the Desert Fathers.

This patriarchate, honored as "the first among equals," has thus been known as the Ecumenical Patriarchate since the sixth century. Unity among the patriarchates is facilitated by the experiential approach to spirituality that characterizes the Orthodox Church. His All Holiness Ecumenical Patriarch Bartholomew extends this sense of oneness to encompass all creation: "For us at the Ecumenical Patriarchate, the term ecumenical is more than a name; it is a worldview, and a way of life. The Lord intervenes and fills His creation with His divine presence in a continuous bond."[64]

The Patriarchate of Constantinople also includes islands in the Aegean and the precipitous Mount Athos peninsula. The latter was historically a great center of Orthodox monasticism, but its population of monks declined considerably in the twentieth century when emigration of monks was prohibited by communist regimes. Now declared a World Heritage site, Mount Athos encompasses twenty Eastern Orthodox monasteries, plus caves and hermitages. Entrance to the area is highly restricted, to allow the monks to concentrate on their spiritual practices in silence.

The Patriarchate of Alexandria is based in Egypt and includes all of Africa, where Orthodoxy arose independently in Uganda and has been embraced with considerable enthusiasm. The Patriarchate of Antioch consists mostly of Orthodox Christian Arabs in Syria and Lebanon. The Patriarchate of Jerusalem is charged with guarding the Holy Places of Christianity.

The Greek Orthodox Church dominates religious life in Greece and is assisting in the revival of interest in the classical books and arts of Orthodox spirituality. In the Church of Cyprus, the archbishop is also traditionally the political leader of the people.

Extensive emigration, particularly from Russia during the first few years of communist rule, also created large Orthodox populations in Western countries. Some retain direct ties to their home patriarchate, such as the New York-based Archdiocese of the Greek Orthodox Church in North and South America. Alongside that, the Orthodox Church in the United States was granted its independence in 1970, and now claims more than four million members in a country where Protestantism and Roman Catholicism are the predominant forms of Christianity. Missionary activity by the Russian Orthodox Church also established Orthodoxy in China, Korea, Japan, and among the indigenous peoples in Alaska.

Distinctive features of Orthodox spirituality

Over the centuries, the individual Orthodox Churches have probably changed less than have the many descendants of the early Western Church. There is

Orthodox priests conduct Easter Mass in Moscow.

a strong conservative tradition, attempting to preserve the pattern of early Christianity. Even though the religious leaders can make local adaptations suited to their region and people, they are united in doctrine and sacramental observances. Any change that will affect all churches is decided by a **synod**—a council of officials trying to reach common agreements, as did the early Church. Although women are important in local Church affairs, they cannot be ordained as priests or serve in hierarchical capacities.

In addition to the Bible, Orthodox Christians honor the writings of the saints of the Church. Particularly important is a collection called the *Philokalia*. It consists of texts written by Orthodox masters between the fourth and fifteenth centuries. "Philokalia" means "love of the exalted, excellent, and beautiful"; in other words, the transcendent divine source of life and truth. The *Philokalia* is essentially a Christian guide to the contemplative life for monks, but it is also for laypeople. A central practice is called "unceasing prayer": the continual remembrance of Jesus or God, often through repetition of a verbal formula that gradually impresses itself on the heart. The most common petition is the "Jesus prayer": "Lord Jesus Christ, Son of God, have mercy on me, a sinner." The repetition of the name of Jesus brings purification of heart and singularity of desire. To call upon Jesus is to experience his presence in oneself and in all things.

The Orthodox Church has affirmed that humans can approach God directly through faith, as opposed to intellectual knowledge. The seventh-century ascetic Isaac the Syrian said, "Faith requires a mode of thinking that is single, limpidly pure, and simple, far removed from any deviousness. ... The home of faith is a childlike thought and a simple heart."[65] Some may even see the light of God and be utterly transformed by it:

> *He who participates in the divine energy, himself becomes, to some extent, light: he is united to the light, and by that light he sees in full awareness all that remains hidden to those who have not this grace; ... for the pure in heart see God ... who, being Light, dwells in them and reveals Himself to those who love Him, to His beloved.*[66]

Another distinctive feature of Orthodox Christianity is its veneration of **icons**. These are stylized paintings of Jesus, his mother Mary, and the saints. They are created by artists who prepare for their work by prayer and ascetical training. There is no attempt at earthly realism, for icons are representations of the reality of the divine world. They are beloved as windows to the eternal. In addition to their devotional and instructional functions, some icons are reported to have

Most icon painters, such as this monk at Mount Athos, Greece, use the ancient Byzantine style in creating sacred icons, which represent Christian stories and open windows to the divine.

great spiritual powers, to heal illnesses, and to transmit the holy presence. Believers enter into the grace of this power by kissing the icon reverently and praying before it.

Some of the major icons in an Orthodox church are placed on an iconostasis, a screen separating the floor area for the congregation from the Holy of Holies, the sanctuary that can be entered only by the clergy. On either side of the opening to the altar are icons of Jesus and the Virgin Mary ("Mother of God," often venerated in Russia as Protectress and Ruler of the country).

Orthodox choirs sing the divine liturgy in many-part harmony, producing an ethereal and uplifting effect as the sounds echo and re-echo around each other. Everything strives toward that beauty to which the *Philokalia* refers. Archimandrite Nathaniel of the Russian Orthodox Pskova-Pechersky Monastery, which has been a place of uninterrupted prayer for almost 600 years despite repeated attacks on its walls and numerous sieges, speaks of the ideal of beauty in Orthodox Christianity:

> *The understanding of God is the understanding of beauty. Beauty is at the heart of our monastic life. The life of prayer is a constant well of beauty. We have the beauty of music in the Holy Liturgy. The great beauty of monastic life is communal life in Christ. Living together in love, living without enmity, as peaceful with each other as one dead body is peaceful with another dead body, we are dead to enmity.*[67]

Central beliefs in contemporary Christianity

What are the central beliefs in contemporary Christianity?

The history of Christianity is characterized more by divisions than by uniformity among Christian groups. The Church is vast and culturally diverse, and Christian theologies are complex and intricate. Nevertheless, there are a few basic motifs on which the majority of faithful Christians would probably agree today.

A central belief is the divine Sonship of Jesus—the assertion that Jesus is the incarnation of God. According to the Gospel of John, before Jesus' death he told his disciples that he would be going to "my Father's house … to prepare a place for you." When they asked how they would find the way to that place, Jesus reportedly said:

I am the way, and the truth, and the life. No one comes to the Father except through me. … Do you not believe that I am in the Father and the Father is in me?[68]

Throughout most of Christian history, there has been the belief that Jesus was the only incarnation of God. Interestingly, Thomas Aquinas argued that although God could become incarnate in multiple incarnations (as in Hindu belief), in fact he chose to do so only once, in Christ. Theologian Paul Knitter, co-editor of *The Myth of Christian Uniqueness*, is one of the contemporary voices calling for a less exclusive approach that still honors the unique contribution of Jesus:

What Christians do know, on the basis of their praxis of following Jesus, is that his message is a sure means for bringing about liberation from injustice and oppression, that it is an effective, hope-filled, universally meaningful way of realizing Soteria *[human welfare and liberation of the poor and oppressed] and promoting God's kingdom. … "Not those who proclaim 'only Lord, only Lord,' but those who do the will of the Father will enter the kingdom" (Matthew 7:21–23).*[69]

For Christians, Jesus is the Savior of the world, the one whom God sent to redeem people from their sins and reconcile them with God. Matthew reports that Jesus said he "did not come to be served, but to serve, and to give up his life as a ransom for many."[70] His own suffering and death are regarded as a substitute sacrifice on behalf of all those who follow and place their faith in him. Belief in salvation by faith in Jesus is so important to many Christians that they affirm, "Only Jesus Saves." With this exclusive belief, they hope that everyone will turn to Jesus as their personal Savior. According to the Gospel of John:

God loved the world so much that he gave his only Son, that everyone who has faith in him may not die but have eternal life. It was not to judge the world that God sent his Son into the world, but that through him the world might be saved.[71]

According to traditional Christian belief, humanity is inclined to sin, illustrated metaphorically in the Old Testament by the fall of Adam and Eve. We have lost our original purity. Given free will by God, we have chosen disobedience rather than surrender to the will of God. This situation is referred to as **original sin**. We cannot save ourselves from our fallen condition; we can only be forgiven by the compassion of a loving God.

Through fully surrendered faith in Jesus, Christians hope to be washed of their egotistical sinfulness, regenerated, made righteous, adopted by God,

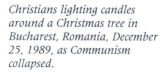

Christians lighting candles around a Christmas tree in Bucharest, Romania, December 25, 1989, as Communism collapsed.

sanctified, and glorified in the life to come. These are the blessings of salvation, which Christians believe Jesus won for them by his sacrifice.

Although Christians worship Jesus as Savior, as the incarnation of a merciful God, they also see him as a human being. His own life is seen as the perfect model for human behaviour. This is the central mystery of Christianity: that God became human in order to lead people back to God.

The human virtue most often associated with Jesus is love. Many Christians say they experience Jesus' love even though he is no longer walking the earth in human form. And in turn, they have deep love for Jesus. Those who are experiencing problems are comforted to feel that Jesus is a living presence in their lives, supporting them spiritually, loving them even in the darkest of times. Reverend Larry Howard, the former pastor of Hopps Memorial Christian Methodist Episcopal Church in Syracuse, New York, declared:

We found a Jesus. A Jesus who came in the midnight hour. A Jesus that was able to rock babies to sleep. A Jesus that stood in the midst and walked the miles when the freedom train rode through the South all the way through Syracuse. Jesus brought us through the mighty trials and tribulations. Why did Jesus do that? Jesus loved us and through that love and because of that love we stand here today. Not because the world has been so good to us. Not because we have been treated fair. Not because we have been able to realize the dream that God has given every man, woman, and child. But we stand here because we love Jesus. We love him more and more and more each day.[72]

The basic thrust of Jesus' message is to invite us into divine union, which is the sole remedy for the human predicament.

Father Thomas Keating[73]

In addition to being the paragon of love, Jesus also provides a model of sinlessness. To become like God, humans must constantly be purified of their lower tendencies. This belief has led some Christians to extremes of penance, such as the monks who flogged themselves and wore hairshirts so that their conscience might always be pricked. In a milder form, confession of one's sinfulness and imperfection is a significant part of Christian tradition. There is an emphasis on repentant examination of one's own faults, self-discipline and prayerful entreaty to guard against temptations, and rituals such as baptism that help to remove the contamination that is innate in humanity. Although one must make these efforts at purification, most Christians believe that it is only through the grace of God— as mediated by the saving sacrifice of Jesus—that one can be delivered from sin and rise above ordinary human nature toward a divine state of sinlessness.

Beyond doctrinal beliefs and model for behavior, Jesus is perceived by many Christians as their companion. Virgilio Elizondo explains his experience as a Mexican Christian:

In our barrios, we never heard anything about the christological doctrines of the church, but we knew Jesus of Galilee very well. From the earliest days of my life, I have known him as a close friend and companion. He was very present in the tabernacle as Jesus Sacramentado, and we easily and frequently visited with him as our most trusted confidant. ... Simple songs, like the corridos of our people, kept him alive among us. Ritual celebrations from the posadas (Jesus and Mary seeking a place to stay where Jesus could be born), the acostada del nino Dios (the laying down of the "Baby God"), and the levantada (presentation of the Child Jesus) of February 2 or the vivid reenactments of Semana Santa (Holy Week) have kept the human Jesus very much present in our lives and communities. ... The Jesus who accompanies us throughout our lives and suffers with us in our afflictions has been a tremendous source of strength in our culture.[74]

Sacred practices

Which seven sacraments are observed by the Roman Catholic and Eastern Orthodox Churches?

Imitation of the model set by Jesus in his own life is the primary practice of Christians. In the widely read fourteenth-century book *The Imitation of Christ*, people are encouraged to aspire to Jesus' own example as well as his teachings:

> *O how powerful is the pure love of Jesus, which is mixed with no self-interest, nor self-love! … Where shall one be found who is willing to serve God for naught?*[75]

In addition to the inner attempt to become more and more like Jesus, Christians have developed a variety of spiritual practices. Although forms and understandings of the practices vary among the branches of Christendom, they may include public worship services with sermons and offering of the sacraments, celebrations of the liturgical year, private contemplation and prayer, and devotions to the saints.

Worship services and sacraments

Christian worship typically takes place in a church building, which may be revered as a sacred space. The late nineteenth-century Russian Orthodox saint Ioann Kronshtadtsky (d. 1908) explained:

> *Entering the church you enter some special realm which is not like the visible one. In the world you hear and see everything earthly, transient, fragile, liable to decay, sinful. In the church you see and hear the heavenly, the non-transient, the eternal, the holy. A temple is the threshold of heaven. It is like the heaven itself, because here is God's throne, the service of angels, the frequent descent of the Holy Spirit. … Here everything from icons to censer and the priests' robes fills you with veneration and prayer; everything tells you that you are in God's shrine, face to face with God himself.*[76]

The word "**sacrament**" can be translated as "mystery." In Roman Catholicism and Orthodoxy, the sacraments are the sacred rites that are thought capable of transmitting the mystery of Christ to worshipers. Roman Catholic and Eastern Orthodox Churches observe seven sacraments: baptism (initiation and symbolic purification from sin by water), confirmation (of membership in the Church), Eucharist (the ritual meal described below), penance (confession and absolution of sins), extreme unction (anointing of the sick with oil, especially before death), holy orders (consecration as a deacon, priest, or bishop), and matrimony. In general, Protestant Churches recognize only baptism and the Eucharist as sacraments and have a somewhat less mystical understanding of their significance.

The ritual of public worship, or **liturgy**, usually follows a set pattern, though in some Churches the actions of the Holy Spirit are thought to inspire spontaneous expressions of faith.

For many Christians, the Eucharist (also called Holy Communion, mass, or the Lord's Supper) is a central part of regular worship. It is a mystery through which the invisible Christ is thought to grant communion with himself. Believers are given a bit of bread to eat, which is received as the body of Christ, and a sip of wine or grape juice, understood as his blood. The priest or minister may consecrate the bread and wine in ritual fashion and share them among the people. While many Protestants consider the bread and wine to be simply reminders of Jesus' last supper, Roman Catholics and Orthodox hold that they are mystically transformed by the Holy Spirit into the blood and body of Christ. They are treated with profound reverence. In sharing the communion "meal" together, the people are united with each other as well as with Christ. Jesus is pictured in the Bible as having set the pattern for this sacrament at what is called the Last Supper, the meal he shared with his inner circle before his capture by the authorities in Jerusalem. The body and blood of Christ are seen as

The sacrament of the Eucharist, celebrated here in Ghana, engages believers in a communal mystical encounter with the presence of Christ.

the spiritual nourishment of the faithful, that which gives them eternal life in the midst of earthly life.

Mother Julia Gatta, an Anglican priest in Connecticut, describes this sacred experience from the point of view of the clergy who preside at the liturgy:

> *To be the celebrant of Eucharist is, I think, the most wonderful experience on earth. In a sense, you experience the energy flowing both ways. … One experiences the Spirit in them offering their prayer through Christ to the Father. But at the same time, you experience God's love flowing back into them. When I give communion to people, I am aware that I am caught in that circle of love.*[77]

The partaking of sacred bread and wine is the climax of a longer liturgy of Holy Communion. The communion service begins with liturgical prayers, praise, and confession of sinfulness. A group confession chanted by some Protestant congregations enumerates these flaws:

> *Most merciful God, we have sinned against you in thought, word, and deed, by what we have done and by what we have left undone. We have not loved you with our whole heart; we have not loved our neighbors as ourselves.*[78]

Catholics were traditionally encouraged to confess their sins privately to a priest before taking communion, in the sacrament of **penance**, meaning "reparation for guilt" (also called "reconciliation"). After hearing the confession, the priest pronounces forgiveness and blessing over the penitent, or perhaps prescribes a penance. Orthodox Christians were also traditionally expected to spend several days in contrition and fasting before receiving communion. The reason for the emphasis on purification is that during the service the church itself is perceived as the Kingdom of God, in which everything is holy. In Orthodox services, the clergy walk around the church, swinging an incense censer to set apart the area as a sacred space and to lift the prayers of the congregants to God.

In all Christian Churches, passages from the Old and New Testaments may be read and the congregation may sing several hymns—songs of praise or thanksgiving to God. The congregation may be asked to recite a credal statement of Christian beliefs, and to make money offerings. There may be an address by the priest or minister (called a sermon or a homily) on the readings for the day. These parts of the liturgy constitute the Liturgy of the Word, in which Christ is thought to be present as the living Word, addressing the people through scripture and preaching. In Protestant Churches, the Liturgy of the Word is often offered by itself, without the communion service.

In both Protestantism and Roman Catholicism, there are now attempts at updating the liturgy to make it more meaningful and personally relevant for contemporary Christians. One innovation that seems to have taken hold everywhere is the "sharing of the peace." Partway through the worship service, congregants turn to everyone around them to hug or shake hands and say, "The Peace of Christ be with you"—"and also with you."

In addition to regular liturgies and the sacrament of the mass or communion, there are special events treated in sacred ways. The first to be administered is the sacrament of **baptism**. Externally, it involves either immersing the person in water or, more commonly, pouring sanctified water (representing purification) on the candidate's head, while invoking the Holy Trinity. The World Council of Churches has defined the general meaning of the practice:

> *By baptism, Christians are immersed in the liberating death of Christ where their sins are buried, where the "old Adam" is crucified with Christ, and where the power of sin is broken. … They are raised here and now to a new life in the power of the resurrection of Jesus Christ.*[79]

Aside from adult converts to Christianity, the rite is usually performed on infants, with parents taking vows on their behalf. There are arguments that infant baptism has little basis in the Bible and that a baby cannot make the conscious repentance of sin and "conversion of heart" implied in the ceremony. Baptists and several other Protestant groups therefore reserve baptism for adults.

A second ceremony—**confirmation**—is often offered in early adolescence in Roman Catholicism and Protestantism. After a period of religious instruction, a group of young people are allowed to make a conscious and personal commitment to the Christian life.

Some Christians observe special days of fasting. Russian Orthodox Old Believer priest Father Appolinari explains fasting as a way of *soprichiastna*, of becoming part of something very large, the spiritual aura of the Lord. He says:

> *More and more ordinary people are seeking a comfortable life. More and more we leave spirituality. We try to fill this vacuum with material things. I told my students that there was a fast coming up. They groaned, "Why?" I said that we fast for spiritual reasons. The rule is that you should fast not with a spirit of suffering but with such elevated spirit that your soul sings.*
>
> *When we limit our physicality, as in limiting our food intake, then we grow in our spirituality. I advise my students to notice whether their brain works better when their stomach is full or when it is almost empty. Monks refuse physical things in order to get spiritual benefits. We look at them and see their lives as dark, but for them, it is light.*[80]

The liturgical year

Just as Christians repeatedly enact their union with Christ through participation in the Eucharist sacrament, Christian Churches celebrate a yearly cycle of festivals, leading the worshiper through the life of Jesus and the gift of the Spirit. As the faithful repeat this cycle year after year, they hope to enter more deeply into the mystery of God in Christ, and the whole body of believers in Christ theoretically grows toward the Kingdom of God.

Christmas and Epiphany First of the major periods in the Church calendar, each associated with a series of preparatory celebrations, is the season of light: **Christmas** and Epiphany. Christmas is the celebration of Jesus' birth on earth as the incarnation of God. "Epiphany" means "manifestation" or "showing forth." The festival celebrates the recognition of Jesus' spiritual kingship by the three Magi (in the Western Church), his acknowledgment as the Messiah and

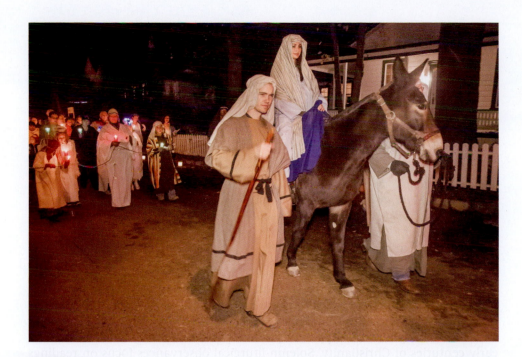

In Sutter Creek, California, people follow the Mexican tradition of posada, going from house to house during the nights before Christmas, re-enacting Joseph and Mary's search for an inn.

the beloved Son of God when he is baptized by John the Baptist, and his first recognized miracle, the turning of water into wine at the wedding in Cana.

In early Christianity, Epiphany was more important than the celebration of Jesus' birth. The actual birth date is unknown, but the setting of the date near the winter solstice allowed Christianity to take over the older "pagan" rites celebrating the return of longer periods of daylight at the darkest time of year. In the Gospel of John, Jesus is "the true light that enlightens every man,"[81] the light of the divine appearing amid the darkness of human ignorance.

Advent, the month preceding Christmas, is supposed to be a time of joyous anticipation. But in industrialized countries, it is more likely a time of frenzied marketing and buying of gifts, symbolizing God's gift of Jesus to the world.

In some countries Churches stage pageants re-enacting the birth story, with people taking the parts of Mary, Joseph, the innkeeper who has no room, the shepherds, and the three Magi. Since the nineteenth century, it has been traditional to cut or buy an evergreen tree (a symbol of eternal life, perhaps borrowed from indigenous ceremonies) and erect it in one's house, decorated with lights and ornaments. On Christmas Eve some Christians gather for a candlelit "watch-night" service, welcoming the turn from midnight to a new day in which Christ has come into the world. Many Christians also celebrate Christmas with the exchange of gifts and feasting.

Easter In terms of religious significance, the most important event of the Christian liturgical year is **Easter**. This is the commemoration of Jesus' death (on "Good Friday") and Resurrection (on Easter Sunday, which falls in the spring but is celebrated on different dates by the Eastern and Western Churches). Like Christmas, Easter is a continuation of earlier rites—those associated with the vernal (spring) equinox, celebrating the regeneration of plant life and the return of warm weather after the cold death of winter. It is also related to Pesach, the Hebrew Passover, the Jewish spring feast of deliverance.

Liturgically, Easter is preceded by a forty-day period of repentance and fasting, called **Lent**. Many Christians perform acts of asceticism, prayer, and charity, to join in Jesus' greater sacrifice. In the Orthodox Church, the last Sunday before Lent is dedicated to asking forgiveness. People request forgiveness from each other, bowing deeply. In the West, Lent begins with Ash Wednesday, when many Christians have ash smudges placed on their foreheads by a priest who says, "Remember, man, thou art dust and unto dust thou shalt return."

On the Sunday before Easter, Jesus' triumphal entry into Jerusalem is honored by the waving of palm or willow branches in churches and the proclaiming of Hosannas. His death is mourned on Good Friday. The mourning is jubilantly ended on Easter Sunday, with shouts of "Christ is risen!"

In Russian Orthodox churches, the Great Vigil welcoming Easter morning may last from midnight until dawn, with the people standing the entire time. Jim Forest describes such a service in a church in Kiev, with 2,000 people crowding into the building and as many more standing outside:

> The dean went out the royal doors into the congregation and sang out, "Christos Voskresye!" [Christ is risen!] Everyone responded in one voice, "Veyeastino voskresye!" [Truly he is risen!] It is impossible to put on paper how this sounds in the dead of night in a church overheated by crowds of people and hundreds of candles. It is like a shudder in the earth, the cracking open of the tomb. Then there was an explosion of ringing bells.[82]

Ascension Ascension may also be celebrated as one of the major holy days in the Christian liturgical calendar, honoring the bodily Ascension of Jesus to Heaven. It is celebrated on the Thursday that occurs forty days after Easter, or on the following Sunday. Apparently this event has been celebrated since the early centuries of Christianity. Solemn liturgical observances focus on readings from biblical accounts and credal statements regarding the religious significance of the Ascension. In medieval England, the Ascension was celebrated by a triumphal torchlight procession with a banner portraying a lion above a dragon, symbolizing the ascended Christ's triumph over Satan.

Pentecost Fifty days after the Jewish Passover (which Jesus is thought to have been celebrating with a Seder meal as the Last Supper with his disciples) comes the Jewish celebration Shavuot (which commemorates the giving of the Torah to Moses, as well as the first fruits of the harvest). Jews nicknamed it Pentecost, which is Greek for "fiftieth." Christians took over the holiday but gave it an entirely different meaning.

In Christianity, Pentecost commemorates the occasion described in Acts when the Holy Spirit descended upon the disciples after Jesus' death, Resurrection, and Ascension, filling them with the Spirit's own life and power and enabling them to speak in foreign tongues they had not known. In early Christianity, Pentecost was an occasion for the baptism of those who had been preparing for admission to the Church.

The Transfiguration and Assumption Some Christian Churches also emphasize two other special feast days. On 6 August, people honor the Transfiguration of Jesus on the mountain, revealing his supernatural radiance. On 15 August, they celebrate the Assumption of Mary, known as "The Falling Asleep of the Mother of God," in which she was thought to ascend body and soul into Heaven at the end of her physical life. These feasts are prominent in the Eastern Church, which generally places more emphasis on the ability of humanity to break out of its earthly bonds and rise into the light, than on the heaviness and darkness of sin.

Contemplative prayer

The contemplative tradition within Christianity is beginning to re-emerge. The hectic pace and rapid change of modern life make periods of quietness essential, if only for stress relief. Many Christians, not aware of a contemplative way within their own Church, have turned to Asian religions for instruction in meditation.

One of the most influential twentieth-century Christian contemplatives was Thomas Merton (1915–1968). He was a Trappist monk who received a special

The Christian monk Thomas Merton and the Tibetan Buddhist Dalai Lama, two great ecumenical figures of the 20th century, met shortly before Merton died in 1968 during a trip to visit the monks of the Asian traditions.

dispensation to live as a hermit in the woods near his abbey in Kentucky. Merton lived simply in nature, finding joy in the commonplace, experienced attentively in silence. He studied and tried to practice the great contemplative traditions of earlier Christianity, and reintroduced them to a contemporary audience through his writings. In meditative "prayer of the heart," or "contemplative prayer," he wrote:

We seek first of all the deepest ground of our identity in God. We do not reason about dogmas of faith, or "the mysteries." We seek rather to gain a direct existential grasp, a personal experience of the deepest truths of life and faith, finding ourselves in God's truths. ... Prayer then means yearning for the simple presence of God, for a personal understanding of his word, for knowledge of his will and for capacity to hear and obey him.[83]

Before he became a Christian monk, Merton had studied Asian mysticism, assuming that Christianity had no mystical tradition. He became friends with a Hindu monk who advised him to read St. Augustine's *Confessions* and *The Imitation of Christ*. These classic works led Merton toward a deep appreciation of the potential of the Christian inner life, aligned with a continuing openness to learn from Eastern monasticism. He died in an accident while in Asia visiting Buddhist and Hindu monastics.

Spiritual renewal through inner silence has become an important part of some Christians' practice of their faith. Syrian Orthodox bishop Paulos Mar Gregorios of India, past president of the World Council of Churches, concluded from the Bible evidence that Jesus himself was a contemplative:

Christ spent seventy percent of his whole life in meditation. He would sleep rarely. All day he gave himself to healing the sick. At night he would pray, sometimes all night. He was not seeking his own self-realization. His meditation and prayer were not for himself but for the world—for every human being. He held the world in his consciousness through prayer, not with attachment but with compassion. He groaned and he suffered with humanity. To follow Jesus in the way of the cross means to say, "I lay aside all personal ambition and dedicate myself to God: 'Here I am, God. I belong to you. I have no idea where to go. It matters not what I am, so long as You lead me.'"[84]

In Orthodoxy, a traditional contemplative practice is centered in repetition of the Jesus Prayer: "Lord Jesus Christ, have mercy on me." Eventually its meaning embeds itself in the heart and one lives in a state of unceasing prayer. An unknown nineteenth-century Russian peasant who lived with continual repetition of the Jesus Prayer described its results:

> The sweetness of the heart, warmth and light, unspeakable rapture, joy, ease, profound peace, blessedness, and love of life are all the result of prayer of the heart.[85]

Veneration of Mary, saints and angels

Roman Catholics and Orthodox and Anglican Christians honor their spiritual heroes as saints. These are men and women who are recognized as so holy that the divine life of Christ is particularly evident in them.

Most venerated of all saints is Mary, mother of Jesus. Devotion to her and to martyrs began in the early years of the Church. Mary serves as a potent and much-loved spiritual symbol.

Some researchers feel that devotion to Mary is derived from earlier worship of the Mother Goddess. They see her as representing the feminine aspect of the Godhead. She is associated with the crescent moon, representing the receptive willingness to be filled with the Spirit. In the story of the **Annunciation**—the appearance of an angel who told her she would have a child conceived by the Holy Spirit—her reported response was "Behold, I am the handmaid of the Lord; let it be to me according to your word."[86] This receptivity is not seen as utter powerlessness, however. Mary, like Christ, embodies the basic Christian paradox: that power is found in "weakness."

Whether or not devotion to Mary is linked to earlier Mother Goddess worship, oral Christian traditions have given her new symbolic roles. One links her with Israel, which is referred to as the daughter of Zion or daughter of Jerusalem in Old Testament passages. God comes to her as the overshadowing of the Holy Spirit, and from this love between YHWH and Israel, Jesus is born to save the people of Israel.

Mary is also called the New Eve. The legendary first Eve disobeyed God and was cast out of the Garden of Eden; Mary's willing submission to God allows the birth of the new creation, in which Christ is in all.

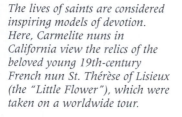

The lives of saints are considered inspiring models of devotion. Here, Carmelite nuns in California view the relics of the beloved young 19th-century French nun St. Thérèse of Lisieux (the "Little Flower"), which were taken on a worldwide tour.

Another symbolic role ascribed to Mary is that of the immaculate virgin. According to the gospels of Matthew and Luke, she conceived Jesus by heavenly intervention rather than human biology. Even in giving birth to Jesus, she remained a virgin. The emphasis on virginity is a spiritual sign of being dedicated to God alone, rather than to any temporal attachments.

In the Orthodox and Catholic traditions, Mary is referred to as the Mother of God. Before he died on the cross, Jesus is said to have told John, the beloved disciple, that thenceforth Mary was to be his Mother. The story is interpreted as meaning that thenceforth all humanity was adopted by Mary.

According to the faithful, Mary is not just a symbol but a living presence, like Christ. She is appealed to in prayer and is honored in countless paintings, statues, shrines, and churches dedicated to her name. Catholics are enjoined to repeat the "Hail Mary" prayer:

A procession of Orthodox nuns carry an icon of St. Elizabeth, a pious nun from the Russian royal family who was killed by the Bolsheviks in 1918 and glorified as a new martyr by the Russian Orthodox Church in 1992.

> *Hail, Mary, full of grace, the Lord is with thee. Blessed art thou among women, and blessed is the fruit of thy womb, Jesus. Holy Mary, Mother of God, pray for us sinners, now and at the hour of our death.*

Theologians point out that veneration of Mary is really directed toward God; Mary is not worshiped in herself but as the mother of Christ, reflecting his glory. If this were not so, Christians could be accused of idolatry.

Be this as it may, Mary has been said to appear to believers in many places around the world. At Lourdes, in France, it is claimed that she appeared repeatedly to a young peasant girl named Bernadette in the nineteenth century. A spring found where Mary indicated it would be has been the source of hundreds of medically authenticated healings from seemingly incurable diseases. In 1531, in what is now Mexico City, Mary appeared to a converted Aztec, Juan Diego. She asked him to have the bishop build a church on the spot. To convince the sceptical bishop, Juan filled his cloak with the out-of-season roses to which she directed him. When he opened the cloak before the bishop, the petals fell away to reveal a large and vivid image of Mary, with Indian features. The picture is now enshrined in a large church with moving walkways to handle the crowds who come to see it, and the "Virgin of Guadalupe" has been declared Celestial Patroness of the New World.

The Virgin of Guadalupe, who reportedly appeared in the 16th century to an indigenous convert to Catholicism, speaking the native language Nahuatl, has been embraced as patron saint of the Americas.

Other famous apparitions of Mary have included sightings by a group of children in Medjugorje in western Herzegovina starting in 1981. They claimed that she appeared, indescribably beautiful, amid brilliant flashes of light. People from around the world continue to make reverent pilgrimages to that site and daily worship goes on there in many languages.

Other saints are also greatly venerated. Roman Catholic and Orthodox Christians pray to saints as intercessors for God's attention to their problems. Orthodox Christians are given the name of a saint when they are baptized. Each keeps an icon of this patron saint in his or her room and prays to the saint daily. Icons of many saints fill an Orthodox church, helping to make them familiar presences rather than names in history books. Saints are often known as having special areas of concern and power. For instance, in the Catholic tradition, St. Anthony of Padua is invoked for help in finding lost things. Relics, usually parts of the body or clothes of saints, are felt to radiate the holiness of the saints' communion with God. They are treasured and displayed for veneration in

Catholic and Orthodox churches. It is said that saints' physical bodies were so transformed by divine light that they do not decay after death, and continue to emit a sweet fragrance.

Roman Catholics and Orthodox Christians also pray to angels for protection. Angels are understood as spiritual beings who serve as messengers from, and adoring servants of, God. They are usually pictured as human figures or faces with wings. In popular piety, each person is thought to have a guardian angel for individual protection and spiritual help.

> *Each saint is a unique event, a victory over the force of evil. So many blessings can pour from God into the world through one life.*
>
> Father Germann, Vladimir, Russia[87]

Contemporary trends

How do evangelicalism and Spirit-oriented movements differ?

At this time, Christianity is gaining membership and enthusiastic participation in some quarters and losing ground in others.

The fall of Communism in the former Soviet Union and its satellites brought reopening and renovation of many churches and a renewed interest in spirituality throughout that large area. Orthodox Christianity has also received a boost from the activist approach of Ecumenical Patriarch Bartholomew, Archbishop of Constantinople, whose position makes him the leading voice in Orthodoxy. He is known as the "Green Patriarch" for his environmental activism, and has also taken an active role in improving Orthodox relations with Roman Catholics and Protestants, and in conflict resolution in areas where people of different religions are at war with each other.

> *There will be an effective, transformative change in our world only when we are prepared to make sacrifices that are radical, painful, and genuinely unselfish.*
>
> Ecumenical Patriarch Bartholomew[88]

In Egypt, Orthodox Coptic Christians believe that Jesus' parents brought him to their area as an infant to escape from King Herod; they are also heirs to the ancient tradition of the Desert Fathers. Copts were long submerged under Muslim rule, but monasteries began to flourish again in the twentieth century. The sixteen million Coptic Christians have their own pope, and they have comprised the largest group of Christians in the Middle East. However, after the Egyptian Revolution in 2011, they have suffered the worst attacks in centuries at the hands of Islamist extremists, and many Copts are leaving the country as the violence continues.

In many parts of the highly volatile Middle East, where Jesus' followers first carried Christianity, Christian minorities are now facing severe persecution from extremist Muslim groups. Many Christians have been murdered by mobs and armed militants; their churches and shops are being attacked, and they face discriminatory laws and attempts to convert them by force. Those who can are fleeing. There are now very few Christians left in Iraq and Libya. In Syria, hundreds of thousands of Christians have been uprooted or have fled the country to escape violence.

In other areas, Christians are facing conflicts among themselves. Roman Catholicism is experiencing divisions between conservatives and liberals. After the liberal tendencies of the Second Vatican Council (Vatican II), Pope John Paul II reaffirmed certain traditional stands and strengthened the position of

The contemporary Coptic Cross. The circle symbolizes the eternal love of God, as manifested in the sacrificial offering of the Son of God.

the right wing of the Church. In 2000, Cardinal Joseph Ratzinger, then head of the Vatican's highly conservative Congregation for the Doctrine of the Faith (the successor to the Inquisition), delivered *"Dominus Jesus,"* a thirty-six-page document proclaiming, "There exists a single Church of Christ, which subsists in the Catholic Church." Other Christian communities "are not churches in the proper sense" and non-Christians are in a "gravely deficient situation" regarding salvation.[89]

The conservative trend in the Vatican was continued with the election of Cardinal Ratzinger in 2005 as the new pope, Benedict XVI. He was known for his defense of traditional Catholic doctrines and values. Nevertheless, he made historic trips to Muslim and Jewish holy sites, and, in contrast to earlier cautions against a focus on social justice, he stated, "Is there anything more tragic, is there anything more opposed to belief in the existence of a good God and a Redeemer of mankind, than world hunger?"[90] Revelations of sexual abuse by priests rocked people's confidence in the priesthood in the Americas and Europe, including Italy, the backyard of the Vatican. Traditions of secrecy protecting the priests and bishops involved have been challenged by public calls for greater transparency and accountability. The required celibacy of priests has been named by some observers as a factor leading to illegal sexual conduct, but the Vatican has not altered this requirement.

In 2013, Pope Benedict became the first pope in almost 600 years to resign, a stunning move that he attributed to being too old and weak to deal with the various crises facing the Church—including sexual abuse by priests, allegations of corruption, and infighting in the Vatican. This surprise was followed by the selection of Pope Francis from Argentina, who quickly became one of the most popular people in the world—the most talked-about person on Facebook and the Internet. He spoke out against the "idols" of money and power, took a non-judgmental stance toward homosexuality and divorce, and urged the Church to return to its mission of protection of the weakest in society. In his message for the World Day of Peace in 2014, he decried the "globalization of indifference," and instead encouraged:

> fraternity which draws us to fellowship with others and enables us to see them not as enemies or rivals, but as brothers and sisters to be accepted and embraced. … Globalization, as Benedict XVI pointed out, makes us neighbours, but does not make us brothers. The many situations of inequality, poverty and injustice, are

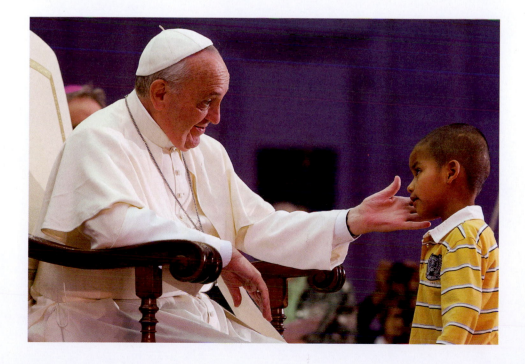

While Pope Francis was speaking about the importance of grandparents during the Pontifical Council for the Family's plenary assembly, a little boy spontaneously came up to him and received a caress from the pontiff.

signs not only of a profound lack of fraternity, but also of the absence of a culture of solidarity. New ideologies, characterized by rampant individualism, egocentrism and materialistic consumerism, weaken social bonds, fuelling that "throw away" mentality which leads to contempt for, and the abandonment of, the weakest and those considered 'useless.'[91]

Pope Francis inherited a Roman Catholic Church in which there is controversy over participation by women (who are not allowed by the Vatican to be priests), and widespread disregard of existing papal prohibitions on effective birth control, abortion, test-tube conception, surrogate motherhood, genetic experimentation, divorce, and homosexuality. These topics are under lively discussion, with considerable resistance to Pope Francis's liberal views from conservative Catholic leaders. Liberals argue that contemporary realities force a rethinking of dogmas such as the traditional Catholic ban on birth control. Sean McDonagh of the Columban Fathers (SSC) asks:

> *Is it really pro-life to ignore the warnings of demographers and ecologists who predict that unbridled population growth will lead to severe hardship and an increase in the infant mortality rate for succeeding generations? Is it pro-life to allow the extinction of hundreds of thousands of living species which will ultimately affect the well-being of all future generations on the planet?*[92]

In Protestantism, traditional denominations in Europe and the United States are declining in membership. According to a Gallup poll, only a minority of those who do not attend church actually disagree with their denomination's teachings. They are more likely to drop away because of apathy, a lack of services, or a lack of welcome on the part of the minister.

On the other hand "megachurches" witnessed phenomenal growth, with congregations of more than 2,000 attending friendly services by charismatic preachers with attractions such as videos and "Christian rock" music, plus add-ons such as restaurants, job-training classes, fitness centers, schools, and support groups for parents, children, families, addicts, people living with HIV/AIDS, people suffering from depression, and so on. But the megachurch phenomenon is waning somewhat, with some congregations turning against their pastors for their perceived moral failures. Rick Warren, "seeker-sensitive" pastor of the huge Saddleback Church, has begun a special mental health ministry after his own son's tragic suicide.

The Anglican Church is in the midst of controversies between traditionalists

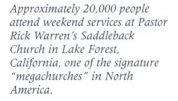

Approximately 20,000 people attend weekend services at Pastor Rick Warren's Saddleback Church in Lake Forest, California, one of the signature "megachurches" in North America.

and modernizers. They threaten to split the global Anglican Communion, which encompasses seventy-nine million people. Conservative Anglican leaders are strongly opposed to liberals' support for the ordination of women and homosexuals as bishops. In 2014 the Church of England did approve ordination of women as bishops, but approximately half of the Anglican fold have declared a state of "impaired communion" with liberal Western churches.

Although many traditional Christian Churches are losing members, other groups and trends are taking vigorous root. These include evangelical and charismatic groups, non-Western Christian Churches, commitment to social justice, Christian feminism, creation-centered Christianity, and the ecumenical movement.

Evangelicalism

A highly active segment of contemporary Christianity falls under the umbrella term "evangelicalism." This dynamic movement encompasses a large group of people who place the "born-again" experience as the central component in a Christian's life. The definition of Scottish historian David Bebbington is often used to define the movement. He proposed that its four defining characteristics are:

1. Biblicism (a particular and constant regard for the Bible).
2. Crucicentrism (a stress on the atoning sacrifice of Jesus on the cross).
3. Conversionism (conviction that lives need to be changed).
4. Activism (the expression of the gospel in effort).

Over time, this tradition has flowered into different groups, including fundamentalists, mainline Protestant evangelicals, the Holiness movement, and Pentecostals.

Contemporary manifestations of evangelicalism are related to the work of eighteenth- and nineteenth-century evangelists, such as the itinerant Methodist preacher John Wesley (1703–1791); George Whitefield (1714–1770), who preached dramatically to large open-air crowds in England and the United States; and Charles Grandison Finney (1792–1875), whose preaching reportedly led hundreds of thousands of people to conversion experiences.

In the United States, dramatic preaching in the 1730s and 1740s by figures such as the Calvinist Jonathan Edwards (1703–1758) brought a religious revival called "the First Great Awakening." Edwards' most famous sermon was "Sinners in the Hands of an Angry God" (1741), in which he exhorted a Connecticut congregation to be wary of God's power "to cast wicked men into hell at any moment."[93]

Another influential factor was the fundamentalist–modernist controversy of the early twentieth century. As discussed earlier, the **fundamentalists** were reacting against the liberal or modern movement in Christianity that sought to reconcile science and religion and to use historical and archaeological data to understand the Bible. This movement had an optimistic view of human nature and stressed reason, free will, and self-determination. In response, a group of Christians called for a return to what they considered the "fundamentals" of Christian faith. In 1911, "fundamentalists" in the United States published as their uncompromising tenets the total inerrancy of the Bible, and Christ's literal virgin birth, substitutionary atonement, bodily resurrection, and anticipated second coming. The controversy between fundamentalism and modernism received its most famous public expression in the Scopes trial in 1925 when John Thomas Scopes, a high school teacher in Tennessee, challenged a state law forbidding the teaching of Darwin's theory of evolution in schools.

During the twentieth century the fundamentalist movement in the United States developed into a powerful political and social force that rejects much of what it considers secular: public education, big government, and social programs run by the government. An attitude of withdrawing from the negative influence of the modern world dominates this movement.

Many evangelicals and other conservative Protestants anticipate the **rapture**—a time when Christians will be transported up to Heaven to live with Jesus in immortal bodies. Popular Christian media in the United States have fanned the belief that the end times are imminent and one should be ready, a belief that has serious ramifications in political decision-making.

Like all Protestants, evangelicals practice the two sacraments of baptism and the Lord's Supper, but they are much more concerned that the sacrament be personal and meaningful than that it be correctly done according to a book of worship. Evangelicals' messages now enjoy widespread visibility through international electronic media. Television programs and websites offer enthusiastic preaching, video and audio material, books, prayers for those in need, and the inevitable appeals for financial contributions to support these huge organizations.

On the ground, evangelicalism is also growing around the world. In South America, in areas that were largely Roman Catholic as a result of colonization by Spain centuries ago, in the early 1990s an average of five evangelical churches were being established each week in Rio de Janeiro. Most of them were in the slum areas, offering to the very poor such incentives as food, job training, and day care, as well as conversion.

Spirit-oriented movements

Overlapping somewhat with the evangelical surge, there is a rising emphasis on **charismatic** experience—that is, divinely inspired powers—among Christians of all classes and nations. While Christian fundamentalists stress the historical Jesus, charismatics feel they have also been touched by the "third person" of the Trinity, the Holy Spirit. These include members of Protestant Pentecostal churches but also Roman Catholics, members of mainline Protestant denominations, and Orthodox churches who are caught up in a widespread contemporary spiritual renewal that harks back to the biblical descent of the Holy Spirit upon the disciples of Jesus, firing them with spiritual powers and faith.

This movement encompasses all those who look for the spiritual gifts mentioned numerous times in the letters attributed to Paul, suggesting that these were common manifestations in the early Church. In I Corinthians, Paul writes:

> To each is given the manifestation of the Spirit for the common good. To one is given through the Spirit the utterance of wisdom, and to another the utterance of knowledge according to the same Spirit, to another faith by the same Spirit, to another gifts of healing by the one Spirit, to another the working of miracles, to another prophecy, to another the discernment of spirits, to another various kinds of tongues, to another the interpretation of tongues. All these are activated by one and the same Spirit, who allots to each one individually just as the Spirit chooses.[94]

There is no typical pattern to the charismatic experience of being endowed with divine powers. Vazhayil Babu is from South India, a nominal Christian by birth. He says he experienced a great void in his life, even as he married and became a successful businessman in the United States. So desperate that he became sick, he prayed, asking, "What should I do?" Then he reportedly experienced a Power in the room and heard a voice say, "Get out from the house now!" He thus took his wife and got on a Caribbean cruise ship. He sat in the hold praying until, he says, "God told me, 'Go to Bible college. Study the Word.'" Being over fifty years old, poor in English, and running a business to support his family, he struggled to obey that command, but at last finished his degree and began preaching. He reports:

> When I speak the word of God, the Bible, when I speak about Jesus, I tell them to come to the altar, and I pray for them. They're blind—they are healed. They are lame and crippled—they walk. I see with my two eyes. Sometimes I speak before 20,000 people. I pray a lot and then speak the word of God. I see miracles after miracles.[95]

One of the streams feeding the charismatic tradition was the nineteenth-century Holiness movement in the United States. It was an outgrowth of John Wesley's concept of "Christian perfection" through a transformational conversion experience. This opened doors to religious empowerment of the poor, women, and minorities. It also brought the element of emotional involvement into worship, in contrast to more formal worship in mainstream Protestant Churches.

A Holiness preacher in Kansas, Charles Parham (1873–1929), was healed of rheumatic fever and thence began a healing ministry and a school in which he proposed to train people for world evangelization, with the Bible as their only textbook. He challenged his students to wait in expectation for the spiritual gift of speaking in tongues, as evidence of baptism by the Holy Spirit.

One who was influenced by Parham was an African American preacher, William Joseph Seymour (1870–1922), whose parents were freed slaves. Given the segregation of races in the South, Seymour was only allowed to listen to Parham's talks through a half-opened door. Seymour was invited to be the pastor of a small African American Holiness church in Los Angeles, but he was locked out of it when he preached that speaking in tongues was a sign of baptism by the Spirit. Several members of the church invited him to pray with them in one of their homes. When the host asked Seymour to lay his hands on him, the man fell to the floor, seemingly unconscious, and began speaking in unknown languages. Seymour and others then had the same experience. For three days and nights they kept praying and rejoicing loudly. As more people joined them, including white people, the house was too small, so they rented an unused church building at 312 Azusa Street. Sitting on planks for benches, they held spontaneous, emotional meetings from morning until late at night. There was no planned worship. People sang in tongues and fell to the ground as they were "slain in the Spirit." These inter-racial revival meetings on Azusa Street eventually drew people from all over the United States and abroad, and as new centers were opened, the movement became known as **Pentecostalism.** Seymour himself was a humble, gracious, prayerful person, and without racial or gender discrimination he developed a core team of leaders who were both male and female, black and white.

The Holiness/Pentecostal movement brought spiritual women to the foreground even in times when women were otherwise excluded from Church leadership. For instance, Aimee Semple McPherson (1890–1944) was told by an inner voice, "Preach the Word!" and had several powerful experiences of the Holy Spirit. With no institutional framework, she simply stood on a chair in the street and prayed silently for an hour, with her arms held in the air. Curious people gathered around her. When she spoke to them afterward, her speech was so compelling that many followed her. This went on until crowds grew so huge that she had to set up an immense tent—her "canvas cathedral." Then she outfitted a large car as her "Gospel car" and traveled around the United States, calling people to Jesus. When she built the Angelus Temple in Los Angeles, her services became so popular that they caused traffic jams. During the Great Depression, she organized a soup kitchen that fed 80,000 people a month, as well as giving blankets and shelter to thousands of homeless people. The International Church of the Foursquare Gospel that she founded has grown to encompass more than five million people in eighty-three countries. It has not, however, emphasized gender equality; there are few women in its leadership roles.

William Joseph Seymour founded the Azusa Street Revival, one of the major sources of Pentecostalism.

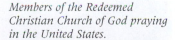

Members of the Redeemed Christian Church of God praying in the United States.

Pentecostalism is now a rapidly growing world movement. Its adherents generally look for a second experience of the Holy Spirit after the initial experience of salvation by belief in Jesus as Savior for the forgiveness of their sins; they require speaking in tongues as a sign of this "second grace" of baptism by the Holy Spirit. Adherents to this tradition affirm that they are under the influence of the Spirit when they speak in tongues (a phenomenon known as glossolalia), stand and gesture as they lovingly sing praises of Jesus and God, pray and utter praises, spontaneously heal by the laying on of hands and prayer, and bear witness to spiritual miracles.

Speaking of the descent of the Holy Spirit, Roman Bilas, Moscow head of the Union of Pentecostal Christians of Evangelical Faith, says passionately:

This moment when you really feel God's power in yourself brings so much peace and joy within you … There comes a sense of total forgiveness for your sins, and the ability in you to forgive others. At that moment, you start to speak in different languages, maybe such that no one can understand. We may also receive the gift of prophecy. … We check to see if the message is consistent with the Bible. If it is, then we will listen … The main thing is that the person should be filled with God's Power. A nice-looking car will not move unless it is fueled. God's Power will only fill those who are pure. That is why in the early Church people went into the wilderness to fast and repent. Then God could fill them with His Power. Each sermon should have this Power of God; then the people will really listen and repent of their sins.[96]

The Yoido Full Gospel Church in South Korea houses one of the largest Protestant Christian congregations in the world, with at least 830,000 members.

The Pentecostal–Charismatic movement is now said to be the fastest-growing religious movement throughout the world. Asia, Africa, and Latin America are experiencing explosive growth of Pentecostal–Charismatic Churches. Many of these Churches are carrying on extensive social work, such as running relief

services, feeding the poor, and building hospitals and schools. In Korea, Pastor David Yonggi Cho developed the immense Yoido Full Gospel Church, which is the world's biggest Christian congregation, with more than 800,000 members and hundreds of pastors promoting "prosperity in all things" as well as spiritual healing and experience of the Holy Spirit. Cho had been highly regarded as the greatest model for Church growth. But in 2014, a group of elders from his Church accused him and his family of embezzling over $500 million in Church funds, and it was also alleged that he had an extramarital relationship with a French singer.[97]

Some Pentecostal Churches are linked to "classical Pentecostalism," with roots in the nineteenth-century revivals in the United States. Others are denominations colored by regional cultural traditions, such as the vibrant **African Instituted Churches**, the umbrella term for Christian Churches in Africa that are not tied to Western denominations. They are usually oriented toward healing and protection from evil, the most prominent aspects of African indigenous religions. There are also independent "Neo-Pentecostal" Churches whose leaders' business sense has helped to market Spirit-oriented traditions to young people and upwardly mobile professionals. Whatever the type, Pentecostals tend to follow a strict code of personal ethics. Because of their conversion experiences, having become "a new creature in Christ," they typically do not drink, gamble, indulge in sex outside of marriage, or spend money and time carelessly.

Mainstream Christian Churches, which have often rejected emotional spiritual experience in favor of a more orderly piety, are gradually becoming more tolerant of it. Among Roman Catholics the movement is often called "Charismatic Renewal," for it claims to bring true life in the Spirit back to Christianity. By broad definition, one-fourth of all Christians today could be considered members of this Spirit-oriented movement,[98] and the percentage is growing.

The great reversal

Although contemporary Christianity was largely shaped in Europe and its North American colonies, the largest percentage of the Christian Church now lies outside these areas. It has great numerical strength and vigor in Africa, Latin America, and parts of Asia, and its strength in these areas is changing the face of Christianity. In 1970, Christianity was about forty-three percent non-Western, whereas today it is about sixty-five percent non-Western. In this short span of time, many independent, indigenous Churches have arisen in the world. Tens of millions of Chinese Christians are now worshiping in their homes or non-church buildings, in addition to those under closer government supervision in churches registered with the government. There are probably more Christians worshiping in China on Sundays than in all of Europe,[99] many of them in congregations of hundreds or even thousands emphasizing charismatic experiences reminiscent of traditional popular culture.

DJ Moz and two other Kenyan DJs bring young people to Jesus through an extremely popular TV program of gospel hip-hop and reggae.

Hundreds of millions of Africans are members of African Instituted Churches. As soon as the Western colonial supports were taken away, Christianity exploded in Africa as an indigenous religion. Africa was twenty-five percent Christian in 1950, whereas it is forty-eight percent Christian today.

When Western missionaries spread Christianity to other regions, they often assumed that European ways were culturally superior to the indigenous ways and peoples. But some of these newer Christians have come to different conclusions. Theologians of the African Instituted Churches, for instance, reject the historical missionary efforts to divorce them from their traditions of honoring their ancestors. This effort tore apart their social structure, they feel, with no scriptural justification:

As we became more acquainted with the Bible, we began to realise that there was nothing at all in the Bible about the European customs and Western traditions that we had been taught. What, then was so holy and sacred about this culture and this so-called civilisation that had been imposed upon us and was now destroying us? Why could we not maintain our African customs and be perfectly good Christians at the same time? ...

We have learnt to make a very clear distinction between culture and religion. ... [For instance], the natural customs of any particular nation or race must never be confused with the grace of Jesus Christ our Saviour, Redeemer and Liberator.[100]

Contemporary perceptions of Jesus have been deeply enriched by those of the inhabitants of poor Third World countries who have brought personal understanding of Jesus' ministry to the outcasts and downtrodden. In Asia, where Christians are usually in the minority, there is an emphasis on a Christ who is present in the whole cosmos and who calls all people to sit at a common table to partake of his generous love. In Latin America, Jesus is viewed as the liberator of the people from political and social oppression, from dehumanization, and from sin. In Africa, the African Instituted Churches have brought indigenous traditions of drumming, dancing, and singing into community worship of a Jesus who is seen as the greatest of ancestors—a mediator carrying prayers and offerings between humans and the divine, and watchful caretaker of the people.

Instead of the old pattern in which the West sent missionaries to spread Christianity to Asia, Africa, and South America, congregations in those areas are now being asked to send volunteers to the West to help spread the gospel in new missionary efforts there. Catholic prayer requests are now being "outsourced" through the Vatican to India from the United States, Canada, and Europe, where there are not enough clergy to handle the requests. Churches in Europe are becoming empty of worshipers as the people become more and more secular in their approach to life. Some of the most active remnants of Christianity in Europe are involved in peace and reconciliation movements.

The vigor of Christianity in the United States can be explained partly by the growth of evangelical and charismatic Churches and a linking of fundamentalist Christianity with right-wing political claims to patriotism and defense of family values. An equally important contribution is immigration. Today, as in the past, the majority of those who migrate to the United States are Christians, and migrants tend to build vital Churches.

Around the globe, many fundamentalists feel they are fighting a cultural war against liberalism, secularism, and materialism—within as well as beyond Christianity. Spiritually diverse, Christianity is also politically and culturally diverse.

Christian faith and justice

Although many Christians make a distinction between the sacred and the secular, some have involved themselves deeply with social issues as an expression of their Christian faith. For instance, the Baptist preacher Martin Luther King, Jr. (1929–1968) became a great civil rights leader. This trend is now called **liberation theology**, a faith that stresses the need for concrete political action to help the poor. Beginning in the 1960s with Vatican II and the conference of Latin American bishops in Colombia in 1968, Roman Catholic priests and nuns in Latin America began to make conscious, voluntary efforts to understand and side with the poor in their struggles for social justice.

The Peruvian theologian Gustavo Gutiérrez (b. 1928), who coined the expression "theology of liberation," explains the choice of voluntary poverty as:

a commitment of solidarity with the poor, with those who suffer misery and injustice. ... It is not a question of idealizing poverty, but rather of taking it on as it is—an evil—to protest against it and to struggle to abolish it.[101]

Volunteers from Feed My Starving Children, a nonprofit Christian organization, pray over food they have packaged for shipment to malnourished children in many countries.

For their sympathetic siding with those who are oppressed, Catholic clergy have been murdered by political authorities in some countries. They have also been strongly criticized by conservatives within the Vatican. The movement has nevertheless spread to all areas where there is social injustice. Bakole Wa Ilunga, Archbishop of Kananga, the Democratic Republic of Congo (formerly Zaire), reminds Christians that Jesus warned the rich and powerful that it would be very difficult for them to enter the kingdom of Heaven. By contrast, writes Ilunga:

> *Jesus liberates the poor from the feeling that they are somehow less than fully human; he makes them aware of their dignity and gives them motives for struggling against their lot and for taking control of their own lives.*[102]

Taking control is not easy for those who are oppressed minorities. In the United States, the Church offers the large African American community of Christians a way of developing an alternative reality in the midst of poverty, urban violence, and discrimination. As theologian Dwight Hopkins observes:

> *The black community has a long tradition of practicing faith as a total way of life. … Within worship, especially, the church is noted for its uplifting preaching, singing, shouting, dancing, and recognition of individual achievements and pain. … The rituals of individual healing and celebration serve to recharge the worshipers' energy to deal with the rigors and racism of a "cruel, cruel world" from Monday through Saturday.*[103]

The practical activities of the Black Church range from building shelters and arranging jobs to treatment for addiction, campaigns against police brutality, voter registration drives, and leadership training. Even without social empowerment, people often feel inwardly empowered and cherished by the presence of Jesus in their lives.

Other Christian denominations are also deeply engaged in social service ministries. For example, Kenyan Pentecostal Florence Muindi undertook training as a doctor because when she was praying she had a shocking vision of sick, starving, and deaf and dumb people. When she went to a very poor village in Ethiopia to serve in conjunction with the local Baptist church, she found health problems so endemic there that she trained a team of "health evangelists" to help eradicate the underlying causes: poor sanitation and hygiene. As they worked with families to improve sanitation in their environment, ministering to people's physical as well as spiritual needs, they also brought greater social

Archbishop Desmond M. Tutu

 During the years of struggle against apartheid in South Africa, one voice that refused to be silenced was that of the Anglican Archbishop of Cape Town, Desmond Mpilo Tutu (b. 1931). Afterward, he served his country as Chairperson of the Truth and Reconciliation Commission, "looking a beast in the eye" to investigate abuses from all sides that were perpetrated during the apartheid era. In this capacity, he still refused to mute his criticisms of those wielding power, no matter what their race and stature. In 1995 he proclaimed:

> The so-called ordinary people, God's favourites, are sick and tired of corruption, repression, injustice, poverty, disease and the violation of their human rights. They are crying out "enough is enough!" It is exhilarating when you are able to say to dictators everywhere: You have had it! You have had it! This is God's world and you will bite the dust! They think it will not happen but it does, and they bite the dust comprehensively and ignominiously.
>
> We will want to continue to be the voice of the voiceless. It is the role of the church to be the conscience of society.[104]

The "Arch's" fearless stance on behalf of truth and justice for the oppressed earned him the Nobel Peace Prize in 1984. He confronted not only those in power but also those who sought change through violence and those in the Church who witnessed the horrors of apartheid but kept silent. He explains, "Our task is to be agents of the Kingdom of God, and this sometimes requires us to say unpopular things."[105] He has continued to speak and act on many issues, including human rights, women's rights, AIDS, homophobia, poverty, racism, and climate change.

The former archbishop feels that faith requires one to be actively engaged in politics because government affects the people, but at the same time to remain independent of political factionalism in order to freely stand for truth. He says of the link between religion and politics:

> Faith is a highly political thing. At the centre of all that we believe as Christians is the incarnation—the participation of God in the affairs of this world. As followers of that God we too must be politically engaged. We need inner resources, however, in order to face the political demands of our time.[106]

How has Archbishop Tutu developed his inner resources? Through meditation, prayer, and fasting. He observes the traditional daily devotions of the Anglican Church, always starts meetings with prayer, and annually takes a long spiritual retreat. He regularly prays for others, and many are also praying for him; he asserts that intercessory prayer has practical effects. His spiritual confessor, Francis Cull, describes Archbishop Tutu's inner life as rooted in the Benedictine monastic discipline that underlies Anglican spirituality. He explains:

> As I ponder on the prayer life of Desmond Tutu I see the three fundamental Benedictine demands that there shall be: rest, prayer, and work and in that order. It is a remarkable fact, and it is one reason at least why he has been able to sustain the burdens he has carried, that he has within him a stillness and a need for quiet solitude. … The "rest" of which St. Benedict speaks is not a mere switching off; it is a positive attempt to fulfill the age-old command to rest in God. … The pattern of Jesus which he follows here: "Come apart and rest awhile," is an urgent need for all those who are caught up in the busyness of church and world.[107]

Desmond Tutu himself insists that spiritual practice is essential in order to know and follow the will of God:

> God's will has to do with what is right, just, decent and healing of the wounds of society. To know what this means we need to cleanse ourselves of ourselves—of our fears, greed, ambitions and personal desires. … We must be vigilant in ensuring that the good that is within all people triumphs over the evil that is also there. … We must commit ourselves to tell the truth. We must identify evil wherever we see it.[108]

cohesion in the community. Muindi explains, "We are the hands of Jesus Christ. The church is the representative of Christ in a suffering world."[109] It is through serving the poor and disenfranchised that people feel connected to Jesus, as they try to carry on his mission.

Feminist Christianity

The issue of taking control of one's life and defining one's identity has also been taken up by feminists within the Christian Church. The Church institution has historically been dominated by men, although there is strong evidence that Jesus had active women disciples and that there were women leaders in the early Churches. Reconstructing their history in the early Christian movement and the effects of patriarchical domination is a task being addressed by considerable in-depth scholarship. The effect of the apostle Paul in shaping attitudes toward women as he guided the developing Christian communities is one area of particular concern. Some of the statements attributed to him in the biblical Epistles seem oppressive to women; some seem egalitarian. He argues, for example, that men should pray or prophesy with their head uncovered but that women should wear a veil:

> For a man ought not to have his head veiled, since he is the image and reflection of God; but woman is the reflection of man. Indeed, man was not made from woman, but woman from man. Neither was man created for the sake of woman, but woman for the sake of man.[110]

Contemporary scholars are trying to sort out the cultural and historical as well as the theological contexts of such statements. Feminist theologian Rosemary Radford Ruether suggests that Paul was trying to preserve something of the status quo, and establish himself as a higher authority than other apostles who had apparently been teaching the Corinthians that, with Christian baptism, all the old separations between people had been erased, "a theological belief that the evil powers that lay behind a world divided by gender, social status, and clean and unclean spheres had already been overcome in the new life in Christ."[111]

Another area of feminist scholarship is the role models for women offered by the Bible. A central female figure in the New Testament is Mary, mother of Jesus. Ivone Gebara and Maria Clara Bingemer of Brazil look at Mary from the perspective of "the great masses of Latin America, the overwhelming majority of whom are poor, [who] enjoy no adequate quality of life, and lack respect, bread, love, and justice." While acknowledging that the dogmas developed by the Catholic Church about Mary may be inflated, they nonetheless reveal a wellspring of hope for women and other oppressed humans: "The exaltation that understandably comes out in dogma cannot … hide what is essential in God's salvation, that is, making God's glory shine on what is regarded as insignificant, degrading or marginal."[112]

A third major area of Christian feminist theology is the concept of God. The divine is commonly referred to as "He" or "Father," but scholarship reveals that this patriarchal usage is not absolute; there also existed other models of God as Mother, as Divine Wisdom, as Justice, as Friend, as Lover. Sallie McFague points out that to envision God as Mother, for instance, totally changes our understanding of our relationship to the divine:

> All of us, female and male, have the womb as our first home, all of us are born from the bodies of our mothers, all of us are fed by our mothers. What better imagery could there be for expressing the most basic reality of existence: that we live and move and have our being in God?[113]

With support from feminist theology, Christian women have won the right to be ordained as pastoral leaders in many denominations. During the past one hundred years, over half of all American Protestant denominations began ordaining women as ministers, and up to half of the students in United States

Reverend Catherine Rumen blesses the communion cup in London.

seminaries are female. In 2014, after a decade of struggles, Anglican women won the right to be ordained as bishops. On the other hand, Roman Catholic and Orthodox churches do not accept women as priests, and under a 2007 ruling, if an attempt is made to ordain a woman as a Catholic priest, both she and the bishop who ordained her will be excommunicated from the Church.

Creation-centered Christianity

Another current trend in Christianity is an attempt to develop and deepen its respect for nature. In the Judeo-Christian tradition, humans are thought to have been given dominion over all the things of the earth. Sometimes this "dominion" was interpreted as the right to exploit, rather than the duty to care for, the earth. Some Christians now feel that the notion of having a God-given right to control has allowed humans to nearly destroy the planet. Historian and passionate earth-advocate Father Thomas Berry (1914–2009) said, "We need to put the Bible on the shelf for twenty years until we learn to read the scripture of life."[114]

A Christianity that would accord greater honor to the created world would also tend to emphasize the miracle that is creation, thus helping to unite science and religion. Creation-centered Christians—such as the Jesuit priest and paleontologist Teilhard de Chardin (1881–1955)—see the mind of God in the perfect, intricate balances of chemistry, biology, and physics that allow life as we know it to exist.

Not only is the earth threatened by our careless exploitation; our spiritual lives suffer as well, according to Father Berry:

What happens to the outer world happens to the inner world. If the outer world is diminished in its grandeur, then the emotional, imaginative, intellectual, and spiritual life of the human is diminished or extinguished. Without the soaring birds, the great forests, the sounds and coloration of the insects, the free-flowing streams, the flowering fields, the sight of the clouds by day and the stars at night, we become impoverished in all that makes us human.[115]

Around the world, many Christian Churches and leaders have taken up the cause of encouraging people and governments to limit environmental destruction. In the United States, a 2006 statement signed by presidents of evangelical colleges, pastors of popular "megachurches," and leaders of social-aid groups such as the Salvation Army urged the government to pass legislation to avert global warming, in accordance with Christian ethics, for "millions of people could die in this century because of climate change, most of them our poorest global neighbors."[116]

The Ecumenical Patriarchate has sponsored many international and inter-disciplinary symposia concerning various aspects of humanity's destruction of its planetary home. Ecumenical Patriarch Bartholomew, the "Green Patriarch," urges: "We are to use its resources in moderation and frugality, to cultivate it in love and humility, and to preserve it in accordance with the scriptural command to serve and preserve (cf. Gen. 2:15). Within the unimpaired natural environment, humanity discovers deep spiritual peace and rest."[117]

Ecumenical movement

Although the followers of Jesus have become split into thousands of denominations, with the explosion of charismatic and African Instituted Churches adding yet more new groups, there is also a contemporary counter-attempt to unify all Christians around some point of agreement or at least fellowship with each other.

The Second Vatican Council (Vatican II) asserted that the Roman Catholic Church is the one Church of Christ, but opened the way to dialogue with other branches of Christianity by declaring that the Holy Spirit was active in them as well. The Orthodox Church likewise believes that it is the "one, holy, Catholic, and Apostolic Church." Although it desires reunion of all Christians and denies any greed for organizational power, it insists on uniformity in matters of faith. Orthodox and Roman Catholic Churches therefore do not share Holy Communion with those outside their respective disciplines. Some Protestant denominations have branches that also refuse to acknowledge each other's validity.

In the attempt to restore some bonds among all Christian Churches, there are dozens of official ecumenical dialogues going on. The World Council of Churches, centered in Geneva, was founded in 1948 as an organizational body allowing Christian Churches to co-operate on service projects even in the midst of their theological disagreements. Its Faith and Order Commission links 300 culturally, linguistically, and politically, not to mention theologically, different Christian Churches in working out the problems of Christian unity. However, the Orthodox Church representatives are always in the minority within the council and therefore typically lose when decisions call for a majority vote. The consensus model for decision-making has been proposed as being closer to the original spirit of Christianity. As Father Denis G. Pereira explains:

> This model may be more difficult and involve more time. But it is inspired by a spirit of love, respect and generosity rather than suspicion and competition. The method supposes that the Church must be always open to the Spirit of God, and that the Spirit often speaks through the least and the last, at times even through a minority of one.[118]

The historic doctrinal and organizational divisions between Churches are not easily bridged. There is also a growing split between liberal and conservative denominations. Instead of doctrinal rapprochement, there are thus some efforts to forge strategic alliances between "Churches of Tradition"—particularly

Pope Francis and Ecumenical Patriarch Bartholomew, respective heads of the Roman Catholic and Orthodox branches of Christianity, in an historic meeting in 2014. They met at the Church of the Holy Sepulchre in Jerusalem, traditionally thought to be the site of the tomb in which Jesus' body was placed after his crucifixion.

Roman Catholics and Orthodox. In 2014, Pope Francis and Ecumenical Patriarch Bartholomew met in Jerusalem to encourage "communion in legitimate diversity." They especially pledged to work together in certain areas of great concern:

> *We acknowledge that hunger, poverty, illiteracy, the inequitable distribution of resources must constantly be addressed. It is our duty to seek to build together a just and humane society in which no-one feels excluded or emarginated...*
>
> *Together, we pledge our commitment to raising awareness about the stewardship of creation; we appeal to all people of goodwill to consider ways of living less wastefully and more frugally, manifesting less greed and more generosity for the protection of God's world and the benefit of His people. ...*
>
> *We invite all Christians to promote an authentic dialogue with Judaism, Islam and other religious traditions. Indifference and mutual ignorance can only lead to mistrust and unfortunately even conflict.*[119]

Ecumenical Patriarch Bartholomew points out that increasing harmony even in the midst of diversity and differences is the mission of Christianity:

> *The growing signs of a common commitment to work together for the well-being of humanity and the life of the world are encouraging. ... It is an involvement that highlights the supreme purpose and calling of humanity to transcend political or religious differences in order to transform the entire world for the glory of God.*
>
> *There will be an effective, transformative change in our world only when we are prepared to make sacrifices that are radical, painful, and genuinely unselfish. ... Unselfishness implies generosity, rendering the world transparent and transforming it into the mystery of communion and sharing between created beings, between human beings, and between earth and heaven.*[120]

Key terms

apocalypse In Judaism and Christianity, the dramatic end of the present age.

Ascension The ascent of Jesus to Heaven forty days after his Resurrection.

baptism A Christian sacrament by which God cleanses all sin and makes one a sharer in the divine life, and a member of Christ's body, the Church.

Christ A reference to Jesus as the "anointed one," the Messiah.

Common Era Years after the traditional date used for the birth of Jesus, previously referred to in exclusively Christian terms as AD and now abbreviated to CE, as opposed to BCE (Before Common Era).

confirmation A Christian sacrament by which awareness of the Holy Spirit is enhanced.

creed A formal statement of the beliefs of a particular religion; in Christianity, especially the Nicene Creed.

crucifixion In Roman times, the execution of a criminal by fixing him to a cross; with reference to Jesus, **Crucifixion**, his death on the cross, symbolic of his self-sacrifice for the good of all humanity.

denomination One of the Protestant branches of Christianity.

dogma A system of beliefs declared to be true by a religion.

ecumenism Rapprochement between branches of Christianity or among all faiths.

Eucharist The Christian sacrament by which believers are renewed in the mystical body of Christ by partaking of bread and wine, understood as his body and blood.

fundamentalism A mostly Protestant movement that began in the late nineteenth century, insisting on biblical literalism and rejecting liberal theological trends.

Gentile Any person who is not of Jewish faith or origin.

Gnosticism Mystical perception of spiritual knowledge, applied to a second-century CE movement arising in Egypt.

gospel The "good news" that God has raised Jesus from the dead and in so doing has begun the transformation of the world; usually now refers to the four books of the New Testament (Matthew, Mark, Luke, and John) chronicling the life and works of Jesus.

Holy Trinity The Christian doctrine that in the One God are three divine persons: the Father, the Son, and the Holy Spirit.

incarnation Physical embodiment of the divine; in Christianity, with particular reference to Jesus' becoming man.

Inquisition The use of force and terror to eliminate heresies and nonbelievers in the Christian Church, starting in the thirteenth century; a specific institution of this name set up in Spain in 1478.

Messiah In Christianity, the "anointed one," Jesus Christ.

New Testament Books of the Christian Bible that were composed after the death of Jesus, including the Gospels, Acts of the Apostles, Epistles, and Revelation.

Old Testament Christian term for the books of the Hebrew Bible that form the first part of the Christian Bible.

original sin A Christian belief that all human beings are bound together in prideful egocentricity. Described mythically in the Bible as an act of disobedience on the part of Adam and Eve.

parable An allegorical story.

Pentecost The occasion when the Holy Spirit descended upon the disciples of Jesus after his death.

pope The Bishop of Rome and head of the Roman Catholic Church.

Resurrection The rising of Christ in his earthly body on the first Easter Day, three days after his crucifixion and death.

sacrament Outward and visible sign of inward and spiritual grace.

synod A council of Church officials called to reach agreement on doctrines and administration.

synoptic Referring to three similar books of the Christian Bible: Matthew, Mark, and Luke.

Suggested reading

Achtmeier, Paul, J., general ed., *The HarperCollins Bible Dictionary*, 1966, New York: HarperCollins, 1996. Extensive contemporary scholarship on the Bible, with its historical contexts and modern interpretations.

Alfeyev, Hilarion, *The Spiritual World of Isaac the Syrian*, Collegeville, Minnesota: Liturgical Press, 2000. An important Russian Orthodox leader delves into the deep spirituality of a seventh century ascetic's teachings of repentance, stillness, faith, and "luminous love."

Anderson, Allen, *An Introduction to Pentecostalism: Global Charismatic Christianity*, Cambridge: Cambridge University Press, 2004. A global picture of the fastest-growing movement in Christianity, in its many different cultural and historical variations.

Bainton, Roland Herbert, *Christianity*, New York: Houghton Mifflin, 2000. A contemporary survey of Christian history.

Balmer, Randall, *Mine Eyes Have Seen the Glory: A Journey into the Evangelical Subculture in America*, fourth edition, New York: Oxford University Press, 2006. Explorations of popular evangelical phenomena across the United States.

Bartholomew, His All Holiness Ecumenical Patriarch, *Encountering the Mystery: Understanding Orthodox Christianity Today*, New York: Doubleday, 2008. Explanations of Orthodox Christianity from a liberal contemporary perspective, by the most influential Orthodox leader.

Bednarowski, Mary Farrell, ed., *Twentieth-Century Global Christianity*, vol. 7 of Denis R. Janz, general ed., *A People's History of Christianity*, Minneapolis: Fortress Press, 2008. Far-ranging articles on how real people are living by, and changing the faces of, Christianity in the contemporary world.

Borg, Marcus J., *The Heart of Christianity*, San Francisco: HarperSanFrancisco, 2003. A major voice in Progressive Christianity discusses the relevance of Christianity to modern life.

Borg, Marcus, J., *Meeting Jesus Again for the First Time: The Historical Jesus and the Heart of Contemporary Faith*, San Francisco: HarperSanFrancisco, 1994. An accessible and appreciative discussion of the Jesus of history, as opposed to the Jesus of faith.

Braybrooke, Marcus, *The Explorer's Guide to Christianity*, London: Hodder & Stoughton, 1998. With the sensitivity of a global interfaith leader, Rev. Braybrooke offers a succinct introduction to Christianity for people of every faith and country.

Brown, Candy Gunther, ed., *Global Pentecostal and Charismatic Healing*, New York: Oxford University Press, 2011. Scholars from many disciplines examine the growing global phenomena of Pentecostalist healings.

Castelli, Elizabeth A., *Martyrdom and Memory: Early Christian Culture Making*, New York: Columbia University Press, 2004. Analysis of ways in which early centuries of martyrdom shaped Christian identity.

Chryssavgis, John, *Light through Darkness: The Orthodox Tradition*, Maryknoll, New York: Orbis Books, 2004. Exploration of the theme of brokenness and healing as central to Orthodox spiritual experience.

Coakley, John W. and Andrea Sterk, *Readings in World Christian History*, Maryknoll, New York: Orbis Books, 2004. Beginnings of Christianity up to the late Middle Ages, with substantial excerpts including ancient roots of Christianity in Asia and Africa.

Crossan, John Dominic, *Jesus: A Revolutionary Biography*, San Francisco: HarperSanFrancisco, 1994. A now classic reconstruction of the life of Jesus through historical and textual analysis.

Crossan, John Dominic and Jonathan L. Reed, *In Search of Paul*, San Francisco: HarperSanFrancisco, 2004. Exploration of Paul's teachings in historical and social context.

Hopkins, Dwight N., ed., *Black Faith and Public Talk*, Maryknoll, New York: Orbis Books, 1999. Essays probing how people of color relate Christian understanding to economic, social, and religious situations and ideals in today's world.

Irvin, Dale T. and Scott W. Sunquist, *History of the World Christian Movement, Volume 1: Earliest Christianity to 1453*. Maryknoll, New York: Orbis Books, 2001. An inclusive view of early Christian history extending to inputs from, and influences on, the cultures and people of Asia, Africa, and West Asia. *Volume 2, Modern Christianity from 1454–1800*, 2012, continues this global study of Christian history up to 1800.

King, Ursula, ed., *Feminist Theology from the Third World: A Reader*, Maryknoll, New York: Orbis Books, 1994. Excellent compendium of the voices of marginalized peoples, which give a special poignance and depth of meaning to efforts to give women a voice in shaping and interpreting Christianity.

Lassalle-Klein, Robert, ed., *Jesus of Galilee: Contextual Christology for the 21st Century*, Maryknoll, New York: Orbis Books, 2011. International scholars consider the meaning of the historical Jesus as seen from their varied social contexts.

Marsden, George M., *Fundamentalism and American Culture*, New York: Oxford University Press, second edition, 2006. Analysis of the political influence of Christian fundamentalism in the United States.

Miller, Donald E. and Tetsunao Yamamori, *Global Pentecostalism: The New Face of Christian Social Engagement*, Berkeley, California: University of California Press, 2007. Perceptive analyses of Pentecostal phenomena and descriptions of social work being done by Pentecostalists in many countries.

Pagels, Elaine, *Revelations: Visions, Prophecy, and Politics in the Book of Revelation*, New York: Penguin Books, 2012. Interesting exploration of meanings attributed to the mysterious last book of the Bible, in context of the history of the early Christian movement.

Robinson, James M., ed., *The Nag Hammadi Library*, San Francisco: Harper & Row, 1977. A fascinating collection of early scriptures that are not included in the Christian canon.

Ruether, Rosemary Radford, *Women and Redemption: A Theological History*, Minneapolis: Fortress Press, 1998. A major feminist theologian traces global and historical threads of women's place in Christian thinking.

Schüssler Fiorenza, Elisabeth, *In Memory of Her: A Feminist Theological Reconstruction of Christian Origins*, New York: Crossroad, 1983, 1994. Extensive scholarship about the role of women in early Christianity.

Schwaller, John Frederick, *The History of the Catholic Church in Latin America: From Conquest to Revolution and Beyond*. New York: New York University Press, 2011. The Church's complex history in Latin America, as intertwined with its political and economic developments.

Sobrino, Jon, *No Salvation Outside the Poor*, Maryknoll, New York: Orbis Books, 2008. Challenging Christian perspectives on the global tragedy of poverty.

Tugwell, Simon, *Ways of Imperfection*, London: Darton, Longman and Todd, 1984, and Springfield, Illinois: Templegate Publishers, 1985. Spirituality as a whole vision of life, as seen by a series of great Christian practitioners.

Wacker, Grant, *Heaven Below: Early Pentecostals and American Culture*. Cambridge, Massachusetts: Harvard University Press, 2001. History and explanation of the growth of Pentecostalism in daily life in the United States.

Ware, Timothy, *The Orthodox Church*, Middlesex, UK, and Baltimore, Maryland: Penguin Books, 1984, 1993. An overview of the history, beliefs, and practices of the Eastern Church.

Wilson, Ian, *Jesus: The Evidence*, Washington, D.C.: Regnery Publishing, 2000. Illustrated survey of historical and archaeological evidence of the life of Jesus.

9.1 Discuss the four gospels on which Christian beliefs about the life and teachings of Jesus are founded

Christian beliefs about the life and teachings of Jesus are especially founded on biblical texts, particularly the first four books of the New Testament. Three of these books, Matthew, Mark, and Luke are so similar that they are called the synoptic gospels, referring to the fact that they can be "seen together" as presenting rather similar views of Jesus' career. The Gospel of John concerns itself less with following the life of Jesus than with confirming his Messiahship.

9.2 Outline the major events in the life of Jesus as described in the gospels

According to the gospels, Jesus was born in Bethlehem (*c.* 4 BCE to 1 CE) where his mother, Mary (a virgin when she conceived him by the Holy Spirit), and Joseph, her husband, had traveled because of a census. Shepherds and Magi (sages from "the east") came to pay their respects. When Jesus was about thirty he was baptized by John the Baptist and then undertook a forty-day retreat in the desert wilderness, fasting. Jesus then gathered his first disciples and traveled, preaching and performing miracles. He was regarded with suspicion by prominent Jewish groups of his time and the anti-institutional tenor of his teachings did not endear him to those in power. Pontius Pilate, the Roman governor, ordered his crucifixion. Jesus rose from his tomb two days later (the Resurrection) and after appearing to his disciples ascended into Heaven.

9.3 Discuss the significance of Paul in the early Christian Church

One of the persecutors of early Christians was Saul, a Pharisee tentmaker. After Jesus' death he helped to throw many of his followers into prison. On the way to Damascus in search of more heretics, Saul met with the risen Christ and was transformed by the experience. He was baptized and immediately began promoting the Christian message under his new name, Paul. His missionary work traveling around the Mediterranean from 46 to 60 CE shaped and expanded the early Christian Church. He tried to convince Jews that Jesus was the Messiah they had been waiting for and also to sway Gentiles (worshipers of the old gods). Paul wrote some of the letters to early groups of Christians in the New Testament.

9.4 Summarize the division between the Eastern and Western Churches in the Middle Ages

Late in the third century CE, the Roman Empire was divided into two: an Eastern section and a Western section. In the fourth century CE, Constantine established a second imperial seat in the East, in Constantinople, which was considered a "second Rome." The two halves of the Christian world grew apart from each other, divided by language, culture, and religious differences. The Eastern part of Christendom did not accept the absolute claims of the papacy, and by the early Middle Ages there were also doctrinal disagreements over the Holy Spirit. In 1054, leaders of the Eastern and Western factions excommunicated each other over this disagreement. When in 1204 Western crusaders entered Constantinople and destroyed the altar and sacred icons in Hagia Sophia, the Orthodox Church ended its dialogue with Rome and proceeded on its own path, claiming to be the true descendant of the apostolic Church.

9.5 Identify the major reforms of the Protestant and Roman Catholic Reformations

With the rise of literacy and printing in the late fifteenth century, many Christians were rediscovering early Christianity and comparing it unfavorably with the Roman Catholic Church. Reformists Martin Luther (1483–1546), Ulrich Zwingli (1484–1531), and John Calvin (1509–1564) in northern Europe challenged some of the doctrines and practices of Roman Catholicism. They believed in salvation by faith alone, the exclusive authority of the Bible, and "the priesthood of all believers." Reform movements branched out in many directions, leading over time to a great proliferation of Protestant denominations.

The Roman Catholic Church was provoked by the Protestant Reformation to clarify its own position through councils of bishops, especially the Council of Trent (1545–63). This council attempted to legislate moral reform among the clergy, to tighten the Church administration, and to recognize officially the absolute authority of the pope as the earthly vicar of God and Jesus Christ. The council also took historic stands on a number of issues, emphasizing that its positions were dogmas, or authoritative truths.

9.6 Describe the distinctive features of Orthodox spirituality

There is a strong conservative tradition in the Orthodox Churches, which attempts to preserve the pattern of early Christianity. Any change that will affect all Churches is decided by a synod (council of officials). Although women are important in local Church affairs, they cannot be ordained as priests or serve in hierarchical capacities.

In addition to the Bible, Orthodox Christians honor the writings of the saints of the Church. Particularly important is a collection called the *Philokalia*—a Christian guide to the contemplative life. A central practice is called "unceasing prayer": the continual remembrance of Jesus or God. The Orthodox Church has affirmed that humans can approach God directly through faith, as opposed to intellectual knowledge. Another distinctive feature is its veneration of icons (stylized paintings of Jesus, his mother Mary, and the saints), believed to be windows to the eternal.

9.7 Summarize the central beliefs in contemporary Christianity

The divine Sonship of Jesus—the assertion that Jesus is the incarnation of a merciful God—is a central belief in Christianity today. For Christians, Jesus is the Savior of the world, the one whom God sent to redeem people from their sins and reconcile them with God. According to traditional Christian belief, humanity is inclined to sin. Through fully surrendered faith in Jesus, Christians hope to be washed of their egotistical sinfulness, regenerated, made righteous, adopted by God, sanctified, and glorified in the life to come. Christians see Jesus as a human being, showing fellow human beings the way to God. His own life is seen as the perfect model for human behavior.

9.8 Define "sacrament" and outline the seven sacraments observed by the Roman Catholic and Eastern Orthodox Churches

Sacrament is the outward and visible sign of inward and spiritual grace in Christianity. In Roman Catholicism and Orthodoxy, the sacraments are the sacred rites that are thought capable of transmitting the mystery of Christ to worshipers. These Churches observe seven sacraments: baptism (initiation and symbolic purification from sin by water), confirmation (of membership in the Church), Eucharist (the ritual meal through which Christ is thought to grant communion with himself), penance (confession and absolution of sins), extreme unction (anointing of the sick with oil, especially before death), holy orders (consecration as a deacon, priest, or bishop), and matrimony. In general, Protestant Churches recognize only baptism and the Eucharist as sacraments and have a somewhat less mystical understanding of their significance.

9.9 Differentiate between evangelicalism and Spirit-oriented movements

Evangelicalism is a dynamic movement that encompasses a large group of people who place the "born again" experience as the central component in a Christian's life. Evangelicals have a particular and constant regard for the Bible and many anticipate the rapture—a time when Christians will be transported up to Heaven to live with Jesus. Like all Protestants, they practice the two sacraments of baptism and the Eucharist.

Overlapping somewhat with evangelicalism, there is a rising emphasis on charismatic experience (divinely inspired powers) among Christians of all classes and nations. Charismatics feel that they have also been touched by the "third person" of the Trinity, the Holy Spirit. The movement encompasses all those who look for the spiritual gifts mentioned numerous times in the letters attributed to Paul. The Pentecostal-Charismatic movement is now a rapidly growing world movement.

CHAPTER 10

ISLAM

"If you at least help one person seriously in your life, then you have learned something in your life. You can show your face to God, that you have helped one of his creatures who was suffering. Otherwise what is life? It won't make any sense." Dr. Syed M. Hussain[1]

10.1 **Describe pre-Islamic Arabia**

10.2 **Explain how the revelations given to Muhammad influenced Islamic belief**

10.3 **Outline the role of the Qur'an in Islam**

10.4 **Summarize the central teachings of Islam**

10.5 **Identify the Five Pillars of Islam**

10.6 **Distinguish between Sunni and Shi'a Islam**

10.7 **Define shari'ah**

10.8 **Describe the key aspects of Sufism**

10.9 **Analyze the reasons for the successful expansion of Islam in the seventh and eighth centuries**

10.10 **Explain the spread of Islam in the West**

10.11 **Discuss the main issues facing contemporary Islam**

In about 570 CE, a new prophet was born. This man, Muhammad, is considered by Muslims to be the last of a continuing chain of prophets who have come to restore the true religion. They regard the way revealed to him, Islam, not as a new religion but as the original path of monotheism, which also developed into Judaism and Christianity.

After carrying the torch of civilization in the West while Europe was in its Dark Ages, in the twentieth century Islam began a great resurgence. It is now the religion of nearly one-fifth of the world's people. Its monotheistic creed is simple: "There is no god but God, and Muhammad is his Messenger." Its requirements of the faithful are straightforward. But beneath them lie profundities and subtleties of which non-Muslims are largely unaware. In fact, ignorance about Islam and perceived targeting of Muslims in general by the U.S.-led "war on terrorism" have exacerbated a dangerous and growing divide between Muslims and non-Muslims in the contemporary world. Therefore it is extremely important to study the origins, teachings, and modern history of this major world religion carefully.

Pre-Islamic Arabia

What was life like in pre-Islamic Arabia?

The Ka'bah in Mecca is Islam's holiest place of worship.

Islam, like Christianity and Judaism, traces its ancestry to the patriarch Abraham (whom Muslims know as Ibrahim). He is said to have fathered two sons. The first was Isma'il, son of Hagar, an Egyptian slave whom Muslims regard as his wife. The second was Isaac, son of his wife Sarah. When Isaac was born, Abraham reportedly took Isma'il and Hagar to the desert valley of Mecca (Makkah) in a mountainous area of Arabia, to establish and maintain prayer to God. According to the Holy Qur'an, the sacred book of Islam, Abraham and Isma'il together built the holiest sanctuary in Islam, the Ka'bah. It was thought to be the site of Adam's original place of worship; part of the cubic stone building is a venerated black meteorite. According to the Qur'an, God told Abraham that the Ka'bah should be a place of pilgrimage. It was regarded as a holy place by the Arabian tribes.

According to Islamic tradition, the region sank into historical oblivion as it turned away from Abraham's monotheism. For many centuries, the events of the rest of the world passed it by, aside from contact through trading caravans. The Arabs of the area were mostly nomadic cattle-breeders, shifting their herds through the desert in search of areas that had some greenery. Robbing caravans and settlements also helped them to sustain themselves, except during three months of the lunar year when raids were forbidden according to tribal religion. Drinking, gambling, and prostitution seemingly were commonplace activities. Mecca was situated along trade routes and was a trading center, but apparently it consisted only of simple palm-branch huts.

The most powerful of the tribes there were the Quraysh, comprising approximately a dozen clans who lived as merchants. Nomadic tribal rules mandated that clan chiefs should take care of their weaker and poorer clan members, but this social rule was not necessarily followed by the merchant clans.

Because of their nomadic traveling, the Arabic tribes were in contact with each other and had a relatively uniform culture and a common language. They worshiped many deities and believed that people's lives were controlled by an impersonal force, called Fate or Time. Their tribal code of ethics held an entire clan responsible for its members' misdoings, and often took a life for a life. Long-lasting blood feuds were therefore common. But violence was prohibited within a large area surrounding the Ka'bah. Before Islam, the Ka'bah is thought to have contained 360 idols of Arabian tribal deities, perhaps including the Daughters of God and Hubal, one of the primary deities worshiped by the Quraysh. Statues of Jesus and Mary were also enshrined there. Pilgrimage to Mecca to honor these deities was an important part of the economy of the city.

The Prophet Muhammad

How did Muhammad's life influence aspects of Islamic belief and practice?

In this unpromising pre-Islamic setting, which Muslims call "the age of ignorance," a child named Muhammad (the praised one) was born into the Hashim clan of the Quraysh tribe. His great-grandfather had been the clan chief and caretaker of the Ka'bah. He was highly respected for organizing large trading caravans with concessions from the Byzantine and Ethiopian emperors and guarantees of safety from surrounding tribes. He was also appreciated for his

Islam

CE c. 570	Birth of Prophet Muhammad
c. 610	Revelation of the Qur'an to Prophet Muhammad begins
622	The hijrah (migration) from Mecca to Medina
630	Prophet Muhammad's triumphant return to Mecca
632	Death of Prophet Muhammad; election of Abu Bakr as first caliph
633	Spread of Islam begins
650	Written text of the Qur'an established
661–750	Umayyad dynasty
680	Karbala massacre of Husayn, grandson of the Prophet, and his relatives
691	Dome of the Rock in Jerusalem
732	European advance of Islam stopped at battle of Tours
750–1258	Islam reaches its cultural peak under Abbasid caliphs
922	al-Hallaj killed
1058–1111	Life of al-Ghazali, leading mystical philosopher
1126–98	Ibn Rushd (Averroes), philosopher of "two truths"—revelation and reason
1187	Salah-al-Din recaptures Jerusalem from crusaders
1300s–1400s	Christians reconquer Spain
1453	Turks conquer Constantinople, renaming it Istanbul
1478–1834	Spanish Inquisition
1492	Surrender of Granada, last foothold of Islam in Spain
1556	Akbar becomes Mughal emperor in India
1800s–mid-1900s	Muslim areas fall under European domination
1947	Partition of Muslim Pakistan from Hindu India
1970s	Oil-rich Muslim states join OPEC and Muslim resurgence begins
2001	Al Qaeda terrorists fly aircraft into U.S. buildings
2003	United States and allies invade Iraq
2011	"Arab Spring" uprisings bring down several governments in Muslim-majority countries
2014	Islamic State declares itself a new caliphate

benevolent care of pilgrims to the Ka'bah. Once, it is said, he prevented starvation from a great famine in Mecca by buying flour and bread in Syria and then killing his own camels to feed the whole tribe daily until the famine ended. Muhammad's grandfather was also renowned for providing food and water to pilgrims to the Ka'bah and for re-digging the well of Zam-Zam, the spring that God is said to have provided for Hagar when she and Isma'il were left alone in the desert. But Muhammad's family fell on hard times, for his father died during a trading journey before he was born. When Muhammad was sent to a Bedouin tribe to be wet-nursed, as was the custom, only a very poor woman took him in. The Prophet therefore grew up amidst poverty, and was always deeply sympathetic with the poor and underprivileged.

Muhammad's mother also died when he was six, and then his grandfather, who had assumed the position of clan chief. Muhammad became the ward of his uncle, who put him to work as a shepherd.

Although Muhammad is not to be worshiped by Muslims, whose faith resides only in God, his life story is considered important as a model. Even in his youth, he was known for his thoughtful and trustworthy character. The stories of Muhammad's life and his sayings are preserved in literature called the **Hadith**, reports of the Prophet's sayings and exemplary actions (**Sunnah**). These are of varying authenticity; the Hadith considered most reliable in the Sunni tradition are those carefully collected by Imam Bukhari (d. 870) and by his student, Imam Muslim (d. 875).

As a young man, Muhammad managed caravans for a beautiful, intelligent, and wealthy woman named Khadijah. When Muhammad was twenty-five, she appreciated his good qualities and offered to marry him. Khadijah became Muhammad's strongest supporter during the difficult and discouraging years of his early mission.

With Khadijah's understanding of his spiritual propensities, Muhammad began to spend periods of time in solitary retreat. These retreats provided opportunities for contemplation, away from the world.

When Muhammad was forty years old, he made a spiritual retreat during the month called Ramadan. An angel in human-like form, Gabriel, reportedly came to him and insisted that he recite. Three times Muhammad demurred that he could not, for he was unlettered, and three times the angel forcefully commanded him. In desperation, Muhammad at last cried out, "What shall I recite?" and the angel began dictating the first words of what became the Qur'an:

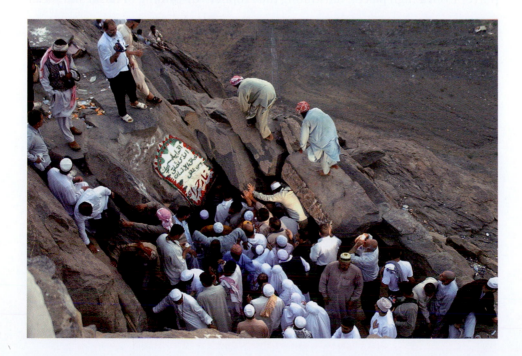

According to tradition, Muhammad undertook spiritual retreats in this cave on Mount Hira outside Mecca. It was here that he received the first revelations of the Qur'an.

Read in and with the Name of your Lord, Who has created—
Created human from a clot clinging (to the wall of the womb).
Read, and your Lord is the All-Munificent,
Who has taught (human) by the pen—
Taught human what he did not know.[2]

Muhammad returned home, deeply shaken and overwhelmed by the profound experience of communion with God. Khadijah comforted and encouraged him. The revelations continued intermittently, asserting the theme that it was the One God who spoke and who called people to Islam (which means complete, trusting surrender to God), emphasizing that they were accountable to God and not their tribes. The revelations in Mecca included other subjects such as rejection of polytheism in favor of pure monotheism, evidence of God in the Creation, belief, repentance, the Last Judgment, social justice, and acceptance of the revelations given through Muhammad as a messenger of God. One of the revelations explained:

> *When Our Revelations, clear as evidence and in meaning are recited (and conveyed) to them, those who have no expectations to meet Us say (in response to Our Messenger): "Either bring a Qur'an other than this or alter it." Say: "It is not for me to alter it of my own accord. I only follow what is revealed to me…"*
> *Say (also): "If God had so willed, I would not have recited it to you, nor would He have brought it to your knowledge. I lived among you a whole life time before it (began to be revealed to me). Will you not reason and understand?"*[3]

The Prophet shared these revelations with the few people who believed him: his wife, Khadijah; his young cousin, 'Ali; his friend, the trader Abu Bakr; Khadijah's Christian cousin Waraqah; and his loyal freed slave, Zayd.

After three years, Muhammad was instructed by the revelations to preach publicly. He was ridiculed and defamed by the Qurayshites, who operated the Ka'bah as a polytheistic pilgrimage center and organized profitable trading caravans through Mecca. While Muhammad was somewhat protected by the influence of his uncle, his followers were subject to persecution. A dark-skinned Abyssinian slave named Bilal, who was among the first converts, was imprisoned and brought out daily under the hot sun, pinned to the ground with a heavy stone on his chest, and ordered to deny the Prophet and worship the old gods. He staunchly refused, saying, "One, one." Once bought by the Prophet's friend Abu Bakr, Bilal became the first **muezzin** (one who calls the people to prayer from a high place), illustrating the Prophet's discarding of racial and social

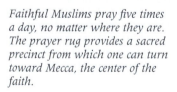

Faithful Muslims pray five times a day, no matter where they are. The prayer rug provides a sacred precinct from which one can turn toward Mecca, the center of the faith.

class distinctions. Finally, according to some accounts, Muhammad and his followers were banished for three years to a desolate place where they struggled to survive by eating wild foods such as tree leaves.

The band of Muslims was asked to return to Mecca, but the persecution by the Qurayshites continued. Muhammad's fiftieth year, the "Year of Sorrows," was the worst of all: He lost his beloved wife Khadijah and his protective uncle. With his strongest backers gone, persecution of the Prophet increased.

According to tradition, at the height of his trials Muhammad experienced the Night of Ascension. He is said to have ascended through the seven heavens to the far limits of the cosmos, and thence into the Divine Proximity. There he met former prophets and teachers from Adam to Jesus, saw paradise and hell, and received the great blessings of the Divine Presence. The Night of Ascension is seen as a confirmation of Muhammad's mission, and also demonstrates Islam's connections to Jewish and Christian tradition.

Pilgrims to Mecca from Yathrib, an oasis to the north, recognized Muhammad as a prophet. They invited him to come to their city to help solve its social and political problems. Still despised by the Qurayshites as a potential threat, Muhammad and his followers left Mecca secretly. Their move to Yathrib, later called al-Medina (The City [of the Prophet]), was not easy. The Prophet left last, accompanied (according to some traditions) by his old friend Abu Bakr. To hide from the pursuing Meccans, it is said that they took refuge in a cave, where the Prophet taught his friend the secret practice of the silent remembrance of God.

This *hijrah* (migration) of Muslims from Mecca to Medina took place in 622 CE. The Muslim era is calculated from the beginning of the year in which this event took place, for it marked the change from persecution to appreciation of the Prophet's message.

In Medina, Muhammad drew up a constitution for the city of Yathrib/Medina that later served as a model for Islamic social administration; the constitution acknowledged the different religious communities in the city. The departure of Muslims from Mecca was viewed with hostility and suspicion by the leaders of Mecca. Their assumption was that Medina had become a rallying point for enemies of the Meccans who, under Muhammad's leadership, would eventually attack and destroy Mecca. To forestall this, Mecca declared war on Medina, and a period of open conflict between the two cities followed.

Muhammad himself directed the first raid against a Meccan caravan. The battle between Muslim emigrants and Meccans took place at Badr near Medina; the small group of Muslims was victorious. According to the Qur'anic revelations, God had sent thousands of angels to help Muhammad. Enraged by the Islamic victory, Mecca made a surprise attack against Medina and routed the Muslims, injuring Muhammad and scattering his forces. Within two years, Mecca had mounted a much larger force, including cavalry and numerous archers, for a siege intended to subdue Medina permanently. Warned by spies, the Muslims defended Medina with a large trench encircling the city. The Meccans were forced to retreat, but rather than continue hostilities Muhammad negotiated a truce between the two warring cities.

In 630 CE the Prophet returned triumphant to Mecca with such a large band of followers that the Meccans did not resist. Reportedly, only thirty people were killed in the historic conquest of Mecca. The Ka'bah was purged of its

Representations of humans, including himself, were discouraged by the Prophet to avoid idolatry, but Persian artists later gave imaginative expression to stories such as the Miraj, *or Ascension, of the Prophet.*

idols, and from that time it has been the center of Muslim piety. Acquiescing to Muhammad's political power and the Qur'anic warnings about the dire fate of those who tried to thwart God's prophets, many Meccans converted to Islam. Muhammad declared a general amnesty. Contrary to tribal customs of revenge, the Prophet showed his unusual gentleness by forgiving those who had been his opponents.

The Prophet then returned to Medina, which he kept as the spiritual and political center of Islam. From there, a number of campaigns were undertaken. In addition to northern Africa, the Persian states of Yemen, Oman, and Bahrain came into the fold. As the multicultural, multiracial embrace of Islam evolved, the Prophet declared that the community of the faithful was more important than the older tribal identities that had divided people. The new ideal was a global family, under God. In his "Farewell Sermon," Muhammad stated, "You must know that a Muslim is the brother of a Muslim and the Muslims are one brotherhood."[4] Distinctions between Arabs and non-Arabs, black and white, were no longer valid.

In the eleventh year of the Muslim era, Muhammad made a final pilgrimage to the Ka'bah in Mecca to demonstrate to the faithful the rites that were to be followed thenceforth. After his return to Medina, he became very ill. As he recognized that the end was near, he gave final instructions to his followers, promising to meet them at "the Fountain" in paradise. Muhammad died in 632 CE. In the circumstances that followed Muhammad's death, his steadfast friend Abu Bakr was elected the first **caliph** (successor to the Prophet). Another possible successor was the trustworthy and courageous 'Ali, the Prophet's cousin and husband of his favorite daughter, Fatima. One tradition has it that the Prophet Muhammad actually transferred his spiritual light to Fatima before his death, but that in the midst of funeral arrangements, neither she nor 'Ali participated in the selection of the first caliph. The Shi'ites would later claim 'Ali as the legitimate heir.

Muhammad's own life has continued to be very precious to Muslims, and it is his qualities that a good Muslim tries to emulate. He always denied having any superhuman powers, and the Qur'an called him "a human being like you," just "a servant to whom revelation has come," and "a warner."[5] The only miracle he ever claimed was that, though unlettered, he had received the Qur'anic revelations in extraordinarily eloquent and pure Arabic. He did not even claim to be a teacher—"God guides those whom He will,"[6] he was instructed to say—although Muslims consider the Prophet the greatest of teachers.

Nevertheless, all who saw the Prophet remarked on his touching physical beauty, his nobility of character, the fragrance of his presence, his humility, and his kindness. Many stories are told of his affectionate compassion toward animals, children, women, widows, and orphans, contrary to prevailing customs. When asked the short cut to heaven, he reportedly said that Paradise lies under the feet of the mother. In his devotion to God, he quietly endured poverty so extreme that he tied a stone over his stomach to suppress the pangs of hunger. He explained, "I eat as a slave eats, and sit as a slave sits, for I am a slave (of God)." Although the Qur'an says that the Prophet is the perfect model for humanity, the purest vehicle for God's message, he himself perpetually prayed for God's forgiveness. When he was asked how best to practice Islam, he said, "The best Islam is that you feed the hungry and spread peace among people you know and those you do not know."[7]

Muhammad's mystical experiences of the divine had not led him to forsake the world as a contemplative. Rather, according to the Qur'an, the mission of Islam is to reform society, to actively combat oppression and corruption, "inviting to all that is good, enjoining what is right, and forbidding all that is wrong."[8] The Prophet's task—which Muslims feel was also undertaken by such earlier prophets as Moses and Abraham—is not only to call people back to faith but also to create a just moral order in the world as the embodiment of God's commandments.

The Qur'an

Why is the Qur'an important in Islam?

The heart of Islam is not the Prophet but the revelations he received, which are revered as the Word of God. Collectively they are called the Qur'an (meaning "reading" or "reciting"). Muhammad received the messages over a period of twenty-three years, with some later messages replacing earlier ones. At first they were striking affirmations of the unity of God and the woe of those who did not heed God's message. Later messages also addressed the organizational needs and social lives of the Muslim community.

After the *hijrah*, Muhammad heard the revelations and dictated them to a scribe; many of his companions then memorized them. They are said to have been carefully safeguarded against changes and omissions. Recited, the passages have a lyrical beauty and power that Muslims believe to be unsurpassed; these qualities cannot be translated. The recitation is to be rendered in what is sometimes described as a serious, subdued tone, because the messages concern God's sadness at the waywardness of the people. Muhammad said, "Weep, therefore, when you recite it."[9]

Recitation of the Qur'an is thought to have a healing, soothing effect, but can also bring protection, guidance, and knowledge, according to Islamic tradition. It is critical that one recite the Qur'an only in a purified state, for the words are so powerful that the one who recites it takes on a great responsibility. Ideally, one learns the Qur'an as a child, when memorization is easiest and when the power of the words will help to shape one's life. Muslim men who have memorized the Qur'an may use the title "Hafiz"; for women, the title is "Hafiza."

During the life of the Prophet, his followers attempted to preserve the oral tradition in writing as an additional way of safeguarding it from loss. The early caliphs continued this effort until a council was convened by the third caliph around 650 CE to establish a single authoritative written text. This is the one still used. It is divided into 114 **surahs** (chapters). The first is the **Fatiha**, the opening surah, which reveals the essence of the Qur'an:

> *In the name of Allah, Most Gracious, Most Merciful.*
> *Praise be to Allah,*
> *The Cherisher and Sustainer of the Worlds;*
> *Most Gracious, Most Merciful;*
> *Master of the Day of Judgment.*

Reading the Qur'an in Java.

Thee do we worship,
And Thine aid we seek.
Show us the straight way,
The way of those on whom
Thou has bestowed Thy Grace
Those whose portion
Is not wrath,
And, who go not astray.[10]

The verses of the Qur'an are terse, but are thought to have multiple levels of meaning. These may not survive translation into other languages, particularly in the case of idiomatic expressions, subtle implications of Arabic grammatical structures, and historic references, unless there are extensive footnotes or bracketed explanations. Furthermore, there are often three layers: (1) a reference to a particular person or situation; (2) a spiritual lesson; and (3) a deeper mystical significance. Some faithful Muslims feel that the mystical level cannot be understood by most people. For instance, noted twentieth-century Iranian scholar Sayyid Muhammad Husayn Tabatabai asserted:

The whole of the Quran possesses the sense of tawil, *of esoteric meaning, which cannot be comprehended directly through human thought alone. Only the Prophets and the pure among the Saints of God who are free from the dross of human imperfection can contemplate these meanings while living on the present plane of existence.*[11]

The Qur'an makes frequent mention of figures and stories from Jewish and Christian sacred history, all of which Muslims consider part of the fabric of

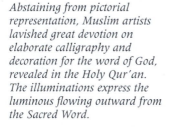

Abstaining from pictorial representation, Muslim artists lavished great devotion on elaborate calligraphy and decoration for the word of God, revealed in the Holy Qur'an. The illuminations express the luminous flowing outward from the Sacred Word.

Islam. Islam is the original religion, according to the Qur'an. Surrender to God has existed as long as there have been humans willing to do so. Adam was the first prophet. Abraham was not exclusively a Jew nor a Christian; he was a monotheistic, upright person who had surrendered to God. Jesus was a very great prophet.

Muslims believe that the Jewish prophets and Jesus all brought the same messages from God. However, the Qur'an teaches that God's original messages have been added to and distorted by humans. For instance, Muslims do not accept the idea developed historically in Christianity that Jesus has the authority to pardon or atone for our sins. The belief that this power lies with anyone except God is considered a blasphemous human interpolation into what Muslims understand as the basic and true teachings of all prophets of the Judeo-Christian-Islamic tradition: belief in one God and in our personal moral accountability before God on the Day of Judgment. In the Islamic view, the Qur'an was sent as a final corrective in the continuing monotheistic tradition. Muslims, citing John 14:16 and 14:26 from the Christian New Testament, believe that Jesus prophesied the coming of Muhammad when he promised that the **Paraclete** (advocate) would come to assist humanity after him.

The Qur'an revealed to Muhammad is understood as a final and complete reminder of the prophets' teachings, which all refer to the same one God, known in Arabic as **Allah** (The God). For example, in Surah 42, Muhammad is told:

> Say: "I believe in whatever Book Allah has sent down; and I am
> commanded to judge justly between you. Allah is our Lord and your
> Lord! For us is the responsibility for our deeds, and for you for your
> deeds. There is no contention between us and you. Allah will bring
> us together, and to Him is our final goal."[12]

The central teachings
What are the central teachings of Islam?

On the surface, Islam is a very straightforward religion. The word "**Islam**" means peace, voluntary surrender to the will of God, and obedience to God's law. It comprises a number of articles of faith.

The Oneness of God and of humanity

The first sentence chanted in the ear of a traditional Muslim infant is the **Shahadah**—"*La ilaha illa Allah Muhammad-un Rasul Allah*" ("There is no god but God, and Muhammad is the Messenger of God"). Exoterically, the Shahadah supports absolute monotheism. As the Qur'an reveals in Surah 2:163:

> Your God is One God:
> There is no god but He,
> Most Gracious, Most Merciful.[13]

Esoterically, the Shahadah means that ultimately there is only one Absolute Reality; the underlying essence of life is eternal unity rather than the apparent separateness of things in the physical world. Muslims think that the Oneness of God is the primordial religion taught by all prophets of all faiths. Muhammad merely reminded people of it.

It has been estimated that more than ninety percent of Muslim theology deals with the implications of Unity. God, while One, is referred to by ninety-nine names. These are each considered attributes of the One Being, such as *al-Ali* (The Most High) and *ar-Raqib* (The Watchful). Allah is the name of God that encompasses all the attributes. Each of the names refers to the totality, the One Being.

Unity applies not only to the conceptualization of God, but also to every aspect of life. In the life of the individual, every thought and action should spring

Muslims express their belief in the Oneness of the divine by saying the Shahadah ("There is no god but God, and Muhammad is the Messenger of God"), the sentence emblazoned on this Turkish plaque.

from a heart and mind intimately integrated with the divine. Muslims theoretically reject any divisions within the Islamic community; all Muslims around the globe are supposed to embrace as one family. All humans, for that matter, are a global family; there is no one "chosen people," for all are invited into a direct relationship with God. Science, art, and politics are not separate from religion in Islam, for ideally they should all involve consciousness of God. Individuals should never forget Allah; the Oneness should permeate their thoughts and actions. Abu Hashim Madani, an Indian Sufi sage, is said to have taught: "There is only one thing to be gained in life, and that is to remember God with each breath; and there is only one loss in life, and that is the breath drawn without the remembrance of God."[14]

> *The "remembrance of God" is like breathing deeply in the solitude of high mountains: here the morning air, filled with purity of the eternal snows, dilates the breast; it becomes space and heaven enters our heart.*
>
> *Frithjof Schuon*[15]

Prophethood and the compass of Islam

Devout Muslims believe that Islam encompasses all religions. Islam honors all prophets as messengers from the one God:

> *Say ye: We believe*
> *In God, and the revelation*
> *Given to us, and to Abraham,*
> *Isma'il, Isaac, Jacob,*
> *And the Tribes, and that given*
> *To Moses and Jesus, and that given*
> *To (all) Prophets from their Lord:*
> *We make no difference*
> *Between one and another of them:*
> *And we bow to God in surrender.*[16]

Muslims believe that the original religion was monotheism, but that God sent prophets from time to time as religions decayed into polytheism. Each prophet came to renew the message, in a way specifically designed for his culture and time. The Qur'anic revelations declared Muhammad to be the "Seal of the Prophets," the last and ultimate authority in the continuing prophetic tradition. The prophets are mere humans, although spiritually powerful and morally perfected; none of them is divine, for there is only one Divinity.

Islam is thought to be the universal religion in its pure form. All scriptures of all traditions are also honored, but only the Qur'an is considered fully authentic, because it is the direct, unchanged, untranslated word of God. Whatever exists in other religions that agrees with the Qur'an is divine truth.

Throughout the history of Islam, Muslims have honored and venerated the prophet Muhammad. Some Muslims, for example, celebrate his birthday, though it is not an obligatory celebration. There are rich traditions of poetry and other writings blessing and honoring Muhammad, and recounting the details of his biography.

Human relationship to the divine

> *We are nearer to [a person] than his jugular vein.*
>
> *The Holy Qur'an, Surah 50:16*

In Muslim belief, God is all-knowing and has intelligently created everything for a divine purpose, governed by laws that assure the harmonious and wondrous working of all creation. Humans will find peace only if they know these laws and live by them. They have been revealed by the prophets, but the people often have not believed. To believe is to surrender totally to God. As the Qur'an states:

> None believes in Our revelations save those who, when reminded of them, prostrate themselves in adoration and give glory to their Lord in all humility; who forsake their beds to pray to their Lord in fear and hope; who give in charity of that which We have bestowed on them. No mortal knows what bliss is in store for these as a reward for their labors.[17]

The Qur'an indicates that human history provides many "signs" of the hand of God at work bestowing mercy and protection on believers. Signs such as the great flood, which was thought to have occurred at the time of Noah, illustrate that evildoers ultimately experience great misfortune in this life or the afterlife. None is punished without first being warned by a messenger of God to mend his or her ways. Creation itself is a sign of God's compassion, as well as of God's omnipotent will.

According to Islam, the two major human sins involve one's relationship to God. One is *shirk* (associating anything else with divinity except the one God). The Qur'an instructs, with reference to People of the Book (Jews and Christians, who are also believed to have received revealed scriptures):

> Say: "Oh People of the book!
> Come to common terms as between us and you:
> That we worship none but Allah;
> That we associate no partners with Him;
> That we erect not from among ourselves
> Lords and patrons other than Allah."[18]

In other words, in Islam's pure monotheism one is enjoined not to worship anything but God—not natural forces, or mountains, or stones, or incarnations of God, or lesser deities, or human rulers. Idol worship is vigorously denounced, as is worship of natural phenomena: "Adore not the sun nor the moon, but adore Allah Who created them."[19]

The other major sin is *kufr* (ungratefulness to God, unbelief, atheism). Furthermore, humans tend to forget God. God has mercifully sent us revelations as reminders. The veils that separate us from God come from us, not from God; Muslims feel that it is ours to remove the veils by seeking God and acknowledging the omnipresence, omniscience, and omnipotence of the divine. Aware that God knows everything and is all-powerful, one wants to do everything one can to please God, out of both love and fear. This paradox was given dramatic expression by the Caliph 'Umar ibn al-Khattab:

> If God declared on the Day of Judgment that all people would go to paradise except one unfortunate person, out of His fear I would think that I am that person. And if God declared that all people would go to hell except one fortunate person, out of my hope in His Mercy I would think that I am that fortunate person.[20]

The unseen life

Muslims believe that our senses do not reveal all of reality. In particular, they believe in the angels of God. These are nonphysical beings of light who serve and praise God day and night. They are numerous, and each has a specific responsibility. For instance, certain angels are always with each of us, recording our good and bad deeds. The Qur'an also mentions archangels, including Gabriel, highest of the angelic beings, whose main responsibility is to bring revelations to the prophets from God. But neither he nor any other angel is to be worshiped,

According to Muslim belief, angels are everywhere; they come to our help in every thought and action. A group of angels is here shown helping the 8th-century Sufi ascetic, Ibrahim ibn Adham.

according to strict monotheistic interpretation of Islam, for the angels are simply utterly submissive servants of God. By contrast, according to Islamic belief, there is a nonsubmissive being called Satan. He was originally one of the **jinn**—immaterial beings of fire, whose nature is between that of humans and angels. He proudly refused to bow before Adam and was therefore cursed to live by tempting Adam's descendants—all of humanity, in other words—to follow him rather than God. According to the Qur'an, those who fall prey to Satan's devices will ultimately go to hell.

Popular Muslim piety also developed a cult of saints. The tombs of mystics known to have had special spiritual powers have become places of pilgrimage. Many people visit them out of devotion and desire for the blessings of the spirit, which is thought to remain in the area. This practice is frowned upon by some reformers, who assert that Muslim tradition clearly forbids worship of any being other than God.

The Last Judgment

In the polytheistic religion practiced by Arabs before Muhammad, the afterlife was only a shadow, without rewards or punishments. People had little religious incentive to be morally accountable. By contrast, the Qur'an emphasizes that after a period of repose in the grave, all humans will be bodily resurrected and assembled for a final accounting of their deeds. At that unknown time of the Final Judgment, the world will end cataclysmically: "The earth will shake and the mountains crumble into heaps of shifting sand" (Surah 73:14). Then comes the terrible confrontation with one's own life:

> *The works of each person We have bound about his neck. On the Day of Resurrection, We shall confront him with a book spread wide open, saying, "Read your book."*[21]

Hell is the grievous destiny of unrepentant nonbelievers—those who have rejected faith in and obedience to God and His Messenger, who are unjust and who do not forbid evil. Hell also awaits the hypocrites who even after making a covenant with God have turned away from their promise to give in charity and to pray regularly:

> *It is a flaming Fire. It drags them down by their scalps; and it shall call him who turned his back and amassed riches and covetously hoarded them.*[22]

Muslim piety is ever informed by this belief in God's merciful judgment of one's actions, and of one's responsibility to remind others of the fate that may await them.

Muslim thought says that what we experience in the afterlife is a revealing of our tendencies in this life. We awaken to our true nature, for it is displayed before us. For the just and merciful, the state after death is a Garden of Bliss. The desire of the purified souls will be for closeness to God, and their spirits will live in different levels of this closeness. For them, there will be castles, couches, fruits, sweetmeats, honey, houris (beautiful virgin women), and immortal youths serving from goblets and golden platters. Such delights promised by the Qur'an are interpreted metaphorically to mean that human nature will be transformed in the next life to such an extent that the disturbing factors of this physical existence will no longer have any effect.

People are asleep, but when they die, they wake up.

Hadith of the Prophet Muhammad

By contrast, sinners and evildoers will experience the torments of hell, fire fueled by humans, boiling water, pus, chains, searing winds, food that chokes, and so forth. It is they who condemn themselves; their very bodies turn against them "on the Day when their tongues, their hands, and their feet will bear witness against them as to their actions" (Surah 24:24). The great medieval mystic al-Ghazali speaks of spiritual torments of the soul as well: the agony of being separated from worldly pleasures, burning shame at seeing one's life projected, and terrible regret at being barred from the vision of God. Muslims do not believe that hell can last forever for any believer, though. Only the evildoers will be left there; the others will eventually be lifted to paradise, for God is far more merciful than wrathful.

The Five Pillars

What are the basic spiritual practices incumbent on all Muslims?

The Five Pillars of Islam are the basic spiritual practices incumbent on all Muslims. They were specified by theologians after the death of the Prophet Muhammad as the actions that define what it means to be a member of the Muslim community. The intention with which a Muslim undertakes each practice is of prime importance. The pillars are not prescribed simply as outer rituals.

Belief and witness

The first pillar of Islam (the Shahadah) is believing and professing the unity of God and the messengership of Muhammad: "There is no god but God, and Muhammad is the Messenger of God," to which Shi'ites add "and 'Ali is the Friend of God." The Qur'an requires the faithful to tell others about Islam and to demonstrate Islam through their character, so that non-Muslims will have the information they need to make an intelligent choice. However, it rules out the use of coercion in spreading the message:

> *Let there be [or: There is] no compulsion*
> *In religion: Truth stands out*
> *Clear from Error: whoever*
> *Rejects Evil and believes*
> *In God hath grasped*
> *The most trustworthy*
> *Hand-hold, that never breaks.*[23]

The Qur'an insists on respect for all prophets and all revealed scriptures.

Daily prayers

The second pillar is the performance of a continual round of prayers (*salat*). Five times a day, the faithful are to perform ablutions with water (or sand or earth if there is no water), face in the direction of Mecca, and recite a series of prayers and passages from the Qur'an, bowing and kneeling. Around the world, this communal facing of Mecca for prayer unites all Muslims into a single world family. When the prayers are recited by a congregation, all stand and bow shoulder to shoulder, with no social distinctions. In a mosque, women and men usually pray separately, with the women in rows behind the men, or in a separate area. There may be an **imam**, or prayer-leader, but no priest stands

Salat

The practice of *salat* (formal prayer) varies somewhat between men and women and by local custom, but nonetheless follows rather standard patterns around the world. No matter what the local language, *salat* is always performed in Arabic.

According to references in the Holy Qur'an, the five obligatory daily prayer times are usually understood to be: (1) early morning after dawn and before sunrise; (2) early afternoon; (3) late afternoon; (4) immediately after sunset; and (5) night before going to bed. Each consists of a certain number of *rak'ahs*, or complete acts of devotion, some of which are congregational (*fardz*) and some of which are individual (*sunnah*). The morning prayer, for instance, consists of two individual *rak'ahs* and then two congregational *rak'ahs*. During the congregational *rak'ahs*, the whole congregation prays side by side, with their movements matching each other, but during the individual *rak'ahs*, people may be praying at their own pace.

There are four parts to each *rak'ah*. The first part is done in standing position, facing the Ka'bah in Mecca. Hands are first raised with open palms, thumbs touching the edge of the ears, and then folded reverently over the waist or breast, with the right hand covering the left. Inwardly, the person should feel that he or she is standing before the Divine Presence. The open palms mean, "I have come empty-handed into this world and I shall leave empty-handed." Hands crossed over the breast or waist may be understood as a gesture to subdue desires and worldly thoughts, so that all attention can be given to God. The worshiper utters *Allahu Akbar* ("God is great," or "God is the greatest"), followed by the Fatiha, and perhaps a traditional prayer and a passage chosen from the Qur'an, all recited softly to avoid disturbing others, who may be reciting different passages at their own speed. In the congregational part of the prayer, however, the imam who leads the prayers recites any passage from the Qur'an audibly while the others listen and perhaps quietly praise or make requests to God according to the content of the passage.

For the second part of each *rak'ah*, the worshiper bows over, standing with hands on knees and praises the glory of the divine by a phrase such as "*Subhana Rabbiy-al-Azim*" ("Glory to my Lord, the Great"), repeated three times. A prayer may also be added thereafter.

In the third part of each *rak'ah*, the worshiper first rises up to standing position with hands hanging down freely, while saying "*Sami' Allahu li-man hamidah*" ("Allah listens to him who praises Him") and "*Rabbana wa la-k-al-hamd*" (Our Lord! All praise is due to Thee"). Then the worshiper drops down to his knees in humble prostration with forehead touching the ground while saying "*Allahu Akbar*." Rising briefly to sitting position, he then prostrates himself again in a gesture of surrender.

The fourth part is a period of sitting with feet tucked under, a posture assumed after two *rak'ahs* have been completed. In this position, the worshiper utters several prayers, such as the following: "My Lord! Make me and my offspring keep up prayer, our Lord! And accept my prayer, our Lord! Grant protection to me and my parents and the believers on the day when the reckoning will take place." Turning their head to the right and then the left, the person then says to the angels on each shoulder, "*As-salamu 'ali-kum wa rahmatu-llah*" ("Peace be on you and the mercy of Allah").

The final prayers usually include the famous *Ayat al-Kursi* (Verse of the Throne) from Surah 2:255, "Allah! There is no god but He: the Living, the Self-subsisting, Supporter of all." The worshiper may also repeat "*subhan-Allah*" ("Glory be to Allah"), "*al-hamduli-ilah*" ("Praise be to Allah"), and "*Allahu Akbar*" ("God is the greatest") several times. Variations in choice of prayers and utterances of praises during the individual *rak'ahs* allow the worshiper to express inner feelings of reverence and submission, while the congregational *rak'ahs* uttered together give a powerful feeling of unity with the global Muslim community.

between the worshiper and God. On Friday noon, there is usually a special prayer service in the mosque. Remembrance of God is an everyday obligation.

Prayer is thought to strengthen one's belief in God's existence and goodness and to carry this belief into every aspect of external life. Praying thus is also expected to purify the heart, develop the mind and the conscience, comfort the soul, encourage the good and suppress the evil in the person, and awaken the innate sense of higher morality and higher aspirations. The words of praise and the bowing express continual gratefulness and surrender to God. During the prayers, one turns to the two recording angels on one's shoulders to say the traditional Muslim greeting—"*Assalamu Alaykum*" ("Peace be on you")—and another phrase adding the blessing, "and mercy of God."

While mouthing the words and performing the outer actions, one should be concentrating on the inner prayer of the heart. The Prophet reportedly said, "Prayer without the Presence of the Lord in the heart is not prayer at all."[24]

In addition to the obligatory prayers five times a day, one may do additional supererogatory prayers, the most valuable of which is prayer offered during the middle of the night. The Prophet reportedly used to stand in prayer so long at night that his feet were swollen. Shaykh Muhammad Hisham Kabbani explains:

This is the time when the world is asleep, but the lovers and seekers of God (al-'ibad) are awake and traveling toward reality and their divine destinations. It is under the veil of the night that the plane of consciousness is clear from the chaos of worldly affairs, for it is a time when the mind and heart operate most effectively.[25]

Ideally, in Islamic spirituality, one should be constantly remembering God inwardly, and one's whole life should become a means of worship.

Women usually pray separately from men. In this portion of the women's prayer hall in the Grand Mosque in Abu Dhabi, United Arab Emirates, women are saying their prayers privately rather than participating in communal prayer at a specified time.

Congregational prayer ends with private prayer requests, as in this scene from Namaz at Nur-ih-illahi Mosque, Gobind Sadan, India.

Zakat

The Qur'an links prayer with **zakat**, charity or almsgiving, the third pillar. One's prayer is accepted only if one also shares with others. Accordingly, at the end of the year, all Muslims must donate at least two and a half percent of their accumulated wealth to needy Muslims. This provision is designed to help decrease inequalities in wealth and to prevent personal greed. Its literal meaning is "purity," for it purifies the distribution of money, helping to keep it in healthy circulation.

Saudi Arabia devotes fifteen percent of its kingdom's GDP to development and relief projects throughout the world. The Islamic Relief Organization that it funds makes a point of helping people of all religions, without discrimination, where there is great need following disasters. Many stories from the life of the Prophet Muhammad teach that one should help others whether or not they are Muslims. For example, the Prophet's neighbor was a non-Muslim. The Prophet reportedly gave him a gift every day, even though the neighbor daily left garbage at his door. Once the neighbor was sick, and the Prophet visited him. The neighbor asked, "Who are you to help me?" The Prophet replied, "You are my brother. I must help you."

Fasting

The fourth pillar is fasting. Frequent fasts are recommended to Muslims, but the only one that is obligatory is the fast during Ramadan, commemorating the first revelations of the Qur'an to Muhammad. For all who are beyond puberty, but not infirm, sick, menstruating, pregnant, or nursing children, a dawn-to-sunset abstention from food, drink, sexual intercourse, and smoking is required for the whole month of Ramadan. The fasting also extends to abstaining from negative emotions such as anger.

Because Muslims use a lunar calendar of 354 days, the month of Ramadan gradually moves through all the seasons. When it falls in the summer, the period of fasting is much longer than in the shortest days of winter. The hardship of abstaining even from drinking water during these long and hot days is an unselfish surrender to God's commandment and an assertion of control over the lower desires. The knowledge that Muslims all over the world are making these sacrifices at the same time builds a special bond between haves and have-nots, helping the haves to experience what it is to be hungry, to share in the condition

Celebrating the end of Ramadan with a communal meal in Houzhou, Anhui Province in eastern China.

An Interview with Dr. Syed M. Hussain

Dr. Syed M. Hussain is a nephrologist —a specialist in kidney disorders, dialysis, and kidney transplants—at a major hospital in New Delhi. His manner with patients is very kind and concerned. He may be called for emergencies at any time, night or day, and yet he also observes the rules of fasting, particularly during Ramadan. He explains:

Ramadan is a very holy month in the Muslim calendar, because the Holy Qur'an was sent to the Prophet Muhammad during this month. It is a ritual for Muslims to fast during this month so that you become a little more spiritual and healthier. At the same time, you also have the pinch of hunger. Many people in their lifetime who are very wealthy will never experience what is hunger and what is thirst. A king, for instance, will never experience hunger and thirst. Fasting will make you understand what a hungry person is going through. Altogether, such sacrifices make you closer to life. You see that God has given you such beautiful things. Whether you have a penny or not, you are still able to enjoy those things—you see how valuable they are for life.

During this holy month of Ramadan, Muslims usually take something in the morning between 4 and 4.30 a.m., and after that, they say their morning prayer at 5 to 5.30 a.m. They will fast until sunset, and then they will have their meal. The logic is that if 100,000 people are missing one or two meals, then 100,000 people are receiving their meals [when that money is given in charity]. This is also a philosophy of equality.

Many people misunderstand Islam, but the religion is not bad. It gives you very good values. It is people who sometimes misuse and misunderstand it.

As a doctor I myself practice, and I see that if you are fasting your system gets toned up. Your physical fitness increases and you become healthier. Your mental alertness rises. When I fast during Ramadan my mind becomes very, very clear. I am relieved of bad thoughts, and when I see patients I feel closer to them. If a patient is not able to take his meal because of sickness you feel closer to him and try your best to see that he is being helped in all respects. When you see someone who suffers you recognize what he is going through. Then you cannot be cruel. If you are cruel, you are not doing religious practice from the bottom of your heart—you

are doing it just for show. There is no place for such things in any religion.

If you fast for some time your digestive tract—which otherwise produces so many secretions all the time—gets a rest. When you give a rest to your digestive system, you also give rest to your brain and heart. If you are fasting, you are giving a rest to your entire system. Your system gets lightened, and if you do it on a spiritual level there is more strength. More natural rays come within the body so you become not only more fit and healthy but also more compassionate and more softhearted. If you are not taking a meal, your metabolism will be low and you will not have anger; you will not fight or be cruel.

If other people are eating when I am fasting, I feel nothing. In the hospital some of my colleagues will say, "You are fasting, so let me hide and take my food." I say, "Don't worry—if I get upset when I see food, then my motive is defeated. Instead, you should get all the best food which I like, and I'll be happier, because that will give me more strength to control my nafs *(inner passions)." That makes me a better person. All religions are religions of sacrifice. The more you sacrifice, the more you become a better person in all respects. People used to trouble the Prophet Muhammad, but when he heard that one of those people was sick he would go to his house and serve him in every way. He would even help him go to the toilet. After that, the person would become a changed person. You can't win a person by fighting. He may be stronger than you, but with love you can capture anybody.*

In modern times I don't know what is going on that people are becoming so aggressive. I don't think any religion has any place for fighting and killing. No religion has a place for terrorist actions. Many people think that Islam is a fundamentalist religion, but no. Look at the basics in the Book. If ten people are practicing the wrong things, that doesn't make the system wrong. The system is right. Some people may have deviated, but if you practice from the heart, then you are compassionate, you are soft, you are helping, and you are generous to all the people around you, whatever little you can do during your lifetime. If you at least help one person seriously in your life, then you have learned something in your life. You can show your face to God, that you have helped one of his creatures who was suffering. Otherwise what is life? It won't make any sense.[26]

of the poor. Those who have are encouraged to be especially generous in their almsgiving during Ramadan.

Fasting is thought to bring great spiritual rewards. The great mystic poet Jalal al-Din Rumi (1207–1273) wrote:

> There's hidden sweetness in the stomach's emptiness. We are lutes, no more, no less. If the soundbox is stuffed full of anything, no music. If the brain and the belly are burning clean with fasting, every moment a new song comes out of the fire. The fog clears, and new energy makes you run up the steps in front of you. Be emptier and cry like reed instruments cry. Emptier, write secrets with the reed pen. ... When you fast, good habits gather like friends who want to help. ... A table descends to your tents, Jesus' table. Expect to see it, when you fast, this table spread with other food, better than the broth of cabbages.[27]

Many people indeed feel that they are spiritually more sensitive and physically more healthy during Ramadan fasting. Fasting liberates a person's body from the heaviness of food and it is also a lesson for the soul, teaching it not to allow anything into the mind and heart that would distract one from God. It is believed that control of the body's desires builds the patience and mastery needed to control the lower emotions, such as anger and jealousy. Fasting can also help a person develop humility. The mystic teacher Abu Madyan (1126–1198) of Algeria emphasized this ascetic practice because "One who is hungry becomes humble, one who becomes humble begs, and one who begs attains God."[28]

The holiday of Eid al-Fitr marks the end of the month of fasting. It begins with a special prayer, and then is typically celebrated with gift-giving, charity, and visits to family and friends.

Hajj

The fifth pillar is **hajj**, the pilgrimage to Mecca. All Muslims who are physically and financially able to do so are expected to make the pilgrimage at least once in their lifetime. It involves a series of symbolic rituals designed to bring the faithful as close as possible to God. Male pilgrims wrap themselves in a special garment of unsewn cloths, rendering them all alike, with no class distinctions. The garment is like a burial shroud, for by dying to their earthly life they can devote all their attention to God. Women who perform hajj are not required to wear unsewn cloth, but their dress should be modest. For all pilgrims, it is a time for dhikr, the constant repetition of the Shahadah, the remembrance that there is no god but God.

The Prophet's Mosque in Medina has been enlarged to allow room for more than one million praying pilgrims.

The pilgrimage to Mecca.

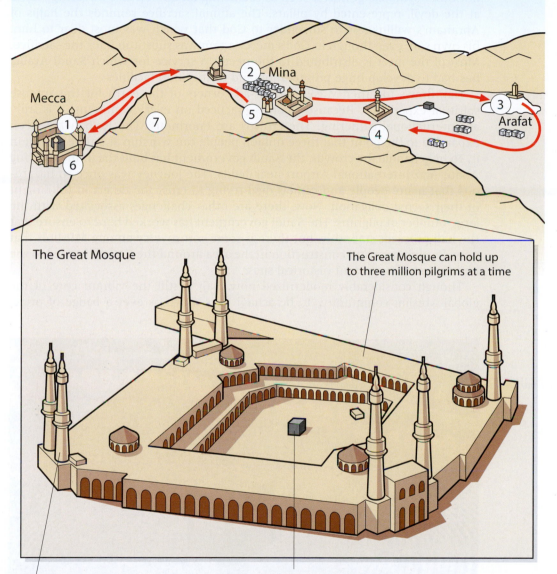

1. Pilgrimage begins at the Great Mosque, with seven circumambulations of the Ka'bah

2. Pilgrims stop at Mina

3. They pray from noon to evening in the Arafat valley. The Prophet Muhammad gave his last talk here

4. Pilgrims gather forty-nine stones

5. They throw their stones at three pillars which represent the devil. Three days of ritual sacrifice begin

6. They return to the Great Mosque and again circle the Ka'bah seven times

7. Pilgrims walk seven times between hills near the Great Mosque and then drink from the sacred spring Zam-Zam

Mecca

Mina

Arafat

The Great Mosque

The Great Mosque can hold up to three million pilgrims at a time

Seven minarets, 300 feet (ninety meters) tall

The Ka'bah is a black cubic structure fifty feet (fifteen meters) high, draped in black silk, embroidered in gold thread with the sacred names of Allah. Pilgrims walk around it seven times until they reach the center and touch the Ka'bah itself

Pilgrims walk around the ancient Ka'bah seven times, like the continual rotation around the One by the angels and all of creation, to the seventh heaven. Their hearts should be filled only with remembrance of God. Pilgrims also run between two hills near the Ka'bah to commemorate the time when Hagar, Abraham's wife, ran in search of water for her son Isma'il; the angel Gabriel appeared, touched the ground, and water appeared at the site now known as the well of Zam-Zam.

Another sacred site on the pilgrimage is the field of Arafat. It is said to be the place where Adam and Eve were taught that humans were created solely for the worship of God. Here pilgrims pray from noon to sunset to be forgiven of anything that has separated them from the Beloved. In addition, pilgrims carry out other symbolic gestures, such as sacrificing an animal and throwing stones at the devil, represented by pillars. The animal sacrifice reminds the hajjis of Abraham's willingness to surrender to God that which was most dear to him, his own son, even though in God's mercy a ram was substituted for the sacrifice. Most of the meat is distributed to the needy, a service for which Saudi Arabia has had to develop huge preservation and distribution facilities.

Hajj draws together Muslims from all corners of the earth for this intense spiritual experience. Because Islam is practiced on every continent, it is truly an international gathering. The crowds are enormous. The Ka'bah has been expanded to the point that three million people can worship at a time within in it. To help handle the crowds, the Saudi government has built the immense King Abdul Aziz International Airport near Jedda. The journey was once so hazardous that many people and camels died trying to cross the desert in fulfillment of their sacred obligation. Now, there are other challenges associated with the large number of pilgrims. The Saudi government has worked hard to ensure that the hajj proceeds smoothly, but there is some controversy among Muslims that new development and construction in the area around the Ka'bah has led to the destruction of important historical sites.

Though considerably modernized now, hajj is still the vibrant core of the global Muslim community. To be a hajji is as much as ever a badge of pride.

During hajj, huge numbers of pilgrims sort themselves out into orderly rows as circumambulation of the Ka'bah takes place.

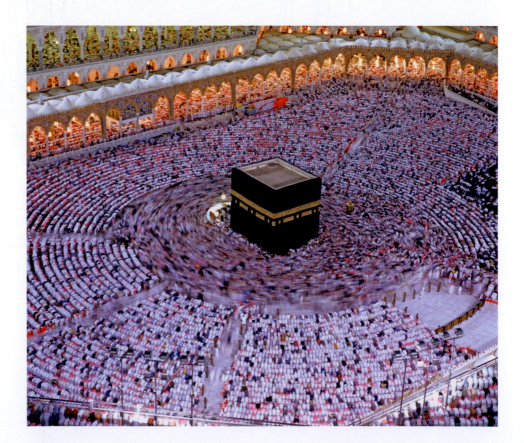

Throughout Muslim history, hajj has brought widely diverse people together, consolidating the center of Islam, spreading information and ideas across cultures, and sending pilgrims back into their communities with fresh inspiration. Hajji Ibrahim Keskin Hafiz, a fisherman from Turkey, says:

When you reach the holy places, you feel as though you are just in front of God. When you change your clothes and put on the white sheet (ehraam), your identity changes. In those huge crowded places, you feel as though everyone has collected and you are waiting for the Judgement. When I visited those places we knew from Islamic history, I was just crying. Whatever we learned from our parents, whatever we learned from books—we are seeing all those things. Wherever you go, you have to try to identify yourself with those historic people. When you are standing near the well of Zam-Zam, you have to identify yourself with Hagar and her son Isma'il. She was trying to take care of her son in the desert. And you think of the Prophet Abraham; you remember his good qualities and think how you can follow his good example. At the Hira cave, we remember our Prophet. We go there by buses now, but he was alone. He was walking on that hill, and he had so many enemies around him. Islam started in those conditions, and now it has very huge crowds of followers. When you enter the Ka'bah, you become very emotional and enthusiastic. In one of the prayers there, you say, "Oh Lord, we are in front of you. We have promised that we are going to follow Your rules. Whatever mistakes we made, we are ready to leave all of them, and we are not going to repeat the same mistakes again and again."[29]

One of the most important holidays for Muslims, Eid al-Adha or "The Feast of Sacrifice" occurs during the month in which pilgrims undertake the hajj. This holiday commemorates Abraham's willingness to sacrifice his son Isma'il. Because God provided a sheep to sacrifice in place of his son, Muslims celebrate Eid al-Adha by sacrificing a sheep or other animal and giving some of the meat to the poor.

Sunni and Shi'a

How do the Sunni and Shi'a groups differ?

The preceding pages describe beliefs and practices of all Muslims, although varying interpretations of the beliefs have always existed. Groups within Islam differ somewhat on other issues. After Muhammad's death, disagreements over the issue of his succession began to divide the Muslim community. The two main groups have come to be known as the **Sunni**, who now comprise about eighty percent of all Muslims worldwide, and the **Shi'a** (adj. Shi'ite).

To decide who would be successor, there were two customs of the times: A hereditary leader was chosen for general purposes, but a designated leader might be preferred in times of crisis or necessary action. As discussed earlier, designation was used at first after Muhammad's death: A caliph was elected to lead the Muslim community. The office of caliph became a lifetime appointment. The first three caliphs, Abu Bakr, Umar, and Uthman, were elected from among the Prophet's closest companions. The fourth caliph was 'Ali, the Prophet's closest male relative, as his cousin and son-in-law. The Shi'a think that Ali should have been the first caliph. Not only was he the most appropriate hereditary successor, but also he was known for his holy and chivalrous qualities. Nevertheless, the dynasty of Umayyads never accepted him as their leader, and he was assassinated by a member of his own party. 'Ali's son Husayn, grandson of the Prophet, challenged the legitimacy of the fifth caliph, the Umayyad Mu'awiyya. When Mu'awiyya designated his son Yazid as his successor, Husayn rebelled and was massacred in 680 C.E. by Yazid's troops in the desert of Karbala along with many of his relatives, who were also members of the Prophet's own family. This martyrdom unified Shi'ite opposition to the elected successors and they broke away, claiming their own legitimate line of succession through the direct descendants of the Prophet, beginning with 'Ali. The two groups are still separate. While Sunni Muslims are in the majority in most Islamic countries, Syria and Iraq have more mixed populations of Sunnis and Shi'as. The major Shi'a-majority country is Iran.

Sunnis

Those who follow the elected caliphs are "the people of the Sunnah" (the sayings and practices of the Prophet, as collected under the Sunni caliphs). They consider themselves traditionalists, and they emphasize the authority of the Qur'an and the secondary authority of the Hadith. They believe that Muhammad died without appointing a successor and left the matter of successors to the **ummah**, the Muslim community. They look to the time of the first four "rightly guided caliphs" (Abu Bakr, Umar, Uthman, and 'Ali) as the golden age of Islam. Sunnis regard not only the life of the Prophet but also the lives of the rightly guided caliphs—who had heard the revelations of the Prophet firsthand and been inspired by his personal example—and a few other close companions of the Prophet as the models for the ideal Muslim. The line of caliphs as temporal rulers nonetheless continued until the end of the Ottoman Empire, when Mustafa Kemal Ataturk disbanded the institution in creating a secular state.

Shi'a

The initial difference between Sunnis and Shi'a occurred over the issue of leadership. The Shi'a believe that 'Ali was the rightful original successor to the Prophet Muhammad. Several weeks before his death, the Prophet reportedly took 'Ali's hand and said, "Whoever I protect, 'Ali is also his protector. O God, be a friend to whoever is his friend and an enemy to whoever is his enemy." This is construed by the Shi'a as a veiled way of designating 'Ali as his successor. They believe that spiritual power was passed on to 'Ali, and that the caliphate is based on this spiritual as well as temporal authority. They are ardently devoted to the memory of Muhammad's close relatives: 'Ali, Fatima (the Prophet's beloved daughter), and their sons Hasan and Husayn. The martyrdom of Husayn at Karbala in his protest against the alleged tyranny, oppression, and injustice of the Umayyad caliphs is held up as a symbol of the struggle against human oppression. It is commemorated yearly as 'Ashura, a memorial on the tenth day of the month of Muharram. Participants in mourning processions cry and beat their chests or, in some areas, offer cooling drinks to the populace in memory of the martyred Husayn. Shi'ite piety places great emphasis on the touching stories told of 'Ali and Husayn's dedication to truth and integrity, even if it leads to personal suffering, in contrast to the selfish power politics ascribed to their opponents.

Rather than recognize the Sunni caliphs, the Shi'a pay allegiance to a succession of seven or twelve **Imams** (leaders, guides). The first three were 'Ali, Hasan, and Husayn. According to a saying of the Prophet acknowledged by both Sunni and Shi'a:

> I leave two great and precious things among you:
> the Book of Allah and my Household.
> If you keep hold of both of them,
> you will never go astray after me.[30]

"Twelver" Shi'a believe that there were a total of twelve Imams, legitimate hereditary successors to Muhammad. The twelfth Imam, they believe, was commanded by God to go into an occult hidden state to continue to guide the people and return publicly at the Day of Resurrection as the Mahdi. A minority of the Shi'a, the Nizari Isma'ilis, recognize a different person as the seventh Imam. This line of Imams has continued to the present forty-ninth Imam, HRH Prince Karim Aga Khan IV.

THE TWELVE SHI'A IMAMS:

1. 'Ali (600–661)
2. Hasan (625–669)
3. Husayn (626–680)
4. 'Ali ibn Husayn (Zayna'l-abeeden) (658–713)
5. Muhammad ibn 'Ali (676–743)
6. Ja'far ibn Muhammad (703–765)
7. Musa ibn Ja'far (745–799)
8. 'Ali ibn Musa (765–818)
9. Muhammad ibn 'Ali (810–835)
10. 'Ali ibn Muhammad (827–868)
11. Hasan ibn 'Ali (846–874)
12. Muhammad ibn Hasan (868–[?])

Unlike the Sunni caliph, the Imam combines political leadership (if possible) with continuing the transmission of Divine Guidance. This esoteric religious knowledge was given by God to Muhammad, from him to 'Ali, and thence from each Imam to the successor he designated from 'Ali's lineage. It includes both the outer and inner meanings of the Qur'an.

Shari'ah: Islamic law and ethics
What role has shari'ah played in Muslim communities?

In the second century of Islam, when the Abbasid dynasty replaced the Umayyads, there was a great concern for purifying and regulating social and political life in accord with Islamic spiritual tradition. Mechanisms for establishing the **shari'ah**, which incorporates both law and ethics, were developed. The shari'ah is based chiefly on the Qur'an and Sunnah of Muhammad, who was the first to apply the generalizations of the Qur'an to specific life situations. Muslims also developed **fiqh**, or jurisprudence, the process of understanding, interpreting and implementing the shari'ah. Fiqh may incorporate different forms of reasoning such as analogy in determining shariah-compliant norms. Shari'ah may be understood as divine guidelines for how Muslims ought to live their lives, and fiqh as the human attempt to know this.

Shari'ah pertains to many areas of life. For example, it specifies patterns for worship (instructions pertaining to the Five Pillars of Islam) as well as detailed prescriptions for social conduct, to bring remembrance of God into every aspect of daily life and practical ethics into the fabric of society. These prescriptions include injunctions against drinking intoxicating beverages; eating certain meats; gambling and vain sports; sexual relations outside of marriage; and sexually provocative dress, talk, or actions. They also include positive measures, commanding justice, kindness, and charity. Women are given many legal rights, including the right to own property, to divorce (according to certain schools of law), to inherit, and to make a will. These rights, divinely decreed during the time of the Prophet 1,400 years ago, were not available to women in the West until the nineteenth century. Polygyny is allowed for men who have the means to support several wives, to bring all women under the protection of a husband. Women are allowed to inherit only half as much as men because men have the obligation to support women financially. The faithful are enjoined to exercise justice and honesty in their relationships and business interactions, to manage their wealth carefully, and to avoid arrogance.

The shari'ah is said to have had a transformative effect on Muhammad's community. As we have seen, before Muhammad, the people's highest loyalty was to their tribe. Tribes made war on each other with few restraints. Women had few rights. Children were often killed at birth either because of poverty or because they were females in a male-dominated culture. People differed widely in wealth. Drunkenness and gambling were commonplace. Within a short time, Islam altered these traditions, shaping tribes into a spiritual and political unity with a high sense of ethics.

Different schools of fiqh (jurisprudence) developed as Islam spread beyond Arabia. Within Sunni Islam, there are four major schools of fiqh, and there are several Shi'a schools. The schools, which developed in different geographical regions, have different views on how best to exercise reason and analogy in reaching legal decisions, particularly when a specific issue is not addressed within the Qur'an or Sunnah. Thus in actual practice there may be multiple legal opinions on a particular question, although contemporary media accounts of shari'ah in the West may portray it as monolithic and unchanging.

Sunnis have felt that as life circumstances change, laws in the Qur'an, Hadith, and Sunnah should be continually interpreted by a consensus of opinion and the wisdom of learned people and jurists. For instance, divorce has always been addressed by the shari'ah. Traditionally, men have possessed the sole prerogative to initiate divorce, but in recent times, the conditions for divorce have been reconsidered so that women, too, are accorded similar rights. For Shi'a, the shari'ah is interpreted by the jurists.

Careful study of the Qur'an and Sunnah as the basis for legal opinions is undertaken by the *ulama*, scholars who devote their lifetimes to developing this knowledge. The most renowned school for the training of the *ulama* is al-Azhar in Cairo. Founded in the tenth century, it is the world's oldest university. A **fatwa**, or legal opinion, from the scholars of al-Azhar is considered authoritative (but not binding, since fatwas are generally not enforced) by Sunni Muslims around the world. There are also now fatwa websites on which Muslims may seek guidance on questions pertaining to shari'ah.

Sufism

What are the key aspects of Sufism?

In addition to the two orthodox traditions within Islam—Sunni and Shi'a—there is also an esoteric tradition, which is said to date back to the time of the Prophet. He himself was at once a political leader and a contemplative with a deep prayer life. Around him were gathered a group of about seventy people. They lived in his Medina mosque in voluntary poverty, detached from worldly concerns, praying night and day.

After the time of the first four caliphs, Muslims of this deep faith and piety, both Sunni and Shi'a, were distressed by the increasingly secular, dynastic, wealth-oriented characteristics of Muhammad's Umayyad successors. The mystical inner tradition of Islam, called **Sufism** (Arabic: *tasawwuf*), also involved resistance to the legalistic, intellectual trends within Islam in its early development.

Sufis have typically understood their way as a corrective supplement to orthodoxy. Rather than rejecting Islamic law, Sufism has added to and deepened adherence to the law. Sufis consider their way a path to God that is motivated by longing for the One. In addition to studying the Qur'an, Sufis feel that the world is a book filled with "signs"—divine symbols and elements of beauty that speak to those who understand. The intense personal journeys of Sufis and the insights that have resulted from their truth-seeking have periodically refreshed Islam from within. Much of the allegorical interpretation of the Qur'an and devotional literature of Islam is derived from Sufism.

The early Sufis turned to asceticism as a way of deepening their piety. The Prophet had said: "If ye had trust in God as ye ought He would feed you even as He feeds the birds."[31] Muhammad himself had lived in poverty, reportedly gladly so. Complete trust in and surrender to God became an essential step in the journey. **Dervishes** (poor mendicant mystics) with no possessions, no attachments in the world, were considered holy people, like Hindu sannyasins. But Sufi asceticism is based more on inner detachment than on withdrawal from the world; the ideal is to live with feet on the ground, head in the heavens.

To this early asceticism was added fervent, selfless love. Its greatest exponent was Rabi'a (*c.* 713–801). A famous mystic of Iraq, she scorned a rich man's offer of marriage, saying that she did not want to be distracted for a moment from God. All her attention was placed on the Beloved, which became a favorite Sufi name for God. Rabi'a emphasized disinterested love, with no selfish motives of hope for paradise or fear of hell. "I have served Him only for the love of Him and desire for Him."[32] When no veils of self exist, the mystic dissolves into the One she loves.

> *The Beloved is all, the lover just a veil.*
> *The Beloved is living, the lover a dead thing.*
>
> *Jalal al-Din Rumi*[33]

In absolute devotion, the lover desires *fana*, total annihilation in the Beloved. This Sufi ideal was articulated in the ninth century CE by the Persian Abu Yazid al-Bistami. He is said to have fainted while saying the Muslim call to prayer. When he awoke, he observed that it is a wonder that some people do not die when saying it, overwhelmed by pronouncing the name Allah with the awe that is due to the One. In his desire to be annihilated in God, al-Bistami so lost himself that he is said to have uttered pronouncements such as "Under my garment there is nothing but God,"[34] and "Glory be to Me! How great is My Majesty!"

The authorities were understandably disturbed by such potentially blasphemous statements. Sufis themselves knew the dangers of egotistical delusions inherent in the mystical path. There was strict insistence on testing and training by a sufficiently trained, tested, and illumined *murshid* (teacher) or *shaykh* (spiritual master). Advanced practices were taught only to higher initiates. It was through the *shaykh* that the *barakah* (blessing, sacred power) was passed down, from the *shaykh* of the *shaykh*, and so on, in a chain reaching back to Muhammad, who is said to have transmitted the *barakah* to 'Ali.

A number of *tariqas* (esoteric orders) evolved, one of which traced its spiritual lineage back to Junayd of Baghdad (who died in 910 CE). He knew that it was dangerous to speak openly of one's mystical understandings; the exoteric-minded might find them blasphemous, and those who had not had such experiences would only interpret them literally and thus mistakenly. He counseled veiled speech, and much Sufi literature after his time is couched in metaphors accessible only to mystics.

Hajji Waris Ali Shah (1819–1905) of Deva Sharif near Lucknow, India, was a great shaykh revered by people of all religions. Understanding Islam as ideally encompassing every religion, he said, "All are equals in my eyes."

Despite such warnings, the God-intoxicated cared little for their physical safety and exposed themselves and Sufism to opposition. The most famous case is that of Mansur al-Hallaj (c. 858–922). After undergoing severe ascetic practices, he is said to have visited Junayd. When the master asked, "Who is there?", his disciple answered, *"ana'l-Haqq"* ("I am the Absolute Truth," i.e., "I am God"). After Junayd denounced him, al-Hallaj traveled to India and throughout the Middle East, trying to open hearts to God. He introduced into the poetry of divine love the simile of the moth that flies ecstatic into the flame and, as it is burned up, realizes Reality.

Authorities imprisoned and finally killed al-Hallaj. Now, however, al-Hallaj is considered by many to be one of the greatest Muslim saints, for it is understood that he was not speaking in his limited person. Like the Prophet, who had reportedly said, "Die before ye die,"[35] al-Hallaj had already died to himself so that nothing remained but the One.

> *What's in your head—toss it away! What's in your hand—give it up! Whatever happens—don't turn away from it. … Sufism is the heart standing with God, with nothing in between.*
>
> *Abu Sa'id Abu al-Khayr*[36]

A more moderate Sufism began to make its way into Sunni orthodoxy through Abu Hamid al-Ghazali (1058–1111). He had been a prominent theologian but felt compelled to leave his prestigious position for a life of spiritual devotion. Turning within, he discovered mystical truths, which saved him from his growing scepticism about the validity of religion. Like mystics of all religions, he urged awareness of the certainty of death as an antidote to entanglements in worldly concerns:

Death does not come upon us at a specified time or in a specified way or at a specified age; but come upon us he does, and so preparation for death is better than preparation for this world. You know that you remain here for only a brief

space—perhaps there remains but a single day in your allotted span, perhaps but a single breath. Imagine this in your heart every day and impose upon yourself patience in obeying God daily.[37]

Al-Ghazali's persuasive writings combined accepted Muslim theology, law, and ethics with the assertion that Sufism is needed to keep the mystical heart alive within the tradition. By the fourteenth century, mysticism was generally accepted by the orthodoxy as one of the sciences of religion, along with theology and jurisprudence.

Over the centuries, other elements have been added to Sufism. Some Sufis have embraced teachings from various religions, emphasizing that the Qur'an clearly states that the same Voice has spoken through all prophets. Shihabuddin Suhrawardi (1153–1191), for instance, combined many currents of Islam with spiritual ideas from the Zoroastrians of ancient Iran and the Hermetic tradition from ancient Egypt. His writings are full of references to the divine light and hierarchies of angels. We humans have descended from the angels and realms of light, he wrote; we are in exile here on earth, longing for our true home, searching for that radiant purity, dimly remembered, in this dark world of matter.

Although Sufi teachings and practices have been somewhat systematized over time, they resist doctrinal, linear specification. They come from the heart of mystical experiences that defy ordinary logic. Paradox, metaphor, the world of creative imagination, of an expanded sense of reality—these characteristics of Sufi thought are better expressed through poetry and stories. A favorite character in Sufi teaching tales is Mulla Nasrudin, the wise fool. An example, as told by Idries Shah:

One day Nasrudin entered a teahouse and declaimed, "The moon is more useful than the sun." Someone asked him why. "Because at night we need the light more."[38]

These "jokes" boggle the mind, revealing the limitations of ordinary thinking at the same time that they offer flashes of metaphysical illumination for those who ponder their deeper significances.

Poetry has been used by Sufis as a vehicle for expressing the profundities and perplexities of relationship with the divine. The Turkish dervish Jalal al-Din

Sufi dancers and musicians in Gaza City.

Rumi (*c.* 1207–1273), by whose inspiration was founded the Mevlevi Dervish Order in Turkey (famous for its "Whirling Dervishes" whose dances lead to transcendent rapture), was a master of mystical poetry. He tells the story of a devotee whose cries of "O Allah!" were finally answered by God:

> *Was it not I that summoned thee to service?*
> *Did not I make thee busy with My name?*
> *Thy calling "Allah!" was My "Here am I,"*
> *Thy yearning pain My messenger to thee.*
> *Of all those tears and cries and supplications*
> *I was the magnet, and I gave them wings.*[39]

The aim of Sufism is to become so purified of self that one is a perfect mirror for the divine attributes. The central practice is called dhikr, or "remembrance," in which the Sufi recites, sings, or sometimes dances while repeating a prayer over and over, such as the phrase *"la ilaha illa Allah."* Sufis understand this phrase in its esoteric sense: "There is nothing except God." Nothing in this ephemeral world is real except the Creator; nothing else will last. As the seventy thousand veils of self—illusion, expectation, attachment, resentment, egocentrism, discontent, arrogance—drop away over the years, this becomes one's truth, and only God is left to experience it.

The development of Islam

Which factors contributed to the successful expansion of Islam?

In the time of Muhammad, Islam combined spiritual and secular power under one ruler. This tradition, which helped to unify the warring tribes of the area, was continued under his successors. Islam expanded phenomenally during the centuries after the Prophet's death, contributing to the rise of many great civilizations. The ummah became a community that spread from Africa to Indonesia. Islam was not usually spread by the sword. The Qur'an forbids coercion in religion, recommending instead that Muslims invite others to the Way by their wisdom, beautiful teaching, and personal example. Islam spread mostly by personal contacts: trade, attraction to charismatic Sufi saints, appeals to Muslims from those feeling oppressed by Byzantine and Persian rule, and unforced conversions. There were some military battles conducted by Muslims over the centuries, but they were not necessarily for the purpose of spreading Islam, and many Muslims believe that wars of aggression violate Muslim principles. Non-Muslim citizens of newly entered territories were asked to pay a poll tax entitling them

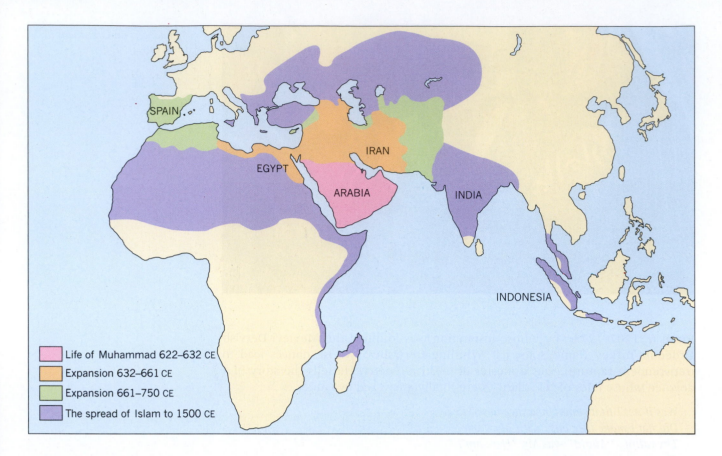

Life of Muhammad 622–632 CE
Expansion 632–661 CE
Expansion 661–750 CE
The spread of Islam to 1500 CE

Only 100 years after Muhammad's death, Islam had spread around the Mediterranean. Its diffusion continued for centuries and the numbers of converts are still increasing, making Islam the fastest-growing religion today. Of areas previously converted to Islam, all remain Muslim except Spain, Greece, and the Mediterranean islands.

to Muslim defense against enemies and exempting them from military service.

Muhammad's nonviolent takeover of Mecca occurred only two years before he died. It was under his successors that Islam spread through West Asia and far beyond. Only a year after Muhammad died, a newly converted Qurayshite, Khalid ibn al-Walid (d. 642), commanded a series of campaigns that within seven years had claimed the entire Arabian peninsula and Syria for Islam. Newly Islamic Arab armies quickly swept through the Sassanian Persian Empire, which had stood for twelve centuries. Defeated in battle in 637 CE, the Persian emperor fled, leaving the capital in Arab hands. Within ten years of the Prophet's death, a mere 4,000 horsemen commanded by Amr ibn al-As took the major cities of Egypt, centers of the Byzantine Empire. Another wave of conquest soon penetrated into Turkey and Central Asia, North Africa, and north through Spain, to be stopped in 732 CE in France at the battle of Tours. At this point, only 100 years after Muhammad died, the Muslim ummah under the Umayyad caliphs was larger than the Roman Empire had ever been.

Muslims cite the power of the divine will to establish a peaceful, God-conscious society as the reason why this happened. By contrast with their strong convictions, the populations they approached were often demoralized by border fighting among themselves and by grievances against their rulers. Many welcomed them without a fight. For example, the Christians of Damascus expected Muslim rule to be more bearable than Byzantine rule, so they opened the city gates to the Muslim armies. Jerusalem and Egypt accepted the Muslims in similar fashion. Syrian Christians at Shayzar under Byzantine rule reportedly went out to meet the Muslim commander and accompanied him to their city, singing and playing tambourines. In Spain, Visigoth rule and taxation had been oppressive; the persecuted Jews were especially glad to help Islam take over. Both Christians and Jews often converted to Islam.

Some historians cite economic factors as an underlying motive for Arabs' expansion beyond their original territory. However, although Islamic civilization did become quite opulent, the central leadership did not always support the far-reaching adventures. The conquered peoples were generally dealt with in the humane ways specified in the Qur'an and modeled by Muhammad in his negotiations with tribes newly subjected to Muslim authority. The terms offered by Khalid to the besieged Damascans were these:

> In the name of God, the merciful, the compassionate. This is what Khalid would grant the inhabitants of Damascus when he enters it. He shall grant them security for their lives, properties and churches. Their city wall shall not be demolished, neither shall any Moslem be quartered in their homes. Thereunto we give them the pact of God and the protection (dhimmah) of His Messenger, upon whom be God's blessing and peace, the caliphs and the Believers. So long as they pay poll-tax nothing but good shall befall them.[40]

Monotheistic followers of revealed traditions, Christians and Jews, who like Muslims were "People of the Book," were treated as *dhimmis*, or protected people. They were allowed to maintain their own faith, but not to try to convert others to it. The Dome of the Rock was built on the site of the old temple of the Jews in Jerusalem, honoring Abraham as well as Muhammad in the city that is still sacred to three faiths: Judaism, Christianity, and Islam.

The Umayyad caliphs had their hands full administering this huge ummah from Damascus, which they had made its capital. They tended to focus more on organizational matters than on the spiritual life. Some were also quite worldly; Walid II, for example, is said to have enjoyed a pool filled with wine so that he could swim and drink at the same time. In 747 CE a rival to the caliphate is said

TEACHING STORY

Transformation by Islam

From the beginning, Islam ended old tribal conflicts and racial discrimination, and radically changed individuals. The Prophet put the freed black slave Zayd in command of the Qurayshi chiefs. Another freed slave, Tariq ibn Ziyad, led the army of 90,000 warriors who conquered Spain and established one of the greatest civilizations in world history. When he entered the defeated king's treasury, he was not tempted to take anything, for he said to himself:

> Be careful, Tariq. Yesterday you were a slave with a chain around your neck. God emancipated you, and today you are a victorious commander. However, you will change tomorrow into flesh rotting under earth. Finally a day will come when you will stand in the Presence of God.[41]

He continued to live simply. His greatest victory was not his conquest of Spain, but his defeat of his own desires.

'Abd Allah ibn Mas'ud was a weak little shepherd. Nobody paid any attention to him until he converted to Islam. Soon he became one of the greatest of the Companions of the Prophet. The Caliph 'Umar sent him to Kufa in Iraq as a teacher. He helped to create such a thriving intellectual climate there that Kufa became one of the major centers of Islamic jurisprudence, Qur'anic interpretation, and even a beautiful script for the writing of Arabic.

Among many other examples of personal transformation, perhaps none is greater than that of 'Umar, who became the second caliph. He was a Meccan who firmly and cruelly opposed Muhammad's monotheistic path as a threat to Quraysh unity. It is said that he intended to kill the Prophet. According to one traditional account, on the way to do so he met a Muslim who told him to first put his own house in order, since his own sister and brother-in-law were secret converts to Islam. On entering their house, he found them reciting the Qur'an. He began brutally beating his brother-in-law, and then his sister as well when she tried to protect her husband. When they bore his blows patiently, he asked to see what they were reading. His sister showed him a portion of the Surat Ta Ha, which describes the Qur'an as "A revelation from Him Who created the earth and the heavens on high" [Holy Qur'an 20:4]. 'Umar was so struck by the beauty of the passage they had been reading that he proceeded to find the Prophet, offered him the sword with which he had planned to kill him, and accepted Islam on the spot. He became one of the most powerful Muslim leaders and was so renowned for his justice toward both Muslims and non-Muslims that he was called *Al-Farooq* (the one who distinguishes between good and bad).

to have invited eighty of the princes of the line to a banquet, where he had them all killed. Three years after "the bloodshedder," a new series of caliphs took over: the Abbasids. They held power until 1258 CE.

Under the Abbasids, Muslim rule became more Persian and cosmopolitan and Islamic civilization reached its peak. The capital was moved to the new city of Baghdad. No more territories were brought under centralized rule, and merchants, scholars, and artists became the cultural heroes. A great House of Wisdom was built, with an observatory, library, and an educational institution where Greek and Syriac manuscripts on subjects such as medicine, astronomy, logic, mathematics, and philosophy were translated into Arabic. In Cairo, under the Fatimid Ismaili caliphate, Muslims built in 972 CE the great university and mosque, Al-Azhar, still important in Muslim scholarship and legal decisions.

In its great cities, Islam went through a period of intense intellectual and artistic activity, absorbing, transmitting, and expanding upon the highest traditions of other cultures. For instance, from Persia, which was to become a Shi'ite stronghold, it adopted a thousand-year-old tradition of exquisite art and poetry. To these avid cultural borrowings Islam added its own innovations. The new system of nine Arabic numerals and the zero derived from Indian numbers revolutionized mathematics by liberating it from the clumsiness of Roman numerals. A love of geometry and a spiritual understanding of numbers, from the One to infinite divisions, provided the basis for beautifully elaborated art and architectural forms. Muslim philosophers were highly interested in Aristotelian and Neo-Platonic thought, but in their unique synthesis these intellectual ways were harmonized with revealed religion. Muslim scholars' research into geography, history, astronomy, literature, and medicine lifted these disciplines to unprecedented heights.

The *ulama* were not only guardians of the faith but were also the pervasive force holding together Islamic society. They were *qadis* (judges), muftis (jurisconsultants), guides and pastors of the artisans' guilds, spiritual leaders, mosque imams, teachers of the civil and military schools, state scribes, and market inspectors. They received their mandate and power from the people and not from any political authority. The major sources of their economic power and their independence from the state were religious and private endowments, run and controlled by the *ulama*.

Although Baghdad was the capital of the Abbasids, independent caliphates were declared in Spain and Egypt. Muslim Spain was led by successors to the Umayyads and became a great cultural center. Córdoba, the capital, had 700 mosques, seventy libraries, 300 public baths, and paved streets. Europe, by contrast, was in its Dark Ages; Paris and London were only mazes of muddy alleys. Spanish Muslim scientists developed a prototype of a flying machine, mechanical clocks, and highly accurate astronomical clocks, many centuries before such inventions were introduced into Europe through translations of Arabic manuscripts.

Tunisia and Egypt comprised a third center of Islamic power: the Shi'ite Fatimid caliphate (so named because they claimed to be descendants of Muhammad's daughter Fatima). While otherwise known for their brilliant cultural and scientific accomplishments, under the troubled Fatimid caliph, al-Hakim (985–c. 1021), the Fatimids broke with Islamic tradition and persecuted *dhimmis*; they also destroyed the Church of the Holy Sepulcher in Jerusalem, provoking European Christian crusades to try to recapture the Holy Lands.

Crusading Christians fought their way to Jerusalem, which they placed under siege in 1099. When the small Fatimid garrison surrendered, the crusaders slaughtered the inhabitants of the holy city. Eyewitnesses recount the beheading of 70,000 captives at the al-Aqsa mosque, near the altar site of the ancient Jewish Temple. Severed hands and feet were piled everywhere. Anti-crusading Muslims led by the famous Salah-al-Din (known in the West as Saladin) retook Jerusalem in 1187 and treated its Christian population with the generous leniency of Islam's highest ideals for the conduct of war. But widespread

Court of the Lions in the Alhambra, Granada, an example of the heights to which architecture evolved in Muslim Spain.

destruction remained in the wake of the crusaders, and a reservoir of ill-will against Christians lingered, to be exacerbated centuries later by European colonialism in Muslim lands.

The Islamic period in Spain was known for its tolerance of Judaism. But during the twelfth and thirteenth centuries, Christians took Spain and later instituted the dread Inquisition against those not practicing Christianity. By the beginning of the sixteenth century, an estimated three million Spanish Muslims had either been killed or left the country.

Eastward expansion

Its westward advance stopped at Europe, Islam carried its vitality to the north, east, and south. Although Mongol invasions from Central Asia threatened, the Mongols were converted to Islam; so were the Turks. While Uzbek Khan, Mongol leader from 1313 to 1340, zealously desired to spread Islam throughout Russia, he nonetheless maintained tolerance toward the Christians in the conquered lands. He granted a charter to the Orthodox Metropolitan concerning the treatment of Christians: "Their laws, their Churches; their monasteries and chapels shall be respected; whoever condemns or blames this religion, shall not be allowed to excuse himself under any pretext but shall be punished with death."[42]

Similar tolerance toward other religions was practiced by the Muslim Turks, but in 1453 the Turks conquered Constantinople, the heart of the old Byzantine Empire, and renamed it Istanbul; Hagia Sophia was turned into a mosque even though it did not face Mecca. At its height, the Turkish Ottoman Empire dominated the eastern Mediterranean as well as the area around the Black Sea.

Farther east, Islam was carried into northern India, where Muslim conquerors destroyed some Hindu idols and temples but allowed the Hindu majority a protected *dhimmi* status. The Chishti Sufi saints drew people to Islam by their great love for God. Under the Muslim Mughals, the arts and learning flourished in India. In the ecumenical spiritual curiosity of the emperor Akbar, who rose to the Mughal throne in 1556, representatives from many traditions—Hindu, Zoroastrian, Jain, Christian—were invited to the world's first interfaith dialogues.

Under British colonization of India, tensions between Hindus and Muslims were inflamed, partly to help Britain divide and rule. India gained its independence under the influence of Mahatma Gandhi, who was unable to devise a political solution to the concerns of Muslims fearing domination by a Hindu-majority government. In 1947, West and East Pakistan (the East section became the independent nation of Bangladesh in 1971) were partitioned off to be Muslim-ruled and predominantly populated by Muslims, while India would become a Hindu-majority state. The creation of Pakistan was one of the major contemporary attempts to create a model nation based on the principles of Islam. Mohammed Ali Jinnah, the London-educated lawyer who is regarded as the founder of Pakistan, conceived of Pakistan as a modern and democratic state in which women, minorities, and human rights would be respected, according to Islam's true tenets of tolerance, compassion, and justice. However, the entrenched powers and ethnic and cultural divisions within the country have prevented realization of his dream. At its inception, the partition of India into Muslim majority and Hindu majority nations turned into a violent and chaotic nightmare. Millions lost their lives trying to cross the borders. The strife between the two faiths continues despite recurrent attempts to renew peaceful

The Taj Mahal, the beautiful 17th-century Mughal tomb built by Akbar's grandson, Shah Jahan, as a monument to his beloved wife, who died in childbirth, is embellished with passages from the Holy Qur'an, though it is mostly visited as a tourist attraction.

In Muslim-majority Malaysia, where gender discrimination was outlawed in 2001, the reality TV show Solehah *(pious female) features competition among female preachers of Islam.*

relationships between the peoples of Pakistan and India, who, though divided into different religions, actually share a similar culture. In India, Hindus and Muslims had long lived side by side in relative harmony, but communal tensions have sometimes been reignited. For example, in December 1992, militant Hindus set off renewed communal violence by destroying a mosque in Ayodhya, India, in the belief that it had been built by the Mughals on the site of an ancient temple to Lord Rama.

The greatest concentration of Muslims developed even farther east, in Indonesia, where Muslim traders and missionaries may have first landed as early as the tenth century CE. Nearly ninety percent of the people are now Sunni Muslims, but the government has thus far preserved a secular, pluralistic society rather than establish Islam as the state religion, as some Islamist groups have sporadically tried to do.

China and the former Soviet Union encompass tens of millions of Muslims. To the south, Islam spread into Africa along lines of trade. In competition with Christianity, Islam sought the hearts of Africans and eventually won in many areas. Many converted to Islam; many others maintained some of their indigenous ways in combination with Islam. The prosperous Mali Empire was headed by a Muslim, who made an awe-inspiring pilgrimage to Mecca with a gold-laden retinue of 8,000 in 1324. As the spread of Islam encompassed an increasing diversity of cultures, hajj became important not only for individuals but also as a meeting ground for scholars and the religion as a whole, holding its center in Mecca in the midst of worldwide variations.

Relationships with the West
What are the key issues facing Muslims in the modern world?

Although Islam honors the prophets of all traditions, its own religion and prophet were denounced by medieval Christian Europe. Christianity had considered itself the ultimate religion and had launched its efforts to bring the whole world under its wings. Muslims felt the same way about the mission of their own religion. In the struggle for souls, the Church depicted Muhammad as an idol-worshiper, an anti-Christ, the Prince of Darkness. Islam was falsely portrayed as a religion of many deities, in which Muhammad himself was worshiped as a god (thus the inaccurate label "Muhammadanism"). Europeans watched in horror as the Holy Lands became Muslim and the **"infidel"** advanced into Spain and elsewhere in Europe. Even though Muslim scholars and artists preserved, shared, and advanced the classic civilizations while Europe was benighted, the wealth of Arabic culture was interpreted in a negative light.

By the nineteenth century, Western scholars began to study the Arabic classics, but the ingrained fear and loathing of Muhammad and Muslims remained. The ignorance about, and negative stereotyping of, Muslims continues today. Annemarie Schimmel, late Professor of Indo-Muslim Culture, Harvard University, explained:

> *The idea that the Muslims conquered everything with fire and sword was unfortunately deeply ingrained in the medieval mind. All these misconceptions about Islam as a religion and the legends and lies that were told about it are really unbelievable. I have often the feeling that this medieval image of Islam as it was perpetuated in ever so many books and even scholarly works is part of our subconscious. When someone comes and says, "But real Islam is something completely different," people just will not believe it because they have been indoctrinated for almost fourteen hundred years with the image of Islam as something fierce and something immoral. Unfortunately, some of the events of our century have revived this medieval concept of Islam.*[43]

> *Borrow the Beloved's eyes. Look through them and you'll see the Beloved's face everywhere. …*
> *Let that happen, and things you have hated will become helpers.*
>
> *Jalal al-Din Rumi*[44]

Although it had enjoyed great heights of culture and political power, the Muslim world fell into decline. It seems that the Mongol invasions were at least partly responsible, for they eradicated irrigation systems and libraries and killed scholars and scientists, erasing much of the civilization that had been built up over 500 years. Some Muslims today think that spiritual laxness was the primary reason that some of the previously glorious civilizations became impoverished

Dome of the Rock, Jerusalem. In an area held sacred by Jews, Christians, and Muslims, the dome was completed in 691–692 C.E. as the first major Muslim monument. The rock had been associated with Abraham's sacrifice of his son. Muslim tradition identified it as the place of the Prophet's ascension to heaven during his Night Journey.

underdeveloped countries. Another theory is that Muslims were simply overtaken by stronger military and economic powers better equipped than they were, such as the Mongols in the thirteenth century, and subsequently the Europeans.

During the late eighteenth and early nineteenth centuries, many Muslim populations fell under European domination. From the mid-twentieth century onward, most gained their independence as states that had adopted certain Western ideals and practices. In many cases, they let go of some aspects of their Muslim heritage, considering it a relic that prevented them from success in the modern world. Arabic was treated as an unimportant language; Western codes of law replaced the shari'ah in social organization. But yet they were not totally Westernized, and they resumed local rule with little training for self-government and participation in a world economy dominated by industrial nations.

Societies that had been structured along traditional lines fragmented from the mid-nineteenth century onward, as wide-ranging programs of modernization were unleashed throughout the Muslim world. The local autonomy of the traditional Islamic society was swept away and replaced by centralized regulations of Western origin. Traditional schools, markets, guilds, and courts into which the societies had been organized lost much of their reason for being. The legacy of this social fragmentation continues to be felt today, and is often a part of the conflicts among Muslims about how to shape contemporary social structures, legal systems, and governments.

Before the colonial forces moved out, foreign powers led by Britain helped to introduce a Jewish state in West Asia. After long and terrible persecution in many countries, Jewish Zionists sought resettlement in Palestine, which they considered their ancient homeland. But some historians allege that the chief motive of the countries supporting this claim was to protect European interests. Lord Palmerston of Britain suggested that a wealthy Jewish population transplanted to Palestine, and highly motivated to protect itself, would prop up the decaying Ottoman Empire so that it could serve as a bulwark against Russian imperialism; the new Jewish presence in Palestine would also serve as a check against the attempts of Egypt to create a pan-Islamic state encompassing Egypt, Syria, and the Arabian peninsula. In 1948 Jordan and Egypt annexed twenty-two percent of Palestinian territory—the West Bank and the Gaza Strip; in 1967, this territory was occupied by Israel. Decades of violence and counterviolence have followed, with Palestinians in the disputed area suffering from appropriation of their lands, destruction of their houses, severe curtailing of their material supplies, and restrictions on their movements; and Israelis living in fear of terrorist attacks.

Islam in the West

Even as Muslims were feeling humiliated by foreign domination elsewhere, they were growing in numbers and self-pride within the United States. Islam is the fastest growing religion in the United States, and may now be the second largest religion in the country. Two-thirds of American Muslims are immigrants; one-third of American Muslims are converts, most of them African Americans.

Conversion to Islam by African Americans was encouraged early in the twentieth century as a form of separatism from white oppression. Awareness grew that many of the slaves who had been brought from West Africa had been of Muslim faith. A number of movements developed to bring the former slaves back to their suppressed ancestral faith, although the teachings of these movements were not always fully in accord with orthodox Islamic traditions. For instance, in 1913 Noble Drew Ali (1886–1929) began the Moorish Science Temple, a movement that was designed to begin teaching the elements of the faith to African Americans and thus give them a strong sense of their own identity. Members were encouraged to adopt Noble Drew Ali's understanding of Muslim lifestyles, with modest dress, gender separation, traditional family structure, and community solidarity.

Worshipers in a mosque in the United States.

Some other early Muslim communities in the United States were based on missionary efforts, such as that of the Ahmadiyyah Movement from India, which was active in publishing tracts and English translations of the Qur'an and in helping African American converts learn Arabic. However, some Muslims do not accept the Ahmadiyyah Movement as Muslim, for the movement's prophet proclaimed himself the Mahdi and Messiah, contrary to mainstream understanding of Muhammad as the "seal of the prophets."

Other movements had a strong nation-building character. In particular, under the leadership of Elijah Muhammad (1897–1975), who proclaimed himself a messenger of God, tens of thousands of African Americans became "Black Muslims," calling themselves the Nation of Islam. However, faith in Elijah Muhammad himself was shaken by allegations about his sexual relationships with his secretaries. Some followers—especially the influential leader Malcolm X and Warith Deen Muhammad, son of Elijah Muhammad—developed contacts with mainstream Muslims in other countries and came to the conclusion that Elijah Muhammad's version of Islam was far removed from Muslim orthodoxy. They steered converts toward what they perceived as the true traditions of Islam and alliance with the world Muslim community.

Others of African American heritage, especially Minister Louis Farrakhan, current leader of the Nation of Islam, maintain Elijah Muhammad's more political focus on unifying against white oppression, despite Islam's strong tradition of nonracism. However, politicization of Islamic identity is probably not the main factor encouraging the growth of Islam. Many American Muslims embrace their religion as a bulwark of discipline and faith against the degradations of materialism.

The homes of African American Muslims become places of refuge from the surrounding culture, with Qur'anic inscriptions, provisions for prayer spaces, cleanliness and lack of clutter, and windows covered as privacy screens. Soon after birth, children are placed with their mothers on their prayer rugs and gradually learn to recite portions of the Qur'an. They are carefully trained in politeness to elders, modest dress, and proper behavior. The environment these children encounter in public schools is a great contrast to this traditional upbringing. Young Muslim girls are taunted about their headscarves, and sex education classes, which begin at an early age, are offensive to Muslim parents who do not accept dating and extramarital sexuality for their children. Some African American Muslim parents thus attempt to home-school their children. Overall, the American Muslim population is extremely diverse, made up of African American converts as well as immigrants and descendants of immigrants from South Asia and various Arab countries. A 2011 Gallup report found that Muslim Americans are one of the most tolerant religious groups in the United States, more so than Protestants, Catholics, and Jews.[45]

In Europe, decades of immigration from formerly French and British colonies in Africa and Asia have expanded the Muslim presence considerably. There are now over twenty million Muslims in western Europe. There they have often maintained their traditional cultures rather than adopting European behaviors. Unlike the diverse Muslim population in the United States, Muslim communities in European countries are typically primarily composed of immigrants from only one or two countries (often former colonies). The secular policies of the French government have prompted a legal ban since 2004 on overt display of religious symbols, including the headscarves traditionally worn by Muslim women. Refusal to allow wearing of headscarves in school has led some Muslim girls to leave public schools and pursue education through home schooling or religious schools, causing further separation between Muslim and non-Muslim populations. In 2011, face veils were banned in France in all public places.

In Switzerland, construction of new minarets (tall towers) on mosques was also banned by a 2009 public referendum. Such restrictions of religious symbols have been linked with various kinds of fears, including concerns about security and political power, as well as resentment in European welfare states that Muslim immigrants are benefiting from their welfare systems. Negative right-wing and nationalistic responses are thus accompanying the growth of Islam in Europe. As an Austrian researcher into this trend observed, "resentments, fears and constructions of the enemy, which have formed in response to historic burdens and a lack of information, [have] now come to the surface."[46]

Muslim resurgence

The Muslim world had lost its own traditional structure and was also generally helpless against manipulations by foreign nations until many Muslim-majority countries found power in oil. In the 1970s, oil-rich nations found that by banding together they could control the price and availability of oil. OPEC (the Organization of Petroleum Exporting Countries) brought greatly increased revenues into previously impoverished countries and strengthened their self-image as well as their importance in the global balance of power.

As the wealth suddenly poured in, it further disrupted established living patterns. Analysts have concluded that some people may have turned back to a more conservative version of Islam in an effort to restore a personal sense of familiarity and stability amid the chaos of changing modern life. Moreover, the increase in literacy, urbanization, and communications helped to spread revived interest in Islam. There was also the hope that Islam would provide the blueprint for enlightened rule, bringing spiritual values into community and politics as Muhammad had done in Medina. It is thought that the Prophet had intentionally tried to create a united community in which each Muslim is responsible for his or her fellow human beings, in which no one should be hungry or unfairly treated, and in which the leader of the community is a just and religious person. This ideal has perhaps never been fully realized, but it continues to inspire committed Muslims today as the best defense against social decadence and, perhaps, as the salvation of the world.

Traditionally, Muslims have seen the world as divided into *dar al-Islam*, "the abode of Islam" (those places where Muslims are a majority and shari'ah governs worldly life), *dar al-sulh*, "the abode of peace" (where Muslims are a minority but can live in peace and freely practice Islam), and *dar al-harb*, "the abode of conflict" (where Muslims are in the minority and are struggling to practice Islam).

As overt colonialism wanes, the world has become divided into autonomous nation-states with strong central governments. In this process, forty-three primarily Islamic nation-states have been created. They differ greatly in culture and in the degree to which each society is ruled by Islamic ethics. But all are now being reconsidered as possible frameworks for *dar al-Islam*, within which the Muslim dream of religion-based social transformation might be accomplished. Those who seek to establish Islamic states in which the sovereignty of God is supreme are often now referred to as **Islamists**.

In the past few centuries, modern industrial societies separated religion from politics. Social, political, and economic issues were treated without any reference to a higher authority or to the values taught by the prophets; religion has been considered a largely private matter, even within some Muslim-majority states such as Turkey, where separation of religion from government became law after reformist President Ataturk led his people in abolishing the Ottoman sultanate and establishing the secular Republic of Turkey in 1923. By contrast, the re-emerging ideal among some Muslim social reformers is that cultures oriented toward the sovereignty of God, acting according to divine commands, can create a new world order of peace.

Contemporary Islam in public and private life

Much of the discourse regarding Islam, particularly in the Western world, focuses on shari'ah, especially with respect to women's roles in public and private life. Media accounts often oversimplify the complex and diverse nature of shari'ah and Islamic jurisprudence, treating it as a single, static entity rather than a complex, sophisticated system comprising different legal schools with longstanding traditions of legal reasoning. There are many different voices within Islam regarding the practice of the faith in the modern world, and many different attitudes regarding the role that shari'ah should play in contemporary Muslim life. Some Muslim thinkers have argued that Islamic jurisprudence already has within it the basis for ongoing reform and reinterpretation through *ijtihad* (reasoned interpretation, independent judgment by a qualified scholar). Others have called for a return to a particular form of shari'ah (sometimes envisioning this revived shari'ah as more monolithic than it has traditionally been), rejecting secular law derived from European codes. The feeling of the orthodox is that the world must conform to the divine law, rather than diluting the law to accommodate it to the material world. In Iran, for instance, an attempt has been made to shape every aspect of life according to shari'ah. Fasting during Ramadan is strictly enforced in Saudi Arabia and Iran, and restaurants in many Muslim countries choose to close during the fasting hours. In Muslim-dominated northern Nigeria, a 1999 shari'ah ruling barred men and women from traveling in the same public vehicles, in an effort to combat immorality and crime.

Private behaviors are also changing. In particular, to honor the Qur'anic encouragement of physical modesty to protect women from being molested, many Muslim women have adopted **hijab** (veiling), covering their bodies except for hands, face, and feet, as they had not done for decades. In Saudi Arabia, where women have been ordered to be "properly covered" outside their homes, some wear not only head-to-toe black cloaks but also full veils over their faces without even slits for their eyes. Some Muslim women assert that they like dressing more modestly so that men will not stare at them. Semaa Abdulwali, a medical science student in Australia who chose to begin wearing the veil, explains:

> *I feel liberated by the fact that I choose what you see. We pass judgement on how a person looks before we know them. When you deal with me, you deal with my mind, my personality, my emotions and what I have to offer as a person—and that's it.*[47]

In some Muslim-majority countries, women are allowed to join the workforce only if they are veiled. In Iran, the replacement of more Westernized customs with Muslim moral codes, including veiling of women, has allowed women from conservative backgrounds to leave their homes and enter public life without

Even when wearing veils for modesty, Muslim women are often exposed to different lifestyles, as in this shopping mall in Dubai, United Arab Emirates.

antagonizing their families. Now that a great number of Iranian Muslim women have been educated and have entered the workforce and politics, they are a formidable part of reformist efforts to challenge the control of the male clerical elite over social life. They have also become active participants in contemporary Iranian attempts to reconcile Islam with human rights and democracy.

Women's rights to divorce and to choose their own marriage partners are among the hotly debated issues in contemporary attempts to define shari'ah. Shari'ah has been locally adapted to various societies over the centuries; some feel that to attempt to restore its original form is to deny the usefulness of its flexibility. Certain customs thought to be Muslim are actually cultural practices not specified in the basic sources; they are the result of Islamic civilization's assimilation of many cultures in many places. Muhammad worked side by side with women, and the Qur'an encourages equal participation of women in religion and in society. Veiling and seclusion were practices absorbed from conquered Persian and Byzantine cultures, particularly their upper classes; peasant women could not carry out their physical work under encumbering veils or in seclusion from public view.

Muslim women scholars are now carefully re-examining the Qur'an and Hadith to determine the historical realities and principles of women's issues that have long been hidden behind an exclusively male interpretation of the traditions. African American Muslim and Qur'anic scholar Amina Wadud, for instance, asserts that the Qur'an is potentially a "world-altering force" that offers universal moral guidance for all believers, be they male or female:

> The more research I did into the Qur'an, … the more affirmed I was that in Islam a female person was intended to be primordially, cosmologically, eschatologically, spiritually, and morally a full human being, equal to all who accepted Allah as Lord, Muhammad as Prophet, and Islam as din [religious way]. … Conservative thinkers read explicit Qur'anic reforms of existing historical and cultural practices as the literal and definitive statement on these practices for all times and places. What I am calling for is a reading that regards those reforms as establishing precedent for continual development *toward a just social order.*[48]

Another challenge with applying shari'ah as civil law is that some ethical issues that arise today, such as cloning and climate change, either did not exist in their present form at the time the legal codes were created or were not specifically addressed by the Qur'an or Hadith. According to Islamic legal reasoning, the accepted method for determining ambiguous issues is to weigh all the benefits and disadvantages that might result from a course of action and then discourage it if the likely disadvantages outweigh the advantages. For those Muslim intellectuals who want to retain their faith within the context of modern life, this process of *ijtihad* is critical.

Shari'ah forbids the practice of usury, or accepting interest for loans, making it problematic for Muslims to make use of the dominant banking models in much of the world. As a result, Muslims have established alternate systems of finance, including banks, mutual funds, and alternative mortgage systems that allow them to conduct business according to shari'ah. Another challenge, particularly for those in areas without a significant Muslim population, is eating a diet made up of halal, or permissible, foods. Muslim student groups have worked with dining services on many college campuses to provide meals that are halal.

While Muslims have continually sought to apply Islamic principles to an ever-changing world, the global family of Islam is not a political unit; its unity under Arab rule broke up long ago. There is as yet no consensus among Muslim-majority states about how to establish a peaceful, just, modern society based on basic Muslim principles. But there is widespread recognition that there are problems associated with modern Western civilization that should be avoided, such as crime, drug abuse, corruption of values, and unstable family life.

> *Today everyone cries for peace but peace is never achieved, precisely because it is metaphysically absurd to expect a civilization that has forgotten God to possess peace.*
>
> Seyyed Hossein Nasr[49]

Outreach and education

Islam is the fastest growing of all world religions, with more than 1.2 billion followers. New mosques are going up everywhere. Some Muslims who constitute a minority in their countries are trying to assert their rights to practice their religion by praying five times a day, leaving work to attend Friday congregational prayer at noon, and wearing traditional head-coverings. Special Islamic satellite channels offer alternatives to Western-oriented programming that some Muslims find offensive because of an emphasis on sexuality and violence and lack of emphasis on family values. These channels also act as a force for international Muslim unity. The channel Iqraa, for instance, is financed by a Saudi Arabian millionaire, offering free broadcasting of what it describes as "entertaining programmes that are devoid of decadence and impropriety and are appropriate for viewing by Muslim families."[50]

Another sign of Muslim resurgence is the increasing attention being given to developing educational systems modeled on Islamic thought. Islam is not anti-scientific or anti-intellectual; on the contrary, it has historically bridged reason and faith and placed a high value on developing both in order to tap into the fullness of human potential. Much of Western education has omitted the spiritual aspects of life, so many Muslims consider it incomplete and imbalanced.

While there are many excellent Muslim educational institutions, there are some **madrasas**, or traditional religious schools, that teach a narrow version of Islam, ignoring its sophisticated cultural and scientific heritage and nuanced philosophy. Because some of these schools have proved to be breeding grounds for militants, fanning hatred of the West, particularly among the poor rural students, they are now coming under closer scrutiny. Muslims have also debated the content of texts used in government-run schools. The Sustainable Development Policy Institute in Islamabad released a report in 2003 which identified a number of troubling features of textbooks and curricula in Pakistan:

RELIGION IN PUBLIC LIFE

Malala Yousafzai

 In 1997, Malala Yousafzai was born in the town of Mingora in the beautiful Swat valley of Pakistan. She attended a school for girls established by her father, Ziauddin Yousafzai, and was a dedicated student, hoping to become a doctor. The Taliban, however, began trying to take control of the Swat region, and schools for girls came under attack. In 2009, at the age of eleven, Malala Yousafzai began speaking out in favor of girls' education, and began blogging for BBC Urdu using a pseudonym. In her blog, she explained what it was like to live in an environment in which the Taliban (see p.420) was trying to stop girls from pursuing their education and had banned television and music. She described her feelings of sadness as the number of young women attending her school dwindled. After her identity as the blogger was revealed later that year, Malala continued to speak out publicly in favor of education for girls, becoming the subject of a 2009 documentary film commissioned by *The New York Times* called "Class Dismissed: Malala's Story." But as the situation in Swat became more unstable and dangerous, Malala's school closed, and Malala and her family had to flee from their beloved Swat, reciting surahs from the Qur'an and prayers to protect their home and the school. They became "internally displaced persons" within their own country.[51]

When Malala and her family returned to Mingora several months later, the town was scarred by the battle between the Pakistani army and the Taliban. Soon, her father was able to re-open Malala's school. But the Taliban was still active. In 2011, as Malala continued to speak publicly in favor of education for girls, she received Pakistan's National Peace Prize, later renamed the Malala Prize. But Malala and her father began receiving threats from the Taliban. In her book *I Am Malala*, she explains how the threats frightened her so much that she could not sleep without checking all the locks in her home each night:

Then I'd pray. At night I used to pray a lot. The Taliban think we are not Muslims but we are. We believe in God more than they do and we trust him to protect us. I used to say the Ayat al-Kursi, *the Verse of the Throne from the second surah of the Quran, the Chapter of the Cow. This is a very special verse and we believe that if you say it three times at night your home will be safe from* shayatin *or devils. When you say it five times your street will be safe, and seven times will protect the whole area. So I'd say it seven times or even more. Then I'd pray to God, "Bless us. First our father*

and family, then our street, then our whole mohalla [neighborhood], *then all Swat." Then I'd say, "No, all Muslims." Then, "No, not just Muslims; bless all human beings."*[52]

In October 2012, while returning home on a school bus after one of her exams, Malala and two schoolmates were shot by the Taliban. Malala was shot in the head; her injuries were initially treated in Pakistan, and she was later taken to England for treatment. Across Pakistan, people held vigils and rallies in support of her. A group of more than fifty Muslim leaders in Pakistan issued a fatwa condemning the shooting as un-Islamic.

The attack on Malala garnered worldwide attention and she became an international symbol of the struggle for girls' access to education. Malala and her family now live in England; her two schoolmates who were also shot are now also attending school there.

Malala Yousafzai has continued to speak publicly as an advocate for girls' education around the world. She and her father started the Malala Fund, which now works in Pakistan, Nigeria, Jordan, and Kenya, providing support to local efforts to expand access to education. On her sixteenth birthday in 2013, named "Malala Day," she addressed the United Nations Youth Assembly, calling for free education for children worldwide.

In 2014, Malala became the youngest person to be awarded the Nobel Peace Prize. She shared the prize with Kailash Satyarthi, an Indian activist fighting child slavery. The announcement of the prize noted, "The Nobel Committee regards it as an important point for a Hindu and a Muslim, an Indian and a Pakistani, to join in a common struggle for education and against extremism."[53] In a public address after learning she had received the prize, and would share it with Satyarthi, Malala said:

He received this award and we both are the two Nobel award receivers. One is from Pakistan, one is from India, one believes in Hinduism and one strongly believes in Islam; and it gives a message to people. Here's a message to people of love between Pakistan and India and between different religions, and we both support each other. It does not matter what's the color of your skin, what language do you speak, what religion you believe in. It is that we should all consider each other as human beings and we should respect each other, and we should all fight for our rights, for the rights of children, for the rights of women, and for the rights of every human being.[54]

- inaccuracies and omissions of facts that lead to distorted interpretations of national history
- insensitivity to the diversity of religions in the country
- glorification of violence
- encouragement of prejudices toward women, religious minorities, and other countries
- omission of material and perspectives for developing critical thinking
- outdated teaching practices that fail to stimulate interest and insight.[55]

Pakistani government officials called for the revisions of textbooks to correct such points. Saudi Arabia has also come under criticism for giving distorted religious messages through its schools, and is now revising its curricula and textbooks to promote peace and harmony. To increase educational opportunities for women, a large university for women encompassing fifteen colleges was opened in Riyadh in 2011.

At the same time, efforts are being made in some countries to increase the accuracy and sensitivity of portrayals of Islam in the education of non-Muslims. Western textbooks have tended to present history as the progress of Western civilization, from which perspective Islam is described mainly as an adversary rather than a high civilization in its own right which has made great contributions to science and culture, not to mention philosophy. Vincent Cornell, editor of the five-volume series *Voices of Islam*, writes:

> *It has long been a truism to say that Islam is the most misunderstood religion in the world. However, the situation expressed by this statement is more than a little ironic because Islam is also one of the most studied religions in the world, after Christianity and Judaism. ... Why is it that most Americans and Europeans are still largely uninformed about Islam after so many books about Islam have been published? Even more, how can people still claim to know so little about Islam when Muslims now live in virtually every medium-sized and major community in America and Europe? ... Scholars of Islam in American universities still feel the need to humanize Muslims in the eyes of their students. A basic objective of many introductory courses on Islam is to demonstrate that Muslims are rational human beings and that their beliefs are worthy of respect.[56]*

At higher levels of academic research, some efforts are now being made by Western scholars to understand Islamic beliefs and practices in their own terms, rather than through Western lenses such as feminist theory or secular-liberal thinking.

A class of women in Izmir, Turkey, are learning to read the Qur'an in Arabic so that they can understand it themselves. These professional women have donned white veils for the class, out of respect for the holy scripture.

Philanthropic projects funded by Muslims are also on the increase. Most notably, the Ismaili Shi'a Muslim community, under the contemporary direction of its current imam, His Highness the Aga Khan, has organized many award-winning public service projects under the aegis of the extensive Aga Khan Development Network, from rebuilding historic cultural sites to projects in improving health, education, urban and rural development, microfinance, and food security for people of all faiths in many countries. Under the Aga Khan's guidance, Ismailis are trying to make positive contributions to society, understanding that this is a central way of being good Muslims. Noordin Kassam, a chartered accountant from England who serves as a regional officer in the network, explains:

> The impetus that spurred this development derives from the Muslim ethic to serve one's fellow man in the spirit of brotherhood. ... We serve because we want to. Over ninety-five percent of the work of the network across twenty-five countries is undertaken by volunteers—people of all walks of life.[57]

Islam in politics

At present, one facet of Islam that is of great concern around the world to both Muslims and non-Muslims is the nature of the relationship between Islam and politics, and especially the political use of Islam by extremist groups. The roots of this trend lie in recent history. From the eighteenth to the twentieth centuries, European powers asserted control of parts of northern Africa, the Middle East, and Asia, areas with substantial Muslim populations, many of which had been under the rule of Muslim leaders. At the end of World War I, European powers set up protectorates and mandates in states that had been part of the Ottoman Empire, even though they had promised those states full independence in exchange for their co-operation with the Allies during the war. As a result, many Muslim populations felt betrayed, and this led to a period of instability during which people resorted to political and armed struggle to achieve full independence for their nations. In the Middle East, for example, many leaders looked to nationalist, socialist, and Marxist thought as suitable ideologies of liberation.

However, these various approaches were not always successful, and Muslim leaders searched for other solutions. There were many Muslims who grew increasingly discontented with what they understood to be the creeping secularization and growing moral decline of their societies, including corruption in government, as well as the ubiquity of authoritarian rule. Many Muslims saw these trends as contrary to Islamic values and, increasingly, they sought a solution to their problems in the Islamic faith itself rather than other ideologies. This state of affairs gave rise to leaders who promised to bring about a renaissance of the Islamic way of life.

Those who sought to restore a way of life guided by Islam did so in an environment in which there were many who did not have a solid knowledge of the religion. In part, secular and colonialist policies in the Middle East after the collapse of the Ottoman Empire had led to a decline in traditional Islamic learning. For example, in his effort to modernize Turkey, President Kemal Ataturk (1881–1938), a secularist, changed the alphabet of the Turkish language from Arabic to Roman. Since Arabic is the language of the Qur'an, the change made it harder for Turks to read their sacred text. In Algeria, which was occupied by the French, French became the official language of the country. Those who wanted to study their religion had to attend religious schools whose endowments had been reduced by the French. As a result of such developments, competency in the language of the Qur'an dropped, and there were fewer Muslims who could read and understand the Qur'an and the rich Islamic legal traditions on their own. Thus, they turned to their elders and imams to learn the religion. In the process, new interpretations of Islam began to emerge.

Muhammad ibn 'Abd al-Wahhab (1703–92), a legal scholar and reformer, urged the discarding of all practices not specifically approved by the Qur'an and

Sunnah. **Wahhabi** thought, which spread to many parts of the Sunni Muslim world, is highly conservative culturally as well as religiously. It called for a return to a simple, unadorned life of piety, and flourished in the area that is now Saudi Arabia, promoted by the leaders of the Saudi regime.

Another voice, which emerged in the twentieth century, was that of the Egyptian scholar and activist Sayyid Qutb (1906–66). After World War II, he saw most Muslim countries being controlled either by corrupt monarchies or by cruel military dictatorships. He had also visited the United States, but was disgusted by its culture. Devoutly religious, he saw the sex, violence, and selfish greed in Western culture as the headwaters of evil that was spreading around the world. Compared with the ideal example of the life of the Prophet Muhammad, he described Westernization thus:

> *Humanity today is living in a large brothel! One has only to glance at its press, films, fashion shows, beauty contests, ballrooms, wine bars, and broadcasting stations! Or observe its mad lust for naked flesh, provocative postures, and sick-suggestive statements in literature, the arts, and the mass media! And add to all this the system of usury which fuels man's voracity for money and engenders vile methods for its accumulation and investment, in addition to fraud, trickery, and blackmail dressed up in the garb of law.*[58]

Qutb's writings during years of imprisonment by the Egyptian government before they eventually executed him have been pivotal in the thinking of later Islamists. There have been many situations in recent history in which Muslim leaders, such as Sayyid Qutb, have stereotyped the West as a source of evil and moral decline, while at the same time many people in the West have stereotyped Islam as advocating and promoting violence, a dynamic exemplified by varied understandings and misinterpretations of the concept of **jihad**. Western media accounts of Islam have often mistranslated jihad as "holy war," thereby suggesting that Muslims are encouraged to wage war against others.

All Muslims are indeed enjoined by the Qur'an to carry on jihad, but it means "striving," not "holy war." The Prophet Muhammad is said to have distinguished between two types of jihad. Of these, he said, the Greater Jihad is the struggle against one's lower self. It is the internal fight between wrong and right, error and truth, selfishness and selflessness, hardness of heart and all-embracing love. This inner struggle to maintain peaceful equilibrium is then reflected in outer attempts to keep society in a state of harmonious order, as the earthly manifestation of Divine Justice. The Lesser Jihad is an external effort to protect the Way of God against the forces of evil. This jihad is the safeguarding of one's life, faith, livelihood, honor, and the integrity of the Muslim community. The Prophet Muhammad reportedly said that "the preferred jihad is a truth spoken in the presence of a tyrant."[59]

Jihad is not to be undertaken for personal gain. The Qur'anic revelations that apparently date from the Medina period when the faithful were being attacked by Mecca make it clear that believers have the right to resist oppression:

> *To those against whom*
> *War is made, permission*
> *Is given (to fight) because*
> *They are wronged; —and verily,*
> *God is Most Powerful*
> *For their aid;*
>
> *(They are) those who have*
> *Been expelled from their homes*
> *In defiance of right,*
> *(For no cause) except*
> *That they say, "Our Lord*
> *Is God."*[60]

The Qur'an gives permission to fight back under such circumstances, and Islamic shari'ah gives detailed limitations on the conduct of war and the treatment of captives, to prevent atrocities.

Muhammad is considered the prototype of the true **mujahid**, or fighter in the Path of God, one who values the Path of God more than life, wealth, or family. He is thought to have had no desire for worldly power, wealth, or prestige.

By fasting and prayer, he continually exerted himself toward the One, in the Greater Jihad. In defending the Medina community of the faithful against the attacking Meccans, he was acting from the purest of motives. It is believed that a true mujahid who dies in defense of the faith goes straight to paradise, for he has already fought the Greater Jihad, subjugating his ego.

The absolute conviction that characterizes jihad derives from the recognition of the vast disparity between evil and the spiritual ideal, both in oneself and in society. Continual exertion is thought necessary in order to maintain a peaceful equilibrium in the midst of changing circumstances. Traditionalists and radicals have differed in how this exertion should be exercised in society.

In terms of the Lesser Jihad, support can be found in the Qur'an both for a pacifist approach and for active opposition to unbelievers. The Qur'an asserts that believers have the responsibility to defend their own faith as well as to remind unbelievers of the truth of God and of the necessity of moral behavior. In some passages, Muslims are enjoined simply to stand firm against aggression. For example, "Fight for the sake of God those that fight against you, but do not be aggressive. God does not love the aggressors."[61] Some Islamist groups, however, have seen the world situation as so dire that they have advocated for an understanding of jihad that may involve violent struggle against those seen as enemies of Islam.

In addition to varying interpretations of Qur'anic passages regarding jihad, contemporary use of violence in the name of Islam involves a complex of varying historical, cultural, and political circumstances in different countries. In modern times, there is as yet no political unity among Muslim states—indeed there are deep disagreements within some Muslim states—but persistent antagonism toward the West is tending to create a certain political unity in opposition to pre-emptive use of American military power against Muslim countries. Just as the legacy of European colonialism influenced developments in Muslim thought in the early twentieth century, so too have American and Western involvement in the governments of Muslim nations in more recent times, from the fall of a government in Iran to the "war on terror" launched by the United States after the September 11, 2001 attacks.

In 1953 in Iran, a predominantly Shi'a country, the democratically elected government of Muhammad Mosaddegh was overthrown by a coup reportedly planned by Great Britain and the United States, since Mosaddegh intended to nationalize Iran's oil production. The country was returned to the authoritarian rule of the Pahlavi Shah, and the gap between the rich and poor grew. At the same time, the Shah tried to rapidly modernize his country, turning it into a major military and industrial power. In the process, he eroded the respected authority of the *ulama*, the clerics and expounders of the shari'ah. A revolutionary leader emerged from this disempowered group, the Ayatollah Khomeini (c. 1900–89). From his Paris exile he led mass demonstrations in Iran against the Shah, who was removed from power in 1979.

Khomeini insisted that social transformation should be linked with spiritual reformation, with the government headed by a ruler "who acts as trustee and maintains the institutions and laws of Islam."[62] Despite the fact that he was a Shi'ite Muslim, his revolutionary zeal began to influence even Sunni Muslims in the region. Neighboring governments were concerned and accused him of

Men gathered for Eid al-Fitr celebration at end of Ramadan in Qinghai province, China.

trying to export his revolution to them. This started a new era of tensions in the region between Sunni and Shi'ite Muslim governments, which ultimately spread to these populations.

Khomeini's call for governmental change was not heeded. Radicals resorted to sabotage and terrorism as their most powerful weapons in what Khomeini described as a great world battle between Islam and the Satanic forces of Western imperialism and Zionism. When the radicals attacked the American Embassy in Tehran and took hostages, the crisis with the West reached its highest level. It also tended to turn world opinion against Islam. In time, however, demonstrators returned to their homes, and the government metamorphosed into a new political system with a unique blend of theocracy and democracy.

Reformers proposed that the government should be founded on Islamic law, but that this law should be interpreted in ways that allow a considerable degree of individual freedom and free expression rather than authoritarianism. In 2009, Iran witnessed unprecedented citizen protests over a contested presidential election in which eighty-five percent of the population had voted. The protests themselves have been interpreted as a sign of the growing freedom and confidence of Iran's educated citizenry. Hassan Rouhani, elected President of Iran in 2013, is considered a moderate who has sought better relations between Iran and other countries.

Iraq, a country neighboring Iran, was thrown into chaos at the end of the twentieth century. Iraq's president Saddam Hussein had tried to re-annex neighboring Kuwait. Kuwait then requested help from the United States and other Western countries. The United States launched massive bombings of Iraq in 2003 using tactics that sought to "shock and awe" the Iraqi regime. The United States government's stated purpose was to liberate the people from the tyrannical rule of Saddam Hussein. The attacks on Iraq were initially justified by claims, later proven unfounded, that the Iraqi regime held massive stockpiles of weapons of mass destruction. Although he had not emphasized Islam in the early years of his rule, Saddam Hussein resorted to using religious language and symbolism in order to rally support among his people after the American-led invasion.

Despite their dislike for Saddam Hussein, many Muslims around the world nevertheless perceived the American-led attacks and occupation of the country as an unprovoked attack on innocent Muslim civilians as well as an attempt to control the oil resources of Muslim-majority nations. A branch of Al Qaeda (see below) emerged in Iraq, and terrorist activity increased there and elsewhere in protest at the American-led invasion. Hundreds of thousands of Iraqi civilians have been killed in the chaotic aftermath of the American-led intervention, including casualties of Sunni–Shi'a conflicts in the destabilized country. When Saddam Hussein was hanged at the end of 2006, many Muslims regarded him as a martyr for his resistance to American power. The United States removed its ground forces from Iraq in 2011, but continues to have military advisors in the country.

The **Taliban** in Afghanistan is another example of a group that had a radical vision of the ideal Islamic state and society. The Taliban came to the world's attention in the 1980s. Initially it was one of various groups supported by the United States as freedom fighters battling the Soviet Union, which had invaded Afghanistan in 1979. The Taliban viewed its role in this war as critical in the collapse of the Soviet Union. After the Soviets left Afghanistan in 1989, Western nations did little to help Afghans rebuild their war-torn country, which collapsed into factional fighting and chaos, from which emerged the authoritarian rule of the Taliban from 1996 to 2001.

The Taliban rejected all secular laws and replaced them with its interpretation of Islamic shari'ah. To deter crime, for instance, it organized public spectacles in which the hands of thieves were amputated and adulterers were whipped. To legitimize these actions, it conducted trials that violated shari'ah's exacting requirements of due process, and contradicted Muhammad's insistence on compassion.

Although the Sunnah of Islam is replete with examples advocating tolerance of other religions, Taliban leaders had very little tolerance either for other religions or for interpretations of Islam other than their own. For example, they bombed the huge ancient cliff-hewn statues of the Buddha at Bamiyan, which had remained safe under Muslim rule for centuries, claiming that the statues were idolatrous. They also placed severe restrictions on women, keeping them out of the workplace, denying them education, and insisting that they wear head-to-toe burqas. This was a substantial setback for Afghan women who were educated and counted among their ranks scholars, doctors, and judges.

American law professor Azizah Y. al-Hibri commented on the Taliban's interpretation and use of shari'ah:

> While there is no central interpretive authority in Islam, an acceptable interpretation must satisfy a minimum number of requirements. For example, the interpretation must be based on the Qur'an and Sunnah. It must be based on knowledge and motivated by Piety. It must also serve (rather than harm) maslaha, the public interest of Muslims in particular and humanity in general. … The Taliban seems to have no such concerns. This is consistent with their rejection of other basic Islamic principles, such as shura (consultation with other Muslims) and bay'ah (a system of elective non-authoritarian governance). It is also consistent with their rejection of the Islamic injunction that the pursuit of education is the duty of every Muslim, male and female. Finally, it is consistent with their rejection of the overarching Islamic model of harmonious gender, racial, religious, and general human relations.[63]

During the same time that the Taliban emerged in Afghanistan, Osama bin Laden, a wealthy Saudi from an aristocratic family, had established camps in rural Afghanistan to train fighters for the struggle against the Soviet Union. In the late 1980s, he played a key role in establishing Al Qaeda, a global terrorist organization, which became infamous after the September 11, 2001 attacks on the United States. Its members were opposed, as a matter of faith, to the Westernization of Saudi society and the military presence of the United States in the Arab Peninsula, home of the central sacred sites of Islam. Shortly after the September 11 attacks, bin Laden issued a videotaped address that included the following insights into his way of thinking:

> What America is tasting now is only a copy of what we have tasted. Our Islamic nation has been tasting the same for more than eighty years of humiliation and disgrace, its sons killed and their blood spilled, its sanctities desecrated. …
>
> They have been telling the world falsehoods that they are fighting terrorism. In a nation at the far end of the world, Japan, hundreds of thousands, young and old, were killed and this is not a world crime. … But when a few more than ten were killed in Nairobi and Dar es Salaam, Afghanistan and Iraq were bombed and hypocrisy stood behind the head of international infidels: the modern world's symbol of paganism, America, and its allies.
>
> I tell them that these events have divided the world into two camps, the camp of the faithful and the camp of infidels. May God shield us and you from them.
>
> Every Muslim must rise to defend his religion. The wind of faith is blowing and the wind of change is blowing to remove evil from the Peninsula of Muhammad, peace be upon him.[64]

After September 11, United States President George W. Bush demanded that the Taliban government in Afghanistan hand over Osama bin Laden and other Al Qaeda members who had participated in the planning of the attacks. When the Taliban refused, the United States and allies including Great Britain launched airstrikes and began sending troops into Afghanistan. Under military attack by the United States and its coalition forces, the Taliban's political power in Afghanistan receded. The United States helped convene the traditional Afghan consultative body, called the Loya Jirga, in Kabul, and this body adopted a new constitution that attempted to pair Western and Islamic values. Viewing it as subject to Western influences, the Taliban rejected the Loya Jirga whose work established an alternative government in Kabul. Under the new government, Afghan life in Kabul returned slowly to its earlier ways. For example, women regained some of their rights and some women occupied positions of responsibility. However, while this alternative body remains functional today, the country remains war-torn and people remain poverty-stricken. The Taliban may have even gained influence recently as a result in part of Western-inflicted casualties in Afghanistan and neighboring Pakistan.

Osama bin Laden was found and killed by U.S. commandos in 2011 in his villa near the Pakistani capital city of Islamabad. In his extremist mixture of religion with politics, martyrdom was heroic, the world was strictly divided into good and evil, destruction of property and lives was justified, and the faithful were urged to undertake jihad on a global, militant scale. The September 11 and other Al Qaeda attacks set in motion a sea change in relationships between Muslims and non-Muslims everywhere, especially in the West.

The porous border between Afghanistan and Pakistan, and the steady stream of Afghan refugees settling in camps in Pakistan created an environment in which the Taliban was able to extend its influence into neighboring tribal areas of Pakistan, and there is now a Pakistani Taliban movement. The United States has been combatting its presence there through drone attacks, which have generated controversy both within the United States and elsewhere. Civilian casualties in these drone attacks have also led to hostility towards the United States.

Another destabilizing factor in many Muslim countries, especially in the Arab world, has been the pervasive presence of authoritarian rule, either in the form of absolute monarchies or military regimes. Many Muslims are of the view that in Islam such regimes are oppressive and illegitimate because they were not freely chosen by the people. Many of these regimes have not sought to improve the welfare of their people. This state of affairs resulted in severe poverty in some areas, lack of employment and housing, and deep discontent. It was in this environment that the broad movement known as the "Arab Spring" began in 2010. People took to the streets demanding better conditions and a greater voice in their own affairs. These demonstrations were spontaneous, and had no designated leaders. They were, therefore, easily usurped by organized political groups and led to intervention by foreign powers. The turmoil and violence that followed quickly turned the "Arab Spring" into a hard fall.

In Syria for example, what started as a small youth protest in the border town of Dar'a metamorphosed into several well-funded, well-organized, and well-armed terrorist groups with members from at least 84 countries. New terrorist organizations sprouted from Al Qaeda. They engage in behavior that a majority of Muslims consider criminal and reprehensible. Indeed, the main victims of these groups have been Muslim civilians, especially women and children. These groups have encouraged innocent youth to engage in suicidal terrorist attacks against peaceful civilian targets, an activity clearly prohibited in Islam. The youth are promised a quick entry to paradise, despite the Qur'anic passages condemning suicide and upholding the value and sanctity of each human life.

In the midst of these developments, Saudi Arabia remains a powerful force due to its geographic, economic, political, and religious influence in the Middle East and beyond. Since 1932, Saudi Arabia has been under the monarchical control of the al-Sa'ud family. The country continues to be religiously conservative, with its legal system based on shari'ah and harkening to Wahhabism. Wealthy from its oil, the Saudi regime has provided funding and support to mosques and Islamic schools throughout the Muslim world, expanding the influence of its particular brand of Islam. The regime has been criticized by some Muslims for exposing the populace to Western culture by allowing Western troops on its soil.

In 2008, Saudi Arabia sponsored an interfaith conference in Mecca to showcase Islam's message of tolerance and encouragement of peaceful co-existence. But Saudi Arabia has also been the focus of criticism on matters such as women's rights. Saudi women continue to wear the traditional 'abaya, which is an outer garment that covers them from head to toe. They are banned from driving cars or leaving home unless accompanied by a close male relative. These restrictions, which stem from local customs, have been slow to change. In 2011, King Abdullah announced that women would at last be given the right to vote, and also to run in municipal elections and to help choose candidates in 2015, for "The Muslim woman must not be marginalized in opinion or advice."[65] However, the death of King Abdullah in 2015 may delay these developments.

Another issue in which religion and politics mix is the situation of the Palestinian people in Israel. Various movements have arisen among Palestinians to reclaim a secure homeland in the face of Israeli settlement. The two major factions are Fatah and Hamas. Fatah was founded in the 1950s to end Israeli control of Palestine. More recently, it has supported a "two-state" solution through a peace process. "Hamas" means "zeal" in Arabic. It was formed in 1987 as the Palestinian branch of the Muslim Brotherhood, an Islamist organization based in Egypt. Its charter calls for the destruction of Israel, and it has supported suicide attacks against Israeli settlements. Conflicts between Israel and the Hamas-ruled Gaza Strip have erupted repeatedly.

Turkey, long home to Ataturk's secular vision, is now engaged in power struggles between secularists, devout Muslims, and hardline Islamists. This conflict leads to paradoxical situations. For instance, women are prohibited from wearing traditional headscarves in universities. Religiously observant women who do not want to give up their headscarves and expose their hair publicly are now resorting to an unusual protest measure: Some students are wearing their headscarves and then jamming wigs over them when they attend classes.

Debates about the role of Islam in modern nation-states persist. Islamist groups seeking radical reformulations of legal, social, and political structures have emerged in places torn by political instability and conflict, particularly areas that were earlier under European colonial control. For example, a group known as Boko Haram is violently opposed to Western education, which it regards as sinful. It declared a Sunni caliphate in northern Nigeria in 2014.

Also in 2014, the so-called Islamic State [IS], a violent, militant group under the leadership of Abu Bakr al-Baghdadi, declared itself a new caliphate. It is an offshoot of Al Qaeda. Taking advantage of instability in Iraq and the ongoing fighting in Syria, the group began claiming control of territories in Iraq and Syria, imposing its particular interpretation of Islamic law, and carrying out executions and other forms of violence. IS has actively recruited members and promoted its agenda using social media. Young men and some young women from around the world, including Europe and North America, have traveled to Syria to join the group.

Some observers suggest that IS appeals to young people whose knowledge of Islam is limited, and are moved by its pleas to Muslims to help their fellow Muslims who are suffering in Iraq and Syria. IS has drawn heavy criticism from Muslims around the world. A group of 126 international Islamic scholars wrote a lengthy open letter to al-Baghdadi, using classical Islamic texts to refute the group's tactics.[66] The scholars argue, for example, that Islam rejects forced conversions and slavery, oppression of women, and the killing of innocent civilians. In the fall of 2014, the United States government formed a coalition with countries including Saudi Arabia and the United Arab Emirates to carry out airstrikes against IS on Syrian and Iraqi territories.

As a result of wars in various Muslim countries, such as the devastating internal fighting in South Sudan, wars between nations, military attacks led by the United States in Iraq and Afghanistan, natural disasters, and climate change, millions of Muslims now live as refugees or internally displaced persons. Muslims account for a significant percentage of all refugees and internally displaced persons in the world. The human misery is staggering.

There is increasing tension between Muslims and non-Muslims, particularly in the West. Terrorist activities that have killed civilians have brought a backlash of anti-Muslim sentiments, with growing perception of Islam as a religion

Because they are involved in conflicts around the world, many Muslims are mourning the loss of their loved ones, becoming refugees, or being attacked or killed. This scene of grief occurred in Falluja, Iraq.

encouraging violence and fanaticism. The United States' "war on terrorism" has brought an increase in acts of terrorism and made it more difficult for moderate Muslim leaders to hold their ground against critics within their countries. As Islamophobia grows among non-Muslims, many leading Muslims are trying to explain to them, and to the gullible youth being courted by IS, that Islam does not equal violence.

The Qur'an permits the jihad of violence only under very specific conditions. To fight, people must have been deprived of their right to live and support themselves. The action must be undertaken not by individuals but by the collective wisdom of the Muslim community. Jihadis are never allowed to harm women, children, or unarmed civilians. They cannot willfully destroy property. The tactics of terrorists are therefore not permitted by the Qur'an. In general, relations with people of other religions are to be as tolerant as possible. It is written in the Qur'an:

> *Do not argue with the followers of the earlier revelations otherwise than in a most kindly manner—unless it be such of them as are bent on evil-doing—and say: We believe in that which has been bestowed from on high upon us, as well as that which has been bestowed upon you; for our God and your God is one and the same, and it is unto Him that we all surrender ourselves.*[67]

Some people argue that there has been a deliberate Western policy of portraying political conflicts as religion-based struggles in order to fan fear of a threat to the Western way of life from Islam, thus steering Western electorates to support a "war on terror," with an underlying agenda of controlling oil-rich lands belonging to Muslims.

Islam for the future

Challenged to explain Islam to its critics, Muslim scholars and intellectuals are meeting at global conferences to formulate unified responses to current issues. There is a tendency toward rapprochement between Sunnis and Shi'as at some levels, with the understanding that their differences are not so much matters of religious doctrine as of historical conflicts over leadership. Religious modernists, Islamists, and secularists are all trying to understand the roots of

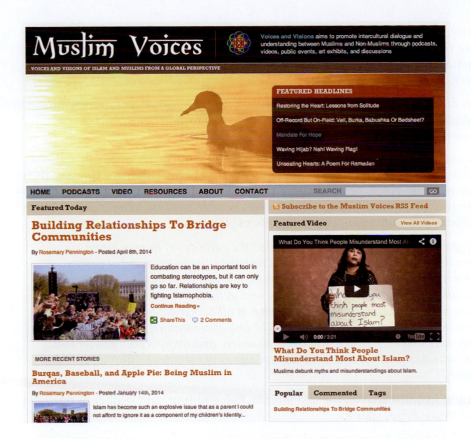

Screenshot of Muslim Voices, one of the present-day attempts to encourage a more nuanced and positive view of Islam. This website, www.muslimvoices.org, "aims to promote intercultural dialogue and understanding between Muslims and Non-Muslims through podcasts, videos, public events, art exhibits, and discussions."

extremism and to seek new ways of relating to and even shaping the rapidly changing world. They feel that extremism is undermining Islam by contradicting its principles and spreading hatred for the religion.

While media attention is centered on sensational manifestations of Islamism in present-day societies, these deeper currents of thought are forward-looking, exploring how Islam can help to shape a new social order in the world. Professor Asaf Hussain of the University of Leicester, England, points out that the goal of a just society inspires but still eludes Muslim resistance movements:

> *Today many Islamic fundamentalist movements have declared war on their own people and are trying to transform their states on the model of the First Islamic state. But the conditions of the seventh century do not obtain today. A new model of the Islamic state has to be devised. The dominating civilization of the present day is Western and its models control the Third World, including the Muslim world. Islamic movements have revolted against this but their strategies have not been well thought out. They do not have to dominate Western civilization but create a parallel which excels it. This will be a long, arduous task but the struggle has just begun.*[68]

Nobel Peace Prize winner Malala Yousafzai (see Box, p. 415), a young Pakistani activist who was shot by the Taliban for being an outspoken advocate for girls' education, explains that for her, Islam means compassion:

> *I am not against anyone. Neither am I here to speak in terms of personal revenge against the Taliban or any other terrorist group. I am here to speak up for the right of education of every child. I want education for the sons and the daughters of the Taliban, and all the terrorists and extremists. I do not even hate the Talib who shot me. Even if there is a gun in my hand and he stands in front of me, I would not shoot him. This is the compassion that I have learnt from Muhammad—the prophet of mercy—Jesus Christ and Lord Buddha.*[69]

Mahmoon-al-Rasheed, founder of the Comprehensive Rural Educational, Social, Cultural and Economic Center in Bangladesh, maintains that there is violence within and between nations because people have not developed a sense of duty toward each other and have not recognized how inseparably all people of the earth are related to each other. He proposes that Islamic values are not aimed at creating a political state but rather a harmoniously integrated world society, for:

> We cannot begin to realize our full potential until we have achieved a community which knows no limit but that of human society and renders all obedience to a Law common to all.[70]

Omid Safi, Professor of Islamic Studies at the University of North Carolina, speaking on behalf of many contemporary progressive Muslims, expresses their desire to bring about positive social change in the fluid, globally hybrid, post-modern world by supporting social justice, gender equality, religious and ethnic pluralism, and nonviolent resistance. He explains:

> Progressive Muslims perceive themselves as the advocates of human beings all over the world who through no fault of their own live in situations of poverty, pollution, oppression, and marginalization. A prominent concern of progressive Muslims is the suffering and poverty, as well as the full humanity, of these marginalized and oppressed human beings of all backgrounds who are called mustad'ifun in the Qur'anic context. The task of progressives in this context is to give voice to the voiceless, power to the powerless, and confront the "powers that be" who disregard the God-given human dignity of the mustad'ifun all over this Earth.[71]

Shirin Ebadi, a lawyer, the first woman judge in Iran, and winner of the 2003 Nobel Peace Prize, states:

> I am a Muslim. In the Qur'an the Prophet of Islam has been cited as saying, "Thou shalt believe in thy faith and I in my religion." That same divine book sees the mission of all prophets as that of inviting all human beings to uphold justice. … If the twenty-first century wishes to free itself from the cycle of violence, acts of terror and war, and avoid repetition of the experience of the twentieth century—that most disaster-ridden century of humankind—there is no other way except by understanding and putting in practice every human right for all mankind, irrespective of race, gender, faith, nationality, or social status.[72]

Key terms

Allah The one God, in Islam.

caliph In Sunni Islam, the successor to the Prophet.

fatwa A legal opinion issued by an authority according to a particular school of law; often erroneously defined as an edict against someone or something.

fiqh Jurisprudence; the process of understanding, interpreting, and implementing the shari'ah.

hajj The holy pilgrimage to Mecca for Muslims.

Hadith Traditional report about the sayings and actions of the Prophet Muhammad.

hijab The veiling of women for the sake of modesty.

hijrah Muhammad's migration from Mecca to Medina.

Imam In Shi'ite Islam, the title for the person carrying the initiatic tradition of the Prophetic Light.

Islam In its original meaning, complete, trusting surrender to God.

Islamist A person seeking to establish Islamic states in which the rule of God is supreme.

jihad The Muslim's struggle against the inner forces that prevent God-realization and the outer barriers to establishment of the order.

madrasa Traditional religious school teaching a narrow version of Islam.

muezzin In Islam, one who calls the people to prayer from a high place.

Shahadah The central Muslim expression of faith: "There is no god but God, and Muhammad is the Messenger of God."

shari'ah The divine law and ethics in Islam.
Shi'a The minority branch of Islam, which tells that Muhammad's legitimate successors were 'Ali and a series of Imams; a follower of this branch.
Sufism The mystical path in Islam.
Sunnah The behavior of the Prophet Muhammad, used as a model in Islamic law.
Sunni A follower of the majority branch of Islam, which tells that successors to Muhammad are to be chosen by the Muslim community.
surah A chapter of the Holy Qur'an.
ummah The Muslim community.
zakat Spiritual tithing.

Suggested reading

Ahmed, Akbar S., *Discovering Islam: Making Sense of Muslim History and Society*, revised edition, London and New York: Routledge, 2002. A well-known Pakistani diplomat and scholar teaching in the United States offers keen insights into the spirituality and history of modern Muslim cultures.

Ahmed, Akbar, S., *Islam Under Siege*, Cambridge: Polity Press, 2003. Careful explanation of Islamic ideals and concerns in the context of contemporary violence in the name of Islam.

Ahmed, Leila, *Women and Gender in Islam: Historical Roots of a Modern Debate*, New Haven, Connecticut: Yale University Press, 1992. Detailed analysis of historical conditions within which oppression of Muslim women developed.

Allen, Roger and Shawkat M. Toorawa, eds, *Islam: A Short Guide to the Faith*, Cambridge, U.K.: Wm. B. Eerdmans Publishing Co., 2011. Clear, insightful contemporary scholarship about history, beliefs, institutions, and social issues in Islam.

Armstrong, Karen, *The Battle for God*, New York: Alfred A. Knopf, 2000. A monumental study of the development of fundamentalism in the United States, Israel, and Egypt in response to modernity.

Capan, Ergu, ed., *Terror and Suicide Attacks: An Islamic Perspective*, Somerset, New Jersey: The Light, Inc., 2006. Turkish scholars carefully examine written and oral traditions which clearly refute terrorism in the name of Islam.

Delong-Bas, Natana J., *Wahhabi Islam: From Revival and Reform to Global Jihad*, Oxford: Oxford University Press, 2004. Careful examination of the writings of Ibn 'Abd al-Wahhab, with the thesis that they do not fit the stereotypical notion of Wahhabism as a major source of extremist movements.

Esposito, John L., *Islam: The Straight Path*, third edition, New York and Oxford: Oxford University Press, 2004. A scholarly, clear introduction to historical and contemporary Islam.

Gülen, M. Fethullah, *The Messenger of God: Muhammad*, Somerset, New Jersey: The Light, Inc., 2006. A loving spiritual analysis of the life of the Prophet.

Haddad, Yvonne Yazbeck and Barbara Freyer Stowasser, *Islamic Law and the Challenges of Modernity*, Walnut Creek: AltaMira Press, 2004. A collection of essays addressing specific examples of issues related to shari'ah and contemporary life.

Hallaq, Wael B., *The Origins and Evolution of Islamic Law*, Cambridge: Cambridge University Press, 2005. A thorough and accessible exploration of the early development of Islamic law.

Hefner, Robert W. and Patricia Horvatich, eds, *Islam in an Era of Nation-states: Politics and Religious Renewal in Muslim Southeast Asia*, Honolulu: University of Hawaii Press, 1997. Detailed analyses of Muslim reformist movements in Southeast Asia with reference to modern governmental structures.

The Holy Qur'an. Although the Qur'an is considered untranslatable, numerous translations from the Arabic have been attempted. Many Muslims' favorite English translation is by Abdullah Yusuf Ali (Durban, South Africa: Islamic Propagation Center International, 1946). Thomas Ballantine Irving (Al-Hajj Ta'lim'Ali) has prepared "The First American Version" of the Qur'an (translation and commentary, Brattleboro, Vermont: Amana Books, copyright © 1985).

Lawrence, Bruce, *The Qur'an: A Biography*, New York: Atlantic Monthly Press, 2007. Insightful exploration of the life of the Qur'an, as it has been transmitted, recorded, translated, and understood during its 1,400-year history.

Lings, Martin, *Muhammad*, London: George Allen & Unwin, and Islamic Text Society, 1983. A highly regarded biography of the Prophet.

McCloud, Aminah Beverly, *African American Islam*, New York and London: Routledge, 1995. An accessible inside view of contemporary African American Muslim communities and issues they face in a contrasting cultural context.

Nasr, Seyyed Hossein, *Ideals and Realities of Islam*, second edition, London: Unwin Hyman, 1985. Thoughtful presentation of both esoteric and exoteric features of Islam.

Nasr, Seyyed Hossein, ed., *Islamic Spirituality I: Foundations*, New York: Crossroad Publishing Company, 1987 and London: SCM Press, 1989. Excellent chapters on key features of Muslim spirituality, from fasting to angels, with sections on Sunnism, Shi'ism, and Sufism.

Nasr, Seyyed Hossein, *Traditional Islam in the Modern World*, London and New York: Kegan Paul International, 1990. Religiously sensitive discussions of varied topics in attempts to bring forth traditional Muslim values within contemporary social settings.

Nasr, Seyyed Hossein, Hamid Dabashi, and Seyyed Vali Reza Nasr, *Shi'ism: Doctrines, Thought, and Spirituality*, Albany, New York: State University of New York Press, 1988. A set of thoughtful essays on aspects of Shi'ite spirituality.

Paige, Glenn D., Chaiwats Satha-Anand, and Sarah Gilliatt, *Islam and Nonviolence*, Honolulu: University of Hawaii, Center for Global Nonviolence Planning Project, 1993. Strong essays on theories and practice of nonviolence stemming from Muslim values.

Pinault, David, *The Shiites: Ritual and Popular Piety in a Muslim Community*, New York: St. Martin's Press, 1992. Sensitive discussions of Shi'ite interpretations of Muslim history and how these inform communal life and action.

Rashid, Ahmed, *Taliban: Militant Islam, Oil and Fundamentalism in Central Asia*, New Haven, Connecticut: Yale University Press, 2000. A Pakistani journalist chronicles the Taliban's rise to power, including global politics and economics as well as religion.

Ruthven, Malise, *Islam in the World*, third edition, Oxford: Oxford University Press, 2006. Explanations of mixtures of Islam with politics and culture throughout history, especially modern history.

Safi, Omid, ed., *Progressive Muslims: On Justice, Gender, and Pluralism*, Oxford: Oneworld Publications, 2003. Scholars and activists explore progressive ways of interpreting Islam in the context of modern issues.

Safi, Omid, *Memories of Muhammad: Why the Prophet Matters*, New York: HarperOne, 2009. An engaging account of the many ways Muslims and non-Muslims have understood the Prophet, from early biographies to contemporary depictions in cyberspace.

Sajoo, Amyn B., ed., *Civil Society in the Muslim World: Contemporary Perspectives*, London: I. B. Tauris, 2004. Essays exploring the intimate relationships between secular, sacred, and state realms in Muslim society, both existing and ideal.

Schimmel, Annemarie, *And Muhammad is His Messenger: The Veneration of the Prophet in Islamic Piety*, Chapel Hill, North Carolina: University of North Carolina Press, 1985. Extensive exploration of Muslims' love for the Prophet.

Schimmel, Annemarie, *Mystical Dimensions of Islam*, Chapel Hill, North Carolina: University of North Carolina Press, 1975. A classic survey of Sufi history, teachings, and saints.

Tibi, Bassam, *The Challenge of Fundamentalism: Political Islam and the New World Disorder*, Berkeley, California: University of California Press, 1998, 2002. A Syrian scholar analyzes Islamist movements as manifestations of Islam's confrontation with modernity.

Wadud, Amina, *Qur'an and Woman*, New York and Oxford: Oxford University Press, 1999. Probing hermeneutic analysis of the Qur'an, revealing its principles of social justice, including gender equality.

Webb, Gisela, *Windows of Faith: Muslim Women Scholar-Activists in North America*, Syracuse, New York: Syracuse University Press, 2000. Articles revealing the depth of feminist scholarship within Islam, particularly with reference to the ideal of social justice as seen from the point of view of women of faith.

Zaman, Muhammad Qasim, *The Ulama in Contemporary Islam*, Princeton, New Jersey: Princeton University Press, 2002. Study of the evolution and contemporary importance of the *ulama* in several countries where these religious scholars have reemerged as a significant factor in religiopolitical activism.

10.1 Describe pre-Islamic Arabia

The people of pre-Islamic Arabia were mostly nomadic cattle-breeders who were in contact with each other and had a relatively uniform culture and common language. They worshiped many deities and believed that people's lives were controlled by an impersonal force, called Fate or Time. The Ka'bah in Mecca, a trading center, was regarded as a polytheistic holy place and violence was prohibited within a large area surrounding it.

10.2 Explain how the revelations given to Muhammad influenced Islamic belief

With the support of his wife, Muhammad (c. 570-632 CE) began to spend periods of time in spiritual retreat and when he was forty years old the angel Gabriel reportedly came to him and insisted that he recite. These revelations continued, asserting the theme that it was the One God who spoke and who called people to Islam, emphasizing that they were accountable to God and not their tribes. The revelations in Mecca included other subjects such as rejection of polytheism in favor of pure monotheism, evidence of God in the Creation, belief, repentance, the Last Judgment, social justice, and acceptance of the revelations given through Muhammad as a messenger of God.

10.3 Outline the role of the Qur'an in Islam

The heart of Islam is not the Prophet but the revelations he received, which are referred to as the Word of God. Collectively they are called the Qur'an (meaning "reading" or "reciting"). Muhammad received the messages over a period of twenty-three years. At first the messages were striking affirmations of the unity of God and the woe of those who did not heed God's message. Later messages also addressed the organizational needs and social lives of the Muslim community. Recitation of the Qur'an is thought to have a healing, soothing effect, and also to bring protection, guidance, and knowledge. The Qur'an revealed to Muhammad is understood as a final and complete reminder of the prophets' teachings, which all refer to the same one God, known in Arabic as Allah.

10.4 Summarize the central teachings of Islam

The Shahadah ("There is no god but God, and Muhammad is the Messenger of God") supports absolute monotheism. Devout Muslims believe that Islam encompasses all religions and honors all prophets as messengers from the one God, with Muhammad as the last and ultimate authority in the prophetic tradition. In Muslim belief, God is all-knowing and has intelligently created everything for a divine purpose, governed by fixed laws.

Muslims believe that our senses do not reveal all of reality. In particular, they believe in the angels of God and in Satan. According to the Qur'an, evildoers will ultimately go to hell. Muslim piety is informed by belief in God's impartial judgment of one's actions, and of one's responsibility to remind others of the fate that may await them.

10.5 Identify the Five Pillars of Islam

The basic spiritual practices incumbent on all Muslims are known as the Five Pillars of Islam. The first pillar (the Shahadah) is believing and professing the unity of God and the messengership of Muhammad. The second pillar is prayer (salat): Five times a day, the faithful are to recite a series of prayers and passages from the Qur'an. The third pillar is zakat, charity or almsgiving: Muslims must donate at least two and a half percent of their accumulated wealth each year to needy Muslims. The fourth pillar is fasting; the only obligatory fast is during Ramadan. The fifth pillar is hajj, the pilgrimage to Mecca.

10.6 Distinguish between Sunni and Shi'a Islam

After Muhammad's death, disagreements over the issue of his succession began to divide the Muslim community into different groups. The two main groups have come to be known as the Sunni (who now comprise about eighty percent of all Muslims worldwide) and the Shi'a.

Sunnis follow the elected caliphs, believing that Muhammad died without appointing a successor and left the matter of successors to the ummah, the Muslim community. They consider themselves as traditionalists, and emphasize the authority of the Qur'an and the secondary authority of the Hadith (the stories of Muhammad's life and sayings).

The Shi'a believe that 'Ali (the Prophet's cousin and son-in-law) was the rightful original successor to Muhammad. Rather than recognize the Sunni caliphs, the Shi'a pay allegiance to a succession of seven or twelve Imams. Unlike the Sunni caliph, the Imam combines political leadership (if possible) with continuing transmission of Divine Guidance.

10.7 Define shari'ah

Shari'ah is the sacred law and ethics of Islam and is based chiefly on the Qur'an and Sunnah of Muhammad, who was the first to apply the generalizations of the Qur'an to specific life situations. Shari'ah specifies patterns for worship (instructions pertaining to the Five Pillars of Islam) as well as detailed prescriptions for social conduct, to bring remembrance of God into every aspect of daily life, and practical ethics into the fabric of society.

10.8 Describe the key aspects of Sufism

Sufism is an esoteric tradition. Sufis consider their way a path to God that is motivated by longing for the One. In addition to studying the Qur'an, they feel that the world is a book filled with "signs"—divine symbols and elements of beauty that speak to those who understand. Sufi asceticism is based more on inner detachment than on withdrawal from the world; the ideal is to live with feet on the ground, head in the heavens.

10.9 Analyze the reasons for the successful expansion of Islam in the seventh and eighth centuries

In the time of Muhammad, Islam combined spiritual and secular power under one ruler. This tradition helped to unify the warring tribes of the area and was continued with waves of successful conquest under Muhammad's successors. In contrast to their strong convictions, the populations Muhammad's successors approached were often demoralized by border fighting among themselves and by grievances against their rulers. Many welcomed the Muslims without a fight. Conquered peoples were generally dealt with in the humane ways specified in the Qur'an, and Christians and Jews were treated as *dhimmis* (protected people) and allowed to maintain their own faith.

10.10 Explain the spread of Islam in the West

In Europe, decades of immigration from formerly French and British colonies in Africa and Asia have expanded the Muslim presence considerably. There are now more than twenty million Muslims in western Europe.

In the United States, Islam is now the fastest-growing religion. Two-thirds of American Muslims are immigrants; one-third are converts, most of them

African Americans. Conversion to Islam by African Americans was encouraged early in the twentieth century as a form of separatism from white oppression. Some early Muslim communities were also based on missionary efforts, such as the Ahmadiyyah Movement from India. Other movements had a strong nation-building character, such as the Nation of Islam.

10.11 Discuss the main issues facing contemporary Islam

The role that shari'ah should play in contemporary Muslim life is one of the main issues facing Islam in the modern world. Some Muslim thinkers have argued that Islamic jurisprudence already has within it the basis for ongoing reform and reinterpretation, but others have called for a return to a particular form of shari'ah, rejecting secular law derived from European codes.

Islam's association with politics is also an issue of concern around the world both to Muslims and non-Muslims. There is as yet no political unity among Muslim states—indeed there are deep disagreements within some Muslim states—but there are debates about relationships with the West, and at times tensions between Muslims and non-Muslims. Terrorist activities that have killed civilians have brought a backlash of anti-Muslim sentiments in some parts of the world, leading to a stereotype of Islam as a religion encouraging violence and fanaticism, despite the efforts of Muslims to present a more balanced view of their tradition.

CHAPTER 11

SIKHISM

"The universal kinship of humankind found in Guru Granth Sahib, which is the living Guru of the Sikhs, serves as a model for harmony and world peace." Sheena Kandhari[1]

> 11.1 **Describe the life and teachings of Guru Nanak**
>
> 11.2 **Summarize the development of Sikhism during the time of the Gurus**
>
> 11.3 **Outline what happened to Sikhism in India after the death of Guru Gobind Singh**
>
> 11.4 **Identify the central beliefs of Sikhism**
>
> 11.5 **Explain how the teachings of Sikhism are put into practice**
>
> 11.6 **Discuss the tensions and challenges faced by Sikhism in India and the diaspora**

Another great teacher made his appearance in northern India in the fifteenth century: Guru Nanak. His followers were called **Sikhs**, meaning "disciples, students, seekers of truth." In time, he was succeeded by a further nine enlightened Gurus, ending with Guru Gobind Singh (1666–1708). Despite the power of these Gurus, the spiritual essence of Sikhism is little known outside India and its **diaspora** (dispersed communities), even though Sikhism is the fifth largest of all world religions. Many Sikhs understand their path not as another sectarian religion but as a statement of the universal truth within, and transcending, all religions. In the past, scholars sometimes characterized Sikh beliefs and practices as an offshoot of Hinduism or a synthesis of the Hindu and Muslim traditions of northern India, but Sikhism has its own unique quality, independent revelation, and history. As awareness of Sikh spirituality spreads, Sikhism is becoming a global religion, although it does not actively seek converts. Instead, it emphasizes the universality of spirituality and the relevance of spirituality in everyday life.

Guru Nanak

What are the three central teachings of Guru Nanak?

Guru Nanak (1469–1539) began to give shape to Sikhism in an environment in which the sant movement was challenging many conventional religious beliefs and practices. The sants, or "holy people," were north Indian poets who rejected most outward forms of ritual expression in favor of deep internal devotion and repetition of the name of God, and were typically critical of caste distinctions. Guru Nanak shared these ideas, but also had a vision of an organized community.

When Guru Nanak was born, the area of northern India called the Punjab was inhabited by both Muslims and Hindus, and ruled by a weak Afghan dynasty. For centuries, the Punjab had been the lane through which outer powers had fought their way into India. In 1398, the Mongolian leader Tamerlane had slaughtered Punjabis and sacked their towns on his way both to and from Delhi. During Guru Nanak's time, it was the Mughal emperor Babur who invaded and claimed the Punjab. This casting of the Punjab as a perpetual battleground later became a crucial aspect of Sikhism.

What Sikhs believe about the life of Guru Nanak is based not so much on historical records as on *janam-sakhis*—traditional stories about his life. The earliest collection of these was probably written down late in the sixteenth century; others were written during the seventeenth to twentieth centuries. Historians view these stories as reflecting the biases and concerns of their times, such as early seventeenth-century opposition to the ritualism of Brahmanic Hinduism; they recount many miraculous happenings that cannot be historically verified. The picture of Guru Nanak that has been handed down is thus a record of how he has been remembered by the faithful.

According to the *janam-sakhis*, Nanak was little concerned with worldly things. As a child he was of a contemplative nature, resisting the formalities of his Hindu religion. Even after he was married, it is said that he roamed about in nature and gave away any money he had to the poor. At length he took a job as an accountant, but his heart was not in material gain.

When Nanak was thirty, his life was reportedly transformed after immersion in a river, from which it is said he did not emerge for three days. He could not be found until he suddenly appeared in town, radiant. According to one account, he had been taken into the presence of God, who gave him a bowl of milk to drink, saying that it was actually nectar (amrit) which would give him "power of prayer, love of worship, truth and contentment."[2] The Almighty sent him back into the world to redeem it from **Kali Yuga** (the darkest of ages). J. S. Neki, Sikh psychiatrist and professor of religious studies, explains that the *sakhi* of Guru Nanak's disappearance in the river is rich in symbolic meaning:

> The word "sakhi" means evidence—evidence of some truth in the form of a story. ... First of all the legend signifies that in order to attain the Lord, one is required to drown—drown in love and devotion and into the depths of meditation. ... The second requirement is to die—die towards the world. Our relationship with the world is ego-oriented and self-nourishing. Such orientation does not permit one to become oriented towards God. Breaking one's bonds with the world signifies the symbolic death in the legend. The third symbol is that of returning. One who loses himself in himself, returns renewed. When he dives, he is a seeker. When he emerges, he is a seer—impregnated with the Beatific Vision. He has been saved. Now he has the task of salvaging others.[3]

According to the *janam-sakhis*, after Nanak's disappearance in the river, he began traveling through India, the Himalayas, Afghanistan, Sri Lanka, and Arabia, teaching in his own surprising way. When people asked him whether he would follow the Hindu or the Muslim path, he replied, "There is neither Hindu nor Mussulman [Muslim], so whose path shall I follow? I shall follow God's path. God is

Guru Nanak holding spiritual dialogue with Hindu ascetics. (Illustration from Biography of Guru Nanak *by Kartar Singh.)*

neither Hindu nor Mussulman."[4] Nanak mocked the Hindu tradition of throwing sacred river water east toward the rising sun in worship of their ancestors—he threw water to the west. If Hindus could throw water far enough to reach their ancestors thousands of miles away in Heaven, he explained, he could certainly water his parched land several hundred miles away near Lahore by throwing water in its direction. Another tradition has it that he set his feet toward the holy sanctuary of the Ka'bah when sleeping as a pilgrim in Mecca. Questioned about this rude conduct, he is said to have remarked, "Then kindly turn my feet toward some direction where God is not."

Guru Nanak emphasized three central teachings as the straight path to God: working hard in society to earn one's own honest living (rather than withdrawing into asceticism and begging, as was the practice of many yogis of his time); sharing from one's earnings with those who are needy; and remembering God at all times as the only Doer, the only Giver. Encouraging people to stay in the world and to help others rather than renounce the world in search of spiritual fulfillment, Guru Nanak himself settled with his family as a farmer in the new community he developed at Kartarpur (Town of the Creator). The multitude of Sikhs who came to him contributed foods or labor to the **langar**, a free community kitchen in which there were no caste distinctions. The Guru encouraged them to live a disciplined life of rising early in the morning to praise God and working hard to support themselves and share with those in need. To a society that stressed distinctions of caste, class, gender, and religion, Guru Nanak introduced the idea of a social order based on equality, justice, and service to all, in devotion to the One God, whom Guru Nanak perceived as formless, pervading everywhere.

Nanak's commitment to practical faith, as opposed to external adherence to religious formalities, won him followers from both Hinduism and Islam. Before he died, they argued over who would dispose of his body. According to the *janam-sakhis*, he told Muslims to place flowers on one side of his body, Hindus on the other; the side whose flowers remained fresh the next day could bury or cremate him. The next day they raised the sheet that had covered his body and reportedly found nothing beneath it; all the flowers were still fresh, leaving only the fragrance of his being.

> *Oh my mind, love God as a fish loves water:*
> *The more the water, the happier is the fish,*
> *   the more peaceful his mind and body.*
> *He cannot live without water even for a moment.*
> *God knows the inner pain of that being without water.*
>
> *Guru Nanak[5]*

The succession of Gurus

How did the activities of the Sikh Gurus help structure and shape the Sikh community and its practices?

There was eventually a total of ten Sikh Gurus, all of whom were thought to be transmitting the spiritual light of Nanak. Before he passed away, Guru Nanak passed his spiritual authority to Lehna, previously a devotee of the Hindu goddess Durga. Lehna had become so dedicated to Guru Nanak's mission that the Guru gave him the name Angad—a limb of his body (*ang*). Although the spiritual transmission from Guru Nanak reportedly made him so powerful that he became famous for healing incurable diseases such as leprosy, Guru Angad (1504–1552) was a model of humility and service to the poor and needy. He continued the tradition of langar and served the people with his own hands. One of the many stories told of his humility concerns an ascetic who was jealous of

TIMELINE

Sikhism

CE 1469–1539	Life of Guru Nanak, the first Sikh prophet
1563–1606	Life of the Fifth Guru, Arjun Dev
c. 1621–1675	Life of the Ninth Guru, Tegh Bahadur
1666–1708	Life of the Tenth Guru, Guru Gobind Singh
1699	Guru Gobind Singh founds the order of Khalsa
1708	Guru Granth Sahib installed as Eternal Guru
1780–1839	Maharaja Ranjit Singh rules the Sikh kingdom, respecting all religions
1849	British rule in Punjab; Sikh rule comes to an end
1947	Partition of India and Pakistan; 2 million Sikhs forced to leave Pakistani territory for India
1984	The Indian army, seeking to overthrow Sikh separatists, takes the Golden Temple at Amritsar; Indira Gandhi, Indian prime minister, assassinated by her Sikh bodyguards, triggering Hindu violence against Sikhs
1999	Millions of Sikhs converge on Anandpur Sahib to celebrate the 300th anniversary of the founding of the Khalsa
2000	Quadricentenary of installation of Adi Granth in Golden Temple
2008	Celebrations of 300 years of Guru Granth Sahib as Eternal Guru

the Guru's popularity. The monsoon rains that were essential for the crops had not come, so the ascetic used the opportunity to turn the poor farmers against Guru Angad. He taunted them that if the Guru was so powerful, he should call for rain. The desperate villagers begged Guru Angad to do so, but he peacefully replied that one should not interfere with God's ways; rain would come only when God so willed. The ascetic persisted in turning the people against Guru Angad, telling them that he himself would magically bring the rains if they would get rid of the Guru. Thus the simple people drove Guru Angad away. Agreeably, he left the village. Refused shelter anywhere nearby, he settled in a forest. Thereafter the ascetic fasted and tried all his mantras, but the rains did not come. At last, Amar Das (1479–1574), who later became the third of the Sikh Gurus, learned of the situation and reproached the villagers for forsaking the sun for the light of a small lamp. Recognizing their mistake, the villagers begged Guru Angad to forgive them and return to the village. He did so, amid great rejoicing, and the rains came.

The Third and Fourth Gurus, Amar Das and Ram Das (1534–1581), developed organizational structures for the growing Sikh **Panth** (community) while also setting personal examples of humility. Ram Das founded the holy city of Amritsar, within which the Fifth Guru, Guru Arjun Dev (1563–1606), built the religion's most sacred shrine, the Golden Temple. The Fifth Guru also compiled the sacred scriptures of the Sikhs, the **Adi Granth** (original holy book, now known as the **Guru Granth Sahib**), from devotional hymns composed by Guru Nanak, the other Gurus, and Hindu and Muslim saints, including many spiritual figures from social castes considered lowly. Among the latter are holy people such as Bhagat Ravi Das, a low-caste Hindu shoemaker who achieved the heights of spiritual realization. His powerful poetry incorporated into the Guru Granth Sahib includes this song:

> When I was, You were not.
> When You are, I am not.
> As huge waves are raised in the wind in the vast ocean,
> But are only water in water,
> O Lord of Wealth, what should I say about this delusion?
> What we deem a thing to be,
> It is not, in reality.
> It is like a king falling asleep on his throne
> And dreaming that he is a beggar.
> His kingdom is intact,
> But separating from it, he suffers. …
> Says Ravi Das, the Lord is nearer to us than our hands and feet.[6]

Emperor Akbar visited the Third, Fourth, and Fifth Gurus and was very pleased with the teachings of the Gurus. But his son and successor, Jehangir, was jealous of Guru Arjun Dev's popularity among Muslims, and thus had him tortured and executed in 1606 on a false charge. It is said that Guru Arjun Dev remained calmly meditating on God as he was tortured by heat, with his love and faith undismayed. His devotional hymns include words such as these:

> Merciful, merciful is the Lord.
> Merciful is my master.
> He blesses all beings with His bounties.
> Why waverest thou, Oh mortal? The Creator Himself shall protect you.
> He who has created you takes care of you. …
> Oh mortal, meditate on the Lord as long as there is breath in your body.[7]

TEACHING STORY

Guru Arjun Dev's Devotion

Throughout his life, Guru Arjun Dev, the Fifth Sikh Guru, responded with calm faith in God to jealous plots against him.

Whereas the open-minded Mughal emperor Akbar was so pleased with the Adi Granth—the sacred scripture that Guru Arjun Dev had compiled—that he made an offering of gold to it, the son who took over his throne, Jehangir, was of a different nature. Akbar had actually nominated his grandson Khusrau to be his successor. Soon after Jehangir took Akbar's place, Khusrau visited Guru Arjun Dev briefly during his travels. Once Khusrau's bid for the throne was quashed, Jehangir blamed Guru Arjun Dev for siding with his rival and ordered that he pay a heavy fine. Guru Arjun Dev refused, saying that monies were not his own property but rather belonged to the Sikh community, to be used for the welfare of those in need. Even though his Sikhs started collecting money to pay the fine, the Guru stopped them, saying that he had not done anything wrong and that compromising with wrong is irreligious.

Ostensibly for his refusal to follow the emperor's orders—but more likely to end his popular influence—the Guru was arrested and subjected to torture by heat, during the already terrible heat of summer. He was made to sit on a hot iron sheet. Hot sand was dumped onto his body and he was placed into boiling water.

As these tortures were being inflicted, Mian Mir, an established saint of Islam who reportedly laid the foundation stone of the Golden Temple at Amritsar, pleaded with the Guru to let him use his mystical power against the persecutors. Guru Arjun Dev refused, telling Mian Mir that he was allowing the torture in order to set an example for others of patiently accepting the reality that everything is under God's control; every leaf that moves does so by God's will.

The daughter-in-law of Chandu, the rich man of Lahore who had turned the emperor against the Guru, tried to offer sherbet to the Guru to ease his agony. But just as he had refused attempts to wed his son to Chandu's daughter, saying that a rich man's daughter would not be happy in the home of a dervish, he refused her food, saying that he would accept nothing. Nonetheless, he blessed her for her devotion.

Through five days of torture, Guru Arjun Dev persisted in calm faith in God. His torturers then forced him to bathe in the river alongside the Mughal fort. His followers wept to see the blisters covering his body. As he walked on blistered feet, he repeated again and again, "Your will is sweet, Oh God; I only seek the gift of Your Name." Calmly, he walked into the water and breathed his last.

To protect Sikhism and to defend the weak of all religions against tyranny, the Sixth Guru, Hargobind (1595–1644), established a Sikh army, carried two swords (one symbolizing temporal power, the other spiritual power), and taught the people to defend their religion. The tenderhearted Seventh Guru, Har Rai (1630–1661), was a pacifist who never used his troops against the Mughals. He taught his Sikhs not only to feed anyone who came to their door, but also to:

> do service in such a way that the poor guest may not feel he is partaking of some charity but as if he had come to the Guru's house which belonged to all in equal measure. He who has more should consider it as God's trust and share it in the same spirit. Man is only an instrument of service: the giver of goods is God, the Guru of us all.[8]

The Eighth Guru, Har Krishan (1656–1664), became successor to Guru Nanak's seat when he was only five years old and died at the age of eight. When taunted by Hindu pandits (teacher-scholars) the "Child Guru" reportedly touched a lowly deaf and dumb Sikh watercarrier with his cane, whereupon the watercarrier expounded brilliantly on the subtleties of the Hindu scripture the *Bhagavad-Gita*.

The ninth master, Guru Tegh Bahadur (*c.* 1621–1675), was martyred. According to Sikh tradition, he was approached by Kashmiri Hindu pandits who were facing forced conversion to Islam by the Mughal emperor, Aurangzeb. The emperor viewed Hinduism as a totally corrupt, idolatrous religion, which did not lead people to God; he had ordered the destruction of Hindu temples and mass conversion of Hindus throughout the land, beginning in the north with Kashmir. Reportedly, one of the Kashmiri pandits dreamed that only the Ninth Guru, the savior in Kali Yuga, could save the Hindus. With the firm approval of his young son, Guru Tegh Bahadur told the Hindu pandits to inform their oppressors that they would convert to Islam if the Sikh Guru could be persuaded to do so. Imprisoned and forced to witness the torture and murder of his aides, the Ninth Guru staunchly maintained the right of all people to religious freedom. Aurangzeb beheaded him before a crowd of thousands. But as his son later wrote, "He has given his head, but not his determination."[9]

The martyred Ninth Guru was succeeded by his young son, who became the tenth master, Guru Gobind Singh (1666–1708). It was he who turned the intimidated Sikhs into saint–soldiers. In 1699 he reportedly told an assembly of Sikhs that the times were so dangerous that he had developed a new plan to give the community strength and unity. Total surrender to the master would be necessary, he said, asking for volunteers who would offer their heads for the cause of protecting religious ideals. One at a time, five stepped forward. Each was escorted into the Guru's tent, from which the Tenth Guru emerged alone with a bloody sword. According to the story, after this scene was repeated five times the Guru brought all the men out of the tent, alive and dressed in new clothes. Some say the blood was that of a goat, in a test of the people's loyalty; others say that Guru Gobind Singh had killed the men and then resurrected them.

Whatever actually happened that day, Sikhs believe that the reported willingness of the five men to sacrifice themselves for the Guru's mission was dramatically proven, and the **amrit** (nectar-like holy water) prepared by Guru Gobind Singh is thought to have turned his followers into heroes, with sugar added by his wife symbolizing the ideal that they would also be compassionate. The Guru called them his Five Beloved Ones

Five devotees representing the Five Beloved Ones walk barefoot out of respect as they escort the Dasam Granth (writings of the Tenth Guru) from the place of his death to Gobind Sadan gurdwara in New Delhi.

(*Panj Piaras*). The Five Beloved Ones became models for Sikhs. It is noteworthy that they came from the lowest classes and from different geographic areas.

After initiating the first five, the Guru (whose name up to that time was Gobind Rai) established a unique Guru–Sikh relationship by asking that they initiate him—thus underscoring the principle of equality among all Sikhs. The initiated men were given the surname Singh (lion); the women were all given the name Kaur (princess) and treated as equals. Guru Gobind Rai took the name of Guru Gobind Singh. He called the initiates **Khalsa** (Pure Ones), a community pledged to a special code of personal discipline. According to Sikh belief about what happened in 1699, Sikh men and women were sworn to wear five distinctive symbols of their dedication: unshorn hair, a comb, drawstring underbreeches, a sword in a sheath, and a steel bracelet. These **"Five Ks"** (so called because all the words begin with a "k" in Punjabi) have been interpreted as proud hallmarks of Sikh identity dating from the birth of the Khalsa in 1699. There are many explanations of what each symbolizes. Not cutting one's hair shows respect for what God created, and keeping it neat with the comb distinguishes the Sikh from Hindu renunciates who let their unshorn hair grow long and matted. The drawstring underbreeches ensure modesty, and were also practical for Sikhs riding horses in battle. The sword symbolizes the willingness to stand up for justice and protection of the weak, and the steel bracelet is worn as a personal reminder that one is a servant of God, and perhaps also offers some protection to the wrist in hand-to-hand combat.

The Five Ks clearly distinguished Sikhs from Muslims and Hindus, supporting the assertion that Sikhism constituted a third path with its own right to spiritual sovereignty. All of these innovations are thought to have turned the meek into warriors capable of shaking off Mughal oppression and protecting freedom of religion; the distinctive dress made it impossible for the Khalsa to hide from their duty by blending with the general populace. In Sikh history, their bravery was indeed proven again and again.

However, to interpret the Five Ks only as symbols of power and separate identity is to overlook the spiritual and egalitarian aspects of Sikhism. By mandating the same symbolic dress for people of all castes, both women and men, Sikhs gave both genders and all castes equal importance, contrary to Indian cultural traditions. There may also be significant spiritual symbols embedded

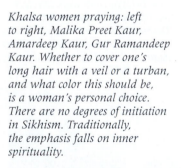

Khalsa women praying: left to right, Malika Preet Kaur, Amardeep Kaur, Gur Ramandeep Kaur. Whether to cover one's long hair with a veil or a turban, and what color this should be, is a woman's personal choice. There are no degrees of initiation in Sikhism. Traditionally, the emphasis falls on inner spirituality.

in the Five Ks. The sword, for instance, is often used in the Guru Granth Sahib as a metaphor for divine wisdom that cuts through ignorance and egocentrism. The devotee who wields it—and even the sword itself—is commonly referred to in female terms. For example, "By taking up the sword of knowledge, she fights against her mind and merges with her self."[10] Feminist scholar Nikky-Guninder Kaur Singh sees the steel bracelet (*kara*) as a metaphorical reminder of the total integration of material and spiritual realities:

> *With neither a beginning nor an end, the circular bracelet is a reminder of the Infinite One. Like the sword, it is a means of centering the self as the person is engaged in various activities; like her, it is not a means for high-handed aggression. Worn around the right wrist, the* kara *participates in all physical functions and gestures, thereby reminding men and women that the timeless moment touches upon each moment, that sacred action touches upon every action. Dressing up, hugging, cooking, reading the holy book, working in the farm or at a computer—all actions are equally validated by the* kara.[11]

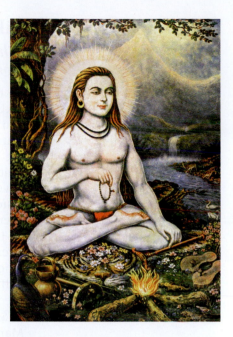

Baba Siri Chand, elder son of Guru Nanak, combined the power of intense meditation with the power of hard work.

Uncut hair is important to observant Sikhs because through it they feel a close inner relationship to Guru Gobind Singh, who called it his "divine stamp."

It is thought that Guru Gobind Singh also commanded his Khalsa to follow a particular disciplinary code, including eschewing hair-cutting, adultery, tobacco, and the meat of animals slowly bled to death in Muslim fashion. Scholars debate the historicity of various versions of the code of conduct now in use, some of which contain hundreds of rules.

Guru Gobind Singh ended the line of bodily succession to Guruship. As he was passing away in 1708, he took the unique step of transferring his authority to the Adi Granth rather than to a human successor. Thenceforth, it was called the Guru Granth Sahib—the living presence of the Guru embodied in the sacred scripture, to be consulted by the congregation for spiritual guidance and decision-making.

After the succession of human Gurus came to an end, Sikhs continued to remember and commemorate events in the Gurus' lives. The stories of the Gurus are full of miracles that reportedly happened around them, such as the Eighth Guru's empowering a lowly watercarrier to give a profound explanation of the *Bhagavad-Gita*. Neither age, nor caste, nor gender is thought to have any relevance in Sikh spirituality.

> *God is like sugar scattered in the sand. An elephant cannot pick it up. Says Kabir, the Guru has given me this sublime secret:*
> "*Become thou an ant and partake of it.*"
>
> *Kabir*[12]

Although the Sikh Gurus gave their followers no mandate to convert others, their message was spread in a nonsectarian way by the **Udasis**, renunciates who do not withdraw from the world but rather practice strict discipline and meditation while at the same time trying to serve humanity. Their missionary work began under Baba Siri Chand, the ascetic elder son of Guru Nanak. He had a close relationship with the Sikh Gurus and was highly respected by people of all castes and creeds because of his spiritual power, wisdom, and principles. During the reign of the Mughal emperor Shah Jahan, a census showed that Baba Siri Chand had the largest following of any holy person in India. Nevertheless, he directed all attention and praise to his father, and never claimed to be a Guru himself. Udasi communities and educational institutions are still maintained in the subcontinent, and old Udasi inscriptions have been discovered in Baku, Azerbaijan.

Sikh rule and India's independence movement

Why did resistance to oppression become a hallmark of Sikhism from 1700?

As the Mughal Empire began to disintegrate and Afghans invaded India, the Sikhs fought for their own identity and sovereignty, as well as to protect Hindu and Muslim women from the attackers, and to protect freedom of religion in the country. In the eighteenth century, they began establishing small states within the Punjab, and at the beginning of the nineteenth century these states were united under Maharaja Ranjit Singh, forming the Sikh Empire, a nonsectarian government noted for its generous tolerance toward Muslims, despite the earlier history of oppression by the Muslim rulers. Maharaja Ranjit Singh is said to have been unusually kind to his subjects and to have humbly accepted chastisement by the Sikh religious authorities for moral lapses on his part. The Sikh Empire attempted to create a pluralistic society, with social equality and full freedom of religion. It also blocked the Khyber Pass against invaders. The empire lasted only half a century, for the British, already in power throughout much of the rest of the India, subdued it in 1849.

Sikhs made substantial contributions to the Indian independence movement. Many were arrested, deported, or executed for their actions. Many Sikhs set heroic examples of nonviolent resistance to oppression, despite their military abilities. One famous story concerns Guru ka Bagh, a garden and shrine that had been used by Sikhs for cutting wood for the community's free kitchen. In 1922, British police began arresting and then beating and killing Sikhs who went to the garden to collect firewood. Every day a new wave of 100 Sikhs would come voluntarily to suffer fierce beatings and perhaps even be killed, without a murmur except for the Name of God on their lips, to resist injustice.

At one point, Sikh political prisoners arrested at Guru ka Bagh were being transported by train. The Sikh community in Hasanavdal asked the stationmaster there to stop the train so they could offer food to the prisoners. He refused, saying that it was a special train and would not stop at Hasanavdal. Determined to care for the prisoners, three leading Sikhs told the *sangat* (congregation) to bring food, and then they courageously lay down on the tracks to force the train to stop. The driver was unable to brake in time; the train ran over them, crushing their bodies, and then stopped. As the *sangat* tried to help the dying martyrs one of them ordered, "Don't care for us. Feed the prisoners." Thus the langar (community meal) was served to the prisoners on the train, and the Sikhs who had laid their bodies on the track died.

The British left India in 1947, creating the new nations of Indian and Pakistan. The partition of India affected Sikhs profoundly. Approximately two-thirds of the Punjab, Sikhism's homeland, became part of West Pakistan. The two million Sikhs living there were forced to migrate to the eastern side of the border under conditions of extreme hardship, leaving behind land, possessions, and some of their most sacred sites, including Nankana Sahib, Guru Nanak's birthplace.

Resistance to oppression has remained a hallmark of Sikhism. High praise for Guru Gobind Singh's military effect has been offered by Dr. S. Radhakrishnan, the respected second president of India:

> For one thousand years, after the defeat of Raja Jaipal, India had lain prostrate. The raiders and invaders descended on India and took away the people, to be sold as slaves. ... Guru Gobind Singh raised the Khalsa to defy religious intolerance, religious persecution and political inequality. It was a miracle that heroes appeared out of straws and common clay. Those who groveled in the dust rose proud, defiant and invincible in the form of the Khalsa. They bore all sufferings and unnamable tortures cheerfully and unflinchingly. ... India is at long last free. This freedom is the crown and climax and a logical corollary to the Sikh Guru's and Khalsa's terrific sacrifices and heroic exploits.[13]

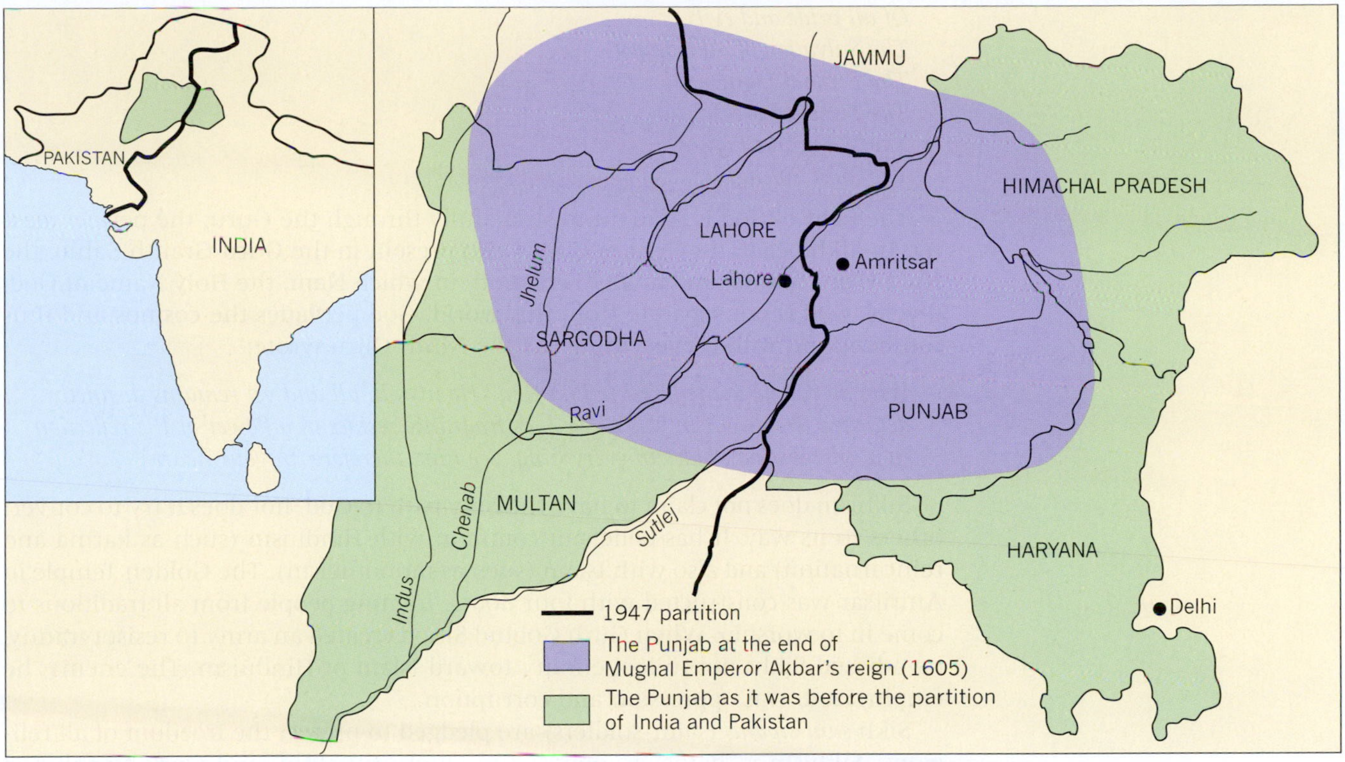

The Punjab at the end of the reign of the Mughal emperor Akbar. The 1947 partition of India left two-thirds of the Punjab, including many of its Sikh temples, inside Pakistan, a Muslim state.

Central beliefs

What are the main beliefs of Sikhism?

Sikhism's major focus is loving devotion to one God, whom Sikhs recognize as the same One who is worshiped by many different names around the world. God is formless, beyond time and space, the only truth, the only reality. This boundless concept was initially set forth in Guru Nanak's *Mul Mantra* (basic sacred chant), which prefaces the Guru Granth Sahib, and *JapJi*, the first morning prayer of Sikhs:

> There is One God
> Whose Name is Truth,
> The Creator,
> Without fear, without hate,
> Eternal Being,
> Beyond birth and death,
> Self-existent,
> Realized by the Guru's grace.[14]

Following Guru Nanak's lead, Sikhs often refer to God as *Sat* (truth) or as *Ik Onkar*, the One Supreme Being. God is pure being, without form.

Guru Gobind Singh, a great custodian of scholars who kept many poets in his court, offered a litany of praises of this boundless, formless One. His inspired composition, *Jaap Sahib*, includes 199 verses such as these:

> Immortal
> Omnipotent
> Beyond Time
> And Space
> Invisible
> Beyond name, caste, or creed
> Beyond form or figure
> The ruthless destroyer

Of all pride and evil
The Salvation of all beings …
The Eternal Light
The Sweetest Breeze
The Wondrous Figure
The Most Splendid.[15]

The light of God is thought to shine fully through the Guru, the perfect master. In Sikh belief, the light of God is also present in the Guru Granth Sahib, the Holy Word of God, and in all of creation, in which **Nam**, the Holy Name of God, dwells. God is not separate from this world. God pervades the cosmos and thus can be found within everything. As the Ninth Guru wrote:

Why do you go to the forest to find God? He lives in all and yet remains distinctly detached. He dwells in you as well, as fragrance resides in a flower or the reflection in a mirror. God abides in everything. See him, therefore, in your heart.[16]

Sikhism does not claim to have the only path to God, nor does it try to convert others to its way. It has beliefs in common with Hinduism (such as karma and reincarnation) and also with Islam (such as monotheism). The Golden Temple in Amritsar was constructed with four doors, inviting people from all traditions to come in to worship. When Guru Gobind Singh created an army to resist tyranny, he advised Sikhs not to feel enmity toward Islam or Hinduism. The enemy, he emphasized, was oppression and corruption.

Sikh *sant-sipahis* (saint-soldiers) are pledged to protect the freedom of all religions. Sikhism is, however, opposed to empty ritualism, and Guru Nanak and his successors praised sincere inner faith, while sharply challenging hypocritical religious practices. "It is very difficult to be called a Muslim," said Guru Nanak. "A Muslim's heart is as soft as wax, very compassionate, and he washes away the inner dirt of egotism."[17] By contrast, said Guru Nanak, "The Qazis [Muslim legal authorities] who sit in the courts to minister justice, rosary in hand and the name of *Khuda* (God) on their lips, commit injustice if their palm is not greased. And if someone challenges them, lo, they quote the scriptures!"[18]

According to the Sikh ideal, the purpose of life is to realize God within the world, through the everyday practices of work, worship, and charity, of sacrificing love. All people are to be treated equally, for God's light dwells in all and ego is a major hindrance to God-realization. From Guru Nanak's time on, Sikhism has refused to acknowledge the traditional Indian caste system. In their social services, such as hospitals, leprosariums, and free kitchens, Sikhs observe a tradition of serving everyone, regardless of caste or creed. A special group of Sikhs, known as Seva Panthis, place great emphasis on this aspect of Sikhism, refusing to accept any offerings to support their services to the needy. They are inspired by the example of Bhai Kanhaiya, who in the time of Guru Gobind Singh was found offering water to the fallen opponents as well as to Guru Gobind Singh's wounded soldiers. The Guru's people complained about his behavior to the Guru, who questioned Bhai Kanhaiya about what he was doing. Bhai Kanhaiya reportedly said that he was obeying the Sikh Gurus' teaching that one should look upon all with the same eye, whether friend or foe. Guru Gobind Singh praised him and gave him ointment, with the instruction not only to give water but also to soothe the wounds of soldiers from both armies.

In contrast to the low status of women in Indian society, the Gurus accorded considerable respect to women. Guru Nanak asked: "Why denounce her, who even gives birth to kings?"[19] Many women are respectfully remembered in Sikh history. Among them are Guru Nanak's sister Bibi Nanaki, who first recognized her brother's great spiritual power and became his first devotee. A group of Guru Gobind Singh's soldiers deserted him in the face of seemingly impossible odds when his citadel at Anandpur was being besieged, but their women refused to allow them to return to their homes. The women threatened to dress in the men's clothes and return to fight for the Guru, to expunge the shame of the men's cowardice. One woman—Mai Bhago—did so and helped to lead forty of the deserters back to battle on the Guru's side against Aurangzeb's army. The men all died on the battlefield, asking the Guru to forgive them, but Mai Bhago survived and remained in the Guru's personal security guard, dressed as a man, with his permission. When amrit was first prepared for Khalsa initiation, it was Guru Gobind Singh's wife who added sugar crystals to make the initiates sweet-tempered as well as brave. In Brahmanic Hindu tradition, such an action by a woman would have been considered a defilement. Women were active as missionaries carrying Guru Gobind Singh's program. During the terrible Mughal persecutions of the eighteenth century, Sikh women were noted for their courage and steadfast faith.

A preference for sons nonetheless persisted, in part because of the heavy dowry burden traditionally expected of females in India. To counter this trend, Guru Gobind Singh reportedly forbade female infanticide, and in 2001 the chief Sikh authorities issued an order that anyone practicing female feticide would be excommunicated from the faith.

In developing the military capabilities of his followers in order to protect religious freedom, Guru Gobind Singh set forth very strict standards for battle. He established five stringent conditions for "righteous war": (1) Military means are a last resort to be used only if all other methods have failed; (2) Battle should be undertaken without any enmity or feeling of revenge; (3) No territory should be taken or captured property retained; (4) Troops should be committed to the cause, not mercenaries fighting for pay, and soldiers should be strictly disciplined, forswearing smoking, drinking, and abuse of opponents' women; and (5) Minimal force should be used and hostilities should end when the objective is attained.

Like Hinduism, Sikhism conceives a series of lives, with karma (the effects of past actions on one's present life) governing transmigration of the soul into new bodies, be they human or animal. The ultimate goal of life is mystical union with the divine, reflected in one's way of living.

> I was separated from God for many births, dry as a withered plant,
> But by the grace of the Guru, I have become green.
>
> *Guru Arjun*[20]

Sacred practices

How are the teachings of Sikhism put into practice in the Khalsa, gurdwara, and langar?

To be a true Sikh is to live a very disciplined life of surrender and devotion to God, with hours of daily prayer, continual inner repetition of the Name of God (Nam), and detachment from negative, worldly mind-states. In Sikh belief, Nam carries intense spiritual power, capable of making a person fearless, steady, inwardly calm and strong in the face of any adversity, willing to serve without any reward, and extending love in all directions without any effort. Why is it so powerful? It comes from the Guru as a transmission of spiritual blessing that automatically transforms people and links them with God. Some feel that Nam is the essence of creation, the sound and vibration of which the cosmos is a material manifestation. The mystics and Gurus whose writings are included in the Guru Granth Sahib refer to many Names of God, such as *Murari* (a reference to Krishna), *Narain* (the One present in water), *Allah*, and Rama. Some Sikhs recite "*Wahe Guru*" (God wondrous beyond words), some say "*Ik Onkar Sat nam Siri Wahe Guru*" (God is One, the Truth Itself, Most Respectful, Wondrous beyond words), some recite the whole *Mul Mantra*, a key verse by Guru Nanak summarizing his philosophy, used at the beginning of the Guru Granth Sahib and in many other places in it.

In the Sikh path, at the same time that one's mind and heart are joined with God, one is to be working hard in the world, earning an honest living, and helping those in need. Of this path, the Third Sikh Guru observed:

The way of devotees is unique; they walk a difficult path.
They leave behind attachments, greed, ego, and desires, and do not speak much.
The path they walk is sharper than the edge of a sword and thinner than a hair.
Those who shed their false self by the grace of the Guru are filled with the
fragrance of God.[21]

The standards set by Guru Gobind Singh for the Khalsa are so high that few people can really meet them. In addition to outer disciplines, such as abstaining from drugs, alcohol, and tobacco, the person who is Khalsa, said the Guru, will always recite the Name of God:

The Name of God is light, the Light which never extinguishes, day or night.
Khalsa recognizes none but the One. I live in Khalsa; it is my body, my
treasure store.[22]

Those who are Khalsa renounce anger and do not criticize anybody. They fight on the front line against injustice and vanquish the five evils (lust, anger, greed, attachment, and ego) in themselves. They burn their karmas and thus become egoless. Not only do they not take another person's spouse, they do not even look at the things that belong to others. Perpetually reciting Nam is their joy, and they fall in love with the words of the Gurus. They face difficulties squarely, always attack evil, and always help the poor. They join other people with the Nam, but are not bound within the forts of narrow-mindedness.[23]

The Sikh Gurus formed several institutions to help create a new social order with no caste distinctions. One is langar, the community meal, which is freely offered to all who come, regardless of caste. This typically takes place at a **gurdwara**, the building where the Guru Granth Sahib is enshrined and public worship takes place. Community worship is highly recommended throughout Guru Granth Sahib. Guru Arjun Dev, the Fifth Guru, wrote, "As one lost in a thick jungle rediscovers one's path, so will one be enlightened in the company of the holy."[24] The congregation is called the sangat, in which all are equal; there is no priestly class or servant class. During community worship as well as langar, all strata of people sit together, though men and women usually sit separately, as is the Indian custom. People of all ethnic origins, ideologies, and castes, including untouchables, may bathe in the tank of water at Sikh holy places. Baptism

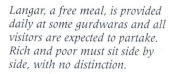

Langar, a free meal, is provided daily at some gurdwaras and all visitors are expected to partake. Rich and poor must sit side by side, with no distinction.

Amrit Ceremony on Baisakhi

The natural exuberance of Punjabis bursts forth every spring in the festival of Baisakhi. Traditionally this was a harvest festival, celebrating the wheat harvest on the first day of the solar month of Baisakh (or Vaisakh), on April 13 or 14. In anticipation of a happy period of plenty, and reportedly also to protect the crop from damage by ill fortune, the people of the Punjab used to gather and perform folk dances. Of these, the most well-known is the *bhangra* dance—a jubilant, athletic dance by men wearing colorful long wrapped skirts and costume jewelry, stamping their feet to the strong backbeat of drums, raising their arms overhead, and shaking their shoulders independently of their torsos. In the time of Guru Amar Das, this jubilant harvest festival became the occasion for a gathering of the Sikh community around the Guru. It was when many Sikhs had gathered in Anandpur Sahib around Guru Gobind Singh for the Baisakhi festival in 1699 that the Guru is said to have dramatically initiated the first Khalsa members.

Sikhs now celebrate Baisakhi with great enthusiasm every year as the birthday of the Khalsa. In gurdwaras around the world, *Akhand Paths*—continuous readings of the Guru Granth Sahib—are held, culminating in a community prayer, kirtan, and special langar. There may also be displays of martial arts, such as adept swordplay.

Baisakhi is also a favorite occasion for initiation of new Khalsa members, via the Amrit Ceremony. In some private area, in the presence of the Guru Granth Sahib, those to be inducted appear in clean dress, wearing the Five Ks. They may or may not be Sikhs, but they agree to follow the principal teachings of the Gurus and to live according to a strict code of outer discipline. Initiates may also dedicate themselves to developing the inner qualities defining Khalsa, such as defeating the five evils within themselves. Formerly initiated Khalsa who have lapsed from the disciplinary code may also appear to be reinitiated after carrying out some specified spiritual punishment.

The ceremony is conducted by five baptized people representing the first Five Beloved Ones (*Panj Piaras*) who offered their heads to Guru Gobind Singh. They are expected to be exemplary members of the Khalsa who know the daily prayers by heart. The ceremony begins with a prayer to the Guru Granth Sahib and reading of guidance from it for the would-be initiates. The officiants then recite the five daily prayers—a process that may take up to two hours—while slowly stirring sugar-sweetened water in an iron bowl to turn

Kirtan on Baisakhi by a sangat *from Gurdaspur, Punjab.*

it into amrit (nectar). The amrit is stirred with a *khanda*, a double-edged sword symbolizing the disintegration of egotism and demolishing of social barriers such as caste and gender discrimination. When the amrit is prepared and prayed over, five handfuls are given to each initiate to drink, it is sprinkled five times on their hair, and it is splashed five times into their eyes. After each time, the initiate is told to say, "The Khalsa is God's, and the victory is God's." Each then drinks from the bowl, turn by turn. Drinking from the same bowl by people of all castes was a revolutionary practice in 1699, and to a certain extent it still is, because of strong caste prohibitions in India and taboos about contamination of food. After amrit initiation, the Khalsa are considered to be in such a pure state that they can share food with each other, but not with anyone else. At the end of the ceremony they are told that they are all children of the same family, with Guru Gobind Singh as their father and his wife Mata Sahib Kaur as their mother, and that they are spiritual residents of Anandpur Sahib.

The Amrit ceremony ends as it began, with the central prayer of Sikhs, but now with new meaning for the initiates. In part:

Bestow upon the Sikhs the boon of Sikhism, of preserving hair, of observing Sikh code of conduct, of divine wisdom, of firm faith, of unshakable belief, the supreme boon of the Name of God, and of the holy bath in the pool of nectar in Amritsar. May the kirtan *choirs, flags, and shrines last till eternity, and may righteousness triumph. … May the mind of the Sikhs be humble and their wisdom profound. … In the name of [Guru] Nanak, may everyone be in high spirits! By Thy will, may all prosper. The Khalsa is of God; all victory is the victory of God!*[25]

Guru Gobind Singh writing Jaap Sahib, *a hymn praising the attributes of God, "without form, beyond religion." (Painting by Mehar Singh.)*

into the Khalsa is thought to do away with one's former caste and make a lowly person a chief. At least one-tenth of one's income is to be contributed toward the welfare of the community. In addition, the Sikh Gurus glorified the lowliest forms of manual labor, such as sweeping the floor and cleaning shoes and dirty pots, especially when these are done as voluntary service to God.

The morning and evening prayers take about two hours a day, starting in the very early morning hours. The first morning prayer is Guru Nanak's *JapJi. Jap*, meaning "recitation," refers to the use of sound, especially the Name of God (Nam), as the best way of approaching the divine. Like combing the hair, hearing and reciting the sacred word is used as a way to comb all negative thoughts out of the mind. Much of the *JapJi* is devoted to the blessings of Nam. For example:

> *The devotees are forever in bliss, for by hearing the Nam their suffering and sins are destroyed.*
> *Hearkening to the Nam bestows Truth, divine wisdom, contentment.*
> *By hearing the Nam, the blind find the path of Truth and realize the Unfathomable.*[26]

"The Lord is stitched into my heart and never goes out of it even for a moment."

Guru Arjun Dev[27]

Reading a large handwritten copy of Guru Granth Sahib in the Golden Temple.

The second morning prayer is Guru Gobind Singh's universal *Jaap Sahib*. It names no prophet, nor creates any religion. It is sheer homage to God. The Guru addresses God as having no form, no country, and no religion but yet as the seed of seeds, song of songs, sun of suns, the life force pervading everywhere, ever merciful, ever giving, indestructible. Complex in its poetry and profound in its content, *Jaap Sahib* asserts that God is the cause of conflict as well as of peace, of destruction as well as of creation; God pervades in darkness as well as in light. In verse after verse, devotees learn that there is nothing outside of God's presence, nothing outside of God's control.

In addition to recitation of these and other daily prayers, passages from the Guru Granth Sahib are chanted or sung as melodies, often with musical accompaniment. This devotional tradition of **kirtan** was initiated by Guru Nanak. But great discipline is required to attend the predawn hymns and recitations every day, and in contrast to the self-respect developed by Guru Gobind Singh in the Khalsa, worshipers humble themselves before the sacred scriptures. The Guru Granth Sahib is placed on a platform, with a devotee waving a whisk over the sacred book to denote the royalty of the scripture. Worshipers bow to it, bring offerings, and then sit reverently on the floor before it. Every morning and evening, the spirit of God reveals its guidance to the people as an officiant opens the scripture at random, intuitively guided, and reads a passage that is to be a special spiritual focus for the day. For many occasions, teams of people carry out *Akhand Path*, reading the entire Guru Granth Sahib from start to finish within approximately forty-eight hours, taking turns of two hours each.

Some gurdwaras, including the Golden Temple in Amritsar, have previously allowed only men to read publicly from the Guru Granth Sahib, to preach, to officiate at ceremonies, or to sing sacred hymns. This has been a cultural custom, however, for nothing in the Sikh scriptures or the Code of Conduct bars women from such privileges. Indeed, Guru Gobind Singh initiated women as well as men into the Khalsa and allowed women to fight on the battlefield. In 1996, the central body setting policies for Sikh gurdwaras ruled that women should be allowed to perform sacred services.

In addition to group chanting, singing, and listening to collective guidance from the Guru Granth Sahib, devout Sikhs are encouraged to begin the day with private meditations on the name of God. As one advances in this practice and abides in egoless love for God, one is said to receive guidance from the inner Guru, the living word of God within each person.

Sikhism today

What are the main issues faced by Sikhs today?

An enterprising and adventurous community, the Sikhs have done well at home and abroad. Though they constitute less than two percent of India's population, they have played a leading role in government of the nation. Dr. Manmohan Singh served as the country's first Sikh prime minister from 2004 to 2014, and his economic expertise was sought-after in world forums after the global financial meltdown.

The center of Sikhism remains the Punjab, though the area of this territory, which is under Indian rule, was dramatically shrunk by the partition of India in 1947. Through emigration, there are also large Sikh communities in Britain, Canada, the United States, Italy, Malaysia, Singapore, the United Arab Emirates, and Kenya.

In India, Sikhs and Hindus lived side by side in mutual tolerance until 1978 to 1992, when violent clashes occurred over some of the policies of the Indian government. Sikh separatists wanted to establish an independent Sikh state, called Khalistan, with a commitment to strong religious observances and protection for Sikhs from oppression and exploitation by the much larger Hindu community. In 1984, Prime Minister Indira Gandhi chose to attack the Golden Temple, Sikhism's holiest shrine, for Sikh separatists under the leadership of Sant Jarnail Singh Bhindranwale were thought to be using it as a shelter for their weapons. The attack seemed an outrageous desecration of the holy place, and counter-violence increased. The prime minister herself was killed later in 1984 by her Sikh bodyguards. In retribution, terrible mob killings of thousands of Sikhs followed.

Many Sikhs "disappeared" in the Punjab, allegedly at the hands of both separatists and police terrorists. Violence has now ended, but tensions are kept alive by Sikhs living outside India who persist in demanding the formation of Khalistan and promoting a militant, rigid version of the religion.

Historical tensions have also arisen within Sikhism as it has been institutionalized and used by some factions for their own ends, such as acquiring the landholdings of the gurdwaras. Leadership of gurdwaras is democratic, by elected committees, but this provision has not stopped fractiousness even within these organizations. In 1998, factions of a Canadian gurdwara had a bloody fight over the issue of using chairs and tables in the langar rather than the tradition of sitting in rows on the ground.

From time to time, self-styled Sikh "saints" or "gurus" have claimed to have special powers and have set themselves up as spiritual guides, thus antagonizing mainstream Sikhs, who believe that the Tenth Sikh Guru turned over the role of guru to the Guru Granth Sahib, and that there will therefore be no more worldly successors to the position. Some of the new gurus have split off from—or been ostracized by—the mainstream tradition and have formed their own new religious movements, such as Nirankaris, Namdharis, and Radhasoamis.

There is also growing tension between orthodox Sikhs and *deras* (communities) composed largely of lower-class Dalits who have converted to Sikhism but worship their own leaders as gurus and perhaps also worship saints from lower classes whose hymns are included in the Guru Granth Sahib. Such tensions are inflamed by political rivalries and sometimes erupt into violence. In 2007 and

Baba Virsa Singh

For decades, Baba Virsa Singh (c. 1934–2007) developed farms and communities in India in which people are trying to live by the teachings of the Sikh Gurus. Not only Sikhs but also Hindus, Muslims, and Christians, literate and illiterate, live and work side by side as brothers and sisters there. Baba Virsa Singh himself, the son of a village farmer, had no formal education. From childhood he had an intense yearning for communion with God. He related:

> From childhood, I kept questioning God, "In order to love Jesus, must one become a Christian or just love?" He told me, "It is not necessary to become a Christian. It is necessary to love him."
>
> I asked, "To believe in Moses, does one have to observe any special discipline, or just love?" The divine command came: "Only love." I asked, "Does one have to become a Muslim in order to please Muhammad, or only love?" He said, "One must love." "To believe in Buddha, must one become a monk or a Buddhist?" He replied, "No. To believe in Buddha is to love." God said, "I created human beings. Afterward, human beings created sectarian religions. But I created only human beings."[28]

Intense spirituality is the base of Baba Virsa Singh's communities, which are known collectively as Gobind Sadan (The House of God). Volunteers work hard to raise record crops on previously barren land. The harvests are shared communally and also provide the basis for Gobind Sadan's continual free kitchens (langar) for people of all classes, free medical services, and celebrations of the holy days of all religions. Devotions are carried on around the clock, with everyone from gardeners and pot-washers to governors and professors helping to clean the holy areas and maintain perpetual reading of the Sikh scriptures. Everyone of all ages and conditions is encouraged to do useful work. Thus under Baba Virsa Singh's guidance, a living example has been developed of the power of Guru Nanak's straightforward, nonsectarian spiritual program: Work hard to earn your own honest living, share with others, and always remember God.

Another social effect of the work of Baba Virsa Singh is an easing of the tensions that have arisen between people of different religions. Even the most rigid proponents of their own religions have been gently convinced to open their eyes toward the validity of other faiths. He taught Sikhs that their own scripture repeatedly praises and invokes the "Hindu" gods and goddesses. He taught Hindu extremists that there is no one tradition that can be called "Hinduism" and that to take the name of Rama is to invoke the heights of moral character and selfless service to humanity. He taught Muslims to appreciate the spiritual depths of their religion.

To religious leaders, he highly recommended the method used at Gobind Sadan—celebrating the holy days of all prophets with great enthusiasm—as a way to combat religious intolerance. The blame, he said, lies with religious leaders:

> When religious leaders speak, the issue is not whether they have read books. The question is whether or not they themselves have awakened spiritually. Dharma is very powerful. It transforms people's minds, transforms their lives, and transforms their inner habits. It is only spirituality that changes people.
>
> If priests, pujaris, or granthis are sitting in temples, mosques, churches, or gurdwaras, it does not necessarily mean that they have realized God. They are managers. Religious leaders will know whether they themselves are spiritual or not. Do we have the forgiveness of Jesus, who from the cross prayed, "Forgive them, for they know not what they do"? When the prophets were here, they had no gold-covered buildings. They built a beautiful inner temple where peace prevailed. If we are spiritual, we will be contemplating all prophets, loving their messages, loving their commandments, loving their ethical codes.
>
> Throughout the world, religion has become a great fort made of hatred. All the prophets have taught us otherwise. All prophets, messiahs, and nabis have come in love, and all have in common the same thing: Love.[29]

Another area in which Baba Virsa Singh influenced public life is his effect on government officials. He urged them to attend to the practical needs of the people and to uphold order and justice in society.

Baba Virsa Singh also gave people spiritual hope for a new world order. To a Russian magazine, he explained:

> Truth is always tested. Who tests it? Evil—evil attacks the truth. But truth never stops shining, and evil keeps falling back. Truth's journey is very powerful, with a very strong base. It never wavers. It is a long journey, full of travails, but evil can never suppress the truth.[30]

2009 there were violent conflicts between followers of certain *dera* leaders and mainstream Sikhs over issues such as the publishing of a photo of one such leader apparently dressed like Guru Gobind Singh.

Another issue is authority over the Sikh community. The Sixth Guru started a tradition of sitting on a high platform or takht (throne) in Amritsar opposite the Golden Temple and issuing *hukamnamahs* (edicts) to Sikhs. This place, the Akal Takht (Eternal Throne), remains the highest seat of both worldly and spiritual authority for Sikhs. In time, four more takhts associated with the life of Guru Gobind Singh were recognized as additional seats of authority, as wielded by their *jathedars* (leaders), but the *jathedar* of the Akal Takht is still the most eminent. This system of control over the affairs of the Sikh Panth is being challenged by some Sikhs as contrary to the original spirit of Sikhism. The challengers argue that Sikhism rejects clergy and rigid authorianism in favor of the direct relationship between the devotee, the Guru, and God.

There are also tensions between those Sikhs who favor a more spiritual and universal understanding of their religion and those who interpret it more rigidly and exclusively. From the late nineteenth century onward, some Sikhs have been concerned to assert their distinct identity and try not to be subsumed under the rubric of Hinduism. In this effort, the ecumenical nature of Sikhism was downplayed. There were no forcible attempts to convert anyone else to Sikhism, but Sikhs became proud of their heroic history and tended to turn inward.

The question of "Who is a Sikh?" was dealt with by the Sikh Gurdwaras Act of 1925, which defined a Sikh as "a person who professes the Sikh religion" but then went on to specify that a person claiming to be Sikh could be required to make the following declaration: "I solemnly affirm that I am a Sikh, that I believe in the Guru Granth Sahib, that I believe in the Ten Gurus, and that I have no other religion."[31] The ancient pluralism that had characterized Indian society was thus cast aside in favor of a more Western idea of definite boundaries between religions. The Delhi Gurdwara Act of 1971 made the definition even

Surrounded by a sacred pool, the Golden Temple at Amritsar houses the Guru Granth Sahib. It has a door on each of its four sides, symbolizing its openness to people of all faiths.

more restrictive, adding the specification that only a person with unshorn hair can be considered a Sikh.

One manifestation of the "Sikhs are not Hindus" agenda has been a re-evaluation of the contents of the **Dasam Granth**, writings attributed to Guru Gobind Singh. In some gurdwaras, this volume is reverently placed in the same room as the Guru Granth Sahib and considered the second most sacred scripture of Sikhs. But its contents are controversial, for it contains many positive references to Hindu deities and moreover is sexually explicit in places. Some scholars, therefore, maintain that it was not entirely written by Guru Gobind Singh and speculate that much of it was written by his court poets or even later writers who wanted to discredit Sikhism. This emotionally charged battle continues in books, journals, and Internet postings.

Major conflicts have also arisen over calendar dates for Sikh holidays, with rejection by some factions of the traditional—and somewhat inaccurate—Hindu way of accommodating differences between solar and lunar calendars. Such complex debates get mixed up with politics, with the Akal Takht, the Sikh Gurdwara Management Committee, and the Sant Samaj (a new coalition of contemporary *dera* leaders) at loggerheads. Having their own separate calendar dates for celebrations is for some Sikhs part of a proud identity as a separate and significant world religion.

Several million Sikhs have emigrated from India and settled in other countries, usually for the sake of economic progress. In the diaspora, many Sikhs have attempted to resist assimilation to the surrounding cultures and to raise their children according to their Indian traditions. Many are sent to Sikh camps to learn Punjabi, sacred music traditions, and scriptural readings. Whenever communities of Sikhs have collected in the diaspora, they have tried to build a gurdwara for their own worship services. One of the chief personal issues over assimilation—not only outside India but also within India, in modern society—is the dilemma over keeping long hair and wearing a turban or veil.

In the effort to stem Islamic fundamentalism, some countries are implementing laws against wearing religious garb to schools, so wearing a traditional turban or veil has become problematic for Sikh students. Turbans are also being searched in many airports now as part of routine security measures. Sikh men have also been subjected to crude verbal abuses about their head coverings. The insults are particularly hard to bear since in Sikh tradition, the turban has sacred meaning. Some Sikh men feel that they cannot fit into the modern world while wearing a turban, but their families may feel strongly that they should not break with sacred tradition and put great pressure on them not to cut their hair.

Wearing the **kirpan** (small sword) on a sling openly is also perceived as a problem in some non-Sikh environments, where others would view it with alarm, so some Khalsa initiates wear miniature symbols of the kirpan, comb, and *khanda* (symbolic double-edged sword) on a necklace, while nonetheless wearing their drawstring underwear and keeping their long hair bound under a turban or veil. In the wake of terrorist attacks, many Sikhs in the diaspora who kept their traditional dress and long hair with beards and turbans have found themselves the mistaken victims of hate crimes, sometimes because they were confused with Muslims. In August 2012, a man with ties to white supremacist groups killed six people and wounded four others in a shooting at the gurdwara in Oak Creek, Wisconsin.

In the wake of such incidents, the Sikh community has found it necessary to explain the religion publicly, and speakers are stressing its universality, democratic nature, and spirit of religious tolerance. Proponents of the traditional symbols were encouraged by a bill unanimously passed in California in 2009 by the state legislature mandating training of policemen about the religious meaning of the kirpan. Positive public-relations and education campaigns are also being waged by groups such as the Sikh Coalition and United Sikhs, who enlist Sikhs as volunteers and donors for disaster relief, economic development, and inter-religious harmony projects.

LIVING SIKHISM

An Interview with Sheena Kandhari

 There are now many Sikhs living outside India but trying to maintain their religious traditions wherever they are. Sheena Kandhari was born in Kenya to Sikh parents of Indian origin and now lives with her family in London, where she has completed a doctorate in Sikh Studies. She recounts:

Growing up in Mombasa as a child in the 1970s–80s, there was only a small Sikh community of maybe 150 families. There was only one gurdwara in the town. We used to go there as a family quite regularly. As children, we were excited to go as we would get to meet our friends and play around the compound. We were never forced to sit in the Darbar Sahib [room of Guru Granth Sahib] because we did not understand the language and what was being said during the service.

Nowadays there are numerous Sikh Youth Camps where children are encouraged to learn about their faith. But in our days, there wasn't any such thing. Whatever little activity that was available at the gurdwara, my parents encouraged us to participate in. For example, there were essay-writing competitions on Sikh history, participation in kirtan, and learning the Gurmukhi script [in which Punjabi is written]. We didn't have many Sikh friends, as the community was really small.

Eight years ago my family shifted to London, where the Sikh community is much bigger and more widespread. We try to go to gurdwara once a week as a family, so that we can do some seva [volunteer service] and listen to kirtan and be in the sadh sangat [community of followers]. There are many gurdwaras here, so we have a choice as to which one to attend.

Every day I spend two and a half hours reading the daily Sikh prayers and other scriptural passages. It has been recommended in the Sikh Code of Discipline that 10 percent of our time should be spent in contemplation of God and/or His service, so I try my best to fulfill this. I find that by doing path [reading the prayers] I have great peace of mind. I am able to go about my daily tasks with a positive attitude. I started doing path from the age of ten. It has become a part of me. The human soul is a tiny spark of God's light which must reunite with God. This is the ultimate aim for every human being, and the Sikh scriptures provide valuable life lessons on how to attain this union.

I also encourage those around me who do not do any path to do so as they will gain the magical effect from it. With today's technology, there are many applications for the cell phone and computers which have the path on them. This gives access and provides those new to the path arena the ability to listen to the correct pronunciation and follow the meanings.

Hair is a big issue for some of us diaspora Sikhs [since Sikh tradition forbids cutting hair]. Growing up in Kenya I never cut my hair. However, when I came to the UK, the water here was really hard. This caused a lot of damage to my hair, which began to fall out gradually. I was recommended to trim it, which would make the hair follicles stronger. At the time I was bewildered, as it was unquestionable to cut my hair. But circumstances changed my opinion about it. I first started with just a trim and then over the years have experimented with various hairstyles. At present I now have long hair again, and have an occasional trim when necessary. My brothers have never cut their hair, and they both wear pagris [turbans]. However, for a female Sikh, cutting of hair is more common.

Regarding the outward symbols of the Sikh faith, it is not necessary to comply with all of them as it may be difficult to do so in present-day society. As long as the individual has a clean, pure soul, that is what is of importance. You may find a proper kesdhari [with full hair] or even amritdhari [Khalsa-initiated] Sikh who may not have a clean heart and has many vices. On the other hand, you may come across a Sikh with cut hair who has more virtues in his character. So now the symbolism of the Khalsa Sikh may not be held in such high regard as at the time it was first introduced by Guru Gobind Singh Ji when he established the Khalsa Panth.

I am now in my late thirties and would like to get married and settle down. Both my family and I prefer that I marry a Sikh. It is important to find someone from a similar background who has similar values. Coming from a religious Sikh family, the Sikh identity has a lot of meaning to me.

I can emphatically say that Sikhism is a universal religion and not just a religion for the Sikhs. The universal kinship of humankind found in Guru Granth Sahib, which is the living Guru of the Sikhs, serves as a model for harmony and world peace. It shines with pristine purity in its originality, authenticity, and the love of all true lovers of God, irrespective of their religion, caste, color, creed, and status.[32]

Controversies concerning Sikhism also persist in the academic world. Some Western scholars of Sikhism have come to conclusions that are rejected by many Sikh scholars as being academically unsound, as well as offensive to the faithful. These conclusions include the work of the New Zealand scholar W. H. McLeod (1932–2009), who asserted that stories about some of the journeys of Guru Nanak are fictitious and questioned the traditional history of the creation of the Khalsa.

Without going so far as to deny the uniqueness or continuing tradition of Sikhism, many contemporary Sikh and non-Sikh scholars are appreciating the message of the Sikh Gurus as supporting the underlying unity of people of all religions. Baba Virsa Singh (see Box, p. 448) expressed the universality of the Gurus' teachings:

> That which we call dharma, that which we call Sikhism, that which we call the religion of Guru Nanak, that which we call the command of Guru Gobind Singh is this: That we should not forget God even for one breath.
> Guru Nanak prepared a lovely ship, in which all the seats were to be given to those who were doing both manual work and spiritual practice.
> The religion of Guru Gobind Singh, of Guru Nanak was not given to those of one organization, one village, one country. Their enlightened vision was for the whole cosmos. Guru Granth Sahib is not for some handful of people. It is for everyone.[33]

In the words of Guru Gobind Singh:

> Same are the temple and the mosque
> And same are the forms of worship therein.
> All human beings are one though apparently many,
> Realize, therefore, the essential unity of mankind.[34]

Key terms

amrit Nectar made with sugar and water, symbolizing the sweetness of compassion.
Dasam Granth The collected writings attributed to Guru Gobind Singh.
Five Ks The symbols worn by Khalsa members.
gurdwara A Sikh place of worship.
Guru Granth Sahib (Adi Granth) The sacred scripture compiled by the Sikh Gurus.
Jaap Sahib The second morning prayer of Sikhs, written by Guru Gobind Singh.
janam-sakhis Traditional biographies, especially stories of the life of Guru Nanak.
JapJi The first morning prayer of Sikhs, composed by Guru Nanak.
Khalsa Order of Sikhs who have undergone special initiation and observe a strict code of conduct.
kirpan Small sword worn by Khalsa initiates.
kirtan Singing of sacred hymns from Guru Granth Sahib.
langar Community meal for all, regardless of caste or position.
Nam The holy Name of God, as recited by Sikhs.
Panth The religious community in Sikhism.
sangat A Sikh congregation.
Udasi An ascetic Sikh order.

Suggested reading

Cole, W. Owen, and Piara Singh Sambhi, *The Sikhs: Their Religious Beliefs and Practices*, second edition, Sussex, UK: Academic Press, 1995. A clearly written survey of the Sikh tradition.

Duggal, K. S., *Secular Perceptions in Sikh Faith*, New Delhi: National Book Trust, revised edition, 1999. Clear and touching presentation of aspects of Sikh history and belief promoting universalist thought.

Jakobsh, Doris R., ed., *Sikhism and Women: History, Texts, and Experience*, New Delhi: Oxford University Press, 2010. Essays by Sikh and non-Sikh scholars on a variety of women's issues in Sikhism.

Macauliffe, Max Arthur, *The Sikh Religion: Its Gurus, Sacred Writings, and Authors*, Oxford: Oxford University Press, reprinted in Delhi: S. Chand and Company, 1963. The most respected general account of Sikhism in English, even though its author was not Sikh.

McLeod, W. H., *Exploring Sikhism: Aspects of Sikh Identity, Culture, and Thought*, Oxford: Oxford University Press, 2000. An influential non-Sikh scholar brings historical method and skepticism to bear on traditional Sikh beliefs.

McLeod, W. H., trans. and ed., *Textual Sources for the Study of Sikhism*, Totowa, New Jersey: Barnes and Noble Books, 1984 and Manchester: Manchester University Press, 1984. Interesting compilation of Sikh literature, from selections from the Adi Granth to rules for the Khalsa initiation ceremony, all with explanatory comments.

Shackle, Christopher, and Arvind Mandair, eds, *Teachings of the Sikh Gurus: Selections from the Sikh Scriptures*, Oxford and New York: Routledge, 2005. Translations of selected texts from the Guru Granth Sahib and the Dasam Granth with helpful introductions.

Singh, Dharam, *Sikhism: Norm and Form*, New Delhi: Vision and Venture, 1997. Discussion of Sikhism as a vision of a new social order: a classless and casteless brotherhood of enlightened humans.

Singh, Guru Gobind, *Jaap Sahib*, English translation by Surendra Nath, New Delhi: Gobind Sadan Publications, 1997. Powerful praises of the formless, ultimately unknowable God, without reference to any particular religion.

Singh, Dr. Gopal, *A History of the Sikh People 1469–1978*, New Delhi: World Sikh University Press, 1979. Thorough and scholarly history of the Sikhs to modern times.

Singh, Harbans, ed., *The Encyclopedia of Sikhism*, Patiala: Punjabi University, 1992–1999. Four volumes on all aspects of Sikhism, prepared by leading scholars.

Singh, Khushwant, trans., *Hymns of Guru Nanak*, New Delhi: Orient Longmans Ltd, 1969. Stories about Guru Nanak's life and selections from his sacred songs.

Singh, Manmohan, trans., *Sri Guru Granth Sahib*, eight vols, Amritsar: Shromani Gurdwara Parbandhak Committee, 1962. A good English translation of the Sikh sacred scripture.

Singh, Dr. Mohinder, *Guru Granth Sahib: The Guru Eternal*, New Delhi: Himalayan Books, 2008. A splendidly illustrated history and analysis of the Guru Granth Sahib.

Singh, Nikky-Guninder Kaur, *The Birth of the Khalsa: A Feminist Re-Memory of Sikh Identity*, Albany: State University of New York Press, 2005. Unique feminist interpretations of the birth and significance of the Khalsa.

Singh, Nikky-Guninder Kaur, *The Name of My Beloved: Devotional Poetry from the Guru Granth and the Dasam Granth*, San Francisco: HarperSanFrancisco, 1995. Daily devotional hymns in contemporary English translation.

Singh, Nikki-Guninder Kaur, *Sikhism*, London: I. B. Tauris, 2011. Engaging introduction to Sikh history, art, and contemporary issues.

Singh, Trilochan, Jodh Singh, Kapur Singh, Bawa Harkishen Singh, and Khushwant Singh, trans., *The Sacred Writings of the Sikhs*, New York: Samuel Weiser, 1973. Selections from the Adi Granth and hymns by Guru Gobind Singh in English translation.

11.1 Describe the life and teachings of Guru Nanak

What Sikhs believe about the life of Guru Nanak (1469–1539) is based not so much on historic records as on *janam-sakhis*—traditional stories about his life. He was born in the Punjab, an area of northern India that at that time was inhabited by both Muslims and Hindus. When he was thirty, his life was reportedly transformed after immersion in a river, and after that he began traveling through India, the Himalayas, Afghanistan, Sri Lanka, and Arabia, teaching commitment to practical faith as opposed to external adherence to religious formalities. He later settled with his family as a farmer in the new community he developed at Kartarpur.

Guru Nanak emphasized three central teachings as the straight path to God: working hard in society to earn one's own honest living (rather than withdrawing into asceticism and begging); sharing from one's earnings with those who are needy; and remembering God at all times as the only Doer, the only Giver.

11.2 Summarize the development of Sikhism during the time of the Gurus

There were eventually ten Sikh Gurus, all of whom were thought to be transmitting the spiritual light of Nanak. The Third and Fourth Gurus, Amar Das (1479–1574) and Ram Das (1534–1581), developed organized structures for the growing Sikh Panth (community). Ram Das founded the holy city of Amritsar, within which the Fifth Guru, Guru Arjun Dev (1563–1606) built the religion's most sacred shrine, the Golden Temple. The Fifth Guru also compiled the sacred scriptures of the Sikhs, the Adi Granth, now known as the Guru Granth Sahib.

To protect Sikhism against the Mughals and to defend the weak of all religions against tyranny, the Sixth Guru, Hargobind (1595–1644), established a Sikh army. The Tenth Guru, Guru Gobind Singh (1666–1708), called his initiates Khalsa (Pure Ones), a community pledged to a special code of personal discipline. They were sworn to wear five distinctive symbols of their dedication (Five Ks): unshorn hair, a comb to keep it tidy, drawstring underbreeches for modesty, a small sword in a sheath, and a steel bracelet. Guru Gobind Singh ended the line of bodily succession to Guruship by transferring his authority to the Adi Granth and the panth.

11.3 Outline what happened to Sikhism in India after the death of Guru Gobind Singh

As the Mughal Empire began to disintegrate in the eighteenth century and Afghans invaded India, the Sikhs fought for their own identity and sovereignty, as well as to protect freedom of religion in the country. They began establishing small states within the Punjab, and at the beginning of the nineteenth century these states were united under Maharaja Ranjit Singh, forming the Sikh Empire. This empire lasted only half a century, for the British, already in power throughout much of the rest of the India, subdued it in 1849. The British left India in 1947, and the new nations of India and Pakistan were created. This partition profoundly affected Sikhs, with approximately two-thirds of the Punjab becoming part of West Pakistan. Two million Sikhs living there were forced to migrate to the eastern side of the border under conditions of extreme hardship, leaving behind land, possessions, and some of their most sacred sites.

11.4 Identify the central beliefs of Sikhism

Sikhism's major focus is loving devotion to God, whom Sikhs recognize as the same One who is worshiped by many different names around the world. The light of God (*Sat*, truth) is thought to shine fully through the Guru, the perfect master, and is also present in the Guru Granth Sahib (sacred scripture compiled by the Gurus). Sikhism does not claim to have the only path to God, nor does it try to convert others to its way. It has beliefs in common with Hinduism (such as karma and reincarnation) and also with Islam (such as monotheism).

The Sikh ideal is to realize God within the world, through everyday practices of work, worship, and charity, of sacrificing love. All people are to be treated equally, and considerable respect is given to women. The ultimate goal of life is mystical union with the Divine. Sikhs believe in protecting religious freedom, but there are stringent conditions for "righteous war."

11.5 Explain how the teachings of Sikhism are put into practice

To be a true Sikh is to live a disciplined life of surrender and devotion to God, with hours of daily prayers, continual inner repetition of the Name of God (Nam), and detachment from negative, worldly mind-states. Morning and evening prayers take about two hours a day, starting in the very early morning.

In addition to recitation and prayers, passages from the Guru Granth Sahib are chanted or sung as melodies (kirtan).

Standards set by Guru Gobind Singh for the Khalsa are so high that few people can really meet them. In addition to reciting the Name of God, the ones who are Khalsa must abstain from drugs, alcohol and tobacco, renounce anger and not criticize anybody. They fight on the front line against injustice and must vanquish the five evils (lust, anger, greed, attachment, and ego) in themselves.

Equality and social welfare are important teachings in Sikhism, and to help create a new social order with no caste distinctions, the Sikh Gurus created langar, a community meal that is freely offered to all who come. This takes place at a gurdwara, the building where the Guru Granth Sahib is enshrined and public worship takes place. During this worship all strata of people sit together. At least one tenth of a Sikh's income has to be contributed towards the welfare of the community.

11.6 Discuss the tensions and challenges faced by Sikhism in India and the diaspora

In India, Sikhs and Hindus lived side by side in mutual tolerance until 1978 to 1992, when violent clashes occurred. Sikh separatists wanted to establish an independent Sikh state with commitment to strong religious observances and protection for Sikhs from oppression and exploitation by the much larger Hindu community. Historical tensions have also arisen within Sikhism as it has been institutionalized and used by some factions for their own ends. Self-styled Sikh "saints" or "gurus" have set themselves up as spiritual guides, antagonizing mainstream Sikhs, and there is also growing tension between orthodox Sikhs and *deras* (communities) composed of largely lower-class Dalits who have converted to Sikhism but worship with their own leaders as gurus. There has been conflict too about the system of control over the affairs of the Sikh Panth and calendar dates for Sikh holidays.

Several million Sikhs have emigrated from India and settled in other countries such as the United States, Canada, Britain, Malaysia, Singapore, Kenya, United Arab Emirates, and Italy, usually for the sake of economic progress. In the diaspora, many Sikhs have attempted to resist assimilation to the surrounding cultures. Recent challenges concern the dilemma over keeping long hair and wearing a turban or veil, particularly in the wake of terrorist attacks and the implementation by some countries of laws against wearing religious garb to school.

CHAPTER 12

NEW RELIGIOUS MOVEMENTS

"We are not anti-religion; we are anti-crazy
nonsense done in the name of religion."
Church of the Flying Spaghetti Monster[1]

12.1 *Differentiate between a "sect" and a "cult"*

12.2 *Discuss the role that may be played by a charismatic leader in the development of a new religious movement*

12.3 *Identify three contemporary new religious movements that are offshoots of older religions*

12.4 *Compare and contrast several movements that combine differing beliefs of traditional religions*

12.5 *Summarize the key belief of universalism and give an example of a universalist movement*

12.6 *Outline some of the aspects furthered by new religious movements arising from social trends*

12.7 *Explain the reasons behind the opposition to some new religious movements*

12.8 *Analyze the secular factors that predispose a new religious movement to last*

The history of religions is one of continual change. Each religion changes over time, new religions appear, and some older traditions disappear. Times of rapid social change are particularly likely to spawn new religious movements, for people seek the security of the spiritual amidst worldly chaos. In the period since World War II, thousands of new religious groups have sprung up around the world. In sub-Saharan Africa, there are now more than 7,000 different religions; every Nigerian town of several thousand people has up to fifty or sixty different kinds of religion.[2] In Japan, an estimated thirty percent of the population belongs to one of hundreds of new religious movements. Imported versions of Asian traditions, such as Hinduism and Buddhism, have made many new converts in areas such as North America, Europe, and Russia, where they are seen as "new religions." Internet websites and social-networking sites have greatly increased the speed with which new religious movements can evolve and spread.

To move into a new religious movement may be a fleeting experience or it may signal a deep change in one's life. In religion, as in other life commitments such as marriage, there are potential benefits in dedication and obedience. Many religions, including the largest world religions, teach self-denial and surrender as cardinal virtues that help to vanquish the ego and allow one to approach ultimate reality. The question for a spiritual person is where to place one's faith.

Social context of new religious movements
What is the difference between a "sect" and a "cult"?

New religious movements are often popularly referred to as "cults" or "sects." These words have specific, neutral meanings: a **cult** arises outside other traditions, while a **sect** is a splinter group or a subgroup associated with a larger tradition. Both words have sometimes been used imprecisely and pejoratively to distinguish new religions from older ones, each of which already claims to be the best or only way. The label "new religious movement" seems more neutral and is widely used, particularly in academic circles, to avoid such negative connotations. However, the word "new" is itself imprecise, for many of these groups have a rather lengthy history and have survived long after the death of the original founder.

Much of the research into new religious movements has been undertaken by sociologists, for they are interested in the processes by which new religions arise, attract members, deal with the death of their founders, and then organize themselves into continuing religious traditions that may gradually enter the social mainstream. Several twentieth-century sociological theories looked at the difference between "Churches" and "sects." If seen as ends of a continuum, "Churches" are more established religious traditions; sects or cults are newer and more marginal. In the typology suggested by Professors Rodney Stark and William S. Bainbridge, a Church typically accepts and accommodates itself to the society in which it operates. A sect, by contrast, rejects its social environment as "worldly" and "unbelieving," that is, opposed to its beliefs. Sects usually have previous ties to a religious organization but have broken off from it, often in the attempt to return to what they perceive as its pristine original form. Cults are independent religious traditions, but they may also be in conflict with the surrounding society.

According to Stark and Bainbridge's typology, cults can be further defined by the degree to which they influence their followers' relationship to society.

Students in Moscow learn ancient levitation techniques from India.

What they call "audience cults" do not require conversion, and allow their followers great flexibility—they may sample many religious movements and attend workshops here and there, making their own choices about what to believe and do. New Age groups tend to fall in this category. California-based Dr. Deepak Chopra, for instance, has such a large following that more than ten million copies of his books such as *The Seven Spiritual Laws of Success* have been sold in English and his workshops on subjects such as physical healing, emotional well-being, and spiritual growth are often sold out. However, those who practice his teachings based on ancient Indian ayurvedic principles plus psychological "self-knowledge" do not become members of a distinct religious group.

"Client cults" offer some kind of service, usually some kind of therapy. Involvement with the organization may become deeper and more

Actor Tom Cruise speaks at the inauguration of a Scientology church in Madrid.

socially defining over time. Scientology, which is based on the writings of L. Ron Hubbard (1911–1986), is considered such a group. The initial agenda is therapeutic: "auditing" in order to clear the mind of the negative effects of past experiences and past lives. But once this process begins, clients learn of more complex levels of involvement, and other members may become their primary social group. Auditing often leads to membership in the Church of Scientology. This institution is based on Hubbard's idea that the mind is directed by what he called the *thetan* (self). Hubbard taught that the *thetan* is trapped in the material world but that its freedom can be obtained through a gradual process of detachment. Step by step, following precise directions, the *thetan* can move up "The Bridge" to "total freedom." Higher levels of involvement in this process are said to confer secret wisdom, or gnosis, and the freed "Operating Thetan" begins to have out-of-body experiences. "Advanced Organizations" have been established to offer these higher levels of experience, culminating in the "Sea Org," which consists of members who have committed themselves to work for Scientology by signing the "billion-year contract." They move to one of the Sea Org centers throughout the world, where they undertake a disciplined program of work and study and attempt to abide by a strict code of conduct, "to help get ethics in on this planet and the universe, which is the basic purpose of the Sea Org."[3] Those reaching this Sea Org level—which has been compared to monastic orders in Christianity or Buddhism—are a small subset of the reportedly millions of clients who register for the auditing sessions with Scientology. The organization thus remains primarily what Stark and Bainbridge call a "client cult."

What Stark and Bainbridge call a "cult movement" is a full-fledged organization that requires conversion and does not allow dual allegiances to other organizations. Some offer a total way of life, with community-based lodging and work as well as group worship. Commitment to this way of life ranges from partial, with people still involved with family and friends outside the movement, to total, in which they are largely cut off from the wider social environment. Groups anticipating an imminent time of great changes in the world may take this path of separation.

When members of a new religious movement anticipate that the end times or new world order are coming soon, they tend to be regarded as eccentrics by the rest of their society. To maintain their faith, they may isolate themselves from mainstream society and try to prepare for the coming changes. Alternatively, those who anticipate the end of the present world may accept social scorn and try to share their prophecies with others in order to save them from the anticipated coming destruction or prepare them for the new world order.

The expectation of major world changes appears in many established religions, including Hinduism, Zoroastrianism, Judaism, Christianity, Islam, and some indigenous religions. Hindus, for instance, anticipate that the current depraved age of Kali Yuga will be followed by the return of Sat Yuga (when dharma will again prevail). This anticipation leads periodically to the formation of movements that preach that the time of great changes is imminent. In Christianity, the last book in the Bible, Revelation, predicts an **apocalypse**, or dramatic end of the present world. Revelation foretells a titanic war at Armageddon between the forces of Satan and the forces of God, with great destruction, followed by the **millennium**, a 1,000-year period of special holiness in which Christ rules the earth. Some nineteenth-century Christians developed the idea of the **rapture**, using Paul's letter to the Thessalonians (1 Thess. 4:17) to say that Christians would be caught up in clouds to meet Jesus when he returned to earth. This idea has been revived in our times, with phenomena such as a series of novels entitled *Left Behind*, which were published around the turn of the millennium, purporting to describe the end times in which true believers are taken instantly to heaven, leaving behind a chaotic world in which the Secretary-General of the United Nations turns out to be the Antichrist. Apocalyptic expectations were rife on the eve of the year 2000. Some groups anticipated a final occasion for enlightenment in 2012, because the ancient Maya calendar ends on 21 December 2012.

UFO cults have added their own anticipations of imminent changes. Raëlians, for instance, believe that wise extraterrestrial beings collectively called "Elohim" (an ancient plural name for the supreme deity as "mighty ones," occurring in the Hebrew Bible) came here and created life on earth. With scientific advances we will soon be able to travel to other planets and, like Elohim, create new life. The Raëlians' goal is to prepare humanity for an imminent encounter with the extraterrestrials, an event that a French Raëlian says is "likely to be the most important event in human history."[4]

Charismatic leadership

What role may be played by a charismatic leader in the development of a new religious movement?

Formation of new religious movements often begins in the same way as many established religions: A charismatic figure emerges who develops a dedicated following of people who regard him or her as their spiritual teacher (such as the Buddha), prophet (such as Muhammad), or messiah (such as Jesus). Huge movements have developed around such beings who are thought to be divinely inspired. From time to time, new figures arise and attract a lot of followers, such as the spiritual leaders Rev. Sun Myung Moon and Mata Amritanandamayi. They have developed far-flung and diversified service and propagation organizations, which may help their movements to survive their own physical deaths.

Sociological research suggests that after a charismatic founder dies, those groups who are able to routinize that charisma into the authority of a religious institution survive, and may later produce other charismatic persons. When an institution has grown or allied with other similar institutions to encompass a large part of the civil community, it may begin behaving more like what Stark and Bainbridge call a "Church" rather than a "sect." In general, Churches take responsibility for the larger community and respond to its needs; sects take responsibility for themselves and for their own members.

Unification Movement

The Unification Movement was founded by the charismatic leader Sun Myung Moon (1920–2012), who proclaimed himself and his second wife, Hak Ja Han, to be Messiahs. Moon was born in 1920 in what is now North Korea into a family of farmers. At that time, Christians met underground, hiding first from the Japanese occupation authorities and then from the Communists. Many of the Christian Churches had strong messianic expectations. Moon's parents converted to Christianity, and around Easter 1935, while he was praying in the mountains, Moon said that Jesus appeared to him in a vision. Jesus reportedly told him that it had not been God's desire that he be crucified, for his mission on earth was left unfinished. By Moon's account, Jesus asked him to complete the task of establishing God's kingdom on earth.

To this end, Moon developed the "Unification Principle," according to which God created the universe in order to manifest true love, and the human family is considered the primary institution for the growth of love. Based on spiritual and moral education in the family, people are to live for the sake of others in all situations. However, according to Moon's theology, humans do not live according to God's design; selfishness prevails in human relationships and in relationships between ethnic groups and nations. The misuse of love through illicit sex has led to the "human Fall." From the time of Adam and Eve, false love has been passed down from generation to generation, infecting the whole human race.

Rev. Moon proposed that God has been grieving ever since the Fall of His children, Adam and Eve, but that, as the "Third Adam," Moon brought Restoration of the ideal, partially restored by Jesus (the "Second Adam"):

> God is almighty. It was not due to any shortcoming or lack of ability that He has been imprisoned in great pain and has endured immense suffering behind the scenes of history. Rather, there are provisions in the Principle of Restoration, which He has not been free to disclose, that called him to wait with forbearance until Adam and Eve's positions, lost at the human Fall, were recovered through the appearance of the perfected "Second Adam."[5]

Moon began to teach publicly in North Korea, where communist leaders were seeking to quash religious activity. He was arrested, tortured, and thrown into a snowdrift. After his followers nursed him back to health, he continued preaching in public, was arrested again, and sentenced to hard labor in a concentration camp. Moon was liberated when American forces bombed the prison.

In the 1970s, the Unification Church staged a series of well-publicized rallies in the United States and saw a rapid growth in membership. Middle-class youths put aside their careers, gave up their worldly possessions, broke off from their girlfriends and boyfriends, and devoted themselves to the religious path. They saw their sacrificial and ascetic way of life as a rejection of the materialistic and hedonistic American lifestyle. However, alarmed parents accused the church of brainwashing their adult children. The church was viewed with suspicion by the established Christian Churches and vilified by the political left because of its anti-communist activities. In 1982, Rev. Moon was subjected to criminal prosecution and imprisoned over a tax liability of $7,300, but the ruling was criticized by the National Council of Churches as a denial of religious liberty and a "miscarriage of justice" since several other religions could have been found equally guilty, and the ruling was overturned by the Supreme Court.

Despite controversy and mockery, the Unification Movement began engaging in large-scale international activities reportedly designed to transform the world. For instance, the Unification-sponsored Inter-Religious Federation for World Peace and the Religious Youth Service have created international inter-religious dialogues among scholars of religion and political leaders, and service projects in many countries. Such expensive projects are financially supported by members' door-to-door sales and their establishment of business companies such as industrial-scale fishing ventures. The Unification Church became extremely financially successful.

A unique aspect of the movement's work is massive wedding ceremonies in which thousands of couples matched by the movement or already-wed couples wanting to dedicate themselves to "live for the sake of others" and "create an ideal family which contributes to world peace" were simultaneously "blessed" by Rev. and Mrs. Moon. With Rev. Moon having announced himself as the "Third Adam," Unificationists view these mass weddings as a movement to create one human family, with couples of all races and nationalities being "engrafted" onto "God's lineage of true love." In February 2014, Mrs. Moon presided over a wedding of 2,500 couples in South Korea, and another 20,000 couples who participated online. Rev. and Mrs. Moon also undertook global speaking tours,

Rev. and Mrs. Sun Myung Moon bless couples in a mass wedding ceremony.

giving the same prepared speeches in many countries to announce that they were the True Parents of all humankind.

In addition to Rev. Moon's self-avowed transmissions of revelations from Jesus, it is also said that Mrs. Moon's deceased mother and Rev. and Mrs. Moon's son, who died in a car crash, are assisting Unificationists from the spirit world, through the help of a medium. Hundreds of thousands of members have participated in workshops in which people cite miraculous physical healings and visions of spirits leaving their bodies. The spirits are then said to be given training in the Unification Principle and duly "blessed." There are also liberation ceremonies for ancestors and even historical "infamous personages," such as Hitler, Lenin, and Stalin. A Unification spokesman reports that they have been "blessed as the representatives of all wicked people, thereby opening the gate for the 'liberation of Hell.'"[6]

Among his many projects to "build the kingdom of Heaven on earth," Rev. Moon bought and renovated an inner-city university on the seashore in Bridgeport, Connecticut, and provided funding until 2002. The University of Bridgeport now serves an ethnically diverse body of students from eighty countries and specializes in career-oriented programs. Like the participants in other projects founded by Rev. Moon, these students are not typically Unification members. Moon's charismatic leadership was kept in the background. At conferences such as the Assembly of the World's Religions, the World Media Conference, and the International Conference on the Unity of Sciences, he or his wife appeared perhaps only once to present his philosophy, and many in attendance would not agree with it.

Rev. Moon preached unification, but not in the sense of ignoring all differences. His theology and such aspects as his announcement of support from the spirit world—including the 2001 claim that both Jesus and Muhammad have recognized Moon as the Messiah—antagonize Christian Churches and Islam. In addition to being attacked by Christian anti-cult groups, the Unification movement as it matures is encountering issues common to the evolution of religious groups. Problems became evident concerning succession as Rev. Moon tried to organize the future of his movement. In the mid-1990s, when the Moons' eldest son demonstrated his interest in media and communications rather than Church leadership, their next living son—Preston—was trained and given leadership of much of the movement's activities. In 2008, when the eldest son passed away at a young age, Preston expected to lead the movement as a whole, including its spiritual dimensions. Instead, the Moons appointed their youngest son, Sean

(Hyung Jin Nim), to represent the position and guidance of "True Parents." Since Rev. Moon's death, there has been controversy within the family and the Unification movement as a whole over questions of succession, but Mrs. Moon has assumed leadership.

Sathya Sai Baba

Another charismatic leader with a huge following was Sathya Sai Baba of India (1926–2011). International crowds coming for his darshan (contact with the divine) became so large that spaces were allotted according to a lottery system.

Sathya Sai Baba claimed to be the reincarnation of Shirdi Sai Baba, a saint who was greatly loved by people of all religions, and furthermore claimed that he was an Avatar, an earthly manifestation of the divine. According to biographical material written by devotees, his mother believed he was divinely conceived when a "big ball of blue light"[7] rolled toward her and seemed to enter her body. When the boy was fourteen, he was reportedly stung by a large scorpion, after which he went into silence broken occasionally by spiritual songs and discourses, weeping or laughing. Spiritual phenomena, his personal magnetism, and his claims of being Shirdi Sai Baba drew people to him. His center in Puttaparthi became a world pilgrimage center including a massive ashram, an educational system from primary schools to a free accredited university with three campuses, a museum of world religions, a planetarium, indoor and outdoor stadiums, free super-specialty hospitals, a railway station, and an airport. Sathya Sai Baba gave darshan daily to hordes of followers, moving among them to accept letters and materialize objects such as rings, necklaces, watches, or sacred ash in his hand to give them; he would choose some for private interviews about matters in their personal lives. His followers also claim that he manifested things in their homes far away, such as turmeric powder, holy ash, holy water, Shiva lingams, fruits, and gems. Many other miracles are attributed to him, such as controlling the weather, changing the color of his clothing, disappearing physically, appearing in two places at the same time, bringing a dead man back to life, and healing people. Such apparent spiritual magic is not unique in India, but it added to his charismatic appeal. He refused to allow scientists to study his materializations of objects, so he was subject to accusations that he was simply a magician. He himself said that the miracles were trivial compared to "my glory and majesty,

When Sathya Sai Baba died in 2011, many top Indian officials came to his death ceremonies. Here the case bearing his body is being draped with the Indian flag before his cremation.

as a mosquito is in size and strength to the elephant upon which it squats."[8] On another occasion he said, "I teach that no distinction should be made between the names Rama, Krishna, Ishwara, Sai—for they are all My names."[9]

Despite attributing Godhead to himself, Sathya Sai Baba did not claim to be starting a new religion, but rather preached the simple universal message of truth, righteousness, nonviolence, love, and peace. His Sai Organization has study circles around the world and runs values-based free schools, medical institutions, digital radio networks, and large-scale projects to provide drinking water to drought-prone areas of India. Its centers also encourage their members to provide selfless service in their communities through projects such as food banks, feeding of the homeless, tree planting, park cleanups, medical camps, blood donation, and collecting old spectacles to be donated to the poor. Sathya Sai Baba's reputation for charitable work was nonetheless marred after his death by the discovery of millions of dollars worth of cash, gold, and silver in his private residence. There have been some allegations of sexual abuse as well, but Sathya Sai Baba was never formally charged.

Offshoots of older religions

Which contemporary new religious movements are offshoots of older religions?

Since newer offshoots of older religions are often sufficiently different from the parent religion to be considered new religious movements—whether they regard themselves as such or not—we will examine three contemporary examples below: the Mormon Church, Jehovah's Witnesses, and Radhasoami.

Mormon Church

The chief feature of the Mormon Church, more formally known as the Church of Jesus Christ of Latter-day Saints, that distinguishes it from the many variations of mainstream Christianity is that Mormons believe not only in the Bible but also in another scripture, the Book of Mormon. Mormons believe that in 1822, under angelic guidance, Joseph Smith found the book in New York State, engraved on golden plates. The Book of Mormon purports to be the account of several of the lost tribes of Israel, who crossed the ocean to become the ancestors of the American Indians, and the appearance of Jesus to them in the Americas after his death and resurrection. Mormon was one of the faithful who is believed to have survived tribal conflict and managed to write down the teachings about Jesus in the Americas for posterity. In 3 Nephi of the Book of Mormon, for instance, it is written that Jesus appeared to the Nephites as "a Man descending out of heaven; and he was clothed in a white robe; and he came down and stood in the midst of them." Jesus reportedly gave them teachings very similar to the Sermon on the Mount from the New Testament, and urged them to practice baptism by immersion and not to quarrel over doctrine.

Convinced of the authenticity of the Book of Mormon, followers of Joseph Smith moved from one place to another to escape persecution and try to build a "New Jerusalem," "the land of Zion." With much effort, they built a great city in Illinois that they called Nauvoo, Hebrew for "beautiful place," and began to develop some political power, but then Joseph Smith was assassinated by angry area residents. In the struggle for succession, several separate groups of Latter-day Saints developed, the largest of which was led by Brigham Young (1801–1877) to Salt Lake City, Utah, to build "Zion in the Wilderness" and restore what the Mormons consider true Christianity, as opposed to the **apostasy** (abandonment of principles) that they think characterizes the Christian Churches.

The Mormon Church now reports fifteen million followers worldwide. Its members control great material wealth and also exercise considerable political influence in the United States, especially in Utah; the 2012 Republican

Mormons have become politically powerful and well established, and the Mormon Tabernacle Choir in Salt Lake City, Utah, is world-famous.

presidential candidate, Mitt Romney, is a member of the Mormon Church. The Mormon Church's success is perhaps due partly to the efforts of its 65,000 volunteer missionaries (usually young men giving two years of their lives), and partly to the appeal of its emphasis on clean living and strong family values in contrast to the prevailing Western culture. In a recent "Proclamation to the World," the President and Council of the Twelve Apostles of The Church of Jesus Christ of Latter-day Saints wrote, "We warn that the disintegration of the family will bring upon individuals, communities, and nations the calamities foretold by ancient and modern prophets."[10]

All Mormon men are ordained to the priesthood, and authority resides in fathers as the heads of the family households. Bishop Thomas Thorkelson from California explains:

> *The father at the head of his household holds the priesthood of God. That father can baptize his child when the child reaches the age of accountability. When the child gets sick, the father can heal it. When the children go off to school, the father gives them a blessing just like Abraham blessed his sons. He is the patriarch of his family and lays his hands upon their heads and gives them a blessing.*
>
> *The Church also teaches that a father should periodically interview each of his children. As holder of the priesthood, the father calls his children in and they kneel down in prayer, and he asks for discernment as he talks with his kids. He talks with them about everything in their lives. If they are old enough, they talk about dating, about their relationships with the opposite sex. They talk about honesty. Or what happens if there is a child in school who is not accepted by the other members of the class ... [or] how do you maintain what you know is right and honest, and still maintain your status as a welcome person within the community?*[11]

Following the revelations given to Joseph Smith, Mormons typically eschew alcohol, tobacco, coffee, and tea, and eat meat only sparingly, thus focusing on a healthy diet of vegetables, fruits, and grains. They have developed a strong social-welfare system to help families in need but also make them self-sufficient. Using volunteer labor alone, they have developed large-scale farms, ranches, peanut-product factories, coal mines, and the like, using the symbol of the hive, in which honey bees co-operate in order to meet the needs of all the members. Children are trained in preaching from a young age, as part of the system of shared responsibility. Sexual relations outside marriage are strongly discouraged.

Mormon theology is still evolving, thanks to its principle of continuing reve-lation. The head of the Church is specially empowered to receive guidance from God on contemporary issues that are not clearly addressed in the Bible and the Book of Mormon. Theological beliefs are also subject to change, the most contro-versial of which—from the point of view of other Christians—may be the nature of God. For some time, Mormons believed that the "Heavenly Father" was orig-inally a man but that he had risen to exaltation, and that humans can likewise become like gods. This belief still exists, but the recent prophet President Gordon Hinckley (1910–2008) restated it: "We believe in the progression of the human soul. We believe in the eternity and the infinity of the human soul, and its great possibilities."[12]

Because Mormons believe that baptism is essential in order to enter the Kingdom of God, since humans are innately sinful, they may baptize not only living humans but also those who have died without being baptized—a ceremo-ny in which a proxy is baptized on their behalf—no matter what their religion was. In response to protests from non-Mormons, the Church of Jesus Christ of Latter-day Saints explains that the dead person can choose to accept the proxy baptism or not.

Jehovah's Witnesses

Whereas Mormons turn to both the Book of Mormon and the Bible for guid-ance, Jehovah's Witnesses place their faith squarely and decisively in the Bible alone and do not have ancillary creeds. Their belief structure and their reli-gious life refer constantly to biblical passages, and their missionaries traverse the globe, going door to door to invite people to study the Bible with them as the inspired and accurate Word of God. They think that mainstream Christian Churches began to deviate from the Bible in the second and third centuries CE by developing untrue doctrines: that God is a Trinity, that the soul is resurrected after death, and that the unrepentant wicked endure eternal torment rather than the everlasting unconsciousness that the Witnesses predict for them when God's kingdom appears. They foresee a new world in which people of all races (including many raised from the dead) will experience paradise on earth. They believe that this will happen only after the majority of humanity is destroyed for not obeying the Bible. In the understanding of Jehovah's Witnesses, God will not let anyone, including "nominal Christians," ruin the earth. Those who are of

A Jehovah's Witness shares Bible study lessons.

the true religion will be saved from the general destruction, reunited with their dead loved ones in a paradise on earth (except for 144,000 who will live with God in Heaven). According to the teachings, in the earthly paradise there will be no pain, no food shortages, no sickness, no death.

The founder of Jehovah's Witnesses, Charles Taze Russell (1852–1916), supported a prediction that in 1873 or 1874 the anointed ones would take their places in Heaven under Christ's rule. When that period passed uneventfully, the anticipated date was changed to 1878, then 1914, and then 1975. As the dates came and went without any apparent change in the present system of things, Russell and his successors developed the idea that Christ had arrived, but was invisibly present. Only the faithful "Jehovah's Witnesses" would recognize his presence. Their mission is to warn the rest of the populace about what is in store. They thus go from house to house, encouraging people to follow their program of studying the Bible as an infallible announcement of the millennium and to leave politics and "false religions." The latter include mainstream Christian Churches, as above. They explain that prevailing problems such as crime, terrorism, social violence, pollution, deforestation, and global warming will soon come to an end because God has made biblical promises to save the planet, as no human institutions can:

> Soon our anxieties about the future will be over, for God will take charge of planet Earth by putting in place his own government, called God's Kingdom. Jesus Christ had that wonderful prospect in mind when he taught his followers to pray: "Let your kingdom come. Let your will take place, as in heaven, also upon earth." (Matthew 6: 9–10).[13]

Not recognizing worldly authorities and being involved in a global movement, Jehovah's Witnesses were severely persecuted in Nazi Germany as "subversives." They refused to give the Nazi salute, display Nazi flags at their homes, or be drafted for military service, and they kept distributing printed materials about their faith. Many were arrested and more than 3,000 were sent to concentration camps, where almost half of them died from the harsh conditions. Another 250 were executed for their refusal to perform German army service. In the concentration camps, they were pressured to save themselves by signing a document refuting their faith, submitting to government authority, and supporting the German military, but few did.

During the 1930s and 1940s, many Jehovah's Witnesses in the United States were also persecuted and arrested for their refusal to engage in military activities. Their trials became tests of the preservation of freedom of speech, press, assembly, and worship, and ultimately they won forty-three Supreme Court cases. They have been similarly successful in high courts of other countries.

Another issue that has arisen is the refusal of Jehovah's Witnesses to have blood transfusions. They cite biblical texts forbidding eating blood, and believe that only the blood shed for them by Jesus can save them. Any Jehovah's Witness who accepts a blood transfusion, even from his own stored blood, is regarded by others as having abandoned his religion. This belief has raised difficult legal issues in cases of children whose parents refuse to allow them to have blood transfusions.

Jehovah's Witnesses now count over eight million active followers—those who are engaged in proselytizing efforts to recruit people for Bible study and thereafter baptism of new members who have committed themselves to active membership.[14]

Radhasoami

The Radhasoami movement is an outgrowth of Sikhism in India. Its leaders often have Sikh backgrounds, but while orthodox Sikhs believe in a succession of masters that stopped with the Tenth Guru and was transferred to the holy scripture, Radhasoamis believe in a continuing succession of living masters.

LIVING TRANSCENDENTAL MEDITATION

An Interview with Wolfgang Hecker

In 1958, Maharishi Mahesh Yogi began teaching the practice of Transcendental Meditation (TM) based on ancient Vedic knowledge. Maharishi's extensive travels and worldwide organization introduced the TM technique to millions of people. For most, TM is a practical part of the daily routine to enrich one's personal life. But for a select few, including Wolfgang Hecker of Germany, TM has become a way of life. Since 1999 he has been living in the Valley of the Saints in the Indian Himalayas as one of a hundred advanced practitioners chosen by Maharishi Mahesh Yogi to practice TM for the sake of bringing greater harmony to the world. Wolfgang has been meditating for so many years that he seems to be in a constant state of inner happiness, and even his skin appears to be translucent and radiant. Wolfgang recounts:

I came to TM like almost everyone has—through the recommendation of a friend. I was very much attracted to Maharishi's technique because I saw on the face of my friend that inner peace and happiness that radiates from people who practice TM.

Right in the very first instruction, I had exactly the experience I was always looking for. I was nineteen and interested in spiritual development. Immediately I had that experience of pure transcendental consciousness. The mind became more quiet, and more quiet, and more quiet, completely effortlessly, completely naturally, completely without any doing. The activity of the mind settled down. I was resting deeply within my own self, silent and yet fully awake at the same time, like the teacher had told me in the introductory lecture. I had that experience right away in the first meditation.

After the personal instruction, you come again for an hour on three consecutive days. You discuss further experiences with the teacher so that you are completely self-sufficient and can meditate on your own. You start practicing twenty minutes in the morning and twenty in the evening, sitting comfortably with eyes closed.

What I found very attractive was that you are not joining a club or an organization. It's not a religious practice, it's not a philosophy. There are Buddhists, Muslims, Christians, Hindus, people who don't believe in anything. All kinds of people practice Transcendental Meditation—housewives, doctors, anyone.

Maharishi always encouraged scientific research on the TM technique, showing that its results could be proved scientifically and would be repeatable and reliable. In the early 1970s, a scientist named Dr. Robert Keith Wallace did the first research on brain wave coherence. Every state of consciousness—waking, sleeping, dreaming—has its own very specific brain waves and biochemistry. During TM, a fourth major state of consciousness occurs in which the brain's functioning is more orderly. Any parameter you can measure on the body at that time is pointing to greater orderliness in the physiology, and a deep level of rest.

There are advanced techniques, of which the most well known is Maharishi's yogic flying technique. This technique also has its origin in the ancient Vedic tradition. It is a very powerful tool to enhance mind–body coordination, which brings benefits on all levels of life to the individual who is practicing it. But above that it was found by scientific research that if large groups practice yogic flying together, not only the individual consciousness of every practitioner is enlivened but also the coherence and orderliness in collective consciousness is increased. It was found that a larger number—6,000, 7,000, 10,000 people—practicing yogic flying together in one place would so dramatically increase the orderliness in the collective consciousness of everyone on the globe that positive trends would be increasing and negative trends would be decreasing.

Yogic flying is one of many siddhi [spiritual power] techniques that Maharishi has been teaching. You first practice TM in order to come to that peaceful, very, very silent, unbounded level of pure consciousness inside. And then you begin the technique of yogic flying. It is like dropping a pebble into a silent lake. Ripples appear. So you can observe how from silent, abstract nothingness, a wave of creation arises. Here the laws of nature begin the process of creation. And as a meditator you can experience the mechanics of creation within your own consciousness.

In the case of the yogic flying siddhi, the body lifts up and the person makes a hop, so to say, in the air. His body moves up and there is a transformation from heavy to something light. But for the practitioner, all his attention is on the inner, rather than the outer. When the unbounded quietness wells up in waves of life and living, then the experience is one of bubbling up of bliss. On the individual level, the yogic flying technique is the most powerful tool to transform the personality. Inner silent happiness nourishes one's daily life. And with mind and body coordination enhanced, scientific research has shown greater effectiveness and joy in life.[15]

The first of the Radhasoami gurus was Shiv Dayal Singh. In 1861, he offered to serve as a spiritual savior, carrying devotees into "Radhasoami," the ineffable Godhead. Some 10,000 took initiation under him. After his death in 1878, the movement eventually split into what are now more than thirty branches, each with its own living master, although there is theoretically only one of these at a time on the earth. The Punjabi branches are known collectively as Sant Mat, or Path of the Masters.

The most popular of the branches is Radhasoami Satsang Beas, with its well-organized center in Punjab near the river Beas. A biographer of Baba Sawan Singh (1858–1948), the saint through whom many of the branches trace their lineage, describes the typical Radhasoami attitude that contemporary Sikhism suffers from lack of a living guru who would guide them in inner spiritual practice:

> In the course of time ... the emphasis of the [Sikh] teachings gradually shifted from spiritual practice under the guidance of a living master to the practice of rituals and external observances. Many devout Sikhs began to confine their religious activities to reading and reciting the holy book, little realizing that it enjoins upon the readers the necessity of internal practice of the sound current to attain ultimate salvation.[16]

Radhasoami is primarily an esoteric path, without exoteric (external, public) ceremonies. Initiates are taught a secret yoga practice of concentrating on the third eye with attention to the inner sound and inner light. "Radha" refers to the Prime Spirit Current; "Soami" means the Prime Sound Current. The two are said to have mingled at the beginning of creation, and the primal sound continues to reverberate. Initiates aspire to ascend to pure spirit, home of the Supreme Creator, where sound and spirit currents intermingle. They are told that the experience must be both initiated and guided by a perfected being "who is possessed of all the powers of the purely spiritual regions."[17]

The Radhasoami movement now claims an estimated two million initiates. Those in the Agra area of India have created whole spiritual suburbs where they live and work as well as worship together. Outside of India, devotees gather in satsangs (spiritual congregations) and are supposed to support each other in the path. They are required to be vegetarians, to meditate every day, to forgo alcohol and, if possible, tobacco, and to be employed.

Combinations of older religions

How do Caodaism, Santeria, and Agon Shu combine differing beliefs from traditional religions?

Mixtures of more than one religion have historically arisen in many places. As we have seen, Buddhism, Confucianism, and Daoism have long intermingled in China, to the extent that it is difficult to sort out the threads as distinct traditions. This process of combining normally differing beliefs produces what seems to be a new religion of sorts.

Caodaism

One of the most extreme contemporary examples of intermingling components from different religions arose in Vietnam early in the twentieth century. The new religious movement Caodaism was formed in 1926 in Vietnam by several people who understood that God was instructing them that religious leaders such as Moses, Buddha, Laozi, Confucius, and Jesus had all been God-inspired to start religions in their home regions. However, these all became distorted by local customs, and through lack of communication between different regions the religions went their separate ways. According to the revelations, this multiplicity of religions kept people from living together harmoniously. Caodaists thus practice a religion made from parts of many world religions, including Judaism, Christianity, Islam, Buddhism, Confucianism, and Daoism, plus the indigenous Vietnamese religion Geniism. For instance, Caodaists believe that before God there was the Dao. God was born in the Big Bang, and then created yin and yang, with the "Mother Buddha" presiding over yin aspects of the cosmos. Such a mixture of religious elements is supposed by Caodaists to be the basis for the "Third Alliance between God and Man," a self-description that is written in many places in Caodaist temples.

Caodaist beliefs have been developed through the process of spiritual mediumship, or "channeling." By various means that have precedents in both Asian shamanistic practices and European spiritualist séances, spirits in Caodaism are thought to convey written messages between heaven and earth. Typically, the medium goes into trance and writes messages received from the spirits. Above a Caodai altar, a great eye with lines radiating from it represents this communication from Cao (high) Dai (palace), where God reigns. Many of the spirits who are thought to carry these communications to earthly mediums are from French culture, such as poet and novelist Victor Hugo, reflecting the strong French influence in Vietnam since its colonization by France in the nineteenth century. Other spirits are Chinese gods, such as Li Po, who reportedly revealed the architecture of the Great Divine Temple in Tay Ninh, center of the faith. In the early years of the religion, séances were held throughout Vietnam, with miracles, healing of the sick, and direct orders to individuals by name to join the new religion. But because there was already a strong tradition of individual channeling of spirits, there was a perceived threat to the institutionalization of Caodaism. In 1936 a decision was taken that official Caodai séances could only be held in the Holy See at Tay Ninh. Having become thus centralized and institutionalized, Caodaism played a prominent role in Vietnamese society during the turbulent war years and became the third largest religion in Vietnam, after Buddhism and Roman Catholicism. Now its central management is under the control of a communist-appointed committee and official séances have stopped, though worship continues in the Holy See temples. Outside Vietnam, members of Caodaism are left with the dilemma of trying to understand what Tay Ninh would likely advise if it were officially guiding them through its link with Cao Dai.

African-inspired religions

In contrast to the institutionalization of spiritualism in Caodaism, other mixtures that have emerged more organically include a variety of new religious movements in the Caribbean and Latin America. These have evolved from mixtures of Catholic traditions implanted there earlier, and African religions carried by slaves. They are characterized by a prevailing interest in contacting and co-operating with spirits. **Santeria** ("way of the saints," or Lukumi, as its practitioners increasingly prefer) blends some of the deities and beliefs of slaves from Dahomey, Bakongo, and Yoruba cultures with images of Catholic saints. Since the slaves were prevented from openly practicing their ancestral faiths, they continued to do so in symbolic ways, such as hanging a white cloth from a doorway or tying bananas with red string, and also by worship of the African *orisa* in the form of Catholic saints. For instance, the female *orisa* Oshun is worshiped in Nigeria as the patron of love, marriage, and fertility, and is associated with river water. In Cuba and in areas of the United States with large Cuban populations, devotions to Oshun have merged into reverence of the Virgin Mary as Our Lady of Charity, the patron saint of Cuba. She is said to have appeared to three shipwrecked fishermen at sea.

Santeria specialists have techniques for "magical" intervention in people's lives to help solve problems that cannot be fixed by ordinary means. The santeros (priests), for example, say they are able to clear away negative spiritual influences around people, help them get jobs, heal sickness, attract mates, block their enemies, and get ahead financially. They see the world as a mesh of

In Santeria, the Yoruba river goddess Oshun is merged with the Christian Our Lady of Charity, patron saint of Cuba.

interconnections among all beings, linked by the energy known as *ashe*. Human efforts are required to keep the *ashe* flowing properly through creation and to nourish the *orisa*. Then, by knowing how to feed and communicate with the *orisa* and understanding the principles of energy, practitioners are thought to be able to wield some control over the environment.

Where remnants of slave populations have coalesced, the renewed practice of African traditions has given the people a link with their cultural heritage, a sense of inner integrity, and a means of sheer survival. But these African traditions have been viewed with some suspicion by the dominant societies. For instance, traditional African methods of communicating with the spirits include divination and the consecrated slaughter of animals, in the context of a community meal. The latter practice was outlawed in Hialeah, Florida, as "animal sacrifice," but in a landmark judgment in 1993 the United States Supreme Court overruled the ban as an unconstitutional barrier to religious freedom. According to a majority of the Supreme Court justices: "Religious beliefs need not be acceptable, logical, consistent, or comprehensible to others in order to merit First Amendment protection."[18] Santeria has become very popular in Latin America and the United States, and there are pilgrimages to Nigeria for people seeking to explore the roots of their religion. It is strengthening its ties to Africa as it gains legal and social acceptance and feels less need to mask its practices as Catholic variants.

A number of "new" religions in West Africa combine ritual elements of indigenous and Christian traditions that had been brought by missionaries. The missionaries regarded worship of ancestors as religiously invalid, but communications with ancestors and spirits had been a major aspect of the indigenous religions. The new religions take seriously problems with the spirit world, such as retaliations from spirits who have not been treated respectfully, and mix Christian prayers and incense with fetishes, talismans, divining, chanting, and drumming. This mixture gives a sense of power against evil spirits and is also applied to contemporary, this-worldly problems. These groups are most popular in urban areas, where they offer a refuge from unpleasant aspects of city life. Those such as the Brotherhood of the Cross and Star are deeply committed to serving the people in areas where governments have failed them. They operate their own schools, food shops, industries, healthcare centers, and transportation services. Those who once felt like nobodies, alienated within modern impersonal culture, now feel recognized as important individuals within a loving group. The movements revive the traditional African community spirit as a stable support network within a changing society. They may also build a sense of African pride and spiritual destiny. Rev. William Kingsley Opoku of Ghana, International Co-ordinator of the African Council of Spiritual Churches and member of the Brotherhood of the Cross and Star, asserts:

> African Scriptures confirm that the world peace process will finally be founded in Africa, and the whole world will come and help build it, to signify the unity of mankind under the Government of God on earth.[19]

Agon Shu

New religious movements have proliferated in Japan, with such porous boundaries between the older religions that various blended forms have evolved. One of the newest of these is Agon Shu, which combines Buddhist, Shinto, and Daoist beliefs and practices in dramatic ceremonies at its central community on a mountaintop in Kyoto. Its founder is Seiyu Kiriyama, who bases his way on the Agamas (*Agon* in Japanese), ancient Chinese scriptures that he encountered among Shingon Buddhists in his personal spiritual search. He asserts that the Shingon sect has become too formalistic and far from its origins, but that esoteric Buddhism is in fact highly transformational, so that everyone can become a Buddha:

> Esoteric Buddhist practice is capable of engendering ordinary and advanced supernormal powers. Divine siddhi are obtained through practicing the methods that the Buddha taught in the Agama Sutras. The highest power of the Buddhist dharma is the power to attain liberation from karma, the power to attain Buddhahood. The liberation from karma is the greatest miracle in the universe.[20]

Rev. Kiriyama also combines esoteric Shinto and Daoist practices with Buddhism in developing regimes for laypeople who climb into the mountains to engage in mental and physical disciplines. At the Agon Shu center above Kyoto, these "mountain ascetics" act as assistants who don symbolic costumes and carry on dramatic fire rituals on two huge pyres, one to help realize the hopes of the living, and the other to liberate the souls of the dead. The fires are fueled by wooden prayer sticks upon which participants have written their wishes. Rituals are conducted both by Rev. Kiriyama and by Shinto priests, with the playing

Agon Shu Shinto-Buddhist ceremony in which prayer requests written on pieces of wood are ritually burned in huge fires.

of large Japanese drums, the performance of ancient dances of the Japanese imperial court in honor of Shinto deities and ancestors, and ceremonies featuring axes, bows and arrows, and swords. Visitors can also get their fortune told by "esoteric Buddhist" astrologers, and are encouraged to visit the shrine of the "Sixty Guardian Deities" of Daoism, each of which is said to guard those born during a particular year in the traditional Chinese and Japanese sixty-year cycle. It is recommended that visitors buy and keep a talisman of their own guardian deity with them "to avoid evil and to invite good luck."[21]

In addition to staging such blended spiritual dramas in Kyoto, Seiyu Kiriyama has traveled to various countries—including China, Taiwan, India, the United States, Poland, and France—to conduct prayer ceremonies for propitiation of departed souls. In 2006, for instance, he held a fire ritual next to the Auschwitz-Birkenau concentration camp, in honor of holocaust victims and in hopes of world peace. His movement, founded in 1978, now claims half a million followers. Some believe that the Agon Shu techniques have brought relief from severe psychological and physical problems thought to be caused by their dead ancestors. Rev. Kiriyama explains:

> *The Buddhist path has the power to destroy all negative attachments, delusions, and illusions and can bring both living and dead beings to liberation. In fact, the dissolution of a dead person's attachments may actually be easier than those of the living. A living person's mind burns like wildfire from one deluded conception to the next, so the roots of their attachments are all over the place. The negative attachments of a dead person, on the other hand, may be very strong but have usually cohered into a single stalk.*[22]

Universalism

What is the key belief of universalism?

Some new religious movements take a broader view, not just blending together components of different religions, but encompassing all religions. Typically they teach that all prophets have brought essentially the same messages to humanity, though in different times and places.

Theosophical Society

A prime example of universalist beliefs is the Theosophical Society, founded by the Russian aristocrat Madame Helen Blavatsky (1831–1891). "Theosophy" means "divine wisdom," as revealed to Madame Blavatsky by unseen "Ascended Masters." Madame Blavatsky was a fierce character with notable psychic powers. She claimed to have traveled around the globe studying with masters of esoteric schools and to have undergone initiations with Tibetan masters. She founded the Theosophical Society with the motto "There is no religion higher than truth." It was an attempt, she said, "to reconcile all religions, sects and nations under a common system of ethics, based on eternal verities."[23]

The Theosophical Society introduced ancient Asian ideas to Western seekers, especially Hindu beliefs such as karma, reincarnation, and subtle energies. Madame Blavatsky was particularly interested in the secret esoteric teachings of each religion, which collectively she called the "Wisdom Religion" or the "secret doctrine." Madame Blavatsky insisted that:

> *Theosophy is not a Religion. Theosophy is Religion itself. A Religion in the true and only correct sense, is a bond uniting men together—not a particular set of dogmas and beliefs. Now Religion, per se, in its widest meaning is that which binds not only all MEN, but also all BEINGS and all things in the entire Universe into one grand whole. … Theosophy is RELIGION, and the Society its one Universal Church; the temple of Solomon's wisdom,—in building which*

Madame Blavatsky, mystic and founder of the Theosophical Society.

In Pearl of Searching, *the Russian painter Nicholas Roerich depicted a spiritual seeker and his guru in the Himalayas, a magnet for spiritual aspiration.*

"there was neither hammer, nor axe, nor any tool of iron heard in the house while it was building" (1 Kings, 6); for this "temple" is made by no human hand, nor built in any locality on earth—but, verily, is raised only in the inner sanctuary of man's heart wherein reigns alone the awakened soul.[24]

The Theosophical Society now has members in seventy countries. The movement has splintered into several factions, which use the same name, and has also spawned other groups, such as the Agni Yoga Society founded by Nicholas Roerich (1874–1947), a Russian painter, philosopher, and humanitarian. When he traveled in the Himalayas with his wife, Helena, he painted the spiritual light he perceived in those mountains and placed in his paintings holy figures from many religious traditions. After his death, Helena encouraged students to revere unseen masters from India as well as Jesus. Now a steady stream of Russian pilgrims visit Roerich's mountain home in Kullu, India, seeking to establish the same connection with Indian spirituality that they see in his paintings.

Baha'i

Universalist beliefs have also manifested in a "new" global religion, the Baha'i faith, which attempts to unite all of humanity in the belief that there is only one God, the foundation of all religions. The Baha'i faith was foreshadowed in Persia in 1844 when a young man called the Bab (the Gate) announced that a new messenger of God to all the peoples of the world would soon appear. Because he proclaimed this message in a Muslim state, where Muhammad was considered the Seal of the Prophets, he was arrested and executed in 1850. Some 22,000 of his followers were reportedly massacred as well. One of his imprisoned followers was said to be Baha'u'llah (1817–1892), a member of an aristocratic Persian family. He was stripped of his worldly goods, tortured, banished to Baghdad, and finally imprisoned in Palestine by the Turks. From prison, he revealed himself as the messenger proclaimed by the Bab. He wrote letters to the rulers of all nations, asserting that humanity was becoming unified and that a single global civilization was emerging.

Despite vigorous initial persecution, this new faith has by now spread to more than five million followers in 233 countries and territories around the world, involving people from a wide variety of racial and ethnic groups. They have no priesthood but they do have their own sacred scriptures, revealed to Baha'u'llah. Baha'is compare this new messenger to previous great prophets, such as Abraham, Moses, Jesus, Muhammad, Krishna, and the Buddha. In fact, they see Baha'u'llah as the fulfillment of the prophecies of all religions. He did not declare himself to be the ultimate messenger, however. Rather, he prophesied that another would follow in a thousand years.

The heart of Baha'u'llah's message appears in the *Kitab-i-Iqan* (The Book of Certitude). God, Baha'u'llah says, is unknowable. Mere humans cannot understand God's infinite nature with their limited minds. However, God has become known through divine messengers, the founders of the great world religions. All are manifestations of God, pure channels for helping humanity to understand God's will. The spiritual education of humans has been a process of "progressive revelation," said Baha'u'llah. Humanity has been maturing, like a child growing in the ability to grasp complex ideas as it grows in years and passes through grade school and college. Each time a divine messenger appeared, the message was given at levels appropriate to humanity's degree of maturity. Baha'u'llah proclaimed his own message as the most advanced and the one appropriate for this time. It contains the same eternal truths as the earlier revelations, but with some new features, which humanity is now ready to grasp, such as the oneness of all peoples, prophets, and religions, and a program for universal governance for the sake of world peace and social justice. Contemporary Baha'is are active in trying to develop a just order in the world, creating projects such as schools promoting global awareness, the European Business Forum encouraging business ethics, environmental awareness campaigns, and rural development projects.

Baha'i Houses of Worship, which are open to all, have nine doors and a central dome symbolizing the diversity and oneness of humanity. Devotional services include readings from the scriptures of all religions, meditations, unaccompanied singing, and prayers by the Bab, Baha'u'llah, and his successor 'Abdu'l-baha, his oldest son. 'Abdu'l-baha describes the unified world that Baha'is envision:

> *The world will become the mirror of the Heavenly Kingdom. ... All nations will become one, all religions will be unified ... the superstitions caused by races, countries, individuals, languages and politics will disappear; and all men will*

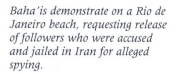

Baha'is demonstrate on a Rio de Janeiro beach, requesting release of followers who were accused and jailed in Iran for alleged spying.

The Baha'i Model for Governance of the World

One of the most unusual features of the Baha'i faith is its own organization, which it sees as a good model for democratic governance of the whole world. Everywhere that people have converted to Baha'i faith, there is a highly organized framework designed not only to propagate the faith but also to democratize its leadership. Campaigning, electioneering, and nominations are prohibited, thus avoiding the empty promises to voters, corruption, and negative campaigning that tarnish elections in contemporary worldly democracies.

In the Baha'i "administrative order," each local group yearly elects nine or more people to a local Spiritual Assembly. Each local member is asked to pray and meditate and then write down the names of nine adults from the local Baha'i community who seem best qualified to lead the community. The necessary qualities are those of "unquestioned loyalty, of selfless devotion, of a well-trained mind, of recognized ability and mature experience."[25] By this simple and unusual process, Baha'is feel they choose leaders who are mature and humble rather than politically bold and egotistical. By the same process, the Local Spiritual Assemblies elect the National Spiritual Assemblies, and again by the same process, the National Spiritual Assemblies choose the nine members of the Universal House of Justice,

seated in Haifa, Israel. Baha'is feel that this framework allows both grassroots access to decision-making and a superstructure for efficient international coordination of activities. However, women are not seated at the Universal House of Justice, and this omission is currently the subject of intense debate.

Within these elected groups—and also within business, school, and family settings—Baha'is attempt to reach decisions by a nonadversarial process of "consultation." The point of the process is to investigate truth in depth and to build consensus rather than struggle for power. Participants are enjoined to gather information from as many sources as possible and to be at once truthful and courteous to each other. Any idea once proposed is thereafter considered group property; it does not belong to one person or group, but rather is investigated impartially. As Svetlana Dorzhieva, formerly Executive Secretary of the National Spiritual Assembly of Baha'is of Russia, Georgia, and Armenia, explains: "What is wonderful is that when a person says his opinion, he just forgets that it belonged to him. It is offered and then it is discussed."[26] Attempts are made to reach unanimous consensus, but failing that, a majority vote may be taken. The success of this process is demonstrated in the fact that people from very diverse backgrounds manage to work and worship together.

attain to life eternal under the shadow of the Lord of Hosts. … The relations between the countries, the mingling, union and friendship of the people … will reach to such a degree that the human race will be like one family. … The light of heavenly love will shine, and the darkness of enmity and hatred will be dispelled from the world.[27]

In the Qur'an Muhammad is referred to as the Seal of the Prophets, a title that was often understood to preclude the emergence of further prophets. The assertion of Baha'u'llah that he bore a divine revelation for the present age challenged such interpretations. This, along with other Baha'i teachings such as the equality of women and men, the abolition of the priesthood, and the affirmation of the divine origin of Hinduism and Buddhism, drew the ire of Muslim clergy and sometimes provoked hostility and oppression. Baha'is in Iran, for example, have been subjected to persecution since the inception of the religion and more recently since the 1979 revolution and establishment of the Islamic Republic of Iran.

Baha'is believe that the challenges facing humanity today call for spiritual transformation in the hearts and minds of individuals, but also in the systems of structures of society. They therefore work to contribute to the formulation of thought and public policy at levels ranging from the village council or neighborhood association to international commissions held under the auspices of the United Nations. They seek to lay the foundations for a unified, peaceful global society through the practical application of principles such as:

1 The end of prejudice in all forms.
2 Equality for women.
3 Acceptance of the relativity and unity of spiritual truth.
4 Just distribution of wealth.
5 Universal education.
6 The individual responsibility to seek truth.
7 Development of a world federation.
8 Harmony of science and true religion.[28]

Social trends

What elements have been furthered by new religious movements arising from social trends?

New religious movements can also be seen as arising from social trends, with or without connections to previous religions or singular charismatic leadership. Examples of such general movements that have arisen in the past hundred years or so include movements furthering racial/ethnic identity, affection for nature, deep ecology, the "New Age" movement, and self-improvement. Since they are rooted in present concerns, these may or may not survive into the future. Some examples are explored below.

Ethnic identity: Rastafari

As descendants of African slaves in the Americas struggled to build better lives for themselves, religious ideals developed that mirrored their hopes. In 1895, Alexander Bedward of the Baptist Free Church in Jamaica prophesied a coming holocaust in which all the white people would be killed, leaving the Blacks, "the true people," to celebrate the new world. He sat in his special robes as the predicted date came and went; eventually he was placed in an asylum for the insane. A more generalized hopeful vision was spread by Marcus Garvey (1887–1940), who saw a fundamental change in society that would be led by Blacks. Garvey linked these dreams to the return of Blacks to Africa, from which their ancestors had been taken as slaves; there they would rebuild a great civilization. A prophecy attributed to Garvey—"Look to Africa when a black king shall be crowned, for the day of deliverance is near"[29]—was thought to have

Rastafari male musicians carry the message of reasserting Black spiritual and social rights.

been realized when Ras (Prince) Tafari of Ethiopia was crowned as Haile Selassie, emperor of Ethiopia. An elaborate mystique was built up around Haile Selassie as the living God (though neither Selassie nor Garvey shared this view). Hopeful lore was based on interpretations of Selassie's statements and passages from the Old Testament and the New Testament Book of Revelation. Poor Jamaicans (who likened themselves to the Jews in captivity in Babylon) repeatedly prepared to be given free passage back to Africa.

Haile Selassie's reign (until his death in 1974) did nothing to liberate Jamaican Africans, but Blacks in Jamaica nevertheless developed a new religious movement around these ideals. They intend to revive the "Way of the Ancients," their concept of the lost civilization of precolonial Africa, and to free people of African extraction from subservience. "Babylon," the oppressor, is collectively the United States, Britain (the former colonial power in Jamaica), the state of Jamaica, and the Christian Church. In protest against Babylon, Rastafarians wear their hair in long uncombed curls, called "dreadlocks," a lion-like mane symbolizing the natural nonindustrial life. Some give use of marijuana (ganja) religious significance as a sacrament. A distinctive music, reggae, evolved as an expression of Black pride, social protest, and Rastafarian millenarian ideals, with the legendary Bob Marley as its musical prophet. In many areas the movement has developed mostly through men; they consider women incapable of experiencing Rasta awareness except through their husbands. However, by the end of the twentieth century women had begun to play more significant roles in the movement.

The Rastafari movement spread beyond Jamaica to Blacks and a few whites elsewhere in the Caribbean, North America, Europe, southern Africa, Australia, and New Zealand. It is very localized and diverse. Some Rastas insist that the truths they espouse are not just for people of African descent. Thus in some places it has been adopted by other ethnic groups such as Native Americans, Indonesians, Maoris, and Thais. And after the Soviet Union fell, during the 1990s a Rasta subculture developed among Slavic youths in some formerly communist states. They adopted reggae music and marijuana and some let their hair grow into dreadlocks, in protest against the values of "Babylon." On the other hand, some insist that Rastafari is only for Blacks. For instance, Ras Charles and French Dread write:

> Rastafari is a movement of black people who know Africa is the birthplace of mankind, all mankind. … We must re-culture ourselves so we can have a sense of pride, in the turning from occidental culture, and taking into ourselves the power of our African culture, which has been hidden from us for so long.[30]

Nature spirituality

One of the strongest trends in our time is that of the religion of nature. Many who are experiencing a reconnection with the natural world do not think of this path as a religion, for it has no clear structure. It seems to be growing spontaneously, cropping up here and there in diverse forms.

Reinvention of old practices Some who seek to practice a nature-oriented spirituality look to the past for models. This trend is sometimes called Neo-Paganism, with reference to pre-Christian spiritual ways that are thought to have been practiced in Europe. Some call their way "Witchcraft," despite the negative connotations associated with this label. As Starhawk, a Neo-Pagan leader and co-founder of the witchcraft tradition Reclaiming, explains:

> Modern Witches are thought to be members of a kooky cult, … lacking the depth, the dignity and seriousness of purpose of a true religion. But Witchcraft is a religion, perhaps the oldest religion extant in the West … and it is very different from all the so-called great religions. The Old Religion, as we call it, is closer in

Russian Neo-Pagans create a ritual celebration of the summer solstice in a forest outside Moscow.

spirit to Native American traditions or to the shamanism of the Arctic. It is not based on dogma or a set of beliefs, nor on scriptures or a sacred book revealed by a great man. Witchcraft takes its teachings from nature, and reads inspiration in the movements of the sun, moon, and stars, the flight of birds, the slow growth of trees, and the cycles of the seasons.[31]

Some Neo-Pagans try to reproduce some of the sacred ways of earlier European peoples, such as the Celts in the British Isles or the ancient Scandinavians. Reconstructing these ways is difficult, for they were largely oral rather than written traditions. After religions such as Christianity were firmly established, the remaining practitioners of the old ways were often tortured and killed as witches and blamed for social ills such as the plague. They were said to be in league with the devil against God, although the pagan pantheons had no devil—he was introduced by the Jewish–Christian–Muslim traditions.

In the 1940s, the writings of Gerald Gardner, a retired civil servant in England, began reintroducing Pagan ways. Gardner claimed to have been initiated into a secret coven of witches who allowed him to write about some of their practices as well as their historical persecutions by Christians, and added other rituals and "magickal" practices from various sources to replace those that had been lost because of the isolation and secrecy of the few remaining covens. He called its practitioners the "Wica." As the ceremonial magic practices spread, the path became known as **Wicca**. This label may now also refer to Neo-Pagans from non-Gardnerian witchcraft lineages.

Another attempt to return to old models is **Goddess spirituality**. Archaeological evidence from many cultures around the world was reinterpreted during the twentieth century as suggesting that worship of a female high goddess was originally widespread. Although there were, and are now, cultures that did not ascribe gender or hierarchy or personality to the divine, some that did may have seen the highest deity as a female.

A reverent address to Ishtar, an important Mesopotamian goddess, dating from some time between the eighteenth and seventh centuries BCE, suggests some of the powers ascribed to her:

Unto Her who renders decision, Goddess of all things. Unto the Lady of Heaven and Earth who receives supplication; Unto Her who hears petition, who entertains prayer; Unto the compassionate Goddess who loves righteousness; Ishtar the Queen, who suppresses all that is confused. To the Queen of Heaven, the Goddess of the Universe, the One who walked in terrible Chaos and brought life by the Law of Love; And out of Chaos brought us harmony.[32]

Temples and images that may have been devoted to worship of the goddess have been found in almost every Neolithic and early historic archaeological site in Europe and West Asia. She was often symbolically linked with water, serpents, birds, eggs, spirals, the moon, the womb, the vulva, the magnetic currents of the earth, psychic powers, and the eternal creation and renewal of life. In these agricultural cultures women frequently held strong social positions. Hereditary lineages were often traced through the mother, and women were honored as priestesses, healers, agricultural inventors, counselors, prophetesses, and sometimes warriors. Goddess spirituality has thus been adopted by some contemporary feminists as their preferred religious way.

Scholars are now trying to piece together not only the possible characteristics of goddess worship, but also the circumstances of its demise. In Europe and West Asia, worship of the goddess may have been suppressed throughout the third and second millennia BCE by invading Indo-European groups in which dominant males worshiped a supreme male deity, often described as a storm god residing on a mountain and bringing light (seen as the good) into the darkness (portrayed as bad and associated with the female).

In replacing the goddess, patriarchal groups may also have devalued the "feminine" aspect of religion—the receptive, intuitive, ecstatic mystical communion that was perhaps allowed freer expression in goddess worship. Women have been the major victims of this devaluation of the feminine, but there has also been distrust of mystics of both sexes.

To revive appreciation of the goddess, including the goddess within themselves, as well as women's spirituality, contemporary women have pieced together and invented rituals for both individual and group use. Diane Rae Schulz writes in *Awakened Woman* e-magazine:

The practice of goddess spirituality can take many forms, from constructing a small altar or meditation space in one's home, to participating in ritual circles with other women, to large seasonal celebrations which include men and children. My first experience of the practice of goddess spirituality was an all women's Samhain (Halloween) spiral dance. The ritual involved meditation on the goddess Hecate, the dark aspect of the triple goddess, the goddess of death and rebirth, and it culminated in a whirling spiral dance—scores of women of all ages holding hands and singing, weaving in and out, re-enacting an ancient celebration of the power of women. I left the gathering feeling uplifted, energized, and reassured of women's unique spiritual unity.[33]

Yet other people seeking to return to old models are members of new religions known collectively as **ethnic religions**, as distinguished from "indigenous religions" with a long history of earth-centered practices in their ancestral environment. What are called "ethnic religions" have emerged since the fall of Communism as revivals of pre-Christian ethnic traditions in countries such as Russia and in eastern Europe. In Estonia, pagan rituals are now celebrated in a rather happy, mocking fashion as a form of entertainment. In other places such as the Udmurt Republic in Russia, faith in pre-Christian prayer and ceremony had been maintained at least up to communist times, only partially replaced by Christian worship. Special groves were reserved for communal prayers to

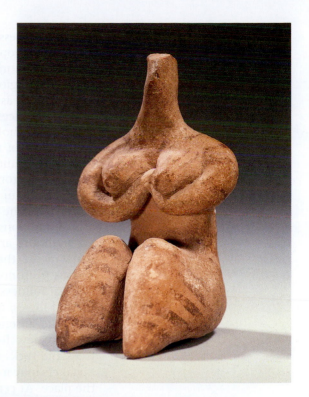

An early female figurine, representing the Great Mother or Goddess (Halaf style, c. 4500 BCE, Paris, Louvre).

the Progenitress in summer and late autumn. Now that freedom of religion is permitted, people are returning to the traditional agrarian rites for the earth's fertility and human links with the cosmic rhythms and energies. Some members of ethnic religions question why they should revere the myths of West Asian desert tribes, as in Judeo-Christian tradition, rather than the ethnic myths of their own ancestors and native lands. Though newly revived on the basis of folklore, mythology, and ethnic pride and given the label "ethnofuturism," the antecedents of these ways may be very ancient. Images of animal guardians have been found in peat bogs that date back as far as the eighth millennium BCE.

Teachers from earth-affirming religions that were never totally destroyed, such as certain Native American sacred ways, are highly valued as guides to worship for the natural world. From them, contemporary seekers have learned to use traditions such as vision quests, sweat lodges, and medicine wheels. But the traditions are complex, requiring lifelong training, and are interwoven with ways of life that have passed or developed in different environments. Neo-Pagans from non-native backgrounds usually cannot experience them in their original fullness. What remains is the intent: to honor and co-operate with the natural forces, to celebrate the circle of life rather than destroy it.

In the absence of sure knowledge of ancient traditions, Neo-Pagans often develop new forms of group ritual. Usually they are held outside, with the trees and rocks and waters, the sun, moon, and stars as the altars of the sacred. Speakers may invoke the pantheistic Spirit within all life or the invisible spirits of the place. At ceremonies dedicated to a phase of the moon or the change of the seasons, worshipers may be reminded of how their lives are interwoven with, and affected by, the natural rhythms. Prayers and ritual may be offered for the healing of the earth, the creatures, or the people.

Certain spots have traditionally been known as places of high energy, and these are often used for ceremonies and less structured sacred experiences. Ancient ceremonial sites in the British Isles, such as Stonehenge and Glastonbury Tor, draw a new breed of tour group wanting to experience the atmosphere of these places.

Neo-Pagan festivals are popular gatherings where participants shed their usual identities and perhaps their clothes, create temporary "kinship groups," and enjoy activities such as ritual fires, storytelling, dancing, and drumming, and workshops on subjects ranging from astrology to old methods of herbal healing.

Deep ecology In addition to groups that are looking to replicate or reinvent past ways of earth-centered worship, many people in nontraditional societies are now seeking new ways of connecting themselves with the cosmos. What is called deep ecology is the experience of oneness with the natural world. By contrast, most Western religions have cast humans as controllers of the natural world, of a different order of being than bears and flowers, mountains and rivers. Australian deep ecologist John Seed refers to this attitude as **"anthropocentrism"**—"human chauvinism, the idea that humans are the crown of creation, the source of all value, the measure of all things."[34]

> *What is man without the beasts? If all the beasts were gone, men would die from a great loneliness of spirit. For whatever happens to the beasts soon happens to the man. … The earth does not belong to man; man belongs to the earth. This we know. All things are connected like the blood which unites one family.*
>
> *Attributed to Chief Seattle[35]*

During the twentieth century, many people came to a new awareness of our planetary home when they first saw it photographed from space. Rather than a globe divided by natural political boundaries, it appeared as a beautiful being, its surface mostly covered by oceans, wreathed in clouds, floating in the darkness of space. Some scientists have taken up this metaphor of the earth as a being and are finding evidence of its scientific plausibility. Biogeochemist James Lovelock (b. 1919) proposed that the biosphere ("the entire range of living matter on Earth, from whales to viruses, and from oaks to algae") plus the earth's atmosphere, oceans, and soil can be viewed as "a single living entity, capable of manipulating the Earth's atmosphere to suit its overall needs and endowed with faculties and powers far beyond those of its constituent parts."[36] Lovelock named this complex, self-adjusting entity Gaia, after the Greek name for the Earth Goddess. In elaborations of his Gaia hypothesis, Lovelock emphasizes the "feminine" and divine characteristics of this being:

> *Any living organism a quarter as old as the Universe itself and still full of vigour is as near immortal as we ever need to know. She is of this Universe and, conceivably, a part of God. On Earth she is the source of life everlasting and is alive now; she gave birth to humankind and we are part of her.*[37]

A corollary to the Gaia hypothesis is the concept that humans are becoming the global brain of the planet, its mode of conscious evolution. In the "body" of Gaia, the tropical rainforests function as the liver and/or lungs, the oceans as the circulatory system, and so on. As the evolving brain of the planet, we are becoming conscious of the dangers our activities pose to these other parts of "our body." Peter Russell, author of *The Global Brain*, warns that we have little time to become fully conscious of our potential destructiveness, our connectedness to everything else, and to take appropriate action to forestall environmental disaster:

> *As a species we are facing our final examination; … it is in fact an intelligence test—a test of our true intelligence as a species. In essence we are being asked to let go of our self-centred thinking and egocentric behaviour. We are being asked to become psychologically mature, to free ourselves from the clutches of this limited identity, and express our creativity in ways which benefit us all.*[38]

Those who perceive a oneness of all life may be inspired to take political action to protect other members of the earth's body. Many support "green" political agendas on behalf of the environment. In Australia, Britain, and the northwest coast of the United States, people have chained themselves to giant

Since the 1970s, Chipko tribespeople of India have been protecting trees with their bodies and also planting new trees. Their movement has helped to limit deforestation, increase environmental awareness, reveal vested interests, change government forest policies, and demonstrate the power of marginalized tribal people.

trees to try to keep loggers from cutting them down. Julia Butterfly Hill spent 736 days living high in a 1,000-year-old redwood tree to protect it from loggers. She braved winter storms, high winds, and harassment by helicopter, refusing to come down until an agreement was negotiated with the logging company to protect the tree and the surrounding virgin forest. She was sustained by spirituality. As she wrote:

> One day, through my prayers, an overwhelming amount of love started flowing into me, filling up the dark hole that threatened to consume me. I suddenly realized that what I was feeling was the love of the Earth, the love of Creation. Every day we, as a species, do so much to destroy Creation's ability to give us life. But that Creation continues to do everything in its power to give us life anyway. And that's true love.[39]

Similarly, in 1974, the women and children of Reni, a Himalayan village, wrapped themselves around trees to protect them from woodcutters seeking wood for the cities. They knew that the trees' roots were like hands that kept the hillside from washing away, that they shaded the plants they used for medicine and homes for the animals and birds. They said, "The trees are our brothers and sisters."[40] Although some view such actions as romantically naive and hopeless, the "Tree-Hugging" movement grew to such proportions in northern India that the government banned commercial woodcutting in Uttar Pradesh.

New Age spirituality

A great variety of spiritual movements developed in the West in the 1970s and 1980s that drew on many characteristics of other "new" movements mentioned already—progressive millennialism, interest in the supernatural and "channeled" revelations from invisible beings, reverence for nature, and universalism. In addition, they are often characterized by a quest for self-improvement but in highly individualistic, anti-institutional formats. Collectively, these ways, rather than being called "religions," are therefore often called "New Age spiritual movements."

A special working group in the Vatican studying New Age groups concluded that they are among the "contemporary signs of the perennial human search for happiness, meaning, and salvation," which people from mainstream institutions may not have found in their own religion due to clergy's lack of attention to such central spiritual themes as "the importance of man's spiritual dimension and its integration with the whole of life."[41] As promoted in books and workshops, this amorphous but widespread movement anticipates that a network of personally transformed individuals will eventually lead to the transformation of the planet. Author Marianne Williamson voiced this hope in 1994:

> A mass movement is afoot in the world today, spiritual in nature and radical in its implications. After decades of declining influence on the affairs of the world, there is once again a widespread consideration of spiritual principles as an antidote to the pain of our times. Like flowers growing up through pieces of broken cement, signs of hope and faith appear everywhere. These signs reflect the light of a transcendent force at the center of things, present in our lives in a corrective and even miraculous manner, a light we can reach personally through internal work of a devotional nature. We are experiencing now an alteration of collective consciousness, centered not in government or science or religion per se. It is the rising up of our true divine nature, a reassertion of God in the consciousness of modern man.[42]

The roots of New Age spiritual movements are many, including Western esotericism, Spiritualism, Theosophy, astrology, and introduction of the Asian religions to the West. Another antecedent is found in discoveries about spiritual healing, developed into a full-fledged religious movement by Mary Baker Eddy (1821–1910) as Christian Science. In her *Science and Health with Key to the*

Scriptures, Eddy proposed that negative inner states such as hatred, fear, self-ishness, and envy obscure one's relationship with God's love. When they are surrendered, healing occurs naturally as one's true spiritual being emerges. Only God is real; the physical body, with its ailments, is not. Christian Scientists may refuse medical treatment, feeling that God is the healer.

A related trend is New Thought, which emphasizes the power of positive thinking. This diverse movement spread widely thanks to the efforts of Emma Curtis Hopkins (1849–1925). At first such groups were quite open to female leadership, but during the twentieth century some tended to revert to patri-archal male structures, with women only in supporting roles. Some are based on the teachings of a single charismatic leader, with organizations that support dissemination of their teachings without church buildings, a priesthood, or other features of organized religions.

One of the manifestations of New Thought that has proved relatively long-lived is the Unity School of Christianity, which dates back to 1886. Its inspirational publication, *Daily Word*, is now available in twelve languages. Like many other new religious movements, the Unity School makes extensive use of the Internet for sharing its teachings and practices. On *Daily Word*'s website, each day a different positive affirmation is posted for reflection, such as this one:

> *Life-giving energy flows throughout my body. I am renewed.*
>
> *Divine energy flows in and through God's creations, renewing, restoring, uplifting. I see this energy in the exuberance of a child, in the beauty of a flower blossom and in the vibrant display of autumn's colors. I feel it in the warmth of the sun's rays, the freshness of a gentle breeze.*
>
> *As I align my thoughts with life and wholeness, I feel divine energy in my own body as well. I am in the flow of life-giving energy, and it is in me. …*
> *I am renewed in mind, body and spirit, Thank You, God.*[43]

New Age spirituality is often mystical, favoring direct communion with the unseen. The Findhorn community is a striking example. One of its leaders, Dorothy Maclean, studied with Sufi masters, learning how to receive "inner guidance," before joining with Eileen and Peter Caddy in developing Findhorn, a transformation of desolate dunes on the coast of Scotland into a lush farming community. Dorothy's role was to receive communications from the energies that she called the plant *devas*, after the Hindu term for the invisible "shining ones." Dorothy developed a co-operative relationship with the *devas*, asking for their "advice" on matters such as what nutrients the plants needed. The Findhorn community receives thousands of visitors every year, has its own eco-village, and hosts workshops on many topics designed to elevate human consciousness.

The main thrust of the 1970s and 1980s New Age movement was the belief that a new era was arising in which poverty, war, racism, and despair would give way to a new feeling of global human community, with peace, harmony, and happiness prevailing. Since this was not to be accomplished through any religious or political organization, the idea developed that groups of people could act as receivers for positive cosmic energies so that their effects would create a "planetary consciousness" that would spread to the rest of the world. This belief was strengthened by widespread distribution of a book, *The Hundredth Monkey*, which described what later turned out to be a false report that monkeys on a Japanese island were affected by behavioral changes

Group meditation in the Findhorn community.

of monkeys on another island. Many New Age groups thus gathered to receive the cosmic energies and try to create enough critical mass to change the world.

The longed-for era of peace and harmony did not emerge, and talk of a "New Age" gradually faded away. However, the many professionals who were making a living as workshop leaders, holistic health practitioners, publishers of New Age literature, and the like were still on the scene. Collectively they shifted to emphasizing transformation in individual consciousness, perhaps coupled with the longer-term goal of global transformation.

While part of the New Age movement lost its millennial nature and focused instead on personal growth and the search for mystical communion through techniques such as meditation, a different millennial thrust developed in some circles: the idea that gradually "higher consciousness" will spread among enough humans for others to be drawn into the same enlightened worldview and thus the whole world will "ascend." This idea was popularized by the bestselling 1993 novel by James Redfield, *The Celestine Prophecy*, which claimed to be true and presented "nine key insights into life itself—insights each human being is predicted to grasp sequentially, one insight then another, as we move toward a completely spiritual culture on earth." The Ninth Insight is this:

> As we humans continue to increase our vibration, an amazing thing will begin to happen. Whole groups of people, once they reach a certain level, will suddenly become invisible to those who are still vibrating at a lower level. ... It will signal that we are crossing the barrier between this life and the other world from which we came and to which we go after death. This conscious crossing is the path shown by the Christ. ... At some point everyone will vibrate highly enough so that we can walk into heaven, in our same form.[44]

Sequels to the novel followed, including *The Tenth Insight*, in which spiritually evolved people create a new global spiritual culture.

Sociologists note that many people who participate in nature rituals and New Age movements are nomads, dabbling here and there without any deep commitment to what Stark and Bainbridge called "audience cults." In countries allowing freedom of religious choice, they may wander through a growing supermarket of spiritual offerings, taking a bit here and there according to their needs of the moment. Sandra Duarte de Souza describes "spiritual nomadism" in contemporary Brazil, where most people remain nominally Christian but many are also attracted to nature-oriented New Age groups. As opposed to a "radical change of life, marking the biography of the converted forever and demanding his faithfulness, ... the idea of 'religious transit' admits the 'walk through' several religions, does not demand intestinal changes in the way of life of the 'transilient,' and exempts or attenuates the commitment."[45] Of course, the same can be said of established religions—that many people belong to them without deeply transformational inner commitment.

Invented religions

One of the newest trends in religions is a medley of religion-like movements that mix features reminiscent of traditional religions with aspects of popular culture. This trend is an extreme example of contemporary individualistic mores which give people the freedom to pick and choose among various religious paths. Sociologist and cultural theorist Jean Baudrillard (1929–2007) referred to such pop culture hybrids as "hyper-reality," for in the bewildering array of signs and symbols in postmodern consumer society, the symbols of pop culture take on a life of their own and become more real for the consumer than ordinary reality. These "invented religions" take advantage of a wide range of technological resources, and are often promoted via the Internet and social media sites.

Science-fiction movies, Harry Potter, and role-playing fantasy games have morphed into new religious movements, such as "Jediism," based on the order of Jedi Knights in the *Star Wars* films. According to the website www.jediism.org, the Jedi movement incorporates strands of many older ways, including Hinduism, Confucianism, Buddhism, Gnosticism, Stoicism, Catholicism, Daoism, Shinto, modern mysticism, the way of Shaolin monks, samurai warriors, and the Code of Chivalry of medieval knights. The mission statement of Jediism draws on many of these traditions:

> *We are a caring and supportive spiritual community that helps individuals worldwide to attain and sustain a one-to-one-relationship with the Light of their own true Inner Self and therefore reconnect to their own True Divine Nature to which we refer as Jedi. ... Our intention is to make a difference by helping people rediscover the real values that inspire illumined action and create an atmosphere of enlightenment and peace, internally and simultaneously in our international community.*[46]

The famous line from Star Wars, "May the Force be with you," has been elaborated in Jediism into an explanation of what this Force is: "An energy field generated by all living things, the Force surrounds and penetrates everything, binding the universe together."[47] This hyper-real hybrid was promoted as a parody in 2001, when a grassroots movement urged people to record their religion as "Jedi" when approached by census-takers. Huge numbers of people did so—more than 70,000 in Australia, 21,000 in Canada, 15,070 in Czech Republic, more than 53,000 in New Zealand, and 390,127 in England and Wales. People's motivations for listing themselves as Jedi apparently ranged from amusement to protest over including the question of religious affiliation in census surveys.

The Church of the Flying Spaghetti Monster is another invented religion. Its origins lie in a letter that Bobby Henderson wrote to the Kansas Board of Education in 2005, suggesting that in addition to the theory of evolution and the theory of Intelligent Design, students also be taught that the universe was created by a Flying Spaghetti Monster. Henderson has detailed the Church's views in his 2006 book *The Gospel of the Flying Spaghetti Monster*, as well as on the group's website, www.venganza.org. The Church has no dogma other than to reject all dogma, and welcomes members of other religions. It explains, "We are not anti-religion; we are anti-crazy nonsense done in the name of religion."[48] Members are called Pastafarians. Church members have mocked laws regarding the wearing of religious regalia by attempting to have driver's license photos taken while wearing colanders on their heads. Some view the Church as satire, others as more serious. While there is no doubt an element of humor and occasional mockery in Pastafarian writings, Pastafarianism is in part a sincere commentary on complex debates about the contemporary religious scene, such as religious and secular laws regarding religious headgear, the relationship between religion and science, and the role of dogma versus individual choice in belief.

Opposition to new religious movements

What are some of the reasons for opposition to some new religious movements?

Throughout history, new religious movements have met with opposition from previously organized religions, which perceive them as threats to their own strength or brand them as heresies.

Baha'is claim that after the 1979 establishment of the Islamic Republic of Iran persecution of Baha'is has become official government policy. According to the Baha'i website, since that time:

> *more than 200 Baha'is have been executed or killed, hundreds more have been imprisoned, and tens of thousands have been deprived of jobs, pensions, businesses, and educational opportunities. Formal Baha'i administration had to be suspended, and holy places, shrines, and cemeteries have been confiscated, vandalized, or destroyed.*[49]

Drawing inspiration from the past in order to greet the future, contemporary Russians gather in a Moscow park to celebrate the spring equinox according to ancient Slavic rites.

In Russia, various foreign-based new religious movements are fighting for freedom of worship against a 1997 law, passed at the behest of the Russian Orthodox Church, that restricts the activities of groups that were newly introduced to Russia. Lawyers defending these groups have had some success in court cases with reference to Jehovah's Witnesses and organizations sponsored by the Unification Movement.

With or without prompting by established religions, nations may attempt to suppress new religious movements. China has taken strong measures to stamp out **Falun Gong**. The movement is one of many based on traditional Daoist **qigong** energy practices. During the 1990s, Chinese masters made qigong techniques even more popular by advertising that one could attain supernatural powers through them. The most famous of these claims are made by Li Hongzhi, who in 1992 developed a form of qigong that mixed Buddhism with Daoist energy practices, producing a hybrid known as Falun Gong. He proposed that he would spiritually install a "falun," or Dharma Wheel, in followers' abdomens so that they could perform advanced energy practices. Li, who now lives in exile, claims that practitioners of Falun Gong can attain excellent health, supernatural power, and cosmic enlightenment if they develop the cardinal virtues of truthfulness, benevolence, and forbearance as well as carrying out the daily exercises. These are taught for free by volunteers at thousands of locations around the world. The movement, also known as **Falun Dafa**, now claims millions of followers.

However, in 1999 the Chinese government characterized Falun Gong as an "evil cult." When approximately 10,000 people staged a silent protest in Beijing, the government responded by banning the movement, alleging that it had "been engaged in illegal activities, advocating superstition and spreading fallacies, hoodwinking people, inciting and creating disturbances, and jeopardizing social stability."[50] Subsequent protestors were reportedly jailed and beaten, followed by wave upon wave of peaceful protests by members who met the same fate. Some are said to have died from torture while in police custody. The government has also cracked down on other forms of qigong that it once supported, and legislation has been passed that may be used to suppress any mystical Chinese group and any other religious group that has not been sanctioned by the Chinese Communist Party. This is in keeping with the centuries-old Chinese governmental assumption that it is responsible for controlling every facet of life. Claims of human-rights abuses of Falun Gong practitioners continue. But the

movement still persists in China and other countries, and practitioners claim that Falun Gong has brought them physical healing, inner peace, and answers to the central questions of life.

Falun Gong members doing their meditation practices.

In addition to negative reactions from governments and established religions, new religious movements frequently meet with opposition from family members of those who join. They may be worried about violence that has sometimes been associated with some new religious movements and widely reported in the media. A catastrophic example occurred in Waco, Texas, in 1993, when a community of Branch Dravidians was besieged by federal officials: a fire broke out and approximately eighty of the Branch Dravidians died as the fire engulfed their compound. The Branch Dravidians had been anticipating the millennium and trying to obey what they understood to be God's will, preparing for the end of the world as prophesied by their messiah, David Koresh. Another spectacular violent incident occurred in 1995, when members of the Aum Shinrikyo movement launched a poison-gas attack on the Tokyo subway under the leadership of Shoko Asahara.

Religion-related violence is not limited to new religious movements. Religious extremists who claim to be followers of major established religions are resorting to violence in many parts of the globe. Are the followers of new religious movements different? Whether old or new, if movements are sincerely expecting imminent world changes and have isolated themselves to prepare for the end, they distance themselves from other points of view. In isolation and group solidarity, seemingly irrational beliefs—such as the apocalyptic scenario of the biblical book of Revelation—may seem to make perfect sense.

In addition to isolation and group support in their beliefs, religious movements may in rare cases turn violent in response to hostility from the surrounding culture. This response is called "deviance amplification" in the literature. Specialists in new religious movements Massimo Introvigne and Jean-François Mayer have observed that when some groups perceive threats from the outside they encourage their members to feel that they are not of this world. When under attack from the outside and also perhaps shaken by defections of disillusioned members, they may conclude that suicide is their only good option. People enter the group of their own free will, but when the trend toward suicide or violence becomes apparent they may find it difficult to leave if the leader is extremely charismatic or even coercive. Families of those who join unfamiliar religious movements may thus fear that they may be dangerous.

There is also concern that new religious movements may cause psychological damage, especially to vulnerable young people. In the United States, the "anti-cult" movement employed special agents who captured and "deprogrammed" followers of new religions, at the request of their parents. However, the claim that members of new religious movements had been "brainwashed" has been largely discredited. As Professor Catherine Wessinger notes, mainstream social and religious institutions all practice some kind of indoctrination in which people's thinking is molded:

> *Usually the processes utilized by members of NRMs to attract and socialize converts are not different from those used in mainstream families and institutions. Belief in brainwashing offers a simplistic explanation for why people adopt unconventional beliefs. It obscures the fact that people adopt alternative beliefs because those beliefs make sense to them, and that people join groups because those groups offer them benefits. [The new religious movements that she examined] all regarded people in mainstream society as being brainwashed by television, the media, educational institutions, and by the values of materialistic society. They believed that their respective groups taught the truth as opposed to the delusions of the brainwashed people in external society. In most cases, the members willingly undertook the discipline and lifestyle of their unconventional religion, which they believed would lead to achieving salvation, their ultimate concern.*[51]

The "brainwashing" theory has been further undermined by studies showing considerable "voluntary turnover"—most people who are introduced to new religious movements' philosophies choose not to adopt them, and even those who enter new religious movements, or whose parents are followers, are more likely to leave than to stay in them.

In addition to the discrediting of the brainwashing theory of why people join new religious movements, the coercive deprogramming techniques of the anti-cult movement have been deemed illegal in themselves. The Cult Awareness Network went bankrupt in 1996 after one of its deprogramming victims won a multimillion-dollar damage suit against it. Nevertheless, what are now called "anti-cult activities" continue in the hands of other organizations, such as the International Cultic Studies Association. Anti-cult activities are also rampant on the Internet, which is now a hotbed of allegations against new religious movements. These can be posted by anyone, without any editorial control. At the same time, the Internet allows new religious movements to present their own positions, unfiltered by anti-cult prejudice.

There are also governmental efforts to eliminate or control new religious movements in Europe, where governments are struggling with issues of religious freedom versus public safety. France is home to hundreds of new religious groups, including the secret Order of the Solar Temple, some of whose members died in mass suicides and murders during the 1990s. There has been concern that some new religious movements are using a religious front to carry on illegal businesses or to extort money from gullible followers. There is also concern in Germanic countries and the United States about neo-fascist groups in the guise of medieval cults whose intentions seem to involve the propagation of white supremacy ideas and hatred of immigrants.

The French government has enacted secularizing legislation that inhibits the practice of many mainstream religions, in addition to anti-cult legislation and police scrutiny of groups such as Mormons, Jehovah's Witnesses, and Scientologists, as well as evangelical and charismatic Christian groups. In Italy, by contrast, the Supreme Court in 1997 overruled a lower-court judgment that had defined "religion" only as Judaism or Christianity; non-profit recognition and tax exemption was extended to Scientology by the court ruling. Germany grants tax-exempt status only to a few long-established religions, excluding not only new religious movements but also Islam, Hinduism, and Buddhism.

Will new religious movements last?

What are the five secular factors that predispose a new religious movement to last?

All of the major religions were once new and were once resisted by more entrenched institutions. Will any of today's new religious movements last more than a few generations? Those who study the sociology of religion are researching the secular factors that seem to predispose a new religious movement to become widespread and longlasting. One of these is a balance between similarities to existing beliefs (making it attractive and nonthreatening to potential converts) and differences compelling enough for people to convert.

A second factor is organization, personal commitment, and bonds between members that will survive the death of the prophet and the original followers. This factor includes efforts to propagate the new religion, including hagiographies—idealized accounts of the life of the founder designed to interest new members. These may diverge from the known facts, a common occurrence within the process of popular myth-making.

A third factor is the social setting: Times of great social change, places that allow freedom of choice in matters of religion, and societies with fragmented relationships between people are most conducive to the recruitment of new members. Fourth is the status of prevailing religions; if they have become merely institutional with little spiritual life they are susceptible to being supplanted by more vibrant new faiths. Fifth is the younger generations: Children must be continually born or recruited into the faith, taught its values, and given responsible parts to play in keeping the faith alive.

The spiritual aspects of new religions are also of major importance but they cannot easily be quantified. Among these are the genuine spirituality of the founder or spreader of the message, and the ability of the new teachings and their presentation to capture people's hearts, change their lives, motivate them to act collectively, and give them the courage to face social opposition.

Frank Kaufmann, founder of Filial Projects and long-time director of the Unification movement's Inter-Religious Federation for World Peace, offers these insights from his decades of experience within a new religious movement:

> One of my recent observations is the persistent power of religion based in its malleable interpretive power. Believers say with equal peace, "Look! People really like us. This is proof our religion is true," and "Look! Everybody hates us. This is proof our religion is true." You've got opposite facts being used to support the assurance that everything is fine—both giving believers confidence and solace that they are on the right path. Not bad. You can't get away with that selling stocks, or selling socks.
>
> But this kind of self-proving and self-assuring is for those who hold their beliefs at some vague distance, and are happy for postcards of "proof" from the pulpit. What's closer (and in my opinion, more important) is what you love, and what you know. For self-aware believers, the divine comes into your life through some person or another. If you are lucky, by God's grace you remain eternally bound to that person. Over the course of time that person teaches you things he or she believes are true. You try them out, and in the process compile your own affirmations and confirmations, aided each step of the way by God's loving help and hints.[52]

Key terms

apocalypse The dramatic end of the present age.

apostasy The accusation of abandonment of religious principles.

cult Any religion that focuses on worship of a particular person or deity.

ethnic religions New religions that emerged since the fall of Communism as revivals of pre-Christian ethnic traditions in eastern Europe and Russia.

Goddess spirituality Worship of a female high goddess in ancient times, now revived in many places.

millennium One thousand years, a term used in Christianity and certain newer religions for a hoped-for period of 1,000 years of holiness and happiness, with Christ ruling the earth, as prophesied in the Book of Revelation.

Neo-Paganism Nature-oriented spirituality referring to pre-Christian sacred ways.

orisa Yoruba term for a deity.

rapture Nineteenth-century belief among some Christians, using Paul's letter to the Thessalonians, that Christians would be caught up in clouds to meet Jesus when he returned to earth.

Santeria The combination of African and Christian practices that developed in Cuba.

sect A subgroup within a larger tradition.

Wicca Neo-Pagan sect of a secret coven of witches traced to the writings of Gerald Gardner in England in the 1940s.

Suggested reading

Barker, Eileen, *New Religious Movements: A Practical Introduction*, London: Her Majesty's Stationery Office, 1989. A sociological study on the effects of new religious movements on people's lives.

Beckford, James A. and James T. Richardson, eds, *Challenging Religion: Essays in Honor of Eileen Barker*, London: Routledge, 2003. Essays by sociologists exploring how societies and governments respond to new religious movements.

Blavatsky, H. P., *The Key to Theosophy*, Los Angeles: The United Lodge of Theosophists, 1920. A wide-ranging survey of esoterica from many of the world's religions.

Bromley, David G. and Phillip E. Hammond, eds, *The Future of New Religious Movements*, Macon, Georgia: Mercer University Press, 1987. Interesting sociological analyses of the likelihood of long-run success of some contemporary movements.

Cleary, Thomas and Sartaz Aziz, *Twilight Goddess: Spiritual Feminism and Feminine Spirituality*, Boston: Shambhala, 2002. Explorations of feminine principles and Goddess worship in a variety of religions.

Daschke, Dereck and Michael Ashcraft, *New Religious Movements: A Documentary Reader*, New York: New York University Press, 2005. New religious movements speak for themselves in these excerpts from founders and followers.

Dawson, Lorne L., *Comprehending Cults: The Sociology of New Religious Movements*, Oxford: Oxford University Press, 1998. Sociological study of the emergence and members of new religious movements, and predictors of violent tendencies.

Dawson, Lorne L., *Cults and New Religious Movements: A Reader*, Oxford: Blackwell Publishing, 2003. Original source material from a variety of new religious movements.

Esselmont, J. E., *Baha'u'llah and the New Era: An Introduction to the Baha'i Faith*, Wilmette, Illinois: Baha'i Publishing, 2006. First published in 1923 but slightly updated through several editions, this book is still widely used as an introduction to the faith.

Gallagher, Eugene V. and W. Michael Ashcraft, eds, *Introduction to New and Alternative Religions in America*, five vols, Westport, Connecticut: Greenwood Press, 2006. A thorough collection of essays addressing key topics in new religions as well as studies of specific groups.

Hall, John R., Sylvaine Trinh, and Philip Schuyler, eds, *Apocalypse Observed: Religious Movements, Social Order and Violence in North America, Europe, and Japan*, London: Routledge, 2000. Articles analyzing situations within which violent new religious movements have developed.

Melton, J. Gordon, *The Church of Scientology*, Salt Lake City, Utah: Signature Books, 2000. A scholar analyzes the development of Scientology as a movement to clear the mind, a Church, and a social-service organization, and describes controversies it has faced.

Melton, J. Gordon and Christopher Partridge, *New Religions: A Guide*, Oxford: Oxford University Press, 2004. Over 200 groups and new religious movements are described according to their roots in older traditions or New Age alternatives.

Miller, Timothy, ed., *When Prophets Die: The Postcharismatic Fate of New Religious Movements*, Albany, New York: State University of New York Press, 1991. Contemporary case studies of how the followers of strong founders have or have not succeeded in keeping the faith alive.

Miller, Timothy, ed., *America's Alternative Religions*, Albany: State University of New York Press, 1995. A lengthy survey of the major alternative traditions in America, with chapters written by scholars specializing in specific groups.

Pike, Sarah, *New Age and Neopagan Religions in America*, New York: Columbia University Press, 2006. Helpful introduction to a wide range of New Age and Neo-Pagan practices, from nature worship to women's leadership roles.

Plaskow, Judith, and Carol Christ, eds, *Weaving the Visions: New Patterns in Feminist Spirituality*, San Francisco: HarperCollins, 1989. Inclusive, Goddess, feminist, and womanist perspectives from several religions.

Seed, John, Joanna Macy, Pat Fleming, and Arne Naess, *Thinking Like a Mountain: Towards a Council of All Beings*, Philadelphia: New Society Publishers, 1988, 2007. Some of the leaders of the deep ecology movement offer a collection of thoughts and exercises to lead one into the experience of kinship with all life.

Starhawk, *The Spiral Dance: A Rebirth of the Ancient Religion of the Great Goddess*, San Francisco and London: Harper & Row, 1979, 1999. A lyrical, experimental introduction to the interweaving of the God and Goddess principles.

Stark, Rodney and William Sims Bainbridge, *The Future of Religion: Secularization, Revival, and Cult Formation*, Berkeley, California: University of California Press, 1985. Includes a sociological classification of religious groups in relation to their broader environment.

Wessinger, Catherine, *How the Millennium Comes Violently: From Jonestown to Heaven's Gate*, New York: Seven Bridges Press, 2000. Develops the theory that violence is catalyzed by certain types of interactions.

12.1 Differentiate between a "sect" and a "cult"

A sect is a splinter group or a subgroup that has broken ties with a larger religious tradition. A cult arises outside other religious traditions and may also be in conflict with surrounding society. While the terms "sect" and "cult" are in popular use, the label "new religious movement" is considered more neutral and is now widely used to avoid negative connotations.

12.2 Discuss the role that may be played by a charismatic leader in the development of a new religious movement

New religious movements often begin in the same way as many established religions: A charismatic figure emerges who develops a dedicated following of people who regard him or her as their spiritual teacher, prophet, or messiah. New figures periodically arise and attract a lot of followers, such as the spiritual leaders Rev. Sun Myung Moon (Unification Church) and Sathya Sai Baba. These two leaders developed far-flung and diversified service and propagation organizations, which helped their movements to survive when they died.

12.3 Identify three contemporary new religious movements that are offshoots of older religions

Newer offshoots of older religions are often sufficiently different from their parent religion to be considered new religious movements. One example is the Mormon Church, which distinguishes itself from the many variations of mainstream Christianity through its belief in the Book of Mormon as well as the Bible. Jehovah's Witnesses are also an offshoot of Christianity, placing their faith in the Bible and foreseeing a new world in which people of all races will experience paradise on earth. Radhasoami is an outgrowth of Sikhism in India, but unlike Sikhs, who believe in a succession of masters that stopped with the Tenth Guru, Radhasoamis believe in a continuing succession of living masters.

12.4 Compare and contrast several movements that combine differing beliefs of traditional religions

Caodaism, Santeria, and Agon Shu all intermingle components from different traditions. Caodaism, which arose in Vietnam in the early twentieth century, is made from parts of many world religions, including Judaism, Christianity, Islam, Buddhism, Confucianism, and Daoism plus the indigenous Vietnamese religion Geniism. In the Caribbean and Latin America, Santeria blends some of the deities and beliefs of slaves from Dahomey, Bakongo, and Yoruba cultures with images of Catholic saints. In Japan, Agon Shu combines Buddhist, Shinto, and Daoist beliefs and practices in dramatic ceremonies.

12.5 Summarize the key belief of universalism and give an example of a universalist movement

Some new religious movements do not just blend together components of different religions, but see themselves as encompassing all religions. Typically they teach that all prophets have brought essentially the same messages to humanity, though in different times and places. Examples include the Theosophical Society, founded by Madame Blavatsky in the nineteenth century, and Baha'i, a new global religion that attempts to unite all of humanity in the belief that there is only one God, and that he has become known through the founders of the great world religions.

12.6 Outline some of the aspects furthered by new religious movements arising from social trends

Examples of movements arising from social trends within the last hundred years include those that further racial/ethnic identity (Rastafari), affection for nature (Neo-Paganism, Wicca), deep ecology (Chipko Tree-Hugging movement), New Age spirituality (New Age movement, Findhorn community), and popular culture (invented religions such as Jediism and the Flying Spaghetti Monster movement).

12.7 Explain the reasons behind the opposition to some new religious movements

Throughout history, new religious movements have met with opposition from established religions, which perceive them as threats to their own strength or brand them as heresies. In Europe, where governments are concerned about the allegedly illegal business activities and intentions of some movements, as well as struggling with issues of religious freedom versus public safety, efforts have been made to eliminate or control them. In China the government has taken strong measures to stamp out Falun Gong, which it considers an "evil cult" engaged in illegal activities, spreading fallacies, and jeopardizing social stability.

Opposition to new religious movements may also come from family members of those who join, concerned about possible psychological damage or worried about the violence that has sometimes been associated with new movements.

12.8 Analyze the secular factors that predispose a new religious movement to last

The factors that seem to predispose a new religious movement to become widespread and long-lasting are: the balance between similarities with and differences from existing beliefs (making it nonthreatening and yet appealing); organization, personal commitment, and bonds between members (enabling the movement to survive the death of the prophet and the original followers); social setting (times of great social change, places that allow freedom of choice in matters of religion, and societies with fragmented relationships between people are most conducive to the recruitment of new members); the status of prevailing religions (susceptible to being replaced if they have become merely institutional with little spiritual life); the younger generations (to keep the faith alive children must be continually born or recruited into the faith, taught its values, and given responsible parts to play in it).

CHAPTER 13

RELIGION IN THE TWENTY-FIRST CENTURY

"These exclusive ideas propagated by the religious authorities have been repeated so long that it will take some time for people to change their thinking." Baba Virsa Singh[1]

13.1 Define globalization

13.2 Outline the forms of Western secularism described in this chapter

13.3 Identify some of the factors that have led to a hardening of religious boundaries

13.4 Discuss the advantages and disadvantages of religions' involvement in politics

13.5 Summarize the ways in which people of different religions may relate to each other

13.6 Discuss the key social issues religions are dealing with today

13.7 Describe how religious observers have responded to issues of materialism in the contemporary world

13.8 Explain the importance of the study of religions for the future of humanity

As the twenty-first century progresses, religion has returned to the foreground in human history. Political conflicts involving religions are assuming great importance on the world scene, and religious perspectives and influence are being sought to solve pressing global challenges, including the potential for catastrophic climate change. Therefore, as we conclude this survey of religions as living, changing, interacting movements, an overview of religion is necessary to gain a sense of how religion is affecting human life now and what impact it may have in the future.

Globalization

What is globalization?

Human factors in the global landscape are not what they once were. In contrast to earlier centuries, in which regions were relatively isolated from each other, two major world wars and other violent conflicts, technological advances, and population shifts have brought us into much closer contact. Our world has been "shrinking" through increasing urbanization (over half of all people now live in cities) and globalization. Primarily through markets and businesses, regional and national economies have become part of an interconnected global network. Cultural and social connectivity is also increasing, through technological innovations such as the Internet and air travel, political alliances such as the European Union, and the entertainment industry.

Global integration has thus far been largely seen as a one-way process, with Western ways dominating and other cultures and societies tending to be submerged. The 2008 financial meltdown in American banks threatened economies and jobs around the globe. More than eighty percent of all websites are in English, particularly American English. Television programming tends to follow models created in the United States such as quick-bite newscasts. And an estimated eighty-three percent of the film offerings in Latin America and fifty percent in Japan consist of Hollywood movies.[2]

However, globalization of culture is not only one-way. For example, Hindu beliefs have been influencing North American culture since the time of John Adams, who after leaving the presidency in 1801 told Thomas Jefferson that he had been reading "everything I could collect" about "Hindoo religion,"[3] and the nineteenth-century early Transcendentalist philosopher Ralph Waldo Emerson, who was deeply influenced by Vedanta. Popular culture—from The Beatles' encounter with Maharishi Mahesh Yogi to Indian-born American Deepak Chopra's talk-show appearances, seminars, and best-selling books—has also brought Hindu spiritual terms such as "karma" and "guru" into everyday vocabulary in the West, and yoga and meditation have become common aspects of Western lifestyles.

Intermixing or overlaying of cultures is also occurring because of immigration. The United States was built on the basis of immigration from various countries and was known as a "melting pot." Emigration in search of economic gain is still happening around the world, creating myriads of diaspora communities as well as individuals of mixed roots. Political violence and natural disasters also continue to send huge numbers of people from their homelands in search of refuge. Oppressed in Tibet, Tibetan Buddhists established a new homeland in India, and lamas are giving Dharma teachings in many countries. Abject poverty, starvation, political collapse, and civil war in Muslim-majority Somalia forced great numbers of Somalians to seek asylum in neighboring Christian-majority Kenya, and millions of Syrians, Iraqis, and Palestinians have been internally displaced or have sought refuge in neighboring countries because of conflicts in their homelands, creating humanitarian problems of immense proportions. For many people, cultural grounding in a fixed sense of place has been lost because of such dislocations.

In addition to such factors, the speed of change has been increasing. Social media are now accessible to ordinary people everywhere, with even poor people owning cell phones. Small issues can quickly become flashpoints as information travels. *Innocence of Muslims*, an otherwise obscure amateurish video produced in the United States, was uploaded to YouTube in 2012, quickly leading to violent protests, deaths, and injuries around the world because of its anti-Muslim content. Since even powerful governments are unable to control the rapid spread of information, whether true or false, Frank Kaufmann, editor-in-chief of *New World Encyclopedia* and director of the Inter Religious Federation for World Peace, concludes that radical cultural and political reform is now essential:

At the heart of this desperate need for radical reform is a curious blend of our finest avant garde, and a concomitant loss of an indispensable rear guard. The avant garde are the relentless and lightning advances in information technology. The rear guard is the lost glue of human integration, namely the mediating institutions through which we learn the rules and dynamics of being properly human in the world. ... The mediating structures to which I refer, weakened by the force of modernity, are family, church (i.e., my own religious home in whatever religion), and neighborhood. ... With the loss of mediating structures, human affairs crack into ever more centralized governing (increasing the use of force and constantly spying on citizens), and increasingly empowered private citizens with ever greater tools for self governance and decision making. The bridge between the two, structures needed to mediate bonds of mutual care between the ruling and the ruled, have crumbled away.[4]

As we speed into the future, religions have the potential for providing the "glue" of human integration, but also, if misused, could play a major role in social disintegration.

Secularism

What are the forms of secularism described?

Until the Iranian revolution in 1979, which brought Islam to the fore as a potent social force, there was a common assumption by Western intellectuals that "Europe's past is the world's future." That is, just as many Europeans had lost interest in religion since the Enlightenment, the whole world would eventually secularize. This assumption that religion would become irrelevant in people's lives was shared by capitalism, Communism, and liberalism.

Charles Taylor, Professor of Philosophy at McGill University, describes three forms of Western secularism. One refers to "public spaces":

This chart shows the percentage of the world's population that follows each of the various religions, based on statistics compiled by Pew Research Center's Forum on Religion and Public life—Global Religious Landscape, December 2012.

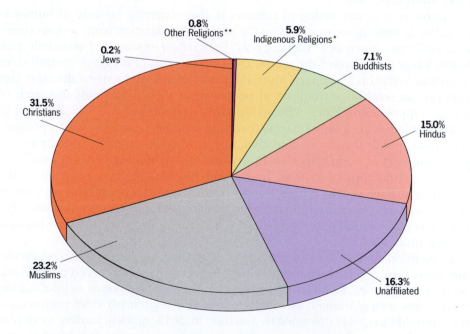

- 0.8% Other Religions **
- 5.9% Indigenous Religions *
- 7.1% Buddhists
- 0.2% Jews
- 15.0% Hindus
- 31.5% Christians
- 16.3% Unaffiliated
- 23.2% Muslims

*   Includes followers of African traditional religions, Chinese folk religions, Native American religions and Australian Aboriginal religions.

**   Includes Bahai's, Jains, Sikhs, Shintoists, Daoists, followers of Tenrikyo, Wiccans, Zoroastrians and many other faiths.

Percentages may not add to 100 due to rounding.

These have been allegedly emptied of God, or of any reference to ultimate reality. … As we function within various spheres of activity—economic, political, cultural, educational, professional, recreation—the norms and principles we follow, the deliberations we engage in, generally don't refer us to God or to any religious beliefs; the considerations we act on are internal to the "rationality" of each sphere—maximum gain within the economy, the greatest benefit to the greatest number in the political area, and so on. This is in striking contrast to earlier periods.

Professor Taylor also describes another form of secularism—its individual dimensions (which he sees mostly with reference to Western Christianity):

In this second meaning, secularity consists in the falling off of religious belief and practice, in people turning away from God, and no longer going to church. In this sense, the countries of western Europe have mainly become secular—even those who retain the vestigial public reference to God in public space.

Yet a third meaning of secularism is the social condition in which religious faith is only one of various possibilities. In Taylor's words:

Belief in God is no longer axiomatic. There are alternatives. And this will also likely mean that at least in certain milieus, it may be hard to sustain one's faith. There will be people who feel bound to give it up, even though they mourn its loss. There will be many others to whom faith never even seems an eligible possibility.[5]

As religion became an option that some have rejected, there was a spate of books by Western authors overtly critical of religion, such as *The End of Faith* by Sam Harris (2005), *The God Delusion* by Richard Dawkins (2006), *When Religion Becomes Evil* by Charles Kimball (2006), and *God Is Not Great: How Religion Poisons Everything* by Christopher Hitchens (2008). Even half a century ago, such literature would have been unthinkable.

Yet a fourth meaning of secularism applies to countries such as the United States, India, and Turkey, where the modern constitutional separation of religion and state may be referred to as "secularism," even though individuals may have strong belief structures. The United States has the largest percentage of church-going people in the industrialized countries of the world, yet its constitution insists on a wall of separation between the state and religion. In a secular democracy, the government is supposed to respect the rights of individuals to their own religious beliefs, thus protecting minority religions from oppression.

In all four senses, secularism is now decreasing. In contrast to the "first generation" of highly skeptical New Atheists, some atheist intellectuals are conceding that religion is an important bearer of social meaning. Many religions are undergoing a strong resurgence, either in their home regions or elsewhere and political secularism is being threatened by politicized religious pressure groups.

Religious pluralism
What factors have led to a hardening of religious boundaries?

Within these social, political, and cultural contexts, the global picture of religion is changing. A major feature of contemporary religious geography is that no single religion dominates the world. Although leaders from many faiths have historically asserted that theirs is the best and only way, in actuality new religions and new versions of older religions continue to spring up and then divide, subdivide, and provoke reform movements. Christianity claims the most members of any global religion, but Christianity is not a monolithic faith. Thousands of forms of Christianity are now being professed.

With migration, missionary activities, and refugee movements, religions have shifted from their country of origin. It is no longer so easy to show a world map in which each country is assigned to a particular religion. In Russia there are not only Russian Orthodox Christians but also Muslims, Catholics, Protestants,

Religions are now practiced far from the countries where they originated. This Tibetan Buddhist nun is practicing on the Holy Island of Lindisfarne in the United Kingdom.

Jews, Buddhists, Hindus, shamanists, and members of new religions. At the same time, there are now sizable Russian Orthodox congregations in the United States. Buddhism arose in India but now is most pervasive in East Asia and popular in Europe and North America. Islam arose in what is now Saudi Arabia, but there are more Muslims in Indonesia than in any other country. There are large Muslim populations in Central Asia, and growing Muslim populations in the United States, with more than fifty mosques in the city of Chicago alone.

Professor Diana Eck, director of the Pluralism Project at Harvard University, describes what she terms the new "geo-religious reality":

> Our religious traditions are not boxes of goods passed intact from generation to generation, but rather rivers of faith—alive, dynamic, ever-changing, diverging, converging, drying up here, and watering new lands there.
>
> We are all neighbors somewhere, minorities somewhere, majorities somewhere. This is our new geo-religious reality. There are mosques in the Bible Belt in Houston, just as there are Christian churches in Muslim Pakistan. There are Cambodian Buddhists in Boston, Hindus in Moscow, Sikhs in London.[6]

Hardening of religious boundaries

As religions proliferate and interpenetrate geographically, one common response has been the attempt to deny the validity of other religions. In many countries there is tension between the religion that has been most closely linked with national history and identity and other religions that are practiced or have been introduced into the country. With the collapse of Communism, Protestant congregations rushed to offer Bibles and religious tracts to citizens of formerly atheistic communist countries, with the idea that they were introducing Christianity there. But Orthodox Christianity, established more than a thousand years ago in Russia, had continued to exist there, even though the Church structures were limited and controlled by the state. The need for immigrant labor to sustain economic activity in Switzerland brought Muslims into the country, but some Swiss people were so afraid that Muslims might take over that in 2009 more than fifty-seven percent voted to ban construction of minarets in the country, a symbolic gesture that was opposed by the government. People from more established religions are struggling to find a balance between freedom of religion for all and the threat they perceive from religious minorities to their traditional values, customs, and sense of national identity.

One issue that arises where there is a diversity of religions is that of legal jurisdiction. Can Muslim minorities in a pluralistic nation-state be governed by their own traditional shari'ah laws, or must they accept the common law of the country? And vice versa: Must other religious minorities in a Muslim-ruled country be subject to the laws of shari'ah? In some northern states of Nigeria, for instance, Muslims and Christians clashed over attempts to implement a particular form of full shari'ah jurisdiction, which could mean applying punishments such as stoning to death in cases of adultery, flogging for those convicted of sexual intercourse outside of marriage, and amputation of the hand of a person convicted of theft.

Another issue arises concerning which religions will receive state funding. Registration requirements are another means

This poster was highly influential in frightening Swiss citizens into voting in 2009 for a ban on minarets for mosques: Minarets designed to look like missiles with their shadows falling across the Swiss flag and a burqa-clad woman evoked negative sentiments.

used to help control or at least track the introduction of religions into countries where they did not originate. Another is outright banning of new or minority religions. In 1997, the Russian parliament passed a law prohibiting religions that had not officially existed in Russia longer than fifteen years from distributing religious materials or newspapers or running schools. The law protects the traditional status of the Russian Orthodox Church and Islam, Buddhism, and Judaism, with some concessions to Protestant and Roman Catholic Christianity.

Religious symbols have become the focus for the French government's attempts to keep religion within bounds. In 2004, a controversial law was passed forbidding the wearing of religious symbols including Muslim veils, Sikh turbans, Jewish yarmulkes, and large Christian crosses in French public schools and colleges. The government also tried to restrict the activities of new religious movements, as well as charismatic and evangelical Christian groups, even though its constitution states "France shall respect all beliefs." Similar legislation has also been passed in other European countries, particularly with reference to the wearing of burqas.

Hardening of religious boundaries has in many places shattered co-existence among people of different religions. In some previously communist countries, old distinctions between people of different ethnic groups resurfaced with great violence once totalitarian regimes toppled. These intense ethnic and political struggles often pitted people of different faiths against each other, as in former Yugoslavia. Where there had been a seemingly peaceful society, horrifying atrocities arose among largely Orthodox Christian Serbs, Roman Catholic Croats, and Muslims. The United States-led invasion of Iraq in 2003 and then military withdrawal in 2011 opened the door to violent conflicts between Sunni and Shia Muslims in the country, and the political fallout is still spreading. The popular uprisings throughout the Arab world starting in 2011 have in many places been co-opted by violent extremist movements that inflame hatreds between people of different religions or sects of the same religion and promote "identity politics." In the struggles between Israelis and Palestinians, violence by both sides has led to increasing mistrust of the "other."

Boundaries between religions have also hardened in recent times because of the clash between fundamentalism and modernism. Along with the salient features of modernity—complex technologies, globalization, urbanization, bureaucratization, and rationality—have come the values collectively known as "modernism." They include individualism, a preference for change rather than continuity, quantity rather than quality, efficiency rather than traditional skills and aesthetics, and pragmatism and profiteering rather than eternal truths and values. Modernism is perceived by some fundamentalists as threatening the very existence of traditional religious values; contemporary secular culture seems crude, sacrilegious, and socially dangerous.

Some fundamentalists have tried to withdraw socially from the secular culture even while surrounded by it. Others have actively tried to change the culture, using political power to shape social laws or lobbying for banning of textbooks that they feel do not include their religious point of view. As described by the Project on Religion and Human Rights:

> *Fundamentalists' basic goal is to fight back—culturally, ideologically, and socially—against the assumptions and patterns of life that are taken for granted in contemporary secular society and culture, refusing to celebrate them or to embrace them fully. They keep their distance and refuse to endorse the legitimacy of any culture that opposes what they perceive as fundamental truths. Secular culture, in their eyes, is base, barbarous, crude, and essentially profane. It produces a society that respects no sacred order and ignores the possibility of redemption.*[7]

Political leaders have found the religious loyalty and absolutism of some fundamentalists an expedient way to mobilize political loyalties. Thus, Hindu extremists in India were encouraged to demolish Muslim mosques thought to be built on the foundation of older Hindu temples and to rebuild Hindu temples in their place. The United States, which had prided itself on being a melting pot for all cultures, with full freedom of religion and no right of government to promote any specific religion, has witnessed attempts by Christian fundamentalists—the "Religious Right"—to control education and politics, and a simultaneous rise in violence against ethnic and religious minorities. Buddhism, long associated with nonviolence, has become involved in the violent suppression of the Hindu minority in Sri Lanka. The Internet reveals the sentiments and activities of a troubling number of hate groups promoting intolerance, bigotry, hatred, and violence against specific others in the name of religion.

Religion after September 11

The stunning attacks by terrorists on United States targets in 2001 brought instant polarization along religious and ethnic lines. Hundreds of hate crimes were committed in the United States against Muslims and immigrants who were mistaken for Muslims. As some Americans responded in fear and rage, these groups were suddenly seen as "outsiders." With the subsequent bombing of Afghanistan and Iraq, the perpetrators of terrorism such as Osama bin Laden incited Muslims to see the world in terms of Muslims versus the infidels, and to join together to drive the United States out of its strategic positions in Islamic lands. Both sides claimed that God was on their side and their cause a holy one.

While the Christian Identity movement promoted ideas of Christian supremacy in the United States, leaders of Al Qaeda selectively cited passages from the Holy Qur'an to give the appearance of spiritual legitimacy to their militant teachings. After September 11, Osama bin Laden proclaimed:

> These events have divided the world into two camps, the camp of the faithful and the camp of infidels. … Every Muslim must rise to defend his religion. … God is the greatest and glory be to Islam.[8]

Once groups have taken such oppositional standpoints, violence seems inevitable. In search of sensational news that sells, the media often fan local issues into widespread conflicts. Dr. Rosalind Hackett, Professor of Religious Studies at the University of Tennessee, found this true of media coverage of inter-religious tensions in Nigeria:

> There is plenty of evidence of how local conflicts get transformed into national issues by virtue of media coverage, especially if that coverage is particularly biased and provocative, which it often can be. … [Nigeria] represents an interesting case of a country which has moved from being renowned for its religious tolerance up to about 30 years ago to one known the world over for its interreligious tensions and conflict.[9]

In some areas, inter-religious animosities have been stirred up to the point that people are even ready to sacrifice their lives as suicide bombers, kill innocent people in terrorist attacks, conduct assassinations, or bomb populated areas, for the sake of what they consider to be a holy cause. Study of suicide bombers in organizations such as Al Qaeda and Hamas in Palestine shows that the suicide attackers tend to be well educated and to come from relatively well-off families. Theirs is not the easily exploited despair of poverty and ignorance; it is the conviction of ideology. Pilots dropping bombs and soldiers treating prisoners brutally may similarly be motivated by the conviction that they are doing the right thing and attacking evil by "countering terrorism." And some who kill innocent people may not be motivated by any kind of principles. Instead, they may be emotionally angry and callous, or simply hired killers working for money without any scruples. Given the plurality of religions in the world and the extremism that some of their adherents are espousing, is a global "clash of civilizations" inevitable in the future? Some observers are now saying that the real problem is not conflict among religions but rather a "clash of ignorance."[10] Rigid exclusivist positions do not represent the heart of religious teachings.

Whether state-sponsored or incited by militant extremists, violence finds no support in any religion. Thus there has been a strong outcry against fundamentalist violence by the mainstream religions from which militants have drawn their faith. Muslims are trying to point out that jihad must not be confused with terrorism, for jihad (spiritual struggle, particularly against one's own inner flaws) is the holy duty of every Muslim, whereas terrorist killing of innocent people is forbidden by the Holy Qur'an. Likewise, many Christian organizations have come out strongly against violence of any sort, including state terrorism. Roman Catholic theologian Vimal Tirimanna explains:

> Ordinary human experience shows that terrorism can never be a moral good, because of the horrendous evils it causes to human lives and to property. Let us not forget here that terrorism also damages the very existence of the terrorist himself/herself as a human being with others; it is demeaning of his/her own basic human dignity. Terrorism is an evil also because it is always a deliberately planned act to hurt, to damage, to injure other human lives, and also to devastate God's creation. Moreover it is intimidation which seeks to eliminate the basic human freedom of the would-be victims and which tends to impose the will of the terrorists forcefully on those who are at the receiving end. Terrorism, no matter whatever form it takes, no matter who are its perpetrators, and no matter what "noble" goals it seeks to promote, can never be justified by a conscientious person.[11]

Religion in politics

What are the advantages and disadvantages of religions' involvement in politics?

The future of religion is sure to include its engagement with politics. Within countries, pluralism of religions has brought varying responses from governments. In the United States there is constitutional separation of Church and state. This "secularism" is a relatively new Western concept, which is now considered natural and desirable in the West. However, it is not enthusiastically embraced everywhere. Historian of religions Karen Armstrong observes:

Religious fervor is a potent force that has often been tied to political movements.

When secularisation was implemented in the developing world, it was experienced as a profound disruption—just as it had originally been in Europe. Because it usually came with colonial rule, it was seen as a foreign import and rejected as profoundly unnatural. In almost every region of the world where secular governments have been established with a goal of separating religion and politics, a counter-cultural movement has developed in response, determined to bring religion back into public life. What we call "fundamentalism" has always existed in a symbiotic relationship with a secularisation that is experienced as cruel, violent and invasive. All too often an aggressive secularism has pushed religion into a violent riposte. Every fundamentalist movement that I have studied in Judaism, Christianity and Islam is rooted in a profound fear of annihilation, convinced that the liberal or secular establishment is determined to destroy their way of life. … Very often modernising rulers have embodied secularism at its very worst and have made it unpalatable to their subjects. Mustafa Kemal Ataturk, who founded the secular republic of Turkey in 1918, is often admired in the west as an enlightened Muslim leader, but for many in the Middle East he epitomised the cruelty of secular nationalism. He hated Islam, describing it as a "putrefied corpse," and suppressed it in Turkey by outlawing the Sufi orders and seizing their properties, closing down the madrasas and appropriating their income. He also abolished the beloved institution of the caliphate, which had long been a dead-letter politically but which symbolised a link with the Prophet. For groups such as al-Qaeda and ISIS [also known as IS or Islamic State], reversing this decision has become a paramount goal.[12]

At the other extreme from secularism, in which theoretically no religion is privileged by the government, everyone in Saudi Arabia is subject to the austere imposition of Wahhabi shari'ah law. Between these two extremes, there are forms such as the Pancasila system in Indonesia, which favors limited tolerance for five religions, but not all religions.

In many countries, religious groups have become associated with political parties or political interest groups—such as the linkage of Hindu religious fundamentalists with exclusivist nationalist political movements in India, and the linkage between neo-conservative politicians in the United States and evangelical Christian beliefs. Such politicians then frequently legitimate their agendas by giving them a religious color or by claiming they are defending religion. When religious groups are mobilized for political purposes, people oriented toward power rather than toward spirituality thus tend to be propelled into leadership roles, while still justifying their actions in religious terms. In 2014, the militants fighting to take over Iraq and Syria by provocative terrorist tactics, such as video-taped beheadings, announced that they were establishing an Islamic caliphate named the Islamic State (IS) with an extremist version of shari'ah, even though Muslims around the world have denounced the methods as totally un-Islamic, including massive peace demonstrations by Muslims in Europe and a "notinmyname" Twitter campaign. Describing Al Qaeda, the network from which IS sprouted, Bruce Lincoln, Professor of the History of Religion, observed:

The Al Qaeda network … understands and constructs itself as simultaneously the militant vanguard and the most faithful fragment of an international religious community. The goal it articulates is the restoration of Islam in a maximalist form and its consequent triumph over its internal and foreign enemies. Those enemies include, first, the Western powers, who are not only non-Muslims, but non-, even anti-religious ("infidels"); second, postcolonial state elites, whose Islamic commitments have been egregiously compromised ("hypocrites"); third, that part of the Enlightenment project committed to religious minimalism and ascendancy of the secular state.[13]

After September 11, U.S. President George Bush had proclaimed a global politico-religious agenda: to attack any nation suspected of harboring terrorists and thus presumably bring peace, with God's blessings resting securely upon America:

In the face of today's new threat, the only way to pursue peace is to pursue those who threaten it. We did not ask for this mission, but we will fulfill it. The name of today's military operation is Enduring Freedom. We defend not only our precious freedoms, but also the freedom of people everywhere to live and raise their children free from fear. ... The battle is now joined in many fronts. We will not waver; we will not tire; we will not falter; and we will not fail. Peace and freedom will prevail. May God continue to bless America.[14]

Some international observers feel that this triumphalist policy has increased rather than decreased terrorism and violent deaths, and many religious leaders have questioned its ethics, as well as its political usefulness. Ignorance of politico-religious issues in the particular area, such as negative perceptions of secularism, has complicated the effects of this kind of thinking. While separation of religion and state is one of the defining principles of modern democracy and also of some totalitarian states, certain religious beliefs and symbols are so deeply ingrained in people's minds as part of their culture that they may still influence policies and worldviews. In Israel, for instance, even totally secular Jews beset by violence on their borders and terrorism within may subconsciously harbor the ancient Jewish dream of a world at peace—and thus rule out any consideration of ending the Zionist political experiment. As Charles Liebman, Professor in Religion and Politics at Bar-Ilan University, writes about Israeli hopes:

Surely the dream of the Jewish prophets, the notion of "the wolf shall dwell with the lamb and the lion shall lie down with the kid, and nation shall not lift up sword against nation, neither shall they know war anymore" is for many, whether they call themselves religious or secular, an important vision of the future and, therefore, a source of how we behave in the present.[15]

Christian Bishop David Niringere of Uganda proposes that "tribalism" is still a problem, and not only in Africa. He notes that politics is a matter of access to public space and public resources, and typically involves the exclusion of others by groups in power:

Tribal-based spirituality does not make a distinction between religious and political ends. Tribal religion is about belonging: All belong, none are non-believers. A few professionals carry it on. Tribal religion enables structuring of power for exclusion, escalating conflict.[16]

For religious cultures such as Islam and Sikhism, the combination of religion and polity is perceived as a positive goal—the possibility of the mundane world reordered according to spiritual ideals. Even Buddhism has become engaged in politics, and to some Buddhists' thinking, a proactive approach to political change is desirable.

Interfaith movement

In what ways may people of different religions relate to each other?

What can religions do to end political deadlock and hatred between followers of various religions? There is already an existing countercurrent in the world, as globalization is increasing friendly person-to-person cross-cultural contacts. In addition, there are many formal efforts at **interfaith dialogue**, in which people of varying religions meet, explore their differences, and appreciate and find enrichment in each other's ways to the divine. This approach has been historically difficult, for many religions have made exclusive claims to being the best or only way. Professor Ewert Cousins, editor of an extensive series of books on the spiritual aspects of major religions, commented: "I think all the religions are overwhelmed by the particular revelation they have been given and are thus blinded to other traditions' riches."[17]

Religions are quite different in their external practices and culturally influenced behaviors. There are doctrinal differences on basic issues, such as the cause of and remedy for evil and suffering in the world, or the question of whether the divine is singular, plural, or nontheistic. And some religions make apparent claims to superiority that are difficult to reconcile with other religions' claims. The Qur'an, for instance, while acknowledging the validity of earlier prophets as messengers of God, refers to the Prophet Muhammad as the "Seal of the Prophets" (Sura 33:40). This description has been interpreted to mean that prophecy was completed with the Prophet Muhammad. If he is believed to be the last prophet, no spiritual figures after he passed away in *c.* 632 CE—including the Sikh Gurus and Baha'u'llah of the Baha'is—could be considered prophets, though they might be seen as teachers. Similarly, Christians read in John 14:6 that Jesus said, "I am the way, the truth, and the life; no one comes to the Father but by me." But some Christian scholars now feel that it is inappropriate to take this line out of its context (in which Jesus' disciples were asking how to find their way to him after they died) and to interpret it to mean that the ways of Hindus, Buddhists, and other faiths are invalid. Relationships with other faiths was not the question being answered.

Many people of broad vision have noted that many of the same principles reappear in all traditions. All religions teach the importance of setting one's own selfish interests aside, loving others, harkening to the divine, and exercising control over the mind. What is called the "Golden Rule," expressed by Confucius as "Do not do unto others what you do not want others to do unto you," and by the Prophet Muhammad as "None of you truly have faith if you do not desire for your brother that which you desire for yourself," is found in every religion.

The absolute authority of scriptures is being questioned by contemporary scholars who are interpreting them in their historical and cultural context and thus casting some doubt upon their exclusive claims to truth. Some liberal scholars are also proposing that there is an underlying experiential unity among religions. Wilfred Cantwell Smith, for instance, concluded that the revelations of all religions have come from the same divine source. Christian theologian John Hick suggests that religions are culturally different responses to one and the same reality. The Muslim scholar Frithjof Schuon feels that there is a common mystical base underlying all religions, but that only the enlightened will experience and understand it, whereas others will see the superficial differences.

> *If the religions are true it is because each time it is God who has spoken, and if they are different it is because God has spoken in different "languages" in conformity with the diversity of the receptacles. Finally, if they are absolute and exclusive, it is because in each of them God has said "I."*
>
> *Frithjof Schuon*[18]

Responses to other faiths

With these contrasting views, there are several different ways in which people of different religions may relate to each other. Diana Eck is one of the scholars who have observed that there are three responses to contact between religions. One is **exclusivism**: "Ours is the only true way." Eck and others have noted that deep personal commitment to one's faith is a foundation of religious life and also the first essential step in interfaith dialogue.

Eck sees the second response to interfaith contact as **inclusivism**. This may take the form of trying to create a single world religion, such as Baha'i. Or it may appear as the belief that our religion is spacious enough to encompass all the others, that it supersedes all previous religions, as Islam said it was the culmination of all monotheistic traditions. In this approach, the inclusivists do not see other ways as a threat. Some Sikhs, for instance, understand their religion as actively promoting interfaith appreciation and thus propose that their holy scripture, the Guru Granth Sahib, could serve as a roadmap to harmony among people of all religions, without denying the right of each religion to exist as a respected tradition.

The third way Eck discerns is **pluralism**: to hold one's own faith and at the same time ask people of other faiths about their path, about how they want to be understood. Uniformity and agreement are not the goals—the goal is to collaborate, to combine our differing strengths for the common good. From this point of view, for effective pluralistic dialogue, people must have an openness to the possibility of discovering sacred truth in other religions. Raimundo Panikkar (1918–2010), a Catholic-Hindu-Buddhist doctor of science, philosophy, and theology, wrote of "concordant discord":

> We realize that, by my pushing in one direction and your pushing in the opposite, world order is maintained and given the impulse of its proper dynamism. … Consensus ultimately means to walk in the same direction, not to have just one rational view. … To reach agreement suggests to be agreeable, to be pleasant, to find pleasure in being together. Concord is to put our hearts together.[19]

Professor Arvind Sharma of McGill University, who grew up in India as a Hindu, goes beyond these categories to describe a fourth possibility. From his personal experience, he states that by studying different religions people may learn about the diversity within their own religion and then the diversity of the world's religions, and yet still somehow develop an inner connection with all religions:

> In the end one might emerge with the tacit knowledge of being the legatee of not just one's tradition, however tolerant, or the various religious traditions of humanity, however diverse, but of the entire religious heritage of humanity, in the singular. The experience could be compared to that of geographical discovery, when what one thought was one's separate country turns out to be part of a continent, and then what one thought were different continents turn out to be part of a single globe.[20]

This feeling is sometimes referred to as "religious tolerance," in the sense of respect and even appreciation for all religions. However, the same term can also have negative connotations, as explained by Wendy Brown, Professor of Political Science at the University of California, Berkeley:

> Despite its pacific demeanor, tolerance is an internally unharmonious term, blending together goodness, capaciousness, and conciliation with discomfort, judgment, and aversion. Like patience, tolerance is necessitated by something one would prefer did not exist. … In this activity of management, tolerance does not offer resolution or transcendence, but only a strategy for coping. … As compensation, tolerance anoints the bearer with virtue, with standing for a principled act of permitting one's principles to be affronted; it provides a gracious way of allowing one's tastes to be violated.[21]

Brown proposes that the kind of "religious tolerance" she is referring to becomes possible when religion is already relegated to the background in a society as having no claim on public life, or else as a solution to insolvable conflicts among dueling absolutist approaches to religious belief. It may also stem from the superior and condescending attitude of a religion in power toward religious minorities whom it is in a position to regulate. It typically does not spring from conviction that religions have equal truth claims, or even that religions are dealing with truths.

> Spirituality is not merely tolerance. … It is the absolute recognition of the other's faith in God as one's own.
>
> Sri Chinmoy

Interfaith initiatives

People of all faiths have been intentionally discovering each other for some time now. A major global assembly was held in Chicago in 1893: The World's Parliament of Religions. The figure who most captured world attention was Swami Vivekananda (1863–1902), a disciple of Sri Ramakrishna. He held a philosophy of the complementarity of religions, asserting, "Each religion, as it were, takes up one part of the great, universal truth and spends its whole force in embodying and typifying that part of the great truth."[22] Vivekananda brought appreciation of Asian religions to the West, and made these concluding remarks:

> If the Parliament of Religions has shown anything to the world it is this: It has proved to the world that holiness, purity, and charity are not the exclusive possessions of any church in the world, and that every system has produced men and women of the most exalted character. In the face of this evidence, if anybody dreams of the exclusive survival of his own religion and the destruction of others, I pity him from the bottom of my heart.[23]

After that initiative, ecumenical conferences involved pairs of related religions that were trying to agree to disagree, such as Judaism and Christianity.

RELIGION IN PUBLIC LIFE

The Assembly of the People of Kazakhstan

President Nursultan Nazarbayev (center) addresses a session of the Assembly of the People of Kazakhstan.

In these times of dangerous sectarian divisions, a significant experiment in inter-religious harmony is being carried out by an entire country: Kazakhstan. When it won its independence from the Soviet Union in 1991, Kazakhstan had the potential for being deeply divided along religious and cultural lines. The new nation consisted of a majority of ethnic Russians, who had been sent by the Soviet Union because of Kazakhstan's oil, gas, and mineral wealth, strategic location, and nuclear testing ground (which was dismantled by the president soon after independence). Ethnic Kazakhs were in the minority, but after population shifts, approximately sixty-four percent of the population are ethnic Kazakhs. They comprise many different clans of the steppes, from ancient mixing of Asian and Western cultures along the Silk Route. They are descendants of Arabian, Turkish, Indo-Iranian, Chinese, Byzantine, Mongolian, and Slovenian civilizations, with a tradition of tolerance for people of other cultures.

The new nation granted freedom of religion, a right that had been suppressed during the Soviet era. Kazakhstanis enthusiastically began to search for and revive their spiritual roots in the process of asserting their cultural identities. Now approximately seventy percent profess Islam, followed by Russian Orthodoxy, other Christian denominations, and small numbers of various other religions such as Judaism, Baha'i faith, Buddhism, the Hare Krishna movement, and Scientology. Very few are atheists.

The farsighted president of the new Republic of Kazakhstan, Nursultan Nazarbayev, grasped the importance of harmonizing the various religious and

Now a large number of interfaith organizations and meetings draw people from all religions in a spirit of mutual appreciation. In 1986, Pope John Paul II invited 160 representatives of all religions to Assisi in honor of the humble St. Francis, to pray together for world peace.

Two years later, the Assisi idea was extended to include governmental leaders, scientists, artists, business leaders, and media specialists as well as spiritual leaders. Some 200 of them from around the globe met in Oxford, England, in 1988 at the Global Forum of Spiritual and Parliamentary Leaders on Human Survival. They held their plenary sessions beneath an enormous image of the earth as seen from space. Dr. Wangari Maathai (1940–2011), leader of the Green Belt movement in Kenya, observed:

> All religions meditate on the Source. And yet, strangely, religion is one of our greatest divides. If the Source be the same, as indeed it must be, all of us and all religions meditate on the same Source.[24]

In 1990, another great assembly of spiritual leaders of all faiths, with scientists and parliamentarians, took place in what, until a few years before, would have been the most unlikely place in the world for such a gathering—Moscow, capital of the previously officially atheistic Soviet Union. The final speaker was

ethnic groups of his country. Early in his presidency, he proposed and then created a unique political body: the Assembly of the People of Kazakhstan. Rather than privileging any religion or culture, the People's Assembly is a carefully organized framework for encouraging each group to value its own cultural roots but also to respect all others. One hundred and thirty ethnic cultures send representatives to the Assembly of the People, and all have equal voice in this advisory and consultative body for national policies, seeking public input and unified consent for government decisions.

All people in Kazakhstan have been granted the same rights according to provisions in the national constitution. For example, Article 12:2 states that "Human rights and freedoms shall belong to everyone by virtue of birth…" while according to Article 19:1 "Everyone shall have the right to determine and indicate or not to indicate his national, party, and religious affiliation."[25] Certain groups from abroad that proselytize and are deemed "pseudo-religions," such as Hare Krishnas and Jehovah's Witnesses, are not represented in the People's Assembly. However, the country remains remarkably peaceful, even though it is bordered by areas beset by internal strife. Any attempts to incite tensions between religious/cultural groups are prohibited by Article 39:2 of the constitution—"Any actions capable of upsetting inter-ethnic concord shall be deemed unconstitutional."[26]

Mass media in Kazakhstan are requested to encourage peaceful co-existence in their reporting, and to avoid stirring up divisive sentiments. The structure of the People's Assembly includes a "club" of leading journalists who supervise the mass media, including their own journals and the website of the People's Assembly, www.assembly.kz. Language is carefully tailored to support peaceful co-existence and stability. For instance, according to the journalistic code, no groups may be referred to as "national minorities."

Addressing the tenth session of the Assembly of the People of Kazakhstan in 2003, President Nazarbayev observed that there are three main reasons for the ethnic conflicts that are raging around the world.[27] One is globalization, which brings intercommunication but also fans people's fears of losing their roots in ethnic and religious identities. Second is internal conflicts that are exacerbated by external influences that cannot be controlled, such as international terrorism and religious extremism. Third is unsolved socio-economic problems, creating a great gap between over-affluence and poverty. He pointed out that there is not yet any workable universal formula for inter-ethnic consent. It is the hope of Kazakhstani people that their model will come to the attention of other countries and international organizations and help the people of the world community find similar ways of respecting and accommodating each other, for the sake of world peace and stability.

last president of the Soviet Union Mikhail Gorbachev, who called for a merging of scientific and spiritual values in the effort to save the planet.

Throughout 1993, special interfaith meetings were held around the world to celebrate the hundredth anniversary of the World's Parliament of Religions. The largest 1993 centenary celebration was again held in Chicago. It included an attempt to define and then use as a global standard for behavior the central ethical principles common to all religions. "The Declaration Toward a Global Ethic" included the Golden Rule:

> *There is a principle which is found and has persisted in many religious and ethical traditions of humankind for thousands of years: What you do not wish done to yourself, do not do to others. Or in positive terms: What you wish done to yourself, do to others! This should be the irrevocable, unconditional norm for all areas of life, for families and communities, for races, nations, and religions.*[28]

The global, gathering model has been replicated in various locations, drawing participants from around the world to deliberate how religions can collectively help to solve the world's problems. Many people have had the vision that the United Nations could be home to representatives or leaders from all faiths, jointly advising the organization on international policy from a religious perspective. This was the thrust of the Millennium World Peace Summit of Religious and Spiritual Leaders held at the United Nations in 2000. Another series of interfaith meetings is ongoing in Astana, capital of Kazakhstan, where people of many faiths are participating in the World Forum of Spiritual Culture, with the idea that Kazakhstan, where multiculturalism is intentionally celebrated, can be a global model of interfaith co-operation for the common good.

Questions arise in such efforts, in addition to the necessity for substantial funding. Which religions should be represented? As we have seen, most major religions have many offshoots and branches that do not fully recognize each other's authority. And which, if any, of the myriad new religious movements should be included? If indigenous religions are to be included, could one representative speak for all the varied traditions? Would such an organization reflect the bureaucratic patriarchal structures of existing religions, or would it include women, the poor, and enlightened people rather than managers? If the members of the body were not elected by their respective organizations, but were rather simply interested individuals, what authority would they have?

Sikhs, Hindus, Muslims, and Christians enjoy a children's interfaith education class together in Gobind Sadan, New Delhi.

Jewish and Palestinian Arab children at Oasis of Peace school. The sign they are holding says "Peace" in Arabic and Hebrew.

The Internet conveys the efforts of many organizations to provide accurate information about a variety of religions to help overcome ignorance and intolerance. The Ontario Consultants on Religious Tolerance, for instance, sponsor www.religioustolerance.org, a rich offering of articles and resources on a long list of religions plus essays on interfaith themes.

Some nongovernmental organizations are also attempting to develop curricula for teaching children about the world's religions in classrooms. Materials for values education have also been prepared for universal use by such august institutions as the Oxford University Press. Its Indian series "Living in Harmony: A Course on Peace and Value Education" uses stories and activities drawn from all religions to inculcate virtues such as honesty, nonviolence, interfaith harmony, and respect for the environment. The editors explain:

> *The destiny of a nation depends on the character of its people. Character is not merely the awareness of some values, but also the commitment to uphold them in practice. To our sages and seers, education was incomplete without nobility of character.*[29]

Local and national inter-religious groups and projects are quite active in Britain, with its increasingly multicultural population. The Leicester Council of Faiths' efforts include developing a multifaith Welcome Centre, ensuring that there is balanced representation of all faiths at civic events, providing multifaith counseling and a multifaith chaplaincy service in some healthcare institutions, informing the various faiths about political matters that affect them, and working with the National Health Service on care that is sensitive to people's specific faiths.

In some places, interfaith efforts are being applied directly to difficult real-life situations, such as the conflicts between Protestants and Catholics in Northern Ireland. In Israel, the Interfaith Encounter Association brings Muslims, Christians, and Jews together for intimate sharing of cultural and spiritual experiences from each other's traditions, and over sixty Jewish and Palestinian Arab families are living together with a spirit of mutual respect and co-operation in a community called Oasis of Peace. In Jaffa, amidst tensions between adults of different religions, the Cologne Day Care Peace Center school develops harmonious interfaith relationships among its nursery and kindergarten students, who are chosen from an intentional mixture of Jewish, Muslim, and Christian families, and taught by both Israeli and Arab teachers. There are even groups bringing together the families and friends of those from all sides who have been killed in conflicts.

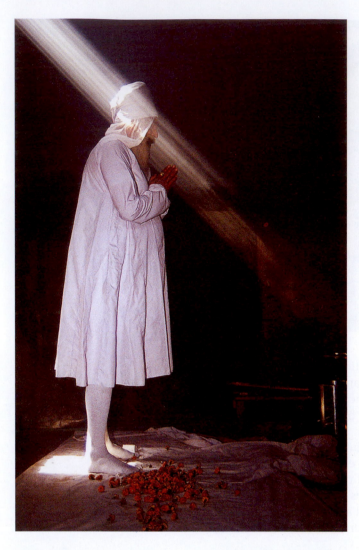

Baba Virsa Singh prays to the Light some perceive as shining through all the prophets and pervading all Creation.

In India, where inter-religious tensions have sometimes been fanned into deadly violence, the Sikh-based interfaith work of Gobind Sadan is bringing together volunteers of all religions in practical farm work on behalf of the poor, and in celebrations of the holy days of all religions. Baba Virsa Singh, the spiritual inspiration of Gobind Sadan, quoted from the words of all the prophets, explaining:

All the Prophets have come from the same Light; they all give the same basic messages. None have come to change the older revealed scriptures; they have come to remind people of the earlier Prophets' messages which the people have forgotten. We have made separate religions as walled forts, each claiming one of the Prophets as its own. But the Light of God cannot be confined within any manmade structures. It radiates throughout all of Creation. How can we possess it?[30]

Although Baba Virsa Singh passed on in 2007, his teachings and his practical approach to interfaith harmony are being carried on by his followers. One new initiative is interfaith education for children. Poor children from the community and surrounding area gather weekly to learn about the teachings of all religions and to act out stories from the lives of all prophets. Sikh, Hindu, and Muslim children happily play the roles of figures from traditions other than their own and regard them all as messengers from the same divine source.

Where people have seen their relatives tortured and killed by fanatics of another faith, reconciliation is very difficult but necessary if the cycle of violence and counterviolent reactions is to be halted. The International Center for Conciliation is training facilitators for conciliation workshops in various hot spots in order to turn "pained memory and hate into empathy."[31] Andreas D'Souza and Diane D'Souza, who have worked to heal hatreds among Muslim victims of violence in India, point out that we tend mentally to divide society into opposing camps:

In our world today, particularly in Western countries, we are tending to demonize the other. It is "us," the sane and balanced, against "them," the demented, violent, and inhuman. We must resist this attempt to polarize "the good" and "the bad," for it leads to complacency at best, and to the rationalization of violence, death, and destruction at worst.[32]

Embedded within religions themselves is the basis for harmony, for all teach messages of love and self-control rather than murderous passions. Yet difficult scriptural passages and histories of antagonism still stand in the way of full harmony among religions. Frank Kaufmann reports that despite over a century of polite interfaith gatherings, these initiatives have yet to address the difficult divisive issues:

Sure, it's okay to year after year to sit through, "That's lovely. I love chapattis. The embroidery on your headscarves is so beautiful. Yes, we too could benefit from your deep respect for and understanding of silence." But what about, "Didn't some countries exterminate innocents in the name of Christ?" "Doesn't your religion teach that if land ever was yours, then it must forever be yours, at any cost, sooner or later?... You know, we have a few passages in our scriptures that SO tend to support violence that we are having a terrible time trying to try to find our way around this. Listen, here are some of these scriptures. ... Do you have any ideas about how we can support the constructive truth implied in these passages, while eroding their great power to serve the perverse ends of violent people?" Will interfaith talk reach this level? It seems increasingly pressing that it must, and must do so sooner than later.[33]

Religion and social issues
What social issues are religions dealing with today?

Within every religion, there are contemporary attempts to bring religious perspectives to bear on the critical issues facing humanity. Today we are having to deal with new issues that were not directly addressed by older teachings, such as climate change. Some are old issues that persist into the present, such as the ethics of abortion and sexual activity outside of marriage. And some issues have reached critical proportions in our times, such as terrorism, HIV/AIDS, global recession, the gap between rich and poor, and the deterioration of the natural environment. Many religious groups are re-examining their scriptures for teachings that would support careful environmental stewardship, in the face of dire warnings about global warming and other looming disasters. Christians are questioning rampant, earth-destructive consumerism. Buddhists are spearheading efforts to ban landmines. Hindus and Muslims are trying to stop the spread of immoral, violent, and cynical mass media communications, to help protect the minds of the young. Racism and violence are challenging people of all faiths to deepen their spiritual understanding and to ponder appropriate responses to these scourges. Poverty, injustice, and human rights abuses in societies are being addressed by many religious groups. The Catholic liberation theologian Gustavo Gutiérrez (b. 1928) asserted:

> *In the last analysis, poverty means an unjust and early death. Now everything is subordinated to market economies, without taking into consideration the social consequences for the weakest. People say, for example, that in business there are no friends. Solidarity is out of fashion. We need to build a culture of love, through respect of the human being, of the whole of creation. We must practice a justice inspired by love. Justice is the basis of true peace. We must, sisters and brothers, avoid being sorry for or comforting the poor. We must wish to be friends of the poor in the world.*[34]

In contrast to this ethic, in today's world there is an increasing gap between rich and poor, and poor people are homeless and dying from malnutrition and starvation in the same countries where many wealthy people are benefiting from their cheap labor and politicians are benefiting from their votes. India, home to the world's largest tribal populations, is also the world's largest democracy, a richly agricultural country with plentiful grain surpluses that are exported or left to rot because of inadequate storage facilities. Urban areas are becoming very smart throughout the country, and many large homes and high-rise apartments are being built with teak and marble decor. However, despite promises of politicians to the tribal peoples languishing out of sight in rural areas, more than eighty percent of them remain below the poverty line, sick, malnourished, ill-educated, lacking basic services, and hungry. Although the central government has legislated many programs designed to alleviate poverty, aid has not reached the people who need it, because of mismanagement, corruption, and a lack of direct participation by tribal people in implementation of poverty alleviation programs. Uneducated and facing extreme poverty, they are easy prey to unscrupulous moneylenders who charge such high interest that poor farmers fall more deeply into debt each year, especially when crops fail. As a result, thousands have committed suicide because they see no other way out. Some faith-based NGOs are trying to help people on a local scale, but there is as yet no concerted, sincere, large-scale effort by religiously conscientious people to change this bleak picture of structural injustice, even though India is home to many of the world's religions. The same widening gap between rich and poor in India is evident in other countries as well. Until individualism gives way to genuine concern for the community, this pattern may persist and worsen in the years to come.

The HIV/AIDS pandemic may continue to grow in the future. More than 35 million of the world's people are carrying HIV/AIDS, and over 36 million people have died so far from this scourge since it was discovered in Africa in the early 1980s. It has been a particularly difficult subject for religions to come to grips with, since in most cases it involves intimate behaviors that they do not usually discuss. However, the response of religions is now growing, with dialogues, debates, and actions being undertaken from local to international levels by religious institutions. In Uganda, one of the worst-hit countries in Africa, the disease was identified in 1982. People thought that those who contracted the disease must be victims of witchcraft, revenge from angry ancestors, or the wrath of God. Once the connections of the disease with sexual promiscuity, homosexual contact, and drug use were made, the issue was shrouded in stigma and denial. But by 1992, the government recognized that its future development could be seriously imperiled by the disease, so it organized the Uganda AIDS Commission. Catholic, Protestant, and Muslim leaders are active members and chairs of the commission, and have helped it to be candid about the problem and also sensitive to the people's religious beliefs and practices. They developed a basic program called "ABC": abstinence, being faithful, and condoms. Since limiting the number of sexual partners is considered the most important way of stopping spread of the epidemic, Ugandans have encouraged "zero grazing" for monogamous, mostly Christian couples, and "paddock grazing" for polygamous relationships among Muslims. But even this simple program, which has apparently shown considerable success, runs into many subtle barriers related to people's religious cultures, such as traditional acceptance of wife-sharing, spontaneous sexuality during celebrations, and allowance for men to "inherit" their relatives' widows. Globally, although condoms can prevent sexual transmission, the most common way that HIV is spread, some religious authorities are opposed to use of condoms on moral grounds.

Reproductive restrictions are proposed by many religious groups, for the sake of safeguarding the family and the preciousness of human life. Same-sex marriages are now legally possible in many countries, but homosexual preferences are not accepted by institutions such as the Roman Catholic Church. The issue of homosexuality in the clergy is a deeply divisive issue within the Anglican Church. Sexual intercourse outside of marriage is discouraged by many religions. Even within marriage, contraception may be subject to religious guidelines. The Roman Catholic Church tries to prohibit contraception by any means other than abstinence during the most fertile days of the woman's monthly cycle, and also forbids abortion and sterilization. Such recommendations do not have the force of law except in theocracies. Many couples make their own sexual choices, including the moral decision not to have large families, to help curb population growth and to use their time and resources to rear a few children as best they can.

Legalized abortion has been a hot issue for decades, with strident conflicts between "pro-life" and "pro-choice" factions, both of which cite ethical principles to support their causes. In-vitro fertilization has also been controversial since its inception. It is seen by infertile couples as a last hope in their efforts to bear children, but some people have religious objections to the procedure. A Sunni Muslim fatwa issued in Egypt in 1980 is still considered valid in many Muslim circles: IVF is permitted if the husband's sperm is used and if the partners are currently married to each other. Because many fertilized eggs die during IVF attempts without becoming viable embryos, the spiritual question arises of whether and when the embryo should be considered a human being, with human rights.

New reproductive-choice issues involve cloning research. Cloned animals of many species, from frogs to camels, already exist. Of various types of cloning procedures, reproductive cloning has the potential for creating a cloned human being. The potential for severe genetic defects is only one of the ethical issues involved, and many countries have banned the reproductive cloning of humans. Another type of cloning, therapeutic cloning, is being researched with the hope of being able to create organs, such as hearts or kidneys, for transplant using a patient's own genetic material, thus thwarting the danger of organ rejection. Some of the ethical issues involved here include the morality of raising genetically modified animals for this purpose, such as pigs, who are genetically similar to humans, from whom organs could then be "harvested" for transplant. People of many religions doubt that humans are wise and restrained enough to use cloning technology carefully. "Bioethics" is becoming a subject of serious consideration by conferences around the world, bringing together religious leaders, scientists, and legal experts to try to shape appropriate policies for use of new technologies.

Climate change is rapidly drawing serious attention, as weather patterns are already becoming more severe, with record-breaking heat and cold, floods, and mega-storms. The concentration of carbon dioxide in the atmosphere is already too high for the planet to bear. Scientists concur that global temperatures will rise by at least two degrees, causing great suffering for all species. Twenty percent of all bird species have already become extinct. If sea levels continue to rise, coastal communities will be inundated, adding millions more to the world's refugee populations. Our ways of life are severely threatening the right to life of future generations. Seyyed Hussein Nasr, Professor of Islamic Studies, warns, "We are marching toward a catastrophe that threatens all human futures."[35] Zen Master Thich Nhat Hanh writes, "All of us know that our beautiful green planet is in danger. … Yet we act as if our daily lives have nothing to do with the condition of the world. We are like sleepwalkers, not knowing what we are doing or where we are heading."[36] Voices from many religions are trying to wake us up, making us aware of our responsibility to future generations. Indigenous peoples are urging us to think in terms of the effects that our current decisions and actions will have on people seven generations—approximately 250 years—from now.

Concerns over these and other social problems, such as drug addiction, overpopulation, and the potential for nuclear catastrophe, have for some people been eclipsed by concern over terrorism. Contemporary terrorist attacks in many countries have brought a sea change in ways of thinking. The future may hold a more serious inquiry into the motives and concerns of people who are willing to risk their lives and kill others, as well as the intentions of those who are interpreting scriptures as supporting such actions.

Religion and materialism

How have religious observers responded to issues of materialism in the contemporary world?

All religions teach that one should not hurt others, should not lie, should not steal, should not usurp others' rights, should not be greedy, but rather should be unselfish, considerate, and helpful to others, and humble before the Unseen. These universal spiritual principles were swamped by the expansion of capitalism in the twentieth century, as the profit motive triumphed as the most important value in economies around the world. The gap between the very rich and the very poor continues to increase. In 2014 Oxfam reported that the wealthiest eighty-five people in the world collectively account for as much wealth as the poorest 3.5 billion people in the world.[37]

Christian theologian Sallie McFague sees an acute spiritual failure in this disparity:

The distinction between "self" and "others" is an exaggeration. The Western paradigm of political and economic theory has built itself on this exaggeration, not only of individual human beings as radically separate from ... other (especially from those less fortunate) human beings, but also of human beings as separate from all other creatures and the cosmos itself. This exaggeration therefore has allowed for the meanest, most unjust form of capitalism to reign as the formula for all behavior toward other human beings and other life-forms.[38]

William J. Byron, who teaches courses in corporate responsibility at Loyola College, observes that integrity has fallen by the wayside in the "new corporate culture." Instead, "secrecy, easy money, and the violation of trust define a framework for the test of character in the world of business."[39] Spiritual principles were notoriously absent in the subprime lending by American banks that led to a severe global recession starting in 2008. Economist Thomas Friedman described the situation as "a near-total breakdown of responsibility at every link in our financial chain."[40]

Some religious observers are re-examining the values of traditional economic systems in light of this situation. Dr. Zhou Qin of the Department of Chinese Studies at the National University of Singapore writes:

In the light of the teachings of Confucian tradition, neoliberalism and the global economy contribute to the moral disorientation and shallowness of our time. Today, it would be absolutely reasonable for one to claim all of one's rights as an individual without any concerns for the rights of others.[41]

From a Buddhist perspective, Professor David Loy of Bunkyo University, Japan, points out that the problem is attachment and uncontrolled desires, rather than wealth per se:

An intense drive to acquire material riches is one of the main causes of our dukkha [suffering]. It involves much anxiety but very little real satisfaction. ... "Wealth destroys the foolish, though not those who search for the goal" (Dhammapada 355). In short, what is blameworthy is to earn wealth improperly, to become attached to it and not to spend it for the well-being of everyone, to squander it foolishly or use it to cause suffering to others.[42]

Some individuals and corporations have now stepped back to consider how to reconcile spiritual motives with earning a living. Books on voluntary simplicity have proliferated on the bestseller lists. Typically, they encourage the relatively wealthy to cut back on their breakneck work pace for the sake of their own spiritual peace, and to cut back on unnecessary individual expenditures for the sake of sharing with others. Liberal capitalism is being reinterpreted not as a means of allowing industrious people to climb out of poverty, but as a potentially amoral system.

A new social consciousness that reflects religious values is beginning to enter some workplaces. Professor Syed Anwar Kabir, a faithful Muslim on the faculty of the Management Development Institute in New Delhi, India, teaches his managerial students to do mind-stilling meditation daily in order to listen to their own conscience and make ethical choices from a base of inner tranquility. He observes:

Businessmen themselves say that the uninhibited, reckless way in which you accumulate wealth will not give you a good name. For a company to survive in a highly competitive world in the long term means creating an image in the mind of the public, creating good will, creating its own impact and niche in the market. ... If you treat human beings not as means but also as ends, naturally it is reflected in your products and services and creates an impact in the world of consumers so that they also come to respect the company's principles and strategies.[43]

However, in the twenty-first century, power-mongering, self-interest, and corruption are at the forefront of economic and political activities; honesty, altruism, service, harmony, justice, and the public good are not the primary motivating forces in most government actions.

Religion and the future of humanity

How can the thoughtful study of religions help in the future of humanity?

The new century has begun with flagrant materialistic greed, crime, amorality, ethnic hatreds, violence, and family crises, together with ignorant demonizing, power-mongering, and moneymaking in religions themselves.

Although there is a global increase in religiosity, this trend includes both polarizing and harmonizing tendencies. New alliances are being forged across old religious lines, but often in the direction of dividing the world into liberal and conservative factions. Many watched the events of the "Arab Spring" in 2011 with hope that people's power to remove oppressive governments would lead to new social models of freedom and harmony. However, the resulting political vacuum gave rise to other restrictive and oppressive regimes and violence. During this process, a Muslim prince from Yemen who is committed to a more humane future cautioned against seeing the world in black and white terms:

> The story of the past is not that of two sides: the good and the bad. Rather it is a story of many sides and many layers, who are good and bad at the same time. There are no angels in this story, nor devils. There are no absolute victims, nor absolute aggressors. The past is ambivalent and complicated, and no one has absolute moral supremacy. Rather, each side has a moral right sometimes, in some situations, with some people, but never always and with everyone. All sides are now suffering, and all have to be sympathetic to the plight of the other. Concessions have to be made based on humanitarian terms, rather than purely legal and political ones. Ultimately, I wish people will decide on building their future not on any moralizing of the past, but rather on moralizing the future. And as a step towards that, I want people to break the monolithic view they have of each other, and to complicate historical process rather than simplify it.[44]

If we are to amicably cohabit the world, we need far more nuanced and educated understandings of each other. The thoughtful study of religions is thus

An estimated 400,000 people joined the People's Climate March in New York in 2014 to call for meaningful resolutions against climate change. The Noah's Ark float with the banner "People of Faith Call for Climate Action" symbolized the desire of religious representatives to prevent extinction of life on the planet.

critical to our shared future. So is deep spiritual awareness and practice of what the prophets of all religions have tried to teach us. The words of the French sage Teilhard de Chardin (1881–1955) are often quoted:

> Some day, after mastering the winds, the waves, the tides, and gravity, we shall harness for God the energies of love. And then, for the second time in the history of the world, man will have discovered fire.

Key terms

exclusivism The idea that one's own religion is the only valid way.
inclusivism The idea that all religions can be accommodated within one religion.
interfaith dialogue Appreciative communication between people of different religions.
modernism Values that developed in the twentieth century including individualism, preference for change rather than continuity, quantity rather than quality, efficiency, pragmatism, and profiteering, all seen by some as threatening the existence of traditional religious values.
pluralism An appreciation of the diversity of religions.

Suggested reading

Adiswarananda, Swami, ed., *Vivekananda World Teacher: His Teachings on the Spiritual Unity of Humankind*, Woodstock, Vermont: Jewish Lights Publishing, 2007. Selected lectures on interfaith unity by a major Hindu thinker.

Braybrooke, Marcus, *Faith and Interfaith in a Global Age*, Grand Rapids, Michigan: CoNexus Press and Oxford: Braybrooke Press, 1998. One of the world's central interfaith co-ordinators surveys the interfaith movement.

Brown, Wendy, *Regulating Aversion: Tolerance in the Age of Identity and Empire*, Princeton, New Jersey: Princeton University Press, 2006. Deep exploration of tolerance as an exercise in power, a means of managing what we actually dislike.

Byron, William J., *The Power of Principles: Ethics for the New Corporate Culture*, Maryknoll, New York: Orbis Books, 2007. A critical survey of cynical, self-serving motives that have taken the place of old ethical principles in business.

Carroll, John E., *Sustainability and Spirituality*, Albany: State University of New York Press, 2004. Inspiring examples of religious communities attempting to live sustainably, and the eco-justice ideals on which they are based.

His Holiness the Dalai Lama, *Beyond Religion: Ethics for a Whole World*, New York: Houghton Mifflin Harcourt, 2011. Thoughts on how basic ethical principles can inform human life, no matter what one's religious orientation, if any.

Fisher, David and Brian Wicker, eds, *Just War on Terror? A Christian and Muslim Response*, Farnham, Surrey, UK: Ashgate, 2010. Christian and Muslim theologians tackle the difficult questions of how democratic states can deal justly with terrorism.

Fisher, Mary Pat and Lee W. Bailey, *An Anthology of Living Religions*, third edition, Upper Saddle River, New Jersey: Prentice Hall, 2012. Readings from the various religions, following the outline of this book, to deepen understanding of the material herein.

Forward, Martin, *Ultimate Visions: Reflections on the Religions We Choose*, Oxford: Oneworld Publications, 1995. Interesting personal essays by scholars and leaders of many religions, reflecting upon why they like their religion and how it can contribute to a future of harmony among all religions.

Johnston, Lucas F., *Religion and Sustainability: Social Movements and the Politics of the Environment*, Bristol, Connecticut: Equinox Press, 2013. Exploration of interrelationships between religious ideals and environmental sustainability movements.

Khan, Hazrat Inayat, *The Unity of Religious Ideals*, New Lebanon, New York: Sufi Order Publications, 1927, 1979. A master of Sufi mysticism explores the underlying themes in the religious quest that are common to all religions.

Knitter, Paul F., *The Myth of Religious Superiority*, Maryknoll, New York: Orbis Books, 2004. Exclusivism, inclusivism, and pluralism as perceived from Hindu, Sikh, Buddhist, and Western perspectives.

Marshall, Katherine and Lucy Keough, *Mind, Heart and Soul in the Fight Against Poverty*, Washington: The World Bank, 2004. Encouraging report from the world's largest development bank as it attempts to work with religions to alleviate poverty, unemployment, debt, and HIV/AIDS.

McFague, Sallie, *Blessed are the Consumers: Climate Change and the Practice of Restraint*, Minneapolis: Fortress Press, 2013. Christian perspectives on sharing and simplicity as antidotes to the climate crisis.

Moe-Lobeda, Cynthia D., *Resisting Structural Evil*, Minneapolis: Fortress Press, 2013. Examination of links between survival of the planet and social justice.

Moore, Kathleen Dean and Michael P. Nelson, eds, *Moral Ground: Ethical Action for a Planet in Peril*, San Antonio: Trinity University Press, 2010. Moral imperatives to deal with environmental crises, as seen by thinkers from all religions.

Nussbaum, Martha C., *The New Religious Intolerance: Overcoming the Politics of Fear in an Anxious Age*, Cambridge, Massachusetts: The Belknap Press of Harvard University Press, 2012. Analysis of fearful knee-jerk reactions based on Islamophobia, with exploration of antidotes.

Smith-Christopher, Daniel L., *Subverting Hatred: The Challenge of Nonviolence in Religious Traditions*, Maryknoll, New York: Orbis Books and Boston Research Center for the 21st Century, 2007. Articles delineating teachings of nonviolence from each of the major world religions.

Snyder, Larry, *Think and Act Anew: How Poverty in America Affects Us All and What We Can Do about It*, Maryknoll, New York: Orbis Books, 2010. The President of Catholic Charities USA urges a new examination of contemporary poverty, grounded in ideals of charity and justice.

Stanley, John, David R. Loy, and Gyurme Dorje, eds, *A Buddhist Response to the Climate Emergency*, Boston: Wisdom Publications, 2009. Well-known Buddhist leaders invoke the principle of awakening to bring attention to actions needed to alleviate climate change.

Taylor, Charles, *A Secular Age*, Cambridge, Massachusetts: Belknap Press of Harvard University Press, 2007. The history of secularization of Western culture from strong belief to disintegration and meaninglessness.

World Scripture: A Comparative Anthology of Sacred Texts, New York: Paragon House/International Religious Foundation, 1991. A thematic compendium of appealing excerpts from the scriptures of all religions

13.1 Define globalization

In contrast to earlier centuries, in which regions were relatively isolated from each other, two major world wars and other violent conflicts, technological advances, and population shifts have brought us into much closer contact. Primarily through markets and businesses, regional and national economies have become part of a global network. Cultural and social connectivity is also increasing through technological innovations such as the Internet and social media, air travel, political alliances such as the European Union, and the entertainment industry.

13.2 Outline the forms of Western secularism described in this chapter

The "public space" form of secularism refers to the fact that within the various spheres of activity (economic, political, cultural, educational, professional, recreational), the norms and principles people follow generally do not refer them to God or to any religious beliefs. The "individual dimension" form consists in the falling off of religious belief and practice, as people turn away from God and no longer go to church. Other forms include the social condition in which religious faith is only one of various possibilities; and the modern constitutional separation of religion and state (such as in the United States, India, and Turkey).

13.3 Identify some of the factors that have led to a hardening of religious boundaries

In many countries there is tension between the religion that has been most closely linked with national history and identity and other religions that are practiced or have been introduced. Where there is a diversity of religions, legal jurisdiction, particularly in relation to Islam, can be an issue. Other factors concern which religions will receive state funding and also the outright banning of new or minority religions. Religious symbols have become a focus for some governments, such as in France. Boundaries have also hardened in recent times because of the clash between fundamentalism and modernism, with some fundamentalists trying to withdraw from the secular culture and others actively trying to change the culture, using political power or violence.

13.4 Discuss the advantages and disadvantages of religions' involvement in politics

For some religious cultures, such as Islam and Sikhism, the combination of religion and polity is perceived as a positive goal—the possibility of the mundane world reordered according to spiritual ideals. In many countries, however, religious groups have become associated with political parties or political interest groups. Politicians of such groups then frequently legitimate their agendas by giving them a religious color or by claiming they are defending religion.

13.5 Summarize the ways in which people of different religions may relate to each other

One way in which people of different religions may relate to each other is exclusivism, the idea that one's own religion is the only valid way. In contrast, inclusivism is the idea that all religions can be accommodated within one religion. Other approaches include pluralism (an appreciation of the diversity of religions), religious tolerance (respect and appreciation for all religions), and interfaith dialogue (appreciative communication between people of different religions).

13.6 Discuss the key social issues religions are dealing with today

Within every religion, there are contemporary attempts to bring religious perspectives to bear on the critical issues facing humanity. Some are old issues that persist into the present, such as the ethics of abortion, reproductive restrictions, and homosexuality. And some issues have reached critical proportions in current times, such as acts of racism and violence, injustice and human rights abuses, the HIV/Aids pandemic, the increasing gap between rich and poor, climate change, and the deterioration of the natural environment.

13.7 Describe how religious observers have responded to issues of materialism in the contemporary world

With the expansion of capitalism in the twentieth century, universal spiritual principles, such as not hurting others, not stealing, and not being greedy, have been swamped. In light of the power-mongering, self-interest, and corruption at the forefront of economic and political activities in the twenty-first century, some religious observers and corporations have now stepped back to consider how to reconcile spiritual motives with earning a living. Some individuals are cutting back their breakneck work pace for the sake of spiritual peace, and reducing their spending on unnecessary expenditures for the sake of sharing with others and reducing the burden on the planet.

13.8 Explain the importance of the study of religions in the future of humanity

Although there is a global increase in religiosity, this trend includes both polarizing and harmonizing tendencies. To amicably cohabit the world, a far more nuanced and educated understanding of each other is needed. The thoughtful study of religions is thus critical to our shared future. Deep spiritual awareness and practice of what the prophets of all religions have tried to teach us are also key.

CHAPTER 1
RELIGIOUS RESPONSES

1 Ivy DeWitt, interviewed 22 May 2014

2 Lisa Bradley, personal communication to author, March 1990, as quoted in Paul Zelanski and Mary Pat Fisher, *The Art of Seeing*, sixth edition, Upper Saddle River, New Jersey: Pearson/Prentice Hall, 2005, pp. 47–48.

3 Christopher Queen, personal communication, 28 November 2011.

4 Thomas A. Tweed, *Crossing and Dwelling: A Theory of Religion*, Cambridge, Massachusetts: Harvard University Press, 2006, pp. 54, 76–77.

5 Pew Research Religion and Public Life Project, "Religion and the Unaffiliated" 2012, http://www.pewforum.org/2012/10/09/nones-on-the-rise-religion/, viewed 30 October 2014

6 Ivy DeWitt, 22 May 2014

7 Karl Marx, from "Contribution to the Critique of Hegel's Philosophy of Right" 1884, *Karl Marx, Early Writings*, translated and edited by T. B. Bottomore, London: C. A. Watts and Co., 1963, pp. 43–44; *Capital*, vol. 1, 1867, translated by Samuel Moore and Edward Aveling, F. Engels, ed., London: Lawrence & Wishart, 1961, p. 79; "The Communism of the Paper 'Rheinischer Beobachter'" *On Religion*, London: Lawrence & Wishart, undated, pp. 83–84.

8 Karl Marx, "Religion as the Opium of the People" in Karl Marx and Friedrich Engels, *On Religions*, Moscow: Foreign Language Publishing House, 1955, p. 42.

9 Robert D. Putnam and David E. Campbell, *American Grace: How Religion Divides and Unites Us*, New York: Simon and Schuster, 2010.

10 Tenzin Gyatso, "The Monk in the Lab" *New York Times*, 26 April 2003, p.A29. Used with permission of The Office of His Holiness the Dalai Lama.

11 Mata Amritanandamayi, *Awaken Children!*, vol. 4, Amritapuri, Kerala, India: Mata Amritanandamayi Mission Trust, 1992, pp. 103–104.

12 Guru Teg Bahadur, Manmohan Singh, trans., *Sri Guru Granth Sahib* (English and Panjabi Translation), p. 633. Amritsar, India: Shromani Gurdwara Parbandhak Committee, vol. 4, p. 2076.

13 Mahatma Gandhi, quoted in Eknath Easwaran, *Gandhi the Man*, Petaluma, California: Nilgiri Press, 1978, p. 121.

14 *The Bhagavad-Gita*, translated by Eknath Easwaran, founder of the Blue Mountain Center of Meditation, copyright © 1985, 2007, pp. 121–122; and from *Gandhi The Man* by Eknath Easwaran, copyright © 1972, 2011. Reprinted by permission of Nilgiri Press, P. O. Box 256, Tomales, CA 94971, www.easwaran.org.

15 C. Brhadaranyaka Upanisad 4.4.18, translated by Patrick Olivelle, *Upanisads*, Oxford University Press, 2008, p. 67 by permission of Oxford University Press, www.oup.com.

16 Jiddu Krishnamurti, *The Awakening of Intelligence*, New York: Harper & Row, 1973, p. 90.

17 Martin Luther, as quoted in Gordon Rupp, "Luther and the Reformation" in Joel Hurstfield, ed., *The Reformation Crisis*, New York: Harper & Row, 1966, p. 23.

18 William James, *The Varieties of Religious Experience*, New York: New American Library, 1958, p. 298.

19 AE (George William Russell), *The Candle of Vision*, Wheaton, Illinois: The Theosophical Publishing House, 1974, pp. 8–9.

20 Kabir, Rabindranath Tagore, trans., *Songs of Kabir*, New York: Samuel Weiser, Inc., 1915, 1977, pp. 96–97.

21 John White, "An Interview with Nona Coxhead: The Science of Mysticism—Transcendental Bliss in Everyday Life" *Science of Mind*, September 1986, pp. 14, 70.

22 Abu Yazid, as quoted in R. C. Zaehner, *Hindu and Muslim Mysticism*, London: University of London, Athlone Press, 1960, p. 105.

23 Dr. I. H. Azad Faruqi, Letter to Dr. Nishat Quaiser, 19 September 2005.

24 Sallie McFague, *Models of God: Theology for an Ecological, Nuclear Age*, Philadelphia: Fortress Press, 1987, p. 133.

25 "Exploring the idea of humanism" http://americanhumanist.org/Humanism, viewed 31 October 2014, American Humanist Association

26 Maimonides, "Guide for the Perplexed" 1, 59, as quoted in Louis Jacobs, *Jewish Ethics, Philosophy, and Mysticism*, New York: Behrman House, 1969, p. 80.

27 Guru Gobind Singh, *Jaap Sahib*, English translation by Surendra Nath, New Delhi: Gobind Sadan, 1992, verses 7, 29–31.

28 Bede Griffiths, *Return to the Center*, Springfield, Illinois: Templegate, 1977, p. 71.

29 Antony Fernando, "Outlining the Characteristics of the Ideal Individual" paper for the Inter-Religious Federation for World Peace Conference, Seoul, Korea, 20–27 August 1995, p. 9.

30 Guy L. Beck, ed., *Sacred Sound: Experiencing Music in World Religions*, Waterloo, Ontario: Wilfrid Laurier University Press, 2006.

31 Edmund Gurney, The Power of Sound, London: Smith, Elder, 1880, pp. 25–26.

32 Quoted in William Dalrymple, *From the Holy Mountain: A Journey in the Shadow of Byzantium*, New Delhi: Penguin Books India Pvt. Ltd., 2004, pp. 300–301. (First published in London by HarperCollins Publishers, 1997.)

33 Akka Mahadevi, in A. K. Ramanujan, quoted in Vijaya Ramaswamy, *Walking Naked: Women, Society, Spirituality in South India*, Indian Institute of Advanced Study, 1997, p. 33. Used with permission of Professor Vijaya Ramaswamy.

34 Joseph Campbell, *The Hero with a Thousand Faces*, second edition, Princeton, New Jersey: Princeton University Press, 1972, p. 29.

35 Manfred Steger, *Globalization: A Very Short Introduction*, Oxford: Oxford University Press, 2009, p. 15.

36 Dr. Syed Z. Abedin, "Let There be Light" *Saudi Gazette*, Jeddah, June 1992, reprinted in *Council for a Parliament of the World's Religions Newsletter*, vol. 4, no. 2, August 1992, p. 2.

37 Quoted in John Gliedman, "Mind and Matter" *Science Digest*, March 1983, p. 72.

38 Murray Gell-Mann, in Kitty Ferguson, Stephen Hawking, *Quest for a Theory of Everything*, London: Bantam Press, 1992, p. 30.

39 Ilya Prigogine, abstract for "The Quest for Certainty" Conference on a New Space for Culture and Society, New Ideas in Science and Art, 19–23 November 1996.

40 Hans-Peter Dürr, talk at World Forum of Spiritual Culture, Astana, Kazakhstan, 18 October 2011.

41 Albert Einstein, *The World As I See It*, New York: Wisdom Library, 1979; *Ideas and Opinions*, translated by Sonja Bargmann, copyright © 1954, Crown Publishers, Inc. Used with permission of Princeton University Press.

42   Paul Davies, excerpted from Bel Mooney, *Devout Sceptics: Conversations on Faith and Doubt*, London: Hodder and Stoughton, 2003, pp. 48–56. Used with permission of Professor Paul Davies.

43   James Lovelock, excerpted from Bel Mooney, *Devout Sceptics: Conversations on Faith and Doubt*, London: Hodder and Stoughton, 2003, pp. 83–84. Used with permission of Professor James Lovelock.

44   Ellen Bernstein, "Creation Theology: Theology for the rest of us" in Rabbi Elyse Goldstein, ed., *New Jewish Feminism: Probing the Past, Forging the Future*, 2009, Woodstock, Vermont: Jewish Lights Publishing, pp. 42–43.

45   Jacqueline Kramer, "Mothering as Practice" in *Sakyadhita*, vol. 8.1, no. 1, Spring 2009, p. 5.

46   His Highness the Aga Khan, address to the School of International and Public Affairs, Columbia University, 15 May 2006.

CHAPTER 2
INDIGENOUS SACRED WAYS

1   Damaris Parsitau, personal communication, 30 June and 1 July 2011.

2   Vine Deloria, Jr., *God is Red*, New York: Grosset & Dunlap, 1973, p. 267.

3   Lorraine Mafi Williams, personal communication, 16 September 1988.

4   Gerhardus Cornelius Oosthuizen, "The Place of Traditional Religion in Contemporary South Africa" in Jacob K. Olupona, *African Traditional Religions in Contemporary Society*, New York: Paragon House, 1991, p. 36.

5   Quoted by Bob Masla, "The Healing Art of the Huichol Indians" Many Hands: Resources for Personal and Social Transformation, Fall 1988, p. 30.

6   Peta Stephenson, *Islam Dreaming: Indigenous Muslims in Australia*. Sydney: UNSW Press, 2010, p. 201

7   Interview with Rev. William Kingsley Opoku, August 1992.

8   Clyde Ford, *The Hero with an African Face: Mythical Wisdom of Traditional Africa*, New York: Bantam Books, 2000, p. 146.

9   Knud Rasmussen, *Across Arctic America*, New York: G. P. Putnam's Sons, 1927, p. 386.

10   Adapted from a Yoruba story told by Deidre L. Badejo. Deidre L. Badejo, "Osun Seegesi: The Deified Power of African Women and the Social Ideal" paper presented at the Inter-Religious Federation for World Peace Conference, Seoul, Korea, 20–27 August 1995.

11   Josiah U. Young III, "Out of Africa: African Traditional Religion and African Theology" in *World Religions and Human Liberation*, Dan Cohn-Sherbok, ed., Maryknoll, New York: Orbis Books, 1992, p. 93.

12   Jo Ag Quis Ho/Oren R. Lyons, spokesman for the Traditional Elders Circle, Wolf Clan, Onondaga Nation, Haudenosaunee, Six Nations Iroquois Confederacy, from the speech to the Fourth World Wilderness Conference, 11 September 1987, p. 2.

13   Quoted in Keith Basso, *Wisdom Sits in Places: Landscape and Language among the Western Apache*, Albuquerque: University of New Mexico Press, 1996, p. 127.

14   Te Urutahi Waikerepuru of Aoeteroa, New Zealand, remarks at the Global Peace Initiative of Women Religious and Spiritual Leaders, Geneva, 7 October 2002. Reproduced with permission.

15   Bill Neidjie, *Speaking for the Earth: Nature's Law and the Aboriginal Way*, Washington: Center for Respect of Life and Environment, 1991, pp. 40–41. Reprinted from *Kakadu Man* by Big Bill Neidjie, Stephen Davis, and Allan Fox, Northryde, New South Wales, Australia: Angus and Robertson, 1986.

16   Jaime de Angulo, "Indians in Overalls" *Hudson Review*, II, 1950, p. 372.

17   Quoted in Matthew Fox, "Native teachings: Spirituality with power" *Creation*, January/February 1987, vol. 2, no. 6.

18   *Lame Deer: Seeker of Visions*, New York: Pocket Books, 1972, p. 116.

19   Tlakaelel, *Talk at Interface*, Watertown, Massachusetts, 15 April 1988.

20   As quoted in Georges Niangoran-Bouah, "The Talking Drum: A Traditional African Instrument of Liturgy and of Meditation with the Sacred" in Jacob K. Olupona, ed., *African Traditional Religions in Contemporary Society*, New York: Paragon House, 1991, pp. 86–87.

21   Leonard Crow Dog and Richard Erdoes, *The Eye of the Heart*, unpublished manuscript, quoted by Joan Halifax, *Shamanic Voices: A Survey of Visionary Narratives*, New York: E. P. Dutton, 1979, p. 77.

22   Yvonne Daniel, *Dancing Wisdom: Embodied Knowledge in Haitian Vodou, Cuban Yoruba, and Bahian Candomblé*, Urbana and Chicago: University of Illinois Press, 2005, pp. 247–248

23   Daniel, ibid., p. 252

24   Cheyenne Peace Chief Lawrence Hart, in "Indigenous Traditions of Peace" by Daniel L. Smith-Christopher, in Daniel L. Smith-Christopher, ed., *Subverting Hatred: The Challenge of Nonviolence in Religious Traditions*, Maryknoll, New York: Orbis Books, 2007, p. 78.

25   Mado (Patrice) Somé, interviewed 14 September 1989.

26   Quoted in John Neihardt, *Black Elk Speaks*, 1932, Lincoln, Nebraska: University of Nebraska Press, 1961, pp. 208–209.

27   Igjugarjuk, in Knud Rasmussen, *Intellectual Culture of the Hudson Bay Eskimos*, report of the Fifth Thule Expedition, 1921–1924, translated by W. E. Calvert, vol. 7, Copenhagen: Gyldendal, 1930, p. 52.

28   From an interview conducted for this book by Tatiana Kuznetsova.

29   Quoted by Black Elk in Joseph Epes Brown, *The Sacred Pipe*, Norman, Oklahoma: University of Oklahoma Press, 2002, p. 71.

30   Mark St. Pierre and Tilda Long Soldier, *Walking in the Sacred Manner*, New York: Simon and Schuster, 1995, pp. 69–70.

31   Leonard Crow Dog and Richard Erdoes, in Joan Halifax, *Shamanic Voices*, op. cit., p. 77.

32   Interview with Wande Abimbola, 6 August 1992.

33   In Jean-Guy Goulet, *Ways of Knowing: Experience, Knowledge, and Power among the Dene Tha*, Lincon, Nebraska: University of Nebraska Press, 1998, p. 73.

34   Tlakaelel, *Talk at Interface*, op. cit.

35   "Aborigine aiming to be first native woman MP" *Asian Age*, 30 September 1998, p. 5.

36   Interviews conducted December 2006 by Savinder Kaur Gill, who gratefully acknowledges the assistance of team members and data providers of the Heritage Garden Project, Kampung Simpai, Pahang, Malaysia.

37   Wilmer Stampede Mesteth (Oglala Lakota), Darrell Standing Elk (Sicangu Lakota), and Phyllis Swift Hawk (Kul Wicasa Lakota), "Declaration of War Against Exploiters of Lakota Spirituality" undated handbill reproduced on http://puffin.creighton.edu/lakota/war.html, 19 April 2001.

38   George Tinker, *Missionary Conquest: The Gospel and Native American Genocide*, Minneapolis: Fortress Press, 1993, p. 122.

39   Rose Mary Amenga-Etego, *Mending the Broken Pieces: Indigenous Religion and Sustainable Rural Development in Northern Ghana*, Trenton, New Jersey: Africa World Press, 2011, p. 29

40   Jace Weaver, in Jace Weaver, ed., *Native American Religious Identity: Unforgotten Gods*, Maryknoll, New York: Orbis Books, 1998.

41   Jameson Kurasha, "Plato and the Tortoise: A Case for the death of ideas in favor of peace and life?" paper presented at Assembly of the World's Religions, Seoul, Korea, August 1992, pp. 4–5. Used with permission of Professor Jameson Kurasha.

42   Damaris Parsitau, personal communication, 30 June and 1 July 2011.

43 Adi Amadiume, "Igbo and African Religious Perspectives on Religious Conscience and the Global Economy" in Paul F. Knitter and Chandra Muzaffar, eds., *Subverting Greed: Religious Perspectives on the Global Economy*, Maryknoll, New York: Orbis Books, 2002, p. 27. Used with permission.

44 "The Hopi Message to the United Nations General Assembly" submitted by Thomas Banyacya, Kykyotsmovi, Arizona, 10 December 1992, reprinted on http://banyacya.indigenousnative.org/un92.html.

CHAPTER 3
HINDUISM

1 Somjit Dasgupta, interviewed 26 February 2006.

2 Sukta-yajur-veda XXVI, 3, as explained by Sai Baba in *Vision of the Divine* by Eruch B. Fanibunda, Bombay: E. B. Fanibunda, 1976.

3 *The Upanishads*, translated by Swami Prabhavananda and Frederick Manchester, The Vedanta Society of Southern California, New York: Mentor Books, 1957, 2009 pp. 30, 68. Used with permission of Vedanta Press.

4 *Chandogya Upanishad*, ibid., p. 46.

5 *Brihadaranyaka Upanishad*, ibid.

6 T. M. P. Mahadevan, *Outlines of Hinduism*, second edition, Bombay: Chetana Ltd., 1960, 1999, p. 24.

7 'A condensation' by Heinrich Zimmer of the *Vishnu Purana*, Book IV, Chapter 24, translated by H. H. Wilson, London, 1840, in *Zimmer's Myths and Symbols in Indian Art and Civilization*, New York: Pantheon Books, 1946, p. 15.

8 Uttara Kandam, *Ramayana*, third edition, as told by Swami Chidbhavananda, Tiriuuparaitturai, India: Tapovanam Printing School, 1978, pp. 198–199.

9 Chapter III:30, p. 57. All quotes from the *Bhagavad-Gita* are from *Bhagavad-Gita as It Is*, translated by A. C. Bhaktivedanta Swami Prabhupada, New York: copyright © 1972, The Bhaktivedanta Book Trust. Quoted courtesy of The Bhaktivedanta Book Trust International, Inc. www.Krishna.com. Used with permission.

10 Ibid., III:30, p. 57.

11 Ibid., IV:3, p. 64.

12 Ibid., IV:7–8, pp. 68–69.

13 Ibid., VII:7–8, 12, pp. 126, 128.

14 Ibid., IX:26, p. 157.

15 Srimad-Bhagavatam, second canto, "The Cosmic Manifestation" part one, chapter 6:3 and 1:39, translated by A. C. Bhaktivedanta Swami Prabhupada, New York: Bhaktivedanta Book Trust, 1972, pp. 59, 275–276. Quoted courtesy of The Bhaktivedanta Book Trust International, Inc. www.Krishna.com. Used with permission

16 Sri Swami Chidananda, *God as Mother, SECOND NIGHT, The Destroyer Of Destructive Forces*, fourth edition, 1991, copyright © The Divine Life Trust Society.

17 *The Thousand Names of the Divine Mother: Sri Lalita Sahasranama*, with commentary by T. V. Narayana Menon, English translation by Dr. M. N. Namboodiri, Amritapuri, Kerala, India: Mata Amritanandamayi Math, 1996, verses 1–2, 8, 158–161, 220–224, pp. 5–6, 11, 82–3, 106–107.

18 Rita D. Sherma, "Sacred Immanence: Reflections of Ecofeminism in Hindu Tantra" in Lance Nelson, ed., *Purifying the Earthly Body of God: Religion and Ecology in Hindu India*, Albany, NY: State University of New York Press, 1998, p. 118., State University of New York Press, copyright © 2005

19 Swami Sivasiva Palani, personal communication, 26 October 1989.

20 Appar, as quoted in R. de Smet and J. Neuner, eds, *Religious Hinduism*, fourth edition, Bangalore, India: St. Paul's Society, 1996, p. 321.

21 *The Patanjala Yogasutra with Vyasa Commentary*, translated from Sanskrit into English by Bengali Baba, second edition, Poona, India: N. R. Bargawa, 1949, pp. 96–97. Used with permission of Motilal Banarsidass Publishers Pvt. Ltd.

22 Swami Sivananda, *Dhyana Yoga*, fourth edition, 1981, p. 67, copyright © The Divine Life Trust Society.

23 Ramana Maharshi, *The Spiritual Teaching of Ramana Maharshi*, Boston: Shambhala, 1972, 2004, pp. 4, 6.

24 Bhakta Nam Dev, as included in Sri Guru Granth Sahib, p. 693, adapted from the translation by Manmohan Singh, Amritsar, India: Shiromani Gurdwara Parbandhak Committee, 1989.

25 *Mirabai and Her Padas*, English translation by Krishna P. Bahadur, Delhi: Munshiram Manoharlal Publishers Pvt. Ltd., 1998, no. 46, pp. 76–77. Reproduced with permission.

26 Swami Vivekananda, *The Complete Works of Swami Vivekananda*, vol. 3, Mayavati, India: Advaita Ashrama, 1948, p. 259.

27 Ramakrishna, quoted in Carl Jung's introduction to *The Spiritual Teaching of Ramana Maharshi*, op. cit., p. viii.

28 Anna Hazare: *The Fakir who Moved a Country*. New Delhi: Reem Publications, 2011, pp. 61–62, 103. Used with permission of Reem Publications Private Ltd.

29 *Thus Spake Sri Ramakrishna*, fifth edition, Madras: Sri Ramakrishna Math, 1980, p. 54.

30 Swami Sivasiva Palani, op. cit.

31 Somjit Dasgupta, interviewed 26 February 2006.

32 William F. Fisher, "Sacred Rivers, Sacred Dams: Competing Visions of Social Justice and Sustainable Development along the Narmada" in Christopher Key Chapple, and Mary Evelyn Tucker, eds, *Hinduism and Ecology*, Boston: Harvard University Press, 2000, p. 413.

33 Ibid., p. 410.

34 Aditi Sengupta De, "The 'holy' mess" c/o editor@ip.eth.net, 31 July 2000.

35 Akka Mahadevi, as quoted in Swami Ghanananda and Sir John Stewart-Wallace, eds., *Women Saints East and West*, Hollywood: Vedanta Press, 1955, 1979, pp. 31–32.

36 Anandamayi Ma, as quoted in Timothy Conway, *Women of Power and Grace*, Santa Barbara, California: The Wake Up Press, 1994, 1996, p. 133.

37 Robert N. Minor, "Sarvepalli Radhakrishnan and 'Hinduism': Defined and Defended" in Robert D. Baird, ed., *Religion in Modern India*, New Delhi: Manohar Publications, 1981, p. 306.

38 Condensed Gospel of Sri Ramakrishna, Mylapore, Madras: Sri Ramakrishna Math, 1911, p. 252.

39 Ramakrishna, as quoted in Swami Vivekananda, *Ramakrishna and His Message*, Howra, India: Swami Abhayananda, Sri Ramakrishna Math, 1971, p. 25.

40 Swami Vivekananda, *Inspired Talks* (recorded by a disciple during the seven weeks at Thousand Island Park), third edition, Chennai: Sri Ramakrishna Math, 1921, p. 53.

41 Lectures delivered by Shastriji Pandurang Vaijnath Athavale at the Second World Religious Congress held at Shimizu City, Japan in October 1954.

42 Shri Pandurang Vaijnath Athavale Shastri, *Nivedanam*, third edition, Bombay, 1973, p. 6.

43 Shri Pandurang Vaijnath Athavale Shastri, discourse on 10 January 1988, Bombay, on the occasion of the Diamond Jubilee Celebration of Shrimad Bhagvad Geeta Pathshala by Sagar-Putras of the Fishing Community, p. 5.

44 *Autobiography of a Yogi* by Paramahansa Yogananda, published by Self-Realization Fellowship, Los Angeles, copyright © 2015 Self-Realization Fellowship. All Rights Reserved.

45 http://www.youtube.com/watch?v=u8zad0cBfSQ. "NarendraModi's Direct Answer on WHAT IS HINDUTVA." Published on 14 June 2013.

46 "Vishwa Hindu Parishad Aims and Objects, Convictions, Guidelines, Motto, and Definition of 'Hindu'" Raghunandan Prasad Sharma, *Vikas Yatra of Vishwa Hindu Parishad*, New

Delhi: Vishwa Hindu Parisad, 2006, p. xix

47   Balkrishan Naik, personal communication, 25 July 2014.

48   Supreme Court of India, Bramchari Sidheswar Bhai, etc. vs State Of West Bengal etc. 2 July, 1995. 1995 AIR 2089, 1995 SCC (4) 646.

49   Excerpted from Mahatma Gandhi, "Hinduism of Today" *Young India*, 8 April 1926, in Mahatma Gandhi, *What is Hinduism?*, New Delhi: National Book Trust, 1994, pp. 24–25.

CHAPTER 4
JAINISM

1   M. P. Jain, interviewed March 2009.

2   *Awashyakchurni*, pp. 304–305, among many fasts listed in Muni Nathmal, *Shraman Mahavir: His Life and Teachings*, New Delhi: Today and Tomorrow's Printers and Publishers, 1980, p. 57.

3   Akaranga Sutra, translated by Padmanabh S. Jaini in *The Jaina Path of Purification*, Berkeley: University of California Press, 1979, p. 26.

4   Padma Agrawal, "Jainism: Mahavira as Man–God" *Dialogue and Alliance*, p. 13.

5   Acharya Kund Kund, *Barasa Anuvekkha (Twelve Contemplations)*, M. K. Dhara Raja, ed., New Delhi: Kund Kund Bharati, 1990, p. 32.

6   Ibid., p. 11.

7   Akaranga Sutra, Fourth Lecture, First Lesson, in *Sacred Books of the East*, F. Max Müller, ed., vol. 22, Jaina Sutras part 1, Oxford: Clarendon Press, 1884, p. 36.

8   Avasyaka Sutra, as quoted in Padmanabh S. Jaini, *Collected Papers on Jaina Studies*, Delhi: Motilal Banarsidass Publishers, 2000, p. 223.

9   Amitagati's Dvatrimsika, 1, as quoted in Padmanabh S. Jaini, ibid., p. 224.

10   R. P. Jain, personal communication.

11   Acharya Tulsi, as quoted in *Anuvibha Reporter*, vol. 3, no. 1, October–December 1997, p. 54.

12   Acharya Tulsi, "World Peace through Self-Restraint" in *Anuvibha Reporter*, vol. 1, nos. 4, 5, July–December 2003, inside front cover.

13   Samani Sanmati Pragya, interviewed 11 December 1993, Rishikesh, India.

14   Gurudev Shree Chitrabhanu, *Twelve Facets of Reality: The Jain Path to Freedom*, New York: Dodd Mead and Company, 1980, p. 93.

15   As quoted by William Dalrymple, *Nine Lives in Search of the Sacred in Modern India*, London/Berlin/New York: Bloomsbury, 2009, p. 19

16   Acharya Mahaprajna, "Without Controlling Desires, No Reform is Possible" from *The Daily Rising Kashmir*, posted on http://www.herenow4u.net/index.php?id=67736, *Raising Kashmir*, 31 January 2009, copyright © 1997–2015 HereNow4U.

17   Acharya Tulsi, in S. L. Ghandi, "Acharya Tulsi's Legacy" *Anuvibha Reporter*, vol. 3, no. 1, October–December 1997, p. 2.

18   Samantabhadra, *Ratnakarandaka Sravakaschara*, quoted by John M. Koller, "Sallekhana" 5 November 2011, unpublished paper.

19   Dr. Shugan C. Jain, interviewed 31 December 2011.

20   Jagdish Prasad Jain "Sadhak""Forgiveness: Its Nature and Significance" *Hindustan Times*, 8 September 2006.

21   Acharya Shri Sushil Kumar, personal communication, 30 October 1989.

22   M. P. Jain, interviewed March 2009.

23   Introduction, Jain Vishva Bharati Institute (Deemed University), Ladnun, Rajasthan, India, p. 3. Reproduced with permission.

24   Acharya Mahapragya, as quoted in Prof. R. P. Bhatnagar, "Acharya Mahapragya: A Living Legend" in *Anuvibha Reporter*, January–March 1995, p. 8.

CHAPTER 5
BUDDHISM

1   Naoyuki Ogi, interviewed 15 December 2011.

2   Majjhima-Nikaya 1.80.

3   Muhaparinibbana Sutta, Digha Nikaya, 2.99f, 155–156, quoted in *Sources of Indian Tradition*, William Theodore de Bary, ed., New York: Columbia University Press, 1958, pp. 110–111.

4   *Parinibbana-sutta*, in *The Teaching of Buddha*, Tokyo: Bukkyo Deno Kyokai, 1966, p. 11, copyright © 1966 by Bukkyo Deno Kyokai.

5   *Digha Nikaya 16, Mahaparinibbana-sutta*, in *The Teaching of Buddha*, ibid., p. 13.

6   "A message from Buddhists to the Parliament of the World's Religions" Chicago, September 1993, as quoted in *World Faiths Encounter* no. 7, February 1994, p. 53, copyright © World Congress of Faiths.

7   Majjhima-Nikaya, "The Lesser Matunkyaputta Sermon" Sutta 63, translated by P. Lal in the introduction to *The Dhammapada*, 162/92 Lake Gardens, Calcutta, 700045 India. Originally published by Farrar, Straus & Giroux, 1967, p. 19. Reprinted by permission of Srimati Lal.

8   Walpola Sri Rahula, *What the Buddha Taught*, revised edition, New York: Grove Press, 1974, p. 17.

9   Ajahn Sumedho, "Now is the Knowing" undated booklet, pp. 21–22.

10   Ajahn Chah, "Our Real Home" Samuel Bercholz and Sherab Chodzin Kohn, *The Buddha and His Teachings*, Boston: Shambhala, 2003, p. 93.

11   Ajahn Sumedho, cited in Satnacitto Bhikku, ed., *Buddhanature*, World Wide Fund for Nature, London, 1989.

12   Maha Ghosananda, *Step by Step*, Berkeley, California: Parallax Press, 1992, p. 42.

13   Sigalovada Sutta, Dighanikaya III, pp. 180–193, quoted in H. Saddhatissa, *The Buddha's Way*, New York: George Braziller, 1971, p. 101.

14   *The Dhammapada*, translated by P. Lal, op. cit., p. 152.

15   Ibid., p. 49.

16   Ajahn Chah, in *A Still Forest Pool*, Jack Kornfield and Paul Breiter, eds, Wheaton, Illinois: Theosophical Publishing House, 1985.

17   Lankavatara Sutra, as quoted in Christopher Key Chapple, "Animals and Environment in the Buddhist Birth Stories" in Mary Evelyn Tucker and Duncan Ryuken Williams, eds, *Buddhism and Ecology*, Cambridge: Harvard University Press, 1997, p. 143.

18   *The Mahavagga* 1.

19   *Suttanipatta* 1093–1094.

20   Majjhima-Nikaya 1:161–164.

21   *The Dhammapada*, translated by P. Lal, op. cit., pp. 71–72.

22   Samyutta Nikaya, quoted in the introduction to *The Dhammapada*, translated by P. Lal, op. cit., p. 17.

23   Chatsumarn Kabilsingh, *Thai Women in Buddhism*, Berkeley, California: Parallax Press, 1991, p. 25.

24   Joko Beck, as quoted in Lenore Friedman, *Meetings with Remarkable Women*, Boston: Shambhala, 1987, p. 119.

25   Mahaparinibbana Sutta ii.142.

26   Interview with Ashin Nyana Dipa, 10 May 2009.

27   *Saddharmapundarika-sutra [Lotus Sutra]* 16, in *The Teaching of Buddha*, op. cit., pp. 22–23.

28   His Holiness the Fourteenth Dalai Lama, speaking on 15 February 1992, in New Delhi, India, Ninth Dharma Celebration of Tushita Meditation Centre. Used with permission of The Office of His Holiness the Dalai Lama.

29 Soen Nakagawa-roshi, as quoted in Lenore Friedman, *Meetings with Remarkable Women*, op. cit., p. 75.

30 Dainin Katagiri, "Emptiness" in Samuel Bercholz and Sherab Chodzin Kohn, *The Buddha and His Teachings*, Boston: Shambhala Publications, 1993, p. 245.

31 David W. Chappell, personal communication, 26 July 1995.

32 As quoted by Joseph A. Adler, *Chinese Religions*, London and New York: Routledge, 2002, p. 86.

33 Platform Scripture of the Sixth Patriarch, Hui-neng, quoted in *World of the Buddha*, Lucien Stryk, ed., New York: Doubleday Anchor Books, 1969, p. 340.

34 Sengtsan "Hsin hsin Ming Verses of the Faith-Mind", translated by Richard B. Clarke, copyright © 1973, 1984, 2001 by Richard B. Clarke. Reprinted with permission of The Permissions Company, Inc., on behalf of White Pine Press, Buffalo, New York, www.whitepine.org.

35 Roshi Philip Kapleau, *The Three Pillars of Zen*, New York: Anchor Books, 1980, p. 70.

36 Bunan, quoted in Lucien Stryk, *World of the Buddha*, op. cit., p. 343.

37 The Most Venerable Nichidatsu Fujii, quoted in a booklet commemorating the dedication for the Peace Pagoda in Leverett, Massachusetts, 5 October 1985.

38 The Most Venerable Nichidatsu Fujii, ibid.

39 Naoyuki Ogi, interviewed 15 December 2011 and 6 October 2014.

40 "Rissho Kosei-kai, Practical Buddhism and Interreligious Cooperation" brochure from Rissho Kosei-kai, Tokyo.

41 "Rissho Kosei-kai, Buddhism for Today" Rissho Kosei-kai pamphlet printed in Japan, 2006.

42 His Holiness the Fourteenth Dalai Lama, *My Land and My People*, New York: McGraw-Hill, 1962; Indian edition, New Delhi: Srishti Publishers, 1997, p. 50. Used with permission of The Office of His Holiness the Dalai Lama.

43 His Holiness the Fourteenth Dalai Lama, evening address after receiving the Nobel Peace Prize, 1989, in Sidney Piburn, ed., *The Dalai Lama: A Policy of Kindness*, second edition, Ithaca, New York: Snow Lion Publications, 1993, p. 114. Used with permission of The Office of His Holiness the Dalai Lama.

44 Lama Drom Tonpa, as quoted in "Gems of Wisdom from the Seventh Dalai Lama" *Snow Lion Newsletter*, vol. 14, no. 4, Fall 1999, p. 14.

45 Venerable Tenzin Dadon interviewed 11 August 2012.

46 Lama Drom Tonpa, as quoted in "Gems of Wisdom from the Seventh Dalai Lama" *Snow Lion Newsletter*, op. cit., p. 14.

47 "Stories and Songs from the Oral Tradition of Jetsun Milarepa" translated by Lama Kunga Rimpoche and Brian Cutillo in *Drinking the Mountain Stream: Songs of Tibet's Beloved Saint, Milarepa*, copyright © 1995 Brian Cutillo and Lama Kunga Thartse Rinpoche. Reprinted by arrangement with Wisdom Publications, Inc., wisdompubs.org.

48 Quoted in Keith Dowman, *Sky Dancer: The Secret Life and Songs of the Lady Yeshe Tsogyel*, Ithaca, New York: Snow Lion Publications, 1996, p. 86.

49 Cue Nguyen, personal communication, 6 July 2003.

50 Angarika Dharmapala, as quoted in Rick Fields, *How the Swans Came to the Lake: A Narrative History of Buddhism in America*, Boston: Shambhala, 1986, p. 122.

51 Thich Nhat Hanh, *Being Peace*, Indian edition, Delhi: Full Circle, 1997, pp. 53–54.

52 Richard B. Clarke, personal communication, 2 October 1981.

53 Alan Wallace in Brian Hodel, "Tibetan Buddhism in the West: Is it working? An interview with Alan Wallace" *Snow Lion Newsletter*, vol. 15, no. 4, Fall 2000, p. 17. Used with permission of B. Alan Wallace.

54 Stephen Batchelor, *Buddhism without Beliefs: A Contemporary Guide to Awakening*, New York: Riverhead Books, 1997.

55 Karma Lekshe Tsomo, personal communication, 14 April 2003.

56 Walpola Rahula, "The Social Teachings of the Buddha" in *The Path of Compassion*, Fred Eppsteiner, ed., Berkeley, California: Parallax Press, 1988, pp. 103–104.

57 Metta Sutta, as translated by Maha Ghosananda, in "Invocation: A Cambodian Prayer" *The Path of Compassion*, ibid., p. xix.

58 Sulak Sivaraksa, "Development as if people mattered" in Stephanie Kaza and Kenneth Kraft, eds, *Dharma Rain: Stories of Buddhist Environmentalism*, Boston and London: Shambhala, 2000, p. 185.

59 Ajahn Pongsak, in Kerry Brown, "In the water there were fish and the fields were full of rice: Rewakening the lost harmony of Thailand", *Buddhism and Ecology*, Martine Batchelor and Kerry Brown, eds., World Wide Fund for Nature, 1992, pp. 94, 90, 98.

60 Maha Ghosananda as quoted by Alan Channer, "Twilight of the Khmer Rouge?" http://www.forachange.co.uk/index.php?stoid=32, 1 June 1997.

61 Maha Ghosananda, *Step by Step*, quoted in "Letter from Cambodia" Coalition for Peace and Reconciliation, January 2001.

62 Aung San Suu Kyi, "In or out of jail, my mind was always free" BBC World Service, in *Asian Age*, 29 June 2011, p. 14.

63 Aung San Suu Kyi, "Freedom from Fear" http://www.dassk.org/contents.php?id=416, accessed 3/5/2006.

64 B. R. Ambedkar, quoted in Namdeo Nimgade, *In the Tiger's Shadow: The Autobiography of an Ambedkarite*, New Delhi: Navayana Publishing, 2010, pp. 184–185.

65 Thich Nhat Hanh, in Christopher Queen, "Engaged Buddhism: Social Service and Public Activism" talk given at Ryukoku University, Kyoto, Japan, 14 December 2011.

66 Sulak Sivaraksa, "Buddhism in a World of Change" in *The Path of Compassion*, op. cit., p. 16.

CHAPTER 6
DAOISM AND CONFUCIANISM

1 Simon Man-ho Wong, interviewed 21 September 2013.

2 Tu Weiming, "The Continuity of Being: Chinese Visions of Nature" in Mary Evelyn Tucker and John Berthrong, *Confucianism and Ecology*, Cambridge, Massachusetts: Harvard University Press, 1998, pp. 106–108.

3 *The I Ching*, translated by Richard Wilhelm (German)/Cary F. Baynes (English), Princeton, New Jersey: Princeton University Press, 1967, pp. 620–621.

4 Excerpt from verse 1 in *Tao-te Ching*, translated by Stephen Mitchell. Translation copyright © 1988 by Stephen Mitchell. Reprinted by permission of HarperCollins Publishers and Pan Macmillan.

5 Lao Tzu, *Tao Te Ching*, translated by D. C. Lau, Penguin Classics, 1963, p. 7, copyright © D. C. Lau, 1963. Reproduced with permission of Penguin Books Ltd.

6 Lao Tzu, ibid., p. 82.

7 Lao Tzu, ibid., p. 82.

8 Chuang Tzu, *Basic Writings*, translated by Burton Watson, p. 40, copyright © 1996 Columbia University Press. Reprinted with permission of the publisher.

9 Lao Tzu, *Tao Te Ching*, op. cit., p. 133.

10 Guanzi, "Inward Training" as quoted in Harold D. Roth, "The Inner Cultivation Tradition of Early Daoism" in Donald S. Lopez, Jr., ed., *Religions of China in Practice*, Princeton, New Jersey: Princeton University Press, 1996, pp. 133–134.

11 Chuang Tzu, *Basic Writings*, translated by Burton Watson, op. cit., p. 36.

12 Lao Tzu, *Tao Te Ching*, op. cit., p. 68.

13 Lao Tzu, ibid., p. 107.

14 Lao Tzu, ibid., p. 139.

15 Liu Zhongyu, translated by Lu Pengzhi, "Daoist Folk Customs: Burning Incense and Worshiping Spirits" http://

www.eng.taoism.org.hk/religious-activities&rituals/daoist-folk-customs, accessed 3/22/2007.

16 *The Secret of the Golden Flower*, translated by Richard Wilhelm/Cary Baynes, New York: Harcourt Brace Jovanovich, 1962, p. 21.

17 *Chuang Tzu: Basic Writings*, translated by Burton Watson, op. cit., p. 74.

18 Excerpted from Huai-Chin Han, translated by Wen Kuan Chu, *Tao and Longevity: Mind–Body Transformation*, York Beach, Maine: Samuel Weiser, 1984, pp. 4–5.

19 Sun Bu-er, "Facing a Wall" in *Immortal Sisters: Secrets of Taoist Women*, translated and edited by Thomas Cleary, Boston: Shambhala Publications, 1989, p. 50, copyright © 1989, 1996 by Thomas Cleary. Reprinted by arrangement with The Permissions Company, Inc., on behalf of Shambhala Publications Inc., Boston, MA. www.shambhala.com.

20 "Taoist Association of China" http://www.eng.Taoism.org.hk/daoist-world-today/contemporary-daoist-organizations, accessed 3/22/2007.

21 Huang Zhi An, interviewed 14 August 2008.

22 Sik Sik Yuen Wong Tai Sin Temple ninetieth birthday brochure, Kowloon, Hong Kong. Used with permission of Wong Tai Sin Temple.

23 Zhou Zhongzhi, "The Significance of Taoist Ethical Thought in the Building of a Harmonious Society" paper for "Continuity+Change: Perspectives on Science and Religion" Metanexus Institute, Philadelphia, Pennsylvania, 3–7 June 2006, p. 3.

24 Quoted in *T'ai-chi, Cheng Man-ch'ing and Robert W. Smith*, Rutland, Vermont: Charles E. Tuttle, 1967, p. 106.

25 "Brooms, Gourds, and the Old Ways, An Interview with Daoist Master An" *Heaven Earth: The Chinese Art of Living*, Howard Dewar, vol. 1, no. 1, May 1991, p. 2, copyright © China Advocates.

26 Yu Yingshi, "A Difference in Starting Points" *Heaven Earth*, ibid., p. 1.

27 *The Analects*, VII:1, in *Sources of Chinese Tradition*, vol. 1, second edition, William Theodore de Bary and Irene Bloom, eds, p. 25, copyright © 1999 Columbia University Press. Reprinted with permission of the publisher.

28 *The Analects*, II:4, as translated by James Legge, in Rodney L. Taylor, *Confucius, The Analects: The Path of the Sage*, Woodstock, Vermont: Skylight Paths, 2011, p. 121.

29 Confucius, *The Analects*, translated by D. C. Lau, Penguin Classics, 1979, copyright © D C Lau, 1979, p. 32. Reproduced with permission of Penguin Books Ltd.

30 Ibid., p. 32, and *The Analects* II: 1, as translated by Ch'u Chai and Winberg Chai in *Confucianism*, Woodbury, New York: Barron's Educational Series, 1973, p. 52.

31 *The Texts of Confucianism, Sacred Books of the East*, Max Müller, ed., Oxford: Oxford University Press, 1891, vol. 27, pp. 450–451.

32 *The Analects*, XI:11, in Ch'u Chai and Winberg Chai, *The Sacred Books of Confucius and Other Confucian Classics*, New Hyde Park, New York: University Books, 1965, p. 46.

33 *The Analects*, XVII:19 in *Confucius, The Analects: The Path of the Sage*, op. cit., p. 131.

34 Ibid., X:25.

35 Ibid., X:103.

36 Mencius, in de Bary, adapted from *Sources of Chinese Tradition*, op. cit., p. 129.

37 Ibid., p. 147.

38 From the Hsun Tzu, Chapter 17, in de Bary, ibid., p. 172.

39 Frederick Streng, *Understanding Religious Life*, third edition, Belmont, California: Wadsworth, 1985, p. 2.

40 Rodney L. Taylor, personal communication, 1 November 2011.

41 Simon Man-ho Wong, interviewed 21 September 2013.

42 Chang Tsai's Western Inscription, in de Bary et al., *Sources of Chinese Tradition*, op. cit., p. 683.

43 "The Tasks of 1945" by Chairman Mao Tse-tung, *Quotations from Chairman Mao Tse-tung*, second edition, Peking: Foreign Language Press, 1967, pp. 172–173, copyright © Foreign Language Press Co, Ltd.

44 *China Daily*, 30 January 1989, p. 1.

45 Yao Xinzhong, "Confucianism and the Twenty-first Century: Confucian Moral, Educational and Spiritual Heritages Revisited" First International Conference on Traditional Culture and Moral Education, Beijing, August 1998, p. 4. Used with permission of Professor Yao Xinzhong.

46 Tu Weiming, "Confucianism" in Arvind Sharma, ed., *Our Religions*, New York: HarperCollins Publishers, 1993, pp. 221–222.

47 Yu Dan, *Confucius from the Heart: Ancient Wisdom for Today's World*, translated by Esther Tyldesley, Pan Books, 2010, p. 16, copyright © Esther Tyldesley 2010.

48 Mary Evelyn Tucker, in Tu Weiming and Mary Evelyn Tucker, *Confucian Spirituality*, New York: Crossroad Publishing Company, 2003, p. 1.

CHAPTER 7
SHINTO

1 Hitoshi Iwasaki, personal communication, April 1990.

2 Survey conducted by Shrine Association. Jinja Honcho Kyogaku Kenkyujo, Jinja ni kansuru ishiki chosa hokokusho, 1997, p. 30

3 Motohisa Yamakage, *The Essence of Shinto: Japan's Spiritual Heart*, Tokyo/New York/London: Kodansha International, English translation 2006, p. 12.

4 Yukitaka Yamamoto, *Way of the Kami*, Stockton, California: Tsubaki America Publications, 1987, p. 75.

5 Sakamiki Shunzo, "Shinto: Japanese Ethnocentrism" in Charles A. Moore, ed., *The Japanese Mind*, Hawai'i: University of Hawai'i Press, 1982, p. 25.

6 *Hitachi-no-kuni fudoki, Nihon Koten Bungatu Taikai* 2: 54–5, quoted in John Breen and Mark Teeuwen, *A New History of Shinto*, Chichester, West Sussex: Wiley-Blackwell, 2010, p. 25.

7 Adapted from the *Nihon Shoki (Chronicles of Japan)*, I:3, in Stuart D. B. Picken, *Shinto: Japan's Spiritual Roots*, Tokyo: Kodansha International, 1980, p. 10.

8 Yamamoto, *Way of the Kami*, op. cit., pp. 73–75.

9 Interviews 15 December 2011 and 11 January 2012, translated by Naoyuki Ogi.

10 *Nihongi, Chronicles of Japan from the Earliest Times to ad 697*, translated by W. G. Aston, Rutland, Vermont: Charles Tuttle, 1985, 2012, 1:176.

11 Kishimoto Hideo, "Some Japanese Cultural Traits and Religions" in Charles A. Moore, ed., *The Japanese Mind*, op. cit., pp. 113–114.

12 Ise-Teijo, Gunshin-Mondo, Onchisosho, vol. 10, quoted in *Genchi Kato*, p. 185.

13 Statistic from Jinja Honcho Kyogaku Kenkyujo, Jinja ni kansuru ishiki chosa hokokusho, 1997, op. cit.

14 Unidentified quotation, Stuart D. B. Picken, ed., *A Handbook of Shinto*, Stockton, California: The Tsubaki Grand Shrine of America, 1987, p. 14.

15 Ibid.

16 Hitoshi Iwasaki, "Wisdom from the night sky" *Tsubaki Newsletter*, 1 June 1988, p. 2.

17 Yamamoto, *Way of the Kami*, op. cit., p. 97.

18 Inoue Nobutaka, *Shinto—A Short History*, op. cit., p. 7.

19 Motoori Norinaga (1730–1801), *Naobi no Mitma*, quoted in *Tsubaki Newsletter*, 1 November 1988, p. 3.

20 Ofudesaki, as quoted in *Aizen Newsletter of the Universal Love and Brotherhood Association*, no. 17, September–October 1997, p. 2.

21 Hitoshi Iwasaki, personal communication, April 1990.

22 http://www.tsubakishrine.com/misogishuho, accessed 5/2/2009, copyright © America Tsubaki Okami Yashiro Kannushi.

23 Jinja-Honcho (The Association of Shinto Shrines), "The Shinto View of Nature and a Proposal Regarding Environmental Problems" Tokyo, 1997.

ZOROASTRIANISM

1   *The Hymns of Zarathushtra*, translated by Jacques Duchesne-Guillemin/Mrs. M. Henning, London: John Murray, 1952, 1993, p. 7.

2   Yasna 33:14, *Songs of Zarathushtra*, the Gathas translated by Dastur Framroze Ardeshir Bode and Piloo Nanavutty, London: George Allen and Unwin, 1952, p. 66.

3   Yasna 34:5,4, ibid., p. 67.

4   T. R. Sethna, *Book of Instructions on Zoroastrian Religion*, Karachi, Pakistan: Informal Religious Meetings Trust Fund, 1980, p. 87.

5   http://fezana.org/return-to-roots-program-report.

CHAPTER 8
JUDAISM

1   Eli Epstein, interviewed 2 March 2009.

2   Genesis 1:1. *Tanakh—The Holy Scriptures: The New JPS Translation According to the Traditional Hebrew Text*, Philadelphia: Jewish Publication Society, 1985. This translation is used throughout this chapter.

3   Genesis 1:28.

4   Genesis 6:17.

5   Genesis 9:17.

6   Genesis 22:12.

7   Personal communication, 24 March 1989.

8   Deuteronomy 7:7.

9   Exodus 3:5.

10 Exodus 3:10.

11 Exodus 3:12, 14–15.

12 Irving Greenberg, "History, Holocaust, and Covenant" in Alan L. Berger, *Judaism in the Modern World*, New York and London: New York University Press, 1994, p. 129.

13 Exodus 34:13.

14 I Kings 9:3.

15 Daniel 7:13–14.

16 From the Talmud and Midrash, quoted in *The Judaic Tradition*, Nahum N. Glatzer, ed., Boston: Beacon Press, 1969, p. 197.

17 Adin Steinsaltz, *The Essential Talmud*, translated by Chaya Galai, New York: Basic Books, 2006, p. vii.

18 *Kaddish Shalem*, English translation by Rabbi Sidney Greenberg in *Likrat Shahhat: Worship, Study, and Song for Sabbath and Festival Services and for the Home*, Bridgeport, Connecticut: Media Judaica/The Prayer Book Press, 1981, p. 251.

19 Maimonides, *The Guide of the Perplexed*.

20 Quoted in S. A. Horodezky, *Leaders of Hasidism*, London: Ha-Sefer Agency for Literature, 1928, p. 11.

21 Moses Sofer, ethical testament cited in W. Gunther Plaut, *The Growth of Reform Judaism: A Sourcebook of its European Origins*, New York: World Union for Progressive Judaism, 1965, pp. 256ff.

22 "From George Washington to the Hebrew Congregation in Newport, Rhode Island, 18 August 1790" *Founders Online*, National Archives. Source: *The Papers of George Washington, Presidential Series*, vol. 6, 1 July 1790–30 November 1790, ed. Mark A. Mastromarino, Charlottesville: University Press of Virginia, 1996, p. 286

23 Elie Wiesel, *Night*, translated by Marion Wiesel, Penguin Books, p. 67. Translation copyright © 1972, 1985, 2006 by Marion Wiesel. Reprinted by permission of Hill and Wang, a division of Farrar, Straus and Giroux, LLC, and Sheil Land Associates Ltd working in conjunction with Georges Borchardt, Inc.

24 Aviezer Ravitzky, *Messianism, Zionism, and Jewish Religious Radicalism*, Chicago: The University of Chicago Press, 1993, p. 1.

25 Paul Johnson, *A History of the Jews*, New York: Harper and Row, 1987, p. 430.

26 Hillel Levine, interviewed 17 July 2011.

27 Jeremy Milgrom, "Let your love for me vanquish your hatred for him" in Daniel L. Smith-Christopher, ed., *Subverting Hatred: The Challenge of Nonviolence in Religious Traditions*, Maryknoll, New York: Orbis Books, 2007, p. 158.

28 Rabbi Michael Melchior, "Jerusalem—A Sacred Space" Chatauqua Institution, YouTube, accessed 8/10/2011. Reproduced with permission of Rabbi Michael Melchior.

29 Statement by Rabbi Michael Melchior, Deputy Foreign Minister of the State of Israel, to Conference against Racism, Racial Discrimination, Xenophobia and Related Intolerance, Durban, South Africa, 3 September 2001. Reproduced with permission of Rabbi Michael Melchior.

30 Michael Melchior, "Bringing Religion back to the Frontlines" *Jerusalem Post*, 16 September 2009, http://www.jpost.com/Opinion/Columnists/Article.aspx?id=742, accessed 12/8/2009. Reproduced with permission of Rabbi Michael Melchior.

31 "Ruh Jedida" document signed by sixty-eight young Mizrahi Jews, circulated on the Internet in May 2011, as received by Hillel Levine. Translated and used with permission of Mati Shemoelof, http://972mag.com/young-mizrahi-israelis-open-letter-to-arab-peers/13695/.

32 Maimonides' "First Principles of Faith" as quoted in Louis Jacobs, *Principles of Jewish Faith*, Northvale, New Jersey: Jason Aronson, 1988, p. 33.

33 Ibn Gabirol, "Keter Malkhut," quoted in Abraham J. Heschel, "One God" in *Between God and Man: An Interpretation of Judaism, from the Writings of Abraham J. Heschel*, Fritz A. Rothschild, ed., New York: Free Press, 1959, p. 106.

34 Abraham Joshua Heschel, *Man is not Alone*, New York: Farrar, Straus & Giroux, 1951, 1976, 1997, p. 112.

35 Abraham J. Heschel, "One God" op. cit., p. 104.

36 Martin Buber, in *The Way of Response: Martin Buber—Selections from His Writings*, Nahum N. Glatzer, ed., New York: Schocken Books, 1968, p. 53.

37 Isaiah 65:25.

38 Eli Epstein, interviewed 2 March, 2009.

39 Ismar Schorsch, "Learning to Live with Less: A Jewish Perspective" in Steven C. Rockefeller and John E. Elder, *Spirit and Nature: Why the Environment is a Religious Issue*, Boston: Beacon Press, 1992, p. 35.

40 *Likrat Shabbat*, translated from the Hebrew by Rabbi Sidney Greenberg, Bridgeport, Connecticut: Media Judaica/The Prayer Book Press, 1981, p. 61.

41 Job 1:20–21.

42 The Jewish Prayer Book, as quoted by Jocelyn Hellig, "A South African Jewish Perspective" in Martin Forward, ed., *Ultimate Visions*, Oxford: Oneworld Publications, 1995, p. 136.

43 Leviticus 11:45.

44 Talmud Berakhoth 11a, in *Ha-Suddur Ha-Shalem*, translated by Philip Birnbaum, New York: Hebrew Publishing Company, 1977, p. 14.

45 Rabbi Nina Beth Cardin, *The Tapestry of Jewish Time*, Springfield, New Jersey: Behrman House, 2000, p. 36.

46 Excerpted from Ruth Gan Kagan, "The Sabbath: Judaism's Discipline for Inner Peace" paper presented at the Assembly of the World's Religions, Seoul, Korea, 24–31 August 1992, pp. 3, 7. Used with permission of Rabbi Ruth Gan Kagan.

47 Sanhedrin 22a, quoted in *The Second Jewish Catalog*, Sharon Strassfeld and Michael Strassfeld, eds, Philadelphia: The Jewish Publication Society, 1976.

48 Rabbi Yochanan ben Nuri, Rosh Hashanah prayer quoted

by Arthur Waskow, *Seasons of Our Joy*, New York: Bantam Books, 1982, p. 11.

49 Prayer quoted by Arthur Waskow, *Seasons of Our Joy*, op. cit., p. 175.

50 Rabbi Maria Feldman, "Why Advocacy is Central to Reform Judaism" Religious Action Center of Reform Judaism, http://rac.org/_kd_items/actions.cfm, accessed 4/14/2007. Reproduced with permission of Religious Action Center of Reform Judaism.

51 Mordecai M. Kaplan, "The Way I Have Come" in *Mordecai M. Kaplan: An Evaluation*, I. Eisenstein and E. Kohn, eds, New York: Jewish Reconstructionist Foundation, 1952, p. 293.

52 Rabbi Karyn D. Kedar, "Metaphors of God" in Rabbi Elyse Goldstein, ed., *New Jewish Feminism: Probing the Past, Forging the Future*, Woodstock, Vermont: Jewish Lights Publishing, 2009, pp. 40–41.

53 Melissa Dinwiddie, Egalitarian Kebutah, http://ketubah-works.com/?s=i+will+be+your+loving+friend. Reproduced with permission.

54 Jewish Orthodox Feminist Alliance from "How the Status of American Jewish Women Has Changed Over the Past Decades" 15 January 2007 by Rela Mintz Geffen, http://jcpa.org/article/how-the-status-of-american-jewish-women-has-changed/#sthash.ziJb5LVz.dpuf. Used with permission of JOFA.

55 Rabbi Tirzah Firestone, "Transforming Our Stories through Midrash" in Rabbi Elyse Goldstein, op. cit., p. 115.

56 Ibid., p. 117.

57 Sarah Meytin, personal communication, 23 June 2014.

58 Rachel Meytin, "Who are you? Who am I?" Shabbat Message 11/1/13, http://meytinink.wordpress.com

59 Susannah Heschel, "The Origin of the Orange on the Seder Plate" April 2001, http://www.miriamscup.com/Heschel_orange.htm. Used with permission of Professor Susannah Heschel.

60 Arthur Kurzweil, ed., *Pebbles of Wisdom from Rabbi Adin Steinsaltz*, San Francisco: Jossey-Bass/Wiley, 2009, p. 109.

CHAPTER 9
CHRISTIANITY

1 David Vandiver, interviewed 1998, 2011.

2 Publishing Department of Moscow Patriarchate, The Russian Orthodox Church, Moscow, 1980, p. 239 in English translation by Doris Bradbury, Moscow: Progress Publishers, 1982.

3 "Origen on First Principles" in Hugh T. Kerr, ed., *Readings in Christian Thought*, Nashville, Tennessee: Abingdon Press, 1966, p. 46.

4 *The Gospel According to Thomas*, Coptic text established and translated by Guilloaumont et al., Leiden: E. J. Brill; New York: Harper & Row, 1959, verse 77, copyright © Koninklijke BRILL NV.

5 Luke 2:47, 49. Most biblical quotations in this chapter are from the *Revised Standard Version of the Bible*, copyright © 1952, second edition 1971 by The Division of Christian Education of the National Council of the Churches of Christ in the USA. Used with permission. All rights reserved.

6 Mark 1:10–11.

7 Dietrich Bonhoeffer, *The Cost of Discipleship*, New York: Simon & Schuster, 1959, 1995, p. 90.

8 Matthew 6:25–27.

9 Matthew 7:7.

10 Luke 9:17.

11 John 6:48.

12 Rosemary Radford Ruether, *Women and Redemption: A Theological History*, Minneapolis: Fortress Press, 2011, p. 15.

13 Matthew 5:21–22.

14 Matthew 5:44–45.

15 David Vandiver, interviewed 1998, 2011.

16 Mark 10:27.

17 Matthew 22:39.

18 Matthew 25:37–40.

19 Luke 10:25–37, *The New English Bible*.

20 Matthew 5:3.

21 Matthew 13:44.

22 Mark 1:15.

23 Matthew 6:10.

24 Matthew 24:29–31.

25 Matthew 15:10, *The New English Bible*.

26 Matthew 23:27–28, *The New English Bible*.

27 Isaiah 56:7.

28 Jeremiah 7:11.

29 Mark 11:15–18, *The New English Bible*.

30 Mark 8:29–30.

31 John 11:27.

32 Matthew 17:2–5.

33 John 7:16, 8:12, 23, 58.

34 Matthew 26:28.

35 Mark 11:10.

36 Mark 14:36.

37 Joachim Jeremias, *New Testament Theology: The Proclamation of Jesus*, translated by John Bowden, SCM-Canterbury Press, 1971, p. 40. Used with permission.

38 Mark 14:41.

39 Matthew 26:64.

40 Matthew 27:11.

41 John 18:35–38.

42 Matthew 28:18–20.

43 Elisabeth Schüssler Fiorenza, *In Memory of Her*, SCM-Canterbury Press, 2009.

44 Acts 4:10–12.

45 Acts 1:10–11.

46 Christos Yannaras, *Elements of Faith: An Introduction to Orthodox Theology*, English translation by Keith Schram, Edinburgh: T & T Clark, 1991, pp. 65–66. Used with permission of Bloomsbury Publishing Plc.

47 Acts 2:36.

48 Acts 26:18.

49 Acts 17:28.

50 Archimandrite Chrysostomos, *The Ancient Fathers of the Desert*, Brookline, Massachusetts: Hellenic College Press, 1980, p. 78.

51 "On Obedience" Chapter 5, Jan. 22–May 23–Sept. 22. Saint Benedict's Rule for Monasteries, translated by Leonard J. Doyle OblSB, of Saint John's Abbey, copyright © 1948, 2001, by the Order of Saint Benedict, Collegeville, MN 56321, p. 80. Used with permission of Liturgical Press.

52 Archimandrite Chrysostomos, The Ancient Fathers of the Desert, op. cit., p.80.

53 From *A Hopkins Reader*, John Pick, ed., New York: Oxford University Press, 1953, quoted in D. M. Dooling, ed., *A Way of Working*, New York: Anchor Press/Doubleday, 1979, p. 6.

54 "St. Francis, Testament" April 1226, p. 3, quoted in Jean Leclerc, Francois Vandenbroucke, and Louis Bouyer, eds, *The Spirituality of the Middle Ages*, vol. 2 of *A History of Christian Spirituality*, New York: Seabury Press, 1982, p. 289.

55 *The Cloud of Unknowing and The Book of Privy Counseling*, Garden City, New York: Image Books, 1973 edition, p. 56.

56 Martin Luther, "A Treatise on Christian Liberty" quoted in John Dillenberger and Claude Welch, *Protestant Christianity*, New York: Charles Scribner's Sons, 1954, p. 36.

57 Ulrich Zwingli, "On True and False Religion" quoted in Harry Emerson Fosdick, ed., *Great Voices of the Reformation*, New York: Random House, 1952, p. 169.

58 John Calvin, "Instruction in Faith" translated and edited by Paul T. Fuhrmann, copyright © 1949, quoted in Fosdick, op. cit., p. 216.

59 John Wesley, "The Repentance of Believers" sermon preached in Londonderry, 24 April 1767, on http://www.

godrules.net/library/wsermons/wsermons14, accessed 7/17/2009.

60 St. Teresa of Avila, *The Interior Castle*, translated by E. Allison Peers from the critical edition of P. Silverior de Santa Teresa, Garden City, New York: Image Books, 1961, p. 214.

61 John Wesley, as quoted in Dillenberger and Welch, *Protestant Christianity*, op. cit., p. 134.

62 Sarah Grimke, "Letters on the Equality of the Sexes and the Condition of Women" (1836–1837), in *Feminism: The Essential Historical Writings*, M. Schneir, ed., New York: Vintage, 1972, p. 38.

63 *The Documents of Vatican II*, Walter M. Abbott, ed., New York: Guild Press, 1966, p. 665.

64 Ecumenical Patriarch Bartholomew, in John Chryssavgis, ed., *Cosmic Grace, Humble Prayer: The Ecological Vision of the Green Patriarch Bartholomew*, Grand Rapids, Michigan: Wm. B. Eerdmans Publishing Co., 2003, p. 61. Reproduced with permission.

65 Isaac the Syrian, in Hilarion Alfeyev, *The Spiritual World of Isaac the Syrian*, Collegeville, Minnesota: Liturgical Press, 2008, p. 257.

66 St. Gregory Palamas, "Homily on the Presentation of the Holy Virgin in the Temple" in Sophocles, *22 Homilies of St. Gr. Palamas*, Athens, 1861, pp. 175–177, quoted in Vladimir Lossky, *The Mystical Theology of the Eastern Church*, New York: St. Vladimir's Seminary Press, 1976, p. 224.

67 Jim Forest, *Pilgrim to the Russian Church*, New York: Crossroad Publishing Company, 1988, p. 50. Used with permission of Jim Forest.

68 John 14: 6–10, *The New Oxford Annotated Bible*, third edition, Oxford: Oxford University Press, 2001, copyright © 2001 by Oxford University Press, Inc.

69 Paul Knitter, in John Hick and Paul F. Knitter, eds, *The Myth of Christian Uniqueness: Toward a Pluralistic Theology of Religions*, Maryknoll, New York: Orbis Books, 1987, pp. 192–193.

70 Matthew 20:28.

71 John 3:16–17, *The New English Bible*.

72 Rev. Larry Howard, interfaith service, Syracuse, New York, 25 October 1992.

73 Thomas Keating, *The Mystery of Christ: The Liturgy as Spiritual Experience*, Continuum, 1994, p. 5, copyright © Thomas Keating. Used with permission of Bloomsbury Publishing Plc.

74 Virgilio Elizondo, "Mestizo Jesus" in Robert Lassalle-Klein, ed., *Jesus of Galilee: Contextual Christology for the 21st Century*, Maryknoll, New York: Orbis Books, 2011, pp. 52–53. Used with permission.

75 Thomas a Kempis, *The Imitation of Christ*, p. 139.

76 F. Ioann Kronshtadtsky, as quoted in F. Veniamin Fedchenkov, *Heaven on Earth*, Moscow: Palmnik, 1994, p. 70.

77 Julia Gatta, personal communication, 22 July 1987.

78 "Brief Order for Confession and Forgiveness" Lutheran Book of Worship, prepared by the churches participating in the Inter-Lutheran Commission on Worship, Minneapolis, Minnesota: Augsburg Publishing House, 1978, p. 56.

79 World Council of Churches, Baptism, Eucharist and Ministry, Faith and Order Paper No. 111, Geneva, 1982, p. 2. Used with permission.

80 Father Appolinari, interviewed 28 October 1994.

81 John 1:9.

82 Jim Forest, *Pilgrim to the Russian Church*, op. cit., p. 72.

83 Thomas Merton, *Contemplative Prayer*, Garden City, New York: Image Classics, 2000, p. 45. Used with permission of Liturgical Press.

84 Bishop Paulos Mar Gregorios, World Congress of Spiritual Concord, Rishikesh, India, 11 December 1993.

85 *The Way of a Pilgrim and The Pilgrim Continues His Way*, translated by Helen Bacovcin, New York/London: Doubleday, 1978, 1992, p. 160.

86 Luke 1:38.

87 Quoted in Jim Forest, *Pilgrim to the Russian Church*, op. cit., p. 63.

88 Patriarch Bartholomew, The Ecumenical Patriarch of Constantinople, *Encountering the Mystery: Understanding Orthodox Christianity Today*, New York: Doubleday, 2008, p. 67. Used with permission of Doubleday, an imprint of the Knopf Doubleday Publishing Group, a division of Random House LLC. All rights reserved.

89 Associated Press, Vatican City: "Only Catholicism 'proper': Vatican" *The Globe and Mail*, 6 September 2000, A14; Philip Pullella (Reuters), "Vatican says no religion equals Roman Catholicism" *Asian Age*, 6 September 2000, p. 5.

90 Pope Benedict XVI, *Jesus of Nazareth*, translated by Adrian J. Walker, Bloomsbury Publishing Plc, copyright © 2008. Used with permission of Bloomsbury Publishing Plc and Penguin Random House LLC.

91 "Message of His Holiness Francis for the Celebration of the World Day of Peace" 1 January 2014, as published in *Tikkun* magazine, Winter 2014. Reproduced with permission.

92 Sean McDonagh, *The Greening of the Church*, Maryknoll, New York: Orbis Books, p. 65.

93 Jonathan Edwards, "Sinners in the Hands of an Angry God" Enfield, Connecticut, July 8, 1741, http://www.ccel.org/ccel/edwards/sermons.sinners.html, accessed 7/20/2009.

94 I Corinthians 12:6–11.

95 Vazhayil Babu, interviewed 11 December 2008.

96 Roman I. Bilas, interviewed 25 October 1994.

97 In Allan Anderson, *An Introduction to Pentecostalism*, Cambridge: Cambridge University Press, 2004, p. 138.

98 Harvey Cox, *Fire from Heaven: The Rise of Pentecostal Spirituality and the Reshaping of Religion in the Twenty-first Century*, Reading, Massachusetts: Addison-Wesley, 1995, 2001.

99 Daniel H. Bays, "Chinese Protestant Christianity Today" in Daniel L. Overmyer, ed., *Religion in China Today*, Cambridge: Cambridge University Press, 2003, p. 7.

100 Members of African Independent Churches Report on their Pilot Study of the History and Theology of their Churches, "Speaking for Ourselves" Braamfontein, South Africa: Institute for Contextural Theology, 1985, pp. 23–24.

101 Gustavo Gutiérrez, *A Theology of Liberation*, New York: Orbis Books, 1973, p. 209. Used with permission.

102 Bakole Wa Ilunga, *Paths of Liberation: A Third World Spirituality*, Maryknoll, New York: Orbis Books, 1984, p. 92. Used with permission.

103 Dwight N. Hopkins, ed., *Black Faith and Public Talk*, Maryknoll, New York: Orbis Books, 1999, pp. 1–2. Used with permission of Professor Dwight N. Hopkins.

104 Desmond Tutu, quoted in *Archbishop Tutu: Prophetic Witness in South Africa*, Leonard Hulley, Louise Kretzschmar, and Luke Pato, eds, Cape Town: Human and Rousseau, 1996, pp. 41–42. Reproduced by permission of Human and Rousseau.

105 Ibid., p. 37.

106 Ibid., p. 38.

107 Francis Cull, "Desmond Tutu: Man of Prayer" in Hulley et al., *Archbishop Tutu*, op. cit., pp. 31–32.

108 Desmond Tutu, in Vila-Vicencio, "Tough and Compassionate" op. cit., pp. 44–45.

109 Florence Muindi, quoted in Donald E. Miller and Tetsunao Yamamori, *Global Pentecostalism: The New Face of Christian Social Engagement*, Berkeley: University of California Press, 2007, pp. 40–41. Used with permission.

110 I Corinthians 11:7–12.

111 Rosemary Radford Ruether, *Women and Redemption*, op. cit., pp. 27.

112 Ivone Gebara and Maria Clara Bingemer, *Mary, Mother of God, Mother of the Poor*, Maryknoll, New York: Orbis Books, 1989, as excerpted in Ursula King, ed., *Feminist Theology from the Third World*, Maryknoll, New York: Orbis Books, 1994, pp. 277, 280–281.

113 Sallie McFague, *Models of God: Theology for an Ecological, Nuclear Age*, Philadelphia: Fortress Press, 1987, pp. 101, 106.

114 Thomas Berry, remarks at "Seeking the True Meaning of Peace" conference in San Jose, Costa Rica, 27 June 1989.

115 Thomas Berry, *The great work: our way to the future*, NY: Bell Tower, 1999.

116 Laurie Goodstein, "Evangelical Leaders Join Global Warming Initiative" *The New York Times*, 8 February 2006.

117 Patriarch Bartholomew, The Ecumenical Patriarch of Constantinople, *Encountering the Mystery: Understanding Orthodox Christianity Today*, op. cit., pp. 99–100.

118 Father Denis G. Pereira, "A New Model for India's Pastoral Clergy" *Vidyajyoti Journal of Theological Reflection*, vol. 67, no. 1, January 2003, p. 67. Used with permission of Vidyajyoti College of Theology.

119 "Full Text: Common Declaration of Pope Francis and Ecumenical Patriarch Bartholomew I" 25 May 2014, catholi-cherald.co.uk, accessed 12/8/14.

120 Patriarch Bartholomew, The Ecumenical Patriarch of Constantinople, *Encountering the Mystery*, op. cit., p. 146.

CHAPTER 10
ISLAM

1 Syed Mousmen Hussain, interviewed 18 October 2006.

2 Surah 96:1–5, Ali Unal, trans., *The Qur'an with Annotated Interpretation in Modern English*, Somerset, New Jersey: The Light, 2007.

3 Surah 10:15–16, Ali Unal, trans., op. cit.

4 Maulana M. Ubaidul Akbar, *The Orations of Muhammad*, Lahore: M. Ashraf, 1954, p. 78.

5 *The Holy Qur'an*, Surah 41:6, translation and commentary by Abdulla Yusuf Ali, Durban, R.S.A.: Islamic Propagation Center International, 1946. Unless noted otherwise, all citations from the Qur'an throughout this chapter are from this translation, by permission.

6 Surah 28:56.

7 Hadith quoted by Annemarie Schimmel, *And Muhammad is His Messenger*, op. cit., 1985, pp. 48, 55.

8 Surah 3:104.

9 Quoted by Mahmoud Ayoub, *The Qur'an and its Interpreters*, Albany: State University of New York Press, 1984, vol. 1, p. 14.

10 Surah 1:1–17. Note that despite the layout of this translation, the Qur'an is not a work of poetry.

11 Sayyid Muhammad Husayn Tabatabai, *Shi'ite Islam*, translated by S. H. Nasr, Albany, New York: State University of New York Press, 1979, http://www.ummah.net/khoei/shia/part1/htm.

12 Surah 42:15.

13 Surah 2:163.

14 Abu Hashim Madani, quoted in Samuel L. Lewis, *In the Garden*, New York: Harmony Books/Lama Foundation, 1975, p. 136.

15 Frithjof Schuon, *Understanding Islam*, translated by D. M. Matheson, London: George Allen & Unwin, 1963, p. 59.

16 Surah 2:136.

17 Surah 32:16–17.

18 Surah 3:63.

19 Surah 41:37.

20 Quoted by Abdur-Rahman Ibrahim Doi, "Sunnism" *Islamic Spirituality: Foundations*, Seyyed Hossein Nasr, ed., New York: Crossroad, 1987, p. 158.

21 Surah 17:13–14.

22 Surah 70:16–18.

23 Surah 2:256.

24 Hadith quoted by Syed Ali Ashraf, "The Inner Meaning of the Islamic Rites: Prayer, Pilgrimage, Fasting, Jihad", *Islamic Spirituality: Foundations*, op. cit., p. 114.

25 Shaykh Muhammad Hisham Kabbani, "The Importance and Meaning of Prayer in Islam" in Vincent J. Cornell, ed., *Voices of Islam*, Westport, Connecticut: Praeger, 2007, vol. 2, pp. 38–39.

26 Syed Mousmen Hussain, interviewed 18 October 2006.

27 Jalal al-Din Rumi, "Fasting" translated by John Moyne and Coleman Barks, *Open Secret: Versions of Rumi*, Putney, Vermont: Threshold Books, 1984, number 1739, p. 42. Used with permission.

28 Quoted by Sadia Dehvi, "God loves the hungry" *Asian Age*, 12 August 2010, p. 7.

29 Ibrahim Keskin Hafiz, interviewed 9 April 2008.

30 Quoted by Muhammad Rida al-Muzaffar, *The Faith of Shi'a Islam*, London: The Muhammadi Trust, 1982, p. 35.

31 Hadith #535 cited in Badi'uz-Zaman Furuzanfar, Ahadith-I Mathnawi, Tehran, 1334 sh./1955, in Persian, quoted in Annemarie Schimmel, *Mystical Dimensions of Islam*, Chapel Hill: University of North Carolina Press, 1975, p. 118.

32 Rabi'a al-'Adawiyya al-Qaysiyya, quoted in Abu Talib, Qut al-Qulub, II, Cairo, A. H. 1310, p. 57, as quoted in Margaret Smith, *Rabi'a the Mystic and her Fellow-Saints in Islam*, Cambridge: Cambridge University Press, 1928, 1984, p. 102.

33 Jalal al-Din Rumi, opening lines of the *Mathnawi*, translated by Edmund Helminski, *The Ruins of the Heart: Selected Lyric Poetry of Jelaluddin Rumi*, Putney, Vermont: Threshold Books, 1981, p. 20.

34 Jalal al-Din Rumi, *Mathnawi-i ma'nawi*, translated and edited by Reynold A. Nicholson, London: 1925–1940, vol. 4, line 2102.

35 Hadith of the Prophet, #352 in Badi'uz-Zaman Furuzanfar, Ahadith-i Mathnawi, in Schimmel, *Mystical Dimensions of Islam*, op. cit.

36 Quoted in Javad Nurbakhsh, *Sufism: Meaning, Knowledge, and Unity*, New York: Khaniqahi-Nimatullahi Publications, 1981, pp. 19, 21.

37 Al-Ghazali, in *The Faith and Practice of Al-Ghazali*, translated by William Montgomery Watt, Oxford: Oneworld Publications, 1953, 1994, pp. 77, 130.

38 Idries Shah, *The Sufis*, London: Jonathan Cape, 1964, p. 76.

39 Jalal al-Din Rumi, *Mathnawi, VI, 3220–3246*, translated by Coleman Barks, *Rumi: We Are Three*, Athens, Georgia: Maypop Books, 1987, pp. 54–55. Used with permission.

40 Treaty cited in Philip K. Hitti, *Islam and the West*, Princeton, New Jersey: D. Van Nostrand, 1962, p. 112.

41 As quoted in M. Fethullah Gulen, *The Messenger of God: Muhammad*, English translation by Ali Unal, Somerset, New Jersey: The Light, 2006, p. 191.

42 Uzbek Khan, 1313 charter granted to Metropolitan Peter, as quoted in *Al Risala*, June 1994, p. 12.

43 Annemarie Schimmel, speaking on "Islam's Hidden Beauty" tape from New Dimensions Foundation, San Francisco, 1989, side 1. Reprinted with permission from the producer, Human Media, www.humanmedia.org.

44 Jalal al-Din Rumi, *Mathnawi, IV*, in *Rumi: We Are Three*, op. cit., p. 52.

45 http://www.gallup.com/poll/148931/presentation-muslim-americans-faith-freedom-future.aspx, 2011.

46 Chris Allen, *Islamophobia*, Farnham, Surrey, UK: Ashgate Publishing, 2010, p. 114.

47 Semaa Abdulwali, "The niqab makes me feel liberated, and no law will stop me from wearing it" *The Guardian*, 6 October 2014, copyright © Guardian News & Media Ltd, 2014.

48 Amina Wadud, *Qur'an and Woman*, New York: Oxford University Press, 1999, pp. ix–x, xiii, xx; Amina Wadud, "Alternative Qur'anic Interpretation and the Status of Muslim Women" in Gisela Webb, ed., *Windows of Faith: Muslim Women Scholar-Activists in North America*, Syracuse: Syracuse University Press, 2000, p. 11.

49 Seyyed Hossein Nasr, "The Pertinence of Islam to the Modern World" *The World Religions Speak on the Relevance of Religion in the Modern World*, Finley P. Dunne Jr., ed., The Hague: Junk, 1970, p. 133.

50 "Islamic TV channel to counter the West" *Asian Age*, 20 October 1998, p. 1.

51 Malala Yousafzai with Christina Lamb, *I Am Malala: The Girl Who Stood Up for Education and Was Shot by the Taliban*, New York: Little, Brown and Company, 2013, pp. 176–77, copyright © 2013 by Salarzai Limited. Used with permission of Little, Brown and Company.

52 Malala Yousafzai with Christina Lamb, *I Am Malala*, op. cit., p. 237.

53 "The Nobel Peace Prize for 2014" http://www.nobelprize. org/nobel_prizes/peace/laureates/2014/press.html, retrieved 15 October 2014, copyright © The Nobel Foundation.

54 Malala Yousafzai's response to the Nobel announcement, copyright © Malala Yousafzai, 2014, https://secure.aworldatschool.org/page/content/the-textof-malala-yousafzais-speech-at-the-united-nations/. Reproduced with permission of Curtis Brown Group Ltd, London on behalf of Malala Yousafzai. http://lybio.net/tag/read-malala-yousafzai-nobel-peaceprize-winner-speech-malala-yousafzai-transcripts/ Reproduced with permission of Curtis Brown Group Ltd, London on behalf of Malala Yousafzai.

55 Ardeshir Cowasjee, "As Pak mocks education" *Dawn*, in *Asian Age*, 8 January 2004, p. 16.

56 Vincent J. Cornell, ed., *Voices of Islam*, Westport, Connecticut: Praeger, 2007, vol. 1, p. vii.

57 Hadith of the Prophet, as quoted in *Fakhr al-Din Al-Razi, Tafsir al-Fakhr al-Razi*, 21 vols, Mecca: al-Kaktabah al-Tijari-yyah, 1990, vol. 7, p. 232.

58 Surah 22:39–40.

59 Surah 2:190.

60 Surah 2:217, 192.

61 Quoted in Karen Armstrong, *The Battle of God: Fundamentalism in Judaism, Christianity and Islam*, London: Harper Collins, 2000, p. 240

62 Imam Khomeini, *Islam and Revolution: Writings and Declarations of Imam Khomeini*, translated by Hamid Algar, Berkeley, California: Mizan Press, 1981, p. 53.

63 Dr. Azizah al-Hibri, "The Taliban and Islamic Teaching" in *Sightings*, an e-mail journal published by the Martin Marty Center at the University of Chicago Divinity School, 14 March 2001. Used with permission from Dr. Azizah al-Hibri.

64 Osama bin Laden, videotaped address, 7 October 2001, in Bruce Lincoln, *Holy Terrors: Thinking about Religion after September 11*, Chicago: University of Chicago Press, 2003, pp. 102–3.

65 King Abdullah, quoted in AFP news service, "Saudi Women at Last Get the Right to Vote" *Asian Age*, 26 September 2011, p. 10.

66 http://lettertobaghdadi.com/, retrieved 24 September 2014.

67 Surah 29:46.

68 Asaf Hussain, "Fundamentalism—An Islamic Perspective" *International Interfaith Center News*, December 2000, p. 7.

69 Malala Yousafzai's speech to the United Nations, 12 July 2013, copyright © Malala Yousafzai, 2013, https://secure.aworldatschool.org/page/content/the-textof-malala-yousafzais-speech-at-the-united-nations/. Reproduced with permission of Curtis Brown Group Ltd, London on behalf of Malala Yousafzai.

70 Mahmoon-al-Rasheed, "Islam, Nonviolence, and Social Transformation" Glenn D. Paige, Chaiwat Satha-Anand, and Sarah Gilliatt, eds, Honolulu: University of Hawai'i, Center for Global Nonviolence Planning Project, 1993, p. 70.

71 Omid Safi, "Introduction: Islamic Modernism and the Challenge of Reform" in Vincent J. Cornell, ed., *Voices of Islam*, Westport, Connecticut: Praeger, 2007, vol. 5, p. xxiii.

72 Shirin Ebadi, http://nobelprize.org/nobel_prizes/peace/laureates/2003/ebadi-lecture-e.html, accessed 8/17/2009, copyright © The Nobel Foundation.

CHAPTER 11
SIKHISM

1 Sheena Kandhari, personal communication, 29 January 2012.

2 Puratan, quoted in Khushwant Singh, *Hymns of Guru Nanak*, New Delhi: Orient Longmans Ltd., 1969, p. 10.

3 J. S. Neki, "Legends of Guru Nanak" *Asian Age*, 2 January 2011, p. 7.

4 Guru Nanak, as quoted in W. Owen Cole and Piara Singh Sambhi, *The Sikhs: Their Religious Beliefs and Practices*, London: Routledge and Kegan Paul, 1978, p. 39.

5 Sri Rag, p. 59, quoted in Trilochan Singh, Jodh Singh, Kapur Singh, Bawa Harkishen Singh, and Kushwant Singh, translators, *The Sacred Writings of the Sikhs*, Unwin Hyman Ltd., 1973, p. 72.

6 Bhagat Ravi Das, Rag Sorath, Guru Granth Sahib, p. 657.

7 Siri Guru Granth Sahib, p. 724.

8 Guru Har Rai, as quoted in Dr. Gopal Singh, *A History of the Sikh People*, New Delhi: World Sikh University Press, 1979, p. 257.

9 Guru Gobind Singh, *Bachittar Natak*, second edition, M.L. Peace and Rattan Kaur, 1967.

10 Siri Guru Granth Sahib, p. 1022.

11 Nikky-Guninder Kaur Singh, *The Birth of the Khalsa: A Feminist Re-Memory of Sikh Identity*, Albany: State University of New York Press, 2005, p. 126, copyright © 2005. Used with permission.

12 Siri Guru Granth Sahib, p. 1377.

13 From Dr. S. Radhakrishnan, letter in the Baisakhi edition of *The Spokesman*, 1956, reprinted as introduction to Giani Ishar Singh Nara, *Safarnama and Zafarnama*, New Delhi: Nara Publications, 1985, pp. iv–v.

14 *Mul Mantra*, quoted in Singh, *Hymns of Guru Nanak*, op. cit., p. 25.

15 *Jaap Sahib*, verses 84, 159, English translation by Harjett Singh Gill, New Delhi: Gobind Sadan Institute for Advanced Studies in Comparative Religion, 2007.

16 *Adi Granth* 684, quoted in Cole and Sambhi, *The Sikhs*, op. cit., p. 74.

17 Guru Nanak, Guru Granth Sahib, p. 141.

18 Ibid.

19 Ibid, p.473.

20 Guru Granth Sahib, p. 102.

21 *Anand Sahib*, verse 14.

22 Excerpt from Guru Gobind Singh, *Rahitnamas*, as translated by Gurden Singh.

23 Ibid.

24 Guru Nanak, Guru Granth Sahib, p. 282.

25 Excerpts from daily Ardas of Sikhs, in English translation.

26 *JapJi* verses 9–10.

27 Siri Guru Granth Sahib, p. 708.

28 Baba Virsa Singh, quoted by Juliet Hollister in *News from Gobind Sadan*, August 1997, p. 1.

29 Baba Virsa Singh, "Challenge to Religious Leaders" *Gobind Sadan Times*, 28 August 2000, p. 1, Gobind Sadan Institute for Advanced Studies in Comparative Religion.

30 Baba Virsa Singh, *Message for the Millennium Peace Summit, Challenge to Religious Leaders*, April 1997, p. 3, Gobind Sadan Institute for Advanced Studies in Comparative Religion.

31 The Sikh Gurdwaras Act 1925, 2 (9), as quoted in W. H. McLeod, "Who is a Sikh?", *Sikhs and Sikhism*, Oxford: Oxford University Press, 1999, p. 93.

32 Sheena Kandhari, personal communication, 29 January 2012.

33 Baba Virsa Singh, in *News from Gobind Sadan*, May 1994, p. 4, Gobind Sadan Institute for Advanced Studies in Comparative Religion.

34 Guru Gobind Singh, *Dasam Granth*.

CHAPTER 12
NEW RELIGIOUS MOVEMENTS

1 Church of the Flying Spaghetti Monster, www.venganza. org, accessed 2 October 2014. Used with permission.

2 Friday M. Mbon, "The Social Impact of Nigeria's New Religious Movements" in James A. Beckford, ed., *New Religious Movements and Rapid Social Change*, Paris and London: Unesco/Sage Publications, 1986, p. 177.

3 "Code of a Sea Org Member" J. Gordon Melton, "A Contemporary Ordered Religious Community: The Sea Organization" paper presented at the 2001 CESNUR conference in London, http://www.cesnur.org/2001/london2001/melton.hem, accessed 9/26/2009. Used with permission of Dr J. Gordon Melton.

4 Damien Marsic, in Anne Berryman, "Who are the Raëlians?" *Time*, 4 January 2003, http://www.time.com.

5 Rev. Sun Myung Moon, "God's Ideal Family and the Kingdom of the Peaceful, Ideal World" http://www.familyfed.org/trueparents, accessed 2/25/2011.

6 Andrew Wilson, "Visions of the Spirit World: Sang Hun Lee's 'Life in the Spirit World and on Earth' Compared with Other Spiritualist Accounts" *Journal of Unification Studies* 2, 1998, p. 123.

7 http://media.radiosai.org/Journals/Vol_04/01DEC06/03-coverstory.htm

8 http://www.sathyasai.org/discour/1974/d740609.htm

9 Sathya Sai Baba, 17 May 1968, *Sathya Sai Speaks*, vol. 8, Chapter 19. On the occasion of the World Conference of Sri Sathya Sai Seva Organization, http://www.srisathyasai.org.in/Pages/SriSathyaSaiBaba/BabaHimself.htm, accessed 9/30/2009.

10 The First Presidency and Council of the Twelve Apostles of Jesus Christ of the Latter-day Saints, "The Family: A Proclamation to the World", https://www.lds.org/topics/family-proclamation, accessed 12/4/2010.

11 Thomas Thorkelson, interviewed 21 February 2004.

12 Gordon B. Hinkley, PBS interview broadcast, 18 July 1997.

13 "A Secure Future under God's Rule" in *Awake!*, May 2008, published by Jehovah's Witnesses, copyright © Watch Tower Bible & Tract Society of Pennsylvania. Used with permission.

14 James Beckford, in David Voas, "The Trumpet Sounds Retreat: Learning from the Jehovah's Witnesses" in Eileen Barker, ed., *The Centrality of Religion in Social Life*, Farnham, Surrey, UK: Ashgate Publishing, 2010, p. 124. Used with permission.

15 Interview with Wolfgang Hecker, 13 November 2009.

16 Julian P. Johnson, *With a Great Master In India*, Beas, Punjab: Radha Soami Satsang Beas, 1934–2002, pp. 88–89.

17 *A Brief Description of Radhasoami Faith and a Short Note on the Holy Samadh*, fourth edition, Agra, India: S. D. Maheshwari, 1984, p. 10.

18 Justice Anthony M. Kennedy, United States Supreme Court majority opinion summation in the Church of the Lucumi vs. The City of Hialeah, 11 June 1993.

19 Rev. William Kingsley Opoku, personal communication, 6 February 1993.

20 Seiyu Kiriyama, *The Marvel of Spiritual Transformation*, translated by Rande Brown, Tokyo: Hirakawa Shuppan, 1996, 2001, p. 65.

21 "35th Fire Rites Festival, Agon Shu's Hoshi Matsuri" 11 February 2008, Agon Shu program, p. 12.

22 Seiyu Kiriyama, The Marvel of Spiritual Transformation, op. cit., p. 190.

23 H. P. Blavatsky, *The Key to Theosophy*, Los Angeles: The United Lodge of Theosophists, 1920, p. 3.

24 H. P. Blavatsky, "Is Theosophy a Religion" *Lucifer*, November 1888.

25 "The Baha'is: A Profile of the Baha'i Faith and its Worldwide Community" "One World, One Faith", National Spiritual Assembly of India, New Delhi: Baha'i Publishing Trust, 1979, p. 42. Used with permission.

26 Svetlana Dorzhieva, interviewed 26 October 1994.

27 "Abdu'l-Baha" as quoted in "One World, One Faith" ibid., p. 3.

28 Adapted from "The Baha'i Faith" New York: Baha'i International Community United Nations Office. Used with permission.

29 Quoted in Ernest Cashmore, *Rastaman*, London: Unwin Paperbacks, 1983, p. 22.

30 "An Introduction to Rastafari" Ras Charles and French Dread, http://www.earthcultureroots.com, accessed 10/6/2009, Earth Culture Roots. Used with permission.

31 Starhawk, *The Spiral Dance: A Rebirth of the Ancient Religion of the Great Goddess*, San Francisco: Harper & Row, 1979, pp. 2–3.

32 Quoted in Merlin Stone, *When God was a Woman*, San Diego, California: Harcourt Brace Jovanovich, 1976, p. x.

33 Diane Rae Schulz, "Discovering Goddess Spirituality" *Awakened Woman* e-magazine, http://www.awakenedwoman.com/goddess_spirituality.htm, accessed 5/9/2007.

34 John Seed, "Anthropocentrism" *Awakening in the Nuclear Age*, Issue #14, Summer/Fall 1986, p. 11.

35 Chief Seattle, "Chief Seattle's Message" quoted in *Thinking Like a Mountain: Toward a Council of All Beings*, John Seed, Joanna Macy, Pat Fleming, and Arne Naess, eds, Santa Cruz, California: New Society Publishers, 1988, p. 71.

36 J. E. Lovelock, *Gaia: A new look at life on Earth*, Oxford: Oxford University Press, pp. 9, 11.

37 James Lovelock, *The Ages of Gaia*, New York: Bantam Books, 1990, p. 206.

38 Peter Russell, "Endangered Earth: Psychological roots of the environmental crisis" *Link Up*, Issue #38, Spring 1989, pp. 7–8.

39 Julia Butterfly Hill, circleoflifefoundation.org/review4.html.

40 David Albert, "A Children's Story: Gaura Devi Saves the Trees" *Awakening in the Nuclear Age*, op. cit., p. 15.

41 "Jesus Christ: The Bearer of the Water of Life: A Christian Reflection on the 'New Age'" Pontifical Council for Culture, Pontifical Council for Interreligious Dialogue, http://www.cesnur.org/2003/vat_na_en.htm, accessed 10/7/2009.

42 Marianne Williamson, *Illuminata*, New York: Riverhead Books, 1994, p. xvii.

43 *Daily Word*, http://www.dailyword.com, accessed 10/8/2009. Reprinted with permission of Unity®, publisher of Daily Word®.

44 James Redfield, *The Celestine Prophecy*, London/New York: Bantam Books, 1994, pp. 276–77.

45 Sandra Duarte de Souza, "Religious Transit and Ecological Spirituality in Brazil" paper presented at "The Spiritual Supermarket: Religious Pluralism in the 21st Century" 19–22 April 2001, London School of Economics, sponsored by the Center for Studies on New Religions, Italy, p. 4.

46 "Mission statement" http://jediismokchap.tripod.com/jedi.html, accessed 3/5/2012.

47 "Force" http://www.jediism.org, accessed 3/5/2012.

48 Church of the Flying Spaghetti Monster, www.venganza.org, accessed 2 October 2014. Used with permission.

49 "Persecution" http://www.bahai.org/dir/worldwide/persecution, accessed 10/5/2009.

50 Xinhua, "China Bans Falun Gong" *People's Daily*, 22 July 1999.

51 Catherine Wessinger, *How the Millennium Comes Violently*, New York: Seven Bridges Press, 2000, p. 6.

52 Frank Kaufmann, personal communication, 6 March 2012.

CHAPTER 13
RELIGION IN THE TWENTY-FIRST CENTURY

1 Baba Virsa Singh, *Loving God*, New Delhi: Gobind Sadan/ Sterling Publications, 2006, p. 83.

2 Jayati Ghosh, "U.S. dominates culture trade" *Asian Age*, 24 June 2008, p. 7.

3 John Adams, letter to Thomas Jefferson, 1813, as quoted in Thomas A. Tweed and Stephen Prothero, *Asian Religions in America*, New York: Oxford University Press, 1999, p. 48.

4 Frank Kaufmann, "Op-Ed: Innocence of Muslims and Rocks in the East China Sea" 28 September 2012, http://digital-journal.com/article/333784#ixzzz27pyOynwu. Used with permission.

5 Charles Taylor, *A Secular Age*, Cambridge, Massachusetts: The Belknap Press of Harvard University Press, 2007, pp. 2–3, copyright © 2007 by Charles Taylor. Used with permission.

6 Diana Eck, "A New Geo-Religious Reality" paper presented at the World Conference on Religion and Peace Sixth World Assembly, Riva del Garda, Italy, November 1994, p. 1. Used with permission.

7 Charles Strozier et al., "Religious Militancy or 'Fundamentalism'" in *Religion and Human Rights*, John Kelsay and Sumner B. Twiss, eds, 1998, New York: Westview Press Inc.

8 Osama bin Laden, videotaped address, 7 October 2001, reprinted in Bruce Lincoln, *A Nation Challenged: Bin Laden's Statement: 'The Sword Fell'*, *The New York Times*, 8 October 2001.

9 Rosalind Hackett interviewed, "The Shari'a Debate: Religion and Politics in Nigeria" Religioscope, 26 April 2002, http://www.religioscope.com/info/articles/ 012_nigeria.htm, accessed 2/2/2009, copyright © 2002 www.religioscope.com.

10 His Highness the Aga Khan, address to the School of International and Public Affairs, Columbia University, 15 May 2006.

11 Vimal Tirimanna, "Can the War against Terrorism be Won?", *Vidyajyoti Journal of Theological Reflection*, July 2004, vol. 68, no. 7, pp. 529–530. Used with permission of Vidyajyoti College of Theology.

12 Karen Armstrong, "The Myth of Religious Violence" *The Guardian*, 25 September 2014, copyright © Guardian News & Media Ltd, 2014.

13 Bruce Lincoln, *Holy Terrors: Thinking about Religion after September 11*, Chicago: University of Chicago Press, 2006, p. 75. Used with permission.

14 George W. Bush, address to the nation, 7 October 2001, *The New York Times*, 8 October 2001.

15 Charles S. Liebman, *Religion, Democracy, and Israeli Society*, Amsterdam: Harwood Academic Publishers, 1997, pp. 7–8.

16 Bishop David Z. Niringere, "Prayer and Public Life" talk for "Politics, Poverty and Prayer: Global African Spiritualities and Social Transformation" conference in Nairobi, 22 July 2010.

17 Ewert Cousins, speech at North American Interfaith Conference, Buffalo, New York, May 1991.

18 Frithjof Schuon, *Understanding Islam*, London: George Allen & Unwin Ltd., translated from French, 1963, p. 41.

19 Raimundo Panikkar, "The Invisible Harmony: A Universal Theory of Religion or a Cosmic Confidence in Reality?" in *Toward a Universal Theology of Religion*, Leonard Swidler, ed., Maryknoll, New York: Orbis Books, 1987, p. 147.

20 Arvind Sharma, *One Religion Too Many*, Albany, New York: State University of New York Press, 2011, p. 1.

21 Wendy Brown, *Regulating Aversion: Tolerance in the Age of Identity and Empire*, Princeton, New Jersey: Princeton University Press, 2006, p. 25.

22 Swami Adiswarananda, ed., *Vivekananda World Teacher: His Teachings on the Spiritual Unity of Humankind*, Vermont: Jewish Lights Publishing, 2007, p. 39

23 Swami Vivekananda, speech for the Parliament of the World's Religions, Chicago, 1893.

24 Wangari Maathai, speaking at the Oxford Global Survival Conference, quoted in *The Temple of Understanding Newsletter*, Fall 1988, p. 2.

25 Tugzhanov, Y. L., A. A. Abdakimov, N. P. Kalashnikova, V. G. Kochenov, S. V. Seliverstov. A. M. Ali, N. Zh. Shaimerdenova, and M. E. Ospanova, *Nursultan Nazarbayev: The Concept of Peace and Public Consent*, Astana, Kazakhstan: Zhasyl Orda, 2014, pp. 174–75.

26 Ibid., p. 175

27 Ibid., pp. 18–19

28 "Towards a Global Ethic" Assembly of Religious and Spiritual Leaders, at the Parliament of World Religions, Chicago, 1993.

29 Valson Thampu, Malini Seshadri, and Prema Raghunath, *Living in Harmony: A Course on Peace and Value Education*, Book 6, New Delhi: Oxford University Press, 2006, p. iv.

30 Baba Virsa Singh, in Mary Pat Fisher, ed., *Loving God: The Practical Teachings of Baba Virsa Singh*, second edition, New Delhi: Gobind Sadan Institute for Advanced Studies in Comparative Religion, 1995, pp. 7–8. Used with permission.

31 International Center for Conciliation, http://centerforconciliation.org.

32 Andreas D'Souza and Diane D'Souza, "Reconciliation: A New Paradigm for Missions", *Islam*, vol. 16, no. 2, Spring 1996, Hyderabad, India: Henry Martyn Institute of Islamic Studies, p. 5.

33 Frank Kaufmann, "Interfaith and the shadows of religion Part 1" http://kaufmannoninterfaith.tumblr.com/post/92445279867/interfaith-and-the-shadows-of-religion-part-i, accessed 21 July 2014. Used with permission.

34 Gustavo Gutiérrez, address to the World Conference on Religion and Peace, Riva del Garda, Italy, November 1994.

35 Seyyed Hussein Nasr, "Our Obligation to Tomorrow" in Kathleen Dean Moore and Michael P. Nelson, eds, *Moral Ground: Ethical Action for a Planet in Peril*, San Antonio, Texas: Trinity University Press, 2010, p. 258

36 Thich Nhat Hanh, "The Bells of Mindfulness" in Moore and Nelson, op. cit., p. 79

37 "85 Richest too Wealthy?" *Asian Age*, 21 January 2014, New Delhi, p. 9, based on 'Working for the Few, 178 OXFAM Briefing Paper', 20 January 2014, Oxfam, http://www.oxfam.org.

38 Sallie McFague, *Blessed are the Consumers: Climate Change and the Practice of Restraint*, Minneapolis: Fortress Press, 2013, p. 98.

39 William J. Byron, *The Power of Principles: Ethics for the New Corporate Culture*, Maryknoll, New York: Orbis Books, 2006, p. 51.

40 Thomas L. Friedman, "All fall down" *New York Times*, 25 November 2008.

41 Zhou Qin, "A Confucian View of the Global Economy" in *Subverting Greed: Religious Perspectives on the Global Economy*, ibid., p. 87.

42 David Loy, "Pave the Planet or Wear Shoes? A Buddhist Perspective on Greed and Globalization" in *Subverting Greed: Religious Perspectives on the Global Economy*, ibid., pp. 60–61.

43 Professor Syed Anwar Kabir, interviewed 12 April 1995.

44 Name withheld, private communication to Hillel Levine, April 2011. Used with permission of the author.

GLOSSARY

In the glossary, most words are accompanied by a guide to pronunciation. This guide gives an accepted pronunciation as simply as possible. Syllables are separated by a space and those that are stressed are underlined. Letters are pronounced in the usual manner for English unless they are clarified in the following list.

a	*as in*	flat
aa		father
aw		saw
ay		pay
ai		there
ee		see
e		let
i		pity
ī		high
o		not
ŏo		book
oo		food
oy		boy
ō		no
ow		now
u		but
ă, ĕ, ŏ, ŭ		about (unaccented vowels represented by "ə" in some phonetic alphabets)
er, ur, ir		fern, fur, fir
ch		church
j		jet
ng		sing
sh		shine
wh		where
y		yes
kh		guttural aspiration ("ch" in Welsh and German)

A

absolutist Someone who holds a rigid, literal, exclusive belief in the doctrines of their religion.

Advaita Vedanta (ăd v̄ī tă ve daan tă) Nondualistic Hindu philosophy, in which the goal is the realization that the self is Brahman.

Adi Granth (Guru Granth Sahib) Sacred scriptures of the Sikhs.

Advent The month of spiritual preparation leading up to Christmas.

African Instituted Churches Christian Churches primarily founded or shaped in Africa.

Agni (ăg nee) The god of fire in Hinduism.

agnosticism (ag nos ti siz ĕm) The belief that if there is anything beyond this life, it is impossible for humans to know it.

ahimsa (ă him să) Nonviolence, a central Jain principle.

Allah (ă laa) The one God, in Islam.

allegory Narrative that uses concrete symbols to convey abstract ideas.

Ameshta Spenta In Zoroastrianism, six divine powers (the Good Mind, Righteousness, Absolute Power, Devotion, Perfection, and Immortality), personified and worshiped as deities with shining eyes and beautiful forms after Zarathustra's death.

Amida (ă mee dă) (Sanskrit: Amitabha) The Buddha of Infinite Light, the personification of compassion whom the Pure Land Buddhists revere as the intermediary between humanity and Supreme Reality; esoterically, the Higher Self.

Amish Remaining members of a Christian denomination with strict discipline, refusal of military service, and maintenance of seventeenth-century customs from their Swiss origins.

amrit (ăm rit) The water, sweetened with sugar, used in Sikh baptismal ceremonies.

Anabaptists Members of a Christian denomination who reject the value of infant baptism.

anatman (Pali: *anatta*) The principle that there is no eternal self.

anekantwad (ă nayk ănt waad) The Jain principle of non-absolutism, because truth has many aspects.

angel In the Zoroastrian, Jewish, Christian, and Islamic traditions, an invisible servant of God.

Anglicanism The Church of England, founded by Henry VIII when he split from Rome and formalized by Elizabeth I in 1559.

anitya (Pali: *anicca*) Impermanence.

Annunciation (ă nun see ay shun) In Christianity, the appearance of an angel to the Virgin Mary to tell her that she would bear Jesus, conceived by the Holy Spirit.

anthropocentrism (an thro po sen triz ĕm) The assumption that the whole universe revolves around the human species.

anti-Semitism A term originating in the nineteenth century referring to expressions of hatred and fear of Jews, not of "Semites" (including Arabs and other people) more generally.

aparigraha (ă pă ree <u>grǎ</u> hǎ) The Jain principle of nonacquisitiveness.

apocalypse (ă <u>paw</u> kǎ lips) In Judaism and Christianity, a narrative account of the predetermined history of humanity, often with emphasis on its dramatic final end in the present day.

apostasy Accusation of abandonment of religious principles.

apostle Missionary follower of Christ who spread his word.

arhant (<u>aar</u> hǎnt) (Pali: *arhat* or *arahat*) A "Worthy One" who has followed the Buddha's Eightfold Path to liberation, broken the fetters that bind us to the suffering of the Wheel of Birth and Death, and arrived at nirvana, the Theravadan ideal.

Ark of the Covenant In Judaism, the shrine containing God's commandments to Moses.

Aryan Invasion Theory Speculation originally advanced by Western scholars that the Vedas were written by people invading India rather than by people already there.

Aryans (<u>Aar</u> ee ǎns) The Indo-European pastoral invaders of many European and Middle Eastern agricultural cultures during the second millennium BCE.

asana (<u>aa</u> sǎ nǎ) A yogic posture.

Ascension The ascent of Jesus to heaven forty days after his Resurrection.

ascetic Austere, detached from worldly comforts; a person who lives in this way.

Ashkenazim An ethnic grouping of the Jews with origins in Italy, France, and Germany.

ashram (<u>Aa</u> shrăm) In Indian tradition, a usually ascetic spiritual community of those who have gathered around a guru.

atheism (<u>ay</u> thee is em) Belief that there is no deity.

atman (<u>aat</u> măn) In Hinduism, the soul.

avatar (ǎ vǎ taar) In Hinduism, the earthly incarnation of a deity.

Avesta Holy text of Zoroastrian teaching and liturgy, only fragments of which have survived.

awakening Awareness of invisible Reality.

B

baptism A Christian sacrament by which God cleanses all sin and makes one a sharer in the divine life and a member of Christ's body, the Church.

Baptists Protestant denomination in which baptism takes place in adulthood.

barakah (<u>bǎ</u> rǎ kǎ) In Islamic mysticism, the spiritual wisdom and blessing transmitted from master to pupil.

Bar Mitzvah (baar <u>mitz</u> vǎ) The coming-of-age ceremony for a Jewish boy.

Bat Mitzvah (baat <u>mitz</u> vǎ) The coming-of-age ceremony for a Jewish girl in some modern congregations.

Beatitudes (bee <u>at</u> ě toods) Short statements by Jesus about those who are most blessed.

Bhagavad-Gita (<u>ba</u> gǎ vǎd <u>gee</u> tǎ) A portion of the Hindu epic *Mahabharata* in which Lord Krishna specifies ways of spiritual progress.

bhakta (<u>bak</u> taa) Devotee of a deity, in Hinduism.

bhakti (<u>bak</u> tee) In Hinduism, intense devotion to a personal aspect of the deity.

bhakti yoga In Hinduism, the path of devotion.

bhikshu (bi kshoo) (Pali: *bhikkhu*; feminine: **bhikshuni** or *bhikkhuni*). A Buddhist monk or nun who renounces worldliness for the sake of following the path of liberation and whose simple physical needs are met by lay supporters.

bodhisattva (bō dee <u>sǎt</u> vǎ) In Mahayana Buddhism, one who has attained enlightenment but renounces nirvana for the sake of helping all sentient beings in their journey to liberation from suffering.

Brahman (<u>brǎh</u> mǎn) The impersonal Ultimate Principle in Hinduism.

Brahmanas (<u>braa</u> mǎ nǎs) The portion of the Hindu Vedas concerning rituals.

Brahmin (<u>braa</u> min) (**brahman**) A priest or member of the priestly caste in Hinduism.

Buddha-nature A fully awakened consciousness.

C

caliph (<u>kay</u> lif) In Sunni Islam, the successor to the Prophet.

Calvinism Protestant denomination founded by John Calvin in the sixteenth century and believing in predestination.

canon Authoritative collection of writings, works, etc., applying to a particular religion or author.

caste (kast) Social class distinction on the basis of heredity or occupation.

Catholic In general, "catholic" means universal, all-inclusive. Christian Churches referring to themselves as Catholic claim to represent the ancient undivided Christian Church.

Celestial Masters Daoist tradition with hereditary lineage of priests representing celestial deities.

chakra (<u>chuk</u> rǎ) Subtle energy centers in the body, recognized in raja yoga.

charisma (kǎ <u>riz</u> mǎ) (adj.: **charismatic**) A rare personal magnetism, often ascribed to a founder of a religion.

Christ A reference to Jesus as the "anointed one," the Messiah.

Christmas Feast on 25 December celebrating the birth of Jesus Christ.

Christology The attempt to define the nature of Jesus and his relationship to God.

Common Era Years after the traditional date used for the birth of Jesus, previously referred to in exclusively Christian terms as AD and now abbreviated to CE, as opposed to BCE, (Before Common Era).

comparative religion Scholarly discipline attempting to understand and compare religious patterns from around the world.

Complete Perfection In Daoism, a monastic tradition combining inner alchemy, meditation, and social morality.

confirmation A Christian sacrament by which awareness of the Holy Spirit is enhanced.

Congregationalism Protestant denomination based on Calvinism, emphasizing the independence of each local congregation.

Conservative Judaism Branch that seeks to maintain traditional laws and practices while employing modern methods of scholarship.

cosmogony (kos <u>mog</u> ǒn ee) A model of the evolution of the universe.

Creationism Belief that all life forms were intentionally created by a Divine Being.

creed A formal statement of the beliefs of a particular religion.

crucifixion In Roman times, the execution of a criminal by fixing him to a cross; with reference to Jesus, his death on the cross, symbolic of his self-sacrifice for the good of all humanity.

crusades Military expeditions undertaken by the Christians of Europe in the eleventh to thirteenth centuries to recover the Holy Land from the Muslims; any war carried on under papal sanction.

cult Any religion that focuses on worship of a particular person or deity.

D

Dao (dow) (also **Tao**) The way or path, in Far Eastern traditions. The term is also used as a name for the Nameless.

Dalits (dǎ lits) A contemporary label used by some Hindus who were previously called "untouchables."

darshan (dǎr shǎn) Visual contact with the divine through encounters with Hindu images or gurus.

Dasam Granth (dǎsam grǎnth) The collected writings attributed to Guru Gobind Singh.

davening (daa věn ing) In Hasidic Judaism, prayer.

deity yoga (dee i tee yō gǎ) In Tibetan Buddhism, the practice of meditative concentration on a specific deity.

denomination (di nom ě nay shun) One of the Protestant branches of Christianity.

dervish (dǎr vish) A Sufi ascetic, in the Muslim tradition.

deva (day vǎ) (feminine: **devi**) In Hinduism, a deity.

Devi In Hinduism, the Goddess in all her forms.

Dhammapada (dǎm ǎ pǎ dǎ) A collection of short sayings attributed to the Buddha.

dharma (dhǎr mǎ) (Pali: *dhamma*) In Hinduism, moral order, duty, righteousness, religion. In Buddhism, **Dharma**, the doctrine or law, as revealed by the Buddha; also the correct conduct for a person according to their level of awareness.

dhimmi (dhimm ee) A person of a non-Muslim religion whose right to practice that religion is protected within an Islamic society.

diaspora (dī ass po ra) Collectively, the practitioners of a faith living beyond their traditional homeland. When spelled with a capital D, the dispersal of the Jews after the Babylonian exile.

Digambara (di gǎm bǎ rǎ) A highly ascetic order of Jain monks who wear no clothes.

dogma (dog mǎ) A system of beliefs declared to be true by a religion.

dukkha (dŏŏ khǎ) According to the Buddha, a central fact of human life, variously translated as discomfort, suffering, frustration, or lack of harmony with the environment.

Durga (door gǎ) The Great Goddess as destroyer of evil, and sometimes as shakti of Shiva.

E

Easter Movable feast in Spring celebrating the Resurrection of Jesus Christ.

ecumenism (ek yoo mě niz ěm) Rapprochement between branches of Christianity or among all faiths.

enlightenment Wisdom that is thought to come from direct experience of Ultimate Reality.

epic A long historic narrative.

Epiphany (ee pi fǎ nee) "Manifestation"; in Christianity, the recognition of Jesus's spiritual kingship by the three Magi.

Essenes (es eenz) Monastic Jews who were living communally, apart from the world, about the time of Jesus.

ethnic religions New religions that emerged after the fall of Communism as revivals of pre-Christian ethnic traditions in eastern Europe and Russia.

Eucharist (yoo kǎ rist) The Christian sacrament by which believers are renewed in the mystical body of Christ by partaking of bread and wine, understood as his body and blood.

evangelicalism Diverse Christian movement calling for a return to biblical faith, personal conversion experience, and spreading of the gospel.

evangelist (i van jě liz ěm) Ardent preacher of the Christian gospel.

exclusivism The idea that one's own religion is the only valid way.

excommunication Exclusion from participation in the Christian sacraments (applied particularly to Roman Catholicism), which is a bar to gaining access to Heaven.

exegesis (ex a jee sis) Critical examination of a religious text.

F

Falun Gong/Falun Dafa A form of qigong mixing Buddhism with Daoist energy practices, and emphasizing ethics—the development of truthfulness, benevolence, and forbearance.

Fatiha (faat i hǎ) The first surah of the Qur'an.

fatwa In Islam, a legal opinion issued by an authority according to a particular school of law.

feng shui (fěng shwee) The Daoist practice of determining the most harmonious position for a building according to the natural flows of energy.

fiqh Jurisprudence; the process of understanding, interpreting, and implementing the shari'ah.

Five Ks In Sikhism, the symbols worn by Khalsa members.

fundamentalism (fun dǎ men tǎl iz ěm) Insistence on what people perceive as the historical form of their religion, in contrast to more contemporary influences. This ideal sometimes takes extreme, rigidly exclusive forms.

G

Gathas In Zoroastrianism, metric verses or hymns which were the words of the prophet Zarathushtra.

Gayatrimantra (gī ǎ tree man trǎ) The daily Vedic prayer of upper-caste Hindus.

Gemara In Judaism, commentaries on the Talmud, additional to the Mishnah.

Gentile (jen tīl) Any person who is not of Jewish faith or origin.

ghetto An urban area occupied by those rejected by a society, such as quarters for Jews in some European cities.

globalization Interdependence of people around the world through contemporary economic, cultural, and technological processes.

gnosis (nō sis) Intuitive knowledge of spiritual realities.

Gnosticism (nos ti siz ěm) Mystical perception of spiritual knowledge.

Goddess spirituality Worship of a high goddess in ancient times, now revived in many places.

gospel In Christianity, the "good news" that God has raised Jesus from the dead and in so doing has begun the transformation of the world.

gurdwara (gŏŏr dwa rǎ) A Sikh place of worship.

guru (gŏŏ roo) In Hinduism, an enlightened spiritual teacher.

Guru Granth Sahib (gŏŏ rŏŏ grǎnth saa hib) The sacred scripture compiled by the Sikh Gurus.

H

Hadith (haa _deeth_) In Islam, a traditional report about a reputed saying or action of the Prophet Muhammad.

haggadah (hă _gaa_ dă) The nonlegal part of the Talmud and Midrash; with capital H, the Seder text.

hajj (haaj) The holy pilgrimage to Mecca, for Muslims.

halakhah (haa laa _khaa_) Jewish legal decision and the parts of the Talmud dealing with laws.

hagiography (_ha_ gee _og_ ra phee) Idealized biography of the life of a saint.

Haredi (Ultra-Orthodox) Favoring detachment from non-Jewish culture, to focus on the Torah.

Hasidism (_haas_ īd iz ĕm) Ecstatic Jewish piety, dating from eighteenth-century Poland.

havan In Hinduism, a sacred fireplace around which ritual fire ceremonies are conducted.

heretic (_hair_ i tik) A member of an established religion whose views are unacceptable to the orthodoxy.

hermeneutics The field of theological study that attempts to interpret scripture.

heyoka (hay _yō_ kă) "Contrary" wisdom or a person who embodies it, in some Native American spiritual traditions.

Highest Purity Daoism In Daoism, an elite tradition of celibates who meditate on purification of the body for spiritual elevation.

hijab (hi _jaab_) The veiling of women for the sake of modesty in Islam.

hijrah (_hij_ ră) Muhammad's migration from Mecca to Medina.

historical-critical studies Objective analysis of scriptures, including historical, cultural, and linguistic factors.

Holocaust (_haw_ lō cawst) The genocidal killing of six million Jews by the Nazis during World War II.

Holy Trinity The Christian doctrine that in the One God are three divine persons: the Father, the Son, and the Holy Spirit.

humanism An approach to life focusing on humans' responsibility to lead ethical lives without belief in the supernatural.

I

icon (ī kon) A sacred image, a term used especially for the paintings of Jesus, Mary, and the saints of the Eastern Orthodox Christian Church.

iconoclast One who attacks cherished beliefs or destroys sacred images.

ijtihad (ij ti _haad_) In Islam, reasoned interpretation of sacred law by a qualified scholar.

Imam (i _maam_) In Shi'ism, the title for the person carrying the initiatic tradition of the Prophetic Light.

imam (i _maam_) A leader of Muslim prayer.

immanent Present in Creation.

incarnation Physical embodiment of the divine.

inclusivism The idea that all religions can be accommodated within one religion.

indigenous (in _dij_ ĕ nĕs) Native to an area.

Indra (_in_ dră) The old Vedic thunder god in the Hindu tradition.

indulgence In Roman Catholic Christianity, granting of a remission of sins.

infidel (_in_ fid ĕl) The Muslim and Christian term for "nonbeliever," which each tradition often applies to the other.

Inquisition (in kwi _zi_ shun) The use of force and terror to eliminate heresies and nonbelievers in the Christian Church, starting in the thirteenth century.

intelligent design The concept that scientific discoveries and recognition of complex life processes prove the existence of a single being, an Intelligent Designer.

interfaith dialogue Appreciative communication between people of different religions.

Islam In its original meaning, complete, trusting surrender to God.

Islamist A person seeking to establish Islamic states in which the rule of God is supreme.

J

janam-sakhis (jă năm _saa_ khees) Traditional Sikh biographies, especially stories of the life of Guru Nanak.

JapJi (jăp jee) The first morning prayer of Sikhs, composed by Guru Nanak.

jati (_jaa_ tee) One of thousands of social sub-castes in India.

Jehovah's Witnesses Movement holding that many modern Christian doctrines are false, and advocating what is regarded as early Christianity.

jihad (ji _haad_) The Muslim's struggle against the inner forces that prevent God-realization and the outer barriers to establishment of the divine order.

Jina (ji nă) In Jainism, one who has realized the highest, omniscient aspect of his or her being and is therefore perfect.

jinn (jin) In Islam, an invisible being of fire.

jiva (_jee_ vă) The soul in Jainism.

jnana yoga (_yaa_ nă _yō_ gă) The use of intellectual effort as a yogic technique.

justified (noun: **justification**) In Christianity, having been absolved of sin in the eyes of God.

K

Kabbalah (kă _baa_ lă) The Jewish mystical tradition.

Kali (_kaa_ lee) In Hinduism, the destroying and transforming Mother of the World.

Kali Yuga (kă lee yŏo ga) In Hindu world cycles, an age of chaos and selfishness, including the one in which we are now living.

kami (_kaa_ mee) The Shinto word for that invisible sacred quality that evokes wonder and awe, and also for the invisible spirits throughout nature that are born of this essence.

kannagara (kă nă gă ră) Harmony with the way of the kami in Shinto.

karma (_kăr_ mă) (Pali: _kamma_) In Hinduism and Buddhism, our actions and their effects on this life and lives to come. In Jainism, subtle matter or particles that accumulate on the soul as a result of one's thoughts and actions.

karma _yoga_ (_kăr_ mă _yō_ gă) The path of unselfish service in Hinduism.

kenotic (ki _not_ ik) In Russian Orthodox Christianity, belief in the monastic pattern of ascetic poverty combined with service in the world.

kensho (ken shō) In Zen Buddhism, sudden enlightenment.

kevala (_kav_ vă lă) The supremely perfected state in Jainism.

Khalsa (_khăl_ să) The body of the pure, as inspired by the Sikh

Guru Gobind Singh.

kirpan (kir paan) In Sikhism, the small sword worn by Khalsa initiates.

kirtan (kir tăn) Devotional singing of hymns from the Guru Granth Sahib in Sikhism.

koan (kō aan) In Zen Buddhism, a paradoxical puzzle to be solved without ordinary thinking.

kosher (kō sher) Ritually acceptable according to Jewish tradition. Applied predominantly to food, but also to ritual objects and practices.

Kshatriya (ksha tree ă) A member of the warrior or ruling caste in traditional Hinduism, Jainism, and Buddhism.

kufr (kōo fer) In Islam, the sin of atheism, of ingratitude to God.

kundalini (kŏon dă lee nee) In Hindu yogic thought, the life force that can be awakened from the base of the spine and raised to illuminate the spiritual center at the top of the head.

L

Lakshmi (lăksh mee) In Hinduism, the consort of Vishnu.

lama (laa mă) A Tibetan Buddhist monk, particularly one of the highest in the hierarchy.

langar (lan găr) In Sikh tradition, a free communal meal without caste distinctions

Lent The forty days of spiritual preparation leading up to Easter.

li (lee) Ceremonies, rituals, and rules of proper conduct, in the Confucian tradition.

liberal Flexible in approach to religious tradition; inclined to see tradition as metaphorical rather than literal truth.

Liberal Judaism see Reform Judaism.

liberation theology Christianity expressed as solidarity with the poor.

lifeway An entire approach to living in which sacred and secular are not separate.

lingam (ling ăm) A cylindrical stone or other similarly shaped natural or sculpted form, representing for Shaivite Hindus the unmanifest aspect of Shiva.

literati The philosophical form of Daoism, followed by intellectuals and artists.

liturgy (lit ĕr jee) In Christianity and Judaism, the rites of public worship.

Lubavich Hasidim Highly structured Orthodox Jewish movement that uses modern technology for propagation but has traditional lifestyles.

Lutheranism Modern denomination of the breakaway Protestant Church founded by Martin Luther in 1517.

M

madrasa (mă draa saa) Traditional religious school teaching a narrow version of Islam.

Mahabharata (mă haa baa ră tă) A long Hindu epic that includes the *Bhagavad-Gita*.

Mahayana (mă haa yaa nă) The "Great Vehicle" in Buddhism, the more liberal and mystical branch of Buddhist schools that stresses the virtue of altruistic compassion rather than intellectual efforts at individual salvation.

mandala (măn dă lă) A symmetrical image, with shapes emerging from a center, used as a meditational focus.

mantra (măn tră) A sound or phrase chanted to evoke the sound vibration of one aspect of creation or to praise a deity.

Mass The Roman Catholic term for the Christian Eucharist.

materialism The tendency to consider material possessions and comforts more important than spiritual matters, or the philosophical position that nothing exists except matter and that there are no supernatural dimensions to life.

maya (mī yă) In Indian thought, the attractive but illusory physical world.

medicine Spiritual power, in some indigenous traditions.

medicine person An indigenous healer.

Mennonites Members of a Christian denomination emphasizing adult baptism and pacifism, dating from the sixteenth century.

Messiah The "anointed," the expected king and deliverer of the Jews; a term later applied by Christians to Jesus.

metaphysics Philosophy based on theories of subtle realities that transcend the physical world.

Methodism An offshoot of the Church of England, originating in the eighteenth century with the evangelist John Wesley, who emphasized personal holiness and methodical devotions.

Midrash (mid rash) "Seeking," "searching," a reference to rabbinic biblical interpretation and the larger rabbinic attitude toward scriptural tradition.

mikveh (mik vă) A deep bath for ritual cleansing in Judaism.

millennium One thousand years, a term used in Christianity and certain newer religions for a hoped-for period of a thousand years of holiness and happiness, with Christ ruling the earth, as prophesied in the Book of Revelation.

minyan (min yăn) The quorum of ten adult Jews (traditionally men) required for the recitation of certain communal prayers.

Mishnah In Judaism, the systematic summation of the legal teachings of the oral tradition of the Torah.

misogi (mee sō gee) The Shinto waterfall purification ritual.

mitzvah (mitz vă) (plural: mitzvot) In Judaism, a divine commandment or sacred deed in fulfillment of a commandment.

Mizrahi Jews from Arab lands.

Modern Orthodoxy Branch of Orthodox Judaism, dedicated to the significance of Israel and Jewish law, which values secular knowledge and integration with non-Jews.

modernism Twentieth-century values including individualism, preference for change rather than continuity, quantity rather than quality, efficiency, pragmatism, and profiteering, all seen by some as threatening the existence of traditional religious values.

moksha (mōk shă) In Hinduism, liberation of the soul from illusion and suffering.

monistic (mon iz tik) Believing in the concept of life as a unified whole, without a separate "spiritual" realm.

monotheistic (mon ō thee iz tik) Believing in a single God.

muezzin (moo ez in) In Islam, one who calls the people to prayer from a high place.

mujahid (mŏo jaa hid) In Islam, a selfless fighter in the path of Allah.

murshid (moor shid) A spiritual teacher, in esoteric Islam.

mystic One who values inner spiritual experience in preference to external authorities and scriptures.

mysticism The intuitive perception of spiritual truths beyond the limits of reason.

myth A symbolic story expressing ideas about reality or spiritual history.

N

Nam (naam) The Holy Name of God reverberating throughout all of Creation, as repeated by Sikhs.

Neo-Confucianism Confucianism stressing the importance of self-cultivation and dedication to becoming a "noble person" established during the Chinese Han and Song dynasties.

Neo-Paganism Nature-oriented spirituality referring to pre-Christian sacred ways.

New Testament Books of the Christian Bible that were composed after the death of Jesus, including the Gospels, Acts of the Apostles, and Revelation.

Nicene Creed Basic profession of faith for many Christian denominations in East and West, including all Orthodox Churches, framed in a council held in Constantinople in 381 CE, and proposed as a basis for unifying all Christians.

nirvana (nir vaa nǎ) (Pali: *nibbana*) In Buddhism, the ultimate egoless state of bliss.

nontheistic Perceiving spiritual reality without a personal deity or deities.

numinous Indicating or suggesting the experience or presence of the "Holy."

O

oharai Shinto purification ceremony.

Old Testament Christian term for the books of the Hebrew Bible that form the first part of the Christian Bible.

OM (ōm) In Hinduism, the primordial sound.

oral Torah (oral tō raa) The rabbinic tradition, including the Mishnah, Talmud, and other texts, whose origins the rabbis assign to the covenant at Mount Sinai.

orisa The Yoruba term for a deity, often used in speaking of West African religions in general.

orthodox Adhering to the established tradition of a religion.

Orthodox Judaism A modern Jewish movement that emphasizes traditional rabbinic authority and *halakhah*.

P

Pali (paa lee) The Indian dialect first used for writing down the teachings of the Buddha, which were initially held in memory, and still used today in the **Pali Canon** of scriptures recognized by the Theravadins.

Pahlavi texts Texts written or translated in Middle Persian from about the ninth century CE with detailed instructions about the rituals and customs of the Zoroastrians in Iran.

Panth In Sikhism, the religious community.

parable (par ǎ bǔl) An allegorical story.

Paraclete (par ǎ kleet) The entity that Jesus said would come after his death to help the people.

Parsis Persian Zoroastrians who avoided conversion to Islam by migrating to western India.

Parvati (paar vǎ tee) Shiva's spouse, sweet daughter of the Himalayas.

passion narratives Descriptions in the gospels of Christ's suffering, betrayal, trial, and death.

patriarchal Of or relating to a group, society, or religion led by men in a fatherly role.

penance An act of self-punishment to atone for wrongdoings.

Pentateuch (pen tǎ took) The five books of Moses; the first section of the three-part Jewish Bible.

Pentecost (pen tě kost) The occasion when the Holy Spirit descended upon the disciples of Jesus after his death.

Pentecostalism Charismatic Protestant denomination experiencing the manifestation of divinely inspired powers by signs such as "speaking in tongues."

Pharisees (fair ě seez) In Roman-ruled Judaea, liberals who tried to practice Torah in their lives.

pluralism An appreciation of the diversity of religions.

pogrom An attack against Jews.

polytheistic (pol ě thee iz ěm) Believing in many deities.

pope The Bishop of Rome and head of the Roman Catholic Church.

prana (praa nǎ) In Indian thought, the invisible life force.

pranayama (praa nǎ yaa mǎ) Yogic breathing exercises.

prasad (prǎ saad) In Indian traditions, blessed food.

Presbyterianism Protestant denomination based on Calvinism, governed by presbyters (governors), or officials of the Church.

profane Worldly, secular, as opposed to sacred.

Protestantism Large branch of Christianity comprising many denominations that believe in a direct relationship with God and Jesus, salvation by God's grace, and understanding scripture by reason and conscience.

puja (poo jǎ) Hindu ritual worship.

Puranas (pǒo raa nǎs) Hindu scriptures composed to popularize the abstract truths of the Vedas through stories about historical and legendary figures.

Pure Land A Buddhist sect in China and Japan that centers on faith in Amida Buddha, who promised to welcome believers to the paradise of the Pure Land, a metaphor for enlightenment.

Purgatory (pur gǎ tor ee) In some branches of Christianity, an intermediate after-death state in which souls are purified from sin.

Q

qi (*chee*) (also ch'i) (chee) The vital energy in the universe and in our bodies, according to Chinese cosmology and the Chinese sciences.

qigong (chee gaang) (also **ch'i-kung**) A Daoist system of harnessing inner energies for spiritual realization.

Quakers Protestant denomination with no liturgy, but the expectation that God will speak through members of the congregation.

R

rabbi (rab ī) An ordained religious authority, who may serve as a teacher, a legal decision-maker, or the spiritual leader of a Jewish congregation.

raja yoga (raa jǎ) Mental concentration yoga (ancient technique for spiritual realization).

Ramayana (raa maa yǎ nǎ) The Hindu epic about Prince Rama, defender of good.

rapture Nineteenth-century belief amongst some Christians, using Paul's letter to the Thessalonians (I Thess. 4:17) to say that Christians would be caught up in clouds to meet Jesus when he returned to earth.

realization Personal awareness of the existence of Ultimate Reality.

Reconstructionism Movement holding that Judaism is an evolving religious civilization.

redaction Editing and organization of a text, including a religious scripture.

Reform Judaism A modern Jewish movement whose emphasis is on the relevance of Judaism for present and future Jews, rather than the *halakhic* tradition.

reincarnation The transmigration of the soul into a new body after death of the old body.

relic In some forms of Christianity and Buddhism, part of the body or clothing of a saint.

religion A particular response to dimensions of life considered sacred, as shaped by institutionalized traditions.

Religious Zionism Holds as central the resettlement of the Jews in Israel.

ren (also *jen*) (yen) Humanity, benevolence—the central Confucian virtue.

Resurrection The rising of Jesus in his earthly body on the first Easter Day, three days after his crucifixion and death.

Rig Veda (rig vay dǎ) Possibly the world's oldest scripture, the foundation of Hinduism.

rishi (rish ee) A Hindu sage.

ritual A repeated, patterned religious act.

Rujiao (rōō jow) The Chinese term for the teachings based on Confucius.

S

Sabbath (sab ǎth) The day of the week set aside for rest and worship in Judaism and Christianity.

sacrament Outward and visible sign of inward and spiritual grace in Christianity. Almost all Churches recognize baptism and the Eucharist as sacraments; some Churches recognize five others as well.

sacred The realm of the extraordinary, beyond everyday perceptions, the supernatural, holy.

sacred thread In Hinduism, a cord worn over one shoulder by men who have been initiated into adult upper-caste society.

Sadducees (saj ǔ seez) In Roman-ruled Judaea, wealthy and priestly Jews.

sadhana (saa dhǎ na) In Hinduism, especially yoga, a spiritual practice.

sadhu (saa dhoo) An ascetic holy man, in Hinduism.

samadhi (sǎ maa dhee) In yogic practice, the blissful state of superconscious union with the Absolute.

Samkhya (saam khyǎ) One of the major Hindu philosophical systems, according to which the interaction of activity, inertia, and equilibrium governs the development of the world.

samsara (sǎm saa rǎ) The continual round of birth, death, and rebirth in Hinduism, Jainism, and Buddhism.

sangat A Sikh congregation, in which all are ideally considered equal.

Sangha (sǎn ghǎ) In Theravada Buddhism, the monastic community; in Mahayana, the spiritual community of followers of the dharma.

sannyasin (sǎn yaa sin) In Hinduism and Buddhism, a renunciate spiritual seeker.

Sanskrit (san skrit) The literary language of classic Hindu scriptures.

Santería The combination of African and Christian practices which developed in Cuba.

Saraswati (sǎ rǎs wǎ tee) Hindu goddess of knowledge.

satori (sǎ tō ree) Enlightenment, realization of ultimate truth, in Zen Buddhism.

scientific materialism School of thought that developed during the nineteenth and twentieth centuries claiming that the supernatural is imaginary; only the material world exists, and from this point of view religions have been invented by humans.

sect A subgroup within a larger tradition.

secularism Personal disregard of religion; government policy of not favoring any one religion.

Seder Ceremonial Jewish meal in remembrance of the Passover.

see An area under the authority of a Christian bishop or archbishop.

Semite (sem ite) A Jew, Arab, or other, of eastern Mediterranean origin.

Sephardim An ethnic grouping of the Jews with origins in Spain and North Africa.

Seventh-day Adventists Protestant denomination or sectarian movement believing in infallibility of the Bible, honoring Saturday as the Sabbath, and anticipating the "end times."

Shahadah (shǎ haa dǎ) The central Muslim expression of faith: "There is no god but God, and Muhammad is the messenger of God."

Shakta (shaak tǎ) A Hindu worshiper of the female aspect of deity.

shakti (shak tee) The creative, active female aspect of deity in Hinduism.

shaktipat (shak ti pǎt) In the Siddha tradition of Hinduism, the powerful, elevating glance or touch of the guru.

Shaiva (shǐ vǎ) A Hindu worshiper of the divine as Shiva.

shaman (shaa mǎn) In indigenous traditions, a "medicine person," a man or woman who has undergone spiritual ordeals and can communicate with the spirit world to help the people.

Shangdi (also **Shang Ti**) In ancient China, a deity (or perhaps deities) with overarching powers.

shari'ah (shǎ ree ǎ) The divine law and ethics in Islam.

shaykh A spiritual master, in the esoteric Muslim tradition.

Shekhinah (she khī nǎ) The presence of God in the world, especially emphasized in Jewish mystical circles.

Shi'a (adj. **Shi'ite**) (shee īt) The minority branch of Islam, which feels that Muhammad's legitimate successors were 'Ali and a series of Imams; a follower of this branch.

shirk (shirk) The sin of believing in any divinity except the one God, in Islam.

Shiva (also **Siva**) (shi vǎ) In Hinduism, the Supreme as lord of yogis, absolute consciousness, creator, preserver, and destroyer of the world; or the destroying aspect of the Supreme.

shudra (shoo drǎ) A member of the manual laborer caste in traditional Hinduism.

shunyata (shoon yǎ taa) Voidness, the transcendental ultimate reality in Buddhism.

Sikh (sikh) "Student," especially one who practices the teachings of the ten Sikh Gurus.

Soma (sō ma) An intoxicating drink used by early Hindu worshipers.

spirituality Any personal response to dimensions of life that are considered sacred.

stupa (stoo pǎ) A rounded monument containing Buddhist relics or commemorative materials.

Sufism (soo fiz ěm) The mystical path in Islam.

Sunnah (sōō nǎ) The behavior of the Prophet Muhammad, used as a model in Islamic law.

Sunni (sŏŏ nee) A follower of the majority branch of Islam, which feels that successors to Muhammad are to be chosen by the Muslim community.

surah (sŏŏ rä) A chapter of the Qur'an.

sutra (soo trä) (Pali: *sutta*) Literally, a thread on which are strung jewels—the discourses of the teacher; in yoga, sutras are terse sayings.

Shvetambara (shwe tăm bä rä) Jain order of monks who are less ascetic than the Digambara.

symbol Visible representation of an invisible reality or concept.

synagogue (sin ä gog) A meeting place for Jewish study and worship.

synod In Christianity, a council of Church officials called to reach agreement on doctrines and administration.

synoptic (sin ŏp tik) Referring to three similar books of the Christian Bible: Matthew, Mark, and Luke.

T

Taiji quan (also T'ai-chi ch'uan) (tī jee chŏŏ an) An ancient Chinese system of physical exercises, which uses slow movements to help one become part of the universal flow of energy.

Taliban Islamic extremists from Afghanistan who promote a harsh interpretation of shariah and reject harmonious Islamic principles.

tallit katan (ta lit kah taan) A shawl traditionally worn by Jewish men during prayers.

Talmud (tal mŏŏd) One of two collections of Jewish law and tradition, compiled in the fifth century CE in Palestine and the sixth century CE in Babylonia.

Tanakh (ta naakh) The Jewish Bible, made up of the Torah, Nevi'im (Prophets), and Ketuvim (Writings).

Tantras (tăn träs) The ancient Indian texts based on esoteric worship of the divine as feminine.

Tantrayana (tăn trä yaa nä) see Vajrayana.

tariqa (ta ree ka) In Islam, an esoteric Sufi order.

tefillin (tĕ fil in) A small leather box containing verses about God's covenant with the Jewish people, bound to the forehead and arm.

thangka (tang ka) In Tibetan Buddhism, an elaborate image of a spiritual figure used as a focus for meditation.

theistic (thee is tik) Believing in a God or gods.

Theravada (The rä vaa dä) The remaining of the early schools of Buddhism, which adheres closely to the earliest scriptures and emphasizes individual efforts to liberate the mind from suffering.

Tipitaka (ti pi tä kä) (Sanskrit: *Tripitaka*) The foundational "Three Baskets" of the Buddha's teachings.

Tirthankaras (tir thaan kär äs) The great enlightened teachers in Jainism, of whom Mahavira was the last in the present cosmic cycle.

Torah (tŏ raa) "Law" or "teaching." The first five books of the Jewish Bible. Can also refer to Jewish teaching or tradition more generally.

transcendent Existing outside the material universe.

Transfiguration The phenomenon that took place when Christ, praying on the mountain, was irradiated with light and God spoke from the heavens.

transubstantiation (tran sŭb stan shee ay shun) In some branches of Christianity, the idea that wine and bread are mystically transformed into the blood and body of Christ during the Eucharist sacrament.

Triple Gem (Three Refuges) The three jewels of Buddhism: Buddha, Dharma, Sangha.

tsumi (tzoo mee) Impurity or misfortune, a quality that Shinto purification practices are designed to remove.

tzaddik (tzaa dik) An enlightened Jewish mystic.

U

Udasi (ŏŏ daa see) An ascetic Sikh order.

ulama (oo lä maa) The influential leaders in traditional Muslim society, including spiritual leaders, imams, teachers, state scribes, market inspectors, and judges.

ummah (ŏŏ mä) The Muslim community.

Unitarianism Protestant denomination holding that God is One rather than Three persons.

universalism Acceptance that truth may be found in all religions; belief in the inner oneness of all religions.

untouchable The lowest caste in Brahmanic Hindu society, now known more respectfully as Dalits.

Upanishads (ŏŏ păn i shăds) The philosophical part of the Vedas in Hinduism, intended only for serious seekers.

Ushas The goddess of dawn in Hindu mythology.

V

Vaishnava (vīsh nä vä) (or **Vaishnava**) A Hindu devotee of Vishnu, particularly in his incarnation as Krishna.

Vaishya (vīsh yä) A member of the merchant and farmer caste in traditional Hinduism.

Vajrayana (väj rä yaa nä) (or **Tantrayana**) The ultimate vehicle used in Mahayana, mainly Tibetan, Buddhism, consisting of esoteric tantric practices and concentration on deities.

varna (vär nä) One of four traditional occupational groupings in Hinduism.

Vedas (vay dä) Ancient scriptures revered by Hindus.

vipassana (vi pas ä nä) In Buddhism, meditation based on watching one's own thoughts, emotions, and actions.

Vishnu (vish noo) In Hinduism, the preserving aspect of the Supreme or the Supreme Itself, incarnating again and again to save the world.

vision quest In indigenous traditions, a solitary ordeal undertaken to seek spiritual guidance about one's mission in life.

Vodou (voo doo) Latin American and Caribbean ways of working with the spirit world, a blend of West African and Catholic Christian teachings.

W

Wahhabism Islamic philosophy founded by Muhammad ibn 'Abd al-Wahhab in the eighteenth century, discarding all practices not specifically approved by the Qur'an and Sunnah.

Wicca Neo-Pagan sect of witches traced to the writings of Gerald Gardner in England in the 1940s.

wu wei (woo way) In Daoism, "not doing," in the sense of taking no action contrary to the natural flow.

Y

yang In Chinese philosophy, the bright, assertive, "male" energy in the universe.

yantra (yăn tră) In Hinduism, a linear cosmic symbol used as an aid to spiritual concentration.

yi (yee) Righteous conduct (as opposed to conduct motivated by desire for personal profit), a Confucian virtue stressed by Mencius.

yin (yin) In Chinese philosophy, the dark, receptive, "female" energy in the universe.

yoga (yō gă) A systematic approach to spiritual realization, one of the major Hindu philosophical systems.

yoni (yō nee) Abstract Hindu representation of the female vulva, cosmic matrix of life.

yuga (yŏo gă) One of four recurring world cycles in Hinduism.

Z

zakat (ză kaat) Spiritual tithing in Islam.

zazen (zaa zen) Zen Buddhist sitting meditation.

Zealots Jewish resistance fighters who fought the Romans and were defeated in the siege of Jerusalem.

Zen (zen) (Chinese: Chan) A Chinese and Japanese Buddhist school emphasizing that all things have Buddha-nature, which can only be grasped when one escapes from the intellectual mind.

zendo (zen dō) A Zen meditation hall.

Zion The original site of the Jerusalem temples, now often used to refer to Jerusalem itself as the heavenly city, the goal of Judaism.

Zionism Movement dedicated to the establishment of a politically viable, internationally recognized Jewish state in the biblical land of Israel.

INDEX

Page numbers in *italics* refer to topics mentioned in illustration captions. When that subject appears in the text on the same page, italics have not been used

CREDITS

CHAPTER 10

375 © Kazuyoshi Nomachi/Corbis 377 ©AP/PA 378 © Mischa Scorer / Hutchison 379 akg-images 381 Getty Images 382 JCK Archives 383 © V&A Images, Victoria and Albert Museum 386 Bodleian Library, Oxford, MS. Pers. B. 1, fol. 33r 389 top © Mary Pat Fisher 389 bottom Photo by Banti Singh 390 REUTRRS/China Daily 392 Getty / KARIM SAHIB 394 © Kazuyoshi Nomachi / Corbis 399 © Mary Pat Fisher 400 © Mark Henley 401 © Christopher Tordai / Hutchison 405 The Art Archive/Dagli Orti 406 © Kent Kobersteen / National Geographic Society, Corbis 407 Ahmad Yusni / epa / Corbis 408 akg-images / Bildarchiv Steffens 410 David Lefranc / Gamma-Rapho / Getty Images 413 © Yadid Levy / Alamy 415 Yui Mok - WPA Pool/Getty Images 416 © Mary Pat Fisher 417 TIM Gurney/www.copix.co.UK 419 © Stringer Shanghai/Reuters/Corbis 424 © Dallas Morning News/Corbis Sygma

CHAPTER 11

433 From *Biography of Guru Nanak* by Kartar Singh, Hemkunt Press, New Delhi 110028 437 © Mary Pat Fisher 438 © Mary Pat Fisher 439 © Mary Pat Fisher 444 © Mary Pat Fisher 445 © Mary Pat Fisher 446 top Painting by Mehar Singh, courtesy of Gobind Sadan, New Delhi 446 bottom STR/AFP/Getty Images 448 Mehar Singh/Gobind Sadan 449 © Ekaterina Sabitova 451 © Mary Pat Fisher

CHAPTER 12

457 © Georges de Keerle / Corbis Sygma 458 ©AP/PA 461 © Ezio Petersen / Bettmann / Corbis 462 Dibyangshu Sarkar / AFP / Getty Images 464 © Paul Schermeister/Corbis 465 © Robert Maass/Corbis 470 © Michael MacIntyre / Hutchison 471 © Tibor Bognar/Corbis 472 Mary Evans Picture Library 473 Nicholas Roerich Museum, New York 474 Ana Carolina Ferandes / AFP / Getty Images 476 © Michael MacIntyre / Hutchison 478 © VIKTOR KOROTAYEV/Reuters/Corbis 479 Bridgeman Art Library 481 © Pallava Bagla/Corbis 483 © Mark Anderson 486 Courtesy Valeriy Lipenkov 487 Stephen Shaver /AFP/ Getty Images

CHAPTER 13

498 top © Nigel Howard / Hutchison 498 bottom Courtesy of GOAL, Switzerland 501 Keith Bedford/Reuters/Corbis 506 Image courtesy of the Assembly of People of Kazakhstan 508 © Mary Pat Fisher 509 © Wahat al-Salam - Neve Shalom 510 © Mary Pat Fisher 515 Jesi Kelley/Noxie Studio